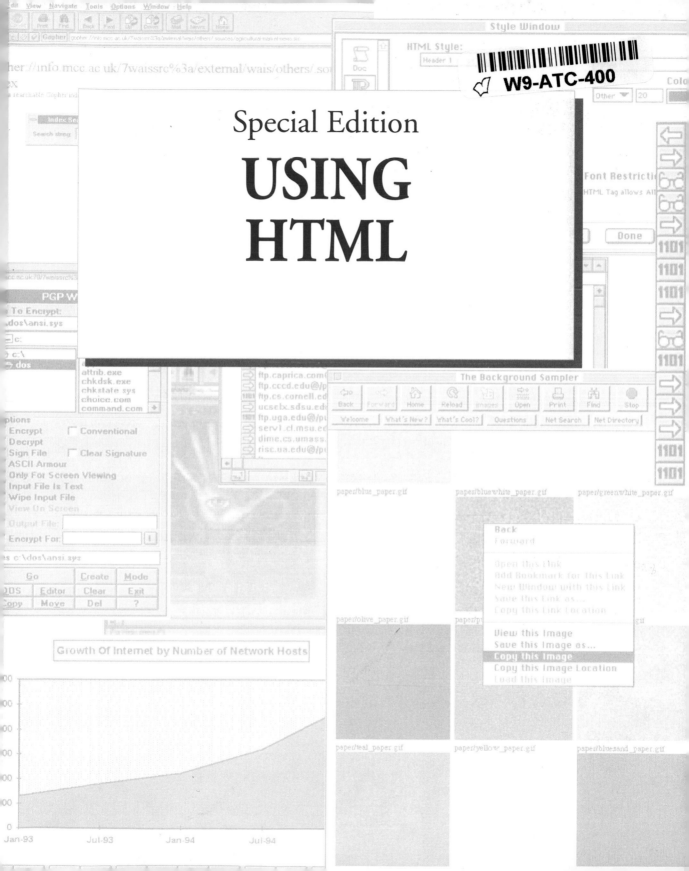

Special Edition

USING
HTML

PLUG YOURSELF INTO...

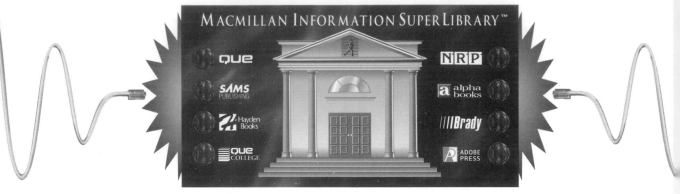

THE MACMILLAN INFORMATION SUPERLIBRARY™

Free information and vast computer resources from the world's leading computer book publisher—online!

FIND THE BOOKS THAT ARE RIGHT FOR YOU!

A complete online catalog, plus sample chapters and tables of contents give you an in-depth look at *all* of our books, including hard-to-find titles. It's the best way to find the books you need!

- STAY INFORMED with the latest computer industry news through our online newsletter, press releases, and customized Information SuperLibrary Reports.

- GET FAST ANSWERS to your questions about MCP books and software.

- VISIT our online bookstore for the latest information and editions!

- COMMUNICATE with our expert authors through e-mail and conferences.

- DOWNLOAD SOFTWARE from the immense MCP library:
  - Source code and files from MCP books
  - The best shareware, freeware, and demos

- DISCOVER HOT SPOTS on other parts of the Internet.

- WIN BOOKS in ongoing contests and giveaways!

TO PLUG INTO MCP: → WORLD WIDE WEB: **http://www.mcp.com**

GOPHER: gopher.mcp.com

FTP: ftp.mcp.com

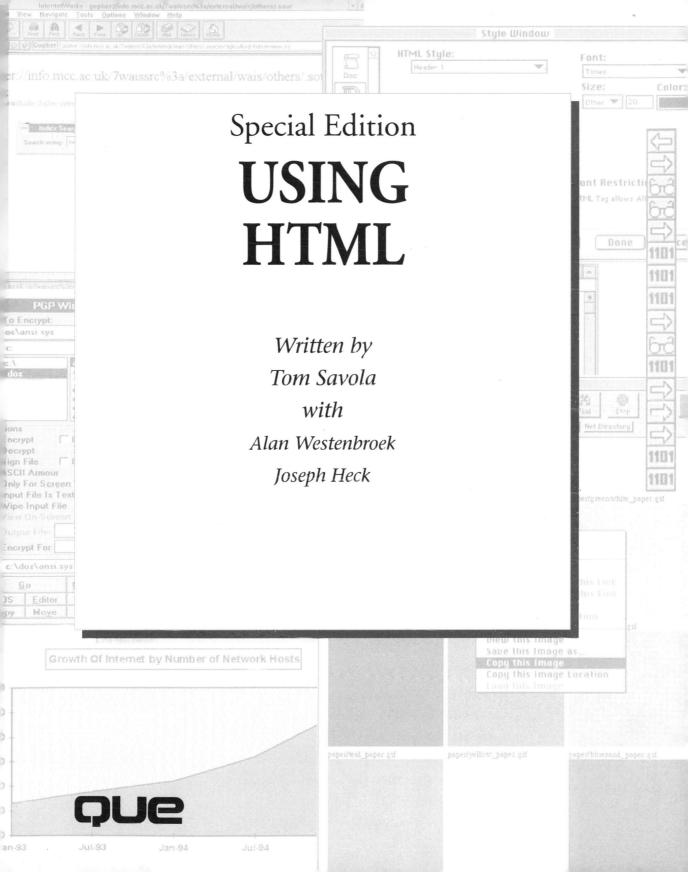

Special Edition
USING
HTML

Written by
Tom Savola
with
Alan Westenbroek
Joseph Heck

Special Edition Using HTML

Copyright © 1995 by Que® Corporation

All rights reserved. Printed in the United States of America. No part of this book may be used or reproduced in any form or by any means, or stored in a database or retrieval system, without prior written permission of the publisher except in the case of brief quotations embodied in critical articles and reviews. Making copies of any part of this book for any purpose other than your own personal use is a violation of United States copyright laws. For information, address Que Corporation, 201 W. 103rd St., Indianapolis, IN 46290. You may reach Que's direct sales line by calling 1-800-428-5331.

Library of Congress Catalog No.: 95-68634

ISBN: 07897-0236-3

This book is sold *as is,* without warranty of any kind, either express or implied, respecting the contents of this book, including but not limited to implied warranties for the book's quality, performance, merchantability, or fitness for any particular purpose. Neither Que Corporation nor its dealers or distributors shall be liable to the purchaser or any other person or entity with respect to any liability, loss, or damage caused or alleged to have been caused directly or indirectly by this book.

97   96   95   4   3

Interpretation of the printing code: the rightmost double-digit number is the year of the book's printing; the rightmost single-digit number, the number of the book's printing. For example, a printing code of 95-1 shows that the first printing of the book occurred in 1995.

Special Edition Using HTML is based on Versions 2.0 and 3.0 of HTML.

Screen Reproductions in this book were created with Collage Complete from Inner Media, Inc., Hollis, NH.

Portions © Microsoft Corporation 1995. All rights reserved.

Publisher: Roland Elgey

Vice President and Publisher: Marie Butler-Knight

Associate Publisher: Don Roche, Jr.

Publishing Director: Brad R. Koch

Editorial Services Director: Elizabeth Keaffaber

Managing Editor: Michael Cunningham

Director of Marketing: Lynn E. Zingraf

Credits

Acquisitions Editor
Jenny L. Watson

Product Director
Kathie-Jo Arnoff

Production Editor
Theresa Mathias

Editors
Thomas F. Hayes
Nancy E. Sixsmith

**Assistant Product
Marketing Manager**
Kim Margolius

Technical Editors
Elizabeth Eisner Reding
Tobin Anthony
Larry Schumer
Chris Negus

Technical Specialist
Cari Skaggs

Operations Coordinator
Patricia J. Brooks

Acquisitions Assistant
Tracy Williams

Editorial Assistant
Jill Pursell

Book Designer
Ruth Harvey

Cover Designer
Karen Ruggles

Production Team
Maxine Dillingham
Chad Dressler
Amy Durocher
DiMonique Ford
George Hanlin
John Hulse
Barry Jorden
Bob LaRoche
Elizabeth Lewis
Paula Lowell
G. Alan Palmore
Dennis Sheehan
Brenda Sims
Mary Beth Wakefield

Indexer
Michael Hughes

Composed in *Stone Serif* and *MCPdigital* by Que Corporation

Dedication

To Laura and Zoe, whose unconditional love keeps me centered in my life, and to Judy, from whose inner strength and courage I continue to learn and measure myself against.

About the Authors

Tom Savola is a freelance writer living in Los Angeles, California, with his wife Laura and their love child Zoe. He also provides multimedia and Internet consulting and is the managing editor for the *UCS Networker,* a bimonthly computer newsletter (**http://www.usc.edu/UCS/userserv /Networker_WWW/**) published by the University of Southern California.

Alan Westenbroek is a technical instructor and developer for Datastorm Technologies, Inc. in Columbia, Missouri. By day, he teaches support technicians about communications and troubleshooting, and catches bugs. By night, he loses sleep surfing the Internet and writing books about surfing the Internet.

Joseph Heck is a Programmer/Analyst for the University of Missouri. He also maintains its World Wide Web site and teaches how to create HTML documents and how to develop applications for the WWW.

Acknowledgments

The opportunity to write this book came at a complicated and unpredictable time in my life. I would like to thank Beverly Eppink for having faith enough to bring me into the project, and Jenny Watson for tightening the reins these last few months to push the book to the finish; Kathie-Jo Arnoff for watching vigilantly over the "big picture" while I scrabbled with the details; Theresa Mathias for early-morning phone calls and a sharp editing eye; and Jim Minatel for compiling a fantastic CD-ROM product to accompany the book.

I would also like to thank Kay Ferdinandsen and Louise Marks at the University of Southern California for letting me loose on the World Wide Web; and Alan Westenbroek, Joseph Heck, and Ian Stokell for stepping up to provide their expertise and talents on this book.

Most of all, I would like to thank my family and friends for supporting me over the course of this project, and for understanding when my attention wandered in conversations or I was otherwise occupied by the writing—and not by the warmth of their company.

Trademarks

All terms mentioned in this book that are known to be trademarks or service marks have been appropriately capitalized. Que cannot attest to the accuracy of this information. Use of a term in this book should not be regarded as affecting the validity of any trademark or service mark.

Contents at a Glance

Overview

How Documents Reach You

Creating Documents

Using Forms

HTML 3.0

Document Aesthetics

Contents

10 Where the Content Is: The Document Body   171

11 Displaying Text in Lists   203

12 Adding Graphics to HTML Documents 221

13 Linking HTML Documents to Other Information Sources 251

14 Point and Click Navigating with Image Maps 271

IX Appendixes — **509**

Introduction

"The bourgeoisie, by the rapid improvement of all instruments of production, by the immensely facilitated means of communication, draws all, even the most barbarian, nations into civilization."

—Karl Marx and Friedrich Engels, *The Communist Manifesto*

I suppose beginning a computer "how to" book with a reference to *The Communist Manifesto* is akin to the Pope beginning a sermon with "you know, a funny thing happened to me on the way to the pulpit..." but the point made almost 150 years ago has a ring of truth in today's global society: the fantastic growth and popularity of one modern form of communication—the Internet—has drawn together over 150 countries around the world into an electronic community. The sheer size of this global market—over 20 million people—is ten times larger than any single commercial online venture.

We are the bourgeoisie of the twenty-first century, the "haves" whose participation in the electronic pageant of digital information separates us from the "have nots." The only difference is, no one owns the store this time. The Internet is not the property of a few, but of the entire community. Each of us pays for our part, and, in turn, benefits from everyones' contributions.

Like any open system that has come before, the Internet is a swift evolving beast. In the last three years, the World Wide Web has taken root on the Internet and excited people as they haven't been in many years. Here is a community—a global marketplace—that is increasing beyond the dreams of its originators.

From a business perspective, this is a virgin market, ripe with opportunity to break ground on a new business paradigm. From a user perspective, the World Wide Web is an endless ocean of data and presentation, complete with text, images, sounds, and moving pictures. From a creative perspective, the World Wide Web is an audience to beat all audiences, with its own whims, interests, and expectations.

Tip
The WWW is about communication. Learning to use it effectively means knowing how to communicate your ideas and information in a way that users around the world will understand.

This book is concerned with all three of these perspectives. The World Wide Web is built on a foundation of documents, and these documents are a combination of content and HTML: the content is whatever you want to bring to the party, and HTML is the way you get it there. HTML, which stands for HyperText Markup Language, is the grammar of the WWW, and your information is the message.

Is HTML Programming?

There is a common perception that HTML is a programming language and is therefore reserved for the technically literate. This perception is endorsed (and often promulgated) by the growing army of HTML programmers, who see the new World Wide Web marketplace as an employment opportunity. And it's an excellent opportunity for these people. But make no mistake, calling HTML a programming language is like calling a janitor a sanitation engineer—it sounds nice but anyone can learn to scrub a floor with a little knowledge and effort.

HTML is a *markup language:* a set of indicators (called *elements*) that define text and document objects and can be incorporated right in your favorite word processor. Remember your high school English class and the red marks you received on your papers indicating missed capitalization and places where new paragraphs were needed? HTML uses the same vocabulary; it "marks up" your existing document with notations to tell the software reading the document where a new paragraph begins, or that certain text is a section heading or has a strong emphasis.

Tip
Using HTML is a lot like using a style sheet in your favorite word processor.

HTML is a versatile language, allowing authors to format text and create relationships (called *hypertext links*) between text and another document (or another portion of the same document). To write HTML, you don't have to work on any one computer platform; it's a neutral language, completely transportable across any flavor of desktop. You can do some pretty sophisticated things with HTML, which are covered throughout this book.

> **What Is "Hypertext?"**
>
> Hypertext is a tool that links information together. Hypertext links (or *hyperlinks*) create associations between disparate sources; a word in one Web document can link with its text definition, a video clip, a sound bite, or a separate document that explores the word as a unique subject. In a hyperlink, the text that provides the link should be related to the information it will access when the link is selected.

For example, the text phrase "Australia" in a Web document can be *hot,* or an available hyperlink that retrieves additional information about Australia and displays it on the user's viewer, regardless of what the original document was about (see fig. I.1).

Hyperlinks don't have to point to other text documents; the WWW supports links to binary file transfers, searchable databases, UNIX sessions on remote computers, e-mail messages, and more. The WWW also supports the use of graphics as links (commonly referred to as *hypermedia,* although the generic *hyperlink* is just as familiar) to the same resources as hypertext links. These links are intuitive interfaces to information and resources on the Internet—a virtual web of connections.

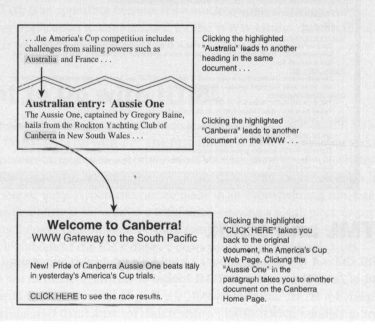

Fig. I.1
Each arrow represents a link to another document or information resource.

HTML as Desktop Publishing

The WWW is generally considered an avenue for electronic publishing; documents that are accessible on a Web site can be viewed by Internet users around the world. A document that appears on a Web host in Los Angeles can almost instantaneously arrive on a London desktop with the click of a mouse button. The document can incorporate text of different sizes, weights, and styles as well as color graphics and links to associated files of practically any media format. HTML is the language spoken by these documents: the combination of nearly any type of content and HTML coding. Figure I.2

> **Note**
>
> URLs, Uniform Resource Locators, are like postal addresses for WWW documents. You must enter them exactly, including capitalization or the lack thereof. URLs are further described in Chapter 8.

Paris Home Page (**http://meteora.ucsd.edu:80/~norman/paris**). Tour the City of Lights, from its monuments and museums to the Metro. Includes a theater season calendar.

Pathfinder (**http://www.timeinc.com/pathfinder/welcome. html**). Time Warner's gateway to the Web includes links to magazines such as *Time*, *Vibe*, and *Sports Illustrated*. Daily editions of *Time* and *Money Watch* are online here.

Internal Revenue Service (**http://www.ustreas.gov/treasury/ bureaus/irs/irs.html**). Includes tax forms, a Frequently Asked Questions resource, and filing locations for around the country.

Games Domain (**http://wcl-rs.bham.ac.uk/GamesDomain**). The most comprehensive collection of computer game tips and archives, including game walk-throughs (in HTML) and links to hundreds of other game resources.

The Electronic Gourmet Guide (**http://www.deltanet.com/2way/ egg**). A full-color online magazine devoted to gourmet food, including recipes, columns, news, and links to other food-related resources.

A Tourist Expedition to Antarctica (**http://http2.sils.umich.edu/ Antarctica/Story.html**). Ride along with a voyage to Antarctica, complete with high-quality photographs and daily trip updates.

Apple World Wide Web Home Page (**http://www.info.apple.com**). Apple Computer's page with product information and links to other Mac-related resources.

Internet Shopping Network (**http://www.internet.net/**). The Home Shopping Network's online shopping service.

Powell's Technical Books (**http://www.technical.powells. portland.or.us/**). Search their extensive database of books for sale by subject from one of the finest bookstores in the country.

MGM/Stargate (**http://www.earthlink.net:80/STARGATE/**). Behind the scenes look at MGM's 1994 hit film, including effects sketches and cast and crew biographies.

The Nine Planets (**http://seds.lpl.arizona.edu/nineplanets/ nineplanets/nineplanets.html**). Tour the Solar System and explore each planet; browse through statistics for each planet and its moons.

When creating HTML documents, consider the audience you expect will view your work. A recent article on executive travel to foreign countries gave some advice I think applies very well to creating HTML documents for wide distribution over the WWW: *when writing World Wide Web documents, be careful to get your message across*. Don't assume your audience has a perfect understanding of the English language, and anticipate the direction of your content so you can "frame" it properly—or present it in the most accessible format and manner. Clearly state your purpose and your relationship to the information you are presenting. If it's important enough for you to publish for a worldwide audience, take the time to do it well.

What This Book Is

This book is intended to provide a comprehensive reference and guide to developing effective World Wide Web applications using HTML and its related tools. Although the majority of Internet and WWW users are accessing the Net from Windows, this book emphasizes HTML's greatest strength: its platform-independence. Tools and procedures for Windows, Macintosh, and (to a lesser extent) UNIX system users are presented as they apply.

Who should use this book? Anyone with an interest in "electronic publishing" via the World Wide Web, either for personal or commercial purposes. Users who need a simple information distribution system in-house will want to take a close look at HTML, as will companies ready to get connected to the Internet and reach out to a new global audience. The WWW, as well as HTML, exist to make using the Internet easier. To use this book, you only need a basic understanding of the Internet and the willingness to apply your creativity to a new and exciting medium.

Here is a brief overview of the contents of the book with a short description of each part:

Part I, "The Internet and the World Wide Web," takes a look at the histories and philosophies behind the Internet and its various information systems (including the newest system, the World Wide Web).

Part II, "How HTML Documents Reach Your Desktop," discusses the components of the system, from the host server to the desktop, and gives a general overview of HTML. After all, HTML is pretty useless without a distribution system.

Part III, "Creating HTML Documents," includes chapters that explore the common "standard and practices" in HTML and creating HTML documents from top to bottom.

Part IV, "Using Forms in HTML Documents," teaches you how to incorporate forms into documents for collecting user input and activating scripts and programs on your Web server.

Part V, "HTML 3.0," describes the "next generation" of HTML, including some of the advanced features already finding support in today's environment.

In Part VI, "Document Aesthetics," you see why HTML is not just a programming tool, it's an artistic expression. This part discusses how to enhance your use of text and graphic elements in Web pages.

Part VII, "Sample HTML Applications," describes how building well-designed Web sites is often best seen as a development process by presenting two sample applications from start to finish.

Part VIII, "HTML Editors and Style Sheets," shows you the tools of the trade, from stand-alone editors to style sheets for popular word processors.

Appendix A, "HTML Elements Reference," lists every HTML 2.0 element, plus Netscape extensions and selected HTML 3.0 elements, with their proper usage and syntax.

Appendix B, "WWW Bibliography," includes an extensive reference list of Internet, WWW, and HTML resources available over the Internet and the World Wide Web.

Appendix C, "What's on the CD-ROM?," provides a list of the bundled software on the HTMLCD disk included in this book. Many of the primary tools and utilities are described in detail to help you find the ones that best suit your needs.

Appendix D, "HTML Level 2 Definition Type Document," prints the official description (written in SGML) for the current HTML standard, version 2.0.

Appendix E, "HTML Level 3 Definition Type Document," is the "rough draft" SGML description of the upcoming revision to HTML.

Appendix F, "The Bare Bones Guide to HTML," was written by Kevin Werbach, and provides quick-and-dirty descriptions of all the HTML tags. It's a concise "cheat sheet" to virtually all of the HTML 2.0 tags, as well as the popular—but not standard—Netscape extensions.

What This Book Is Not

This book does not provide more than a brief overview of the Internet and the information systems other than the World Wide Web. It is not a tutorial about getting connected to the Net, nor is it a guide for setting up your own World Wide Web server. However, the necessary tools are included on the CD-ROM as an added value.

For further information regarding the Internet and its related tools, pick up a book such as "Special Edition Using the Internet" (a comprehensive reference) or "Using the Internet" (a shorter, user-friendly reference), both available from Que.

Conventions Used in This Book

Certain conventions are used in *Special Edition Using HTML* to help you more easily use this book and understand HTML concepts.

Text that is representative of on-screen messages will look like this. New terms are introduced in *italic* type, and text that you type appears in **boldface**. World Wide Web URLs (essentially document addresses) are also presented in **boldface**. HTML code elements, tags, and tag attributes are always in FULL CAPS. (HTML is not case-sensitive—this is purely a convention that makes the HTML examples and text easier to read.)

Tip

This paragraph format suggests easier or alternate methods of executing a procedure.

Part I

The Internet and the World Wide Web

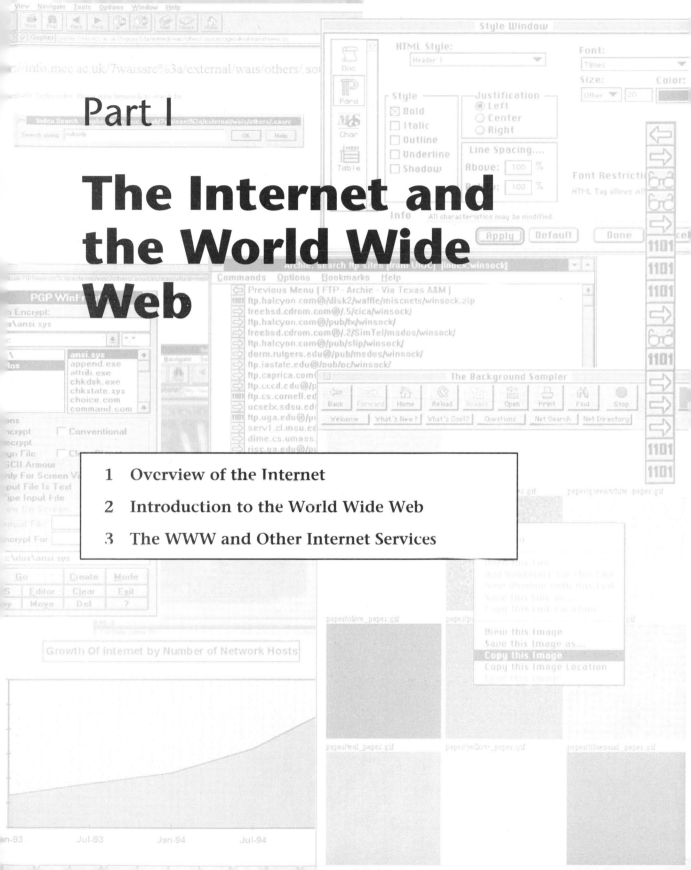

Chapter 1

Overview of the Internet

"The Internet is awash with information, both useful and banal. In a very real sense, the entire Internet is becoming one extremely large, globally distributed, and mostly public electronic library, post office, and discussion forum. The Internet evolved with a strong and explicit philosophy of sharing information (mail, documents, programs, data, and graphics), and that perspective has dominated how the system works today."

—Thomas F. Mandel, "Surfing the Wild Internet"
(at **gopher://sepa1.bio.cmu.edu/**)

In "computer years" (a measurement very close to "dog years," for what that's worth), the Internet has had a long history of public service. It was born as ARPANET, the Department of Defense's internetwork created to simplify the exchange of information between government-contracted developers and defense researchers. At the time, no one suspected how large ARPANET (and its associated networks) would become.

Today, the *Internet* is an all-encompassing term that describes a complex interconnection of international networks. These smaller networks connect to the "backbone," or NSFNET, and serve well over 20 million users in more than 80 countries around the world (over 150 countries have at least e-mail service).

This chapter answers the following questions:

- How did the Internet get started?
- When did the Internet move into public and commercial use?
- What distribution services have emerged?
- Who uses the Internet today?

Growth of the Internet

Figure 1.1 shows how fast the Internet has grown in just the last two years. (You can find this information at **http://www.nw.com/zone/WWW /report.html**.)

Fig. 1.1
The tremendous increase in the number of Internet *hosts* (the computers attached to the Internet's physical network) has shown no signs of slowing.

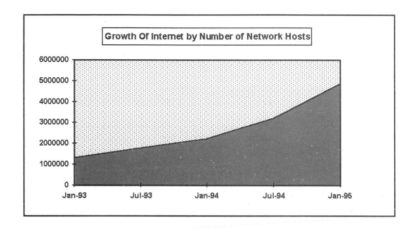

Other statistics also point out the fantastic worldwide growth of the Internet's infrastructure. Table 1.1 shows the results of a recent survey of Internet resources.

Table 1.1 Internet Growth: Number of Hosts, Domains, and Nets					
Date	Hosts	Domains	Class A Networks	Class B Networks	Class C Networks
Jan 95	4,852,000	71,000	91	4,979	34,340
Jul 94	3,212,000	46,000	89	4,493	20,628
Jan 94	2,217,000	30,000	74	4,043	16,422
Jul 93	1,776,000	26,000	67	3,728	9,972
Jan 93	1,313,000	21,000	54	3,206	4,998

From the "Internet Domain Survey, January 1995," produced by Network Wizards (http://www.nw.com/)

> **Note**
>
> The Internet is composed of thousands of computers—*hosts*—and subnetworks worldwide. Three types of networks are registered: Type A (the largest), Type B, and Type C (the smallest). *Domains* identify unique top-level Net addresses, such as "nw.com". Subdomains, such as "www.nw.com" organize the network structure within a domain.

In fact, the Internet Index reports that a new network connection (Class A, B, or C) occurs an average of every 30 minutes, and over 1,500 new domains are registered a month. It has even been estimated that, at the current pace, every person on the planet will have access to the Internet by 2003—*less than 10 years from now*. If there were ever a time to take a serious look at the direction the Internet is taking, and how users—and consumers—will be using these resources, it's now.

▶ See "Defining URLs in HTML Documents," p. 143

> **Note**
>
> Many of the statistics mentioned in this chapter are drawn from the Internet Index, a regular electronic publication inspired by Harper's Index. You can find the current Internet Index (and all archived issues) at the URL **http://www.openmarket.com /info/internet-index/**.

A Commercial Internet

A few years ago, all of this growth presented a slight problem for the architects of the Internet. Public use was at an all-time high and continuing to grow dramatically. A restless user base began asking for public and consumer services on the Net. Corporations eyed the swelling user base and began champing at the bit to get at that mass of consumers.

The National Science Foundation, which provided the critical funding for NSFNET (the backbone that carries the bulk of the data between hosts on the Internet), had policies that forbid commercial use of the Internet. To meet the expectations of both users and businesses, the government has reconsidered its financial support of NSFNET. As the uses of the Internet have changed, so has come a changing of the guard.

First, the Commercial Internet Exchange (CIX) pieced together a redundant backbone to duplicate NSFNET's services. CIX offered memberships to businesses and for-profit organizations to carry their traffic over their backbone, sidestepping the NSFNET's restrictions.

When the government began to sell the idea of a National Information Infrastructure, the overhyped Information Superhighway, the NSF began shifting its data load over to commercial carriers, such as MCI (who had already been providing much of the wire for the Internet for years). Soon, NFSNET will no longer be a part of the Internet infrastructure, and the commercialization of the Net will be complete. Business consortiums like CommerceNet are already working to provide a streamlined virtual marketplace and business park to promote secured commerce on the Internet.

What does this mean to end users and content providers (such as Web page authors)? There will be a new way of looking at the Internet. It won't be the domain of computer geeks and tech-heads for much longer. As communications services (like real-time voice and video) come online and are widely embraced, the Internet will become as familiar in our lives as another commonplace household appliance. As writer Peter Huber (**72643.2211@ compuserve.com**) recently commented in an article in the December 19, 1994 issue of *Forbes,* "The Internet is like telephone, not television. Viewers have the equivalent of *TV Guide* and the whole phone directory at their fingertips—not just Oshkosh stations and listings, but New York's and Tokyo's, too."

> **Note**
>
> Real-time voice communications is not a goal for the future of the Internet—it's here today. A World Wide Web application uses personal computer sound hardware to record and play packets of live audio data. Today, users on different sides of the globe are talking to each other for no more than the cost of their Internet connections.
>
> The application is InterPhone (**http://www.vocaltec.com/**). A shareware version of the software is available, letting you talk to your party for 10 minutes at a time. The commercial version is available for around $50; check with the home page for more details.

And it won't be cheap, either. As the government shifts control into the private sector, and as the hardware that connects the Internet (and Internet hosts themselves) is improved to support faster data rates—you do want "Internet video on demand," don't you?—the support costs will climb. Corporations and universities that were accustomed to spending $50,000 to $100,000 a year to maintain their Internet hardware are going to see those costs climb into the range of $500,000 or more. Facility costs will not just trickle downhill, they will cascade onto the user base. It may come to pass that usage is measured per minute or per transaction, and the consumers will begin to bear much more of the cost to support the Internet than they do today.

The Internet's Information Systems

As I pointed out, the *Internet* is a description of the infrastructure of the Net: the vast array of international computer networks. But there's another side to the term Internet, one which describes the function of this supernetwork and deals with the real equity in the system: the software.

The Internet supports a wide assortment of software *protocols,* or communication rules and structures, to traffic information from host to desktop, desktop to host, and host to host. These protocols often work together to get the job done. For instance, one protocol may manage the transfer of data between two points (like TCP/IP) while another handles the format of the data and its use (like Gopher).

Protocols such as Gopher, which deal mainly with the delivery and management of information, are called *distributed information systems.* Other protocols, such as UseNet, are derived from networks that are not a part of the Internet but that are accessible to Internet users.

The Internet supports a variety of protocols, each with their particular strengths and weaknesses. These include:

- *File Transfer Protocol,* a protocol for transferring binary and ASCII text files to and from Internet-connected host and desktop computer systems.

- *Gopher,* a protocol that uses a menu hierarchy to organize and access information from any Internet host running Gopher servers.

- *World Wide Web,* a protocol that distributes information via hypertext-capable documents to users running WWW client software, such as Lynx and Mosaic. See Chapter 3 for more information on the WWW.

> **Note**
>
> New Internet providers sprout up every day. Services and prices change rapidly as the market matures (no wonder there's a resource for looking up Internet providers). Point your WWW client to the URL **http://www.teleport.com/~cci/directories/directories.html**. The Internet Directory provides a list of current providers searchable by area code. A second resource, Commercial Sites Index (**http://www.directory.net/**) lists additional resources for the user looking to get set up online.

Deciphering Internet Addresses

It's one thing knowing someone is online on the Internet or on another commercial online service—it's another to find them and figure out how to contact them. The Internet uses a standard naming format (to manage the rapidly growing user and host base) known as the *Domain Name System,* or DNS. DNS addresses are composed of two halves: the user's account name and the host address. The format looks like

> *username@hostname.subdomain.domain*

where:

- *username.* The account name, such as tsavola and prez.

- *hostname.* The host (or computer) on which that account is maintained, such as darmok and www.

- *subdomain.* The organization's name in DNS, such as uoregon and whitehouse.

- *domain.* The base DNS category or branch, such as edu, com, or gov.

For its simplicity, the DNS will meet the needs of Internet users well into the foreseeable future.

Other services often use their own naming schemes. As the DNS addressing scheme becomes more popular, other network systems are converting to its naming constructs.

"What's Your Domain?"

You can tell a lot about a user based on the domain value of his address. There are standard domains for different types of organizations, and these are adhered to fairly strictly. Table 1.2 lists the most common domains and their related organization categories.

Table 1.2 DNS Domain Branches		
Domain	**Organization Type**	**Example**
edu	Educational institutions	**www.usc.edu**
com	Commercial entities	**ibm.com**
org	Common organizations	**w3.org**
net	Network providers	**holonet.net**
mil	Military organizations	**dt.navy.mil**
gov	Government institutions	**nasa.gov**
ca	Canadian computing sites	**mcgill.ca**
uk	United Kingdom computing sites	**leeks.ac.uk**
au	Australian computing sites	**ulas.edu.au**

Other non-US networks also have unique domains based on their country of origin (like Germany and Taiwan). There is even an implementation of a .US domain for regional network addresses in the United States, but it is used very infrequently.

A DNS address can include more than one subdomain, depending on the organization's computer system hierarchy.

Reach Out and Mail Someone

It's easy to send mail to another Internet user—just plug his Internet address into your mail message's Recipient line and away it goes. It's already possible to send e-mail directly to proprietary network systems via Internet gateways. For instance, to send a mail message to user P Johnny on America Online (AOL), the DNS address would be pjohnny@aol.com. (Note: all characters must be in lowercase when sending mail from the Internet to AOL; sending mail to an AOL user while on the AOL system will follow AOL's mail conventions). Similar constructs exists for other services, as shown in Table 1.3.

Table 1.3	Electronic Mail Conversions	
Service	**Recipient Account**	**Internet Mail Format**
CompuServe	74262,3171	74262.3171@compuserve.com
Prodigy	wxyz99a	wxyz99a@prodigy.com
GEnie	toady	toady@genie.geis.com
Applelink	toady	toady@applelink.apple.com
ATT mail	toady	toady@attmail.com
MCI mail	Albert Toady (555-1234)	5551234@mcimail.com
MCI mail (alt.)	Albert Toady (if "AToady" is unique)	AToady@mcimail.com
Fidonet	Albert Toady at 1:2/3:4	albert.toady@p4.f3. n2.z1.fidonet.org

Note

Information services use a variety of formats for user IDs. CompuServe, for instance, still relies on an outdated 7-bit ID system—resulting in the unusual "two-part" numbered user IDs. Your mail program should allow you to create *recipient* listings or address book entries to automate hard-to-remember mail addresses.

For mail exchange formats for many more networks, as well as instructions on sending mail from other networks to each other and the Internet, see Scott Yanoff's "Inter-Network Mail Guide," available by FTP from **ftp.csd.uwm.edu** or from the WWW URL **http://alpha.acast.nova. edu/cgi-bin/inmgq.pl**.

Finding an Internet Address

Sending e-mail is easy if you know where to send it. But what if you don't have a person's e-mail address? Is there an easy way to get it?

The answer is both yes and no. While there are a few standard directories and services you can refer to, their listings are not comprehensive or even up to date (and some are voluntary, requiring users to register their e-mail addresses with the service). And unless you have direct access to any of the proprietary online services, you won't be able to access their member directories.

Note

Sometimes finding out the e-mail address of a colleague or friend on another online service is as easy as asking. Internet users often post open requests for e-mail addresses in UseNet public discussions. Each online service has its own "special interest group" newsgroup. Refer to the following table to find the newsgroup associated with a particular service, and don't be afraid to ask for help!

Service	Network News Newsgroup
America Online	**alt.online-service.america-online**
CompuServe	**alt.online-service.compuserve**
Prodigy	**alt.online-service.prodigy**
GEnie	**alt.online-service.genie**
Delphi	**alt.online-service.delphi**
Imagination	**alt.online-service.imagination**

The most comprehensive address search facility is Netfind, available via Telnet (the Internet's remote login application). By connecting to **eis.calstate.edu** and logging in as **netfind**, you can locate users on Internet-connected network hosts around the globe. All you need to know is their name and their domain. Figure 1.2 shows a Netfind session in progress.

Fig. 1.2
When entering the search parameters for Netfind, replace the separating periods with regular spaces.

A second Telnet option is to connect to **info.cnri.reston.va.us,** and use the Knowbot Information Service. The Knowbot has access to a wide variety of address lists, and may be able to locate your user by name alone. Figure 1.3 shows a typical query on the Knowbot.

Fig. 1.3
You can also query the Knowbot by mail at **kis@cnri. reston.va.us**; include your query statements in the body of your mail message (such as **query Tom Savola**).

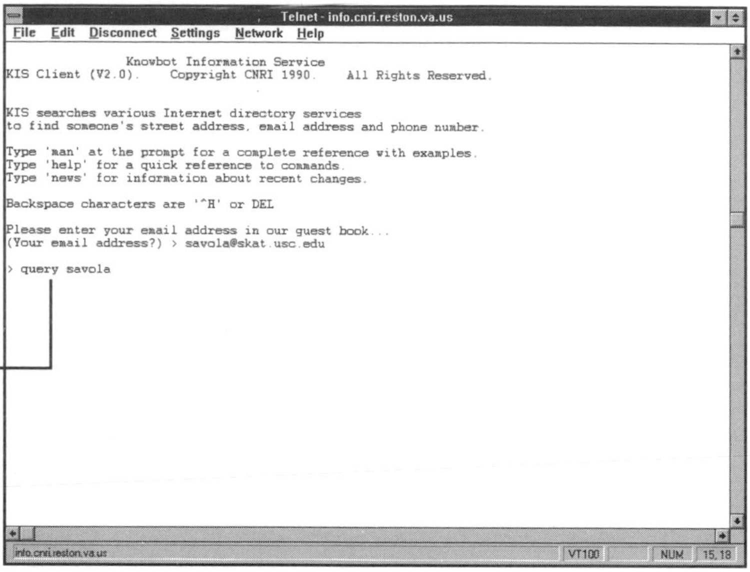

Knowbot query
statement

```
┌──────────────────────────────────────────────────────────────────────────┐
│ ▫                    Telnet - info.cnri.reston.va.us              ▾ ♦     │
│ File  Edit  Disconnect  Settings  Network  Help                          │
│ ┌──────────────────────────────────────────────────────────────────┬───┐ │
│ │                  Knowbot Information Service                      │ ▲ │ │
│ │KIS Client (V2.0).    Copyright CNRI 1990.    All Rights Reserved. │   │ │
│ │                                                                  │   │ │
│ │KIS searches various Internet directory services                 │   │ │
│ │to find someone's street address, email address and phone number. │   │ │
│ │                                                                  │   │ │
│ │Type 'man' at the prompt for a complete reference with examples.  │   │ │
│ │Type 'help' for a quick reference to commands.                    │   │ │
│ │Type 'news' for information about recent changes.                 │   │ │
│ │                                                                  │   │ │
│ │Backspace characters are '^H' or DEL                              │   │ │
│ │                                                                  │   │ │
│ │Please enter your email address in our guest book...              │   │ │
│ │(Your email address?) > savola@skat.usc.edu                       │   │ │
│ │                                                                  │   │ │
│ │> query savola                                                    │   │ │
│ │                                                                  │   │ │
│ │                                                                  │ ▼ │ │
│ │◄ ▯                                                               │   │ │
│ ├──────────────────────────────────────────────────────────┬──────┴───┤ │
│ │info.cnri.reston.va.us                          │VT100│      │NUM│15,18│ │
│ └──────────────────────────────────────────────────────────┴──────────┘ │
└──────────────────────────────────────────────────────────────────────────┘
```

The WWW also has an e-mail address search alternative. The Four11 Online User Directory is a searchable directory that also allows users to add themselves to the directory via e-mail. After you're entered in the directory, Four11 allows you to search the database (they provide you a password for access). Figure 1.4 shows a search session on Four11's Web page.

Caution

Depending on your Web viewer, the search form may look slightly different: however, all of the appropriate input fields and the Submit button will be available for entering your search criteria.

Four11 will eventually offer additional services, like a PGP public key database for use with sending encrypted information to other users across the Internet.

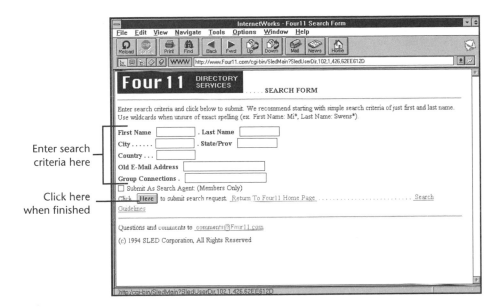

Enter search criteria here

Click here when finished

Fig. 1.4
Searches on the Four11 database are currently free, although in the future they may charge a transaction fee.

Overview

From Here...

Now that you've got a general understanding of the Internet and how people use it, it's time for a closer look at the information distribution system that delivers HTML documents, the World Wide Web, and how it relates to other Internet services. Refer to the following chapters and sections to learn about the HTML distribution and document creation:

- Chapter 2, "Introduction to the World Wide Web," provides an overview of the development and goals of the World Wide Web, the Internet's busiest information service.

- Chapter 3, "The WWW and Other Internet Services," looks into the relationship between the World Wide Web and the rest of the Internet's information distribution systems, including Gopher and File Transfer Protocol.

- Chapter 7, "Distributing Information with HTML," describes the advantages and disadvantages of using HTML documents for distributing and retrieving information across the Internet and on your own local area network (LAN).

- Part III, "Creating HTML Documents," is the place to go if you're ready to get down to business. Includes chapters on common standards and practices in HTML and creating HTML documents from top to bottom.

Chapter 2

Introduction to the World Wide Web

"For fifty years, people have dreamt of the concept of a universal information database—data that would not only be accessible to people around the world, but information that would link easily to other pieces of information so that only the most important data would be quickly found by a user. It was in the 1960's when this idea was explored further, giving rise to visions of a "docuverse" that people could swim through, revolutionizing all aspects of human-information interaction, particularly in the educational field. Only now has the technology caught up with these dreams, making it possible to implement them on a global scale."

—Kevin Hughes, "Entering the World-Wide Web: A Guide to Cyberspace" (at **http://epics.aps.anl.gov/demo/guide www.guide.html**)

Hang around the Internet long enough and you'll come across the catch phrase, "information wants to be free." Regardless of whether information can have desires of its own, the Internet culture has grown around this concept of free and readily available information. The World Wide Web, born out of much of the same philosophical beliefs, provides the greatest opportunity for creating a truly global information society.

This chapter answers the following questions:

- When did the World Wide Web begin?

- What is its purpose?

- How does it distribute information across the Internet?

- What resources are available on the Web?

- Who uses the WWW?

Origins of the Web

In March, 1989, Tim Berners-Lee at the European Laboratory for Particle Physics (more popularly known as CERN), proposed a new set of protocols for an Internet information distribution system to be used among various high energy physics research groups. The World Wide Web protocols were soon adopted by other organizations and a consortium of organizations was formed, called the W3 Consortium, to pool their resources for the continued development of WWW standards. (For more information, see Chapter 19, "Extending the Standard.")

▶ See "HTML's DTD," p. 67

The consortium is led by the Massachusetts Institute of Technology (MIT), CERN, and INRA (the French National Institute for Research in Computer Science and Control). This consortium proposes new and more sophisticated features for HTML, evaluates suggestions and alternate implementations, and publishes new *levels* or versions of the HTML standard. The current standard is Level 2; Level 3 will be published in late 1995. Many features that will be new in Level 3 are already implemented by client software, and authors can use the proposed HTML features with this audience in mind. See Part V, "HTML 3.0," for more information about upcoming changes to HTML.

▶ See "The Internet's Information Services," p. 38

The WWW is officially described as a "wide-area hypermedia information retrieval initiative." It's an information system that links data from many different Internet services under one set of protocols (called the World Wide Web). Web clients (also called *browsers* or *viewers*) interpret HyperText Markup Language documents delivered from Web servers.

These documents use hypertext links to connect different documents and information resources together; click a link and the client software retrieves the linked document or jumps to a specific position in the current document. These links can access Web pages, Gopher menus, File Transfer Protocol (FTP) file directories, Wide Area Information Service (WAIS) databases, and more.

Web servers and Web viewers communicate with each other using a protocol called the HyperText Transmission Protocol (HTTP). This protocol associates certain characteristics about the documents they are sending so that the client software interprets the data correctly. If this relationship between the function of the data and protocol did not exist, a viewer wouldn't know it was supposed to translate the document from its ASCII text format into the intended HTML-coded format.

Note

HTTP is the great equalizer: it lets you create HTML documents on any platform (such as UNIX) and deliver them in a consistent manner to any other platform (such as the Macintosh). If your server can deliver the document, anyone can view it as you created it.

Note

HTML documents use elements to "mark up," or identify, sections of text for different purposes or display characteristics. These elements are invisible to the user; they are not displayed in the viewer's text window when the page is retrieved.

It's easy to take a look at a Web page's HTML formatting. Many viewers provide a feature that allows the user to view the "source" of the current document; nearly all allow you to save the current document as an HTML type document (saving as a text file may save the information as it is displayed in the viewer's window without including the HTML elements). The HTML source view (or document) includes all of the page's hidden codes, as well as any author comments and additional document-level information not displayed by the client software.

Tip
If you're anxious to see how HTML 3.0 will work (and you use a networked UNIX system, or any environment running X Windows), point your Web viewer to the home page for Arena, the HTML 3.0 test bed viewer (**http:// www. w3.org/ hypertext/ WWW/Arena/**).

The WWW's protocol support is easily modified to incorporate new data formats and uses. The Web model successfully unites the diverse Internet resources under a single system, relying on servers and Web viewers to "negotiate" or handle data compatibility. Basically, Internet data formats and ways they are transported and handled by the software goes on "behind the scenes," invisible to the user. This strength of HTTP (and the associated advantages it provides HTML) will lead to new and creative uses of WWW technology in the protocol's original design limits.

▶ See "The Client/Server Relationship," p. 123

▶ See "Using NCSA Mosaic," p. 84

Mosaic Made It Simple

Soon after CERN developed the basic protocols for the WWW, the National Center for Supercomputing Applications (NCSA) undertook the task of creating an interface for the service. The goal of the interface was to provide a graphical, easy-to-use application that would stimulate commercial development and support of the WWW. NCSA developed their front-end simultaneously for three platforms: UNIX (running the X Window graphical environment), the Macintosh, and Microsoft Windows. They dubbed their interface Mosaic (see fig. 2.1). Its release, in 1993, further spurred on the Internet revolution that has made the WWW the most popular Internet service in use today.

Note

Operating systems on PC computers are in the midst of evolving to 32-bit environments. To use the upcoming 2.0 release of NCSA Mosaic, Windows users must install the Win32s 32-bit extensions. Netscape users have a choice between 16- and 32-bit products for Netscape 1.1.

Fig. 2.1
NCSA Mosaic brought the familiarity of a graphical interface, complete with pull-down menus and an icon bar, to the WWW. Due to its ground-breaking success, many people mistakenly call the World Wide Web "Mosaic."

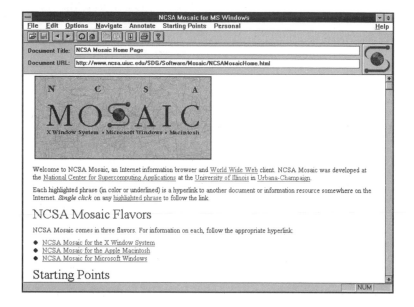

▶ See "Using Netscape Navigator," p. 96

Note

While Mosaic may be the most recognizable viewer for the WWW, it isn't the most popular. According to *The New York Times,* a study of more than 72,000 WWW users has found that about four out of five use a competing product, Netscape Communications Netscape Navigator. Only 14 percent of the respondents said they used Mosaic as their primary Web browser.

Why is Netscape so popular? Its developers pushed the Web viewer envelope from the beginning, delivering a product that can load HTML documents faster and that will use a series of versatile "non-standard" HTML commands to enhance document layout and design.

Netscape has encouraged users to utilize the new HTML extensions to persuade the WWW architects to adopt the changes in the upcoming new HTML standard through common usage (sort of like "voting with your dollars"). With some of the concessions to Netscape's extensions in early drafts of HTML 3, it looks like a "mandate of the masses" approach can be successful with the right product.

What and Who Are on the Web?

The World Wide Web distributes information and links to resources via Web pages. These documents are often called *home pages,* because many represent a starting point from which to explore Web sites; home pages can incorporate formatted text, color graphics, digitized sound, and digital video clips. WWW clients can display Web pages with the various data, using external utility programs to *view* or handle data formats they do not process themselves.

The WWW is capable of accessing data on many different Internet services. The following list of WWW resources was originally provided by Kevin Hughes of Honolulu Community College in his online publication "Entering the World-Wide Web: A Guide to Cyberspace" (**http://epics.aps.anl.gov /demo/guide/www.guide.html**).

- Anything served through Gopher
- Anything served through WAIS
- Anything served through anonymous FTP sites
- Full Archie services (an FTP search service)
- Full Veronica services (a Gopher search service)
- Full CSO, X.500, and "whois" services (Internet phone book services)
- Full Finger services (an Internet user lookup program)
- Any library system using PALS (a library database standard)
- Anything on UseNet
- Anything accessible through Telnet
- Anything in Hytelnet (a hypertext interface to Telnet)
- Anything in techinfo or texinfo (forms of campus-wide information services)
- Anything in hyper-g (a networked hypertext system in use throughout Europe)
- Anything in the form of man pages
- HTML-formatted hypertext and hypermedia documents

> **Note**
>
> Although the WWW lacks a common index for every resource available over the Web, search engines are becoming increasingly sophisticated. For a look at the "next generation" engine, see the home page for the University of Colorado's Harvest tools (**http://harvest.cs.colorado.edu**).

Most users will be familiar with the Web through the final item, HTML-formatted documents. They are the "programming" for the WWW network; by opening the appropriate URL (see the following note), Web sites deliver the requested document to the user desktop.

> **Note**
>
> HTML documents use Uniform Resource Locators (URLs) to describe the absolute or relative locations of information. A URL is like a street address; it can be to-the-letter exact (1212 Main Street, Oakville, California), or it can be a reference from an assumed location (the third house down the street and on the left). URLs are the key to the WWW hypertext support and can point to information on any Internet service. They can also be used to read UseNet newsgroups and send e-mail to a specified recipient.

Where cable can deliver hundreds of channels of programming, the Web can deliver hundreds of thousands of documents, with thousands more coming online every week.

Tip
To see the depth of available Web sites, or to browse for something new and interesting, go to the Yahoo Web Guide (**http://akebono.stanford.edu/yahoo/**). This site links to an impressive number of Web resources in dozens of categories.

Web pages can serve many functions. They can be purely informative, they can be entertaining, they can even be completely irrelevant. Like other publications (or even advertising), Web pages are representative of their creators. Companies, like Sun, express their casual and loose corporate culture through their home pages (URL: **http://ww.sun.com/**). Others, like *Time,* Inc., strive to maintain the same level of professionalism on the Web that they deliver through their magazines (URL: **http://www.timeinc.com/pathfinder/Welcome.html**).

People tend to create personal home pages that express their individualism. There's probably a psychological study being done somewhere about identity and the Internet, but I'll save you the theory and jargon and just say this: self-publishing is liberating, it's novel, and it's conducive to creativity. It's the outlet every frustrated writer has dreamed of. Create your own documents with whatever content you want. Publish them to an audience of millions. Get instant gratification through e-mail feedback.

The Web's commercial aspect is growing rapidly. Services from flower delivery to book and music catalogs to corporate-image consulting are all available on the Web. Business is going to drive the Internet (and the WWW) in new and interesting directions. The WWW is definitely a consumer's market because, unlike broadcast media, this time *users* control the access. They choose what links they access, which ones they add to their lists of bookmarks (so they can return to them later), and which ones they promptly forget, letting the URLs fade into the rising tide of Web sites. Companies are just beginning to find out what this market will support and how to make it work for them.

▶ See "Commercial Applications in HTML," p. 121

> **Note**
>
> The WWW is a relative infant compared to other information-distribution systems, but it has caught the interest and imagination of millions of Net residents. More than 13 million Internet users can access the Web (not every Internet user has either the proper connection, access account, or software to use the Net's interactive services). Traffic on the Web (the amount of data that passes across the Internet's infrastructure between WWW servers and clients) grew an astounding 1713 percent in 1994, nearly 10 times as fast as the growth in Gopher traffic, the next most popular Internet service.

From Here...

The WWW is a rich environment for users and authors alike. To find out more about how the Web relates to other Internet services, or to get down to creating your own HTML documents and applications, see the following chapters and parts:

- Chapter 3, "The WWW and Other Internet Services," looks at the relationship between the World Wide Web and the rest of the Internet's information distribution systems, including Gopher and File Transfer Protocol.

- Chapter 7, "Distributing Information with HTML," describes the advantages and disadvantages of using HTML documents for distributing and retrieving information across the Internet and on your own local area network (LAN).

- If you're ready to get down to business, Part III, "Creating HTML Documents," is the place to go. These chapters include common "standards and practices" in HTML and creating HTML documents from top to bottom.

Tip
Internet wire travels in the same phone wire bundles as regular long distance wires. Internet data traffic is also transmitted by satellite and, as will become more common in the next few years, cable television services.

◄ See "Origins of the Web," p. 30

Tip
For recent Web usage and site statistics, point your Web viewer at the Network Wizard's Internet Domain Survey (**http://www. nw.com/zone/ WWW/top. html**) or to the List of Sites (**http://www. netgen.com/ cgi/comprehen- sive**).

The Internet's Information Services

There is a great human need for collective distribution of data. Remember libraries? They've been around since the Mesopotamian Empire. Aristotle's "teaching library" inspired the creation of the Egyptian library at Alexandria (perhaps the greatest library that ever existed). Information is at the heart of our civilizations and we're still distributing it.

It's no different on the Internet. The system was designed for sharing information between separate research groups (in a redundant system, providing backup pathways for data connections that are disrupted due to an enemy attack—this system *was* born in the Cold War era). Since the end of the Cold War, this redundancy has been most effective at shoring up pathways overloaded by the volume of traffic or those down due to phone service disruptions.

The Internet's information distribution services, the WWW, Gopher, FTP, WAIS, and e-mail, comprise the vast majority of the Internet's traffic. And this volume is growing; the NSFNET (the National Science Foundation's network backbone) saw an increase in traffic in 1994 of 110 percent—even as its use is being phased out. Overall traffic on all backbones is up substantially over the last two years, with no signs of slowing.

The World Wide Web as a "Super Service"

As the newcomer of the Internet services, the World Wide Web is in a position to learn from its elders—file-format support, menu navigation, search features, hypertext capabilities. But one of the things that the WWW seems to do best is imitate its predecessors; the Web can act like a Gopher client, an FTP client, and even provide a WAIS interface. The Web could be called a "super service" as in the prefix "super," meaning "above" or "beyond." Or it could be painted with a cape and a red "S" on its chest. Either way, the WWW can handle just about anything the other services can provide, and sometimes it can even go them one better.

Caution

What the Web supports and what your Web client software supports may be different. More than two dozen different viewers and add-ons are available (or are being developed) that will process HTTP-delivered data, the Web's primary content.

Overview

To increase their marketability, some of these viewers go beyond the basics, incorporating editing tools (such as the Microsoft Internet Assistant) and support for non-traditional data types (such as native WordPerfect documents in Novell's WordPerfect add-on).

Some viewers also lack support for some of the less-popular Internet services (such as Hyper-G). Know the capabilities of your own software before you assume you can access all of the content out on the Web.

WWW and Gopher

Gopher is a distribution system that uses a series of menu lists to connect to resources around the globe. Gopher's menus can contain items that represent text files, binary files, other menu lists for information at the same location (or on a remote computer), Telnet sessions, and searchable databases. Figure 3.1 shows a common Gopher client.

Shows additional documents

Shows information about this Gopher menu

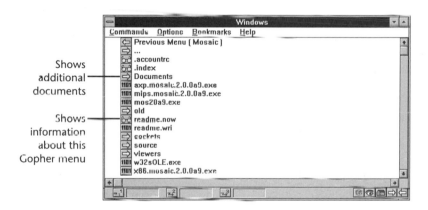

Fig. 3.1
Gopher menu icons represent different types of resources: text and data files, other lists of items, Telnet sessions, and so on.

Gopher is a poor man's WWW: it supports most of the same protocols (except HTTP) but can't handle the graphical and multimedia data types, like bitmap graphics and digital video clips. What Gopher does, it does well, including displaying, saving, and printing ASCII text files and retrieving binary files via FTP.

Gopher is also adept at using searchable databases such as Archie and Veronica. *Archie* is a searchable database of the file directories of nearly every large anonymous FTP file site on the Internet. (An *anonymous FTP site* allows you to connect as a guest, browse any public file directories, and upload or download files from the server to your desktop.) Give Archie a search text string based on the name of a file and Archie will display a list of FTP sites that have a file matching your query (see fig. 3.2).

Tip
Files ending in ZIP are compressed and need to be expanded.

Fig. 3.2
Archie returns a list of all available file listings that match your query; Gopher lets a user choose to connect to a service by selecting the menu item.

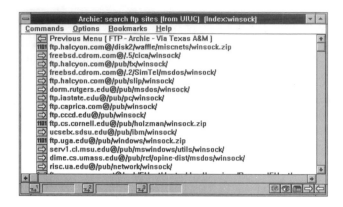

Tip
Not all Web providers have Gopher, Archie, and Veronica, but you can use the Web to access other Internet computers that do provide these services.

Archie query is integrated into Gopher's FTP engine, so an Archie search from within Gopher that returns a file list will also connect to one of the FTP sites, so you can download the file if desired.

Gopher supports searches on *Veronica* as well. This isn't as kinky as it sounds. Veronica is a utility that indexes the titles of menus from a large number of Gopher sites on the Internet. By entering a search string, which can be a single topic or a group of topics, Veronica searches for the appearances of these keywords and creates a menu list of the search results (see fig. 3.3).

Fig. 3.3
Select any menu item in a "search results" menu to connect directly to that Gopher menu or retrieve the item's data file (as you would from a standard Gopher menu).

Gopher also supports WAIS searches, ph (phone book) searches, and Netfind searches. The Gopher protocol and Gopher desktop clients are still active technology; many users who can't use a WWW viewer (due to connection, hardware, or software limitations) can still run a Gopher session. The WWW is designed to support all of Gopher's capabilities; WWW servers can process Gopher service requests. Web viewers display Gopher data in a close approximation to a standard Gopher application (see fig. 3.4). Integration is the key for the Web's Gopher support.

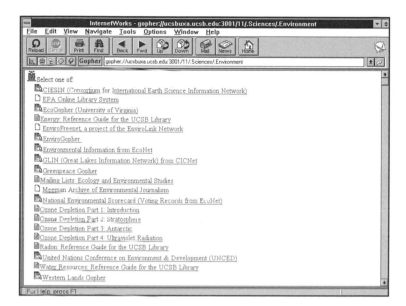

Fig. 3.4
A Gopher menu in a Web viewer looks and responds as if it were in a native Gopher application.

Troubleshooting

When I try to access a particular Gopher site from my Web viewer, I get the message `cannot locate gopher host` *and it doesn't connect. I know the address is correct—what's happening?*

If you're having problems connecting to non-Web resources, you may be using the wrong URL. Not only must the particular Internet address for the server be correct, but the header must also agree with the resource type. A gopher URL must begin with **gopher://** or your viewer won't recognize the Gopher server.

A second possible problem may be that the Gopher server is not located on the host's default network port. Think of a network port as a switchboard channel for users to "plug in" to the proper server software on the host machine. If the Gopher site doesn't use the standard port 70, you must specify what port your viewer connects to (such as **gopher://gopher.rabies.com:80/**).

WWW and FTP

File Transfer Protocol, or *FTP,* is a simple set of protocols. It handles one thing and one thing only: the transfer of files from desktop to server, and vice versa. With that in mind, FTP is a rugged service. File transfer activity has been estimated at up to half of the total data transfer activity on the Internet, which isn't surprising. FTP is adept at handling multiple transfers on the same host (or the same desktop, depending on the client software), and file sizes can range all the way up into the megabytes. Even the WWW, transferring pages at sizes up to a few hundred kilobytes (if they are designed well), still accounts for less activity than FTP.

Tip
Evaluate the range of FTP programs available for your computer system before choosing the one that is best suited to your needs and computing habits.

As a simple protocol, FTP has a single view: the file directory (see fig. 3.5). Clients travel into and out of a directory structure from the command line. In a graphical environment, they navigate file directories and issue FTP commands using buttons.

> **Note**
>
> In its native form, FTP is a text-only "enter a command at the prompt" system. There is no standard design for graphical FTP front-end utilities. Some provide a list of both your local file and directory structures, as well as those of the remote FTP server; others only show the remote files and automatically store retrieved files in a pre-configured folder or directory. Some clients simplify using FTP by displaying buttons that issue the text command for each FTP action; others give you a command field for you to enter the commands for actions you want to perform.

Active location on remote system

Fig. 3.5
File directories display in a list, are sorted alphabetically, and are case-sensitive (if located on a UNIX server).

File transfers can be initiated in either ASCII text or binary file format; the user is generally required to specify the type of transfer, or let the client software figure out the data type on its own. Most FTP clients do a good job of transferring files in the proper format, but sometimes the user must set the mode manually.

As the WWW supports the FTP protocol, Web viewers provide the same file directory view as FTP clients (see fig. 3.6).

◄ See "Origins of the Web," p. 30

> **Note**
>
> Because the WWW has been designed to transfer data and negotiate file types between the client and the server "behind the scenes," Web viewers are much better at handling multiple data types than FTP clients. In fact, users rarely have to manually identify a file format before the Web client software will retrieve or display it properly.

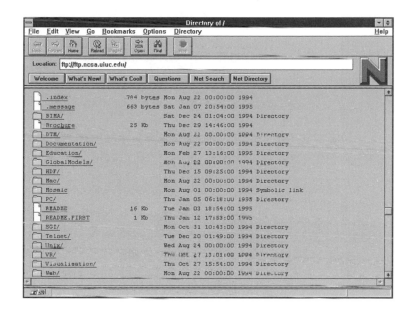

Fig. 3.6
FTP listings in a Web viewer follow the same linear file-directory structure.

Navigation through the directory tree is the same as with other graphical FTP clients. For example, clicking a list name with a folder icon (representing a subdirectory) issues the Change Directory command to the FTP server, which then sends the new file list to the Web viewer. Clicking the ".." (double-periods) line tells the viewer to travel back up a tree level, and the previous list is retrieved from the viewer's stored data cache. If no cached information is available, the appropriate command is sent, and the new list is again retrieved.

Clicking a listed file initiates the file transfer—no typing is required, because WWW is smart enough to determine the data format of the incoming file. Different viewers handle how and where to save an incoming file differently.

► See "Overview of Common Web Viewers," p. 77

WWW and WAIS

WAIS, or Wide Area Information Servers, is a protocol for distributing searchable databases. Like FTP, WAIS is a one-note service that performs its function well. It's a popular protocol for users (especially in university environments) who want to create databases on focused topics; that's its primary use. Hundreds of databases exist across the Internet, spanning the breadth of academic research and other subjects.

There are a few master WAIS lists that are useful as jumping-off points for database searches. One such site is the Gopher site at the University of Manchester, **gopher://info.mcc.ac.uk/11/external/wais**. From this list, you can initiate a WAIS search.

As far as I can tell, there are no stand-alone WAIS clients, but many services (such as Gopher) support WAIS searches (see fig. 3.7).

Fig. 3.7
WAIS provides a basic search command line as its simple interface (this database is being accessed from a Gopher client).

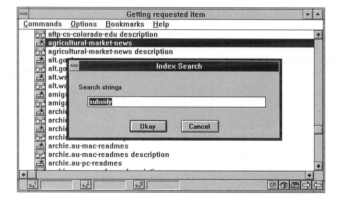

The WWW protocol integrates WAIS search support and can access WAIS servers anywhere on the Internet. This support is identical to the support provided by a Gopher client (see fig. 3.8).

As long as the user community relies on WAIS for extended database reference, the World Wide Web protocol will support it.

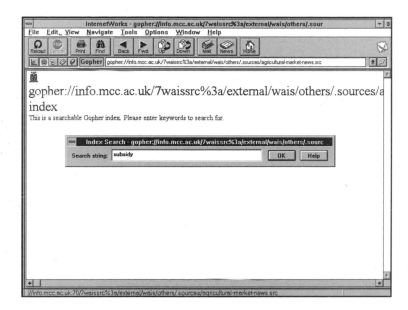

Fig. 3.8
WAIS database
searches are
straightforward:
just enter your
search text and
click OK.

From Here...

The World Wide Web is a versatile set of protocols, providing seamless support for the Internet's other primary services. How do Web viewers and servers interact: What is fundamentally different about the World Wide Web model in comparison to the other information services? Refer to the following chapters and parts to learn about the WWW-client relationship or skip ahead to begin learning about HTML:

- Chapter 4, "The Power of the Desktop Client," explains the process of information distribution from a WWW server to the desktop; it is a look at how the client software determines how information is handled.

- Chapter 5, "Building Blocks of HTML," provides a general overview of the HTML, the markup elements, and text entities it uses to modify document text.

- Chapter 7, "Distributing Information with HTML," describes the advantages and disadvantages of using HTML documents for distributing and retrieving information across the Internet and on your own local area network (LAN).

- If you're ready to get busy, Part III, "Creating HTML Documents," is the place to go. This part includes chapters on common "standards and practices" in HTML and creating HTML documents from the top to the bottom.

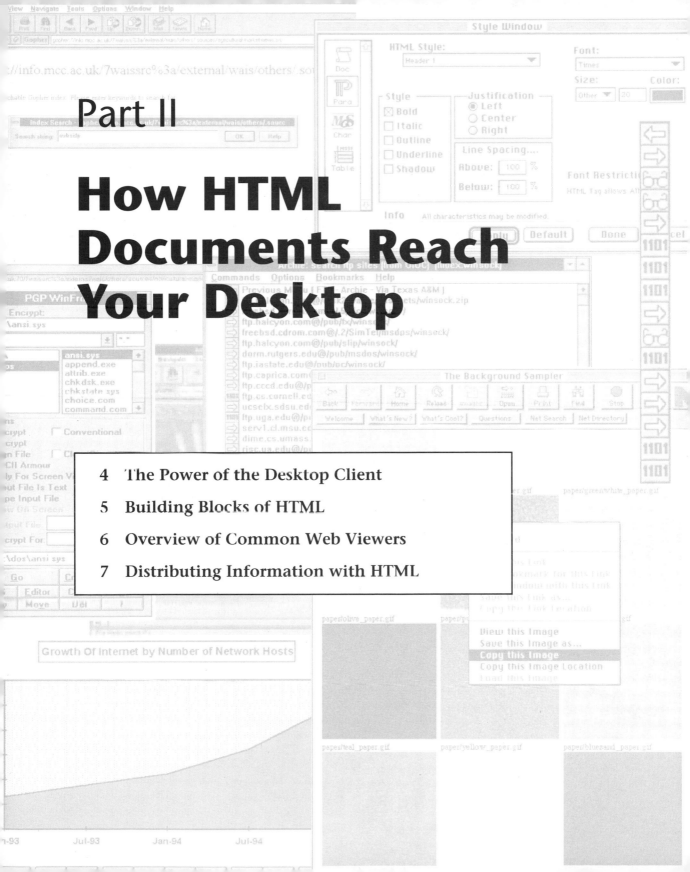

Part II

How HTML Documents Reach Your Desktop

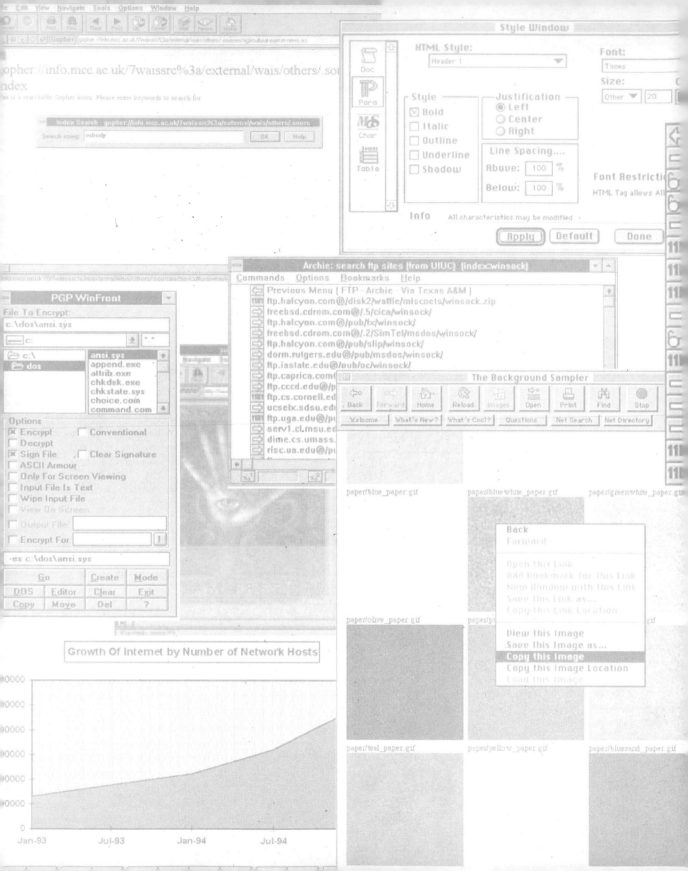

Chapter 4

The Power of the Desktop Client

In the World Wide Web, the relationship between the Web *server* (on the host) and the Web *viewer* (on the desktop) is somewhat different from other Internet services. With FTP, for example, the FTP client is responsible for sending files to or retrieving files from the FTP host to which it is currently connected. The FTP server sends or receives files in the format specified by the client.

In Gopher, the client is responsible for displaying the menu lists and initiating a new link with the Gopher server whenever an item is selected. The server connects the client to menus on other hosts, initiates FTP downloads and Telnet sessions, and sends text files to the client to be displayed in the application's window.

In the WWW relationship, the server functions much like a Gopher server: managing various protocol requests (FTP, Gopher, and so on) and sending text files to be displayed by the client. But where FTP servers assume that clients expect a certain type of file when downloaded, and Gopher servers know that a menu list will be displayed as text in a client's window, a Web server doesn't make these assumptions. It's concerned only with recognizing different protocols and handling data formats correctly. What the client does with this information is irrelevant. The server doesn't even stick around to see what happens with the data it sends; after completing a transmission the server drops the connection with the client.

This chapter answers the following questions:

- Why don't Web pages look the same in every WWW client?
- Can users change the way HTML documents look?

- How do viewers handle non-supported data types?

- Is there a "standard" for viewer compatibility?

Understanding the WWW Distribution Method

The "one transaction and out" feature of the WWW is actually a tremendous benefit. Where FTP and Telnet sessions maintain constant connections to their hosts, which consume Net bandwidth and occupy a connection to the server, the WWW does not use any more server time or bandwidth than it takes to transfer a requested document. The distinction between these connection methods may best be understood through the following analogy:

- *The prevalent information distribution system method.* You are in the process of reading a book. You always have the book with you, open to the page you are currently reading. Even when you have stopped reading, you still have the book in your hands, open to the most recent page, until you consciously close it and put it down. At this point, someone else can pick up the book and begin reading (there are only so many copies to go around and they had to wait for one to become available).

- *The World Wide Web method.* You want to read a book so you ask for the first page. It appears in your hands. When you're finished with it you ask for another. It appears in your hands. Each successive page is available to you as you request it, yet you never pick up the whole book. While you are reading, many others are also able to ask for pages. Because no one has the book to themselves, these requests are granted and any waiting is minimized.

◀ See "Origins of the Web," p. 30 This model shares the burden of how information is presented to the user between both the server and the client; it is up to the server to send the proper document in the proper format, and it is the client's job to process the information for the user.

The Viewer Controls the Image

On the Web, the client software has to interpret incoming data to determine how to process it. Because HTTP (or Web) servers can send many different types of data, clients have to be intelligent enough to recognize different data types and know what to do with them.

The majority of documents that Web viewers receive are in the HTML format. These files are text-based, with formatting commands embedded in the data to define how the data is to be displayed. Viewers are in complete control when it comes to interpreting HTML commands. Although there is a consensus of formatting standards for many HTML elements, each viewer has its own capabilities and definitions for representing HTML.

For example, figure 4.1 shows a document that is a raw HTML file. It uses a variety of document conventions and standard and non-standard HTML elements. HTML coding is shown within angle brackets; these codes define how the text will be formatted on-screen, or tell the Web viewer to display a graphic file (or what to display if the user has turned off graphics in their viewer). Different viewers may display these images and formatting differently, but the content remains the same for each user.

Tip

Most Web viewers allow you to save your current Web document as either a text file (what you see in the viewer) or as an HTML source.

▶ See "The Elements of HTML," p. 68

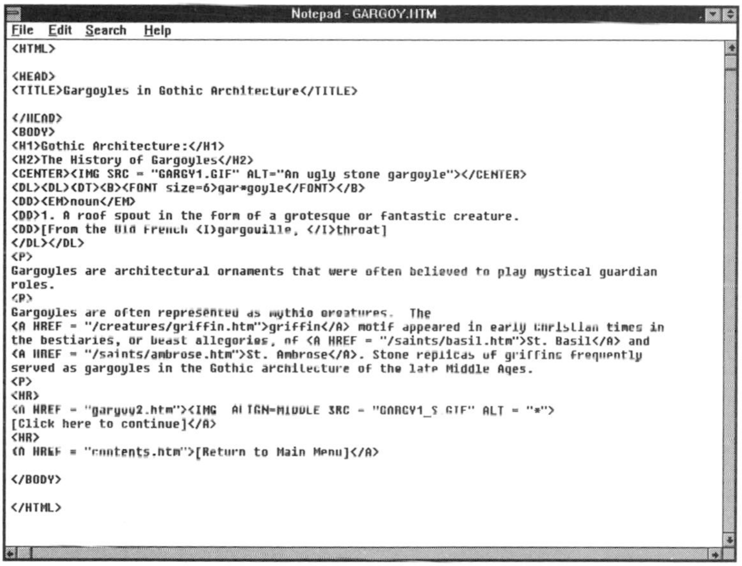

```
                        Notepad - GARGOY.HTM
 File  Edit  Search  Help
<HTML>

<HEAD>
<TITLE>Gargoyles in Gothic Architecture</TITLE>

</HEAD>
<BODY>
<H1>Gothic Architecture:</H1>
<H2>The History of Gargoyles</H2>
<CENTER><IMG SRC = "GARGY1.GIF" ALT="An ugly stone gargoyle"></CENTER>
<DL><DL><DT><B><FONT size=6>gar*goyle</FONT></B>
<DD><EM>noun</EM>
<DD>1. A roof spout in the form of a grotesque or fantastic creature.
<DD>[From the Old French <I>gargouille, </I>throat]
</DL></DL>
<P>
Gargoyles are architectural ornaments that were often believed to play mystical guardian
roles.
<P>
Gargoyles are often represented as mythic creatures.  The
<A HREF = "/creatures/griffin.htm">griffin</A> motif appeared in early Christian times in
the bestiaries, or beast allegories, of <A HREF = "/saints/basil.htm">St. Basil</A> and
<A HREF = "/saints/ambrose.htm">St. Ambrose</A>. Stone replicas of griffins frequently
served as gargoyles in the Gothic architecture of the late Middle Ages.
<P>
<HR>
<A HREF = "gargoy2.htm"><IMG  ALIGN=MIDDLE SRC = "GARGY1_S.GIF" ALT = "*">
[Click here to continue]</A>
<HR>
<A HREF = "contents.htm">[Return to Main Menu]</A>

</BODY>

</HTML>
```

Fig. 4.1
HTML documents can include content such as page titles, text headings, hypertext links to other documents, and graphics.

II

How Documents Reach You

Figures 4.2 through 4.5 show how different clients are initially configured to display this text in slightly different manners.

The variations between how these programs display the document are cosmetic alone; the data is unaltered. What's more important: what you say or how you say it? Many Web users believe that how information is presented is just as crucial as the actual information. Others believe that the message is not in the medium—that presentation is all just eye candy. This debate will surface again in later chapters.

Tip

If the decorative graphics on a Web site are making the download time too long, turn off the inline images option in your Web viewer to limit the documents to their text only.

Fig. 4.2

The Web document aligns text and images along the left-hand margin, unless the text is inside a definition list (such as the definition for "gargoyle" beneath the picture).

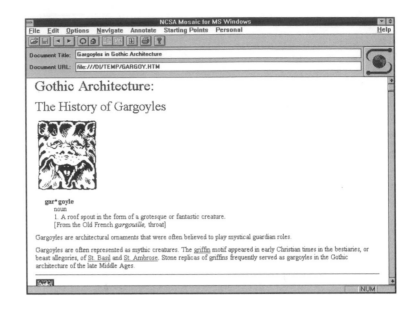

Fig. 4.3

Netscape Navigator, the most popular Web browser, supports centered images and a wider line spacing.

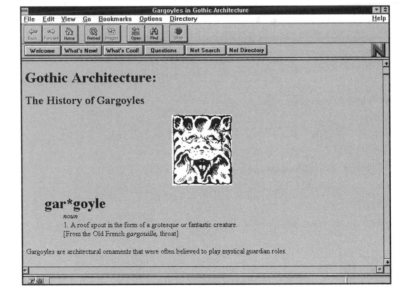

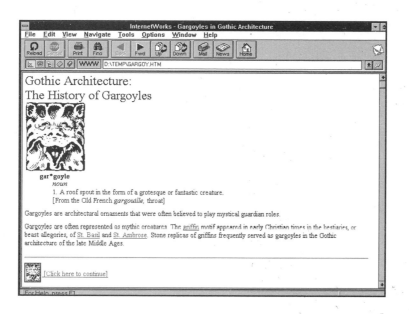

Fig. 4.4
BookLink's
InternetWorks,
a full-featured
WWW viewer, uses
tighter line spacing
to display more
information on-
screen at once.

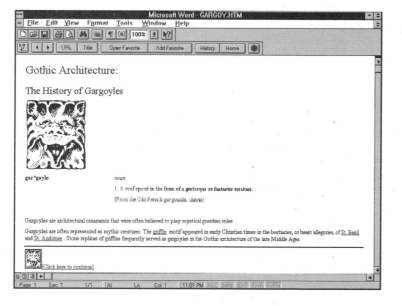

Fig. 4.5
Internet Assistant
can read HTML
documents (and
browse the Web)
from within Word
itself.

II

How Documents Reach You

Tailoring the View

The examples presented in the previous section are representative of how the software developers initially configured the viewers. However, these characteristics are not set in stone; there is no governing body that has declared that an <H1> heading must be a certain font, or of a certain point size and weight. The WWW actively avoids these declarations, leaving it up to users to adjust and customize the interpretation of HTML elements to suit their own tastes.

The primary reason that viewers are as similar "out of the box" is probably due to the original definitions in Mosaic, the first graphical Web viewer. The reasons they're dissimilar vary greatly: from the personal tastes of the programmers to an overt campaign to bring changes to the HTML language. Whatever the intentions of the developers, the one feature they all provide (to some extent) that is consistent with the philosophy of the WWW is the user's ability to customize the way documents are interpreted.

▶ See "Using NCSA Mosaic," p. 84

Depending on the platform you work on, different conventions for making these changes may apply. In NCSA Mosaic for the Macintosh, for example, you choose Options, Styles to reach the Style Window dialog box (see fig. 4.6).

Fig. 4.6
Mosaic for the Macintosh allows users to select characteristics for each text element and display characteristic.

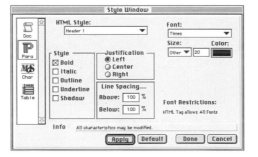

Caution

Although most viewers let you define the text color for styles such as the header levels, be very careful when choosing any color other than black. Your viewer uses colors to identify available hypertext links and to show what links have been retrieved. Defining a text style to one of these colors will create quite a bit of confusion and may obscure available links in the Web pages.

The Style Window dialog box lets the user control everything from the viewer's highlight color for hyperlinks to the display font for each text element. Another Macintosh viewer, Netscape's Netscape Navigator (commonly called Netscape), provides a much more limited custom options dialog box (see fig. 4.7).

▶ See "Using Netscape Navigator," p. 96

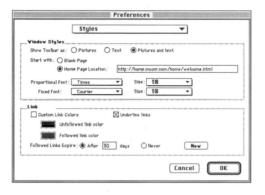

Fig. 4.7
Netscape uses a pull-down menu (here showing the Styles options) to allow users to customize the viewer's settings.

Under Microsoft Windows, customizing conventions are not nearly as broad. Most viewers allow users to redefine how elements are displayed. BookLink's InternetWorks provides a customize dialog box for defining a session's display settings (see fig. 4.8).

▶ See "Using InternetWorks," p. 107

List of available HTML styles

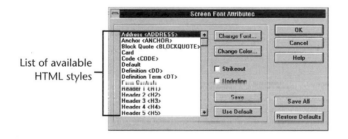

Fig. 4.8
InternetWorks' original text definitions provide little distinction between related elements such as headings and lists; you can change these settings to improve the readability of HTML documents.

OS/2 applications follow a menu format similar to Windows applications. WebExplorer, a native OS/2 WWW viewer, allows you to change individual settings from this series of menus (see fig. 4.9).

Fig. 4.9
Like Netscape,
WebExplorer
supports a wide
variety of non-
standard HTML
elements, but it
provides more user
control over how
they're displayed.

Tip
The Restore De-
faults button resets
the text style
characteristics to
the viewer's pre-
defined settings.

▶ See "Using
WebExplorer,"
p. 115

▶ See "File Nam-
ing Issues in
HTML," p. 146

Tip
Associations are
connections be-
tween data for-
mats and the
software programs
that can process
them in your
WWW client's
helper
configuration.

When You Need a Little Helper

The WWW supports a wide variety of data types, from plain text to digital video clips. The protocol is an open standard, and any future data formats (such as Apple's proposed 3D data format) can be added and be backward-compatible. How can this kind of support be managed so easily, given the huge base of Web clients that exists even today?

Web viewers don't support every data format that can be distributed across the Web. That's just not practical: there are nearly a dozen graphic formats alone that can be accessed from an HTML document link. There are many other data types—sound, video, Encapsulated PostScript, Acrobat PDF—that are in use today across the Web. Viewers support these data files by passing them to external applications, or helper applications.

These applications can range from single function utilities (such as Sound Machine for Macintosh sound support) to sophisticated applications (such as LView Pro, used to provide graphic file support). Web viewers *associate* the file formats with the applications, allowing the clients to automatically launch the helper applications with the data file loaded.

I like the term "helper application" because it connotes the proper relationship between the additional utilities and Web viewers: they're not replacing the viewer, just providing support beyond what the viewer can provide natively. It's a perspective more developers should take, given the communal nature of the Web.

Graphic Helpers

The standard graphic file formats supported by Web viewers are generally limited to GIF (from CompuServe), X bitmap (BMP), and the Joint Photographic Experts Group's JPEG. Other formats, such as TIFF (Tagged Image File Format), TGA (Targa), PCX (PC Paintbrush), and DIB (Device Independent Bitmap), are common, but used to a lesser extent. To support these files, programs like LView Pro are widely used (see fig. 4.10).

Fig. 4.10
LView Pro, like most graphic helpers, will display nearly every major graphic format. It is recommended that users choose one application to meet as many external support options as possible.

Tip
After the helper program displays a data file (such as a graphic image) you can save it to your local hard drive using the **F**ile, Save **A**s menu option.

Other common Windows helpers are Paint Shop Pro and Image Alchemy. Helpers for the Macintosh include JPEG View. UNIX viewers use utilities such as xv for displaying incoming graphics.

Digital Sound Helpers

Few viewers support sound natively. Most rely on helpers for playing all linked sound files. The most well-known digital sound helper is probably SoundMachine, which has been used on the Macintosh since the first Mosaic release. All it does is play Mac-formatted sounds; its interface is simple and clean (see fig. 4.11). Its sparse design almost makes you forget it is not a part of Mosaic, but a separate application.

Tip
VCR-like buttons let you control the sound playback.

SoundMachine
Applause
11.1 kHz   FSSD

Similar applications on the Windows platform include WPlany and Wham. UNIX sound support for X Windows or Open Windows users is provided by audiotool.

Fig. 4.11
SoundMachine's slim design breaks free from the "menu-itis" most graphical applications suffer, making it a great companion for other traditional programs like Mosaic.

II

How Documents Reach You

Digital Video Helpers

Digital video is not a big hit on the Internet; the comparably large file sizes, combined with the slow speed of the current infrastructure, make retrieving any substantial footage a deliberate chore and not something users do on a whim. The promise of useful digital video distribution is quite tantalizing; this includes the ubiquitous "video conferencing on the Internet" that might come to pass.

Tip

When including links to video files in your Web pages, it's a good idea to note the size of the file next to the link so users can gauge the download time before retrieving the file.

However, the Internet (and, consequently, the WWW) does carry video files for those patient enough to wait out the download process. Three file formats have emerged as standards: Microsoft's AVI, Apple's QuickTime, and the Motion Picture Experts Group's MPEG. Both QuickTime and MPEG are cross-platform data formats; AVI is used to a lesser extent, but is supported by a much wider audience (the Microsoft Windows establishment).

There are a few well-established digital-video utilities. QuickTime Player supports viewers primarily on the Windows platform. Apple has made version 2 available for download by the public (in controlled environments, such as CompuServe) and it will be bundled with applications that use QuickTime video.

On the Macintosh, the long-time favorite is Sparkle, a QuickTime viewer. Another popular utility is Popcorn. These share the same advantages as SoundMachine: clean interfaces with the role of utility apparent in their design—as opposed to QuickTime Player, which suffers from looking too much like a full-blown application (see fig. 4.12).

Little Video Windows

As you're probably aware, multimedia has been the hot catchword the past few years. Fueled by an industry that is eager to exploit new technologies, digital video has arrived on the Internet in two forms: live video transmission and digital video data files. Video transmission is in its very early stages, pioneered by such products as CU SeeMe (**ftp://gated.cornell.edu/pub/CU-SeeMe/html/Welcome.html**). It supports a very low frame rate that varies as the local traffic on the Internet increases and decreases. This technology will improve tremendously as the Internet's infrastructure is improved.

The second format for digital video is the data file. The three common formats, Microsoft's AVI, Apple's QuickTime, and the Motion Picture Experts Group's MPEG, all share the same characteristics that have made them less than crowd favorites: low frame rates, small image sizes, low image quality, and limited sound support.

- Frame rates vary from 5 to 30 frames per second, although an image clipping along at 15 fps is doing well by today's standards.

- Image sizes are typically 160 × 120 pixels, or even 320 × 200, but rarely larger (with one exception).

- Image quality is directly proportionate to the frame size and the color depth of the image; most digital video files are recorded in 8-bit color (256 simultaneous colors) or sometimes 16-bit color (65 thousand colors). The more colors, the larger the file size and the lower the frame rate on the user's desktop.

- Sound in digital video files can range from 8 MHz mono all the way to 44MHz stereo, but at a huge cost in file size and playback rates (sound or video often "drop out" or break up when the computer system can't keep up with both the video and audio frame rates).

These factors have dampened the computer community's enthusiasm for video technology, but new technologies are under development to soften these limitations. Each of the popular formats supports the current standard and shares the same limitations.

Microsoft AVI (Audio Video Interleave) is a format that laces picture and sound data together—much like a zipper, with alternating fields of data. AVI files are limited by their reliance on software compression (as opposed to hardware compression), requiring systems to decompress the moving images through the player software. AVI files are supported by the largest audience—about 40 million users can use Microsoft's Video for Windows runtime module—yet it's the most limited of the formats available today.

The current version of Apple's QuickTime supports a larger image size at the same frame rate as either its earlier version or the AVI format. QuickTime also relies exclusively on software to decompress its data files. Apple has incorporated QuickTime support into its current Mac OS software, and a runtime for Windows is distributed with many multimedia programs (QuickTime is the leading video format in multimedia development). A recent advance by Apple has led to a new product, QuickTime VR, a "wide screen" format that allows users to navigate within the image—as in a "virtual reality" environment. QuickTime VR is available for both Macintosh and Windows, and is a further testament to Apple's role as the leader in digital video technology.

The third format, MPEG, is both supported by hardware and software decompression. Software decompression suffers from the same limitations as AVI and QuickTime. However, MPEG hardware assisted decompression is capable of displaying a full-color, 30 fps video image at 640 × 480 pixels—full VGA resolution—with CD-quality stereo sound. Admittedly, the user base with MPEG codec (compression/decompression) hardware is very small, but motherboard manufacturers (and even CPU manufacturers like Intel) are working to integrate this support directly into your standard hardware.

II

How Documents Reach You

Fig. 4.12
QuickTime Movie Player supports multiple windows, each with its own volume controls; as a Windows application, it adheres to standard Windows menu conventions.

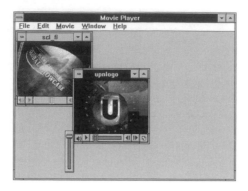

Other Data Helpers

Tip

You can link to batch files to perform simple interactive duties without a script, such as appending documents to create a customized Web page.

Other data formats are less familiar to the ordinary user, but are becoming increasingly more popular. Adobe's Acrobat document exchange format (PDF) can be used to exchange and view documents in their original layout and font without having to use the application that created the document (such as PageMaker or WordPerfect). If desired, these can be printed out to create a hard copy that is exactly like the original document in the original application.

> **Note**
>
> Adobe distributes Acrobat's Reader free on the Internet (it's available at **http://www.adobe.com/**). Users can associate the PDF file format with Acrobat, making it a start-up as a helper application when the viewer retrieves Acrobat files.

◀ See "Origins of the Web," p. 30

Other helpers can display or print out PostScript data files, uncompress downloaded archived files, play MIDI or MOD sound files, or execute batch language files (such as REXX.CMD files). Helpers can be set up in a target audience to handle a specific data format you want to distribute to them, such as daily database file updates or word processor-type files.

HTML and Viewer Compatibility

Like any young software protocol, HTML is still evolving. The W3 Consortium evaluates and implements modifications and enhancements to the markup language. The revision process is very public, and users are encouraged to respond to and suggest new ideas for HTML functionality.

Level 2 is currently the most widely supported version of HTML; the next generation of HTML (Level 3) is well under development. Many features that will be available in Level 3 are already showing up in Web clients today (forms is the most popular new feature).

Other modifications to HTML are also underway at Netscape Communications Corporation (NCC). As the producer of the Web's most popular Web viewer, NCC has promoted a set of non-standard HTML elements and *attributes* (modifiers or function identifiers for HTML codes). These non-standard additions provide a greater amount of control over the look and feel of Web pages, including changing font sizes, aligning graphics and text in relation to each other and to the viewer window, and increasing the speed at which text and graphic information in Web pages are displayed.

The success of Netscape's WWW client, coupled with the growing usage of these extensions to the HTML language, have encouraged other viewer developers to support the non-standard extensions. For example, OS/2's Web Explorer is generally Netscape-compatible, but NCSA's Mosaic is not. These developers are taking different approaches to participating in the public HTML development process.

An understanding about how Web viewers play a primary role in the WWW is essential for Web authors. The WWW is not a reflection of the typical "content provider-consumer" model that exists in entertainment media and in the computer software market.

Users play an important role in defining how content will be presented. If they choose to use a viewer that follows strict HTML compatibility, they will miss out on any non-standard enhancements to Web documents. If they choose to change the standard configuration for HTML's elements, the resulting documents will not match the author's original intentions. Knowing that the way HTML documents are displayed can be changed will allow authors to anticipate their audience to a better degree.

Tip

To see how development of the next version of HTML is coming along, connect your Web viewer to **http://www. hpl.hp.co.uk/ people/dsr/ html/Contents. html**.

From Here...

You've seen that creating HTML documents is only half the picture; the other is provided through the participation of the Web audience. To get a better idea of what software they may be using to view Web pages, or to begin the authoring process itself, refer to the following chapters and parts:

- Chapter 5, "Building Blocks of HTML," provides a general overview of the Hypertext Markup Language and the markup elements and text entities it uses to modify document text.

- Chapter 6, "Overview of Common Web Viewers," overviews WWW viewers across the range of operating systems, with simple user's instructions.

- Chapter 7, "Distributing Information with HTML," describes the advantages and disadvantages of using HTML documents for distributing and retrieving information across the Internet and on your own local area network (LAN).

- Part III, "Creating HTML Documents," includes chapters on common "standards and practices" in HTML and creating HTML documents from top to bottom for when you're ready to get down to business.

Chapter 5

Building Blocks of HTML

HTML pages are like annotated bibliographies: they give you the opportunity to expand on an endless variety of topics and present additional factual or thematic resources to further explore a subject.

Of course, HTML pages are also like gossip magazines: sooner or later you'll see just about everything on them.

But regardless of how anyone perceives HTML, everyone who uses it speaks the same language. Elements, tags, anchors, hyperlinks, URLs, and attributes: they're all part of the lexicon of the Web's documents. To create inspired Web pages (and to cast a critical eye on those already on the Web), you need to have an intimate familiarity with the building blocks of HTML.

This chapter answers the following questions:

- How is HTML related to SGML?

- What is a DTD?

- What's the difference between empty and container elements?

- What are the basic components of HTML?

Creating the Standards

The HTML standard is constantly under development. Users and developers from around the world contribute to the on-going discourse and testing of new ideas, concepts, and uses for HTML and its component elements. One user who provided an enormous amount of time and energy in this process is Daniel Connolly (**connolly@w3.org**) of the W3 Consortium at MIT. He outlined standards for the

(continues)

(continued)

standards; he provided the following guidelines for the HTML development team to assist them in writing the current and upcoming specifications for HTML.

The goal of any HTML specification should be to promote confidence in the fidelity of communications using HTML. This means specifications need to adhere to the following standards:

- Make it clear to authors what idioms are available to express their ideas.

- Make it clear to implementers how to interpret the HTML format so that authors' ideas will be represented faithfully.

- Keep HTML simple enough that it can be implemented using readily available technology, and then processed interactively.

- Make HTML expressive enough that it can represent a useful majority of the contemporary communications idioms in the WWW community.

- Make some allowance for expressing idioms not captured by the specifications.

- Address relevant interoperability issues with other applications and technologies.

You can get more information about the ongoing HTML standards process from Daniel Connolly's Web page, **http://www.w3.org/hypertext/WWW/People/ Connolly/**, or by reading Chapter 8, "HTML Standards and Practices."

HTML and SGML: A Parent-Child Relationship

HTML is a subset of SGML (Standardized General Markup Language). SGML documents are more complex and programming-like than HTML. Figure 5.1 shows how an SGML document describes the HTML standard (the figure is, in fact, the SGML declaration for HTML).

HTML resembles a simplified SGML. The observation that SGML is to HTML as HTML is to plain text seems reasonable on the surface. When you take a look under the hood, though, it's easy to see how HTML shares the advantages of both systems of marking text.

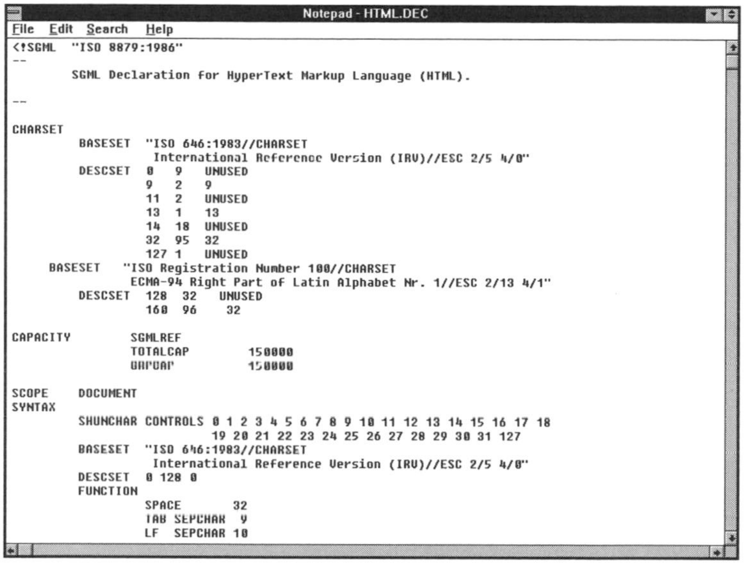

```
[Notepad - HTML.DEC]
File  Edit  Search  Help
<!SGML   "ISO 8879:1986"
--
         SGML Declaration for HyperText Markup Language (HTML).


--

CHARSET
         BASESET  "ISO 646:1983//CHARSET
                   International Reference Version (IRV)//ESC 2/5 4/0"
         DESCSET  0   9   UNUSED
                  9   2   9
                  11  2   UNUSED
                  13  1   13
                  14  18  UNUSED
                  32  95  32
                  127 1   UNUSED
      BASESET  "ISO Registration Number 100//CHARSET
                ECMA-94 Right Part of Latin Alphabet Nr. 1//ESC 2/13 4/1"
         DESCSET  128 32  UNUSED
                  160 96  32

CAPACITY      SGMLREF
              TOTALCAP        150000
              GRPCAP          150000

SCOPE    DOCUMENT
SYNTAX
         SHUNCHAR CONTROLS 0 1 2 3 4 5 6 7 8 9 10 11 12 13 14 15 16 17 18
                           19 20 21 22 23 24 25 26 27 28 29 30 31 127
         BASESET  "ISO 646:1983//CHARSET
                   International Reference Version (IRV)//ESC 2/5 4/0"
         DESCSET  0 128 0
         FUNCTION
                  SPACE        32
                  TAB SEPCHAR  9
                  LF  SEPCHAR  10
```

Fig. 5.1
SGML coding provides machine-level display format and function commands.

Note

SGML is not for the faint of heart, as the code in figure 5.1 suggests. SGML code constructs are not based as much in "plain English" as HTML is. The following text is written in SGML, describing how the HTML element BLOCKQUOTE is used:

```
<!ELEMENT (%blockquote) - - %body.content>
<!ATTLIST (%blockquote)
        %attrs;
        %needs; -- for control of text flow --
        >
```

How would that read in English? The BLOCKQUOTE element is a container for text in the BODY section (%body.content); it does not have any defined arguments that affect its use or how its contents are displayed (no options are listed under the %attrs; or %needs; categories).

SGML is a full-bodied language for defining text function and formatting that many users have remained loyal to with the arrival of HTML. HTML's use of English language editing markup elements is a key reason for the popularity and success of the World Wide Web.

Advantages and Disadvantages

In his World Wide Web Research Notebook (**http://www.w3.org/hyper-text/WWW/People/Connolly/drafts/web-research.html**), Daniel

Connolly outlines the advantages and disadvantages to carrying over SGML practices and constructs into the current HTML standard.

These are the benefits of using SGML to define HTML:

- Based on a written definition of HTML in SGML, whether a document conforms to the current standard can be determined by the viewing or editing software. Document authors can have confidence in their documents that pass automatic verification processes.

- SGML (with a defined HTML standard) defines an abstract parsing model for reducing an SGML document (at the source level) to a form called the Entity Structure Information Set. This form allows a standard interpretation of all HTML documents.

- Like HTML, SGML provides a clear and widely supported standard for creating interchangeable documents.

These are the disadvantages of using SGML to define HTML:

- SGML coding is meant to be interpreted at the machine-level, and SGML documents are difficult for people to read and understand.

- Due to its structural complexity, it's possible to read related SGML documents and come to incorrect assumptions about SGML usage.

- SGML is defined at a level of complexity beyond the function and purpose of HTML, and certain modular capabilities that use SGML are too complex for the level of author manageability HTML strives to provide.

The Strength of the HTML Standard

HTML's strength comes from its combination of SGML machine-level constructs (the tags and elements that tell a viewer the purpose of document text) and standard English text markup notation.

For example, the <B> container tag is mnemonically correct (it stands for bold), and it signals a format change to the document's viewing software, which changes the display format of the following text. When the viewer comes across the </B> closing tag, which tells it to turn off the bold attribute, it returns to the previous text formatting.

The versatility of SGML and HTML is becoming widely acknowledged as they are adopted as hypertext document standards by more content managers, including the federal and many state governments.

HTML's DTD

It's debatable who has contributed more to the "acronymization" of our culture. In a world where ATM can have two totally different meanings (one's great for convenience banking and the other for high-speed data networking), you might expect a language like HTML (itself an acronym) to continue the tradition.

And it does. From its elements—UL stands for, appropriately enough, unordered list—to its parent language SGML, HTML is defined by its use of acronyms. An acronym defines HTML as well—HTML's DTD.

DTD stands for Document Type Definition. It's a document that describes the HTML language, its elements, and their legal uses. The HTML DTD has many levels that pertain to different categories of use or compatibility with the HTML standard. These levels are:

- *Level 0.* Minimal conformance to or use of HTML elements.

- *Level 1.* HTML compatibility with (or use of) HTML with Level 1 extensions.

- *Level 2.* HTML compatibility with (or use of) HTML with Level 2 extensions.

The HTML DTD is written in SGML and can be difficult to interpret. Figure 5.2 shows a portion of the HTML DTD for Level 0 (for the complete DTD, see Appendix A, "HTML Elements Reference"). The document coding is complex and difficult to read; it's not meant entirely to be read by people, but by SGML interpreters. Don't be surprised if it makes no sense to you—it doesn't to the vast majority of people.

Annotated versions of the HTML DTD make it easier for developers and end users to verify conformity issues. Daniel Connolly maintains one popular version, and you can find it at **http://www.w3.org/hypertext/WWW/ People/Connolly/**. The Web sites listed in Appendix B, "WWW Bibliography," collect other descriptions of the various HTML standards.

Fig. 5.2
The document for each level defines a measure of compatibility to the HTML specification.

```
                           Notepad - HTML.DTD
 File  Edit  Search  Help
<!ENTITY % list " UL | OL | DIR | MENU ">
<!ENTITY % literal " XMP | LISTING ">

<!ENTITY % headelement
         " TITLE | NEXTID |ISINDEX" >

<!ENTITY % bodyelement
         "P | HR | %heading |
          %list | DL | ADDRESS | PRE | BLOCKQUOTE
          | %literal">

<!ENTITY % oldstyle "%headelement | %bodyelement | #PCDATA">

<!ENTITY % URL "CDATA"
         -- The term URL means a CDATA attribute
            whose value is a Uniform Resource Locator,
            as defined. (A URN may also be usable here when defined.)
         -->

<!ENTITY % linkattributes
         "NAME NMTOKEN #IMPLIED
          HREF %URL;  #IMPLIED
          REL CDATA #IMPLIED -- forward relationship type --
          REV CDATA #IMPLIED -- reversed relationship type
                                to referent data:

                                PARENT CHILD, SIBLING, NEXT, TOP,
                                DEFINITION, UPDATE, ORIGINAL etc. --

          URN CDATA #IMPLIED -- universal resource number --

          TITLE CDATA #IMPLIED -- advisory only --

          METHODS NAMES #IMPLIED -- supported public methods of the object:
                                TEXTSEARCH, GET, HEAD, ... --
```

The Elements of HTML

HTML is composed of elements, or instructions, to WWW viewers to perform a defined task (make text bold, insert a paragraph break, or format and number a list in a predetermined manner). HTML tags consist of individual elements inside angle brackets. Figure 5.3 shows a few typical elements and how they are written in tag format.

Fig. 5.3
HTML tags are "invisible" when the WWW viewer displays the document.

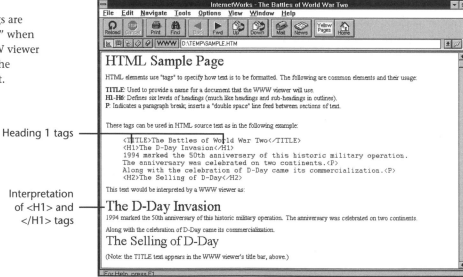

Troubleshooting

If WWW viewers read HTML tags as instructions, how did you show them in figure 5.3? Why didn't the viewer just mark up the text in the tags?

Displaying the HTML tags in the previous figure was not as easy as it looks. Because Web viewers look for tags as signals to format text, all occurrences of tags are supposed to be interpreted. To get around this handicap (after all, the software is just doing its job), HTML provides a list of text entities that viewers will interpret as certain ASCII characters. For example, to write a line that the viewer will display as

    <TITLE>The Battles of World War Two</TITLE>

you must use entities for the angle bracket characters. HTML defines the "less than" bracket (<) as < and the "greater than" bracket (>) as >. Therefore, the previous line would be written in the HTML document as

    <TITLE>The Battles of World War Two</TITLE>

As the name implies, HTML marks up text in a document by defining the specific formatting for sections of the document. HTML is a hybrid, using some elements to define the abstract value of text (such as "emphasized") and others to define the actual on-screen representation in the WWW viewer's window (such as "italicized"). This "split personality" created quite a controversy in the authoring community, spawning two camps of thought that support the different uses of HTML markup.

▶ See "The Great Debate: Formatting Text in HTML," p. 140

Unlike the file systems of some operating systems, HTML element names are case independent. You can write tags with any mixture of upper- and lower-case characters. For example, you can write one tag that defines the formatting of a section of text as <BLOCKQUOTE>, <blockquote>, <BlockQuote>, or any capitalization combination. Some authors use unorthodox capitalization schemes, such as <bLocKquOtE>, but that doesn't make for easy-to-read HTML, and your site administrator probably discourages this brand of "net.hipness."

Note

This book's convention of using all uppercase characters in HTML tags is for legibility only; feel free to use whatever scheme you're most comfortable with in your own documents, or whatever conforms to your Web site's HTML document style sheet—if there is one.

Empty and Container Tags

HTML uses two types of elements: *empty* (or open) and *container* tags. These tags differ because of what they represent. Empty tags represent formatting constructs, such as line breaks, horizontal rules, and paragraph breaks. These tags indicate "one time" instructions that WWW viewers can read and execute without concern for any other HTML construction or document text.

Container tags define a section of text (or of the document itself) and specify the formatting or construction for all of the selected text. A container tag has both a beginning and an ending: the ending tag is identical to the beginning tag, with the addition of a forward slash. Most containers can overlap and hold other containers or empty tags (see fig. 5.4). Specific restrictions apply in some cases, which are described in Part III, "Creating HTML Documents."

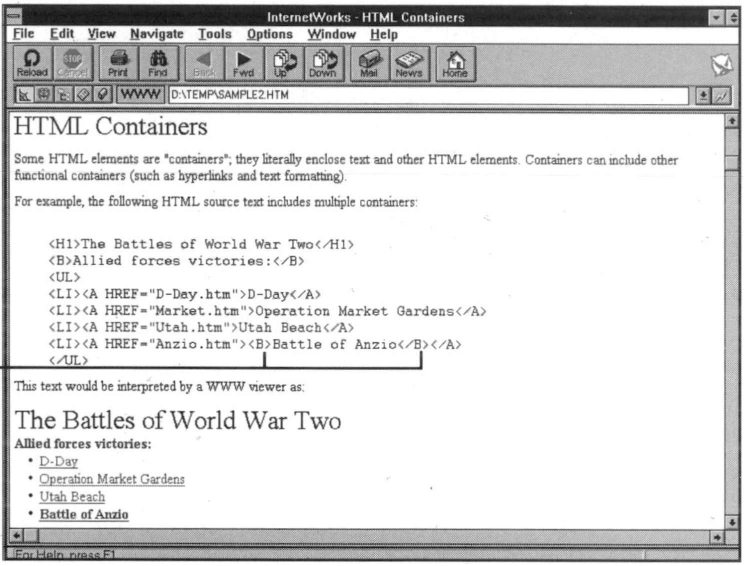

Fig. 5.4
Containers can hold other elements—the entire HTML document is actually one large container, defined by the tag <HTML>.

Container tags ———

HTML Tag Arguments

I'm not talking about disagreements between tags in HTML documents. Like command-line applications, many HTML elements use additional parameters (known as *arguments*) to increase their functionality. These arguments pass on to the client software and affect the way the element is applied to the section of text (or, with empty tags, how the tag's construct is displayed in the viewing software's window).

For example, the anchor element uses arguments to define the function of the anchor (whether it's a marker or a hypertext link to another document or anchor). So, a document can contain links to specific sections of text and named anchors at those text locations (see fig. 5.5). Notice that the parameters are contained in the tag's angle brackets.

Fig. 5.5
You use anchors as both the starting and ending points of hypertext links in HTML documents.

Links to other documents   Anchor tags

In this example, the first line in the list, `<LI><A HREF="#D-DAY">D-Day</A>`, is an anchor that points to a named anchor somewhere else in the document. The named anchor it points to is found in the line `<A NAME="D-Day"><H1>D-Day: The Invasion of Normandy</H1></A>`. When the user clicks the list item `D-Day` in the viewed document, the WWW viewer jumps immediately to the associated named anchor at `D-Day: The Invasion of Normandy`.

Figure 5.6 shows how a WWW viewer displays the sample HTML document.

Caution

Underlining and colored borders (such as red or green) are used in some Web pages to indicate hyperlink text and graphics, but these don't print well.

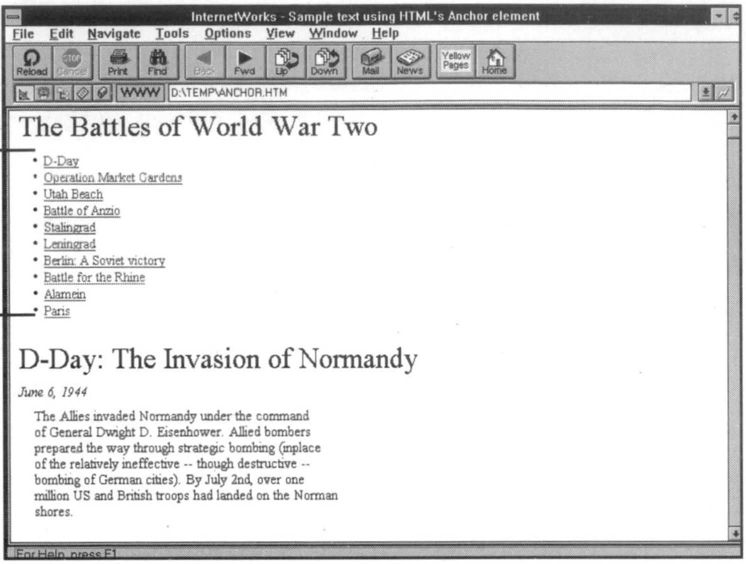

Fig. 5.6
Hypertext links display in color—usually blue or green—and underlined (as defined by the WWW viewer) to make it easier for the user to see the available links.

Hypertext links ——

Some WWW viewers, notably Netscape, provide support for non-standard arguments that primarily affect the display of the HTML text in the viewer's window. WWW viewers that don't support non-standard elements or arguments just ignore them. Non-standard usage is noted in Part III, "Creating HTML Documents."

> **Note**
>
> If you incorporate Netscape's non-standard HTML in your own documents, let users know with a simple statement at the head of your "entry-point" document (usually the "Welcome" or introduction page). This way, they know that Netscape displays your Web pages as you intended them to be seen.

An Overview of HTML Elements

Tables 5.1, 5.2, and 5.3 provide a brief overview of the HTML elements found in different sections of HTML documents. These tables don't include arguments but they do include the element's tag type. For a complete description of each element and its associated arguments, see Appendix A.

Table 5.1 HTML Elements for Head Sections in HTML Documents

Element	Element Type	Description
BASE	empty	Base context document
HEAD	container	Document head
HTML	container	HyperText Markup Language Document
ISINDEX	empty	Document is a searchable index
LINK	empty	Link from this document
NEXTID	empty	Next ID to use for link name
TITLE	container	Title of document

Table 5.2 HTML Elements for Body Sections in HTML Documents

Element	Element Type	Description
A	container	Anchor: source and/or destination of a link
ADDRESS	container	Address, signature, or byline for a document or passage
B	container	Bold text
BLOCKQUOTE	container	Quoted passage
BODY	container	Document body
BR	empty	Line break
CITE	container	Name or title of cited work
CODE	container	Source code phrase
DD	empty	Definition of term
DIR	container	Directory list
DL	container	Definition list, or glossary
DT	empty	Term in definition list
EM	container	Emphasized phrase
H1	container	Heading, level 1

(continues)

II

How Documents Reach You

Table 5.2 Continued

Element	Element Type	Description
H2	container	Heading, level 2
H3	container	Heading, level 3
H4	container	Heading, level 4
H5	container	Heading, level 5
H6	container	Heading, level 6
HR	empty	Horizontal rule
I	container	Italic text
IMG	empty	Image; icon, glyph, or illustration
KBD	container	Keyboard phrase, such as user input
LI	empty	List item
LISTING	container	Computer listing
MENU	container	Menu list
META	container	Generic meta-information
OL	container	Ordered or numbered list
P	empty	Paragraph
PLAINTEXT	container	Plain-text passage
PRE	container	Preformatted text
SAMP	container	Sample text or characters
SELECT	empty	Selection of option(s)
STRONG	container	Strong emphasis
TT	container	Typewriter text
UL	container	Unordered list
VAR	container	Variable phrase or substitutable
XMP	container	Example section

Note

As the HTML standard changes, elements will be *deprecated*, or replaced by new elements with greater functionality. Deprecated elements will still be supported by existing WWW viewers but may not be in the future. Be prepared to review your older HTML documents for deprecated elements that may no longer be useful.

Table 5.3 HTML Elements for Forms in HTML Documents

Element	Element Type	Description
FORM	container	Fill-out or data-entry form
INPUT	empty	Form input datum
TEXTAREA	empty	Area for text input
OPTION	empty	Selection option

From Here...

Now that you're familiar with the basics of HTML, it's time to look at how you can use HTML to distribute information to end users and how to build the HTML documents themselves. Refer to the following chapters and parts to learn about HTML distribution and creation:

■ Chapter 6, "Overview of Common Web Viewers," looks at WWW viewers across a range of operating systems, and provides simple user instructions.

■ Chapter 7, "Distributing Information with HTML," describes the advantages and disadvantages of using HTML documents for distributing and retrieving information across the Internet and on your own local area network.

■ Part III, "Creating HTML Documents," includes chapters on common standards and practices in HTML and creating HTML documents from top to bottom.

■ Chapter 13, "Linking HTML Documents to Other Information Sources," describes how, through the use of hypertext links, HTML documents can connect directly to other HTML documents or to a wide range of Internet applications.

Chapter 6

Overview of Common Web Viewers

The World Wide Web can be like a complex woven tapestry: documents link together, taking you along intuitive pathways of interest and curiosity, until you eventually end up somewhere unexpected and illuminating. This journey takes place while you're stationary; the world is brought to *your* desktop and interpreted through *your* agent, the Web client software or viewer.

Since the arrival of the groundbreaking NCSA Mosaic Web software, more than a dozen competitors of varying levels of excellence have reached the user community.

The future of WWW commerce and communication depends on the continued enthusiasm and support for the software that will bring the Web into our homes and businesses.

This chapter covers the following topics:

- What services are supported by most Web viewers?

- What's in the future for Web clients?

- Lynx, a UNIX text-based viewer

- Mosaic for the Macintosh and Windows

- Netscape Navigator for the Macintosh and Windows

- InternetWorks for Windows

- MacWeb for the Macintosh

- WebExplorer for OS/2 Warp

Viewer-Supported Services

◄ See "WWW and Gopher," p. 39

The information support for WWW clients can be broken into three categories: information distribution, communication, and remote access services.

Information Distribution Services

◄ See "WWW and WAIS," p. 44

◄ See "WWW and FTP," p. 41

Information distribution services are those Internet services that allow data to be transported from host to desktop or from desktop to host. Those supported on the Internet today are Gopher, WAIS (Wide Area Information System) searchable databases, and FTP (File Transfer Protocol). Because support for these services is a standard feature in every WWW server, all viewers can send and process the response to a call to one of these services *natively* (that is, without the help of any additional software or Internet servers).

Communication Services

Tip

The Internet community is the largest segment of UseNet users.

Communication services available via the data infrastructure used by the Internet (and many other networks around the world) include e-mail and UseNet newsgroups. You can send e-mail to nearly any global network from any other network—it's the most universally supported and accessible network service. UseNet is a piggyback network that provides discussion groups.

◄ See "Reach Out and Mail Someone," p. 23

◄ See "What Is UseNet?" p. 20

To use both of these services, Web viewers require external assistance. To send and retrieve e-mail, viewers need access to a mail server with an active user account. To send and retrieve UseNet news posts, viewers need to access a valid NNTP news server. Network News Transfer Protocol (NNTP) is the protocol used to specify how UseNet news articles are distributed and posted on news servers.

Remote Access Services

The third category of Internet services supported by WWW viewers is remote access. The primary protocol used on the Internet to connect to a remote computer and access a public or private user account is called Telnet. Telnet protocols support text-only sessions across the Internet. For all intents and purposes, a user connected to another UNIX account on a remote server has all of the "look and feel" as though they were actually sitting at a local terminal attached to the remote host, or at the remote desktop itself. These Telnet sessions are supported natively by Web viewers. Telnet is useful for Web applications that want to provide a "real time" connection in addition to the distributed Web pages (see fig. 6.1).

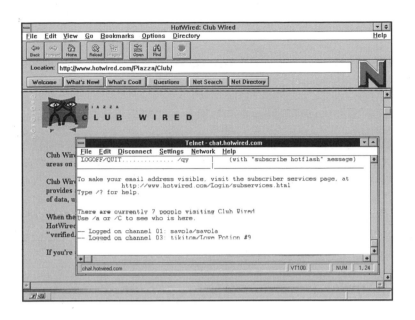

Fig. 6.1
The Club Wired section of *Wired* Magazine's Hot Wired Web site provides a real-time chat service via a separate Telnet window so users can participate in live online discussions.

What's in the Future for Web Clients?

The WWW and HTML are under continual development. As new features are incorporated into the network protocol and document language, viewers will adapt to accommodate them.

Security

The hottest topic on Web development today is security. The Internet is an open system, and as such, provides virtually no protection to data while in transit from one host to another. This data is vulnerable to theft at many points along the way, including at the hosts themselves.

While the W3 Consortium (which administers development efforts for the WWW) can't enforce security measures for host computers, it can implement a standard security protocol for data communication between Internet servers and client desktops. The commercial interests of the WWW have been held up while the Consortium settles on a standard solution. A few potential candidates are already well-publicized, including the SSL software protocol from Netscape. At this time, the W3 Consortium is aware of the critical nature of net security and is working quickly to develop a security solution.

Tip
The overwhelming majority of connections are not secure and most likely will never be, unless they connect to commercial Web sites.

When a security method is finally implemented, Web viewers will be modified to support the authentication procedure that will be necessary to guarantee the integrity of any client/server data transmissions. Netscape Navigator 1.0N already incorporates basic security features, and will notify the end user when a connection is secure (see fig. 6.2).

Fig. 6.2
Netscape provides a pop-up notification and changes the viewer interface to reflect a secure connection.

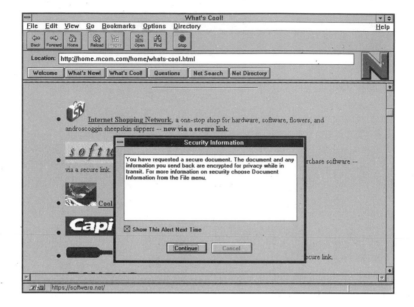

The Current Desktop Climate

Despite continuing advances in the WWW and its client software, the current computing desktop environment includes a wide range of hardware and transmission capabilities, some of which can be viewed as restrictive to effective "web crawling":

- A data infrastructure with variable transmission rates (from 56K to 10M per second),

- User serial access rates as slow as 2,400 baud (for particularly patient users) through a maximum of 28.8 K per second,

- Desktops running minimum hardware configurations (PCs using 80286 and 80386 technology and Macintosh machines running on 68020 processors) through Sun Microsystems workstations,

- Web clients with no graphics support through viewers with full graphics and digital video capabilities.

With the state of Web client development today, and the common practice of making at least provisionally free versions available, no choice of viewer is permanent. Each of the viewers described in this chapter carry pros and cons—weigh them against your own hardware and data connection capabilities when deciding on the best solution for you.

Using Lynx

Although the WWW is a multimedia environment, users who don't have the access or hardware to support graphics-based access to the Web are not without access. Lynx provides a text-based interface to the WWW (see fig. 6.3).

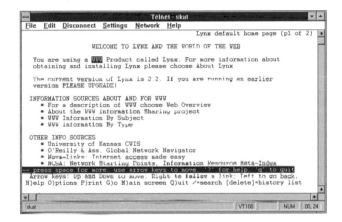

Fig. 6.3
Lynx provides options at the bottom of the screen.

Lynx supports the entire range of Internet services, including FTP, Gopher, WAIS, and UseNet News. It can also display the source of a loaded HTML document, and can act as an editor for local files. It's a versatile and fast performer on the WWW.

The Lynx interface is somewhat quirky to users accustomed to mouse-driven environments. Use the cursor keys to navigate, and perform Lynx commands with single character keystrokes. The up- and down-arrow keys allow you to cycle through the available links on a Web page, and the left- and right-arrow keys allow you to travel your link history (left takes you back to the previous link, and right takes you forward to the link currently highlighted).

The Lynx Options menu (type **O**) allows you to customize the Lynx environment, including selecting a default text editor, entering your e-mail address for Web mail messages, and choosing the current user mode.

Tip
In Lynx, type **H** to display the online help. Most UNIX-based programs use extensive help or man page systems to assist users from the command prompt, and Lynx is no different.

Lynx provides three user modes depending on the amount of guidance the user needs. First-time users should leave the mode setting at Novice because full navigation controls and Lynx command keys are listed on each page. The Intermediate setting removes the visible Lynx commands, leaving the navigation commands. The Advanced setting removes all on-screen command text, allowing Web pages to use the full session window (see fig. 6.4).

Fig. 6.4
In addition to the Web page text, the Advanced mode displays only the document's URL.

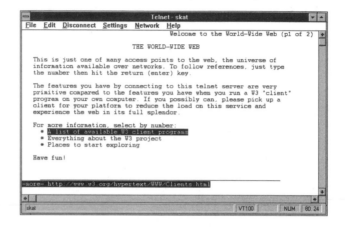

Tip
Lynx uses colored text to represent links, just as in graphical viewers.

Lynx depends on the Web documents to use the ALT attribute when incorporating graphics, or to alternate text-only menus where ALT values can't provide the necessary links to navigate the Web site. Unfortunately, too many authors overlook this courtesy or are unfamiliar with text-based Web users. For example, the Napa Valley Virtual Visit provides a link from its graphics-based Web page (see fig. 6.5) to a page based on text menus (see fig. 6.6).

Fig. 6.5
Lynx users can't use this page...

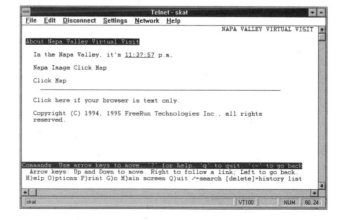

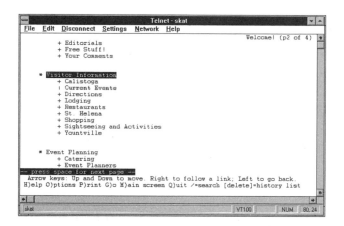

Fig. 6.6
...but this page
allows full access
to the site's
information links.

Many Web sites provide Mailto: links that allow users to send e-mail to the
contact person for the Web site. Lynx supports the Mailto: feature, providing
a sparse—and rather unfriendly—message interface (see fig. 6.7).

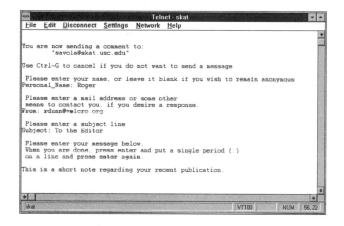

Fig. 6.7
Mail messaging
from Lynx is
command-line
based with
no on-screen
enhancements.

For users with a slow data connection to the Web (such as a modem connection into a UNIX account), or for those who prefer to avoid the lengthy retrieval times for graphics-based Web pages, Lynx is an excellent choice that
deserves better support from HTML document authors.

II

How Documents Reach You

Using NCSA Mosaic

When CERN began developing the WWW back in 1989, it had little idea how popular the Web would become. It took the arrival of NCSA Mosaic four years later to make that a reality.

The National Center for Supercomputer Applications, at the University of Illinois, spent years developing the graphical front end to the WWW that became Mosaic. When it arrived in 1993 on the three primary educational platforms (UNIX, Windows, and Macintosh), it ushered in a revolution in the way people approached the Internet. In less than a year, the archaic commands and less-than-intuitive text interfaces of Internet services (including Gopher, which had already established its dominance in the distributed information field) were replaced by a graphical, link-driven "super client." The Internet has been moving out of the realm of research and education and into the popular culture ever since.

In the past year, the Mosaic team has seen the competition arrive—mostly clones providing the same features and service support. But there are others, primarily Netscape Navigator, that have propelled enhancement and feature development forward at a quicker pace than NCSA. This isn't surprising, given that the competition has been using commercial salaries to lure away the programmers who originally designed and created Mosaic. Netscape Communications was founded by a former Mosaic team member, who turned his expertise into a runaway favorite consumer product.

What Mosaic Can Do

As the original WWW client, Mosaic supports the entire range of Internet services and document capabilities. These include HTTP, FTP, Gopher, WAIS, Telnet, and NNTP (Network News Transport Protocol) services from UseNet and e-mail. Some of the services are fully supported, such as Gopher; others are still not completely implemented, such as e-mail and UseNet News (see fig. 6.8). Mosaic also does not let you upload files via FTP, although that capability might be added in the future.

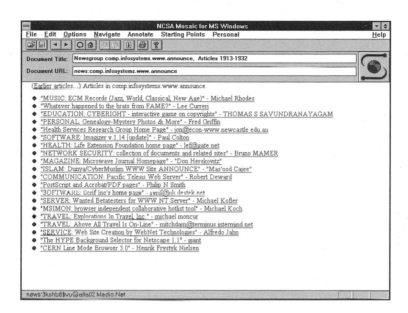

Fig. 6.8
Mosaic can read News postings, but can't post new articles to the groups.

Note

As with any new technology, Mosaic is always under development. The current software is fairly limited in its capability to handle features like e-mail and News posts. The limitations are being addressed to "catch Mosaic up" to the feature levels of other browsers.

Also, the primary advantage to using Mosaic and other Web viewers is to access the HTTP services—Web servers can't deliver documents to clients for other Internet applications, such as Gopher clients (although those capabilities are being pursued by the Gopher team). Lesser-known network information systems like Hyper-G may also integrate support for WWW data to enhance usefulness and attract a wider user base.

Mosaic uses external utilities to process data formats it can't understand itself. These helper applications process information such as digital sound, video, and documents that require their own viewers, such as Adobe Acrobat or Common Ground. Mosaic uses a table of file extensions to associate these data types with the proper players (see fig. 6.9).

II

How Documents Reach You

Fig. 6.9
This list (found
under the
Preferences dialog
box) allows you to
create new data
file types and
their respective
associations, and
to make changes
to current
associations.

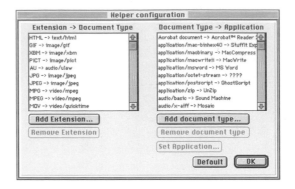

One feature found on Mosaic that isn't commonly available in other viewers
is the Annotate feature. This lets you attach a text note or record a digital
sound file associated with the current Web document (see fig. 6.10 and fig.
6.11). The sound annotation feature is available only on the Macintosh version of Mosaic at this time. Whether sound or text, a note referring to the
annotation appears at the bottom of the page you have displayed. You can
view the annotation, which is saved as a file on a local drive, the next time
you access the page. Just click it the same way you click any other hyperlink.

Fig. 6.10
Text annotations
are used much like
margin notes to
attach comments
to HTML
documents.

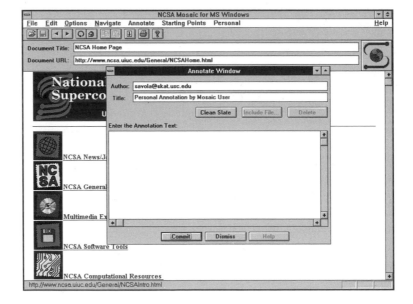

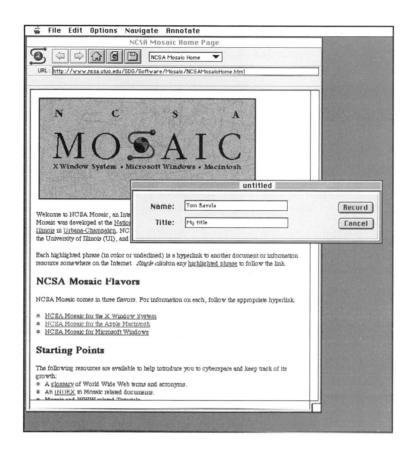

Fig. 6.11
Sound annotations use the built-in sound capabilities of the Macintosh for recording and playback.

NCSA is developing Mosaic for three platforms: Windows, Macintosh, and UNIX systems (running the X Window graphic environment). The Mosaic interface has been standardized across these platforms, but a few program functions are system-specific.

Mosaic for Windows

Mosaic's interface is straightforward and uncluttered, as shown in figure 6.12.

Mosaic uses the standard Windows menu conventions as a starting point (the Print option is appropriately on the File menu) and then it detours to provide application-specific menu options. The interface has a simple toolbar, document title field, and URL field. Each of these components is optional; the Options menu lets you select and deselect any component you want (see fig. 6.13).

II

How Documents Reach You

Fig. 6.12

The Mosaic default layout offers a wide window for the display of document text and images.

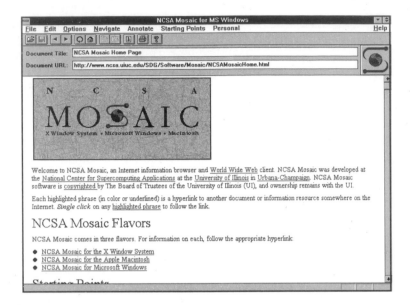

Fig. 6.13

To select an option just pull down the Options menu.

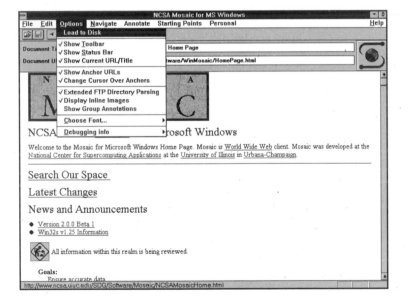

The toolbar icons are fairly self explanatory, with the exception of a couple. The Open button opens a dialog box that allows you to enter a new URL or choose a URL to access from a pull-down list. The Save button, which looks like a floppy disk, lets you save your next link to your hard drive as a text or source file. The Back (left arrow) and Forward (right arrow) buttons allow you to move backwards and forwards in your current session's document history, retrieving information from the data cache and reducing the amount of time it takes to retrieve a document again.

> **Note**
>
> If you ever need to do an impromptu demonstration of the WWW, and do not have a network or serial connection to access the Internet, use the data cache to store a series of Web pages. As you give your demonstration, use the history arrows or document links to travel between them, creating the illusion that you're "surfing the Net."

The Reload button resembles a recycle icon. It lets you reload the current document and not use the data stored in Mosaic's data cache. This is great for browsing pages that change quickly, or local documents that you're editing and previewing in Mosaic, to see how they'll look before being published on the WWW.

When you choose the Home button, it retrieves your default home page. The next two buttons are generally not found on the toolbar of many viewers: the Copy and Paste buttons.

The Find button resembles a thermometer. Click this button to open a search field; enter your text string and press Enter to search the current document. This search function is bare bones—it doesn't allow for different types of searches (such as with or without case-sensitivity, forwards or backwards in the document from the cursor position).

The last two buttons are the Print button, which starts a print job for the current document, and the Help button, which loads the Mosaic Windows Help file. Mosaic provides documentation with the viewer, giving users a readily available reference in case they are having problems and can't access the Windows Mosaic home page for answers.

Tip
Click and hold any button and a text description will appear in the status bar at the bottom of the Mosaic window.

II

How Documents Reach You

Unlike the Macintosh version of Mosaic, the Windows version uses hierarchical menus to customize different settings, such as the text representation of various HTML elements (see fig. 6.14). This pull-down paradigm is less user-friendly, making it necessary to repeatedly access the menu system when modifying more than one setting.

Fig. 6.14

Choose your own fonts to customize how HTML text containers in Web documents display text.

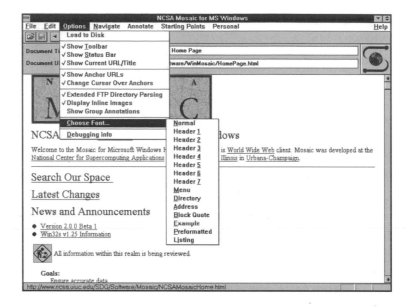

Note

The Options menu reveals that Mosaic supports up to seven header levels, while the HTML standard specifies only six levels. You can ignore the seventh header because most authors won't create documents with more than six levels.

The **N**avigate menu echoes the button controls with the additional options for viewing the current session's document history and managing a *hot list,* a list of saved document URLs that point to Web pages you want to keep track of for future use. The hot list editor lets you change the list order, create subgroups of URLs, and edit item names and URL text (see fig. 6.15).

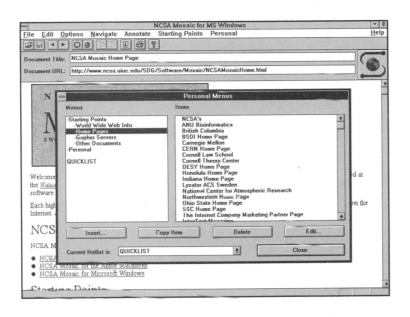

Fig. 6.15
The hot list menu
editor lets you
manage more than
one hot list; the
different lists are
available from the
dialog box pull-
down arrow.

The Starting Points and Personal menus give you a hierarchical menu of your
current hot list. The submenus that are defined in your hot list show up as
arrows in your menus; select the menu choice and the submenu is displayed
next to the first menu list (see fig. 6.16).

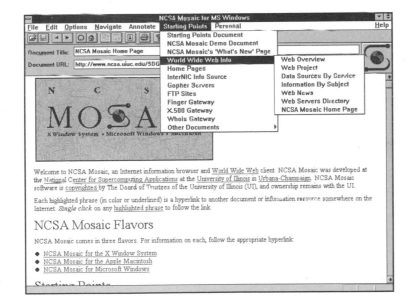

Fig. 6.16
Hot list menus
only support a
hierarchy of one
sublevel.

II

How Documents Reach You

Recently, NCSA Mosaic entered the beta stage for its Mosaic 2.0 product. The new version adds support for many of the deficiencies of the current "gold" version (the version this overview is closer to in terms of features and functions). The first beta level has demonstrated support for advanced HTML features, such as tables and delayed and interlaced inline image display. NCSA has made a commitment to WIN32s, the 32-bit extension for Windows, and version 2.0 will only be able to run on systems running Windows 3.1 and WIN32s (or systems using Windows NT).

Mosaic for the Macintosh

Like the Windows version, Mosaic for the Macintosh is a product in development. The version used for this overview, 2.0b1, includes many of the advanced features talked about in the previous section.

The program's interface is very similar to the Windows version: some of the toolbar buttons look different but they function the same; and the menu options have been rearranged in a more logical manner. The Reload button looks like a document page with the same "recycle" circle on it. The document title is not displayed in a Title field with the page URL—it's displayed in the Mosaic title bar above the menu bar (see fig. 6.17).

Tip

Mosaic uses a nifty animation to indicate that the program is busy: the lights spin around the globe icon. To interrupt the current document or graphic being downloaded, click the globe.

With the Macintosh version, buttons on the toolbar are: Backwards, Forwards, Home, Reload, and Save.

Mosaic for the Macintosh incorporates a pull-down history window on the toolbar; click and hold the current page name to display a list of previous pages. Scroll to a specific entry to have Mosaic reload that document for you.

The Starting Points and Personal menus found in the Windows version have been incorporated under the Navigate menu. The Personal menu has been replaced with a Hotlist menu item (see fig. 6.18).

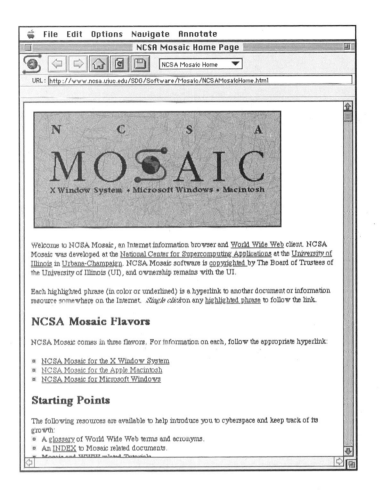

II

How Documents Reach You

Fig. 6.17
Mosaic for the
Macintosh does
not have a "status
bar" to indicate
the viewer's
progress in its
current activity.

The current level of Mosaic for the Macintosh has a few features not found
on the Windows version. The new features are found under the Options
menu (see fig. 6.19). The Use This Page for Home option changes your designated home page to the one you're currently viewing. The Flush Cache option deletes your existing cache data, requiring Mosaic to download every
previous page again.

Fig. 6.18
The Navigate menu items are condensed for easier use; the Custom Menu option opens the hot list in edit mode.

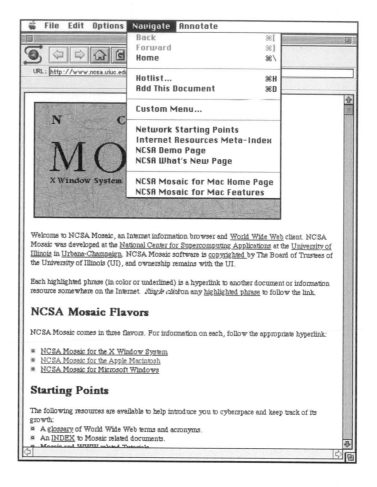

> **Note**
>
> There are reasons to define the data in Mosaic: because it forces the viewer to re-trieve every document again, loading them in a fresh state with no indication that the pages have been visited before, it forces a user to enter user authentication infor-mation for Web sites such as Hot Wired.

A newly supported feature is Enable View Source in the Options menu, which, when selected, allows you to view a document's source HTML code when you choose File, View Source. Mosaic for the Macintosh also provides a

Preferences option. When you choose this option, the Preferences dialog box opens. Here, you can customize your personal settings, mail and news servers, and define external helper application data formats.

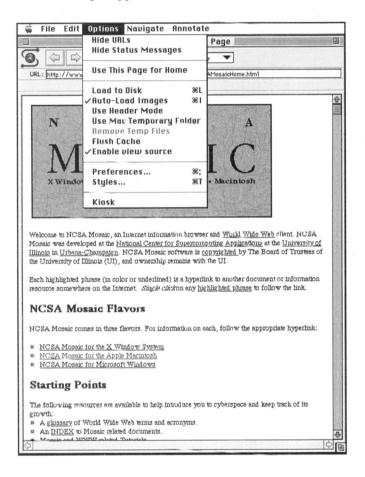

Fig. 6.19
Mosaic for the Macintosh uses "hide" and "show" to turn on and off features like the current URL field and the status messages.

II

How Documents Reach You

The final new feature is the Kiosk option. Choosing Kiosk removes the application window controls and strips out the application commands from the menus. What's left looks very much like a kiosk application; with this feature, Mosaic has taken a strong step towards integrating the WWW and HTML development into certain areas of multimedia development like kiosks and computer-based training (or CBT).

NCSA is moving quickly to regain some of the user base it lost to faster developing products like Netscape Navigator. With the cutting-edge features and HTML support emerging in the beta program for 2.0, and the development for Microsoft Windows (with WIN32s), Macintosh 680 × 0 machines, Power Macintosh machines, and UNIX graphical workstations, NCSA Mosaic is making a strong bid to be the definitive World Wide Web application once again.

Using Netscape Navigator

In the early months of 1994, Jim Clark (former chairman of Silicon Graphics) and Marc Anderssen (formerly of the NCSA Mosaic development team) came together to start up a commercial business focusing on Web interface development. Their flagship product is Netscape Navigator, which has made Netscape Communications nearly a household name. In the last year, the product's popularity has soared; it's estimated that 70 percent of the Web community uses Netscape (compared to just over 20 percent who use Mosaic as their Web browser).

Why Is It So Popular?

Netscape earned its share of the user market by outperforming Mosaic. Netscape is noticeably faster than Mosaic; it was the first viewer to support delayed and interlaced inline graphics. This allows users to see the text of a Web document while the images are still being downloaded, and to see the images in increasing resolutions as they are retrieved—like a picture being focused from fuzzy to sharp. You can get the gist of the image before it's completely transferred and then you can interrupt the transfer with another link on the page or with a viewer command, speeding up your Navigator session.

Netscape also blazed a solitary trail defying the sacrosanct domain of the W3 Consortium HTML development team by supporting a set of non-standard (but very popular) extensions to HTML 2.0. These extensions provide authors much more control over the look of a Web page in the viewer window. The underlying philosophy behind HTML is that the author should have very little control of a document's display, but every control over the intentions of the document's contents. How the intentions are interpreted is up to the end user's software.

Netscape's new controls allow authors to center text and graphics, increase the size of text fonts, scale graphics in a page, make text blink, align images against either margin, and control the spacing of text and graphic document elements.

What Netscape Can Do

Netscape is a full-featured viewer. Besides HTTP, it supports e-mail, Gopher, FTP, Telnet, WAIS, and UseNet News (see fig. 6.20).

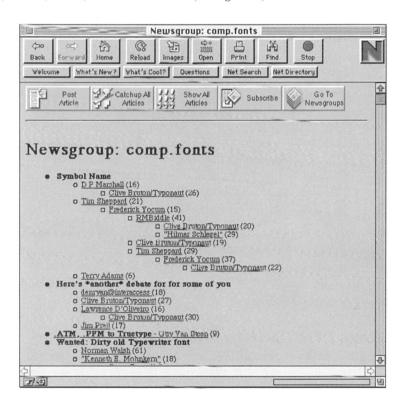

Fig. 6.20
Netscape provides a remarkably robust interface for reading UseNet News.

Netscape can use FTP to retrieve files from remote file servers, issue searches on WAIS databases, support standard Gopher functions, and even launch Telnet sessions for remote host access over the Internet. Netscape doesn't replace some of your stand-alone utilities, such as Fetch or WS_FTP (after all, it can't upload files or perform file management via FTP). But it's very adept at making these different services invisible on your desktop—Navigator can be the single application to use if you have to choose just one.

As with other Web clients, Netscape supports external viewers (helper applications) to process data formats the software does not handle natively. Popular viewers include digital audio and video players and the Adobe Acrobat Reader. The end user is generally required to find and install helper programs, and configure Netscape to use them with files having the proper extension, as shown in figure 6.21.

Fig. 6.21
The Preferences dialog box lists all current helper applications and the file extensions they are associated with.

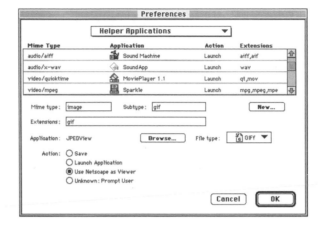

Netscape provides all of its documentation online via its home pages. While this is great for users who can access their Web sites, others who might need troubleshooting tips or other help can have problems receiving support (Netscape does not support non-paying customers). Figure 6.22 shows the Netscape Frequently Asked Questions page.

Netscape HTML Extensions

The most controversial issue surrounding Netscape Navigator is its support and promotion of non-standard HTML usage. These extensions create incompatibilities between Netscape-specific formatting and the majority of Web viewers (if a client doesn't recognize an extension, it should ignore it and format the data without the additional characteristics). A few browsers, including OS/2 WebExplorer, also support Netscape's non-standard HTML.

The extensions have been hugely popular with the authoring community. Some Web sites go so far as to discourage non-Netscape users from viewing their documents. The heavy usage of Netscape extensions, and the demand for additional author control over the desktop display of Web documents, have pressured the W3 Consortium to adopt many Netscape features for the upcoming HTML 3.0. Some element uses were already under development for HTML 3.0 when Netscape implemented them, and others that Netscape introduced have been accepted by the development consortium. Figures 6.23 and 6.24 show a Web site that uses extensive Netscape formatting, viewed by Navigator 1.0N and Mosaic Alpha 2, respectively.

Netscape produces three versions of Navigator. They are all virtually identical, adapted to the operating environment's standards.

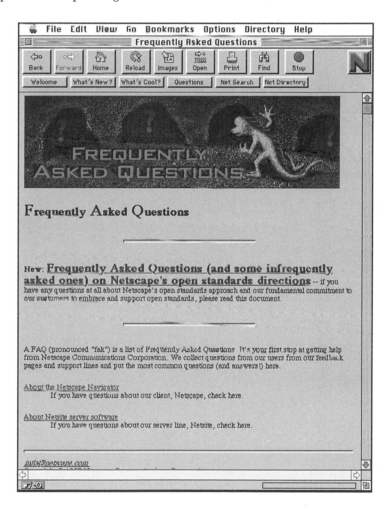

Fig. 6.22
Netscape also publishes the Navigator end-user manual and basic guidelines for using Netscape HTML extensions online.

Fig. 6.23
Netscape Naviga-
tor interpretation
of this sample
home page.

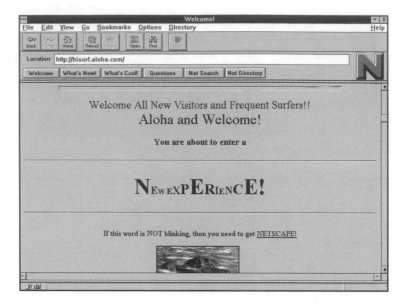

Fig. 6.24
NCSA Mosaic
interpretation
of the same
document.

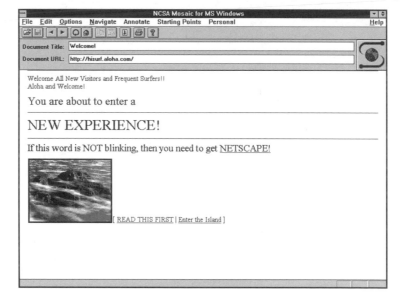

Netscape Navigator for Windows

Netscape follows the standard Windows conventions regarding menu items and window controls. Navigator's interface provides a toolbar with buttons for the most commonly used actions (see fig. 6.25).

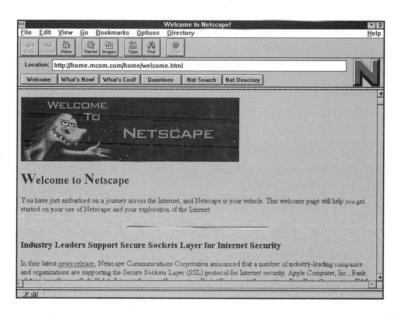

Fig. 6.25
Netscape grays out buttons that are not supported by the current Options configuration or that are not yet available (such as the page history arrow buttons).

The right- and left-arrow buttons allow you to move forward and backwards through your page history. The Open button lets you retrieve a URL by entering it into a pop-up dialog box. The Find button provides a typical text search for the current document (the text string can be case-sensitive or case-insensitive and the search can progress either up or down the document). The Stop button is useful for interrupting the current viewer action, such as retrieving a particularly slow document. The Reload button lets you retrieve the current document again.

> **Note**
>
> If an initial document access is interrupted, or the text or graphics don't load correctly, use the Reload function to prompt the Web server to send the same document again. This is also handy when previewing your own pages; after you modify and save the current test page, Reload lets you see the changes in a snap.

Tip

You can remove the toolbar, Directory buttons, and current URL location to allow more room. Open the Options menu and deselect these options.

The Home button loads the Web page designated as your "home page" in the Preferences Styles dialog box; by default, Netscape opens the Welcome to Netscape page. The Images button lets you manually retrieve inline images in a document; turning off document graphics improves the performance dramatically, especially when there are multiple images on the same page. The Images button lets you selectively view the pages you want to see with images.

The Directory buttons, beneath the URL location field, give you an on-screen shortcut to various Netscape home pages.

Configuring Navigator is very easy; Navigator borrows a convention from Macintosh browsers and uses the Preferences dialog box for all configuration categories—as opposed to the collapsing menu structure that is more common with Windows applications (see fig. 6.26).

Fig. 6.26

You can access Netscape Navigator categories through the pull-down list in the Preferences dialog box.

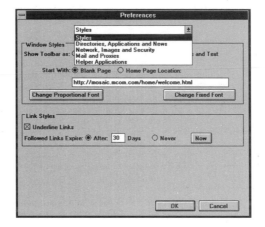

Navigator lets users save a list of their favorite or most frequently traveled WWW pages in a *bookmark* list. This list is manageable; users can reorder items, insert line breaks and headings to subdivide the list, and create a pull-down menu structure to the bookmark list. Netscape provides two methods for accessing your bookmark list. You can open the **B**ookmarks menu to display a vertical list or hierarchy that you create. To edit your bookmark list, or to organize and categorize your listings, select the second viewing method. Choose the View Bookmarks option from the **B**ookmarks menu. This opens the Bookmark List dialog box (see fig. 6.27).

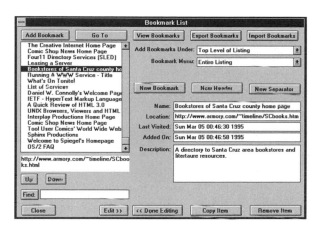

Fig. 6.27
The extended
Bookmark List
dialog box can
display attached
comments to help
you keep track of
the content of
each entry (these
comments are not
visible from the
main Navigator
interface).

Lists with subheadings then look different when viewed with the Bookmark
menu. See figure 6.28 for an example of a formatted Bookmark List.

Fig. 6.28
Headings and
lined dividers help
make an extensive
Bookmark List
easier to read.

One feature available with the Windows version of Navigator, that isn't available in the Macintosh version, is Print Preview (choose File, Print Preview).
Figure 6.29 shows the Welcome to Netscape home page as it would be
printed.

Fig. 6.29
Print Preview
allows you to see a
document layout
before printing it
to your currently
selected printer.

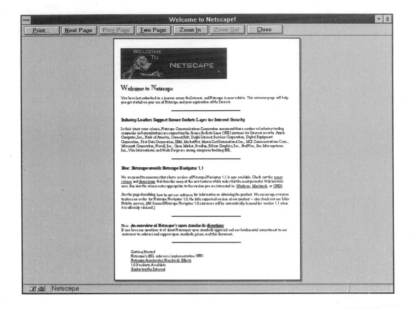

Preview allows you to zoom in and out of the displayed document, display two pages at once, and issue the Print command from within the preview page. This feature is consistent with applications like Microsoft Word and Excel, which have similar preview windows and document display controls.

Netscape Navigator for Windows is currently available as a 16-bit application (running under the standard Microsoft Windows 3.1 software); the next version, 1.1, will be offered as both a 16-bit application and a 32-bit application (for users of the WIN32s extensions or Windows NT).

Netscape Navigator for the Macintosh

Netscape for the Macintosh shares in the advantages of standard Macintosh applications: sharp and bright on-screen images, select and copy viewer window text (a feature available in all platform versions), and a consistent menu interface. In fact, one advantage all versions of Navigator share is a consistent interface and nearly identical feature set (with exceptions as noted in this chapter).

Note

To indicate that Netscape is busy retrieving a document, the N icon "pulses" in and out. Unlike Mosaic, clicking the N not only stops retrieval of the current document, but also tells Netscape to load the Netscape home page. To only interrupt the current program action, click the Stop button.

Navigator for the Macintosh shares all of the interface button functions and options described in the Windows version. As shown previously, Navigator uses a common Preferences dialog box to display all customization options (choose Options, Preferences). Helper applications are also defined in this dialog box.

The bookmark list customization capability is also the same here as in the Windows version. Figure 6.30 shows an example of a Bookmark list that has been customized with pull-down menus and categories.

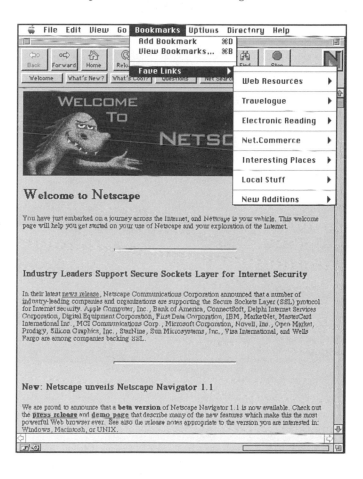

Fig. 6.30
Arrows indicate where additional drop-down menus are available in the Bookmark list.

One feature available on the Macintosh version that was not incorporated into the Windows version is the Save Next Link As option on the File menu (see fig. 6.31). When you choose this option before selecting a hypertext link in the current document, you're prompted with a Save As dialog box.

You can save HTML documents as text-only or as source, including the HTML codes. Links to graphics will prompt you for a local file name and save the location for the image being retrieved.

Fig. 6.31
Choosing Save Next Link As changes your cursor to a double-line crosshair cursor.

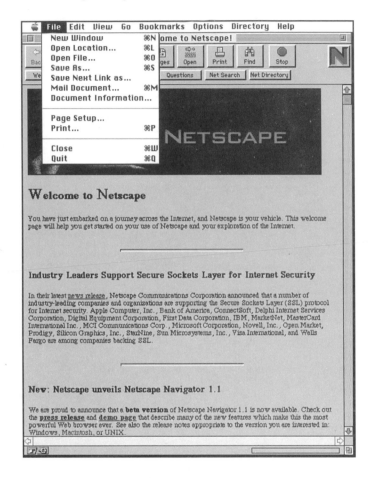

The next version of Netscape for the Macintosh will be available in either a 680 × 0 version (for Quadras, Centris, and other older Macintosh systems) or a PowerMac version for PowerPC-based machines.

New Version on the Way

Netscape has already begun the beta program for Version 1.1, which will include many additions to the current extensions and support the HTML Level 3 elements, as well as improve many of Navigator's basic functions. The expected features and improvements include:

- Support for HTML-based tables

- Dynamic backgrounds (authors can define either the color or a graphic image as the page background)

- Author-defined font colors

- Pop-up menus for viewer windows

- Drag and drop links in Web documents to your desktop to save them in a text file

- Improved e-mail and UseNet newsreaders

- Additional security options for Web documents

See Chapter 19, "Extending the Standard," for more information and a sneak peek at the upcoming Navigator 1.1.

Using InternetWorks

NCSA Mosaic has spawned an entire industry of developers who want to get into the WWW client business. InternetWorks Lite, available at no charge from BookLink, is a lesser known product, but one that ranks among the best in terms of features and support. It supports all of the primary Internet services (FTP, Gopher, WAIS, UseNet News, and e-mail) with the exception of Telnet. This single deficiency aside, InternetWorks Lite is a good choice for the new Web user. The commercial version of InternetWorks provides additional capabilities and end-user support.

InternetWorks is an OLE 2.0 application; when you install the viewer software you also are prompted to install the OLE extensions if they don't exist on your system.

> **Note**
>
> Check your Windows configuration to find out whether OLE 2.0 is installed. Note the date of the OLE files (such as OLE2.DLL in your Windows\System subdirectory)—you don't want to overwrite more recent files with an older distribution of OLE 2.0. In the past, the InternetWorks installation program has crashed during installation, which I was able to track to a conflict with OLE files. This problem might be resolved by the time you read this.

InternetWorks is comprised of two applications: the WWW viewer and an e-mail and UseNet newsreader called InternetWorks Messaging System. This is actually a nice benefit—if you are not already using programs for these purposes (or don't like your current tools), the InternetWorks package is well-suited for day-to-day use.

Unlike other WWW clients, which default to a home page usually on their own Web site, InternetWorks installs a home page on your local system, using an extensive collection of HTML documents with well-designed graphics and Web links (see fig. 6.32). The local home page is the default for the viewer; you can change the default by choosing **F**ile, Set As **H**ome Page.

Fig. 6.32
InternetWorks uses a graphical map interface to navigate the wealth of home pages installed with the software.

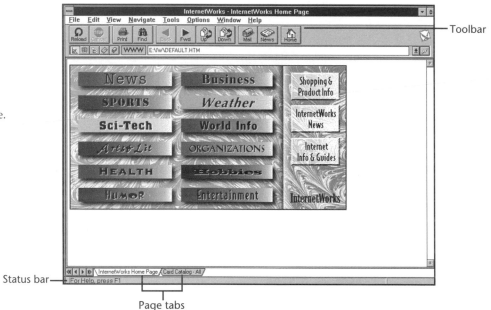

Toolbar

Status bar

Page tabs

Tip
WWW viewers share a common set of functions and use standard terminology when referring to viewer actions. The Reload button acts the same on every Web client.

The InternetWorks interface is fairly busy, but provides a great deal of functionality without having to navigate the applications menu system. The interface proves three optional features: the toolbar, page tabs, and status bar. InternetWorks uses text labels on each button of the toolbar to quickly identify the function of the button.

In addition to the standard actions, the toolbar also provides a quick link to the InternetWorks Messaging System; the Mail and News buttons open the Messaging System in the specific modes. The Toolbar also has two additional document navigation options: Up and Down. These move to the next or previous linked document for the current page (as opposed to traveling your document history, which only accesses documents you've already seen). To remove the toolbar from the viewer window, open the View menu and deselect the Toolbar option.

Another optional window feature is the page tabs (see fig. 6.33). This feature is unique to InternetWorks.

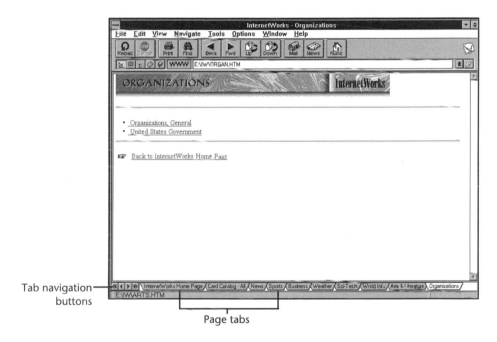

Tab navigation buttons

Page tabs

Fig. 6.33
The page tabs and tab navigation buttons resemble notebook tabs and list the document history of the current session.

II

How Documents Reach You

The page tabs represent recent Web documents. Clicking a tab takes you directly to the page (similar to the history function on Netscape and Mosaic). If the page tabs "run off" the window, the tab navigation buttons will scroll the list either one tab at a time or a page of tabs at a time. If you want to see a complete representation of the Web documents from this session, select the Card Catalog - All tab (see fig. 6.34).

You can scroll through this stack. To see information on a link and retrieve the associated document, click the card once. The card "expands" and displays the URL, the type of link it represents (such as a web document—text/html), the size (in bytes) of the document, when it was last accessed, and its current download status (the percentage finished that is in the data cache). If you want to add your own information about the document, a Note field is provided for your comments. To close the card (shrink it back into the stack) click the card's face again.

Fig. 6.34

The Card Catalog - All window displays each recent document as a stacked card with an arrow button that links back to the retrieved document.

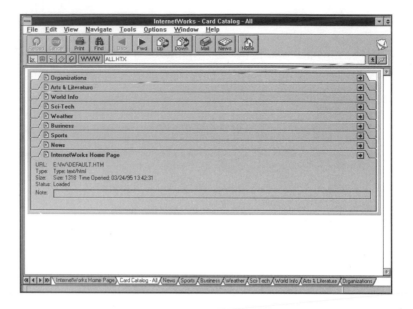

> **Note**
>
> To save a current tab stack without having to create a new catalog, choose File, Save As. Name the document using the HTX (hypertext) document type. While it's only readable by InternetWorks the file is a transportable "home page" and can be shared with other InternetWorks users.

To remove the page tabs from the viewer window (freeing up space for Web document text and images), open the View menu and deselect the Tabs option.

Beneath the toolbar is a set of Internet service icons, a URL command line, and a lightning bolt button. This feature provides a shortcut to accessing new or previous documents; clicking the Gopher button, for example, enters the Gopher URL type in the command line field, ready for you to enter the rest of the Gopher address (see fig. 6.35).

After you have entered the URL information, or used the pull-down list to select a previous document, click the lightning bolt icon to launch the URL. The InternetWorks icon spins while the document is being retrieved.

InternetWorks supports an unlimited number of *panes,* or document windows. Each window can contain a different Web page, allowing you to maintain multiple sessions (see fig. 6.36). Use the commands under the Window menu to open horizontal and vertical panes, or to close the current pane.

Fig. 6.35
Five services are
available using the
command line
shortcuts: WWW,
Gopher, FTP,
UseNet News,
and e-mail.

Like the Windows version of Netscape Navigator, InternetWorks also supports Print Preview. This feature allows you to see a document layout before
printing it to your selected printer.

Preview allows you to zoom in and out of the displayed document, display
two pages at once, print text in either one or two columns (to save paper),
and issue the Print command from within the preview page (see fig. 6.37).

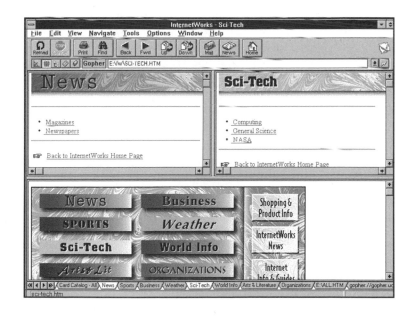

Fig. 6.36
The viewer
window title
changes to reflect
the title of the
active pane.

BookLink was purchased by America Online in 1994, a tribute to the quality of the InternetWorks products. Expect to continue to see this product on the market (or in some form or another, perhaps as the basis for America Online's own Web support).

Fig. 6.37
Choose File, Page Layout to set your document margins and the number of columns.

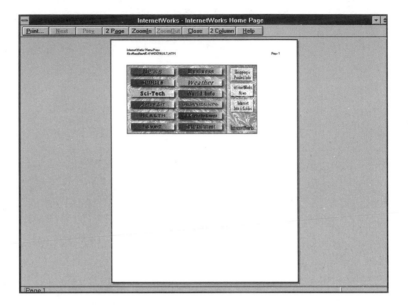

Using MacWeb

Tip
MacWeb's small memory footprint (it loads in under 800K) makes it a great choice for systems with limited memory resources, such as 2M models and portable systems.

WWW viewers on the Mac, like the Macintosh platform in general, are scarcer than on the PC and the quality can vary widely. After Mosaic and Netscape, one viewer worth mentioning is Microelectronics and Computer Technology Corporation's EINet MacWeb. MCC has developed this product for use on both the WWW and its enterprise networking platform, EINet. MacWeb is notable for a few innovative design features and HTML element definitions, yet it still lacks key functions available on other applications.

The MacWeb interface is clean and elegant, a commendable quality in the face of viewers who attempt to add every feature and "button comfort" to their viewers (see fig. 6.38).

The button interface is simple: two navigation arrow buttons for moving forward and backward along your document history and a Home Page button to return to your designated home page. The URL field is active; you can edit the URL text, press Return, and MacWeb will try to access the new URL. This feature saves you the time of having to pull down a menu or click a button to get the Open URL dialog box (as in Mosaic and Netscape).

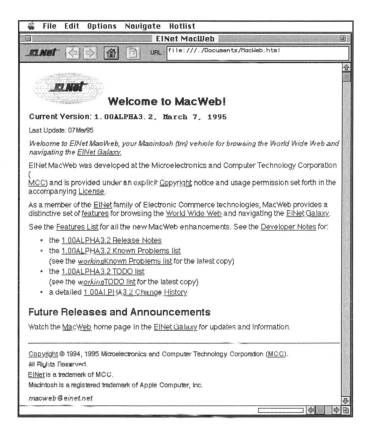

Fig. 6.38
The simple four-button design of MacWeb is especially comforting to first-time WWW users.

Note

One of the really nice touches in MacWeb is the default font for the HTML text elements and document body text. Nearly every other viewer uses a serif font, usually Times Roman, for their data. MacWeb uses Helvetica, a common font, and the difference is good on the eyes. Serif fonts can be tiring to read for extended periods of time, especially at different weights (and with Netscape, often at variable, non-standard point sizes). The Helvetica text is light and clean, a perfect choice for MacWeb's similar design.

The File menu does provide a manual method for opening a URL, as well as reloading the current document and bringing up the Preferences dialog box, where you can define your default home page and the viewer's background color. Only use the third option, enabling blank lines in HTML, if you're accessing documents where the author was unaware that sequential paragraph breaks are generally not recognized by WWW clients.

Tip
You can export
your MacWeb
hotlist for use by
another viewer by
saving it as an
HTML document.
Choose Hotlist,
Hotlist Operations.
Then choose
HTML as the Save
As option.

Also under the File menu is the Save URL item, a feature only available on MacWeb. Save URL allows you to save the current document URL to a file, which can be organized on your local hard drive. By dragging and dropping the URL file onto MacWeb, you will launch the viewer and it will automatically open the specified resource.

The Edit menu includes items for the Styles dialog box and the Helpers helper applications dialog box. The Styles drop-down lists let you modify the current definition for any HTML element (see fig. 6.39).

In the same manner, when you choose Edit, Helpers, it brings up the Helper dialog box for associating helper applications to file types and file name extensions (see fig. 6.40).

Fig. 6.39
The Element pull-down menu lets you select an HTML element to define.

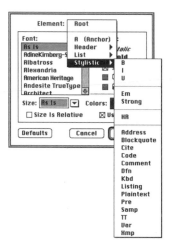

Fig. 6.40
The Helper dialog box lets you add, delete, and change MIME (or file data types) associations.

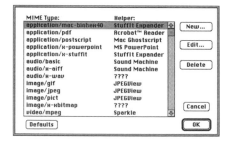

The Options menu provides the toggle for automatically loading inline images, a choice to flush the data cache, and a choice to view the current document's source (either as it is generated or as it has been retrieved, and without the document headers).

The Navigate menu offers the standard complement of navigation options: forward to the next page, back to the previous page, go to the home page, and a document history.

The Hotlist menu provides a list of documents on the hot list, plus a series of submenus for modifying the list and adding new items (see fig. 6.41).

Fig. 6.41
The Hotlist Operations includes the option to create and retrieve multiple hotlists.

MacWeb supports a number of advanced features, including forms, user authentication, and transparent inline images. But it's missing others that are mandatory on a Web viewer, including a mechanism that lets you interrupt the current viewer download (especially necessary as more and more Web pages rely on complex graphics). There's nothing more frustrating than having to wait for a painfully slow document to complete its download, especially when you've already chosen the viewer's next link or action to perform!

Tip
Convert your existing Mosaic hotlist to MacWeb by dragging and dropping it onto the MacWeb icon or alias.

MacWeb, like many Web viewers and Web pages, is still under construction; this version is less than a month old and it is a seventh-generation alpha product (meaning it has not even reached the beta stage in its development). For an alpha, it's very solid and stable. If you're a Mac user, keep an eye on the MCC MacWeb product.

Using WebExplorer

WWW viewer development primarily centers around the Windows and Macintosh platforms—after all, they probably make up more than 90 percent of the Web audience. The rest of the platforms, hardware or software, generally have to contend with little or no selection of native WWW clients.

II

How Documents Reach You

The OS/2 platform is no exception. Since the arrival of version 2, the OS/2 user base has grown considerably. Because it's compatible with the vast majority of hardware in use today, OS/2 has been measured as a minor success compared to the Windows monolith. OS/2 Warp, the latest iteration, lept beyond other operating systems by shipping with Internet tools and a related provider. (IBM's move was probably the deciding factor for Microsoft's plans to integrate Internet access into the long-awaited Windows 95.) The WWW client shipped with Warp is WebExplorer, developed by IBM (you might have to download it from a public FTP site or a service line CompuServe, depending on which Warp you own).

WebExplorer supports the entire range of Internet services: FTP, Gopher, WAIS, Telnet, UseNet News, and e-mail. WebExplorer has the distinct advantage of being one of the first viewers to openly support the Netscape non-standard HTML extensions, providing OS/2 users the full intended effect of Web pages created with Netscape coding.

WebExplorer is also breaking ground on the use of "drag and drop" in regards to Web page content; you can click and drag inline images from the viewer window into a folder on the Workplace Shell desktop, creating a new file containing the image data.

Tip

To get a quick description of a toolbar button, place the cursor over it—the button's function appears in the status bar.

The interface for WebExplorer is straightforward; the viewer window is composed of a toolbar and an optional URL field at the top, and a status bar at the bottom.

Some of the toolbar icons are a little cryptic; fortunately, these tend to be for functions that are not accessed frequently. The first two Arrow buttons move you forward and backward along your document history. The Open File brings up a dialog box so you can open a new URL. The Text button calls up the Configure Fonts dialog box that allows you to customize the font and size for the WebExplorer basic screen font formats: small, normal, large, and very large (see fig. 6.42).

Fig. 6.42

The use of font formats is unconventional for WWW viewers; most users don't have any idea how or when each format is used.

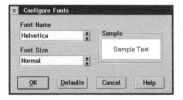

The fifth button is the Colors button, which displays WebExplorer's Configure Colors dialog box. Here, you can customize the color of body text, hyperlinks, accessed hyperlinks, and the viewer background (see fig. 6.43).

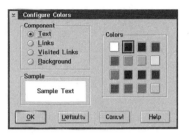

Fig. 6.43

The color palette is limited to six colors, regardless of the system's current color palette.

The next button is the Web Map button. Web Map is a unique method for displaying the document history from the current session. Much like InternetWorks' "card catalog" feature, Web Map displays a graphic list of the Web pages you accessed (see fig. 6.44). You can select the icons to quickly return to the pages.

Fig. 6.44

Icons let you know which documents were successfully accessed (the file folder icon), which documents were not successfully accessed (the red "stop" circle), and where you currently are (the green arrow).

How Documents Reach You

The QuickList button calls up the WebExplorer QuickList (makes sense!). This is the same as a hot list or bookmark list, where you can keep a list of favorite Web pages and their URLs (see fig. 6.45). You can access these during any viewer session.

Fig. 6.45
You can also access the QuickList from the Navigate menu.

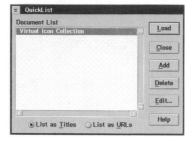

Tip
WebExplorer's Cyberspace icon animates during viewer activity; to interrupt the current process and regain control of the viewer, click the icon.

QuickList provides some customization of the list of Web sites; you can choose to view the documents by their page titles (which you can edit if they're not expressive enough), or by their associated URL addresses. At this time, you can't import or export this list or other lists—a "feature-deficiency" that should be addressed by the developers at IBM in the next version. Clicking the next button, the Page button, adds the current Web page to the end of your QuickList.

The last two buttons are reminiscent of what you'll find on other Web viewers. The Print button prints the current page (there is no Print Preview feature in WebExplorer) and the Home button jumps you back to your designated home page.

Tip
WebExplorer buries the ever-popular Reload function under the Navigate menu; for faster service, press F5 (the keyboard shortcut) to reload the current page from its source.

Other features supported by WebExplorer include letting you view the HTML source of the current document. Just open the File menu and choose View File (HTML). You can also set WebExplorer in Presentation Mode by opening the Options menu and choosing Presentation Mode. This is the same as Mosaic's Kiosk setting—the menu and window controls disappear and the Web pages act as though they're part of a stand-alone interactive application.

To configure external data file viewers, use the Configure Viewers menu item to open the Configure Viewers dialog box (see fig. 6.46). You can scroll through the various data types and associate them to their corresponding utilities.

Fig. 6.46
WebExplorer
doesn't allow you
to enter new data
types for formats
such as Adobe
Acrobat.

WebExplorer definitely has its limitations. It doesn't let a user modify most of the HTML text styles (including headings and text containers). It does allow you to change the background color, which was necessary for the figures you see in this book, but is probably less important for everyday use. WebExplorer version 1.0 seems to have trouble displaying transparent GIF inline images, and it accesses the disk cache quite frequently on Web documents that don't make other viewers blink twice. The QuickList management is poor—there are no import and export capabilities, no support for subheadings and separators, and no provision for adding comments to the documents on the list.

For OS/2 users who prefer to use native applications on Warp, rather than Windows programs from within Warp's Windows emulation, WebExplorer is the only choice today. Users can elect to run the Windows-based programs, such as Mosaic and Netscape, but should expect a period of troubleshooting system and viewer settings to begin to approach the same performance level provided by native Windows or by WebExplorer.

From Here...

Web authors have little control over their audience's software choices. Most users settle into one favored viewer after experimenting with the available software to find which provide the ease of use and feature mix they are looking for. Some users just use what's in front of them, which may be determined by their system administrator or the Internet software bundle from their service provider. This overview should have given you a sense of the most common software your audience may be using to view your Web pages, and you should be able to anticipate their expectations and viewer functionality. To find out more about the HTML distribution process, or to jump right into HTML authoring, refer to the following:

■ Chapter 7, "Distributing Information with HTML," describes the advantages and disadvantages of using HTML documents for distributing and retrieving information across the Internet and on your own Local Area Network.

■ In Chapter 8, "HTML Standards and Practices," you can see how HTML authoring has accumulated a set of common practices for the benefit of both authors and end users. This chapter discusses the "good habits" of HTML development.

■ Part III, "Creating HTML Documents," includes chapters on common standards and practices in HTML and creating HTML documents from the top to the bottom.

■ Part IV, "Using Forms in HTML Documents," teaches you how to incorporate forms into documents for collecting user input and activating scripts and programs on your Web server.

Chapter 7

Distributing Information with HTML

In earlier chapters, I discussed how the World Wide Web excels as the "mother of all information distribution systems" on the Internet. The popularity and growth of the Web is a testimony to the strengths of the Web:

- Its capability to act as a common interface for most Internet services

- HTML's ease of use

- The growing number of authoring and Web management tools

But how do these strengths benefit or aid application development? Is there a role for the World Wide Web as the foundation for personal, commercial, and corporate systems?

This chapter answers the following questions:

- How can you use HTML to create commercial applications?

- What are the advantages of using HTML for applications?

- What are the disadvantages of using HTML for applications?

- Is your privacy assured when using the WWW?

Commercial Applications in HTML

Commercial software development is an art as much as it is a science. As development tools become easier to use (such as Microsoft Visual Basic's "object-oriented" capabilities), software programming is moving out of the domain of the highly trained code writers into the realm of "cottage programming." Like cottage industries of the past few centuries, accessible tools provide an opportunity for people with little or no training to participate in software development. As a consequence, the shareware market is growing steadily.

While some people call this trend the "dumbing down" of application tools, others consider it a liberation from the programming elite. I like to promote the idea that tools such as Visual Basic and HTML are necessary to help socialize computers and their applications. You'll know that computers have reached a new plateau of social integration the day a technophobe (like my father) can create a software agent to monitor the week's Internet content for discussions and news articles that include topics he's interested in.

> **Note**
>
> "Software agents" are not science fiction, but are in use today. Online services like CompuServe and Prodigy offer personalized "newspapers" that are delivered daily with only the new articles on subjects you have selected. These content-tailored services are ushering in a new personalized perspective of the Internet and related services.

▶ See "What Are Hypertext Links?" p. 252

How does HTML compare to other general interest software development tools? In many of these tools, functions and relationships between objects are defined by linking them together and creating a set of *if-then* definitions (*if* the user clicks the left mouse button on this object, *then* open the Settings dialog box). HTML functions in a similar way in Web pages: if the user clicks this inline graphic, then display the CHAPTER1.HTM document.

Tip
Hypertext links are indicated by text that is in color or underlined (or both), and images that display a color border.

As a document format language, HTML is also particularly useful for creating *front-ends* or application interfaces. This is done using mnemonic-type codes (HTML elements) to mark plain ASCII text files. For example,

◀ See "The Elements of HTML," p. 68

> A company's product catalog can be *Webified*, or converted to HTML, to allow the sales team to pull up specific and detailed information about the individual items in the company's product line.
>
> A research statistics database can be given search parameters from a Web page that incorporates a user-input form connected to coded scripts, allowing the management to generate statistical comparisons "on the fly" based on any scenario they define.

HTML should be taken seriously for developing network applications for use across the Internet (on the WWW) and locally on local area networks (LANs).

Advantages of HTML Applications

When I use the term *HTML application,* I am talking about a group of HTML documents and supporting scripts that constitute a Web site and serve a self-contained purpose. Many applications can reside on the same Internet host and be served by the same HTTP server, but as long as they are not connected by hyperlinks, they are independent of each other.

Using HTML for developing applications has a number of inherent advantages. First, these applications are quickly developed, requiring substantially less time than is required when creating stand-alone programs with languages such as C and Pascal. Web applications are easy to maintain and update without disrupting the network's data traffic (or requiring users to install new software on their desktops). HTML's unique characteristics give it a definite advantage over conventional programming languages.

Tip
You can indicate relationships between documents using the HTML element LINK.

> **Note**
>
> Like other networks, the WWW is starting to see tools emerge for maintaining WWW sites. These utilities manage file structures and can make transporting HTML applications easy (they often use "relative" associations between the HTML documents, and must remain in the same location in relation to each other). One such tool is HTML Mapper for Microsoft Windows, by Sean Jepson (**ftp://s850.mwc.edu/pub/pc /htmlmap.zip**).

The Client/Server Relationship

The WWW uses a *client/server* model for delivering information. As a web viewer requests a document from a Web site, its server sends the data, and the connection between the two computers is dropped. The client application does all processing and manipulation of data, conserving the server's CPU (central processing unit) processing power. This relationship greatly reduces the amount of time a server spends serving a client, freeing it to serve other users or let the host system perform other tasks.

> **Note**
>
> The client/server characteristic of the WWW has allowed the system to grow at its current pace, while the Internet's infrastructure has remained relatively the same. Only in the past year or so has a significant effort been necessary to improve the transmission speed of the Net to accommodate future Web growth and usage.

A second advantage to the Web's delivery model, is that it allows businesses with tight budgets to invest in hardware with less horsepower (based on the size of the intended audience and the anticipated amount of document traffic). These smaller servers are cost-effective and work very well serving closed environments, such as a company's LAN.

HTML as Common Ground

◀ See "WWW and FTP," p. 41

◀ See "WWW and WAIS," p. 44

Developing applications in HTML takes advantage of HTML general compatibility. Web applications can access other company data servers, like File Transfer Protocol (FTP) servers and WAIS (Wide Area Information Server) databases. Web viewers are also an interface to Telnet sessions, allowing users to run external command-line programs from within the HTML application.

Data types can be standardized on Web servers as well. They can be converted to types supported internally by the audiences' Web viewers, or they can deliver platform-specific formats to those users whose clients then launch an external helper program to view the data files. Developers can also use HTML documents to distribute Web viewer updates (or revisions of software) to users at their convenience, reducing support costs.

Tip

Web viewers often give users the option of saving retrieved documents to the local hard drive if an associated helper application is not defined.

Best of all, HTML applications become the common interface for the audience, regardless of their platform and operating system. There are no portability issues to tackle.

> **Note**
>
> The creative uses for the WWW just keep coming. A recent development is a utility called Web Chat, developed by the Internet Roundtable Society. *Web Chat* allows a group of users to hold nearly real-time text conversations (limited only by the speed of the network). This is a great application for implementing whiteboard-style conferencing and brainstorming sessions. See Web Chat's home page at **http://www.irsociety.com/webchat.html** for more information and download instructions.

Collecting Information with HTML

▶ See "Linking to E-Mail," p. 267

HTML Level 2 (and its compatible viewers) supports a single method of collecting information from users: e-mail, via the Mailto hyperlink. Level 3 officially introduces support for forms, although most popular viewers have already implemented this support long ago. Forms collect data from author-defined input fields and buttons, and send the results to either an e-mail address or to a CGI (Computer Gateway Interface) script to be processed in the background. See Part IV, "Using Forms in HTML Documents," for more information.

Forms allow Web sites to retrieve data such as customer mailing and payment information. Scripts can perform functions such as verifying user authorizations and generating an output to be displayed in an HTML document based on user inputs.

An excellent example site that incorporates forms, CGI scripting, an external application, and dynamic HTML display is the Interactive Graphics Generation Page at **http://www.cngg.ksu.edu:8872/**. The HTML document acts as a front-end for a "do it yourself" 3D graphics renderer (see fig. 7.1). Web authors can use pre-written commercial scripts (such as Vend) to assist in collecting online purchasing information.

Tip

Another HTML 3 feature, tables, is gaining support among WWW clients such as Mosaic and Netscape Navigator.

Note

Vend can track which products (and the quantity) that customers have selected from a Web catalog. The program requires Perl 5 and can be retrieved from **ftp://gray.maine.com/pub/awilcox/vend-0.1.tar.gz**.

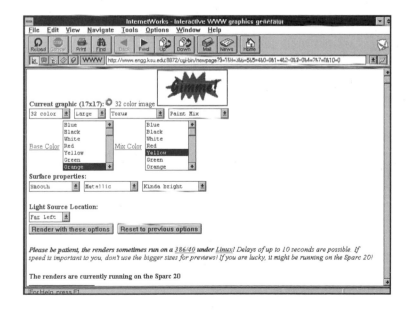

Fig. 7.1

The Interactive Graphics Generation Page generates 3D GIF and PostScript graphic files that you can download for non-commercial use.

II

How Documents Reach You

Disadvantages of HTML Applications

There are disadvantages to creating applications in HTML and distributing them over the Internet. Because HTML is not a compiled data format (HTML is text-based), Web pages can't be locked. Users have free and open access to look at HTML sources; many popular viewers provide a "view source" option. HTML files are easily displayed with any ordinary text editor.

Tip
Access to HTML documents is controlled by the Web server; different server software programs provide varying levels of security privileges.

In the WWW model, the server delivers HTML-marked documents to Web clients, which interpret the coding and display the document according to their own configuration. Using HTML means giving up control over how exactly a document will look to end users, and what HTML features the viewer will support (like forms, tables, and Mailto: URLs).

World Wide Web Acrobatics

There is a strong push from a growing segment of Internet content providers and Adobe Systems Incorporated to make their Acrobat PDF file format a "standard" exchangeable data file format. What's so hot about Acrobat? Its PDF files retain all of their original document layout and fonts even when displayed on a system without the same fonts or software installed. All the end user needs is Adobe's Acrobat Reader. Therein lies the rub.

It's too early in the ball game to declare Acrobat the winner—other products such as Common Ground, provide the same support. And the Reader (although currently provided at no cost by Adobe) is yet another Web helper to be downloaded and installed, consuming a megabyte of hard disk space and making changes to both the Microsoft Windows and Macintosh system settings. There's a cost to supporting PDF files (as my numerous re-installs on both platforms attest to).

Adobe is choosing to sell PDF as a singular "hypertext-based page layout file format" solution. Wait a minute—isn't that what HTML provides? This is another one of those instances where a corporation's interests and those of a "freeware" technology are competing at the track, and the odds-on favorites lay with the horse from the public domain—HTML.

◀ See "When You Need a Little Helper," p. 56

Web clients have their own limits to deal with. The majority handle only a few of the many possible data types and transactions on the WWW. When a data type or function is not supported by a viewer, it has the capability to assign an external application to handle the duties. For more information, see Chapter 17, "Server Scripts and Applications."

HTML's link to CGI scripting as a means of providing "behind the scenes" support to Web pages brings with it the costs of writing the CGI scripts and maintaining them on the server. If a Web author is not trained to write scripts, that cost must be accounted for as well.

> **Caution**
>
> Server-side CGI scripts are a fundamental weakness in the security of a Web host. Before implementing any new scripts, pass them by the site's "security chief" (often the administrator) so the code can be checked for potential holes.

Like every other Internet service, the WWW inherits the problems of an open network environment. The primary concern on the Internet right now is security; another is transmission speed.

How Secure Is It?

The Internet and, by extension, the WWW experience a trade-off as open systems: security for convenience. Using the Internet and the WWW is a snap—few network hosts require anything more than an anonymous login. Information is easily accessible and travels fairly unimpeded between hosts and desktops.

The cost for this freedom is security. For just as you can log onto the port of a remote Web site to retrieve an HTML document for your viewer, so can an unscrupulous user run software to monitor the traffic into and out of that port. These applications are called *sniffers,* and all they do is collect data packets. Hackers can then take those packets and steal insecure information from them. The only solution to this problem requires encrypting the data before it leaves a computer, so the hackers have a much more difficult task of "breaking in" to your data transmissions.

Tip
Both Netscape Communications and NCSA provide a "secure" version of their Web viewers for greater data protection.

Many encryption techniques exist today for use on unsecured networks. Probably the most widely talked about and popular is *PGP* (Pretty Good Protection). By using PGP encryption and a trusted public key server, the chances that your data will be stolen drop to near zero.

How Does PGP Work?

PGP, created by Phil Zimmermann, works by processing data files using a *public key*, a complex and long string of characters, for the person you're sending the file to. This results in a file with a large chunk of encrypted characters, unrecognizable (and, more importantly, unreadable) to the average hacker. The file can only be decrypted by the recipient's private key.

The recipient can double-check that the data file actually came from you by verifying the *digital signature* of the encrypted file with your own public key (it's impossible to forge a digital signature). This system works especially well when sending files anonymously, where both users do not know who the other person is.

The only problem with this public key system is making sure the public key you encode the file with is really the key for the recipient. To make sure the public key information is genuine, get the key from a reliable source. Use a well-known public key server (such as the SLED Public Key Archive at **http://www.Four11.com/**) to discourage hackers from replacing a public key listing with their own key, rendering your secured data an open book to them.

PGP is a command-line executable. There are graphical front ends for most platforms, such as Microsoft Windows PGP WinFront from Ross Barclay (**RBarclay@TrentU.Ca**). WinFront simplifies the PGP file security measure (see fig. 7.2).

Fig. 7.2
PGP WinFront uses no menus to manage PGP file encryption and decryption; all commands are available from the intuitive interface.

When Speed Is Everything

On the WWW, there are two types of speed: data transmission performance and Web page development cycle. If you are looking for high-speed data access, forget the Internet for the meantime. The current infrastructure is undergoing a series of upgrades to faster data hardware (and, in some cases, wire), but chances are that any complex HTML documents are not going to be instantaneously on the users' desktops. The amount of graphical data and how it is incorporated into the Web pages also affects the speed of the Web. For HTML applications on LANs, performance is markedly better (so long as data traffic conditions allow).

One solution to the speed issue is to localize as much of the data traffic as possible; installing the Web server and external scripts and applications on fast hardware and minimizing the *eye candy* (or non-informational text and graphics) in HTML documents will also improve a Web site's performance.

> **Note**
>
> HTML adaptations will speed up the transmission to and display of documents on the end user desktop. One such improvement originally comes from Netscape Communication's non-standard HTML extensions for inline images. By providing the height and width of inline images in the HTML document itself, Web viewers can display the document's text in the viewer window much faster than was previously possible.

HTML is already a fast development platform; the majority of the work comes from the initial conversion of documents to the HTML format. A number of easy solutions are available to help the transition to Web-based documents:

- Recycle pre-existing code; don't create from scratch what can be borrowed from existing HTML documents.

- Select a standard suite of HTML development tools and train the authors to use them. This may sound like common sense, but the recent creation and novelty of good HTML tools is a sure-fire guarantee that authors will experiment, looking for something better than what they currently use.

- Standardize page formats (perhaps with a corporate style sheet) and create templates for easy document generation.

The Right to Privacy Issue

It's possible for Web servers to collect information about a user who is accessing HTML documents—but is it ethical? Many users have argued that the philosophies behind the WWW model actively discourage this practice. Many Web sites also require users to register and maintain "authentication" databases.

Tip
Server-side user authentication (as a means of controlling access to Web pages) is one of the few legitimate uses of the information a viewer broadcasts to a Web server when linking to a document.

How should registration information be managed? Can (or should) a Web site maintainer freely sell lists of e-mail addresses? Services such as Four11 Directory (**http://www.Four11.com/Sled.html**) state emphatically that they will not sell e-mail address lists, and the Directory is configured to make retrieving large numbers of addresses very difficult, if not impossible.

If you are managing a Web site, at one point or another your policies and practices regarding user privacy will be questioned. As a Web author, it may sound nifty to display a user's vital statistics to them as they retrieve your HTML documents, but it's quite alarming when it happens to you the first time. It's very easy to cross the privacy line, so take some simple advice: don't get anywhere near it.

From Here...

Commercial development on the Internet is a new phenomenon; the number of services and products being advertised online is growing as more companies assess the Net as a market. Security issues are still unresolved, but a cautious organization can use the Net (and the WWW) to conduct business with few worries. Now that the playing field has been assessed, refer to the following chapters to begin developing World Wide Web documents:

- Chapter 8, "HTML Standards and Practices," discusses good and bad HTML practices, what universal resource locators are, and an overview of the debate about conventions that attempt to add control to how HTML documents are displayed by Web clients.

- Chapter 9, "At the Beginning: The Document Head," teaches you what the head section in an HTML document includes, and how it links HTML documents to each other and to server functions.

■ Chapter 10, "Where the Content Is: The Document Body," illustrates the style and navigation HTML elements available for the body section of a document.

■ Part IV, "Using Forms in HTML Documents," shows how to incorporate forms into documents for collecting user input and activating scripts and programs on your Web server.

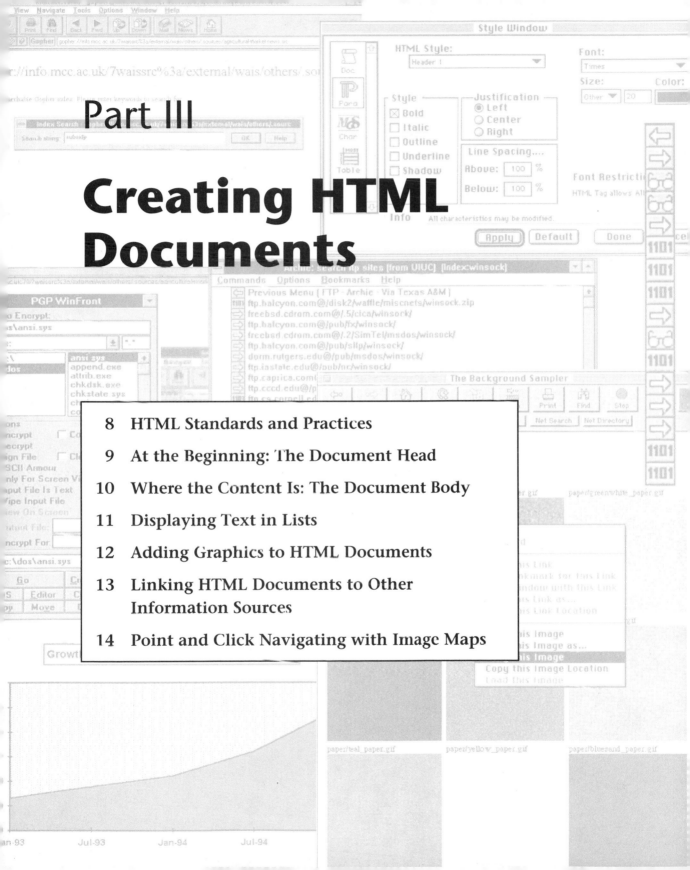

Part III

Creating HTML Documents

Chapter 8

HTML Standards and Practices

"The chains of habit are too weak to be felt until they are too strong to be broken."

—Dr. Samuel Johnson, English author

Like the proverbial old dog, it's easy to fall into patterns of behavior that are just too hard to change. In the case of HTML, picking up bad habits will likely lead to extra work in the future, as HTML specifications get revised and new uses for HTML documents appear. What you learn now—the HTML habits of organization and courtesy—will give you an advantage as you develop, reuse, and adapt HTML documents and additions down the road.

In this chapter, you learn the answers to the following questions:

- What's the difference between good and bad HTML?

- Why should you title a document?

- How do you "sign" a document you create?

- Can you format HTML text to look the way you want it to in the viewer?

- What's a URL and how do you use one?

- How does the "lowest common denominator" rule apply to HTML?

- What is a text entity?

Defining the Good and the Bad in HTML

Tip
Annotated versions of the current HTML DTD help explain the official standard in plain English. A current DTD can be found at **http://www.oac.uci.edu/indiv/ehood/html2.0/DTD-HOME.html**.

"Good" HTML is generally defined as code that follows the most current HTML DTD: a document that describes every element in the HTML specification. This document is written in SGML, the grandfather language of HTML, and is not something the average person would enjoy reading.

HTML coding that follows the DTD closely has the best compatibility with the wide range of WWW viewers. As new clients come to the market and current viewers enhance their functionality, some will promote their own *extensions* (elements and entities unique to their software). Compatibility issues will then become more prevalent. It's always best to err on the side of conservatism and have "good" code.

> **Note**
>
> Unique viewer extensions to HTML were pioneered by Netscape Communications (formerly known as Mosaic Communications) with their Netscape Navigator HTML client software. These extensions enhanced the document author's ability to control the on-screen interpretation of HTML code. These extensions are generally ignored by viewers that don't support them, and allow Netscape users to experience more aesthetic and functional HTML documents. These extensions do not represent the current HTML standard or even the HTML 3.0 currently under consideration (and may never be adopted in their current format), so use them in your own HTML documents with care.

And what's considered "bad" HTML? Those documents that ignore standard practices, use specialized viewer-specific extensions that other viewers can't handle gracefully, load up on a wide assortment of headers, incorporate hundreds of kilobytes of graphics—all of the things you'll know better than to do, after reading this book!

What's in HTML?

This is a literal question, not a metaphysical one. HTML documents contain, by definition, HTML content. WWW viewers interpret any text file with the proper HTML tags and elements as HTML. But there may be times when you need to create a compound document, one with both HTML and non-HTML content. Is this possible?

Under the current HTML standard, yes. The very first tag in an HTML document is exactly that, <HTML>. The container tag defines the beginning and ending of a document's content to be read by WWW viewers. What isn't in the container isn't supposed to be identified by the Web client software as HTML (but the client may read it as another data stream).

> **Note**
>
> Although all WWW viewers recognize the <HTML> tag, they also accommodate files in which the container was left out. This type of "error correction" is very common, and also an issue of debate. This flexibility may change as other Internet applications create other data type containers.

Using the <HTML> tag is an easy habit to pick up. *Always begin a new HTML document with the container.* Always end the document with the closing tag (although, if the document ends at the end of the HTML content anyway, the closing tag may seem redundant).

Figure 8.1 shows the basic use of the HTML container. Making this a regular part of your document creation process saves you from having to edit your existing documents if tighter standards are promoted in the future (and as alternate data containers are promoted for combining data in single documents).

HTML opening tag

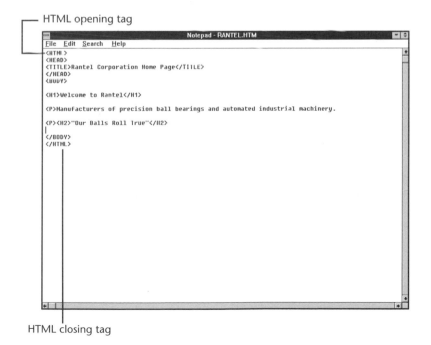

HTML closing tag

Fig. 8.1
The <HTML> container tag bookends all of the HTML content in a document.

III

Creating Documents

Every Good Book Deserves a Good Title

It's the same for HTML documents—every one deserves a title. Titles serve three purposes:

- They're used by other Internet applications (such as WAIS) for document searches and indexing.

- They act as an indicator of what to expect (the contents of "The Electronic Roadkill Diaries" and "Seattle Florists On-line" *should* be quite different).

- They're the opening text in the document—an easy visual clue for identifying the ASCII source files quickly.

When creating an HTML document, choose a title that accurately reflects the function or content of a page. The easier to read you make the document, the larger your audience will be (after all, a satisfied audience is the true measure of a successful Web home page).

Titles are visible in the viewer. In the Microsoft Windows and UNIX versions of Mosaic, the title text is on the ribbon at the top of the viewer (beneath the icon bar) in the Document title field. On the Macintosh version of Mosaic, the title occupies the window's title bar across the top of the window (see fig. 8.2). Avoid long, rambling titles that can overflow a viewer's title field.

Fig. 8.2
Client software programs display the HTML page's title in different places (from the title bar to the ribbon); the Macintosh software standards dictate the placement of the title in NCSA Mosaic for the Macintosh.

Title in Mac window

Sign and Date, Please

Signing and dating documents is a courtesy practice in HTML documents. A signature just displays your e-mail address for the reader's benefit. You do want to be associated with your outstanding work, right? The date stamp lets the reader know how current the page is, and is especially handy for evaluating the worthiness of time-sensitive information (a date stamp is crucial, for instance, on a home page with stock market listings or investment evaluations).

You add signatures to a document by using the LINK element. You can also add a link to a closing <ADDRESS> tag that opens a mail form, allowing readers to send a message to your e-mail address. Figure 8.3 shows how these appear in HTML code, and figure 8.4 shows how a WWW viewer displays the signature and ADDRESS element.

▶ See "Using LINK," p. 164

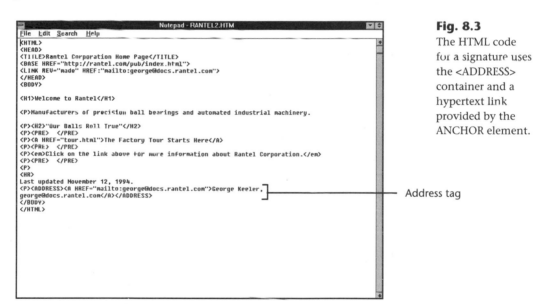

— Address tag

Fig. 8.3
The HTML code for a signature uses the <ADDRESS> container and a hypertext link provided by the ANCHOR element.

Depending on the type of document you create (and for whom), also consider including a pointer to your own personal home page—if you have one. Many readers like to learn more about a document's author, especially if there's a question of authority. Remember, practically anyone can publish any kind information on the Web, and it's a safe bet that you'll see just about anything, the more you explore the reaches of the Web.

III

Creating Documents

Fig. 8.4
Clicking a
signature lets
readers send their
comments about
your work or
information to the
e-mail address
listed in the LINK
element.

Interpretation of HTML
<ADDRESS> tag

The Great Debate: Formatting Text in HTML

Historically, although it's been a short history up to this point, HTML is an offshoot from SGML (Standard Generalized Markup Language). The philosophies behind SGML were passed down to HTML, and the SGML motto is to trust the client. In practical terms, this means to provide only the information necessary for the client to interpret your intentions regarding the information in your document. The rest, including the specific manner in which those intentions are carried out (such as how the viewer displays the information) is determined by the client software.

The reason behind this separation of data and interpretation is clear: SGML documents are designed to be platform and device independent. They're meant to be read and displayed by an unlimited number of systems using any software designed to read them.

SGML versus HTML

This hands-off attitude works very well under controlled conditions—when the authoring community is in sync with this philosophy. The platform independence begins to break down as the authoring community grows, and segments start asking for more control over the eventual display of their data. This is the debate between the SGML school and what can be called the

Author school: what can be pre-determined for the viewing software, and what should be left to the discretion of the various clients.

What's Logical to You Is Physical to Me

No HTML debate is more heated than the discussion of physical and logical text styles. SGML advocates stress the use of logical text styles in HTML documents. These styles describe the relative strength of emphasis to be applied to text, thus defining a relationship between different text strings.

For example, the first logical level of emphasis for text uses the HTML container <EM>, for emphasis. To make a stronger case, the second level uses the container <STRONG>, for stronger emphasis. SGML purists don't describe nor do they care how the end user's software displays these relationships; all that's important are the relationships. The text could be italicized, bold, underlined, or in bright red for all they care.

▶ See "Formatting Text in HTML: Physical versus Logical," p. 190

To the Author school of thought, these issues do matter. Drawn from the user community that is accustomed to readily available desktop publishing and document formatting tools, they're concerned that viewer software may not treat HTML documents properly, or that end users may define certain elements (such as EM or STRONG) as an inappropriate fashion for the delivered data.

These authors want to be able to define the appearance of emphasized text, regardless of the software platform the text is viewed on, using the <B> and <I> tags. Figure 8.5 shows how a typical WWW viewer displays formatted text.

For these two schools of thought, two categories of text formatting elements were created. Logical styles are available using the <EM>, <STRONG>, and <CITE> (citation) tags; physical styles are available using the <I> (italicize), <B> (bold), and <U> (underline) tags. Additional physical styles are being considered for future versions of HTML, such as controlling the display size of text and its alignment in a viewer window.

III

Creating Documents

> ### Note
>
> Many of these additional styles are available as non-standard elements (or extensions) in viewers such as Netscape. Text formatted with these extensions only exhibits the non-standard formatting in viewers that support the extensions; other viewers either ignore the non-standard HTML or display the extension tags or data in unusual ways. Know your audience before choosing to use non-standard HTML elements.

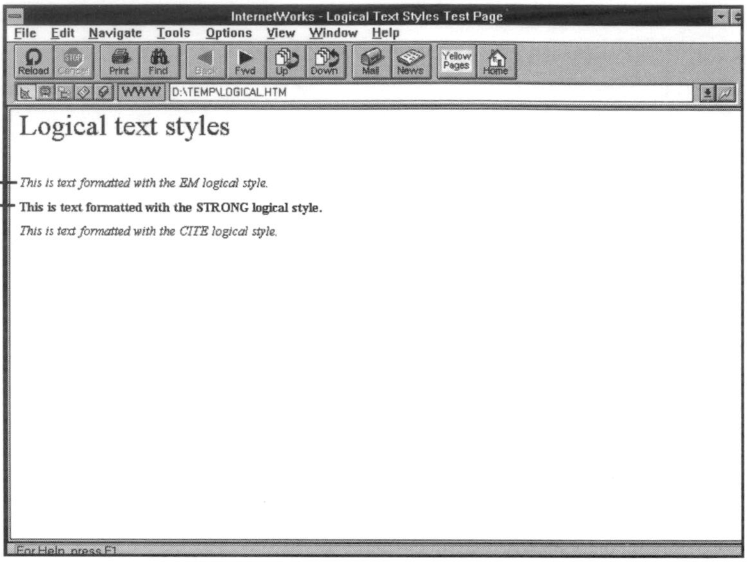

Fig. 8.5
Logical styles display in different ways, depending on the viewer software, whereas physical styles are specific display definitions.

<EM> tags often display in italics

<STRONG> tags often display in bold

Choosing a Camp

So which school of thought should you follow? The answer is neither and both. Common sense dictates when allowing the relationship between text is more important than its screen display, and vice versa. HTML gurus try to stress logical styles over physical styles, and then they use the appropriate one regardless. Remember that not all WWW viewers can display all physical styles. Also remember that logical styles are fairly limited and can't be combined to create new display options.

Here are some guidelines for choosing which text style is appropriate for your documents.

Use logical styles if:

- You don't know what WWW viewers your audience will be using to read your documents; only use physical styles if it doesn't matter whether the style can be displayed.

- The relationship between emphasized text is more important than its appearance.

- You can express every relationship between emphasized text in your HTML document using the current selection of logical style elements.

- Your documents need to adhere to strict SGML guidelines for distribution purposes.

Use physical styles if:

- Your target audience uses one or more WWW viewers that support the exact screen formatting your documents require.

- The display of your information in the client software is more important than the relationship between the text.

- Existing logical style elements can't represent every relationship between emphasized text in your document.

- Your documents need to use physical style containers for accurate conversion to other document formats in which the native software doesn't interpret logical style relationships.

This debate will continue as new HTML standards are proposed and the HTML community swells with new document authors who have their own experiences (or lack of) with SGML, HTML, and electronic document publishing. As more of the desktop publishing generation arrives, they will ensure that an increasing number of physical style options are adopted and put into wide use. A kind of "standard through usage" attitude has already sprung up in the vocal Netscape user community (and it's growing as the popularity of the software soars).

Defining URLs in HTML Documents

URLs (Uniform Resource Locators) are the Internet's all-purpose reference tools. They act much like addresses, not only to actual data, but to any definable resource on the Internet, including the results of application commands. URLs are available for newsgroups on UseNet, Gopher servers, Telnet connections, WAIS server files, and World Wide Web server files (the most common usage in HTML). Any link from an HTML document to another file or application is written in the form of a URL.

How you write a URL is important. A complete (or fully qualified) URL looks like this:

scheme://host.domain [:port]/path/dataname

- **scheme** defines what kind of data the URL points to.

- **host.domain** gives the explicit Internet server on which the data or application is located.

III

Creating Documents

■ **:port** is required if the data server is not located at a default port location (for instance, Gopher servers are assumed to reside on port 70).

■ **path/dataname** defines the specific location and data name of the data on the indicated server.

Table 8.1 lists the most common URLs and their equivalent components.

Table 8.1 URL Definitions and Examples		
Scheme	**Data Type**	**Sample URL**
file	Data files	file://ftp.yoga.com/pub/exercises/techniques.txt
http	HTML files	http://www.calendar.com/pub/monthly/january.html
news	UseNet newsgroup	news:alt.fan.cecil-adams
gopher	Gopher server	gopher://gopher.toolbox.org/
telnet	Telnet connection	telnet://harbor.piedmont.edu
wais	WAIS server	wais://wais.nectar.gods.com:8080

Troubleshooting

*UseNet newsgroup URLs don't conform to the standard URL format. Why don't UseNet newsgroup URLs (such as **news:alt.cdrom**) include the host path to a UseNet news server?*

Most WWW clients do not as yet support the capability to specify UseNet servers in URLs. Instead, they require that a single news server be defined in the software's configuration settings (or in the system variables).

One advantage of being able to specify a UseNet news server would be to point a URL toward a server that carries that particular newsgroup (not all servers carry all groups, at the discretion of the news server administrator or the organization that runs the server). Another advantage would be to point toward a low load server to maximize the connection's performance.

In the future, HTML may support this viewer capability and the current newsgroup URL definition may change as well. Chances are that both the current URL usage and any new format will be supported concurrently to maintain compatibility with the growing number of HTML documents that take advantage of UseNet newsgroup access. See Chapter 3, "The WWW and Other Internet Services."

Each example in Table 8.1 uses fully qualified URLs—every component of the URL is provided to guide any client software to the specific data resource specified. In HTML, after a document is accessed in a particular path, you can reference other documents on the same server using partial or relative URLs. This simplifies writing links in HTML documents that will point to additional local files.

For instance, if an HTML link uses the URL http://www.calendar.com/pub/monthly/january.html to point to a document that provided links to a monthly calendar document, references to other monthly documents would look like http://february.html, http://march.html, or http://april.html. Links to associated weekly documents would look like http://weekly/jan1-7.html or http://weekly/mar13-20.html. Links to daily calendar documents would look like http://daily/january1.html or http://daily/march13.html. The WWW viewer assumes the rest of the URL path is the same as the first document retrieved (see fig. 8.6).

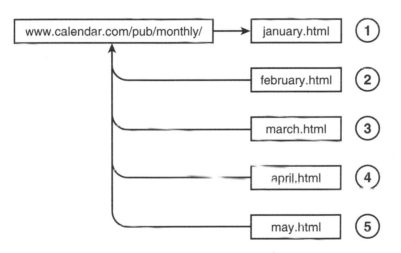

Fig. 8.6
WWW viewers interpret relative links by assuming the path of the document that contains the link.

Of course, you're always allowed to provide the fully qualified URL for any link—the WWW client doesn't care either way. But the advantages to using relative URLs can be substantial. Besides being much shorter (thus saving lots of time entering them in the HTML documents), relative URLs establish a relationship between local documents that can be retained even if the files are moved. So long as all of the relative locations don't change, none of the HTML links will break when the files are relocated.

III

Creating Documents

> **Note**
>
> Only use relative URLs for links between documents that are related to each other; that is, only use them for files that will always be located together or in the same relative directory structure. Do not use them for links to documents such as third-party FAQs and related Web pages. These links may break if the other documents move or you move your own. And the last thing you want is your audience to get `Error 404` messages from broken or unimplemented links in your documents!
>
> If you're trying to access a URL that points to a WWW host (like **www.newbie.net**) and are receiving an error message, check to see if the URL ends with a forward slash (/). If not, add one to the end of the URL and choose the viewer's Reload option; the viewer will attempt to load the host's index.html (or other directory default) document.

File Naming Issues in HTML

Most people think naming files is as simple as choosing Save As and entering a unique name for a data file. For the typical home computer user, that might be true. But HTML requires that users broaden their knowledge of different file naming schemes and learn how to use and reference file names for an Internet audience.

File names come in all shapes and, more importantly, all sizes. Figure 8.7 demonstrates how you can represent the same file differently, depending on the computer system it was created on.

The variations of file naming conventions on different operating systems is enough to give network administrators migraine headaches. Systems such as DOS (and hence its graphical environments like Microsoft Windows) limit file names to an "eight dot three" format. This allows a file name to consist of an eight-character name with a three-character extension. The case of the characters is irrelevant and special characters (such as punctuation and blank spaces) are illegal.

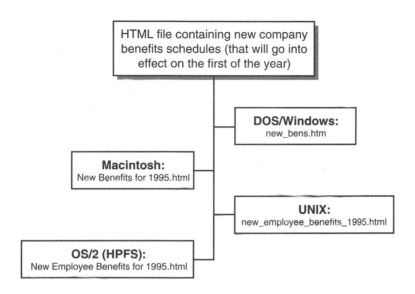

Fig. 8.7
File names differ
greatly depending
on the native
operating system's
file name
conventions.

The Macintosh operating system allows a file name to be up to 32 characters, and you can use characters such as blank spaces and punctuation. UNIX allows names to be up to 255 characters, doesn't allow blanks spaces or special characters, and is case-sensitive. Other operating systems have their own special conditions.

How does HTML untangle the jumble of file name allowances and restrictions and provide support for hypertext documents? The democratic way—through compromise.

HTML dictates that file names, because they're absolute for the platform the file is located on, must obey all of the local restrictions, and enjoy the benefits as well. UNIX files can be 30 (or more) characters of mixed cases and underscores between words. DOS files can be cryptic combinations of eight alpha and numeric characters. Macintosh files can use spaces and punctuation.

The compromise comes in the use of extensions. All HTML files and their related data files (sounds, graphics, and digital video bites) must use a standard set of extensions. Table 8.2 lists the common extensions for HTML-associated files.

III

Creating Documents

Table 8.2 Extensions for HTML and Related Data Files

Extension	File Type	Sample File Name
html	HTML text	broadway_bound.html
htm	HTML text	broadway.htm
text	ASCII text	sample_output.text
txt	ASCII	text sample.txt
gif	compressed graphic	pekinese.gif
jpeg	compressed graphic	Damn_Yankees.jpeg
jpg	compressed graphic	damyanks.jpg
tiff	high-resolution graphic	Applegate_Lola.tiff
tif	high-resolution graphic	app_lola.tif
pcx	bitmap graphic	logo.pcx
bmp	bitmap graphic	design.bmp
mpeg	digital video	nature_walk.mpeg
mpg	digital video	naturewk.mpg
avi	digital video	natural.avi
wav	digital audio	welcome.wav
au	digital audio	first_visit.au
ps	PostScript data	bibliography.ps

Troubleshooting

I'm moving a lot of files from my desktop PC, running DOS and Windows, to my company's UNIX server. Is there a way to convert the extension on my .HTM files to .HTML, as required by my server?

You have two ways to resolve this: pass the buck to your Web administrator or do it yourself. Passing the buck is the easiest and least time-intensive; ask your administrator to configure the Web server to serve HTM files as HTML documents (because it already serves HTML files).

If you do it yourself, you have to do a global file move after the files are copied to your UNIX file directory. A simple csh script that will accomplish this task can be created as follows:

```
#!/usr/bin/csh
for each file (*.htm)
  mv -i $file $file:r.html
end
```

Execute this in the directory with your HTM files to convert them en masse to the HTML extension.

In the future, new data types will be supported in HTML by adding new extensions (in four and three-character variations as necessary). Non-standard support will be added to most WWW viewers by adding the new extensions and helper applications in the software configuration. An advantage of this function of client software is when you're using HTML to deliver documents to a specific target audience.

Most viewers have a configuration option that defines how the software handles each file type. Some are handled in the application itself, especially the HTM, HTML, and GIF files. Many use external or "helper" applications to process the other data formats. For instance, the Macintosh version of NCSA Mosaic uses Sparkle to play MPG and MPEG digital video files, and Sound Machine to play AU digital audio files.

Note

Not all WWW viewers can handle all data types (either natively or through external helper applications). Use common sense when choosing a data type for HTML documents—stick with the most widely supported formats and you guarantee that your audience can handle the majority of the content in your Web pages. For instance, when using inline graphics, GIF files are recommended due to their small file size and native support by nearly all WWW viewers.

Delivery of Linked Files

In HTML, the server where the file is located delivers the requested documents to the WWW client (the "client/server" model once again). When you create links to files, the absolute file names must be accurate within the limitations of the file's own naming scheme; if a file on a UNIX Web server is

III

Creating Documents

called Life_with_Annie.html, then the link must be spelled exactly the same way (because UNIX file names are case-sensitive).

If a file on a DOS Web server is called life_ann.htm, the link is still accurate if it's called LIFE_ANN.HTM—as long as the file stays on the DOS platform. If this file moves to a UNIX server, the link is no longer valid and breaks. The best rule is to always use accurate file names in links, including character cases, spaces, and punctuation.

> ### Note
>
> The World Wide Web spans the globe and supports well over 3,000 registered Web servers. Due to the historical evolution of the Internet, the vast majority of these servers are located on computer systems running a variation of the UNIX operating system. While UNIX is not the friendliest system to learn or use, it does allow for lengthy and unambiguous file names.
>
> Authors who create documents on non-UNIX systems may find that renaming files on the UNIX server makes managing large collections of files easier. By the same token, you must rename some files for proper delivery; some UNIX systems require that HTML documents end with the HTML extension, which DOS users can't create in their native environment. Check with your system administrator to find out what extensions are valid for HTML documents.

Remember, when creating files for use on the World Wide Web, adhering to the common file extensions is mandatory for the documents to be accessible by your intended audience. Unique extensions should only be used when the audience has customized their viewer's support to handle the new data types. File names must adhere to their local platform limitations, and links to these files (in HTML documents) must use the file's absolute name to avoid any ambiguity or broken links.

Accommodating WWW Users and Their Viewers

Estimations of the number of Internet users who can access the WWW with graphical client software range from four million on up. This is a minority of the 20 million plus Internet user base. In these measurements, the graphical user base is defined as users who have the necessary data connections to use desktop WWW tools such as Mosaic and Netscape. The rest of the users access the Internet over modem connections or through text-only terminal connections, and can't run graphical applications fast enough (or at all).

When you create HTML documents, keep the "lowest common denominator" rule in mind. You know how it goes: assume you're writing Web pages for the least capable users in your intended audience to guarantee that everyone gets the message you want them to get.

Accessing the WWW with Lynx

The way users access the Internet is changing as fast as the Internet itself. First, nearly all Internet users already have access to the WWW in their text UNIX sessions via Lynx, a text-only UNIX WWW client application. (To tell whether you have access to Lynx, just type **lynx** at any UNIX prompt.) While Lynx doesn't support inline graphics or many types of text formatting options, it does provide usable and fast access to the growing collection of Web sites.

◀ See "Using Lynx," p. 81

Dialing In with a Graphical WWW Viewer

A second option for the dial-in Internet surfer is using a graphical WWW viewer that runs over an ordinary dial-up modem connection (and doesn't require SLIP or PPP access, only a UNIX shell account). The first out of the gate is SlipKnot from Peter Brooks and MicroMind, Inc. As Brooks describes it, the goal of SlipKnot is to "make the Web accessible for the first time to a very large number of people." This goal is accomplished by providing direct access to HTML resources over a standard modem connection. Your local UNIX account provider must make Lynx or WWW available for SlipKnot to retrieve Web pages and data files.

▶ See "SlipKnot 1.1 (Windows)," p. 583

Using ALT for Non-Graphical Viewers

Depending on your intended audience, keep non-graphical viewers in mind when creating HTML documents. The easiest step you can take—and one that is documented in the HTML standard—is to use the ALT attribute when including inline images. The ALT attribute's function is simple: when a viewer can't display a graphic, it looks for a text string defined in ALT and displays that instead. For example, if you add an inline GIF of your company's corporate headquarters, include the ALT attribute with a description of the headquarters' location (see fig. 8.8). That way a user accessing the Web page from a non-graphical viewer (such as Lynx) will get the text description instead of an empty marker.

Fig. 8.8

The ALT attribute provides text information that a viewer can display instead of a marker for unreadable graphic images.

Compressed graphic file

ALT attribute for non-graphical viewers

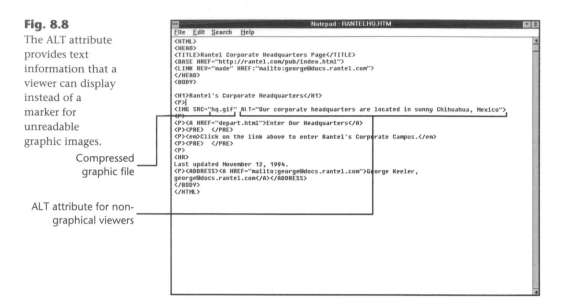

```
                                    Notepad - RANTELHQ.HTM
 File  Edit  Search  Help
<HTML>
<HEAD>
<TITLE>Rantel Corporate Headquarters Page</TITLE>
<BASE HREF="http://rantel.com/pub/index.html">
<LINK REV="made" HREF="mailto:george@docs.rantel.com">
</HEAD>
<BODY>

<H1>Rantel's Corporate Headquarters</H1>
<P>
<IMG SRC="hq.gif" ALT="Our corporate headquarters are located in sunny Chihuahua, Mexico">
<P>
<P><A HREF="depart.html">Enter Our Headquarters</A>
<P><PRE>  </PRE>
<P><em>Click on the link above to enter Rantel's Corporate Campus.</em>
<P><PRE>  </PRE>
<P>
<HR>
Last updated November 12, 1994.
<P><ADDRESS><A HREF="mailto:george@docs.rantel.com">George Keeler,
george@docs.rantel.com</A></ADDRESS>
</BODY>
</HTML>
```

ALT attributes are essential if you incorporate graphic formats that not all viewers can display. For example, native JPEG graphic support is becoming more common but still isn't universal, so you should use ALT attributes. The current drawback to using the ALT attribute is that the majority of graphical viewers don't feel the need to support it. This is the perfect time to push for implementation through usage and by providing feedback to the software developers. The IMG's ALT attribute is too useful to be ignored by the "bleeding edge" WWW clients.

Providing Text-Only Versions for Non-Graphical Viewers

Another way to support non-graphical viewers (or users connected to the WWW via slow data connections and who can't afford to wait for elaborate graphics to download for display) is to provide access to a text-only version of the document. Most often, these are just text menus that offer the same links and data as the full graphics page. Figure 8.9 shows an example of a Web page with the text option, and figure 8.10 shows a text-only page that includes the same information.

Text Transcriptions in Place of Multimedia

Many authors fall in love with the idea of incorporating multimedia elements in their Web pages. When IBM first opened **www.ibm.com**, the home page included a link to an audio file introduction from IBM's CEO, Lou Gerstner.

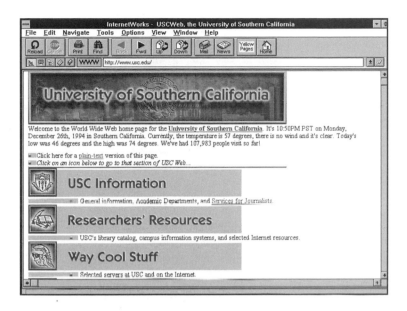

Fig. 8.9
Graphic-oriented
Web pages should
include alternate
viewing options.

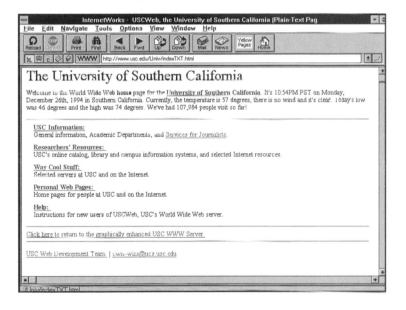

Fig. 8.10
Text-only menus
can give explicit
descriptions to
make up for the
lack of graphics.

The problem with using these data links is that, unless the files provide information that can't be communicated via text, the time it takes to retrieve them can be wasteful.

An alternative for the WWW audience who can't afford to wait, or WWW viewers using slow connections, is to offer text-only options for both digital audio and digital video links. These links provide text transcriptions of the audio and video data and are quickly retrieved and read.

> **Note**
>
> Links to text-only transcriptions provide the same advantages that thumbnail images do for graphics; they allow users to preview data links before committing the time and resources to retrieve them. Even partial quotations on your graphical Web pages provide an inkling of what information the linked data file contains. The smaller and faster your Web pages are, the easier they are to use and enjoy.

Considering the Client Software

It's not enough to know your intended audience; you must also create HTML documents that consider the conditions under which your audience uses the World Wide Web and the capabilities of their client software. Anything you can do to make using your Web site faster and easier—for all of your audience—will contribute to the success of your efforts.

Using Text Entities in HTML

HTML reserves a handful of text characters for special uses. When the characters are identified in their text entity format, WWW viewers can still display these characters without being misinterpreted as language commands. HTML also supports special characters, like those used for accented or non-English alphabet characters. For more information on HTML entities, see Chapter 5, "Building Blocks of HTML."

The HTML entity definitions or ISO Latin-1 character codes can represent these characters. Characters should not be "cut and pasted" into HTML documents (which is an easy solution for graphical environment users), but written in entity format. This is because these characters will not always translate as you see them on your own viewer.

Why? Modern character sets are 8-bit (such as ASCII) and its characters are likewise 8-bit characters. HTTP is a 7-bit network protocol and can't support 8-bit characters directly. It's up to the local platform to translate the incoming 7-bit characters into the supported format, and the outgoing characters into ISO Latin-1 characters (notably for platforms such as the Macintosh).

It's easy to use HTML entities. The standard format is &*name*; (where *name* is the entity label or the ISO Latin-1 character number). You can insert entities in any normal line of text. Figure 8.11 shows how you can use entities in an HTML document, and figure 8.12 shows how a WWW viewer translates the text.

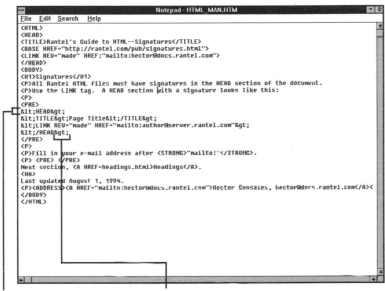

Less than angle bracket   Greater than angle bracket

Fig. 8.11
HTML entities may not look pretty in the code but they're supported by nearly all WWW viewers.

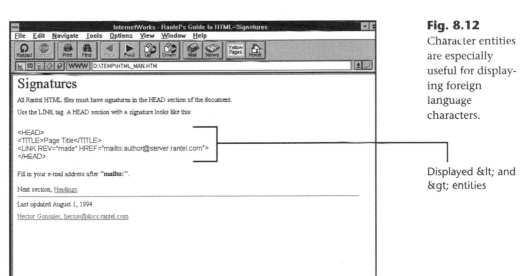

Fig. 8.12
Character entities are especially useful for displaying foreign language characters.

Displayed < and > entities

III

> **Note**
>
> Netscape provides two additional non-standard character entities: the registered trademark symbol, ® (defined as ®), and the copyright symbol, © (defined as ©). These entities are not under consideration for the next HTML standard, but they may be in the future. The current HTML standard defines these symbols as their ISO Latin-1 characters, ™ for the registered trademark symbol and © for the copyright symbol.

From Here...

Now that you're familiar with some of the basic issues surrounding HTML and how to accommodate the teeming mass of World Wide Web users who may access your Web pages, it's time to begin building HTML documents. Refer to the following sections to learn about the various HTML document components and what content is supported:

- Chapter 9, "At the Beginning: The Document Head," teaches you what the head section in an HTML document includes and how it links HTML documents to each other and to server functions.

- Chapter 10, "Where the Content Is: The Document Body," describes the style and navigation of HTML elements available for the body section of a document.

- Chapter 11, "Displaying Text in Lists," provides a range of formatting and sorting options for generated text lists.

- Chapter 12, "Adding Graphics to HTML Documents," shows you how to incorporate eye-catching GIF graphics in a document to provide additional information and style.

- Part IV, "Using Forms in HTML Documents," illustrates how to incorporate forms into documents for collecting user input and activating scripts and programs on your Web server.

Chapter 9

At the Beginning: The Document Head

Creating an accurate document head is the first step to writing good HTML. Fortunately, it's also the easiest.

As the name implies, the *head* section of an HTML document precedes the main content of the document. Similar to the banner page of a magazine, the head provides information for both the viewer software and the end user.

This chapter answers the following questions:

- What is the function of the head section in an HTML document?
- How do I use the HTML element?
- How does the TITLE element function?
- How can I create relationships between HTML documents?
- Can I simplify using relative URLs somehow?
- How can I provide text searches in my documents?

What the Head Section Does

The head section is like a quick reference for WWW viewers and other applications that access HTML files. The head supplies the document title and establishes relationships between HTML documents and file directories. The document head can signal the WWW viewer to use its search capabilities to index the current document.

The HEAD Element

HTML provides the HEAD element to define the head section in a document. The <HEAD> tag encloses or contains the head section (which is enclosed by the <HTML> tag). The closing </HEAD> tag sets the bounds for the head section. The only element in the head section displayed by the end user's viewer is the value of the TITLE element. Figure 9.1 shows a typical document head.

Fig. 9.1

The elements in a document head define its function, and clearly show the relationships between the document and other files.

Writing proper document heads is not only good HTML, it also prepares your documents to be used by additional applications (such as WAIS searches) and other future, undefined uses.

Including the <HTML> Tag

HTML documents are *platform-independent*, meaning that they don't conform to any one system standard. Created properly, you can move home pages to any server platform, or you can access them with any compliant WWW viewer. One reason for this independence is the <HTML> tag.

Because HTML documents are not *compiled* (or processed) for execution, some applications need a hint to know how to interpret the plain text in a home page. That's where the <HTML> tag comes into play.

Note

Technically, the <HTML> tag contains all of the HTML portions of the current document, including the head section. But, for purposes of clarity, the tag is presented here, where users begin to write their HTML code. The tag's closing component, </HTML>, comes at the very end of the document, like the traditional "The End" at the end of a book or movie. Logically, the closing is unnecessary (after all, if there is no more text in the file, the document is ended). But, as a matter of good usage, take the extra second or two to include the </HTML> line.

Although most viewers can handle a home page without the <HTML> tag, it is recommended that all of your HTML documents use it (see fig. 9.2). The end of the HTML container is defined with the end tag </HTML>.

Beginning HTML tag

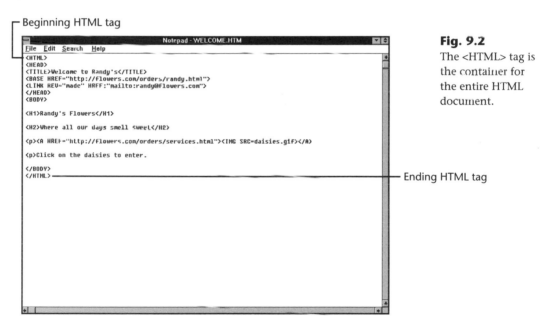

Fig. 9.2
The <HTML> tag is the container for the entire HTML document.

Ending HTML tag

Files without the <HTML> tag can be misinterpreted as text-only documents, and the markup tags as just more text on the page. This is particularly relevant as other applications increasingly access existing HTML documents without the presumption that the document is HTML and not a plain text file (mail and news readers, for instance).

III

Creating Documents

How to Use the TITLE Element

◀ See "Using Text
Entities in
HTML," p. 154

It's as simple as it sounds—the TITLE element "names" your document. The title doesn't assign a file name to a document; it defines a text string that is interpreted as the *HTML title* of the document. The actual file name is incidental (thankfully); most file systems either limit the number of characters in a file name or limit the use of "special" characters that are required by the system (such as the / character). In HTML titles, any character can be displayed.

Caution

The HTML character set does reserve some characters for special uses, such as the "less than" and "greater than" angle brackets. However, these characters can be displayed in your software viewer by using their HTML "entity" equivalents. If you try to use the special characters as normal, the viewer software either ignores them or displays the rest of the document's body text in unexpected (and unwanted) ways.

The TITLE value is used by different viewers in different ways. For instance, Macintosh viewers display the TITLE as the name of the document's window, as shown in figure 9.3.

Fig. 9.3
Macintosh
conventions
define the name of
a window as the
name of the
current document.

Title of file

Many Windows-based viewers display the TITLE text in a title bar, or at the top of the document (see fig. 9.4). You can copy this text from the bar with the standard cut-and-paste actions.

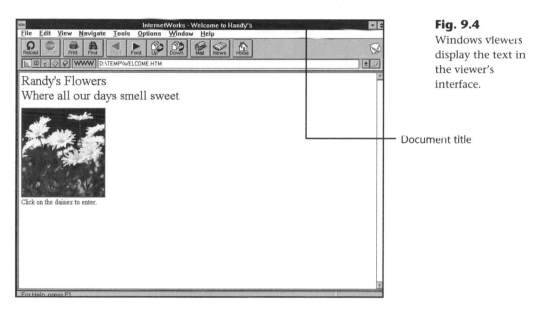

Fig. 9.4
Windows viewers display the text in the viewer's interface.

— Document title

HTML doesn't limit the length of the TITLE element. However, before you rush off to give your documents voluminous and wonderfully expository titles, consider the space where the title is displayed (the viewer's title bar or window label). A good rule of thumb for the length of a title is no more than a single phrase or no longer than 60 characters. See figure 9.5 for an incorrect use of TITLE.

> **Note**
>
> When a user adds your document to her viewer's "hot list" or bookmark list, the TITLE value is saved as the name of your document. Avoid nondescript TITLE values, such as "Page 1," for documents likely to be linked to. Or play with your audience's expectations by providing a tantalizing TITLE for the link.

Tip
Although viewers have a limited capability to display a document's TITLE value, by combining the TITLE text with a lead heading statement, you can effectively create a "1-2" punch with your introductory text.

Fig. 9.5
TITLE values that
are too long might
get cut off by the
viewer's title bar
or window,
decreasing the
effectiveness of
the home page.

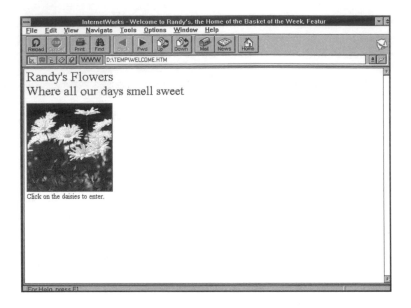

Troubleshooting

I put a TITLE statement in the head section, but some people complain that their viewers display something else. What's happening?

You probably made a mistake in your document's head section, either leaving off an angle bracket or forgetting the closing tag </TITLE>. While some viewers try to catch these errors and display what they think the author intended, others don't. Viewers can display all sorts of nasty text with a TITLE error. Go back and double-check your code, or use an HTML validation service, such as the HalSOFT HTML Validation Service (**http://www/hal.com:80/users/connolly/html-test/service/ validation-form.html**).

Creating Relationships between HTML Documents

Computer files are glorious things: small, lightweight, easily transportable. With a few keystrokes you can relocate entire directories of files, or files with similar names or extensions. It doesn't take a great deal of work (or knowledge) to reorganize a hard disk of files or create copies on a different system. And it doesn't take any effort at all to make havoc of an orderly file system.

As the volume of HTML files under your management increases, you'll be thankful for two elements HTML uses for document heads. These tags serve to connect HTML documents to each other and to their authors.

Using BASE

HTML documents often rely on the physical locations of other HTML files. A document might include a pointer to another document, from a menu list for instance (see fig. 9.6).

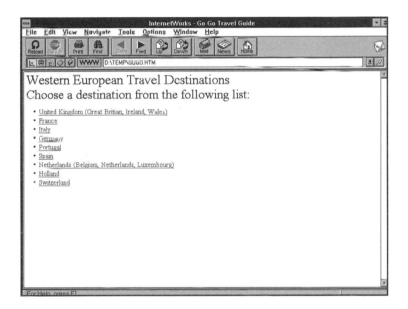

Fig. 9.6
Pointers in HTML documents can point to other locations in the same document or to other documents entirely.

Using <BASE> to simplify URLs

The HTML <BASE> tag acts somewhat like the DOS PATH statement; it provides an additional file directory location for the WWW viewer to refer to when looking up a document link. By specifying a value for <BASE> in your document head, you can shorten the URL statements by using relative URLs in your document's anchor and image links. <BASE> protects relative URL links in the document from "breaking" should the file be physically moved. Figure 9.7 demonstrates a proper BASE statement.

◀ See "Defining URLs in HTML Documents," p. 143

III

If no BASE value exists in a document, the WWW viewer assumes that relative URLs derive from the current directory of the HTML document.

Creating Documents

Fig. 9.7
The value of BASE is a link to the document's absolute URL location written in the form of an anchor link.

```
                              Notepad - DIR.HTM
 File  Edit  Search  Help
<HTML>
<HEAD>
<TITLE>8-bit Color Nature Bitmap Library</TITLE>
<BASE HREF="http://www.studio.com/images/library/256/directory.htm">

</HEAD>
```

Using LINK

▶ See "Using the Anchor Element," p. 253

One problem associated with managing a growing volume of HTML files is often determining which files belong together or who is the proper author of a file. It's very easy to lose track of files when a single home page can use an unlimited number of file links (and these files can be local or on a remote server). Using LINK can easily solve these problems.

> **Note**
>
> Authorship on the Internet is a sticky issue. The WWW and other Internet applications make retrieving and reusing documents easy. One manner of protection is to include a LINK reference to the original author or to the original document (or documents) the file derived from. Using LINK, combined with a text statement in the document's body, provides as much copyright protection as the Internet currently allows.

LINK statements define relationships between the current document and other documents, the author, or Web clients. They generally include a hypertext reference in the form of a URL and an attribute value that explains what the document's relationship with this URL is. Refer to Appendix A, "HTML Elements Reference," for more information about LINK attributes.

A document can include multiple LINK statements using as many attributes as necessary (see fig. 9.8). These attributes are shown in Table 9.1.

Table 9.1	**LINK Attributes and Their Functions**
Attribute	**Function**
HREF	Points to a URL
REL	Defines the relationship between the current document and an HREF value
REV	Like REL, defines the relationship between the HREF value and the document (the opposite association)
NAME	Defines a link from an anchor or URL to this document
URN	Defines a Uniform Resource Number for the current document
TITLE	Same functionally as the <TITLE> tag in the head of the associated HREF
METHODS	List of functions supported by the current document; how it can be used by a viewer

Fig. 9.8
LINK options and attributes apply to the entire HTML document.

III

Creating Documents

In this example, the LINK statements are performing three tasks. The first statement, `<LINK HREF="intro.html" REL="precedes">`, tells the Web viewer that the current document (masters.html) comes before the identified URL document (intro.html). The second statement, `<LINK HREF="http://www. motown.com/blues/intro.htl" TITLE="Introduction to Blues">` identifies the title (Introduction to Blues) for the specified document (intro.html).

The third statement, `<LINK REV="made" HREF:"mailto:parker@motown.com">`, says that the author of this document (REV="made") is described at the following hypertext reference—in this case, an e-mail window that allows you to send a message to the author, **parker@motown.com**.

Of the attributes listed in Table 9.1, HREF, NAME, REL, and REV are most often used. As HTML documents begin to be used by more applications, these values and attributes will become important to assist programs in using HTML documents.

Indexing a Document

HTML documents can be long and complex. Searching for specific information in these documents is a tedious job, especially when the terminology you're looking for varies. What you need is a simple method for doing a difficult job, and in HTML, where there's a need there's often a solution (or two).

Consider the example of an HTML document that lists classical composers and their works with associated music data files and a brief synopsis for each work. Searching such a document for a specific musical composition, or an obscure composer, could take some time. What you want is an efficient way to retrieve this information (especially if you're providing this document for wide use and you want people to come back for more).

HTML provides the ISINDEX element for just such a need. ISINDEX signals the WWW viewer to use its internal capabilities to generate a simple search form, where the user enters one or more search variables (separated by commas) in a blank and presses the Search button. (The viewer can still view and read the document normally if a user doesn't want to perform a keyword search.) The viewer passes the search information to the document's server, which performs the search.

Note

Having the ISINDEX element in a document doesn't guarantee that the document can be searched. WWW viewers don't have the means to perform their own searches, so they rely on the document's server to have a "search engine" program. For this reason most Web sites prefer to run a script that appends the ISINDEX element automatically to its HTML documents if a search engine is available.

ISINDEX requires no additional information or attributes—just add it to the head section of a document you want to make searchable.

Figure 9.9 shows how ISINDEX is included in the head of an HTML document used for searching a long HTML document of classical music. Figure 9.10 shows the resulting search form at the bottom of the Web page; entering text into the form and pressing Enter (or clicking the Submit button that some viewers provide) begins a search for the next occurrence of the text string.

The ISINDEX element

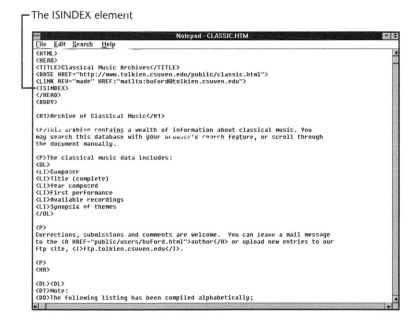

Fig. 9.9
The ISINDEX element requires no attributes or document information; it signals the viewer to provide a search form.

III

Creating Documents

Fig. 9.10
The WWW viewer displays a search field when it finds the ISINDEX element in the document head; press Enter to start a search based on the text string in the search field.

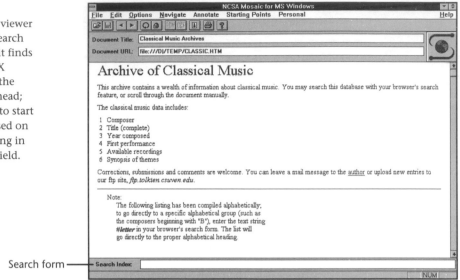

Search form ——

Using an Alternate Indexing Method

▶ See "Using the Anchor Element," p. 253

It's possible that your Web server doesn't have a search engine to make ISINDEX a useful tool. An HTML document author, with sufficient time and desperation (and a Web site administrator who can't provide the necessary search program), can create a "rolodex" or "organizer" effect in a document. This effect is possible using anchors. Figure 9.11 shows an anchored index in a document.

This search function works using the HTML ANCHOR element; by defining each letter as an anchor link to a named anchor, the user can click that letter and jump immediately to the specified point in the document.

For example, in figure 9.11, the list of letters would begin like this in HTML:

```
<A HREF="#A">A</A>

<A HREF="#B">B</A>
```

And so on. Clicking the highlighted B in the viewer window would jump to the line of HTML in the document that includes the following named anchor:

```
<A NAME="B">BACH</A>
```

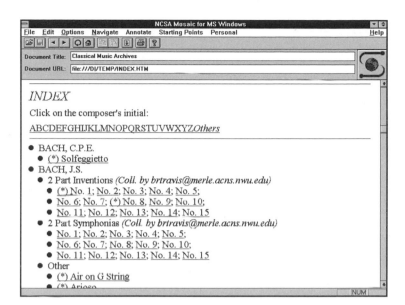

Fig. 9.11
An HTML document can incorporate a rolodex-type search feature using named anchors; click an alphabetical category to jump to that point in the Web page.

From Here...

The next step in creating HTML documents is to add the content that users will read. Refer to the following chapters for instructions on creating and formatting content:

- Chapter 10, "Where the Content Is: The Document Body," describes the style and navigation of HTML elements available for the body section of a document.

- Chapter 11, "Displaying Text in Lists," illustrates the range of formatting and sorting options for generated text lists provided by HTML.

- Chapter 12, "Adding Graphics to HTML Documents," shows you how to incorporate eye-catching GIF graphics in a document to provide additional information and style.

- Part IV, "Using Forms in HTML Documents," teaches you how to incorporate forms into documents for collecting user input and activating scripts and programs on your Web server.

III

Creating Documents

## Chapter 10

Where the Content Is: The Document Body

As you've seen, the World Wide Web and HTML are all about delivering information to end users. The body section is the "cargo carrier" of this international data highway; it's the container that carries the data HTML viewers display to users.

The body is also the blank canvas for your creative energies. This chapter will provide you with some basic tools to bring your HTML documents to life.

This chapter answers the following questions:

- What's the function of the body section in an HTML document?

- How do headings work together in an HTML document?

- How do I break a paragraph or a line of text?

- Can I control how a document displays text?

- How can I indent text?

- How can I emphasize a break between paragraphs?

Think of the Body as a Big Container

The BODY element defines the boundaries of your data to be shown in the viewer software. When WWW viewers see the <BODY> line in your document, they know to display the contents that follow, interpret any HTML formatting or object codes in the contents, until they reach the </BODY> line. Figure 10.1 shows a typical document body following the head section.

The document is an example of how personal information can be presented in a simple manner.

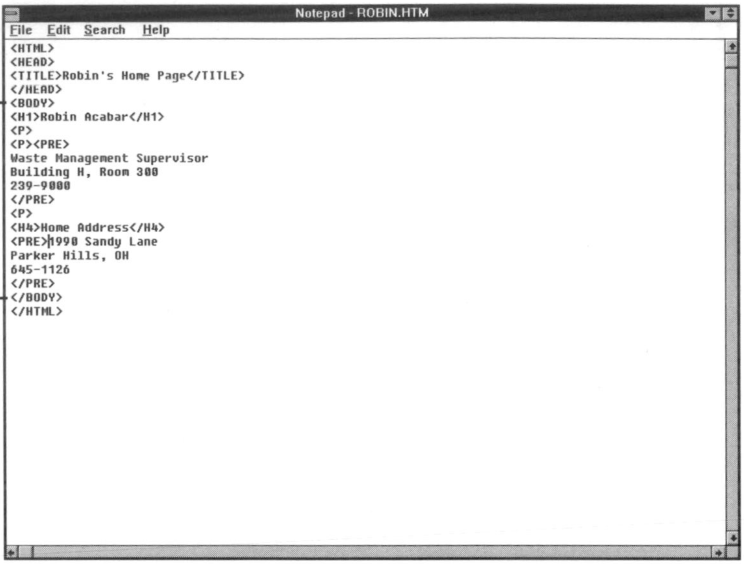

Fig. 10.1
The <BODY> and </BODY> tags act like bookends to a document's information.

Begin body tag ——

End body tag ——

```
                          Notepad - ROBIN.HTM
File  Edit  Search  Help
<HTML>
<HEAD>
<TITLE>Robin's Home Page</TITLE>
</HEAD>
<BODY>
<H1>Robin Acabar</H1>
<P>
<P><PRE>
Waste Management Supervisor
Building H, Room 300
239-9000
</PRE>
<P>
<H4>Home Address</H4>
<PRE>1990 Sandy Lane
Parker Hills, OH
645-1126
</PRE>
</BODY>
</HTML>
```

> **Note**
>
> Although a document can end without the </BODY> closing tag (or even the </HTML> tag), proper HTML dictates that you use them. Sure, the information will display the same either way, but for future uses of the HTML document (by WWW viewers or other Internet applications) these definitions may be necessary. Save yourself the time and effort later of having to edit your inventory of HTML documents just to add the tags!

Using Headings in an HTML Document

The first elements you learn to use, and will eventually find indispensable, are headings. HTML supports six heading levels. To get a real sense of how headings work, imagine an outline format. The relationships between each line or item are shown by the level or indentation of the elements; items on the same levels are considered equals (see fig. 10.2).

Level 1 heading   Level 2 heading   Level 3 heading   Level 4 headings

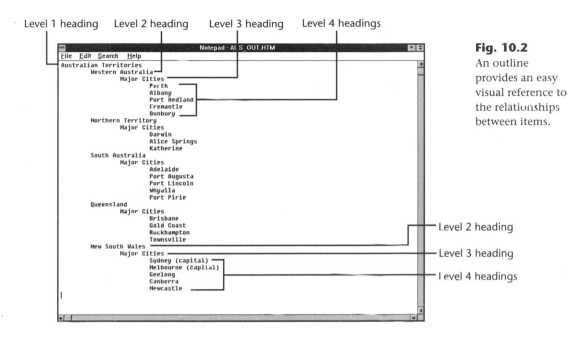

Fig. 10.2
An outline
provides an easy
visual reference to
the relationships
between items.

Level 2 heading

Level 3 heading

Level 4 headings

Headings function in the same manner. Each of the six levels is defined in HTML, and each has its own formatting. Because HTML documents generally don't contain specific font or style information, the end user's WWW viewer defines the on-screen look of the different heading levels.

Headings are defined using the Hn container, where n represents the heading level for the text. For instance, text surrounded by the H1 container element uses the first heading level format. Use headings in a logical order; subheadings in a document should proceed numerically. As a purely functional point, you can use any heading level at any time, but for consistent on-screen formatting, and to represent the relationships between the headings properly, it's best to follow this rule. It doesn't hurt to stick to the convention and it does make using the document in other applications easier (to extract an outline from an HTML document, for instance).

Note

One non-standard use of the heading elements has become a somewhat common practice—using H6 for text that is intended to be "small print." Most viewers display this heading in eight- or 10-point bold characters. Until HTML provides a specific tag for this purpose (perhaps <LEGAL>?), this usage is acceptable.

III

Creating Documents

While HTML doesn't define line feeds (sometimes called carriage returns, for the old-timers) as line breaks, and viewers don't interpret line feeds as the start of a new line, heading tags supply their own break and line spacing. A line of HTML such as

```
<H1>This is my first data set.</H1><H1>This is my second data set.</H1>
```

would be displayed as two separate lines of text. Figure 10.3 shows examples of the proper formatting for a list of headings in an HTML document.

Fig. 10.3

Headings are contained by the <H*n*> and </H*n*> tags; blank spaces and lines are for readability only.

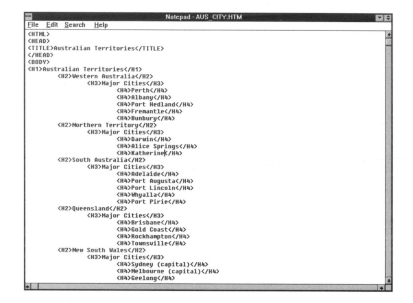

```
Notepad - AUS_CITY.HTM
File  Edit  Search  Help
<HTML>
<HEAD>
<TITLE>Australian Territories</TITLE>
</HEAD>
<BODY>
<H1>Australian Territories</H1>
        <H2>Western Australia</H2>
                <H3>Major Cities</H3>
                        <H4>Perth</H4>
                        <H4>Albany</H4>
                        <H4>Port Hedland</H4>
                        <H4>Fremantle</H4>
                        <H4>Bunbury</H4>
        <H2>Northern Territory</H2>
                <H3>Major Cities</H3>
                        <H4>Darwin</H4>
                        <H4>Alice Springs</H4>
                        <H4>Katherine</H4>
        <H2>South Australia</H2>
                <H3>Major Cities</H3>
                        <H4>Adelaide</H4>
                        <H4>Port Augusta</H4>
                        <H4>Port Lincoln</H4>
                        <H4>Whyalla</H4>
                        <H4>Port Pirie</H4>
        <H2>Queensland</H2>
                <H3>Major Cities</H3>
                        <H4>Brisbane</H4>
                        <H4>Gold Coast</H4>
                        <H4>Rockhampton</H4>
                        <H4>Townsville</H4>
        <H2>New South Wales</H2>
                <H3>Major Cities</H3>
                        <H4>Sydney (capital)</H4>
                        <H4>Melbourne (capital)</H4>
                        <H4>Geelong</H4>
```

Note

HTML doesn't respect empty space. Most programmers are familiar with the practice of indenting code or inserting blank lines to organize lines of code and make the source easier to read. The same can be done in HTML, with the understanding that HTML allows only a single blank character and ignores any consecutive ones (blanks separated by other characters are perfectly legal). HTML completely ignores blank lines. But if you're more comfortable creating "source" HTML that's easier to read, it's okay to use blanks where necessary in your HTML documents.

Figure 10.4 shows how these headings can be displayed by a WWW viewer.

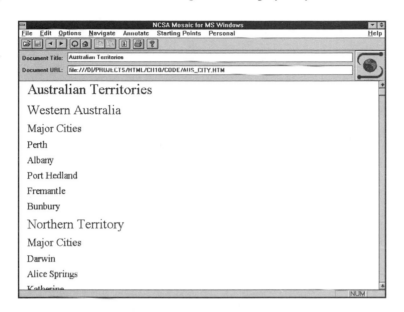

Fig. 10.4
The blank spaces were ignored by the viewer as required by the HTML standard.

Different viewers might have different formatting rules for each heading level. As a comparison, figure 10.5 shows how NCSA Mosaic for the Macintosh displays the same HTML document using its default style settings for the heading elements.

Troubleshooting

I stick to the conventions of using heading elements in their proper order, but my users complain that the headings look too much alike from one level to the next. What can I do?

It's not your fault that they see headings the way they do—it's their software. Tell your users to redefine their viewer's heading formats to make the heading levels easier to distinguish. You can give them specific guidelines (for example, H1 as 24-point normal or H6 as 8-point bold), but it's ultimately up to them to accommodate their own tastes and needs.

III

Creating Documents

Fig. 10.5

A viewer's character font, size, and style differences affect how the text is displayed on-screen.

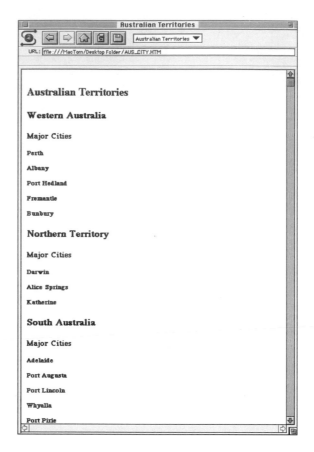

Creating Text and Line Breaks in HTML

One of the foremost concerns in publishing (whether it's distributed in print or electronically) is readability: You want your audience to be able to read the document. Every visual choice, from selecting a font and layout style to designing graphics, affects the quality of the reading experience. You will quickly learn that line and paragraph breaks are crucial for creating effective HTML documents.

Remember, under the markup language concept, HTML authors have little control over the on-screen format of their documents. Two factors play a significant role in this lack of control. First, HTML doesn't display line feeds in documents (except in the PRE container; see the "Using PRE" section later in this chapter for more information). Second, WWW viewers allow you to resize the document window, which affects text wrapping and the visual effect of inline graphics. Figure 10.6 shows an HTML document that doesn't include text breaks, and figure 10.7 shows what the end user sees.

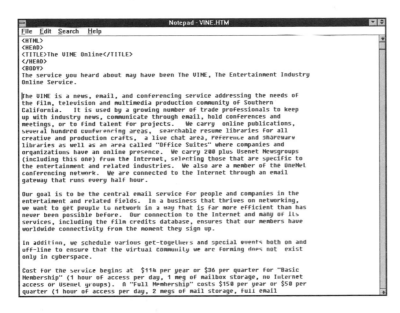

Fig. 10.6
This HTML page is very easy to read as a text document.

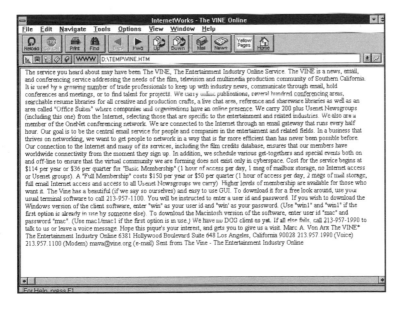

Fig. 10.7
But the document loses its effective-ness when loaded into a WWW viewer.

The Paragraph Break

You use the <P> tag to avoid compressing all of your text into one big paragraph, and to separate your text for easy reading. Although it's technically a container, the current HTML standard doesn't require the closing </P> tag. This will be required under HTML 3.0; see Part V of this book for more information. HTML doesn't allow consecutive <P> tags in a document (it ignores any empty containers after the first one).

> **Note**
>
> The <P> tag is useful to separate text, but what if you want to use multiple line feeds to create a larger space between text paragraphs? One solution is to add a small preformatted container (using the <PRE> tag) with *two* blank spaces inside it after the <P> tag. Viewers interpret this as valid content for the P element, and generate a blank line. Why two spaces? Some viewers, notably Netscape, accept one blank space, while others (such as NCSA Mosaic) treat one blank as if it's no content. Using two provides the greatest compatibility for all WWW viewers.

Paragraph containers can hold any content, including other containers. Figure 10.8 shows an example of the paragraph tag in an HTML document. Figure 10.9 shows how this code is interpreted by a WWW viewer.

Fig. 10.8
Separate text and other HTML elements with the <P> tag to define breaks between paragraphs.

Paragraph tags ——

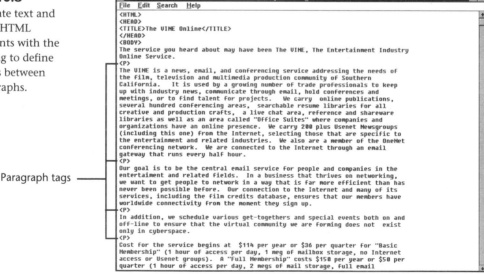

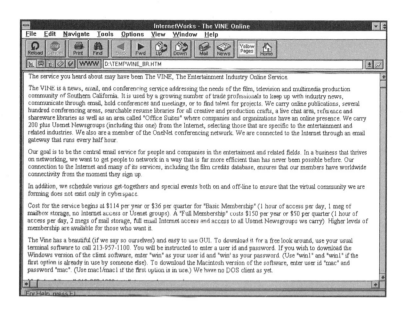

Fig. 10.9
The viewer inserts a "double space" between paragraphs; different viewers define this space differently.

Modifying Paragraphs in Netscape

Netscape's extension to text paragraphs (and document images) is probably the most-often used non-standard HTML that Netscape has promoted. The CENTER container element defines a section of the document body that will be centered within the Netscape-compatible viewer window. Centering is dynamic—if the user resizes the viewer window, the text will wrap accordingly and re-center to the window's new margins. Figure 10.10 shows a document with both centered images and text.

The Forced Line Break

You may intend for a line of text to end at a specific point. One example is if you want to create a text list by hand, in the standard paragraph container text style. Use <BR>, the forced line break tag, to signal the viewer to enter a line feed at the tag and continue with the text on the next line. The lines are single spaced, as opposed to the paragraph break.

Figure 10.11 shows how to use forced line breaks, and figure 10.12 shows how BR tags retain some control over text display in the WWW viewer's window.

Tip
Use the BR element to create a tight vertical text column; preformat your HTML document text to a specific line width with a utility such as Add/Strip and append <BR> tags to each line.

Fig. 10.10
Viewers that don't support the <CENTER> tags will ignore them and align all document information from the left margin.

Fig. 10.11
Like paragraph breaks, you can insert forced line breaks into a line of HTML code at any point to indicate a new line.

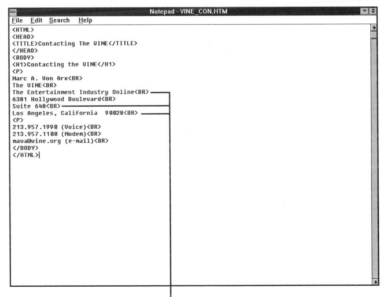

Forced line breaks

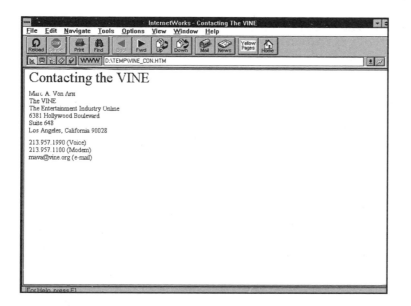

Fig. 10.12
WWW viewers
automatically start
a new line after a

 tag.

Caution

Viewers follow orders, even to the detriment of the text being displayed. A forced break can look unsightly if the text has already wrapped in the viewer window. The shorter you keep lines of text between <BR> tags, the better your chances of the end user's software displaying your document as you intend it to look.

▶ See "Using
Additional IMG
Attributes to
Enhance Text
in Netscape,"
p. 242

Modifying Line Breaks in Netscape

Netscape has added a new level of functionality to the forced line break as an enhancement to the extensions for the IMG element. The BR CLEAR attribute tells the viewer to do the following:

CLEAR=LEFT. Breaks the current line of text and starts the next line of text on the first line available against the left margin.

CLEAR=RIGHT. Breaks the current line of text and starts the next line of text on the first line that has a clear right margin.

CLEAR=ALL. Breaks the current line of text and starts the next line on the first line that has both margins clear (there are no images on or overlapping the line).

III

Creating Documents

Better management of how text interacts with inline graphics allows the author much more control over the desktop display, even when the user resizes the viewer window. (This is the bane of Author school creators who do not have a Netscape audience.)

The advantages may not be so obvious here. Let's look at it from a word processing or desktop publishing perspective. The effect of this extension of the BR element is to provide authors the ability to control how text "wraps around" images in a document. Figure 10.13 shows how these three additions to the <BR> tag can create some interesting effects with floating inline images.

Fig. 10.13
Use the CLEAR attribute to control where images are located in the flow of text.

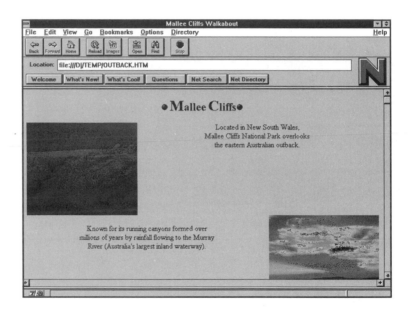

Tip
When using the <NOBR> tag, do not forget to close the text section with </NOBR>. Otherwise, you will wind up with a very long sentence composed of all of your body text.

Netscape also supplies two additions to the HTML text break family: the NOBR and WBR elements. <NOBR> is a container element that stands for "no break," and is used to indicate a section of text that is not allowed to be broken. For instance, a URL address might benefit from using NOBR.

The <WBR> tag is an empty element; it stands for "word break" and is used to indicate specifically where a line can be broken. This is useful when used in a "no break" section to let Web viewers know what break point is allowable. It does not actually force a break, but it gives Netscape-compatible WWW clients the option to do so at that specific location in the text.

Displaying Preformatted Text in Its Original Form

At times, HTML can seem like more work than necessary. For instance, is there a simpler way to re-create a specific section of text without having to use <BR> and <P> tags all over the place? Yes, there is. Preformatted text tags are containers that tell the WWW viewer to display HTML code in its original format, possibly including line feeds and multiple blank spaces as well. This can vastly simplify "cut and paste" procedures if retaining the original text layout is important.

Using PRE

The PRE container is the best known and most versatile preformatted text element. It supports line feeds and blank spaces, and also lets you include other tags and links in the text. Strictly speaking, using emphasis tags (such as <STRONG> or <B>) in a PRE container is frowned upon (it isn't considered "good HTML"). But you can and should take certain liberties if they enhance the readability of your document. For instance, a table created in a PRE container can use <B> tags (to bold text) for its column and row labels, making the displayed text easier to read.

> **Caution**
>
> One consideration when using the PRE container is that WWW viewers display this text in a plain, non-proportional font, which looks much like the text displayed by a non-graphical application (such as Telnet or the DOS command line).

Tip
Don't forget to close the container with the </PRE> end tag.

Take advantage of PRE's use of a non-proportional font to create text-based graphics ("ASCII art") and charts. Be careful when using style tags such as <B> and <EM> because they affect the spacing of the text characters.

Figure 10.14 shows a series of samples using the PRE container.

WWW viewers interpret PRE text exactly as you enter it. The PRE container is handy when re-creating table or multi-column information. Figure 10.15 shows how the sample HTML document is displayed by Web client software.

III

Creating Documents

Fig. 10.14
You can use spaces and line breaks in the PRE container; text modifiers (elements such as U for underlining and EM for emphasis) can also be used.

Creates a horizontal line in a document

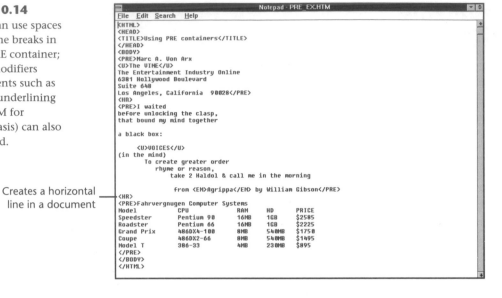

Fig. 10.15
WWW viewers display a non-proportional font for PRE text.

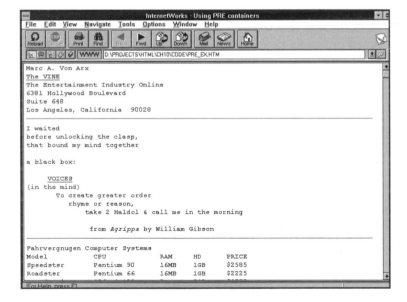

Using XMP

A second HTML container you can use for preformatted text is XMP. The XMP container works just as the PRE container does, with the following differences:

- HTML tags can't be used in an XMP container.

- Viewers display the text in a proportional font, typically the default body text font (this can be different, according to the specific viewer).

- The </XMP> closing tag does not force a line break.

- Not recommended for tables or columns.

XMP is considered obsolete—an element that's no longer defined in the current HTML standard. However, XMP is still supported by WWW viewers, and its limitations do provide certain benefits over using PRE; proportional fonts look less "rigid" and are easier to read; and XMP containers can co-exist on the same line as other text in the viewer (such as hypertext links). Figures 10.16 and 10.17 show how the PRE sample text would be used with XMP.

XMP containers represent the text as it is written by the author, including line breaks, blank lines and HTML codes. In figure 10.17, the <EM> and </EM> tags—normally interpreted as an emphasis container—are displayed as regular text information. Be careful using this element; as WWW viewers are revised to meet new HTML standards and functionality, the XMP support may suffer or disappear.

◀ See "Using Text Entities in HTML," p. 154

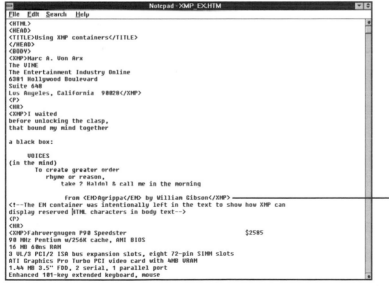

Fig. 10.16
Line breaks and spaces are legal, just like in PRE containers.

The <EM> and </EM> tags display as shown.

Fig. 10.17
However, viewers
ignore embedded
tags and display
them as though
they're body text.

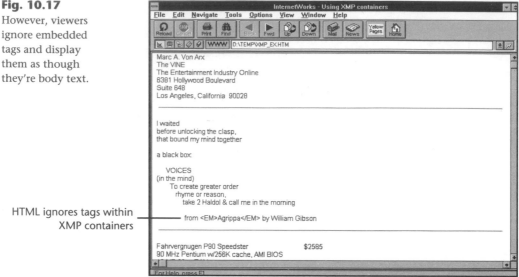

HTML ignores tags within
XMP containers

Note

XMP can be a handy tool for displaying characters that are normally reserved by HTML. This is a way to sidestep using HTML's entities. Of course, this shortcut is generally discouraged as "bad HTML" because the element is obsolete (and may lead you to have to revise older HTML documents as the tag is eventually retired by WWW clients). Use it at your discretion!

Using PLAINTEXT

A third tag you can use to display preformatted text is the PLAINTEXT element. This isn't a container, although few viewers (notably Mosaic) will recognize a </PLAINTEXT> closing tag. An element of the original HTML specification, PLAINTEXT will be obsolete with the coming of HTML version 3. Most viewers will continue to interpret the tag (to support older HTML documents still in circulation).

The current WWW viewers display PLAINTEXT text in varying ways. Unfortunately, the differences can be drastic and point out the difficulty of making your documents as widely compatible as possible. For instance, figure 10.18 shows a typical HTML usage of the <PLAINTEXT> tag. Figure 10.19 shows how NCSA Mosaic interprets the <PLAINTEXT> tag. Figure 10.20 shows how Netscape 1.0 interprets the same HTML document.

Other viewers might display the document in similar ways. It should be obvious that the <PLAINTEXT> tag is dangerous to use, given the unpredictable behavior of WWW clients. For this reason, and because it is an obsolete tag, it's probably best to avoid using PLAINTEXT in favor of PRE.

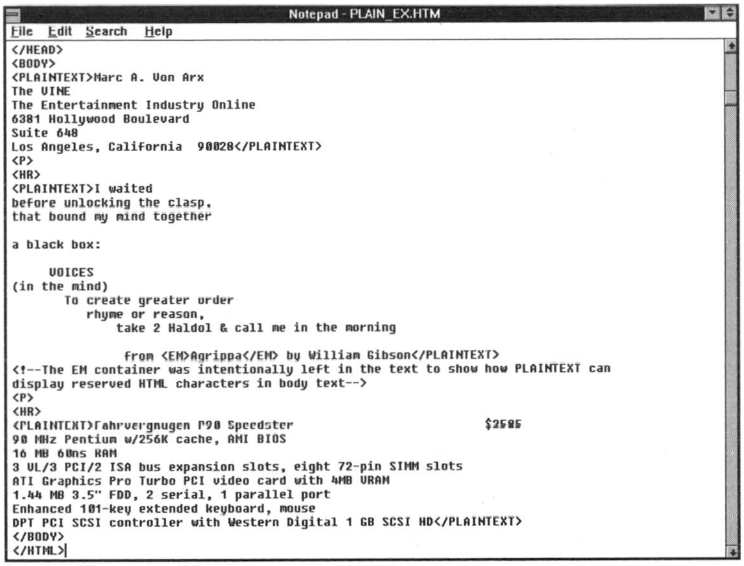

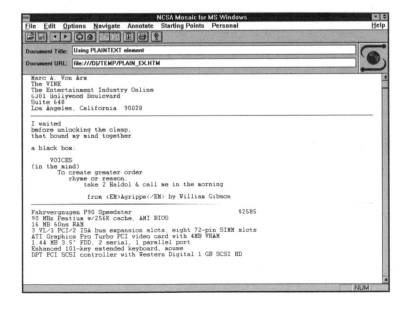

Fig. 10.18
The PLAINTEXT element doesn't require a closing tag but this example uses one for demonstration purposes.

Fig. 10.19
NCSA Mosaic for Windows treats the PLAINTEXT element much like the XMP element, displaying all following HTML coding as normal text.

Fig. 10.20
Netscape treats
<PLAINTEXT> as
an empty tag (it
ignores the
</PLAINTEXT>
closing tags and
displays them as
regular text) and
displays all the
text that follows
(as the XMP
element).

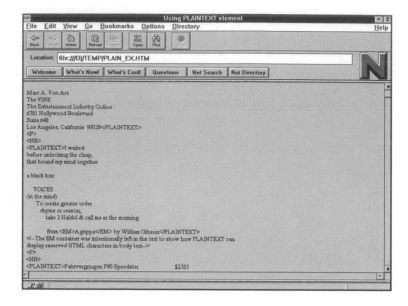

Using BLOCKQUOTE

Often, when printed texts use extended citations from other works, the citations are set apart from the rest of the body text in an indented block. The BLOCKQUOTE container provides this feature for HTML documents. Unlike PRE, BLOCKQUOTE doesn't retain line feeds in the text, nor does it allow additional consecutive blank spaces. What it does provide is a uniform indented format for all citations that simplify reuse of the source HTML document, or the redefinition of the screen format of all citations in BLOCKQUOTE containers.

BLOCKQUOTE containers can include other HTML codes, such as text styles and text breaks. Remember to use the closing tag </BLOCKQUOTE> to signal the end of the container. Figure 10.21 shows examples of BLOCKQUOTE in an HTML document.

Figure 10.22 shows how the preceding document is interpreted by a standard WWW viewer (the on-screen display may vary, depending on the viewer software).

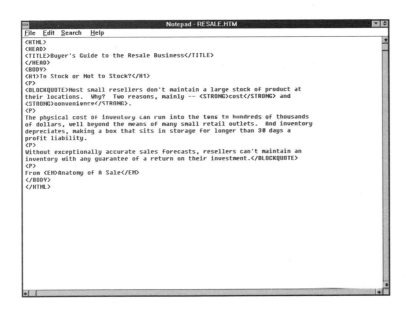

Fig. 10.21
Text formatting in the BLOCKQUOTE container is ignored (unless provided by an HTML element).

Fig. 10.22
BLOCKQUOTE text uses the standard body text font style and a uniform indentation.

Tip

Use BLOCKQUOTE to indent text in a list item—a simple way to create a formatted "aside" or reference for the item's text without having to use a new sub-list container.

The Standards, They Are a Changin'...

All around us, new standards arrive on a constant basis. From music distribution formats to automobile safety codes, revising standards is the process of improving our lives. In the computer industry, these standards seem to change before the previous standards have been ironed out (and the industry often takes heat for this practice). HTML is a young and evolving markup language. In fact, although the HTML 2.0 standard was only published in December, 1994, the HTML 3.0 standard is already well under consideration. Viewers such as Arena already support HTML 3.0 "features."

In HTML, current elements become obsolete as new elements (or better uses of existing elements) are approved. It's important to watch the changes in the language—or participate in the development process—to anticipate what elements will be retired or re-purposed. The best source for information about HTML and WWW development issues is from CERN (the European Laboratory for Particle Physics) at **http://info.cern.ch/hypertext/WWW/**.

Formatting Text in HTML: Physical versus Logical

All communication is based on the notion of a shared understanding. Part of communication is emphasis, whether it's transmitted through tone in a voice, body language behind spoken words, italicized words in a book, or the punctuation that separates sentences. Because the WWW is a mechanism for distributing information, HTML must provide tools for defining various emphases in HTML documents.

Note

Of course, you don't always have to rely on the written word for communication. The WWW supports distribution of video and audio data files; go ahead and record a message in one manner or another. Add a link in your HTML document and presto! Instant clarity. Of course, the size of these data files limits their effective use, but someday users will pull down documents that use these data types extensively. Be prepared!

There are two schools of thought when it comes to providing emphasis in HTML documents. First is the Author school, that allows the creator to be specific in defining what and how to apply emphasis to displayed HTML text.

Second is the SGML school, which stresses the responsibility of the viewer over the creator in providing the proper on-screen formatting of emphasis. The following sections explore these two approaches.

Using Physical Style Elements

Physical style elements are familiar to any word processor user. They consist of HTML containers that provide bold, italic, and underlined emphasis to the text they enclose (see Table 10.1).

Table 10.1	Physical Styles and Their Meanings
Style	**Description**
B	Bold text
I	Italic text
U	Underlined text

These tags are absolute: every viewer software interprets the tags in exactly the same manner. While the limitations of a viewer may prevent the representation of the text style (the text-only Lynx viewer, for example), there is no variable definition a viewer may interpret the tag with. What you expect to see is what you get. Figure 10.23 shows how the physical style tags are used, and figure 10.24 shows how a WWW viewer displays them.

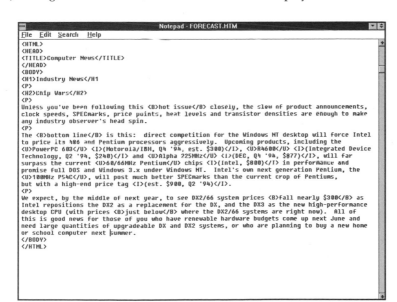

Fig. 10.23
Physical style containers apply their styles to all enclosed text and require closing tags.

III

Creating Documents

Fig. 10.24
Viewers interpret physical styles in a straightforward manner; their effects are cumulative.

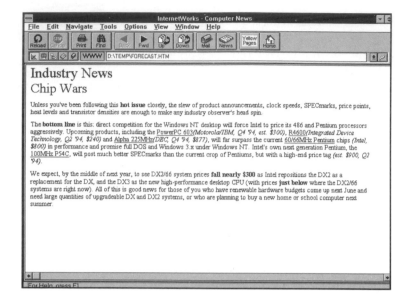

Contrary to the traditional SGML model, there is a place for physical styles in HTML. While some may decry the practice of letting the HTML document tell the client software how to display text, at times it can be vital to have this kind of control.

Consider the use of a preformatted text container to re-create a table (refer to fig. 10.16). To enhance the table (and make it easier to read), use physical styles on the labels and legends. Figures 10.25 and 10.26 show how a detailed table with callout cells and text labels can be written.

Tip
You can combine physical styles for predictable display results in the majority of Web viewers; logical styles generally can't be combined this way.

Using Logical Style Elements

In the SGML school of thought, documents are "device-independent": code can be read on any platform with the appropriate screen formatting applied by the viewing software. Data is defined according to its semantic content (this is the same "relative" philosophy that you see with the heading containers). In the case of logical styles, instead of defining the relationships between tagged headings, the relationship of the tagged text to untagged text is defined. Thus, the tags and definitions given in Table 10.2 apply.

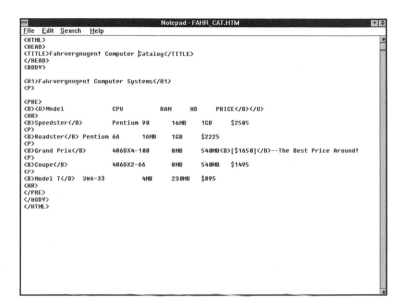

Fig. 10.25
Adjust the table data after formatting with the physical style tags to maintain proper positioning.

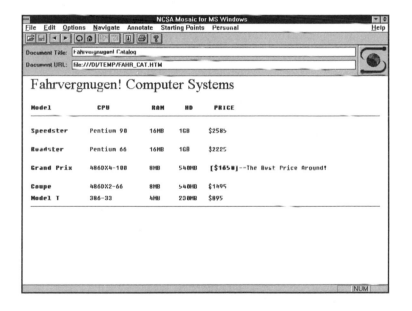

Fig. 10.26
Physical style containers emphasize information and make a table easier to read.

III

Creating Documents

Table 10.2 Logical Styles and Their Meanings	
Style	**Description**
EM	Emphasized text
STRONG	Strongly emphasized text
CITE	Text in a citation
CODE	Text representing an HTML element
DFN	Text in a definition
SAMP	Text in an output sample
KBD	Text representing a keyboard key
VAR	Text defining a variable

Logical style elements provide a measure of consistency for the user; styles can be redefined according to the software and user's needs and applied to all tagged text (whereas physical style elements override the viewer's inclination to define the text's appearance). Figure 10.27 shows how logical styles are written, and figure 10.28 shows how a viewer's default settings interprets them.

Fig. 10.27
Unlike physical styles, you should not use logical styles in combinations.

Use of output sample container

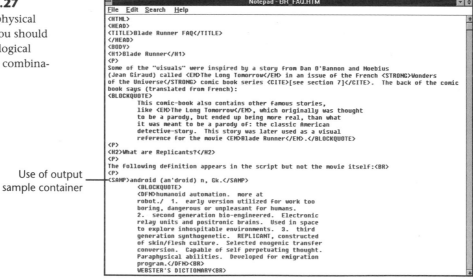

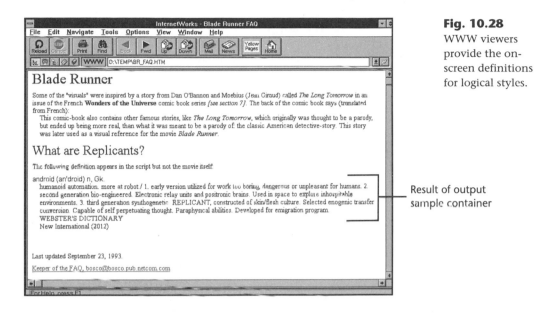

Fig. 10.28
WWW viewers
provide the on-
screen definitions
for logical styles.

Result of output
sample container

Separating Paragraphs with Horizontal Lines

Magazine and newspaper layout often use lines to separate content, making it easier for the reader to follow the flow of one subject, and providing a quick perspective to the size of the current topic. Aesthetically, lines provide variety for the eye. Psychologically, they break text into manageable chunks and avoid overloading the reader with a single overwhelming bulk of text.

Using the <HR> Tag

In document layout, text is often divided by vertical and horizontal lines to separate unrelated material and create a natural flow for the eye. Vertical lines are not available in HTML, but HTML does provide a simple solution for incorporating horizontal lines. The <HR> tag places a fixed-weight shaded line across the width of the viewer (and resizing the viewer's window also resizes the line to match its new width). The <HR> tag is an empty tag, requires no closing tag, and forces both a paragraph break before and after the line. Figure 10.29 shows how the <HR> tag can be used in an HTML document, and figure 10.30 shows how a standard viewer interprets the tag.

III

Creating Documents

Fig. 10.29
The <HR> tag
does not require
paragraph breaks
or a closing tag.

These tags produce
horizontal rules

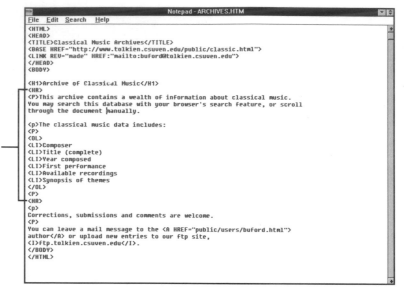

Fig. 10.30
Against NCSA
Mosaic's default
gray background
the shaded lines
would look
"etched" into the
page.

Results of the <HR> tags

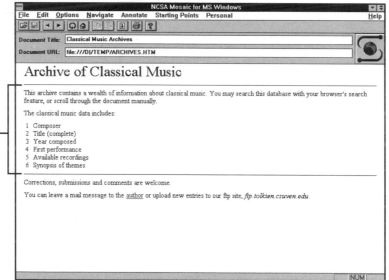

Modifying the HR Element in Netscape

Netscape provides additional attributes for HR. These allow you some control
over the weight of the line, its length, and its placement in the viewer

window. Netscape also provides a way to drop the "etched" look of the line in favor of a solid black line. Table 10.3 lists the non-standard attributes and their functions.

Table 10.3	Netscape Extensions to HR
Extension	**Description**
SIZE	Sets thickness of horizontal line
WIDTH	Sets width as a measure of pixels or percentage of viewer window's width
ALIGN	Allows line to be justified for left, center, or right in the viewer window
NOSHADE	Changes appearance of horizontal line to be solid black with no "etched" effect

Figure 10.31 shows how these extensions are incorporated in an HTML document. Notice that the first horizontal rule has been set to a height of 5 with no drop shadow behind it. The three rules grouped at the bottom of the page are staggered in size and centered, creating a stylish "pyramid" effect. Figure 10.32 shows how Netscape's extensions can enhance a document.

Tip
To the user, a single <HR> tag is the psychological equivalent of a topic break. Multiple horizontal rules become a graphic construct in the text—experiment by using more than one rule in place of an inline graphic to separate text paragraphs.

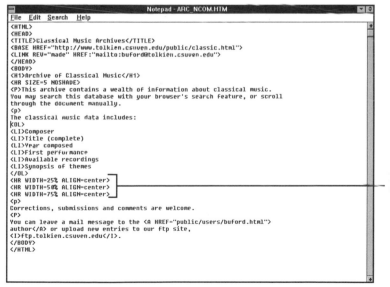

Attributes added
to <HR> tag

Fig. 10.31
Netscape's extensions are ignored by viewers that don't recognize them.

III

Creating Documents

Fig. 10.32

Controlling the appearance of lines adds a creative touch to Web pages.

Horizontal rule, thickened by using attributes

Centered horizontal rules

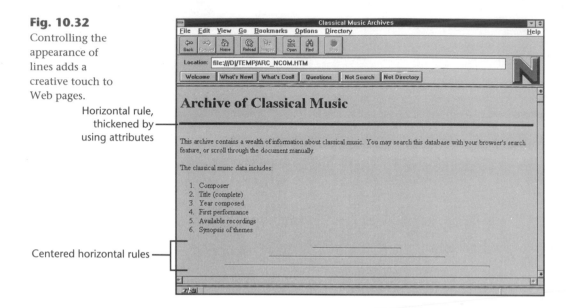

These extensions are an issue for debate between the SGML purists and the authorial control advocates. The SGML school regards the eventual on-screen formatting as the domain of the viewer; if a horizontal line is going to be used, the user's software will determine its size, placement, and appearance. The opposing school regards layout in the way a typesetter would: controlling presentation is important for maximizing the communication of ideas. While the debate continues, there is no denying that Netscape is breaking ground on new applications of existing HTML elements.

Adding Author Comments in HTML Documents

Creating HTML documents is often compared to software programming. One habit that good software programmers develop is including comments and documentation right inside the code itself. You use these sections of hidden text to describe the purpose or function of the following code, or to leave a notation explaining the programmer's intentions with the code or its methods.

Caution

Don't use the comment element to "turn off" HTML code in a document (like "REM" is used in DOS batch files); viewers might still interpret HTML sequences in your comments and display them in your document.

HTML documents benefit from this same practice. Like the head section, HTML provides a means for including embedded comments in the body that are not visible in the WWW viewer. HTML has adopted the standard SGML container of <!-- (an exclamation mark followed by two dashes) to begin the author's comments, and a tag of --> to close the comment container. Comments included inside the container should consist of standard text without using any of HTML's special characters (such as the left- and right-angle brackets).

Caution

Always test a commented document in a viewer to make sure the comments are correctly written before making it widely available—you might not want to share your "behind the scenes" commentary!

Figure 10.33 shows how comments can be embedded in an HTML document. The viewer doesn't display this text.

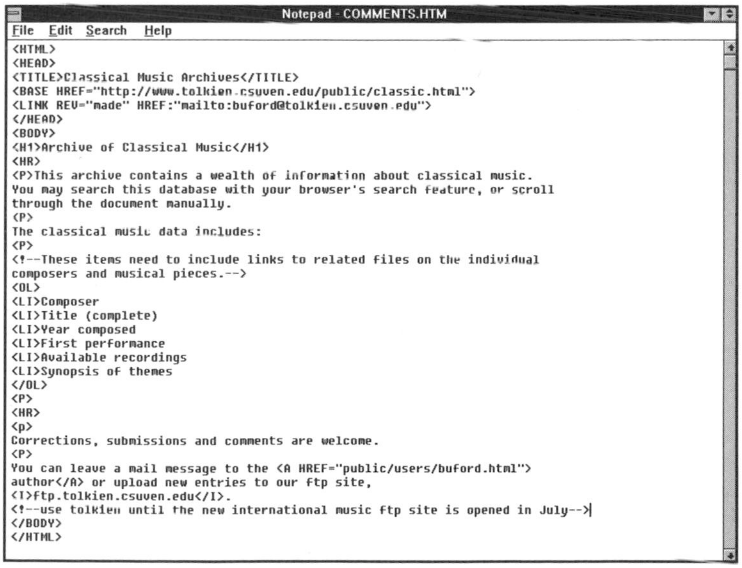

```
<HTML>
<HEAD>
<TITLE>Classical Music Archives</TITLE>
<BASE HREF="http://www.tolkien.csuven.edu/public/classic.html">
<LINK REV="made" HREF:"mailto:buford@tolkien.csuven.edu">
</HEAD>
<BODY>
<H1>Archive of Classical Music</H1>
<HR>
<P>This archive contains a wealth of information about classical music.
You may search this database with your browser's search feature, or scroll
through the document manually.
<P>
The classical music data includes:
<P>
<!--These items need to include links to related files on the individual
composers and musical pieces.-->
<OL>
<LI>Composer
<LI>Title (complete)
<LI>Year composed
<LI>First performance
<LI>Available recordings
<LI>Synopsis of themes
</OL>
<P>
<HR>
<p>
Corrections, submissions and comments are welcome.
<P>
You can leave a mail message to the <A HREF="public/users/buford.html">
author</A> or upload new entries to our ftp site,
<I>ftp.tolkien.csuven.edu</I>.
<!--use tolkien until the new international music ftp site is opened in July-->
</BODY>
</HTML>
```

Fig. 10.33 Comments can be embedded anywhere except in a preformatted text container.

Additional Netscape Text Elements

Besides controlling the behavior of rules and breaks, and providing the capability to center HTML data, Netscape also provides the author with the ability to manipulate the document's font size. Two non-standard extensions control how text is displayed, one locally and one globally. Like URLs, font sizes can be defined in absolute or relative terms.

Tip

Netscape's font elements support sizes ranging from 1 to 7 (1 is the smallest font displayed; 7 is the largest). Use adjacent values to create a "small caps" or initial caps text effect.

The global font element is BASEFONT, a container used to define the font size for a section that all other relative font changes will refer to. The tag <BASEFONT SIZE=n> can be set to a value of 1 to 7, and determines how large the document text will be in the viewer window. All other relative font changes within the section will use this font size as their starting point.

The standard font element is just that: FONT. It is a container, like BASEFONT, that is defined as <FONT SIZE=n>, in which n can be a number from 1 to 7. FONT SIZE can also be defined in relative terms, using a plus or minus sign to indicate the container's font size in relation to the text around it. For example, if you define your <FONT SIZE=+2> in a document section in which <BASEFONT SIZE=3> (the default HTML document font size), your FONT-defined text will be displayed in size 5. The same is possible using the minus sign to reduce the screen font in relation to the surrounding text. Figure 10.34 shows how FONT and BASEFONT are used in an HTML document, and figure 10.35 shows how Netscape-compatible viewers will display text in whatever size the author dictates.

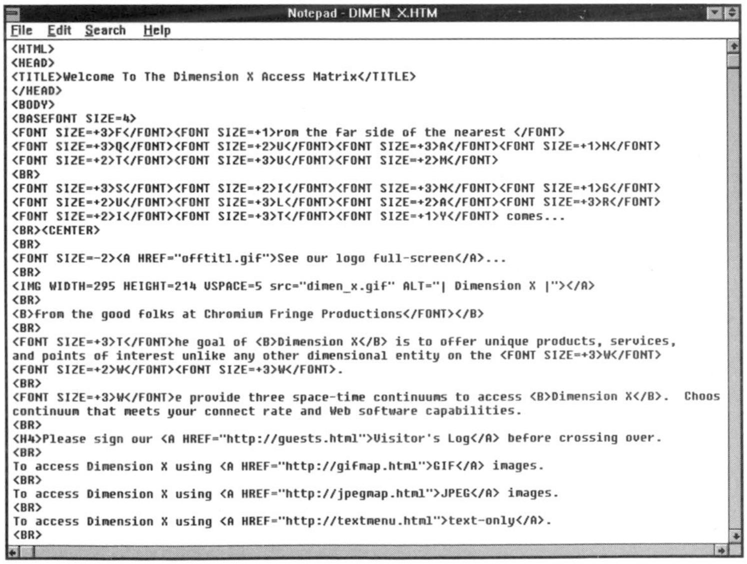

Fig. 10.34

Both FONT and BASEFONT are container elements; remember their closing tags to properly define the text you want to apply your font size to.

```
                              Notepad - DIMEN_X.HTM
 File  Edit  Search  Help
<HTML>
<HEAD>
<TITLE>Welcome To The Dimension X Access Matrix</TITLE>
</HEAD>
<BODY>
<BASEFONT SIZE=4>
<FONT SIZE=+3>F</FONT><FONT SIZE=+1>rom the far side of the nearest </FONT>
<FONT SIZE=+3>Q</FONT><FONT SIZE=+2>U</FONT><FONT SIZE=+3>A</FONT><FONT SIZE=+1>N</FONT>
<FONT SIZE=+2>T</FONT><FONT SIZE=+3>U</FONT><FONT SIZE=+2>M</FONT>
<BR>
<FONT SIZE=+3>S</FONT><FONT SIZE=+2>I</FONT><FONT SIZE=+3>N</FONT><FONT SIZE=+1>G</FONT>
<FONT SIZE=+2>U</FONT><FONT SIZE=+3>L</FONT><FONT SIZE=+2>A</FONT><FONT SIZE=+3>R</FONT>
<FONT SIZE=+2>I</FONT><FONT SIZE=+3>T</FONT><FONT SIZE=+1>Y</FONT> comes...
<BR><CENTER>
<BR>
<FONT SIZE=-2><A HREF="offtit1.gif">See our logo full-screen</A>...
<BR>
<IMG WIDTH=295 HEIGHT=214 VSPACE=5 src="dimen_x.gif" ALT="| Dimension X |"></A>
<BR>
<B>from the good folks at Chromium Fringe Productions</FONT></B>
<BR>
<FONT SIZE=+3>T</FONT>he goal of <B>Dimension X</B> is to offer unique products, services,
and points of interest unlike any other dimensional entity on the <FONT SIZE=+3>W</FONT>
<FONT SIZE=+2>W</FONT><FONT SIZE=+3>W</FONT>.
<BR>
<FONT SIZE=+3>W</FONT>e provide three space-time continuums to access <B>Dimension X</B>.  Choos
continuum that meets your connect rate and Web software capabilities.
<BR>
<H4>Please sign our <A HREF="http://guests.html">Visitor's Log</A> before crossing over.
<BR>
To access Dimension X using <A HREF="http://gifmap.html">GIF</A> images.
<BR>
To access Dimension X using <A HREF="http://jpegmap.html">JPEG</A> images.
<BR>
To access Dimension X using <A HREF="http://textmenu.html">text-only</A>.
<BR>
```

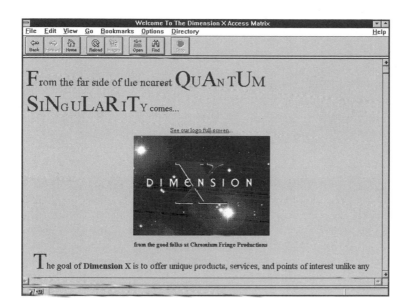

Fig. 10.35
Various text effects
are available when
preparing docu-
ments for a
Netscape audience;
non-Netscape users
will see this text in
their viewer's
standard body
font.

From Here...

Besides blocks of text in physical and logical styles, HTML provides additional
means of organizing and displaying information in HTML documents. Refer
to the following chapters to learn about additional HTML content options:

■ In Chapter 11, "Displaying Text in Lists," you see how HTML provides a
range of formatting and sorting options for generated text lists.

■ Chapter 12, "Adding Graphics to HTML Documents," teaches you how
to incorporate eye-catching GIF graphics in a document to provide
additional information and style.

■ Chapter 13, "Linking HTML Documents to Other Information Sources,"
describes how, through the use of hypertext links, HTML documents
can link directly to other HTML documents or to a wide range of
Internet applications.

■ In Part IV, "Using Forms in HTML Documents," you learn how to incorporate forms into documents for collecting user input and activating
scripts and programs on your Web server.

III

Creating Documents

Chapter 11

Displaying Text in Lists

You can organize information for presentation in many different ways. One of the most effective formats is the list form. Lists are both functional and easy to read; they can define sequential procedures, relevant importance, available decision options, collections of related data, and data ordering. We see lists everywhere and every day. From restaurant menus to encyclopedias to phone books, lists are a fundamental way we organize and assimilate information.

HTML provides container elements for creating lists in HTML documents. The basic list types available are numbered, bulleted, menu, directory, and definition. Mix up these types to create a variety of display and organization effects.

This chapter answers the following questions:

- What types of lists are available?

- How do I create a numbered list?

- How do I develop a bulleted list?

- How do I represent a menu or directory list?

- Is there a way to format a list of definitions?

Creating a Numbered List

A basic list in HTML consists of a list identifier container plus the standard list items tag (in HTML, all list items use one tag, <LI>, and the lists are differentiated by their container tags). The ordered list is also called the numbered list. When a viewer sees the tag for an ordered list, it sequentially numbers each list item using standard numbers, such as 1, 2, 3, and so on.

Using the <OL> Tag

Ordered (or numbered) lists begin with the <OL> tag and each item uses the standard <LI> tag. Close the list with the </OL> tag to signal the end of the list to the viewer. List containers provide both a beginning and ending line break to isolate the list from the surrounding text; it's not necessary (except for effect) to precede or follow the list with the paragraph <P> tag.

Note

Lists support internal HTML elements. One of the most useful elements is the paragraph tag (<P>), which allows you to separate text in a list item. Other useful tags include both logical and physical style tags (like <EM> and <I>) and HTML entities. Headings are *not* appropriate for use in lists; although they're interpreted correctly, their forced line breaks make for an ugly display. SGML purists also object to them because heading tags are meant to define relationships in paragraphs, not lists.

Figure 11.1 shows how you can use the OL list container. Pay particular attention to including closing tags, especially in nested lists. You can use leading blanks and extra lines to make your list code easier to read, but WWW viewers ignore them. Figure 11.2 shows how WWW viewers interpret this HTML code.

Fig. 11.1
Lists can include fixed data as well as links to other information sources.

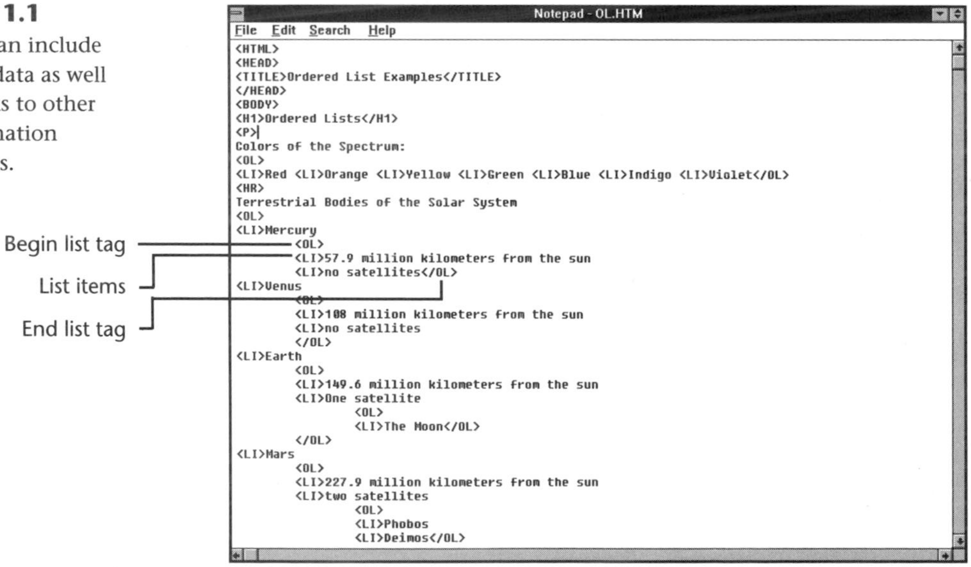

Begin list tag
List items
End list tag

```
<HTML>
<HEAD>
<TITLE>Ordered List Examples</TITLE>
</HEAD>
<BODY>
<H1>Ordered Lists</H1>
<P>
Colors of the Spectrum:
<OL>
<LI>Red <LI>Orange <LI>Yellow <LI>Green <LI>Blue <LI>Indigo <LI>Violet</OL>
<HR>
Terrestrial Bodies of the Solar System
<OL>
<LI>Mercury
    <OL>
    <LI>57.9 million kilometers from the sun
    <LI>no satellites</OL>
<LI>Venus
    <OL>
    <LI>108 million kilometers from the sun
    <LI>no satellites
    </OL>
<LI>Earth
    <OL>
    <LI>149.6 million kilometers from the sun
    <LI>One satellite
        <OL>
        <LI>The Moon</OL>
    </OL>
<LI>Mars
    <OL>
    <LI>227.9 million kilometers from the sun
    <LI>two satellites
        <OL>
        <LI>Phobos
        <LI>Deimos</OL>
```

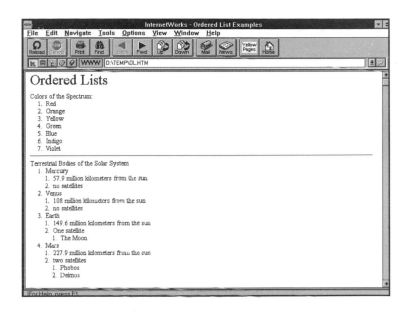

Fig. 11.2
WWW viewers
display internal
HTML elements
according to their
defined usage.
Sublists automati-
cally indent.

Users may wonder how they can create a more classical style of outline, where subheadings use different list numbers (such as roman numerals or letters) from the primary headings. Unfortunately, standard HTML does not allow the author to control how a viewer numbers the list items—only that the items are numbered. In fact, few Web viewers allow the end user to modify how bulleted and numbered lists are displayed in the viewer windows. The following section provides a little relief for "outline purists" who are authoring for the Netscape Navigator audience.

Using Netscape Extensions with the <OL> Tag

Netscape provides useful extensions to the <OL> tag. These give you control over the appearance of the item markers and the beginning marker number. Table 11.1 lists the nonstandard attributes and their functions.

Table 11.1 Netscape Extension to OL	
Extension	**Description**
TYPE=A	Sets markers to uppercase letters
TYPE=a	Sets markers to lowercase letters
TYPE=I	Sets markers to uppercase roman numerals

(continues)

III

Creating Documents

Table 11.1 Continued	
Extension	**Description**
TYPE=i	Sets markers to lowercase roman numerals
TYPE=1	Sets markers to numbers
START	Sets beginning value of item markers in the current list

Varying the marker style lets you create distinctions between numbered lists in the same document. Figure 11.3 shows how an HTML document incorporates these extensions, and figure 11.4 shows how Netscape's extensions can enhance a document.

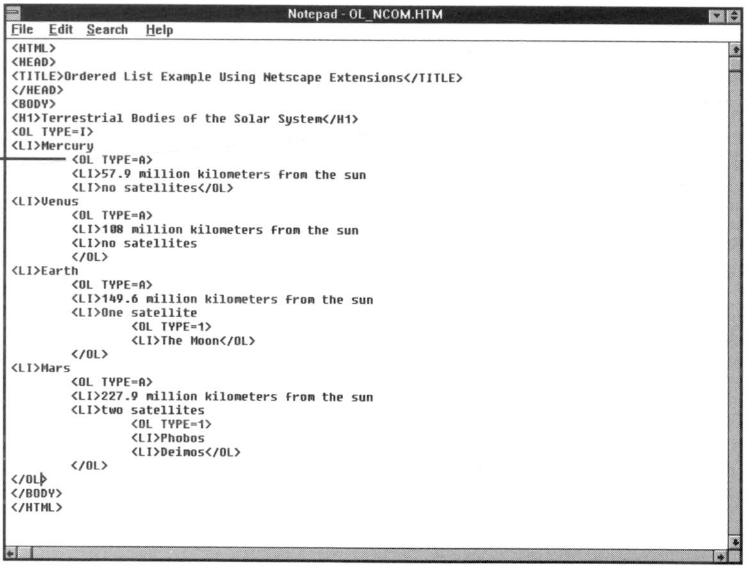

Fig. 11.3
This TYPE attribute changes the marker to upper case letters; viewers that don't recognize Netscape's extensions will ignore them.

New marker type

```
Notepad - OL_NCOM.HTM
File  Edit  Search  Help
<HTML>
<HEAD>
<TITLE>Ordered List Example Using Netscape Extensions</TITLE>
</HEAD>
<BODY>
<H1>Terrestrial Bodies of the Solar System</H1>
<OL TYPE=I>
<LI>Mercury
        <OL TYPE=A>
        <LI>57.9 million kilometers from the sun
        <LI>no satellites</OL>
<LI>Venus
        <OL TYPE=A>
        <LI>108 million kilometers from the sun
        <LI>no satellites
        </OL>
<LI>Earth
        <OL TYPE=A>
        <LI>149.6 million kilometers from the sun
        <LI>One satellite
                <OL TYPE=1>
                <LI>The Moon</OL>
        </OL>
<LI>Mars
        <OL TYPE=A>
        <LI>227.9 million kilometers from the sun
        <LI>two satellites
                <OL TYPE=1>
                <LI>Phobos
                <LI>Deimos</OL>
        </OL>
</OL>
</BODY>
</HTML>
```

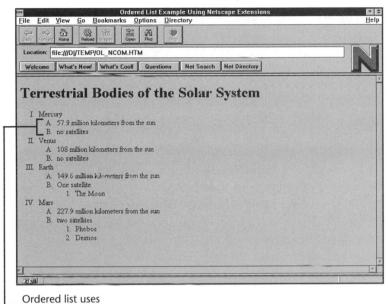

Fig. 11.4
Controlling the appearance of lists is useful for both functional and aesthetic purposes.

Ordered list uses
uppercase letters

Troubleshooting

I'm creating a list of items and I need to interrupt the list for a regular paragraph of text. How can I make the list pick up where it left off and keep numbering the items sequentially?

In standard HTML, you can't. It's impossible to close a list and open a new one without resetting the numbers back to 1. You can't even tell a paragraph in the list to align with the left margin (which might have solved your problem).

What you *can* do is tell your audience to switch to using Netscape as their Web viewer and learn how to use the START extension to OL. This lets you close the list, insert your text paragraph, and start a new list with whatever list number you choose, such as the following:

    <OL START=/>

The number 7 is just an example. Put whatever value you want the numbering to start with.

◀ See "Formatting Text in HTML: Physical versus Logical," p. 190

Tip
This trick also works if you're being creative in Netscape and using a different list marker with the TYPE extension.

Creating a Bulleted List

HTML also supports the bulleted list. You can also call it an unordered list, because the list of items does not define a specific structure or relationship between the data.

Using the <UL> Tag

Bulleted lists use the <UL> container tag (derived from the name "unordered list"). Just like ordered lists, bulleted lists provide beginning and ending line breaks, and support internal HTML elements and sublists. Also, like ordered lists, they require closing tags: include the </UL> tag to signal the end of the list to the viewer. WWW viewers automatically indent these sublists and vary the bullet icon based on the relative level of the list. These icons vary depending on the client software viewing the HTML document. See Table 11.2 for the default bullets provided by various popular viewers.

Table 11.2 Indent Level Bullet Icons for Some Popular Viewers			
Viewer	**First Level**	**Second Level**	**Third Level**
NCSA Mosaic for Macintosh	▫	■	✪
NCSA Mosaic for Windows	●	●	●
Netscape for Windows	●	●	■
Netscape for Macintosh	■	◘	▢
InternetWorks	✦	■	◌
Cello	◉	✛	◉
WebExplorer	●	■	○

Figure 11.5 shows how to use the UL list container. Again, to make the HTML document easier to read, you can include leading blanks and extra lines, but WWW viewers will ignore them. Figure 11.6 shows how WWW viewers interpret this HTML code.

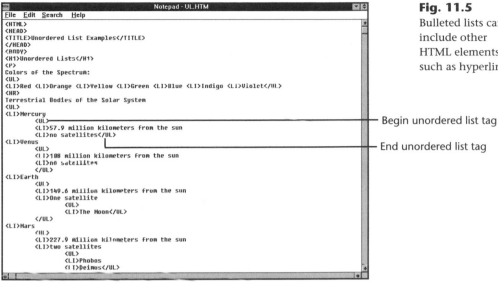

Fig. 11.5
Bulleted lists can include other HTML elements, such as hyperlinks.

Begin unordered list tag

End unordered list tag

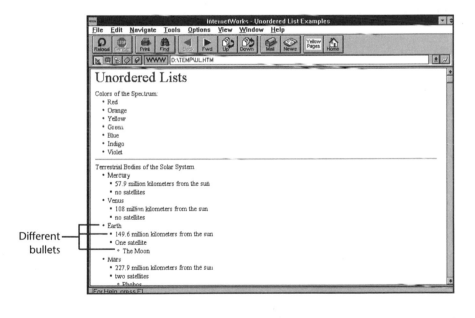

Fig. 11.6
WWW viewers automatically indent sublists and apply the corresponding item markers.

Different bullets

Creating Documents

III

> **Note**
>
> When adding blank lines within an HTML document, use the preformatted text element PRE to create filler for blank lines, as follows:
>
>   <PRE> </PRE>
>
> Remember to put two spaces inside the tags; most viewers will ignore PRE sections with only one.

Using a Netscape Extension with the UL Tag

Netscape allows you to manually control the appearance of item markers as either circles, squares, or discs. This feature is meant to give you more control over the look of bulleted lists.

The <UL> tag extension is TYPE. Figure 11.7 demonstrates its use in an HTML document. Figure 11.8 shows how Netscape displays that document.

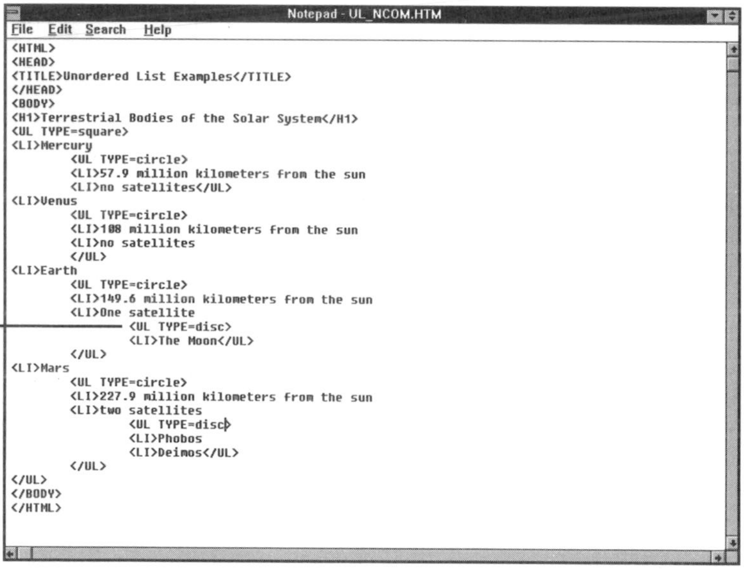

Fig. 11.7
TYPE provides control over the look of list bullets; viewers that don't support its use ignore the <TYPE> tag.

Author-defined bullets

```
Notepad - UL_NCOM.HTM
File  Edit  Search  Help
<HTML>
<HEAD>
<TITLE>Unordered List Examples</TITLE>
</HEAD>
<BODY>
<H1>Terrestrial Bodies of the Solar System</H1>
<UL TYPE=square>
<LI>Mercury
        <UL TYPE=circle>
        <LI>57.9 million kilometers from the sun
        <LI>no satellites</UL>
<LI>Venus
        <UL TYPE=circle>
        <LI>108 million kilometers from the sun
        <LI>no satellites
        </UL>
<LI>Earth
        <UL TYPE=circle>
        <LI>149.6 million kilometers from the sun
        <LI>One satellite
                <UL TYPE=disc>
                <LI>The Moon</UL>
        </UL>
<LI>Mars
        <UL TYPE=circle>
        <LI>227.9 million kilometers from the sun
        <LI>two satellites
                <UL TYPE=disc>
                <LI>Phobos
                <LI>Deimos</UL>
        </UL>
</UL>
</BODY>
</HTML>
```

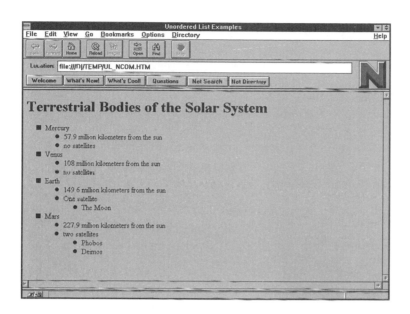

Fig. 11.8
It's easy to control
the display of
bullet markers for
your Netscape
audience.

◀ See "Formatting
Text in HTML:
Physical versus
Logical," p. 190

Caution

There is a reason why HTML and its client software support multiple item markers:
to provide a visual differentiation for sublists. By manually controlling the markers,
however, you're working against the user's expectations and potentially weakening
the communication of your document's information. After all, the less work the user
has to do to recognize subsets of lists, the easier any viewer can read the document.
Use this manual control with care!

Note

Besides the extensions to the OL and UL elements, Netscape also provides non-
standard extensions for individual list items. The extensions are based on those available to the list container the item is in (ordered or unordered). Ordered lists pass on
the capability to change the current TYPE of list items and also the VALUE they begin
with (all subsequent items adopt the extension changes until the list closes). You can
modify unordered list items with the TYPE extension; all subsequent items in the
container use the new item marker.

Tip
Just because HTML
has specific names
for these list types
doesn't mean
you're limited to
how you can use
them. Experiment
with how each list
delivers your infor-
mation, and use
what works best.

III

Creating Documents

Creating Menu Lists

You can create menu lists with another list type supported by HTML and WWW viewers. The distinction here is primarily for HTML identification; most viewers' default display for the MENU container is identical to the font and style used for the unordered list container. The value of this element is enhanced if you select a distinct screen format for the menu paragraph in a WWW viewer's preferences. The container might also be more functional in future versions of HTML and its client software, allowing viewers and other applications to identify the menu sections in your documents.

As with the previous lists, menu lists provide beginning and ending line breaks, and can include other HTML elements in a menu container. The anchor element is the most likely HTML element to use in this type of list, used to link the menu listings to other document resources or Internet applications.

Figure 11.9 shows typical uses of the MENU container.

Fig. 11.9

As a container, the MENU element requires a closing </MENU> tag.

Opening menu container

Closing menu container

Text appears in menu

Again, the current implementation of MENU by most WWW viewers doesn't provide a visual distinction between menu and unordered lists. Figure 11.10 shows how a typical WWW viewer interprets the <MENU> tag.

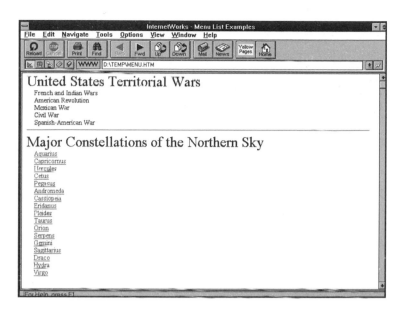

Fig. 11.10
Unlike the <UL>
tag, the MENU
element doesn't
support non-
standard
extensions.

Note

Menu items can contain hypertext links to other documents or Internet resources.
Use the <A> container to create the links, as follows:

    <A HREF="home.htm">Jump to My Home Page</A>

Click the text Jump to My Home Page and the viewer retrieves the document
HOME.HTM.

Creating Directory Lists

The DIR element functions much like the MENU element; it provides HTML
identification to the section of text that has more potential usefulness than
real functionality right now. Similar to MENU, DIR containers display with
the same default settings as unordered lists. As viewers and other applications
begin to support DIR as it's intended, it'll become more common.

The intended use for the DIR container limits items to 24 characters and
displays the items in rows (like file directories in UNIX, or in DOS using the
/W parameter). Current viewers don't support this interpretation. The DIR
element also isn't intended to include other HTML elements, although viewers interpret them correctly. When using <DIR>, remember to close the container with the ending </DIR> tag.

Figure 11.11 shows typical uses of the DIR container.

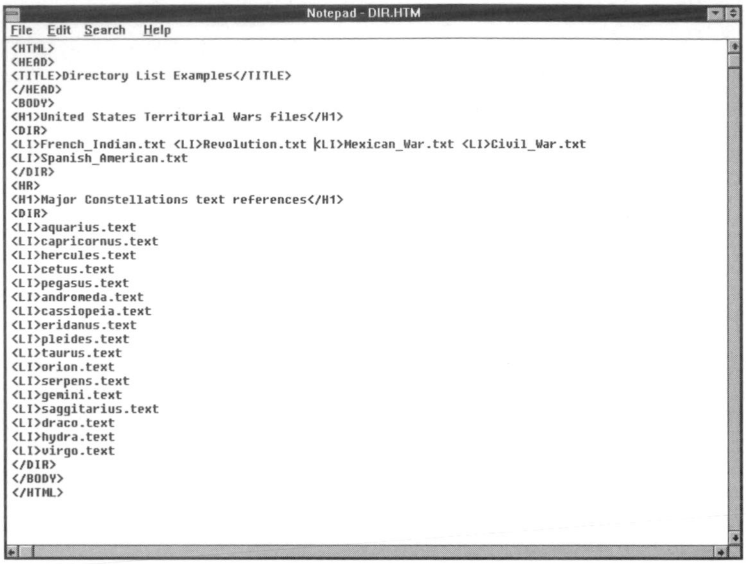

Fig. 11.11
The DIR element
container has few
frills and little
viewer support.

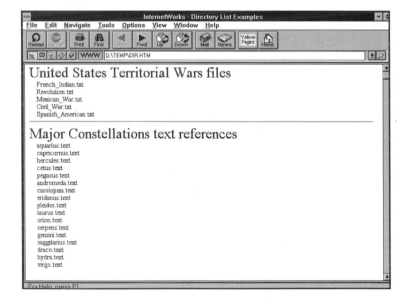

Viewers don't provide, by default, any unique display attributes for the DIR element. Figure 11.12 shows how a typical viewer interprets the <DIR> tag.

Fig. 11.12
Currently, DIR
text displays in a
single vertical
column like an
unordered list.

Creating Definition Lists

Definition lists, also called glossary lists, are a special type of list in HTML. They provide a dictionary entry-like format, with an identifiable term and indented definition paragraph. This format is especially useful when listing items with extensive descriptions, such as catalog items or company departments. The DL element provides both a beginning and ending line break. In the DL container, the <DT> tag marks the term and the <DD> tag defines the paragraph. These are both open tags, meaning they *don't require a closing tag* to contain the text.

The standard format of a definition list is:

```
<DL>
<DT>Term
<DD>Definition of term
</Dl>
```

The <DT> tag's text should fit on a single line, but it will wrap to the next line without indenting if it runs beyond the boundary of the viewer window. The <DD> tag displays a single paragraph, continuously indented one or two spaces beneath the term element's text (depending on how the viewer interprets a definition list).

HTML provides one optional attribute for DL: COMPACT. This attribute is supposed to be interpreted as a list with a different style, presumably with a smaller font size or more compact font and character spacing. This could be useful for embedded definition lists (those inside other definition, numbered, or bulleted lists), or for graphic effect. Most viewers, however, ignore the attribute, displaying the definition list in the standard format.

Definition lists *can* include other HTML elements. The most common are physical and logical styles and other lists containers. Although WWW viewers can correctly interpret elements such as headings, this is bad HTML—their forced line breaks are not pretty to look at, and SGML purists object to this use as, again, heading tags are meant to define relationships in paragraphs, not lists.

◄ See "Formatting Text in HTML: Physical versus Logical," p. 190

III

Creating Documents

Figure 11.13 shows examples of how you can create and combine definition lists with other HTML elements.

Fig. 11.13

You can indent definition lists for easier reading, although viewers apply their own formatting regardless.

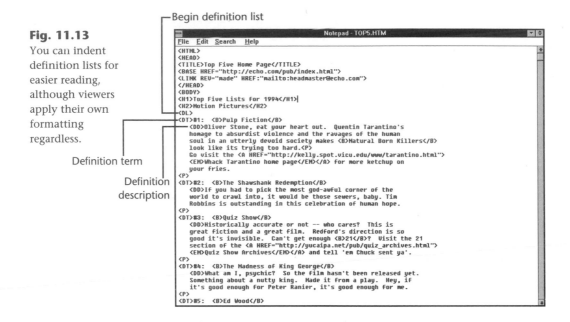

Begin definition list

Definition term

Definition description

Tip
Use a horizontal rule, <HR>, on a <DD> tagged line in a definition list. The rule indents with the rest of the <DD> lines, providing an easy-to-read separator for your definition text.

Figure 11.14 shows how this document displays in NCSA Mosaic. Other viewers may format this text differently; Netscape, for instance, uses two additional spaces when indenting description paragraphs (see fig. 11.15).

In the examples shown in figures 11.3 and 11.4, I created a "Top Five" list using a single definition list. Each movie occupies a <DT> tagged line. The review text is on a single <DD> line. A paragraph break, <P>, separates each view.

On the <DT> lines, I anticipated how viewers will display the definition list text. By using a space after the ranking number and the title of the movie (such as "#1: Pulp Fiction"), I managed to line up the movie title with the indented <DD> text in the viewer window. In a way, this is an example of dumb luck: there's nothing to stop a viewer from indenting the <DD> text five or ten spaces instead of three or four (in fact, the same text in InternetWorks does not line up as nicely). When creating your own HTML documents, look for these chance opportunities to add a little flair to your information.

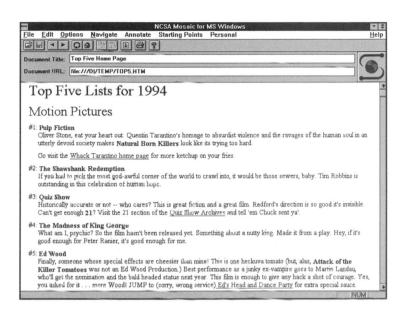

Fig. 11.14
NCSA Mosaic
provides extra
space between
elements to
enhance
readability.

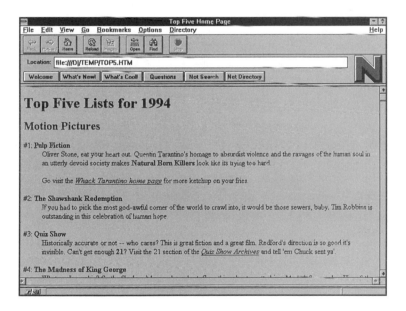

Fig. 11.15
Netscape uses
different defaults
for definition
list elements,
giving a list
distinctive display
characteristics.

III

Creating Documents

Combining List Types

There are times when it's necessary to use more than one list type in a single
paragraph. For instance, you may have a numbered list that includes a list as
one of the numbered elements. Instead of just creating a sublist, which numbers each of the subpoints, you might prefer to display an unordered list to

differentiate the sublist (while avoiding ordering the information as well). HTML supports embedded combinations of all of the list types. Figure 11.16 gives a set of sample uses of combined lists.

Fig. 11.16
Remember to use closing tags for all internal lists to avoid dropping the original list style.

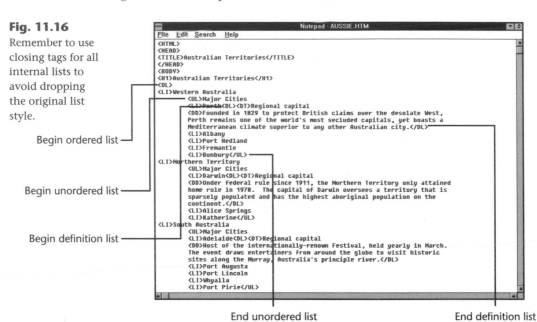

Begin ordered list

Begin unordered list

Begin definition list

End unordered list   End definition list

Tip
Use indentations and blank lines to organize your data when creating HTML documents. Web viewers don't care how the text is aligned or run together, but you will appreciate the extra effort when re-reading and editing the HTML code.

In this example, I used three list types: numbered, bulleted, and definition. The primary list is a numbered list of Australian territories. Each territory has a bulleted sublist of major cities in the territory. The territory's capital has a definition sublist to provide additional information about the city or region. I'm relying on the audience's viewers to indent embedded lists; if I want to force indentation, I can embed the lists in additional lists. See Chapter 21, "Managing Your Text," for more information on forcing layout in Web documents.

Because the primary difference between lists types involves either the list item markers or the screen formatting of the elements, and not the actual text representation itself, combined lists tend to display very well. Figure 11.17 shows how the previous samples display in a typical WWW viewer.

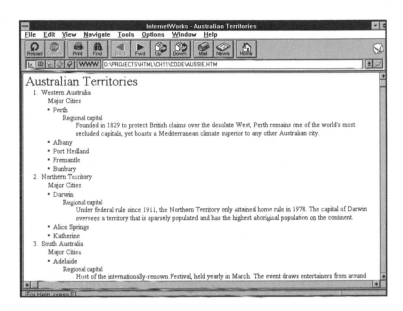

Fig. 11.17
Embedded list
types inherit
certain formatting
characteristics
from the original
list styles.

From Here...

HTML is not limited to methods of organizing and displaying information in HTML documents. Refer to the following sections to learn about additional features of HTML:

- Chapter 12, "Adding Graphics to HTML Documents," incorporates eye-catching GIF graphics in a document to provide additional information and style.

- Chapter 13, "Linking HTML Documents to Other Information Sources," shows how, through the use of hypertext links, HTML documents can link directly to other HTML documents or to a wide range of Internet applications.

- Chapter 14, "Point and Click Navigating with Image Maps," describes how HTML can use image maps to provide links to other documents and Internet services.

- Part IV, "Using Forms in HTML Documents," teaches you how to incorporate forms into documents for collecting user input and activating scripts and programs on your Web server.

III

Creating Documents

Chapter 12

Adding Graphics to HTML Documents

"What is the use of a book," thought Alice, "without pictures or conversations?"

—Lewis Carroll, *Alice's Adventures in Wonderland*

Alice is right. Books and documents are useless without text or illustrations. Without content, the greatest information distribution system in the world isn't worth a cent. The World Wide Web is a rapidly growing system because of its increasing popularity as a distribution system for a wide range of data and services.

The previous chapters have shown how you can format text, order it into lists, and break it up into separate paragraphs and blocks. But HTML's versatility isn't built on text alone—the ability to include information in many types of media ("multimedia," for you buzzword watchers) lets it do much more. The World Wide Web allows authors to create HTML documents in a manner approaching traditional desktop publishing.

This chapter answers the following questions:

- How are graphics "sent" in a document?

- What types of graphics does HTML support?

- How do text and images coexist?

- What happens if a viewer can't display a graphic?

- Is there a way to use other types of graphics?

What's a Picture Worth?

Most people take the strength of the media in our everyday lives for granted. It's easy to do. Print and broadcast technology have advanced to the point where we no longer appreciate the combinations of text, sight, and sound— we expect them. Look at newspapers like *USA Today,* which have set new standards for the use of graphics to deliver news to its readership.

Compared to *USA Today,* the Internet looks like a lumbering dinosaur. As recently as 1991, the standard method for distributing information was in ASCII text format. In fact, Gopher was developed to streamline the organization and access to text and data files. The capability to incorporate graphics in the body of a delivered text document is nothing short of amazing in a traditionally ASCII environment (see fig. 12.1).

Fig. 12.1

Graphics can enhance the communication of ideas, as well as lend an aesthetic quality to a Web document.

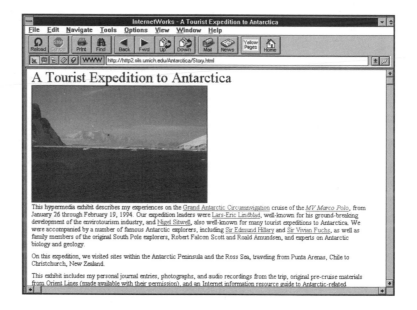

◀ See "When You
Need a Little
Helper," p. 56

In theory, the World Wide Web supports every graphic data format in use today. Due to the limits of current WWW clients and the standard file services they provide, the number of supported file formats is limited to the most popular and versatile. Table 12.1 lists the current commonly-used graphic file formats.

Table 12.1   Graphic File Formats Supported by WWW Viewers

Format	Extension	Support Provided
Graphics Interchange Format	GIF	Native
Joint Photographic Experts Group Bitmap	JPEG, JPG BMP, XBMP, XBM	Native or External
Device Independent Bitmap	DIB	Native or External
Tagged Image File Format	TIFF, TIF	External
PC Paintbrush	PCX	External

Support for each of these formats is not universal. Take care to use graphics you're sure your audience can handle. Other formats can be used as long as the target audience has the proper software for displaying them [formats such as Encapsulated PostScript (EPS)].

> **Note**
>
> File formats are often dictated by the software that creates the graphic files. Photoshop prefers to save its files in its own native format, which isn't supported across the WWW. However, like Photoshop, most graphics programs allow files to be "Saved As" different file formats. Photoshop supports saving files in both GIF and JPEG formats, the two most popular in use on the Web. Chances are your preferred graphics software can save your data files in these formats as well.

Choosing a Format: GIF versus JPEG

While WWW client programs let you use a variety of file formats, making the choice may still be unclear. What are the advantages of one format over another? When do you have to worry about image quality or file size? What format provides the greatest compatibility for end users?

Currently, for general purpose graphics, the choice is between two public standards: GIF and JPEG. These two formats are heating up the graphic developer debates. Both are in use on the WWW, but GIF has the wider viewer native compatibility; all graphical WWW viewers support GIF images without using external viewers. Native JPEG support is less common, but the support is growing.

Tip

When creating graphics, avoid incompatible graphic formats that seem normal, like compressed BMP (bitmaps) and non-standard JPEG files. In general, viewers can't handle them, nor will the standard company of "helper" applications.

III

Creating Documents

Why have more than one "standard" graphic format? Each brings its own inherent strengths and weaknesses to the WWW. Table 12.2 shows the general statistics associated with GIF and JPEG.

Table 12.2 GIF versus JPEG: The Statistics		
	GIF	**JPEG**
Image Type	Bitmap	Bitmap
Color Depth Support	1- to 8-bit color support (256 colors)	1- to 24-bit color support (16.7 million colors)
Compression Scheme	LZW	JPEG
Created By	CompuServe, Inc.	Joint Photographic Experts Group

These formats are *compressed bitmaps,* meaning that the graphic information is stored in the file in a reduced form, making the file smaller and easier to transport.

Putting the Squeeze on Data Compression

As computer systems become more user-friendly, and applications take on additional and more complex tasks, software is reaching enormous sizes. Million-code line programs are commonplace in home and professional applications. IBM's OS/2, for all of its functionality and features, consumes well over 40 megabytes of hard drive storage space; a similarly equipped Microsoft Windows configuration takes even more. Storage requirement is a critical issue in software development.

One solution to the growing size of applications and data files is compression. By reducing the size of application and data files, you can stretch the current storage format resources (such as hard drives and removable media). Three types of compression are available:

- The first scheme, typically used with any data file, retains all of the file's original data and compresses it by replacing strings of data (an example is the GIF LZW compression).

- A second scheme, used primarily with photographic images, uses sophisticated analysis of an image's color data and removes *low priority information,* or information that the human eye can't necessarily distinguish, during the compression process. This is called *lossy* compression; JPEG uses this scheme.

- A third scheme uses mathematical algorithms, similar to those used to generate fractal images, to achieve data compression. This scheme yields the highest compression ratios but takes a tremendous amount of time and processing horsepower. It isn't practical yet for the average user or developer.

The first scheme is the easiest to demonstrate. It handles data compression by replacing a string of characters with a marker pointing to the same string in a *reference table.* Some compression schemes use a standard table and compare all files to it; others create a table based on the information in the file itself, and include the unique table in the file for programs to read when decompressing the data. Different schemes provide varying degrees of compression—depending on the type of information being compressed. For example, the following sentence can be compressed as follows:

Uncompressed data:

> The rain in Spain falls mainly on the plain, while the rain in the Amazon just falls.

Compression table text strings:

> the=W   ain=X   on(space)=Y   falls=Z

Compressed data:

> W rX in SpX Z mXly on W plX, while W rX in W AmazY just Z.

The first sentence consists of 85 characters, the second only 58—about two-thirds the size. This example is very crude: today's replacement data compression can reduce certain types of files up to one fifth their original size. Lossy compression can achieve two to four times better compression (depending on the amount of image degradation allowed).

Is this good compression? Consider that full motion (30 frames per second), 640 x 480 resolution, 24-bit color digital video requires a bandwidth of 216,000 kps (kilobytes per second). The fastest data modems on the market today support transmission rates of 28.8 kps (under continuous, perfect conditions). To support this bandwidth, the video data would have to be compressed at an average ratio of 7,500:1!

Tip
Mac Web authors
should convert
PICT and TIFF
graphic files to GIF
or JPEG format;
most WWW view-
ers don't recognize
them internally,
and non-Mac users
rarely have exter-
nal support for the
PICT bitmap
format.

A more practical video bandwidth might be based on a 320 × 200 image, using 8-bit color at full motion. Quite a compromise, but it still isn't feasible under current technology. This data bandwidth requires compression rations of well over 500:1, believe it or not, but that's the compression target for schemes such as fractal compression. And faster transmission rates (from communication services such as ISDN) will reduce the overhead further and help make live desktop video a reality.

Evaluating Your Data Needs and Audience

What to choose, GIF or JPEG? That depends on what the needs are for your data, and who your audience is. Consider the following strengths and weaknesses of each format:

GIF Advantages:

- Widely-accepted standard with native support in nearly all graphical applications

- Includes multimedia extensions for multi-image GIF files and sound file (MIDI) extensions

- Fast decompression

- Better with images using smaller color palettes

JPEG Advantages:

- Smaller file size, which provides a better image transmission rate

- Supports "true color" 24-bit image representation

- Better with photographic quality (higher color palette) images

- Compression scheme is in the public domain and free to use

GIF Disadvantages:

- *Dithering* (approximating a color by adding a pattern of dots over an-other color) is necessary to create colors beyond the 256 color palette

- Fewer colors create palette conflicts when more than one image has to be displayed at the same time

- GIF users are open to compression scheme copyright infringement claims

JPEG Disadvantages:

- Lossy compression scheme reduces image quality at higher compression levels

- Slower decompression (and therefore display) time

- Fewer graphical applications support JPEG file format

Use GIF when the audience's graphic support is unknown, or when representing graphics with smaller color palettes. Use JPEG when reproducing images over 256 colors, or when using more than a handful in a single document. Figures 12.2 through 12.4 show how a sample 640 × 480, 24-bit graphic image is handled by each compression scheme.

Tip
JPEG compression removes some of the graphic information when compressing a file. Always look at images converted to JPEG to make sure the image degradation is acceptable.

Fig. 12.2
The original photographic-quality image is in 16 million colors (here displayed in an equal number of shades of gray).

Fig. 12.3
Side-by-side comparison shows how GIF dithers complex images...

III

Creating Documents

Fig. 12.4
…while JPEG's
lossy representa-
tion is evident in
the image's slight
degradation.

GIF compressed the file to 200K (reducing the color palette at the same time), while the JPEG file compressed to 45K. Using the same graphics application, the GIF file takes two and a half seconds to decompress and the JPEG file takes almost twelve seconds.

If you were to look at these files in color, you would notice that the original, figure 12.2, is perfectly clean: the colors are solid and continuous, with a sharp "focus" on the sunflowers. The GIF file, figure 12.3, is dithered down to 256 colors: the format does a fairly good job of representing all of the shades in the image, but you can see a "hatched" pattern where the dithering is present. The JPEG image, figure 12.4, shows the most degradation: the edges of the sunflowers are swirled, not crisply sharp, where the compression has allowed the colors to bleed together.

Figures 12.5 through 12.7 show a second example, using a 640×480, 8-bit computer graphic.

GIF compressed the second file to 87K (maintaining the image's color palette), and JPEG reduced the file size to 30K. The GIF file takes less than two seconds to open, and the JPEG file takes eight seconds to be displayed.

Do either of these examples demonstrate a clear advantage of one compression format? Of course not. The circumstances and viewer requirements for any one situation will suggest the appropriate format. But it is important to know what options are available, and serve your data better under specific conditions.

Fig. 12.5
The original computer-generated graphic file is in 256 colors (here displayed in an equal number of grays).

Fig. 12.6
GIF represents the image faithfully...

Fig. 12.7
...as does JPEG, but with some image degradation.

Tip
To improve the quality of JPEG images, create them in an application that lets you control the amount of compression used when creating the file. The lower the compression you choose, the better the image will look.

Troubleshooting

How can I avoid color "shifts" when I display more than one graphic at a time? And what's going on?

When displaying more than one GIF image on the same page, color shifts may occur as each new image asserts its own color palette. This is typical of images that consist of 256 or more colors (and have been reduced and dithered from a higher color depth, such as 16- or 24-bit color palettes). Microsoft Windows also reserves 20 or so colors for its own desktop palette, reducing the number of colors left for image palettes to define.

To reduce the chances of seeing these shifts occur, equalize your color palettes; graphic utilities such as PalEdit can create and apply a single palette to a group of images. A certain amount of color shifting is always possible as other running applications assert their own palettes as well. Equalizing the palettes of your graphics assures that they are not the "color culprits."

CompuServe *Plus* Unisys *Equals* Royalty-Free GIFs?

Sometimes the computer industry goes a long way to show that, for some players, it's all about business. On December 29, 1994, CompuServe announced that they had completed negotiating a licensing agreement with Unisys Corporation, the holder of a patent granted for the LZW compression technology CompuServe used when developing the GIF graphic format. The agreement (called the Graphics Interchange Format (GIF) Developer Agreement) was aimed at software developers who incorporated GIF file support in their products. The agreement specifically limited the license to developers' programs that would be used in conjunction with CompuServe, arguably the largest repository for GIF files. Any GIF encoding development not related to CompuServe has to be negotiated with Unisys. The royalty fee Unisys is charging under this agreement is 1.5 percent per purchased copy of the software program.

The user community's vocal reaction was one of amazement and outrage. Since CompuServe's development of the GIF standard in 1987, it has become the primary graphic format for the online community, and is an integral part of the World Wide Web graphic support. Users accused Unisys of waiting until the format became entrenched in the user and developer communities before enforcing their patent: in essence, taking the common file format hostage and blackmailing developers into paying royalties on new and existing software products.

On January 6, 1995, in the face of a public backlash, Unisys amended their policy and decided not to require licensing fees for non-commercial, non-profit GIF-based applications, including those used in conjunction with online services. Unisys also stated that they would not pursue copyright infringement by developers producing commercial software products before 1995. They do expect developers of commercial software to license the LZW technology in all future products (or enhancements to previous products).

Note

Unisys acknowledged the roll that the public outcry, especially from members of the various online services, had in prompting the revised policies.

What does this mean for the World Wide Web and its users? The GIF format is still non-proprietary and available for public use; new WWW viewer developers will have to negotiate a license with Unisys to be able to support GIF files natively; older WWW viewers that have GIF support added in new versions will have to pay for the usage; existing software products are free from copyright infringement.

At this point, only the applications are subject to the licensing agreement; creating GIF files themselves does not constitute an infringement. If this policy holds for the future, the end user will only see its effect in possible higher costs of the commercial applications; however, it is sensible to keep your graphic file format options open and consider any alternatives that meet your data needs and avoid the potential for future legal action from its usage (JPEG, for example, has no such legal implications).

A copy of the GIF Developer Agreement is available from the Graphics Support Forum on CompuServe's Graphics Support Forum and also on their World Wide Web site at **http:\\www.compuserve.com**.

Using the IMG Element

After you choose a graphic format for your data files and create them, HTML provides a simple mechanism for associating the files with your Web documents. The IMG (image) element is an empty container, meaning it does not require a closing tag. The syntax for the <IMG> tag is

```
<IMG SRC=image_URL>
```

where SRC= indicates the source of the graphic file you want to display, and *image_URL* is the relative or absolute path name for the graphic file. For example, figure 12.8 shows how this element is used in the body of an HTML document, and figure 12.9 shows how a WWW viewer interprets the tag.

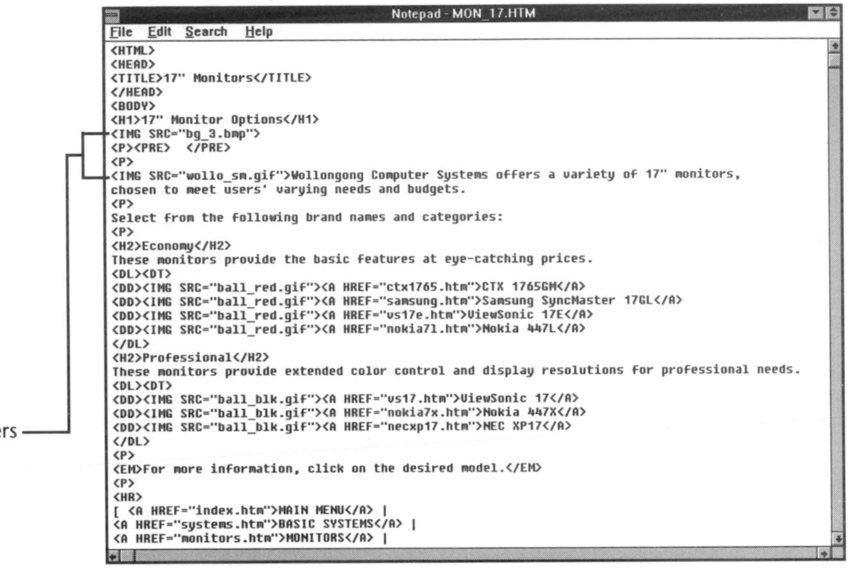

Fig. 12.8
To allow WWW viewers to accurately interpret inline graphics, use the full file name, including the appropriate extension for the image type (such as GIF).

Image containers ————

Fig. 12.9
As a default, WWW viewers align graphics on a line without text along the left-hand margin in the viewer window.

Images ————

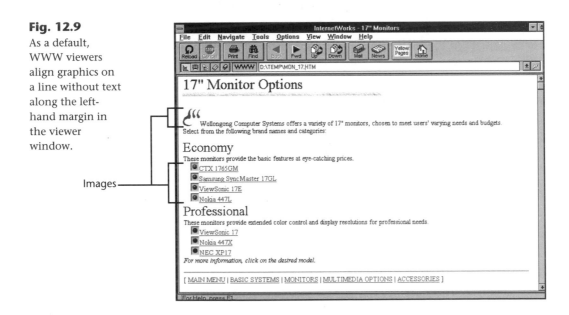

Note

Authors often see nifty buttons and navigation graphics on a Web page and, as human nature often dictates, they wonder how they can get that graphic without having to re-create it with their own artistic talents. The following methods are meant to provide you with the necessary shortcut, although it should be emphasized that photographs and business logos displayed on Web sites are most likely copyrighted material and should only be used with the original author's permission. With that aside, here are two methods for retrieving inline images:

- *Method 1:* If your WWW viewer stores the graphics in temporary files in the cache, you may be able to retrieve the graphic file (under a temporary name) and rename it to a legal name with the proper extension. Netscape is one viewer that stores its cache data in this manner.

- *Method 2:* If that method is unavailable to you, or you don't like the thought of rummaging through a cache (even if its your own), follow these steps:

  1. View the source of the HTML page that contains the graphic you want to retrieve.

  2. Find the IMG statement for the graphic and note its relative or absolute path name.

  3. Recreate the absolute path for the graphic (use the URL for the page itself if you're working with a relative path name).

  4. In your viewer, select the option to load the next link to disk (under the Options menu in Mosaic) or, in Netscape, choose Save Next Link As from the File menu. The next link you open copies to a file on your local hard drive and not into the cache for display.

  5. Choose Open Location or Open URL (generally under your viewer's File menu) and enter the graphic's reconstructed path name. Press Enter and watch your hard drive light flicker away. Some viewers may prompt you for a file name and download destination; others just dump the file into a default folder or directory. Either way, you are now the proud owner of the coveted graphic.

Tip

Inline graphics can be embedded in lists. Add small images before or after text on <LI> tagged list items to emphasize or draw additional attention to particular items.

III

Creating Documents

The current HTML standard provides no modifiers for the SRC component; the image appears in the document where the <IMG> tag is. Like anchors, you can place inline graphics links anywhere in the body of the text; text can come before or after an image (or both). How the image and text display is entirely up to the WWW viewer and the width of the viewer's window.

Similar to text, graphics wrap to the next line if the window is not wide enough to display the image after text on the same line. Graphics on a line by themselves run beyond the border of the viewer window if the window is narrower than the image; authors should be aware that graphics may not be completely visible if they are too wide for the viewer to display. The last thing you want is a Web site's graphics to be cut off, especially because such a large graphic should be more than cosmetic (a clickable menu bar, for example).

Troubleshooting

Although Netscape provides a non-standard extension to IMG to center images across the width of the viewer window, most of the browsers ignore this feature. How can I do this in standard HTML so even Mosaic will center my graphics?

In the current HTML, there are no alignment attributes you can use with either the IMG or P (paragraph) elements. However, HTML viewers do define an indentation for components of a definition list, and resourceful authors can take advantage of this function. Because it's legal to embed other containers in a definition list (DL) container, why not additional DLs? Using a word processing analogy, this would be like inserting multiple tab spaces. Using this trick, the following HTML statement is displayed in figure 12.10:

```
<DL><DL><DL><img src="pan.gif"></DL></DL></DL>
```

The only drawback to using this tip is that the author has no control over where the image will appear relative to the left, or how centered it will be in a viewer window that can be adjusted to suit the needs of the user.

Using the ALT Attribute with IMG

By now, the idea that "there are no guarantees" with how HTML documents will be displayed by end users should be clear. Consider the possibility that some users in your intended audience can't display the particular format of the inline graphics in your Web pages. Consider the chances that they are not even using a graphical viewer, but a text-based WWW client application like UNIX's Lynx. How can you accommodate these users while retaining the custom graphics you have worked so hard to provide for the rest of your audience?

Fig. 12.10
You can use nested definition lists to approximate indented or centered images and text.

HTML provides a simple solution that too many authors overlook these days. IMG supports an attribute called ALT (or alternative) that specifies a string of text that can be displayed in place of an inline graphic. This text takes the place of the image; if it is used in an anchor, the text is clickable just as the graphic is. The ALT string is not limited to any specific length, but the "KISS" principle is a good rule of thumb ("Keep It Short and Simple"). Figure 12.11 shows how to add the ALT attribute to an inline graphic element; figure 12.12 shows what is displayed when the ALT text is displayed in place of the graphic.

> **Note**
>
> Authors who rely on JPEG graphics for incorporating true color images in their documents should not consider ALT attributes an option—they should consider them a requirement. Many WWW viewers do not display JPEG natively, and most of these users do not configure an external viewer to handle JPEG files until they have problems viewing them on Web sites (see "Displaying Associated Graphics with External Applications" later in this chapter for more details about external image file viewers). And authors who use less common graphic formats such as TIFF or CGM had better use ALT attributes religiously.

III

Creating Documents

Fig. 12.11
The ALT text can be as straightforward as a description of the image it represents.

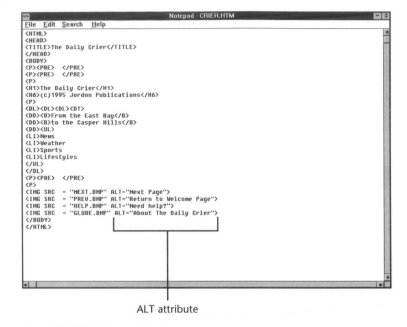

ALT attribute

Fig. 12.12
WWW viewers display ALT text in different ways; InternetWorks places the text in a box frame to distinguish it from other text in the body of the HTML document.

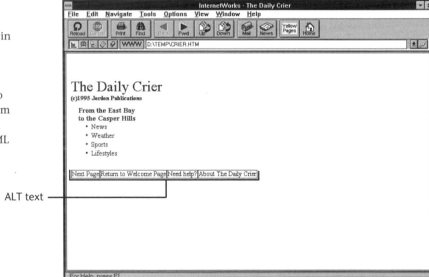

ALT text

ALT text is handy if an associated graphic file is not found by the viewer, or if a user turns off inline graphics to speed up the rate at which a WWW viewer displays Web pages. This is a fairly common practice when dealing with HTML documents that include too much "eye candy," or non-functional inline graphics, or when the user is accessing the WWW over a slow data connection and can't afford to wait for each graphic to come down the pipeline. Images that can't be displayed by a viewer and do not have an ALT text attribute are generally replaced by a generic icon.

> **Note**
>
> I've been talking as though using ALT attributes is a common practice when creating HTML documents and have wide-spread support by WWW viewer applications. After all, the attribute is a part of the current HTML standard, has always been a part of HTML, and will continue to be in the upcoming HTML 3.0. Unfortunately, most authors neglect to include the attribute in their IMG elements. Maybe It's too much work, or perhaps they don't like to see all of this conditional text crowding the rest of their beautiful HTML code. And too many viewers ignore the ALT text and just default to using a generic, uninformative icon for inline graphics they can't display.
>
> While there is little you can do to add this functionality to your WWW viewer (besides encouraging—or even demanding—that software developers provide support for the entire complement of standard HTML elements and attributes), you can do something about using ALT text in your HTML documents. As stressed in Chapter 8, "HTML's Standards and Practices," writing good HTML requires adapting good HTML habits. Using the ALT attribute is a good thing—it provides support for users who can't fully access your documents in the manner you intend. Consider it the Web equivalent of television's "closed captioning" for the hearing impaired—while most users may never see the text, the ones who need it most will have the support when necessary.

Tip
ALT text occupies space on the text line just like any other information in the document. Always review your documents with inline images "off" to see how the ALT text will look to users.

Aligning Graphics and Text

The previous section discussed how inline images and text can be combined in the same document body. Using the default alignment, graphics and text combined are displayed in figure 12.13.

Fine, the SGML purists say, this alignment is acceptable because the function of incorporating a graphic image has been met. Not fine, say those in the Author camp, because it is inflexible and looks awkward under various circumstances—give us more control over how these two content components interrelate.

The HTML development team threw a bone to the authorists, and created the ALIGN attribute. This attribute allows the author to control where text on the same line as an inline graphic aligns along the vertical sides of the image. The attribute is written as:

```
<IMG ALIGN=TOP SRC=image_URL>
```

III

Creating Documents

with the values of TOP or MIDDLE available (the third alignment option, BOTTOM, is the default for IMG and does not need to be specified). The TOP value aligns the body text with the top of the tallest inline graphic on the line, leaving space beneath the text until it wraps beneath the image. The MIDDLE value aligns the baseline of the current line of text with the middle of the inline graphic, leaving slightly more white space beneath the text on the line as above. Incidentally, the default alignment, BOTTOM, leaves white space above the text to the line of text above the top of the inline graphic. Figure 12.14 includes a variety of image alignments used in HTML code.

Fig. 12.13
Text automatically aligns itself with the bottom of an inline image on the same line.

Tip
More than one ALIGN value can be active on a single line in a document. The images will align themselves to the line of text; you can create interesting effects by varying the alignments of images on the same line.

Figure 12.15 shows how a typical WWW viewer interprets the various image alignments.

Nearly all graphical WWW viewers support graphics inline (on the same line as text) in HTML documents. Those that don't will ignore the ALIGN attribute and display the graphic on a separate line from the body text in the document.

Using Extensions to Align Text in Netscape

Netscape's extensions to the ALIGN attribute allow an author greater control over the display of on-screen graphics. In fact, Netscape's additional functionality is so versatile that you might consider this the first step toward integrating desktop publishing with HTML document creation.

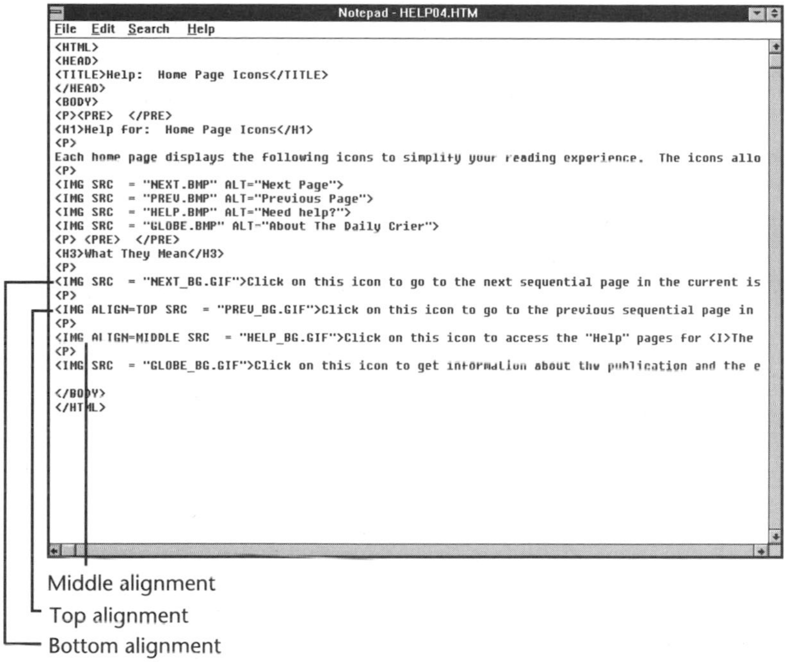

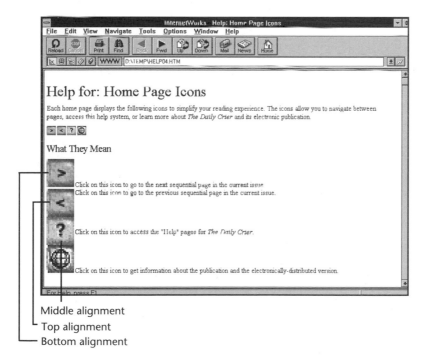

Fig. 12.14
IMG elements
without an ALIGN
attribute default to
aligning text with
the bottom of the
inline graphic.

Middle alignment
Top alignment
Bottom alignment

Fig. 12.15
Only text on
the current line
accommodates the
selected ALIGN
option. Text on
the next line in
the viewer window
drops underneath
the inline image.

Middle alignment
Top alignment
Bottom alignment

III

Creating Documents

> ### Caution
>
> Remember that Netscape's extensions, while skillfully broadening authors' creative control over how HTML elements are displayed by the Netscape viewer, are nevertheless *non-standard* implementations. Some of the extensions are under consideration in the upcoming HTML 3.0 standard; the vast majority are not. HTML 3.0 may incorporate the same functionality through different elements and attributes. The chances of Netscape's extensions being completely adopted are virtually nil. Keep this in mind when using these proprietary extensions to create dynamic and visually stunning Netscape HTML pages: they may be obsolete in the future.

The first two ALIGN values create a new type of graphic called a floating graphic. No longer anchored to one spot in a line of text, this graphic "floats" against a margin while text wraps down its side in *multiple lines*—not just a *single line* of text, as the standard IMG element defines (refer to fig. 12.15). These two values are LEFT and RIGHT, and specify which margin the image will float against. Figure 12.16 shows how these values are represented in HTML code. Figure 12.17 shows how Netscape interprets the floating image attributes.

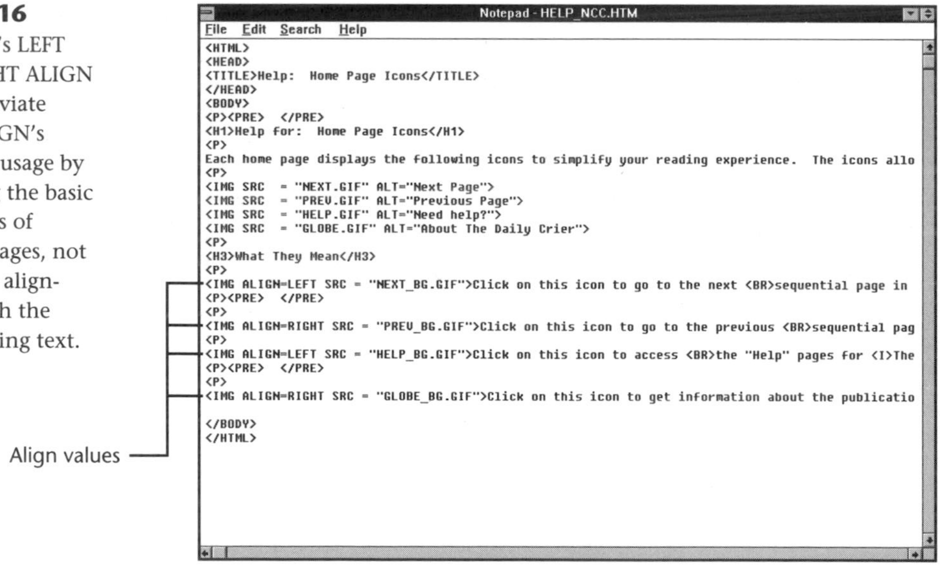

Fig. 12.16

Netscape's LEFT and RIGHT ALIGN values deviate from ALIGN's standard usage by changing the basic properties of inline images, not just their alignment with the surrounding text.

Align values

```
Notepad - HELP_NCC.HTM
File  Edit  Search  Help
<HTML>
<HEAD>
<TITLE>Help:  Home Page Icons</TITLE>
</HEAD>
<BODY>
<P><PRE>  </PRE>
<H1>Help for:  Home Page Icons</H1>
<P>
Each home page displays the following icons to simplify your reading experience.  The icons allo
<P>
<IMG SRC  = "NEXT.GIF" ALT="Next Page">
<IMG SRC  = "PREV.GIF" ALT="Previous Page">
<IMG SRC  = "HELP.GIF" ALT="Need help?">
<IMG SRC  = "GLOBE.GIF" ALT="About The Daily Crier">
<P>
<H3>What They Mean</H3>
<P>
<IMG ALIGN=LEFT SRC = "NEXT_BG.GIF">Click on this icon to go to the next <BR>sequential page in
<P><PRE>  </PRE>
<P>
<IMG ALIGN=RIGHT SRC = "PREV_BG.GIF">Click on this icon to go to the previous <BR>sequential pag
<IMG ALIGN=LEFT SRC = "HELP_BG.GIF">Click on this icon to access <BR>the "Help" pages for <I>The
<P><PRE>  </PRE>
<P>
<IMG ALIGN=RIGHT SRC = "GLOBE_BG.GIF">Click on this icon to get information about the publicatio

</BODY>
</HTML>
```

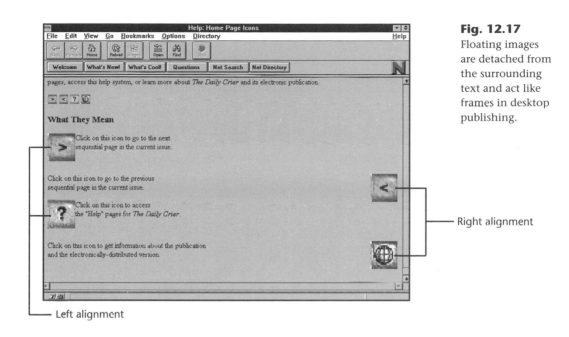

Fig. 12.17
Floating images are detached from the surrounding text and act like frames in desktop publishing.

Right alignment

Left alignment

Netscape also provides new values for ALIGN that effect how inline graphics and text display in the viewing window. While supporting the standard TOP, MIDDLE, and BOTTOM values, Netscape adds the values specified in Table 12.3.

Table 12.3 Netscape ALIGN Values

Value	Definition
TEXTTOP	Aligns the baseline of the current line of text with the top of the tallest text on the line.
ABSMIDDLE	Aligns the middle of the current line of text with the middle of the inline graphic.
ABSBOTTOM	Aligns the bottom of the current line of text with the bottom of the inline graphic.
BASELINE	Just like the BOTTOM value, aligns the baseline of the current line of text with the bottom of the inline graphic.

Figure 12.18 demonstrates HTML code using the non-standard text ALIGN values, and figure 12.19 shows how Netscape displays the various alignment options.

III

Creating Documents

Fig. 12.18
As in standard HTML, ALIGN values only effect the current line of text.

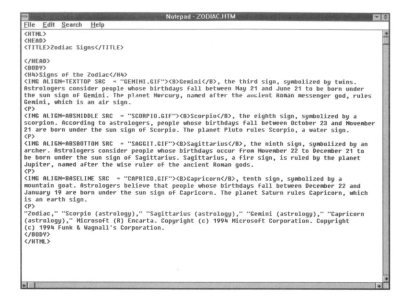

Fig. 12.19
Each ALIGN value provides a different look and distribution of space around the text.

Top alignment ———

Middle alignment ———

Bottom alignment ———

Baseline alignment ———

Using Additional IMG Attributes to Enhance Text in Netscape

Netscape provides additional non-standard attributes for the IMG element. These produce additional aesthetic enhancements when displaying the inline (and floating) images, yet one results in faster image HTML document display and may find its way into the HTML standard (or be generally supported by WWW viewers) at some point.

When an HTML document is being retrieved by a viewer, the software must wait until the image loads and calculates its size before the software can "lay out" the document in the viewer window. This wait adds time to each document access; just measure how long it takes—while the viewer's byte counter clicks over each graphic—before the body text zips on-screen and the viewer begins to display each inline graphic.

Netscape avoids that initial pause in the action by sending the graphic size calculations ahead of the graphic, contained in the IMG element. This is done by defining both the WIDTH and HEIGHT. In figure 12.20 each graphic's size is predetermined in the HTML code.

Note

WIDTH and HEIGHT values that are different from the actual measurements of an image can force the images to "scale" in size to the new dimensions. This doesn't effect the storage size of the image nor its download time.

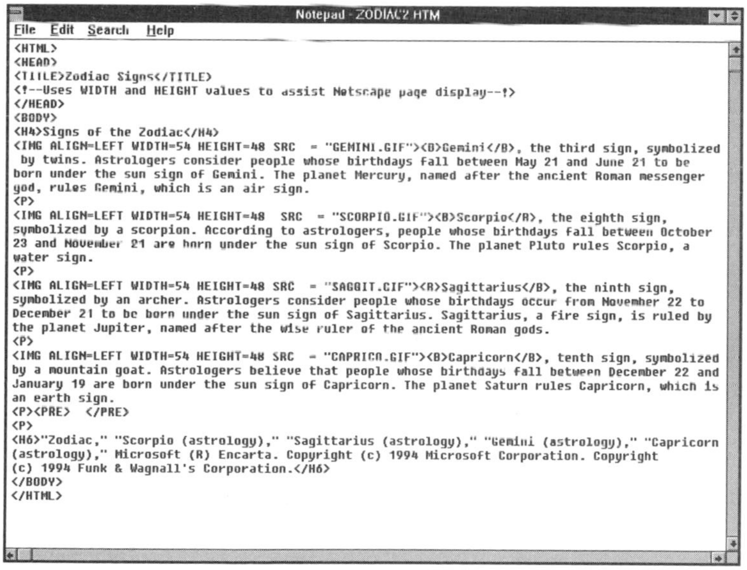

```
Notepad - ZODIAC2.HTM
File  Edit  Search  Help
<HTML>
<HEAD>
<TITLE>Zodiac Signs</TITLE>
<!--Uses WIDTH and HEIGHT values to assist Netscape page display--!>
</HEAD>
<BODY>
<H4>Signs of the Zodiac</H4>
<IMG ALIGN=LEFT WIDTH=54 HEIGHT=48 SRC  = "GEMINI.GIF"><B>Gemini</B>, the third sign, symbolized
 by twins. Astrologers consider people whose birthdays fall between May 21 and June 21 to be
born under the sun sign of Gemini. The planet Mercury, named after the ancient Roman messenger
god, rules Gemini, which is an air sign.
<P>
<IMG ALIGN=LEFT WIDTH=54 HEIGHT=48  SRC  = "SCORPIO.GIF"><B>Scorpio</B>, the eighth sign,
symbolized by a scorpion. According to astrologers, people whose birthdays fall between October
23 and November 21 are born under the sun sign of Scorpio. The planet Pluto rules Scorpio, a
water sign.
<P>
<IMG ALIGN=LEFT WIDTH=54 HEIGHT=48 SRC  = "SAGGIT.GIF"><B>Sagittarius</B>, the ninth sign,
symbolized by an archer. Astrologers consider people whose birthdays occur from November 22 to
December 21 to be born under the sun sign of Sagittarius. Sagittarius, a fire sign, is ruled by
the planet Jupiter, named after the wise ruler of the ancient Roman gods.
<P>
<IMG ALIGN=LEFT WIDTH=54 HEIGHT=48 SRC  = "CAPRICO.GIF"><B>Capricorn</B>, tenth sign, symbolized
by a mountain goat. Astrologers believe that people whose birthdays fall between December 22 and
January 19 are born under the sun sign of Capricorn. The planet Saturn rules Capricorn, which is
an earth sign.
<P><PRE>  </PRE>
<P>
<H6>"Zodiac," "Scorpio (astrology)," "Sagittarius (astrology)," "Gemini (astrology)," "Capricorn
(astrology)," Microsoft (R) Encarta. Copyright (c) 1994 Microsoft Corporation. Copyright
(c) 1994 Funk & Wagnall's Corporation.</H6>
</BODY>
</HTML>
```

Fig. 12.20
The WIDTH and HEIGHT attributes are measured in pixels and correspond to the image's actual pixel measurements.

As you can see in figure 12.21, Netscape pre-determines the positioning of the graphics, accelerating the document retrieval process.

Fig. 12.21
The black borders around the graphics are place markers for the inline graphics, which load after the text is displayed.

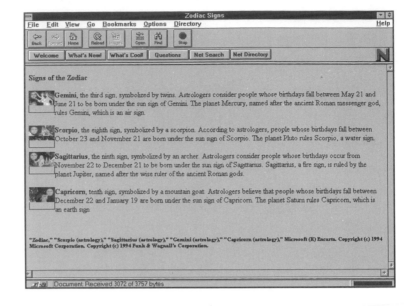

A second pair of attributes effects the layout relationship between the HTML document's body text and floating images. The VSPACE and HSPACE attributes define the space (or gutter size, for those of you familiar with page layout) above and below (VSPACE) and to the right and left (HSPACE) of a floating image. Refer to figure 12.17 to see how floating images display without controlling the surrounding spaces. Figure 12.22 is an example of how to define these attributes in your HTML documents, and figure 12.23 shows how Netscape interprets their values.

Caution

The optional HSPACE attribute allows you to define the gutter size, or blank space, between LEFT and RIGHT aligned floating images and the body text in HTML documents. However, if you don't define this space in your IMG element, Netscape defaults to no gutter, butting the text directly against the image. This generally isn't what you want, so make sure you include the attribute HSPACE=5 (or another gutter size you prefer) for all floating images.

The final nonstandard attribute for IMG controls the weight of the border Netscape places around inline images. The BORDER attribute is used as follows:

```
<IMG BORDER=number SRC=image_URL>
```

where *number* is a relative value for the border width and *image_URL* is the absolute or relative path name for the image file. Figure 12.24 shows how the BORDER attribute is interpreted by Netscape.

Fig. 12.22
The values of VSPACE and HSPACE are relative values; a typical value for creating white space around a floating image is five.

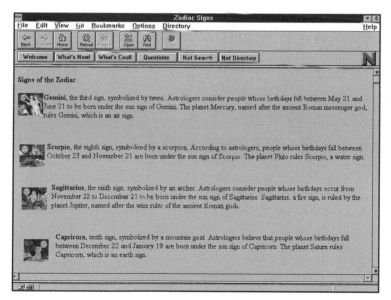

Fig. 12.23
The VSPACE value is used both above and below an image, while the HSPACE value is applied to the left and right gutters; you can't modify the spacing on a single side alone.

III

Creating Documents

Fig. 12.24
Netscape applies a
solid border to
inline and floating
images based on
the BORDER
attribute value (in
this example, its
value is 7).

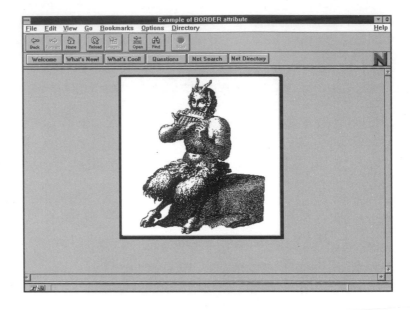

Caution

Be careful not to set BORDER=0 for inline graphics that are hypertext links for anchors: they won't display the default link highlight, and users won't know they're
"clickable" pathways to other documents or Internet services. If you choose to remove the border for aesthetic reasons, consider using text in the anchor link as
well—it will appear in the link highlight color.

Displaying Associated Graphics with External Applications

A project often requires that one HTML document contain many graphic
images, or that many large images be included in a collection of Web pages.
A photography portfolio for example, or a travelogue's photo journal, or even
a menu of photos linked to other HTML pages. It's tempting, when you have
a color scanner and lots of beautiful photographs, to scan them all and create
an endless HTML document sharing your latest Walt Disney World vacation
with the world.

Endless is the key word: depending on the data connection, a 100K image
can take upwards of a half a minute to be sent to your viewer and decoded

for display. Multiply that by five or six and you'll soon find yourself with plenty of time to kill while a Web page loads. Avoid the temptation to use lots of full-sized images.

How can you make your vacation highlights available for display? Think small—think thumbnails.

Using a simple graphics editor program, you can easily resize images of various formats. Reduce that 100K graphic to one sixth its screen size, and you reduce its file size to nearly 5K! This smaller version is called a *thumbnail*, and it's very handy.

Consider the photography portfolio project. A collection of ten or twenty thumbnails can be displayed on one page, each one linked to the full-sized image that users can retrieve and view as they want. Linking thumbnails to their larger images requires combining inline images and anchor elements. Figure 12.25 shows how images and anchors are combined in HTML code.

▶ See "Using the Anchor Element," p. 253

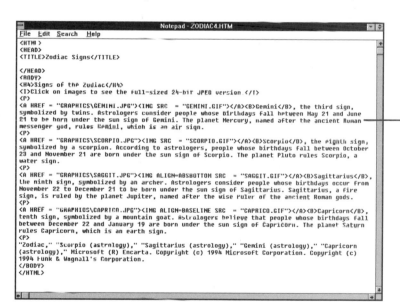

Fig. 12.25
Anchors link the thumbnail to the external associated graphic file.

— Anchor and image

In figure 12.26, these thumbnails are outlined with the viewer's hypertext link color. Through everyday WWW usage, users know that clicking a highlighted image retrieves a file, another document, or an Internet service (like a File Transfer Protocol menu).

You must configure WWW viewers to use an external graphics viewer to display retrieved graphic files, even if they're supported internally by the

III

Creating Documents

viewers themselves. External programs (also called "helper programs" or "external viewers") take the retrieved file and open them as they would any normal file. If the user wants to save the file for future reference, choosing Save As and selecting a destination and name creates the file on the local system. External programs are required for each data type. See Chapter 6, "Overview of Common Web Viewers," for instructions on configuring different WWW viewers.

Fig. 12.26
Link highlighting (color borders around images) separates clickable images from non-clickable ones, just as it does with text links in the body of text.

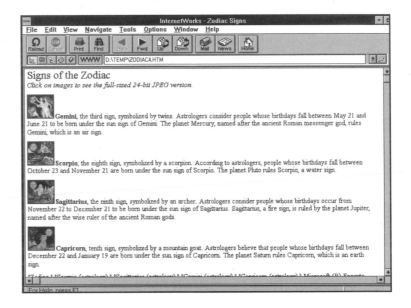

Note

Although most of us want to believe we're creative, we wouldn't know how to create a GIF graphic if our *net.reputations* depended on it (which, as HTML authors, is not an impossibility). Luckily enough, many collections of public domain graphics are available for use in your documents. These are generally available in one of the common file formats (GIF or JPEG).

Here are a few sites that provide access to public domain graphics archives:

http://lal.cs.byu.edu/buttons/gifs.html

http://crab.sp.ph.ic.ac.uk/hobbes/hobbes.html

http://www.di.unipi.it/iconbrowser/icon.html

http://white.nosc.mil/images.html

http://legendre.ucsd.edu/y/icons.html

http://www.csc.ncsu.edu/sanjay/patel/art.html

http://128.172.69.103/bullet.html

http://www.cs.yale.edu/HTML/YALE/CS/HyPlans/loosemore-sandra /clipart.html (Sandra's Clip Art Server)

http://www2.ncsu.edu/bae/people/faculty/walker/ hotlist/graphics.html

http://www.charm.net/~web/

http://gagme.wwa.com/~boba/images.html

Retrieving the files is self-explanatory (generally requires clicking the selected graphic or its associated text link).

From Here...

At this point, you've learned the basics of HTML. This chapter demonstrated how to choose graphic formats and incorporate graphic files into HTML documents. Next comes the advanced use of HTML: what else can HTML do with graphic images? How can a document point to other Internet information services? How can HTML retrieve feedback and information from users? Refer to the following chapters to learn how to incorporate HTML's advanced components:

- Chapter 13, "Linking HTML Documents to Other Information Sources," shows you how to use hypertext links to link HTML documents directly to other HTML files or to a wide range of Internet applications.

- Chapter 14, "Point and Click Navigating with Image Maps," describes how you can use graphics as visual maps for collecting user input and performing pre-determined links to anchors in associated HTML documents.

- Part IV, "Using Forms in HTML Documents," teaches you how to incorporate forms into documents for collecting user input and activating scripts and programs on your Web server.

III

Creating Documents

Linking HTML Documents to Other Information Sources

"All paths lead to the same goal: to convey to others what we are. And we must pass through solitude and difficulty, isolation and silence, in order to reach forth to the enchanted place where we can dance our clumsy dance and sing our sorrowful song—but in this dance or in this song there are fulfilled the most ancient rites of our conscience in the awareness of being human and of believing in a common destiny."

—Pablo Neruda, 1971

To connect, to communicate, is a basic human need. It may even be a subconscious pull that drives us to interconnect, to bridge the space between our thoughts and make our messages clear. On a certain level, the Internet can be seen as an avenue of pursuit for this connectivity. It's worldwide, it crosses language barriers, and it delivers information and knowledge in an immediate, intimate manner.

The World Wide Web is built on many of the same principles. Its fundamental goal is to unite many types of data in a single delivery system. HTML provides the tools that make this delivery possible.

Up to now, I've discussed the components of HTML documents—the elements available to authors as they create individual Web pages. Of course, a single Web page is as effective as a single page of a book by itself: it's only as useful as the information it can contain and successfully manage. For that reason (and because our civilization has a long history in journalism and publishing, with corresponding notions of how to distribute information firmly ingrained in our psyches), we break information into digestible chunks and organize them in relation to each other in order to communicate our ideas. Books are composed of chapters, newspapers of articles and columns, television of distinct programs, and so on.

The practice is no different in HTML. Information is often best delivered in many Web documents—not just crammed into a single mammoth page. How do you establish the relationships between HTML documents so users can access the proper data when they want to (or when it's relevant)? Through hypertext links.

This chapter answers the following questions:

- How can HTML pages link to other Web documents and data sources?

- How can HTML start an FTP transfer?

- Can HTML provide Gopher access to WWW pages?

- Is it possible to use a Web page with a Wide Area Information System network?

- Does HTML support remote login to other network servers?

- How can authors link to e-mail and UseNet News from within a Web page?

What Are Hypertext Links?

Hypertext has existed for decades; the name literally means "excessive or exaggerated text," although the familiar computer slang usage is probably closer to "enabled or interactive text." Hypertext uses *links,* or connections between documents, to allow users to access other documents whenever they activate these links. In HTML, a hypertext link can be a string of text or an inline image (see fig. 13.1).

Tip
The end user can change the color of link highlights for text and image borders (the user's software determines the color, not the HTML document).

> **Note**
>
> You can recognize hypertext links (referred to as just links) because they're a different color or underlined (or both). Hypertext images are displayed with a colored border to separate them from inactive images.

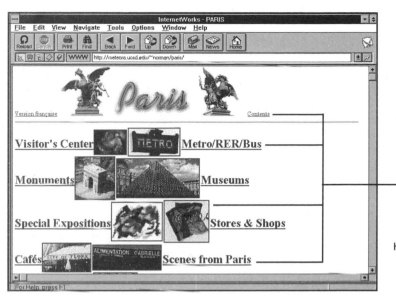

Fig. 13.1
In this Web page, all of the images have colored borders that link them to other documents. The underlined text mimics the behavior of the linked images for viewers without graphics support.

The advantages of hyperlinking are that you can define a path through a series of related documents, or allow the user to choose his own path through the data by connecting not just pages to each other, but concepts (such as topic references in a printed book). This kind of intuitive behavior allows ideas and concepts to be communicated much more effectively, and at the user's discretion.

Using the Anchor Element

You incorporate links into HTML documents similarly to how you use inline graphics. The *anchor element*, A, is a container element; it contains additional information (between its beginning and closing tags) that identifies its current function and the link destination (if appropriate).

◀ See "Using the IMG Element," p. 231

The anchor element is fairly versatile: not only does it signal a link to another document or resource, but it can also define a location to be linked *to*. Figure 13.2 shows a typical HTML document that incorporates the anchor element in both functions.

III

Creating Documents

Fig. 13.2
Anchors can
provide links to
other documents
or locations, or
they can define
locations them-
selves (where the
anchor is called a
"named anchor"
and acts more like
its namesake).

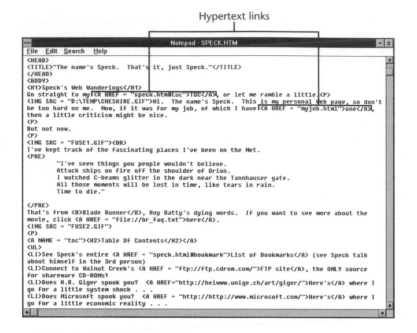

Hypertext links

The anchor element surrounds text that the viewer software displays. If the
anchor defines a link, as in `<A HREF="top.htm">home</A>`, the home text is highlighted to indicate that the user can click it to jump to another resource location (in this case, the document "top.htm"). If the anchor is acting as a place
marker (a named anchor), the text is not highlighted but is the text line displayed at the top of a viewer when a link jumps to that anchor. Figure 13.3
shows the display of the HTML document in the previous figure.

◀ See "Defining
URLs in HTML
Documents,"
p. 143

If the anchor acts as a link, the destination for the link is included in the
enclosed HREF statement. The destination can be either a relative or absolute
URL. If a link is to another information resource *not* associated with the current document (such as a Web site found on a different computer), you need
absolute URLs to include all of the information necessary for a viewer to locate the new resource. If the document is located locally, you can use a relative URL if it preserves the portability of all of the related documents.

Tip
Each URL listed in
figure 13.4 repre-
sents a different
Web site that is
available in the
bookmark list.

You can easily link Web documents to other documents using their URL and
the "http://" URL header. WWW viewer hotlists (or bookmarks, depending
on the terminology your WWW client uses) are composed of a list of URLs
that you can access by selecting them. Figure 13.4 shows how a list of URLs
compiled by your viewer might actually look.

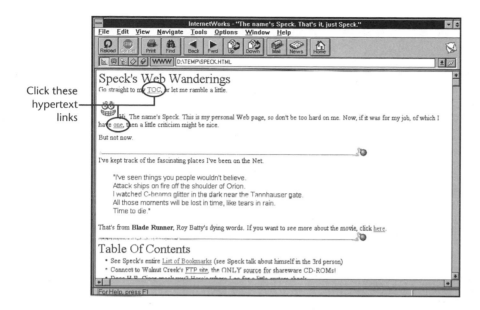

Fig. 13.3
Links and named anchors display the anchor text and inline graphics seamlessly in the rest of the document text.

Click these hypertext links

Fig. 13.4
Netscape lets you create a hierarchy in your bookmark list, that's converted to conventional HTML if you export the list to a file.

◀ See "Using Netscape Navigator," p. 96

Anchors support URLs for many different information resources. Table 13.1 shows how a URL can reference various information distribution systems.

Creating Documents

Tip
If you want to find
WWW sites that
interest you, refer
to a Web page that
indexes Web sites
or searches the Net
for any topic. The
most popular
service is Yahoo
(**http://www.
yahoo.com**).

Table 13.1 URL Definitions for Various Services

URL	Service	Example
http://	World Wide Web document	http://microsoft.com/welcome.html
gopher://	Gopher server	gopher://gopher.spandex.net:80/
ftp://	FTP server	ftp://ftp.asymetrix.com/
file://	FTP file	file://ftp.asymetrix.com/pub/msdos/index.txt
news:	UseNet News group	news:comp.www.announce
mailto:	E-mail message	mailto:weenie@dynamo.com
telnet:	Telnet session	telnet:jocko.dynamo.com

◀ See "Using
BASE," p. 163

Troubleshooting

I'm getting tired of typing in all of these absolute URL addresses. What's the rule for using relative URLs?

Your first link to a new document site will always use an absolute link (for example, a listing in a hotlist). You can format every subsequent link from that page as a relative link; the missing information is supplied from the initial absolute address, which is referred to as the base URL. You can override this base by using the BASE element in the document's head section.

For example, if your original document is **http://www.wip.com/app/top.htm**, subsequent links can be entered as any of the following:

brief.htm (absolute address of **www.wip.com/app/brief.htm**)

/logo.gif (absolute address of **www.wip.com/logo.gif**)

pics/sunset.jpg (absolute address of **www.wip.com/app/pics /sunset.jpg**)

#info (absolute address of **www.wip.com/app/top.htm#info**)

/pres/welcome.htm#press (absolute address of **www.wip.com/pres /welcome.htm#press**)

> **Note**
>
> Certain URLs rely on your WWW server software to provide the necessary server that can handle the requested service. For instance, your viewer must be told where a mail server you have access to (through a user account) is located before you can send a mail message from a Mailto: link. On the same token, a valid news server must be defined before the current Web page you're reading can link you to an associated newsgroup with the News: URL.

Using Links to Access Non-WWW Internet Resources

As discussed in Chapter 3, WWW viewing software programs are designed to access data across the range of standard Internet information systems such as Gopher, WAIS, and UseNet. They also support other standard Internet applications, such as File Transfer Protocol (FTP), Telnet, and e-mail. WWW viewers are of the "jack of all trades" variety—they do a little bit of everything. Sophisticated viewers (such as Netscape and Mosaic) do most things quite well.

To support this "super viewer" perspective, HTML directly supports each of these services in the markup language. Although the support in HTML is undisputed, each viewer may vary in its capability to support the data connection natively or by using an external application.

Why is it important that HTML support pre-existing Internet information services? Consider the promise of the future: NII (National Information Infrastructure), the loudly touted "Information Superhighway." As with any national public system, its goal will be to deliver a wide variety of data and services to end users using one bandwidth.

The services provided today by the Internet will be a subset of the NII's offerings; "grandfathering" will ensure that current information services (like UseNet News) will be virtually the same under the NII, even if only at the desktop, where the user interacts with the system. Behind the scenes, UseNet News may be incorporated into a new national news distribution system, but the old nomenclature (such as the newsgroup **comp.www.announce** used for announcing new Web sites) will still be supported by UseNet News readers. They may be aliases for the equivalent news topic in a new naming system, but they will be there to support the existing habits of the inherited Internet user base.

Tip
Connections to Web pages occasionally fail, usually due to too many users trying to retrieve the page or from heavy Net traffic that can disrupt your file retrieval.

◀ See "The World Wide Web as a 'Super Service,'" p. 38

III

Creating Documents

In much the same way, HTML exists to unite the existing Internet services under a common interface. The notion of a "universal readership" is fundamental to a basic understanding of why HTML exists. According to Tim Berns-Lee, a founding father of the World Wide Web:

Tip
Many Web clients don't provide the extensive support for UseNet News or e-mail found in dedicated stand-alone applications; use the program that best serves your needs.

> *"The W3 principle of universal readership is that once information is available, it should be accessible from any type of computer, in any country, and an (authorized) person should only have to use one simple program to access it."*

HTML serves the body of universal readers by providing an avenue for access to existing Internet services: FTP, WAIS, Gopher, Telnet, UseNet News, and the ubiquitous e-mail.

Linking to FTP

◀ See "WWW and FTP," p. 41

File Transfer Protocol (FTP) is a staple application for Internet veterans. *FTP* is a set of communication protocols that define data transfers from remote Internet servers. Users log in to these remote servers, often as guests using the "anonymous" account, and retrieve or download text and binary files from the site. HTML supports the FTP protocols, and WWW viewers are designed to handle FTP connections and file services seamlessly.

As an end user, you don't have to know anything about FTP or how to connect to a public server. The WWW protocols integrate access to the established Internet system automatically, leaving users (and authors) free to take advantage of the data they contain with minimal instruction. Figure 13.5 shows how a link to a public FTP site is used in an HTML document.

When displayed in a WWW viewer, FTP links look the same as any other hypertext link in an HTML document (refer to fig. 13.3). When the user selects an FTP link, the WWW viewer begins an internal FTP session. After it connects to the file site (provided the site is available; public sites often limit the number of active connections and may refuse your connection requests during peak hours), the viewer displays the FTP file list (see fig. 13.6).

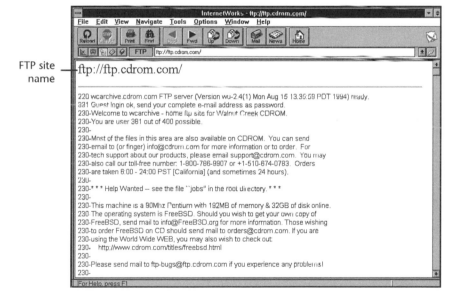

Fig. 13.5
FTP links use the
standard anchor
element; the link's
text description
should identify
the destination as
an FTP file site.

FTP site
name

Fig. 13.6
FTP file lists are
text-only directory
lists and include
both subdirectories
and files in the
current directory.

III

Creating Documents

WWW viewers vary in the manner in which they represent FTP file directories. Many imitate standard FTP applications and only display the current directory's contents. Others provide a visual structure of the FTP file hierarchy, making the user's browsing easier (see fig. 13.7).

Tip
The read and write
notations in figure
13.7 indicate
UNIX FTP sites.

Fig. 13.7
Viewers such as
InternetWorks
display a branch-
ing tree hierarchy
of the site's files
and directories.

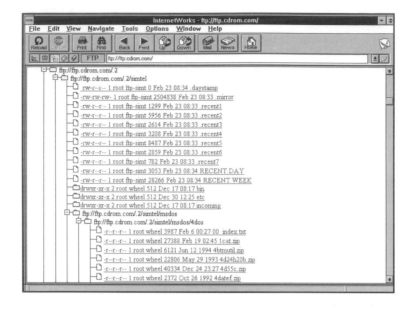

FTP files are *clickable:* by selecting a file on the remote FTP site (usually with a
double-click), your viewer will retrieve the file and save it to your local hard
disk if it's in a binary form, or display it in the viewer window if it's an ASCII
text format (see fig. 13.8).

Fig. 13.8
WWW viewers
can display ASCII
text files; most
viewers can be
configured to
display these files
in a user-selectable
font.

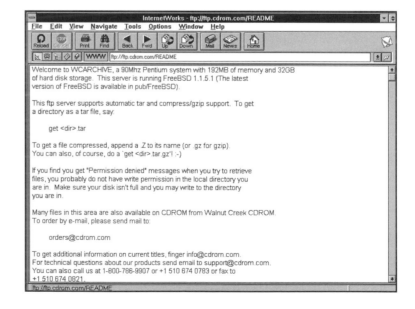

Public FTP sites are still the preferred means of making data files (including the vast bulk of shareware applications) available to the Internet community. Chances are, if you're creating a Web site that also will distribute data files to end users, you will use an FTP site in conjunction with your Web server for your Internet presence.

Troubleshooting

How can I find a file on an FTP site if I don't have the complete URL for the file I want to download?

If you have the FTP server's host name, you might be able to construct a "browsing directory" that will let you progress through the site's directory structure until you find the file you are looking for. Just double-click directory names to move forward into the subdirectory, or double-click the double period line to step backwards one level in the directory tree. When you find the file you want to download, a double-click starts the file transfer.

◀ See "WWW and Gopher," p. 39

Linking to Gopher

Gopher is a distribution similar to the WWW with the exception of hypertext links. It is widely popular and is the second largest distribution system on the Internet (the WWW is the largest and fastest growing). Gopher organizes files and menus in text lists, much like FTP files and directories. In this case, however, Gopher's menu items can act as links to other menus, or can initiate file transfers. Like FTP, selected binary files are retrieved from the remote server and saved to your local hard disk or server, and items that represent other menus open new list windows, displaying the items in the new menu.

HTML supports Gopher's Internet protocols with the standard anchor hypertext links (refer to fig. 13.3). Most WWW viewers can access Gopher resources natively; a few may require an external Gopher application to retrieve Gopher information. Viewers that do support Gopher natively, such as InternetWorks, display the Gopher items in a standard list fashion (see fig. 13.9).

Similar to FTP, WWW viewers can retrieve and display Gopher text files in the viewer window. This text is displayed in a configurable format (see fig. 13.10).

III

Creating Documents

Fig. 13.9
WWW viewers
like InternetWorks
display Gopher
menu lists
similarly to typical
Gopher applica-
tions, using
unique icons for
each item type
(text, binary, or
menu).

Binary file

Text file

FTP site

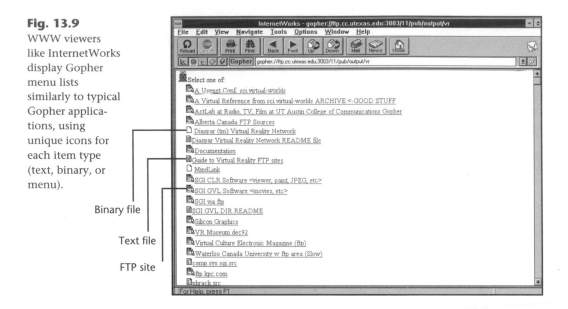

Fig. 13.10
Gopher's list icons
represent the type
of data the item is
associated with,
including links to
other menu lists.
Similar to WWW
links, menu list
icons may
correspond to
menu lists on
other Gopher
servers on the
Internet.

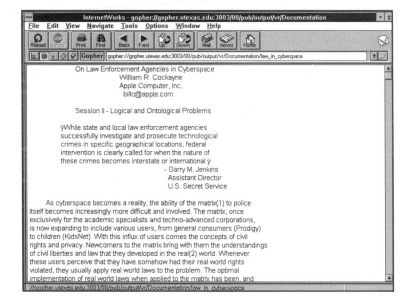

◄ See "WWW
and WAIS,"
p. 44

Again, using Gopher resources requires no additional knowledge or training
for WWW users—the Internet service is integrated seamlessly into the Web.
Until data transmission rates on the Internet increase substantially, many
information providers will continue to use Gopher because it's much faster

than the WWW, especially for users on slower connections and those without graphical support. The WWW and Gopher will continue to coexist on the Internet for years to come.

Linking to WAIS

WAIS (pronounced "ways") stands for Wide Area Information Server, and is yet another Internet protocol for distributing information of many types. WAIS servers allow users to search a collection of data in many forms from a single interface. While less popular than Gopher or the WWW, WAIS is a viable system in use on a great number of Internet servers.

The WWW supports the WAIS protocol seamlessly, and most WWW viewers also support WAIS searches. Figure 13.11 shows a WAIS search of the CIA World Fact Book index for the text string "France."

Tip
WAIS database addresses often make little sense, such as the one in figure 13.11. Rely on the menu choices leading to them to tell you what the index contains.

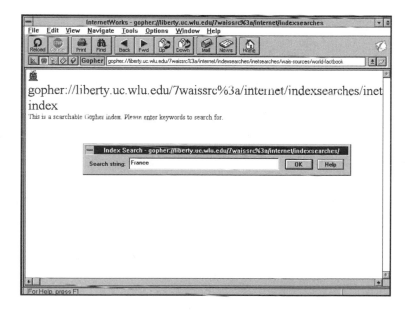

Fig. 13.11
When a WWW link accesses an indexed WAIS database, a search dialog box or form displays to accept the user's search text string.

You can also find WAIS resources in lists on WAIS servers. WWW viewers display these lists in the same manner as Gopher and FTP lists: each item is a clickable link to the associated WAIS database. Figure 13.12 shows how a list of WAIS resources looks in a typical viewer.

III

Creating Documents

Fig. 13.12
World Wide Web
viewers do not
distinguish data
types (as they do
with Gopher lists)
in WAIS lists.

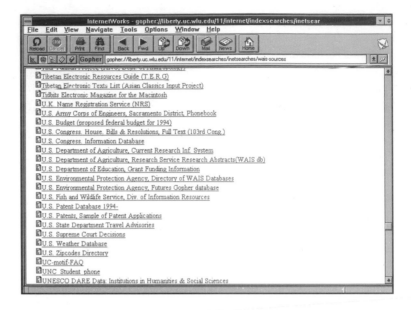

Again, users don't have to understand how to access a WAIS database: the
WWW incorporates its protocols, and HTML anchors provide the necessary
connections to WAIS resources.

Linking to Telnet

Telnet is the Internet application that provides remote login capabilities.
From a UNIX host account, users can log in to other machines on the
Internet by way of the Telnet protocol. These sessions are *text-only*, providing
command-line access to the remote system.

Telnet is useful for running a text-based application on the remote system as
though it were available on your local system. Many Internet sites (primarily
universities) use text applications for maintaining online library card catalogs, central information services, and so on. Users who don't have access to
Gopher on their local system can use a Telnet session to access another system with the application.

Tip
You can use Telnet
to login to an
account you may
have on another
Internet computer
system located
anywhere in the
world.

The WWW supports Telnet's protocols seamlessly. Web pages use anchor
links to initiate Telnet sessions from Web pages. WWW viewers generally use
external Telnet applications to provide the support for these links. When a
Telnet link is clicked, the external application starts up on top of the Web
viewer (see fig. 13.13).

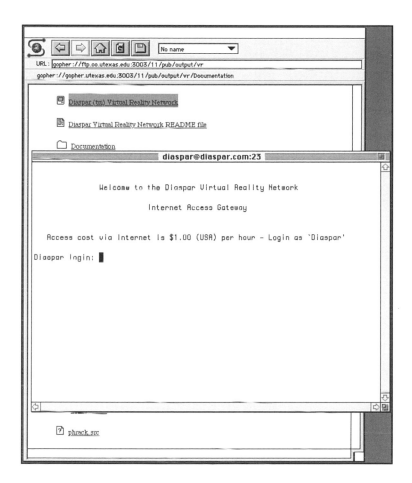

Fig. 13.13
Telnet is run in a
text window.
When the Telnet
session is over, the
user must quit the
external applica-
tion manually.

Telnet links in WWW should be to public Internet servers, unless the Web
application is for a closed audience. Telnet sessions started by WWW viewers
can use guest privileges, or prompt for user names and passwords. As an external application, the HTML link only gives it a "kick start"; the user must
end the Telnet session and application as though he started it himself.

Telnet is a common application for users who don't do their daily work out
of their server accounts. As WWW applications become more common in the
workplace, the WWW will continue to support this flexible work environment and the capability to connect remotely to the growing number of
Internet-connected systems.

◄ See "What Is
UseNet?" p. 20

III

Creating Documents

Linking to UseNet News

UseNet is a network of servers separate from the Internet that distributes public forum discussions and news feeds. UseNet Network News consists of well over 5,500 different newsgroups. The content and participation of these groups varies greatly; a group such as **comp.os.os2.misc** may attract a hundred or so posts a day, while a group such as **alt.binaries.pictures.erotica** might rack up five or six hundred posts daily. As I said, the subject matter and the traffic vary greatly.

UseNet is often a valuable resource for authors who are providing information on a specific subject that is also discussed in a newsgroup; a link to the UseNet resource is often the best way of saying "don't ask me about this subject, but here are the right people to talk to." The number of companies that provide consumer technical support via Internet newsgroups is growing, especially because the commercial online services (where their electronic support has typically been focused) have added direct access to the Internet and UseNet.

Tip

Netscape's Usenet News support lets you click URL links in news posts to go directly to that Web site.

The WWW provides seamless support for Network News. When an HTML document links to a newsgroup, the WWW browser displays the current list of articles (see fig. 13.14).

Fig. 13.14

InternetWorks provides a companion application, InternetWorks Messaging System, to access UseNet newsgroups.

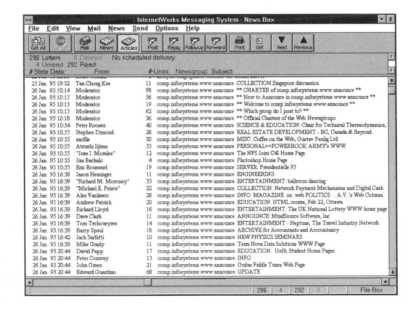

Newsgroup articles often contain references to previous articles. The WWW has been designed to create *instant hypertext links* in newsgroup posts, linking documents to those referenced in the current message. Each message also includes a link back to the newsgroup article list. Automatic management of UseNet articles is greatly appreciated by the user base who venture into UseNet infrequently: the WWW relieves them of having to learn Network News procedures to access newsgroup information.

◀ See "Reach Out and Mail Someone," p. 23

Linking to E-Mail

E-mail is the most widely used network application for a good reason: it's easy and convenient. Most people don't think twice about writing e-mail to someone they may not see or call regularly (and sometimes that's not a good thing). In Chapter 8, "HTML Standards and Practices," I talk about the conventions of HTML such as signing Web pages so users have an identifiable author to respond to. Most signatures are accompanied by e-mail links. See figure 13.15 for an example of an e-mail anchor link.

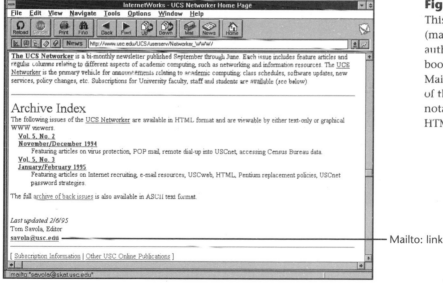

Fig. 13.15
This Web page (maintained by the author of this book) includes a Mailto: link as part of the signature notation in the HTML document.

Mailto: link

The Mailto: URL requires a valid e-mail address, not the author's name (which may be displayed as the link text in the WWW viewer window if you prefer). Most WWW viewers support e-mail natively. When an e-mail anchor is selected, a mail dialog box pops up with both the addressee and the recipient's information inserted into the message (see fig. 13.16).

III

Creating Documents

> **Note**
>
> E-mail addresses can sometimes be valid in more than one format. For example, **savola@usc.edu** and **savola@skat.usc.edu** will both send mail to me because my user name (savola) is unique to the entire "usc" subdomain, making my account's specific host name (skat) optional.

Fig. 13.16
WWW viewers must be configured to know where the user's mail server is located—they can't deliver e-mail by themselves.

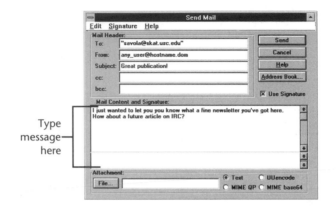

An advantage not to be overlooked with WWW's support for e-mail service is the notion of user feedback. There's an old maxim about the difficulty authors have writing in a vacuum, with no critical feedback to judge their work; this applies to Web authors as well. Readily available avenues for feedback will allow users to comment on your Web information and how you present it. It's imperative to know whether you're doing a poor job with your Web pages; it's even more important to know whether you're doing a good job! This kind of feedback is critical to the development of a successful collection of Web documents.

From Here...

I've examined how HTML can link WWW users to an array of Internet information services. What's next? How else can you use HTML links? Can HTML documents collect information as well as deliver it, or are they just a one-way connection between the author and user? For answers to these questions, and more, refer to the following:

■ Chapter 14, "Point and Click Navigating with Image Maps," teaches you how to use inline graphics as visual maps to retrieve input from users and link HTML documents to other Web pages and Internet services.

■ Part IV, "Using Forms in HTML Documents," describes how to incorporate forms into documents for collecting user input and activating scripts and programs on your Web server.

■ Part V, "HTML 3.0," shows how HTML continues to change and new features give the author more control over the way information is delivered to an audience. Special formatting features, including tables, provide "ease of use" for document creation.

■ Part VI, "Document Aesthetics," teaches you the tricks of the trade for making your HTML documents easier to read, easier to access, and extremely good-looking.

Point and Click Navigating with Image Maps

In Chapter 13, you saw how to use anchors to link together information in different HTML documents. This capability to distribute information in a hypertext paradigm is one of the World Wide Web's strengths. Hypertext linking is intuitive, spontaneous, and non-linear—much like our own thinking process. The next natural step would be to combine this "human nature" hypertext capability with the visual capabilities of the WWW. The result? "Hyper-images," or *image maps*.

Image maps allow an author to create visual navigation maps. By clicking specific locations in a graphic, the WWW viewer grabs a new document (or jumps to an anchor somewhere else in the current document), or executes a program in the background.

Using graphic images as an interface for an application is nothing new. Graphical environments, like Macintosh OS and Microsoft Windows, are large clickable images with associated graphic elements (what you and I call *overlapping windows* and *icons*). The first graphical, mouse-driven interface was developed by Xerox in the late sixties. Computer gaming software has gone to great lengths to advance the science of interactivity with static graphics. Just ask any seasoned game player about the importance of "clicking everywhere" to see what links may be hidden in plain sight. In HTML, the goal is to make the links easy to identify and clear enough to enhance the usage of your data, not to obscure it in puzzles or details. Figure 14.1 shows an example of how graphical an HTML interface can be.

▶ See "Linking Data to Server Applications," p. 311

III

Creating Documents

Fig. 14.1
Time Warner's
Pathfinder Home
Page includes a
"road map," text
lists, and function
buttons—all
contained in a
single image.

Tip
Click the *hot spots,*
or active areas in
an image, to access
additional linked
resources.

▶ See "Linking
Data to Server
Applications,"
p. 311

◀ See "Using
the Anchor
Element,"
p. 253

This chapter answers the following questions:

■ What is an image map?

■ What types of graphical formats are supported as image maps?

■ What happens if a viewer can't display a graphic image?

■ How are images linked to the imagemap program?

■ How do you create image maps?

Just What Is an Image Map?

Image maps are just that—interactive "maps," graphics that allow users to
click specific areas in the graphic to access another HTML document, or to
run a CGI (Common Gateway Interface) process in the background. They're
created with the same graphics you embed in your documents with the anchor element. Through a mapping process, authors define specific shapes in
the image that correspond to defined actions. This mapping process requires
that the author know the pixel coordinates of the boundaries for the *hot
spots,* or clickable areas in the graphic (various utilities exist to automate this
process). See the section "Mapping Image Maps" later in this chapter for more
information.

The ISMAP Attribute

Image maps are a subset of the linked inline images you saw in Chapter 10. They still require the A (anchor) and IMG elements, but with the ISMAP attribute; this signals to the WWW viewer software that this image is a point of input for the user. When the user clicks anywhere in the boundaries of the image, the viewer calculates the pixel coordinates of the click and returns that value to the HTML document source. A server-side program, imagemap, processes the input by comparing it to the specified database of recognized input values. If the input value is found in the database, imagemap returns the associated URL function.

An HTML image map statement is comprised of two parts: the link to the database that is associated with the graphic, and the displayed IMG graphic itself. For instance, the line

<A HREF="http://random.com/bin/oz_toto"><IMG SRC=toto.gif
ISMAP></A>

consists of:

- The hyperlink anchor (A HREF=...</A>)

- An alias that represents the physical database file ("http://random.com/ bin/oz_toto")

- The graphic image to be displayed with the ISMAP attribute, telling the viewer to return the mouse click coordinates (IMG SRC=toto.gif ISMAP)

Figure 14.2 shows an HTML document with an image map; figure 14.3 shows how a typical HTML viewer will interpret the coding.

The Imagemap Program

Support for image maps by WWW viewers is only half the battle: the Web server that services the HTML documents must also know how to interpret the data coming back from the viewer when the user clicks a hot spot. Servers generally need an external program to handle this information. The most common program is NCSA imagemap.

Tip
Web sites can configure the imagemap application to return a generic error document when a mouse click is not recorded on a defined image map hot spot.

◄ See "Using the IMG Element," p. 231

III

Creating Documents

Fig. 14.2
It's good practice to use absolute URLs for image map links, unless portability is required.

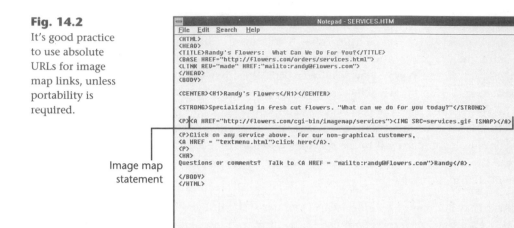

Image map statement

Fig. 14.3
Viewers typically don't display image maps like standard linked images—they don't use high-lighted borders (in the viewer's defined link color) to identify the graphic as clickable.

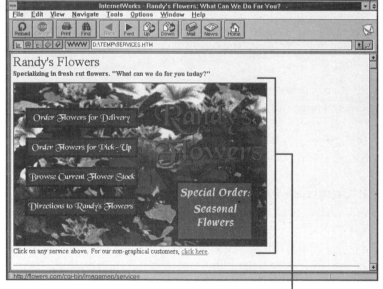

Displayed map statement

NCSA imagemap only does one thing: it takes pixel coordinates and an associated database file and reads the data file to see whether the coordinates were designated as a hot spot with an associated action or not. If imagemap finds the coordinates in a specified hot spot, it sends a "connect to URL" command to the WWW viewer software, which then loads the specified document. If the coordinates do not fall in a designated hot spot, imagemap returns a default URL (or none if not specified) that the viewer loads up. If no default is identified, the viewer receives no response to the screen click, and the user must try a different location in the graphic. The Star Trek Voyager home page only allows you to click the defined button areas (see fig. 14.4).

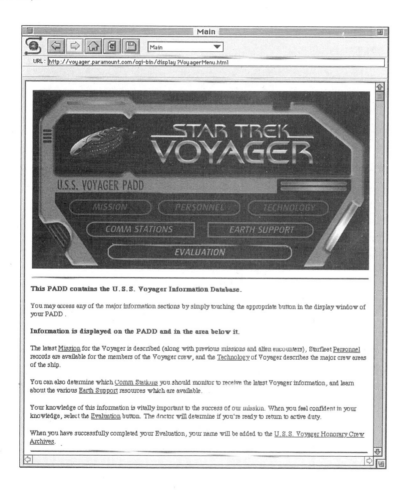

Fig. 14.4
Paramount's home page for the Star Trek Voyager television series incorporates the show's fictional computer controls into the WWW interface.

Some Web sites return a default URL to an HTML document that informs the user that he has not clicked a hot spot. Whether this step is necessary is debatable; end users should be smart enough to figure out for themselves whether they're clicking an image map's hot spots (but this may be necessary if your image's hot spots are not intuitive, or if you're building a WWW interactive game).

On the CD

Note

Imagemap is the most often used image map server program. Other software packages (particularly for other operating systems) also exist. One popular program is MapServe, for the Macintosh. MapServe is designed to be used on systems running Chuck Shotton's MacHTTP 2.0 or greater (available on HTMLCD). MapServe is functionally identical to imagemap, but also supports oval hot spots generated by WebMap. MapServe has a WWW home page, located at:

http://www.spub.ksu.edu/other/machttp_tools/mapserve/mapserve.html

See "For the Macintosh: WebMap" later in this chapter for more information.

Database File: the IMAGEMAP.CONF File

Functional image maps are a team effort, relying on cooperation from both the WWW viewer and the imagemap program to send, process, and retrieve URL data. This team isn't complete without the manager and the players: the IMAGEMAP.CONF and MAP data files. The IMAGEMAP.CONF database stores the actual data files that relate to the image map aliases used by all HTML documents on your site; they translate the nicknames for the data files into the real thing. For example, in the image map statement

<A HREF="http://random.com/bin/oz_toto"><IMG SRC=toto.gif ISMAP></A>

the alias "oz_toto" doesn't have any real meaning on its own, until you refer to imagemap's IMAGEMAP.CONF file and learn the actual data file location. The IMAGEMAP.CONF file entry looks like this:

oz_toto oz/html/protags/toto.map

Each alias is listed with its appropriate MAP data file. Remember, an alias represents one image map, so the IMAGEMAP.CONF file may not be very large, depending on how many HTML documents use image maps on your Web server.

Tip
Imagemap is traditionally installed in a Web site's CGI/bin subdirectory.

The location of IMAGEMAP.CONF is *hardcoded* into the imagemap program; that's why, more often than not, imagemap is distributed as source code, which you must then compile into the executable binary program file.

Application File: the MAP File

Imagemap refers to IMAGEMAP.CONF to determine the actual data file that corresponds to the alias provided by the HTML document link. These files are the players; they're identified by their MAP extension. These files consist of a list of links that correspond to the hot spots in the image map graphic. Comments can also be incorporated into MAP files (using leading # characters, similar to how DOS comments are signaled with the REM statement). Table 14.1 lists the components of a standard MAP entry. This is the syntax statement: method URL x1,y1 x2,y2...xn,yn

Table 14.1	MAP Line Entry Format
Component	**Description**
method	Type of hot spot (circle, rectangle, polygon, oval)
URL	URL action to return to the WWW viewer (an HTML file, FTP connection, gopher connection, and so on)
x1,y1	List of coordinates that describe the hot spot

Hot spot methods use pixel coordinates to define themselves differently (see Table 14.2).

Table 14.2	Defining Hot Spot Methods	
Method	**Type**	**Required Coordinates**
circle	circle	2 pairs: center edge point
oval	oval	2 pairs: upper_left lower_right
rect	rectangle	2 pairs: upper_left lower_right
poly	polygon	polygon means many-sided; up to 100 pairs can define the vertices ("points") of the shape
point	point	1 pair: the_point

The oval description seems illogical: requiring the points of a rectangle for its definition. This is actually the easiest way to define a circular object: by the four-sided box that contains it. Circles can also be defined that way (after all, an oval in a square is just a circle). The point method is useful as a "closest to" input (it's pretty hard to click a specific pixel coordinate). If two points are described, the one accessed is the one that the click is "closest to" as measured by a straight line.

> **Note**
>
> One problem with image maps is the general lack of definition for the hot spots; unless the graphic area (where the hot spot is located) is square, circular, or a straight-line polygraphic shape, a user won't know the precise boundaries of the spot. One solution is to draw physical representations—outlines or buttons—on the graphic to define the hot spots. Many graphic utilities allow you to draw frame outlines in a graphic. One of the best for the job is the UNIX gd1.1 graphics library, written by Thomas Boutell. Visit the URL **http://siva.cshl.org/gd/gd.html** for more information.

Tip

If hot spots overlap in an image map, a mouse click will activate the hot spot that is listed first in the MAP file.

The MAP data files also include a statement indicating the default URL to return for clicks that fall outside the defined hot spots. Be careful, though, to not use a default URL with an image map that has a hot spot defined with the point method: any clicks that are not fully in other hot spots (such as a circle or rectangle) will be interpreted as being "closest to" the point, and the default URL will not be displayed. Points are best used when relative actions (such as clicking anywhere in an image map) are valid inputs; this may have implications in interactive game pages.

In the previous example, the alias "oz_toto" referred to a data file called TOTO.MAP (see fig. 14.5).

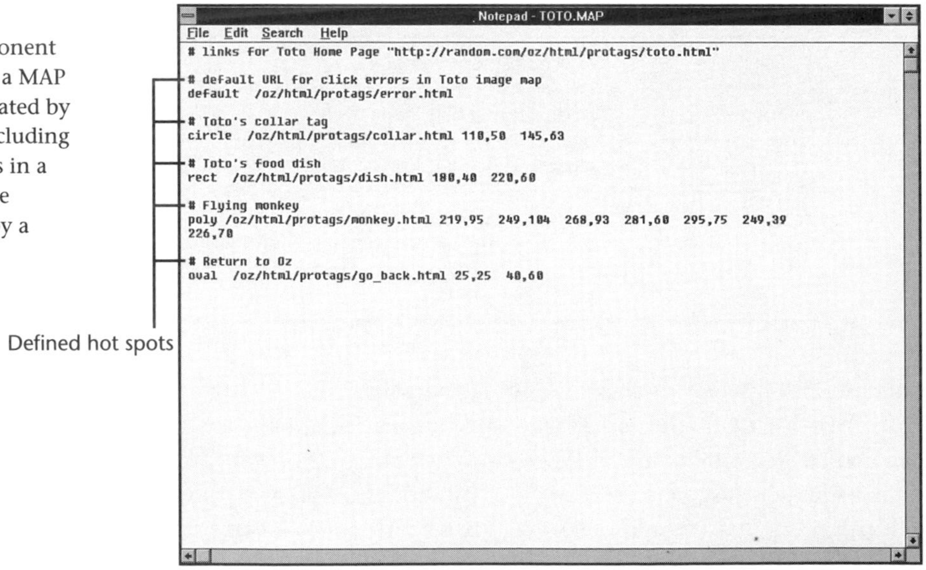

Fig. 14.5

Each component of a line in a MAP file is separated by a space (excluding coordinates in a pair that are separated by a comma).

Defined hot spots

```
Notepad - TOTO.MAP
File  Edit  Search  Help
# links for Toto Home Page "http://random.com/oz/html/protags/toto.html"

# default URL for click errors in Toto image map
default  /oz/html/protags/error.html

# Toto's collar tag
circle  /oz/html/protags/collar.html 110,50  145,63

# Toto's food dish
rect  /oz/html/protags/dish.html 100,40  220,60

# Flying monkey
poly /oz/html/protags/monkey.html 219,95  249,104  268,93  281,60  295,75  249,39
226,70

# Return to Oz
oval  /oz/html/protags/go_back.html 25,25   40,60
```

Graphic Formats Supported

Image maps can consist of any IMG-supported graphic format. The most popular is GIF; it has nearly universal support by WWW viewers. JPEG is also gaining popularity as an image map graphic format.

◀ See "What's a Picture Worth?" p. 222

Troubleshooting

How do I accommodate non-graphical users (such as Lynx users or people with disabled inline graphics in their WWW clients) when using image maps?

Unfortunately, it's impossible to embed a link in an ALT statement (the optional text string displayed when an inline graphic is not supported or viewed). Your best alternative is to include a text-only page that provides the necessary links, and to include a separate line of code with the link pointing to the alternate document. For example, include a link in your HTML document to the text menu page like:

    <A HREF = "http://www.rhino.com/beasley.htm">Click here for users without
    graphic support</A>

to create the link Click here for users without graphic support in the displayed home page.

Tip

HTML 3.0 will allow HTML elements such as hypertext links to be included in an image's ALT statement.

Mapping Image Maps

By far, the most difficult task in creating image maps is defining the boundaries for each hot spot. You can always fire up Adobe Photoshop or any other commercial package that will display a cursor's current pixel location when the mouse pointer is moved over a map. This can get tedious (and confusing), especially when you have multiple hot spots, and hot spots in shapes such as polygons, circles, and ovals.

Thankfully, a few resourceful programmers found it in their hearts to write easy-to-use programs for marking off hot spot locations. The utilities in the following sections are available as shareware (some are included on HTMLCD, and the locations of upgraded versions are noted if known).

On the CD

III

Creating Documents

For Windows: Mapedit

Written by Thomas Boutell (who receives lots of mentions in relation to his fine HTML tools), Mapedit is a Windows WYSIWYG (What You See Is What You Get) image map editor. Load a GIF graphic into the editor, and create a list of hot spots by drawing the figures on the image. Mapedit allows an author to associate URLs and comments to each of these spots. The hot spots are fully editable, and the output MAP files are CERN and NCSA compatible.

For the Macintosh: WebMap

Written by Roland Smith, WebMap allows an author to mark out graphic figures (such as rectangles or circles) onto a GIF or PICT image to denote hot spots in the image map. WebMap lets you enter the "action" URLs for each hot spot. The data is then easily exported to a MAP file format, that is compatible with the NCSA, CERN, and MapServe imagemap formats. Figure 14.6 shows a typical WebMap session in action.

Fig. 14.6
WebMap displays each hot spot as you enter its shape, making it easy to avoid unintentionally overlapping spots.

You can find additional information about WebMap at **http://www.city. net/cnx/software/webmap.html**.

For UNIX: xv

Written by John Bradley, xv is an X Windows UNIX graphics viewer and editor. xv handles format conversions, interlacing, and transparency, as well as describing pixel coordinates in an image to define hot spot locations. While xv does not compile a database of hot spot URLs and associated comments (like WebMap and Mapedit), it is one of the best UNIX graphics tools around.

MapMaker Home Page

The MapMaker Home Page is a WWW page that allows you to create an image map for any inline image that exists on a World Wide Web document. You can find this page at the following address:

http://www.tns.lcs.mit.edu/cgi-bin/mapmaker

MapMaker prompts the author for the URL location of the image (see fig. 14.7). It then creates the image map by mapping the various polygon vertices the author indicates by clicking the displayed image in MapMaker (see fig. 14.8). This Web service is provided by Professor David Tennehouse and the Telemedia, Networks, and Systems Group at the MIT Laboratory for Computer Science.

Tip
A fine Web site for UNIX-based graphics tools and tips for resolving XMosaic's palette issues is **http://rugmd4.chem.rug.nl/hoesel/expo/part2.html**.

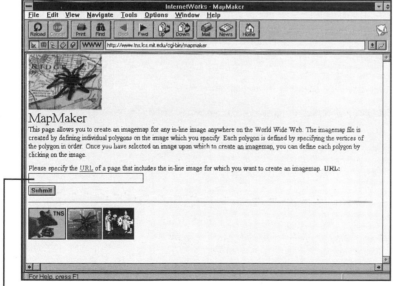

Enter URL here

Fig. 14.7
The inline image must reside on a public URL. MapMaker accesses the graphic the same way a WWW viewer would—it loads the appropriate Web page.

III

Creating Documents

Fig. 14.8
After each polygon is defined, and action URLs are associated with them, choose the Complete Imagemap button to compile the image's MAP file (save this to your local directory).

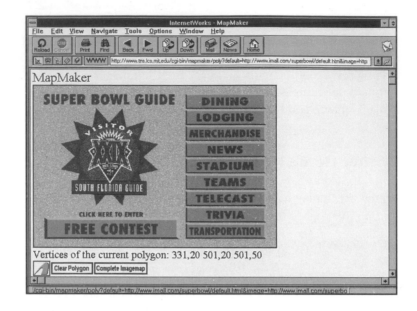

Additional Graphic Resources

Here are additional Web sites that provide archives of images for use as inline graphics in HTML documents. The formats vary from site to site. If you decide to retrieve and use any graphics from these or other sites, make sure your intended use is allowed—some collections have restrictions for commercial use. And, by all means, give credit where it's due: include an acknowledgment (or link) to the file archive.

Graphics Archive Web site:

> **http://www.best.com/~bryanw/index.html**

Syed's Bullets, Buttons, and Other Gizmos:

> **http://coney.gsfc.nasa.gov/www/sswg/gizmos.html**

TIC/MIDS WWW Server:

> **http://www.tic.com/gifs/index.html**

Kansas State University Interactive Graphics Render

If you like the idea of creating your own bullets and icons, link to the following URL:

http://www.engg.ksu.edu:8872/

This Web page, maintained by Patrick Hennessey, provides a form interface for defining raytraced objects. The Web page form sends the chosen characteristics (colors, shape, size, and so on) to a raytracer, which generates a resulting GIF file. You can preview and retrieve these files. Figure 14.9 shows the site's form page.

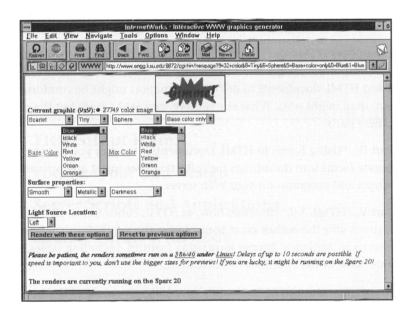

Fig. 14.9
The raytracing application may take several seconds to generate new images, depending on the server-side machine it's currently running on.

Ten different graphic characteristics are user-definable. The variety of combinations is impressive. The raytracer generates anti-aliased graphics that look far superior to non-aliased graphics. Be aware that this service is intended for non-commercial use. I highly recommend it for adding a unique touch to your own Web documents.

A Gallery of Interactive Online Geometry

The address **http://www.geom.umn.edu/apps/gallery.html** links users to a virtual wealth of interactive geometry demonstrations. Each application lets you manipulate the settings and characteristics of the figures and

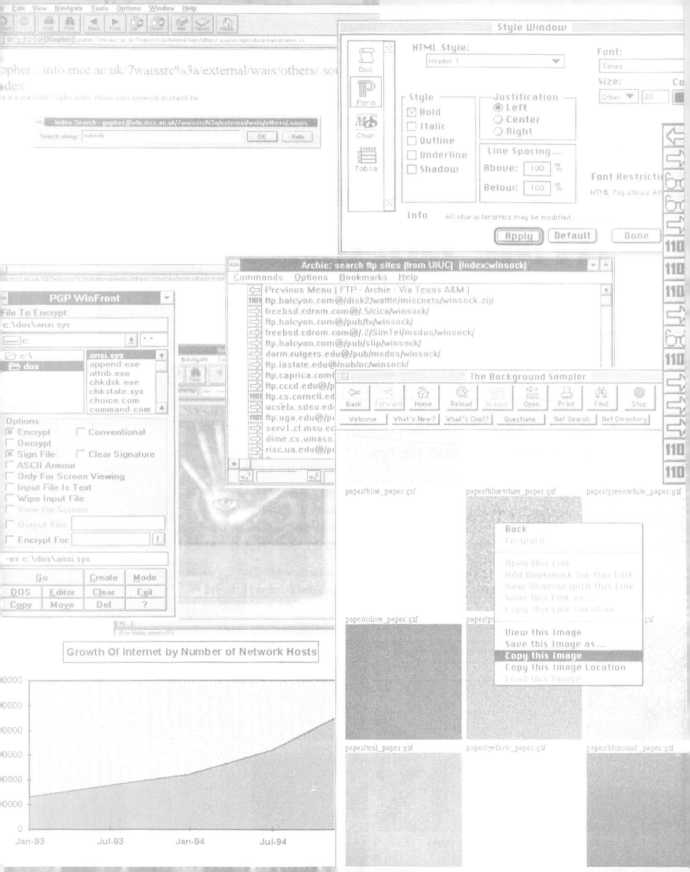

Chapter 15

Elements of Forms

Forms are one of the most popular features on the World Wide Web. They allow you to interact with the text and graphics being displayed on your machine. You can make forms with simple "yes or no" questions, you can make highly complex ordering forms, or you can make a form for people to send you comments.

You create forms by giving a number of fields in which you can enter information or choose an option. Then, when you submit the form, the information is returned to a script. A *script* is a short program that is written specifically for each form. You can create them to do any number of things.

In this chapter, you learn to

- Set up a form

- Create fields to enter information in or to make a choice from

An Overview of HTML Forms Tags

The HTML tags you use to display forms are straightforward. There are three types of tags to create fields: TEXTAREA, SELECT, and INPUT. You can put any number of these tags between <FORM> and </FORM>. The following is a brief description of each tag:

- The TEXTAREA tag defines a field in which the end user can type multiple lines of text.

- The SELECT tag lets the end user choose between a number of choices in either a scroll-box or pop-up menu.

■ The INPUT tag provides all of the other forms of input: single lines of text, radio buttons, checkboxes, and the buttons to submit or clear the form.

FORM

The FORM element comes at the beginning of any form. When you create a FORM element, you also define what script it uses and how it sends data. You do this with the elements ACTION and METHOD:

■ ACTION points the form to a URL that will accept the forms information and do something with it. If you don't specify an ACTION, it sends the information back to the same URL the page came from.

Tip

Use POST for all of your forms unless it's a very simple query. Especially because URLs have a definite length that they can't exceed.

■ METHOD tells the form how to send its information back to the script. The most common method is *POST,* which sends all the information from the form separately from the URL. The other option for METHOD is GET. *GET* tacks on the information from the form to the end of the URL.

The following is an example of a FORM tag:

```
<FORM METHOD="POST" ACTION="/cgi-bin/comment_script">
...
</FORM>
```

This example says I want the form to send the completed form to the script comment_script in the cgi-bin directory on my server, and to use the POST method to send it.

Caution

You can put any number of forms on the same HTML page, but be careful not to nest one form inside another. If you put in a <FORM> tag before finishing that last one, that line is ignored and all the inputs for your second form are assumed to go with the first one.

Tip

TEXTAREA fields are ideal for having someone enter a comment or some lengthy information, because they can type as much as they want in the field.

TEXTAREA

With TEXTAREA, you can provide a field for someone to enter multiple lines of information. By default, a TEXTAREA form shows a blank field four rows long and 40 characters wide. You can make it any size you want by setting

IV

the ROWS and COLS in the tag. You can also put in some text by simply entering or typing it between the <TEXTAREA> and </TEXTAREA> tags.

The options for the TEXTAREA tag are:

- *NAME.* This is required. It defines the name for the data.

- *ROWS.* Sets the number of rows in the field.

- *COLS.* Sets the width of the field (in characters).

- *Default text.* Any text between the <TEXTAREA> and </TEXTAREA> tags is used as default text and shows up inside the field.

> **Tip**
> All input fields—
> TEXTAREA,
> SELECT, and
> INPUT—in a form
> must have a NAME
> defined for their
> information.

Caution

Browsers can't interpret any HTML coding inside <TEXTAREA> tags.

Consider the following tag (TEXTAREA.HTML):

```
<TEXTAREA NAME="comments" ROWS=4 COLS=40>Default text
1  2  3 ...
</TEXTAREA>
```

This result of this tag is shown in figure 15.1.

On the CD

> **Fig. 15.1**
> The default text
> is shown as
> preformatted text
> in the TEXTAREA
> element.

SELECT

The SELECT element shows a list of choices in either a pop-up menu or a scrollable list. It's set up as an opening and closing tag with a number of choices listed in between. Just like the TEXTAREA element, the SELECT tag requires you to define a name. You can specify how many choices to show at once, using the SIZE option.

▶ See "Using Line
Break Tags,"
p. 297

The options for the SELECT element are:

- *NAME.* This is required. It defines the name for the data.

- *SIZE.* Determines how many choices to show. If you omit SIZE or set it to 1, the choices are shown as a pop-up menu. If you set it to 2 or higher, it shows the choices in a scrollable box. If you set SIZE larger

Tip
Most WWW browsers won't properly display a scrollable window if the SIZE is 2 or 3. Leave it as a pop-up menu or think about using the INPUT field's radio buttons if the size is 2 or 3.

than the number of choices you have within SELECT, a "nothing" choice is added. When the end user chooses this, it's returned as an empty field.

■ *MULTIPLE.* This allows multiple selections. If you specify multiple, a scrollable window displays—regardless of the number of choices or the setting of SIZE.

You present the choices the end user will make within the <SELECT> and </SELECT> tags. The choices are listed inside the <OPTION> tag and don't allow any other HTML markup.

The options for the <OPTION> tag are:

■ *VALUE.* The value to be assigned for the choice. The value of the choice is what is sent back to the script, and doesn't have to be the same as what is presented to the end user.

■ *SELECTED.* If you want one of the choices to be a default, use the selected option in the OPTION tag.

On the CD

Consider the following tag (SELECT1.HTML):

```
<SELECT NAME="network">
<OPTION SELECTED VALUE="ethernet"> Ethernet
<OPTION VALUE="token16"> Token Ring - 16MB
<OPTION VALUE="token4"> Token Ring - 4MB
<OPTION VALUE="localtalk"> LocalTalk
</SELECT>
```

The results of this tag are shown in figures 15.2 and 15.3.

Fig. 15.2
The select element will use the default of a pop-up menu (size=1).

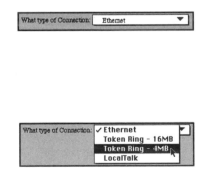

Fig. 15.3
The width of the pop-up menu is determined by the size of the entries listed with the OPTION elements.

IV

Using Forms

Suppose that you set the tag to be the following (SELECT2.HTML):

```
What type of Connection:
<SELECT MULTIPLE NAME="network">
<OPTION SELECTED VALUE="ethernet"> Ethernet
<OPTION VALUE="token16"> Token Ring - 16MB
<OPTION VALUE="token4"> Token Ring - 4MB
<OPTION VALUE="localtalk"> LocalTalk
</SELECT>
```

The results of this tag are shown in figure 15.4.

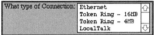

Fig. 15.4
If you use MULTIPLE within the <SELECT> tag, then the field becomes a list of choices.

Troubleshooting

I know the most common choices I want to present, but I want to allow people to enter their own value if they want to. How can I do that?

Your best bet is to display the common choices in a SELECT box or pop-up menu, with one of the options set to Other. Then include an INPUT text field or a TEXTAREA field right after the list of choices (see the code SELECT3.HTML).

```
What type of Connection:
<SELECT MULTIPLE NAME="network">
<OPTION SELECTED VALUE="ethernet"> Ethernet
<OPTION VALUE="token16"> Token Ring - 16MB
<OPTION VALUE="token4"> Token Ring - 4MB
<OPTION VALUE="localtalk"> LocalTalk
<OPTION VALUE="other"> Other...
</SELECT>
<BR>
If other, please specify:<INPUT TYPE="text" NAME="network_other">
```

The results are shown in figure 15.5.

On the CD

Fig. 15.5
This type of form layout provides both a common list and a place for exceptions.

INPUT

INPUT, unlike TEXTAREA or SELECT, is a single tag option for gathering information. INPUT contains all of the other options for acquiring information, including simple text fields, password fields, radio buttons, checkboxes, and the buttons to submit and reset the form.

The options for the INPUT tag are:

- *NAME*. Defines the name for the data. This field is required for all the types of input except SUBMIT and CLEAR.

- *SIZE*. The size of the input field in number of characters for text or password.

- *MAXLENGTH*. The maximum number of characters to be allowed for a text or password field.

- *VALUE*. For a text or password field, it defines the default text displayed. For a checkbox or radio button, it specifies the value that will be returned to the server if the box or button is selected. For the submit and reset buttons, it defines the text inside the button.

- *CHECKED*. To set a checkbox or radio button "on." It has no meaning for any other type of INPUT tag.

- *TYPE*. Sets the type of input field you want to display. (See the types in the following section.)

INPUT TYPE

This section describes the possible choices for INPUT TYPE.

TEXT

TEXT, the default input type, displays a simple line of text. You can use the options NAME (this is required), SIZE, MAXLENGTH, and VALUE with TEXT.

On the CD

For example, consider the following tag, the result of which is shown in figure 15.6 (see the code INPUT1.HTML):

```
A Phone Number: <INPUT TYPE="text" NAME="Phone" SIZE="15"
MAXLENGTH="12">
```

A Phone Number: 555-1212

Fig. 15.6
The INPUT TEXT
element provides a
very flexible input
field.

▶ See "Using Line
Break Tags,"
p. 297

IV

Using Forms

Troubleshooting

*I want to let someone put in a very long URL, but the screen's not that wide. How do I do
that?*

A good way to allow someone to put in an extremely long text line is to simply set
the size to 60 or 80 characters and to not set a maximum length. This will allow
someone to put in a very long string, even if you can't see it all at once.

PASSWORD

PASSWORD, a modified TEXT field, displays typed characters as bullets instead of the characters actually typed. Possible choices to include with the
type PASSWORD include: NAME (this is required), SIZE, MAXLENGTH, and
VALUE.

Consider the following tag, the results of which are shown in figure 15.7 (see
the code INPUT2.HTML):

On the CD

```
Enter the secret word: <INPUT TYPE="password" NAME-"secret_word"
Size="30" MAXLENGTH="30">
```

Enter the secret word: ••••••

Fig. 15.7
Although it will
look different in
different browsers,
the PASSWORD
element hides the
text that is typed.

CHECKBOX

CHECKBOX displays a simple checkbox that can be checked or empty; use a
checkbox when the choice is yes or no and doesn't depend on anything else.
Possible options to include with the TYPE text include: NAME (this is required), VALUE, and CHECKED (which defaults the checkbox as checked).

Consider the following tag (the results are shown in figure 15.8).

On the CD

```
<INPUT TYPE="checkbox" NAME="checkbox1" VALUE="checkbox_value1">A
checkbox
<INPUT TYPE="checkbox" NAME="checkbox2" VALUE="checkbox_value2"
CHECKED>A pre-selected checkbox
```

▶ See "Checkbox
and Radio
Button
Layouts,"
p. 304

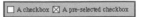

Fig. 15.8
Select the checkboxes that are commonly checked to make the form easier to use.

RADIO

RADIO is a more complex version of a checkbox, allowing only one of a set to be chosen. You can group radio buttons together using the NAME option; keep all buttons in the same group under one NAME. Possible options to include with the TYPE text include: NAME (this is required), VALUE, and CHECKED.

The results of the following tag are shown in figure 15.9.

```
<INPUT TYPE="radio" NAME="choice" VALUE="choice1"> Yes.
<INPUT TYPE="radio" NAME="choice" VALUE="choice2"> No.
```

Fig. 15.9
Without selecting yes or no, the end user can send back a "blank" value for this selection.

The following is another variation on the previous tag. The results are shown in figure 15.10.

```
One Choice:<BR>
<INPUT TYPE="radio" NAME="choice1" VALUE="choice1" CHECKED>(1)
<INPUT TYPE="radio" NAME="choice1" VALUE="choice2">(2)
<INPUT TYPE="radio" NAME="choice1" VALUE="choice3">(3)
<BR>
One Choice:<BR>
<INPUT TYPE="radio" NAME="choice2" VALUE="choice1" CHECKED>(1)
<INPUT TYPE="radio" NAME="choice2" VALUE="choice2">(2)
<INPUT TYPE="radio" NAME="choice2" VALUE="choice3">(3)
<INPUT TYPE="radio" NAME="choice2" VALUE="choice4">(4)
<INPUT TYPE="radio" NAME="choice2" VALUE="choice5">(5)
```

Tip
If you want to give a long list of possible choices, use the SELECT tag so the choice doesn't take up as much space on the page.

Fig. 15.10
The end user has more choices in this variation.

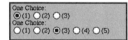

▶ See "Using List Tags," p. 303

Caution

If you don't specify a set of radio buttons or checkboxes with one of the values as SELECTED, then you could receive an empty field for that INPUT name.

RESET

RESET displays a push button with the preset function of clearing all the data in the form to its original value. You can use the VALUE option with the RESET tag to provide text other than "Reset" (the default) for the button.

For example, consider the following tag (RESET.HTML):

```
<INPUT TYPE="reset">
<BR>
<INPUT TYPE="reset" VALUE="Clear that form!">
```

The result is shown in figure 15.11.

On the CD

Fig. 15.11
The top button shows the default text for the RESET element.

SUBMIT

SUBMIT displays a push button with the preset function of sending the data in the form to the server to be processed. You can use the VALUE tag with Reset to provide text other than "Submit Query" (the default) for the button.

Consider, for example, this tag (SUBMIT.HTML):

```
<INPUT TYPE="submit">
<BR>
<INPUT TYPE="submit" VALUE="Send in the data!">
```

The result is shown in figure 15.12.

On the CD

Fig. 15.12
The top button shows the default text for the SUBMIT element.

From Here...

The tags and elements for creating fields on forms are straightforward and flexible. The FORM element details how to send in the completed form. The TEXTAREA element provides a field to enter multiple lines of text. The SE-LECT element gives a list of choices; and the INPUT element covers all the remaining pieces of the forms.

- Chapter 16, "Form Layout and Design," describes how to set up forms to be easy and fun while still getting the needed information.

- Chapter 17, "Server Scripts and Applications," details how to create the scripts and how to make them work with forms.

- Chapter 18, "Sample Forms with Code," shows three sets of forms with different types of fields and the scripts to run them from the server.

Chapter 16

Form Layout and Design

Forms can be easy-to-read, simple one or two entry affairs with little to display; they can also be terrifically complex devices. As forms get more complex, you need to carefully consider the layout of your forms. Think about how to make it obvious that certain titles are connected to certain fields, and think about how to make it easy for anyone to use. People are often put off by complex and hard to understand forms, so it's in your best interest to make them as easy and fun to use as possible.

Regardless of how complex or simple you want to make a form, you need to make it easy to understand.

In this chapter, you learn how to do the following:

- Use line breaks to make a form easier to read

- Mix forms and lists

- Create logical layouts for checkboxes and radio buttons

- Put multiple forms in one HTML document

Using Line Break Tags

When you mark up HTML documents, you usually just let the words wrap across the screen. While this flexibility is wonderful to have for segments of text, it can make reading a form incredibly difficult. A quick and simple solution is to include the line break tag, <BR>, to move something to the next line.

◄ See "Creating Text and Line Breaks in HTML," p. 176

Forcing Fields onto Separate Lines

If you want to have two fields, Name and Email address, you can simply mark it up as:

```
<HTML><HEAD>
<TITLE>Form Layout and Design</TITLE>
</HEAD><BODY>
<H1>Line Break Tags</H1>
<FORM>
Name: <INPUT NAME="name" SIZE="30">
Email address: <INPUT NAME="email" SIZE="40">
</FORM>
</BODY></HTML>
```

While this might look great now, it can wrap strangely on some WWW browsers and look shabby when displayed (see fig. 16.1).

Fig. 16.1
Without some organization, your forms can be very hard to read.

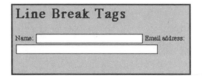

To split these lines and make them more readable, you need to include the line break tag <BR> between them.

```
<HTML><HEAD>
<TITLE>Form Layout and Design</TITLE>
</HEAD><BODY>
<H1>Line Break Tags</H1>
<FORM>
Name: <INPUT NAME="name" SIZE="30"><BR>
Email address: <INPUT NAME="email" SIZE="40">
</FORM>
</BODY></HTML>
```

Adding the <BR> tag between the two fields forces the browser to wrap the field to the next line, regardless of the width of the screen. The end result is shown in figure 16.2.

Fig. 16.2
The <BR> tag allows you to control the placement of form text.

Line Break Tags

Name:
Email address:

> **Note**
>
> The wrapping feature of HTML can work for you to help keep a form small in size. If you have several multiple choice items that could take up huge amounts of space on your form, you can try to keep them small and let them wrap closely together on the page.
>
> If you're using the SELECT tag, the width of the pop-up menu on the screen is directly related to the words in the options to be selected. If you keep it all small, you can provide a relatively large number of choices in a small area.

Working with Large Entry Fields

If you're working with long text entry fields, or perhaps with a TEXTAREA field, it's often easier to put the text just above the field, and then separate the different areas with paragraph breaks.

For example, if you have a text input line that is very long, or a long field description, it doesn't work well to put them side by side. Also, if you want to leave a space for comments, it's easier and looks nicer to have the field description just above the comment area. This makes it appear that there's more space to write in.

Here's an example of this sort of design:

On the CD

```
<HTML><HEAD>
<TITLE>Form Layout and Design</TITLE>
</HEAD><BODY>
<H1>Line Break Tags</H1>
<FORM>
Please enter the new title for the message:<BR>
<INPUT NAME="name" SIZE="40">
<HR>
Your comments:<BR>
<TEXTAREA ROWS="6" COLS="70"></TEXTAREA>
</FORM>
</BODY></HTML>
```

The result of this code is shown in figure 16.3.

> **Note**
>
> Most browsers automatically wrap large fields to the next line, treating it like an image. Because you don't know how wide (or narrow!) the client screen is, ensure the form will look as you want. If you want the field to be on the next line, put in a <BR> tag to make sure it will be!

Fig. 16.3
Using the line break tags allows you to put a label just above the field.

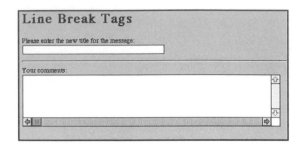

Using the Preformatted Text Tag to Line Up Forms

◀ See "Displaying Preformatted Text in Its Original Form," p. 183

A very common sight on many forms are simple text entry fields aligned haphazardly. A great trick for aligning text fields is to use the <PRE> tag. This ensures that some spaces appear before the field.

Caution

If you're using the <PRE> tags to line up fields, don't use any other HTML tags inside that area. Although the tags won't show up, they'll ruin the effect of lining everything up perfectly.

On the CD

The following is an example of an entry form that just uses line breaks:

```
<HTML><HEAD>
<TITLE>Form Layout and Design</TITLE>
</HEAD><BODY>
<H1>Using PRE tags</H1>
<FORM>
Name: <INPUT TYPE="text" NAME="name" SIZE="50"><BR>
Email: <INPUT TYPE="text" NAME="email" SIZE="50"><BR>
Street Address: <INPUT TYPE="text" NAME="street1" SIZE="30"><BR>
<INPUT TYPE="text" NAME="street2" SIZE="30"><BR>
City: <INPUT TYPE="text" NAME="city" SIZE="50"><BR>
State: <INPUT TYPE="text" NAME="state" SIZE="2"><BR>
Zip: <INPUT TYPE="text" NAME="zip" SIZE="10">
</FORM>
</BODY></HTML>
```

The end result of this code is displayed in figure 16.4.

Fig. 16.4
These fields were just organized with line breaks, so they align haphazardly.

IV

Using Forms

If you space things out and use the tags for preformatted text, you can get a very nice look to the form. The following is an example of aligning fields using the <PRE> tag:

```
<HTML><HEAD>
<TITLE>Form Layout and Design</TITLE>
</HEAD><BODY>
<H1>Using PRE tags</H1>
<FORM>
<PRE>
Name   : <INPUT TYPE="text" NAME="name" SIZE="50">
Email  : <INPUT TYPE="text" NAME="email" SIZE="50">
Street Address: <INPUT TYPE="text" NAME="street1" SIZE="30">
       : <INPUT TYPE="text" NAME="street2" SIZE="30">
City   : <INPUT TYPE="text" NAME="city" SIZE="50">
State  : <INPUT TYPE="text" NAME="state" SIZE="2">
Zip    : <INPUT TYPE="text" NAME="zip" SIZE="10">
</PRE>
</FORM>
</BODY></HTML>
```

Caution

Make sure you keep the size of the fields smaller than the general browser, or your lines will wrap off the screen. If the input fields have to be large, you can still add spaces before them and put them on separate lines.

The previous example code produces the layout shown in figure 16.5.

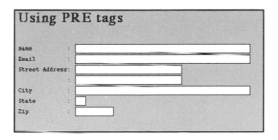

Fig. 16.5
The layout of the preformatted text is organized and easy to follow.

Troubleshooting

When I set up the preformatted text, it doesn't come out aligned in my HTML document! Why doesn't it match up?

In some text editors, the width of each letter on the screen isn't the same. If you're creating HTML documents with a text editor or word processor, make sure you have it set to use a monospaced font (each letter takes up exactly the same amount of space, including spaces), and that should solve the problem.

Using Paragraph Marks to Separate Form Sections

If you have a large form with different sections, it's handy to separate those sections. The paragraph tag, <P>, provides a way of adding some space, without making the delineation so hard that it appears to be another form.

For example, a simple comment form might have places for a name and e-mail address for a response, but these might not be a required part of the form. In this case, separate the "comment" part of the form from the area that's optional. It's also possible to make it more obvious by simply making some comments in the form, such as a small heading titled Optional.

A simple comment form with optional Name and Email fields can have the following code:

```
<HTML><HEAD>
<TITLE>Form Layout and Design</TITLE>
</HEAD><BODY>
<H1>Using &lt;P&gt; tags</H1>
<FORM>
<PRE>
<I><B>Optional:</B></I>
Name : <INPUT TYPE="text" NAME="name" SIZE="50">
Email : <INPUT TYPE="text" NAME="email" SIZE="50">
</PRE><P>
Your comments:<BR>
<TEXTAREA ROWS="6" COLS="70"></TEXTAREA>
</FORM>
</BODY></HTML>
```

This example, using both <PRE> tags and line break tags, produces the layout shown in figure 16.6.

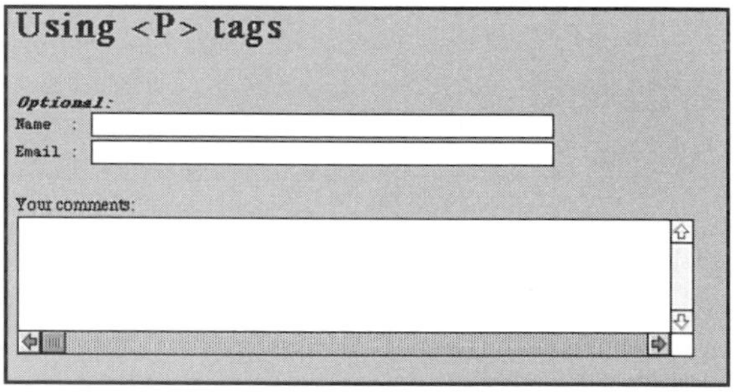

Fig. 16.6
Combining preformatted and wrapped areas can make your form very easy to use.

Using List Tags

There are a few occasions when line breaks and paragraph tags can't set up the form exactly as you'd like. At these times, list tags can provide just the right look! The best examples of using the list tags are when you need something either indented or numbered.

◀ See "Creating Definition Lists," p. 215

Indenting Form Entries with Descriptive Lists

On the WWW, it's common to see an Order form. Finding out what method of payment is wanted is a perfect example for using the descriptive list tags to lay out the choices. Indenting some items more than others makes the choices more obvious and easier to read.

> **Note**
>
> When I lay out lists, I indent the areas in my HTML documents that will be indented on-screen. This makes it easier to remember to finish with the descriptive list tag, </DL>.

For example, the following code shows how to separate a section of credit cards from the rest of the payment methods:

On the CD

```
<HTML><HEAD>
<TITLE>Form Layout and Design</TITLE>
</HEAD><BODY>
<H1>Descriptive List Tags</H1>
<FORM>
<DL>
<DT>How would you like to pay for this?
<DD><INPUT NAME="pay" TYPE="radio" VALUE="cash" CHECKED>Cash
<DD><INPUT NAME="pay" TYPE="radio" VALUE="check">Check
<DD><INPUT NAME="pay" TYPE="radio" VALUE="debit">Debit Card
   <DL>
   <DT>Credit Card
   <DD><INPUT NAME="pay" TYPE="radio" VALUE="mc">Mastercard
   <DD><INPUT NAME="pay" TYPE="radio" VALUE="visa">Visa
   <DD><INPUT NAME="pay" TYPE="radio" VALUE="disc">Discover
   <DD><INPUT NAME="pay" TYPE="radio" VALUE="ae">American Express
   </DL>
</DL>
</FORM>
</BODY></HTML>
```

IV

Using Forms

The result of the previous code is shown in figure 16.7.

Fig. 16.7
Descriptive lists
make the break-
down of choices
very obvious.

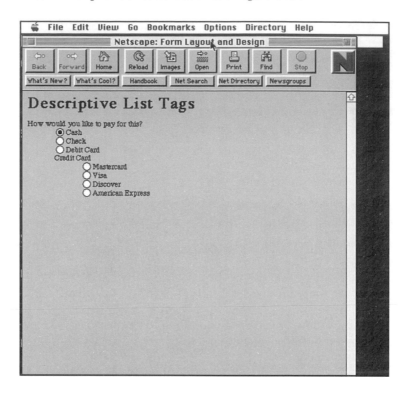

Using Ordered Lists to Number Fields

It's easy to display a numbered list if you use the ordered list tag, <OL>.

◀ See "Creating a
Numbered
List," p. 203

The following code uses the <OL> tag to automatically number the fields.

```
<HTML><HEAD>
<TITLE>Form Layout and Design</TITLE>
</HEAD><BODY>
<H1>Ordered List Tags</H1>
<FORM>
What are your three favorite books?
<OL>
<LI><INPUT NAME="1st" SIZE="20">
<LI><INPUT NAME="2nd" SIZE="20">
<LI><INPUT NAME="3nd" SIZE="20">
</OL>
</FORM>
</BODY></HTML>
```

The result of the code above is shown in figure 16.8.

Fig. 16.8
Using ordered lists, you can reorder fields without retyping all those numbers!

Checkbox and Radio Button Layouts

Checkboxes and radio buttons can provide a great deal of simple yes or no input. They can also be some of the hardest parts of a form to understand if they're not laid out correctly. There are three straightforward methods of layout: setting up the checkboxes and radio buttons in a line horizontally, using a list to order them vertically, or setting them up in a grid pattern.

Setting Up Checkboxes or Radio Buttons in a Line

Probably the easiest method is listing the checkboxes in a line horizontally. It has the benefits of being very simple to set up, relatively compact on the browser, and cohesive in understanding. The only caution with listing items in a horizontal line is to make sure there aren't too many for one line. The intent of the form might not be obvious if you let checkboxes wrap unintentionally.

```
<HTML><HEAD>
<TITLE>Form Layout and Design</TITLE>
</HEAD><BODY>
<H1>Checkboxes and Radio Buttons</H1>
<FORM>
What size would you like?<BR>
<INPUT NAME="size" TYPE="radio" VALUE="sm">:Small
<INPUT NAME="size" TYPE="radio" VALUE="md">:Medium
<INPUT NAME="size" TYPE="radio" VALUE="lg">:Large
<INPUT NAME="size" TYPE="radio" VALUE="x">:X-Large
<INPUT NAME="size" TYPE="radio" VALUE="xx">:XX-Large
</FORM>
</BODY></HTML>
```

The result of the previous code with a horizontal line of radio buttons is shown in figure 16.9.

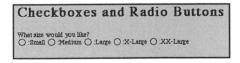

Fig. 16.9
This method works well for checkboxes too!

Lists of Checkboxes

◄ See "Creating Definition Lists," p. 215

When the choices get more complex than a simple line selection, it's best to forgo compactness and spread out the choices in a list.

```
<HTML><HEAD>
<TITLE>Form Layout and Design</TITLE>
</HEAD><BODY>
<H1>Checkboxes and Radio Buttons</H1>
<FORM>
<DL>
<DT>What machines do you work on?
<DD><INPUT NAME="mac" TYPE="checkbox">Macintosh
<DD><INPUT NAME="pc" TYPE="checkbox">IBM Compatible PC
    <DL>
    <DT>UNIX Workstation
    <DD><INPUT NAME="sun" TYPE="checkbox">Sun
    <DD><INPUT NAME="sgi" TYPE="checkbox">SGI
    <DD><INPUT NAME="next" TYPE="checkbox">NeXT
    <DD><INPUT NAME="aix" TYPE="checkbox">AIX
    <DD><INPUT NAME="lin" TYPE="checkbox">Linux
    <DD><INPUT NAME="other" TYPE="checkbox">Other...
    </DL>
</DL>
</FORM>
</BODY></HTML>
```

The result of using a descriptive list in the previous code is shown in figure 16.10.

Fig. 16.10
Complex choices are often easier to understand in a list format.

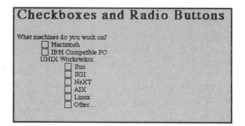

Making a Grid

The most complex method you have for displaying checkboxes is in a grid. Using preformatted text, you can space out the display to create a grid effect. The largest drawback is that it's time consuming to set up, and may not look perfect. You can also create a grid of radio buttons by substituting radio for checkbox in the <INPUT> tags.

On the CD

```
<HTML><HEAD>
<TITLE>Form Layout and Design</TITLE>
</HEAD><BODY>
<H1>Checkboxes and Radio Buttons</H1>
```

```
<FORM>
<PRE>
What combinations?
<!-- 1 checkbox = 2-3 chars in PRE -->
<PRE>
    Red Blue
Small <INPUT NAME="sr" TYPE="checkbox"> <INPUT NAME="sb"
➥TYPE="checkbox">
Medium <INPUT NAME="mr" TYPE="checkbox"> <INPUT NAME="mb"
➥TYPE="checkbox">
Large <INPUT NAME="lr" TYPE="checkbox"> <INPUT NAME="lb"
➥TYPE="checkbox">
</PRE>
</FORM>
</BODY></HTML>
```

Tip
When you're creating grids, try to give any checkbox or radio button two to three "spaces" to match up the grid.

The result of setting up the grid in the previous code is shown in figure 16.11.

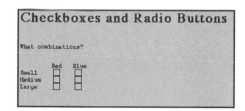

Fig. 16.11
When you're finished, grids provide a very intuitive method of making a choice.

Multiple Forms in a Document

It's quite possible to put multiple forms in a single document; it often makes the document more concise and easier to understand. An example of using multiple forms is a document with a number of different methods for searching. From one form, you can choose to do a search from any of a number of locations, having each <FORM> point to a different search method.

When including multiple forms in a document, visibly separate them to make them easier to understand. A common way to break up a form is to use the horizontal rule tag, <HR>, or a wide image in an <IMG> tag. Put line breaks before and after the tags.

For example, the following code shows how to separate three forms by using <HR> tags to break it up:

On the CD

```
<HTML><HEAD>
<TITLE>Form Layout and Design</TITLE>
</HEAD><BODY>
<H1>Multiple Forms in a Document</H1>

<FORM>
What size would you like?<BR>
```

```
<INPUT NAME="size" TYPE="radio" VALUE="sm">:Small
<INPUT NAME="size" TYPE="radio" VALUE="md">:Medium
<INPUT NAME="size" TYPE="radio" VALUE="lg">:Large
<INPUT NAME="size" TYPE="radio" VALUE="x">:X-Large
<INPUT NAME="size" TYPE="radio" VALUE="xx">:XX-Large
<P>
<INPUT TYPE="submit">
</FORM>

<HR>

<FORM>
<PRE>
Name    : <INPUT TYPE="text" NAME="name" SIZE="50">
Email   : <INPUT TYPE="text" NAME="email" SIZE="50">
Street Address: <INPUT TYPE="text" NAME="street1" SIZE="30">
      : <INPUT TYPE="text" NAME="street2" SIZE="30">
City    : <INPUT TYPE="text" NAME="city" SIZE="50">
State   : <INPUT TYPE="text" NAME="state" SIZE="2">
Zip     : <INPUT TYPE="text" NAME="zip" SIZE="10">
</PRE>
<P>
<INPUT TYPE="submit">
</FORM>

<HR>

<FORM>
<DL>
<DT>How would you like to pay for this?
<DD><INPUT NAME="pay" TYPE="radio" VALUE="cash" CHECKED>Cash
<DD><INPUT NAME="pay" TYPE="radio" VALUE="check">Check
<DD><INPUT NAME="pay" TYPE="radio" VALUE="debit">Debit Card
   <DL>
   <DT>Credit Card
   <DD><INPUT NAME="pay" TYPE="radio" VALUE="mc">Mastercard
   <DD><INPUT NAME="pay" TYPE="radio" VALUE="visa">Visa
   <DD><INPUT NAME="pay" TYPE="radio" VALUE="disc">Discover
   <DD><INPUT NAME="pay" TYPE="radio" VALUE="ae">American Express
   </DL>
</DL>
<P>
<INPUT TYPE="submit">
</FORM>
</BODY></HTML>
```

The result of breaking up multiple forms with the <HR> tag in the previous code is shown in figure 16.12.

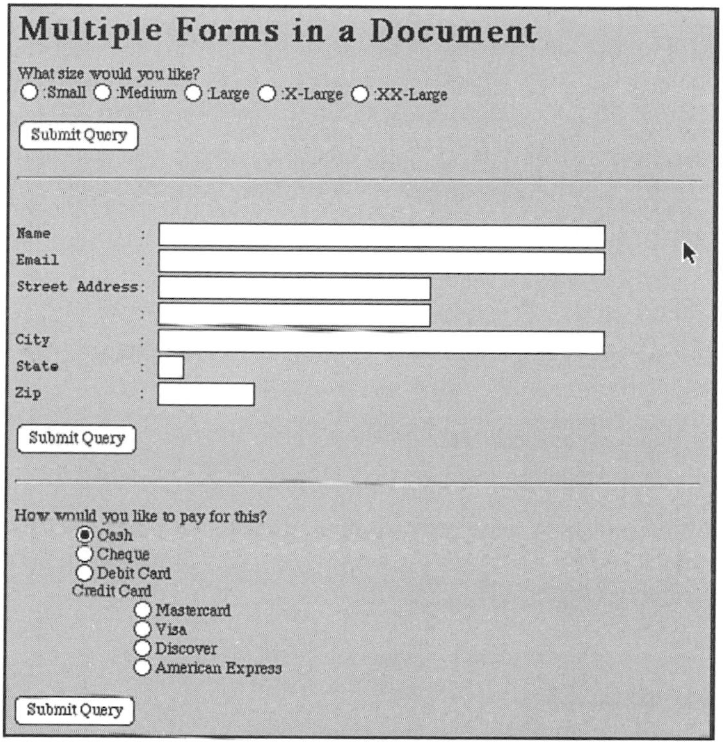

Fig. 16.12
By using horizontal rules to break up the multiple forms in this document, the intent of the form is easily apparent.

Troubleshooting

I put multiple forms in one document, but I only see one. Why aren't both showing up?

Check to make sure you finished one form before beginning another. If you didn't include the </FORM> tag to stop the first form, the second <FORM> tag will just be ignored.

Final Notes on Form Layouts

I have a few final notes on making forms easy to understand and use. When you're creating forms, it's always a good idea to keep the form on a single page. Because you can't control what browser someone uses to look at your pages, you need to use some general guidelines.

- If your form is very short, keep it under 10 or 14 lines. This ensures that it will fit on one page in most browsers. It won't always work, but it does make for a compact page that's easy for most people to see. A good trick for keeping the pages compact is using <SELECT> tags with the size set to one (to show a pop-up menu) or set to three or four (for a small scrolling window for multiple choices) instead of large numbers of checkboxes and radio buttons.

- If your form is large (more than two pages on any browser), don't put the <SUBMIT> or <RESET> buttons in the middle of the form. If you do, someone reading the form might not continue beyond those buttons and might miss an important part of the form.

- Put the fields on your form in a logical order. This sounds obvious, but it's easy to forget.

- Think about your forms well before you start creating them. If you know what you want to provide in the way of choices, it'll make your final layout much easier.

From Here...

There are a number of different layout techniques available for setting up forms on the Web. Regardless of how complex or simple the form, take some time to think about what will be the most intuitive layout and set up the form so it is easy to understand and as compact as possible.

- Chapter 17, "Server Scripts and Applications," details how to create scripts and how to make them work with forms.

- Chapter 18, "Sample Forms with Code," shows three sets of forms with different types of fields and the scripts to run them from the server.

Chapter 17

Server Scripts and Applications

Server scripts and applications are extensions to World Wide Web servers. They present flexibility; allowing the end user to interact with the HTML documents instead of just reading them. You can write scripts that mail the results of a form to an appropriate person, or you can write scripts that present the results of a program through the WWW.

Scripts are run from your server in a number of ways. Usually the scripts are kept in a special directory; the location of this directory is configured in your WWW server. When the server calls the URL that points to your script, it runs your script. The server waits for your script to give it some feedback, and hopefully displays that information.

In this chapter, you learn the following:

- What the Common Gateway Interface is and how it interacts with your scripts

- How to write a script to provide output

- Some of the common pitfalls and applications for scripts

> **Tip**
> If you're familiar with macros, learning about scripts will be easy. They're essentially the same.

Linking Data to Server Applications

The WWW server talks to your program (and vice-versa) through a standard called CGI (Common Gateway Interface). With this standard, you can write programs to provide information through the WWW.

Today, WWW servers come with some CGI programs already written for you—one of the most common being the Imagemap script. The Imagemap

◀ See "The
Imagemap
Program,"
p. 273

script takes information from the server (the coordinates of the place where you clicked an image) and then uses that information to determine which URL it should open.

Giving Information to the Server

The CGI interface accepts a couple of lines of information that tells the server what it should be doing. You can have the server send back data—anything from an HTML document to a sound file; or tell the server to reference a different URL. If your program doesn't tell the server what to do, you get an error.

Sending Out a Document

If you want to send a document through the server, you need to tell the server you're going to do that. Then you need to tell it what kind of document you're sending. The line you send to the server is:

```
Content-type: type/subtype
```

Type and subtype are MIME types for the information you're sending out. If you're sending back a plain text (ASCII) document, the type would be listed as "text/plain." To send back an HTML document, you send "text/html" to the server. After you send the information about what you're sending, you need to include a blank line to let the server know you're done telling it what this stuff is, and to accept whatever comes next as the information you want the end user to see.

If you're writing scripts to send out HTML documents, the first two lines out of that script should be Content-type: text/html followed by a blank line.

Note

MIME stands for Multipurpose Internet Mail Extension. It's an Internet standard (RFC 1521 and 1522, if you're interested) that was originally created to help transfer all sorts of different files across e-mail. Since its creation, it's been used not only for e-mail, but also for Gopher and the Web. It provides a common method to transfer data and then tells your program how to deal with it.

There are hundreds of standard MIME types now registered. Any program might have a MIME type. For example, an Adobe Acrobat document in PDF format would have a MIME type of "application/pdf," while a GIF image has a MIME type of "image/gif" and an AU format sound file has MIME type of "audio/basic." The most common types of output for your scripts files are going to be plain ASCII text and HTML documents, so the ones you're interested in are "text/plain" and "text/html."

Referencing Another URL

The other option that the CGI standard allows is to tell the server to reference another URL. Instead of sending back information from your script, it tells the WWW server to fetch another document and present that. This is exactly the method the Imagemap script uses to tell the server to send out an HTML page.

To tell the server to find another URL and send it out, you write a script to send the line

```
Location: URL address
```

URL can be a partial URL on your server or a full URL to any number of resources on the Internet. Just like the Content-type line, you need to follow the Location: line with a blank line to let the server know you're done, and that it can get the proper resource and present it.

For example, if you want to tell the server to go the WWW server at CERN, you send out Location: http://www.cern.ch/ followed by a blank line.

Getting Information from the Server

The most common reason why you might want to get information from the server is that you've written a form and want the script to do something with the information you're sending.

The way the server passes this information back to the programs is by setting a number of environment variables. Your scripts read them and then determine what to do. Possibly the most important variable that you're going to be interested in is the REQUEST_METHOD variable. The REQUEST_METHOD variable is either GET or POST, depending on the form used to send the information in.

If the REQUEST_METHOD is GET, then you want to check into a different environment variable called QUERY_STRING, which contains the information from the form.

If the REQUEST_METHOD is POST, then you need to look at the variable CONTENT_LENGTH, which is going to contain the number of characters that have been sent back through the program's standard input. You then need to grab that many characters from the standard input to take a look at.

Tip

If you want to do something fun, like create a link to a random URL, you can write a script to choose a URL from a list and have the server find and display that document.

IV

Using Forms

> **Caution**
>
> The server won't send back an end of file character, so you have to be careful grabbing information from the standard input with the POST method. Make sure you check the CONTENT_LENGTH variable for the number of characters and then read in that many.

Finally, you need to figure out what's been sent back to you. Information that's sent back to the script is encoded in a standard URL format. That means the form has automatically changed all the spaces to the + symbol, and any other non-text characters to %##, where ## is a hexadecimal representation of the ASCII character. In some servers, spaces also get sent back as %20 (20 is the hexadecimal code for the space).

Data sent back from a FORM is set up as a bunch of pairs of name=value; the pairs separated by the & symbol. For example, if a form sent back a variable called name with the value Frederick and a variable named age with the value 6, the stream of information you'd see as the data is:

```
name=Frederick&age=6
```

> **Troubleshooting**
>
> *I'm reading the data from a form that's using GET, but I can't seem to find all the information I typed in the form. Where did it go?*
>
> When you use the GET method with forms, it tacks on the information to the end of the URL it sends. In general, URLs have a finite length (some 1024 characters or so, depending on the server). If you're trying to send in more information than can fit, it just gets truncated.

Because you're certainly not the first to have to go through all this trouble, others have made some scripts available. They take the pain out of doing the reading and decoding yourself.

The AA Archie gateway contains the "sh" commands to invoke sed and awk (UNIX comments) to turn this data into a bunch of separate environment variables. The AA Archie gateway is available at **ftp://ftp.ncsa.uiuc.edu/ Web/httpd/UNIX/ncsa_httpd/cgi/AA-1.2.tar.Z**.

If you're a C programmer, you can get the NCSA default strings that turn the query string into a bunch of C structures. The NCSA default strings are available at **ftp://ftp.ncsa.uiuc.edu/Web/httpd/UNIX/ncsa_httpd/ cgi/ncsa-default.Z**.

There's also the PERL CGI library that reads both GET or POST data and turns it into a bunch of key/value pairs. The PERL CGI library is available at **ftp:// ftp.ncsa.uiuc.edu/Web/httpd/UNIX/ncsa_httpd/cgi/cgi-lib.pl.Z**.

Creating CGI Scripts

Scripts can be extremely simple or extremely complex. The programs you write are the limits of what can be produced through the WWW. If you're working on a UNIX platform, the platform probably already has a number of programs that you can use to help you write scripts.

> **Note**
>
> If you're working on a UNIX platform, you can do a great deal with the various available programs. If you don't already have some of these utility programs available to you, you might want to see whether you can find them and get them running on your machine:
>
> ■ *Perl.* A programming language in it's own right, PERL has a great deal of flexibility and is probably easier to learn than C for writing scripts. In addition, there are lots of people out there already writing CGI scripts for PERL, and there are some libraries to help you work with forms.
>
> ■ *Grep, Sed, and Awk.* This trio of standard UNIX utility programs represent some incredibly powerful programming that can save you a lot of time. While using them within PERL scripts probably isn't very efficient, they can be a lot quicker to learn and get going than to learn the intricacies of PERL. In addition, you can create some quick programs by just tacking together a shell script until you have the time to "do it right" in either PERL or C.

On the CD

Creating a Simple Script

If you just want to provide a simple message, the script can be a set of print or echo statements. For example, the following is a basic Bourne Shell script:

```
#!/bin/sh
echo "Content-type: text/plain";
echo;
echo "This is my message.";
```

If you ran this program directly (not through the WWW server), you'd see the output as

```
Content-type: text/plain
This is my message.
```

If you run this script through the server (that is, if you point your browser at the URL), you see what's shown in figure 17.1.

Fig. 17.1

When you output plain text to the browser, it treats it like preformatted text.

Troubleshooting

I keep getting these errors when I try to access my script. What do they mean?

The most common cause is an error in the script. If the script has an error and sends out warning messages, then the server won't understand what to do with the information.

If you're seeing 500 Server Error, your script probably isn't starting out by telling the server what kind of information it's presenting.

If you're seeing 403 Forbidden, then it's probably because the server doesn't have permission to run the program. Most WWW servers are set up so that you have to have permission to execute the program.

Creating a Script that Puts Out HTML

This gets a little more complex when it's an HTML document. To do this, you might add a few lines that send out HTML tags and lets the server know you're sending it an HTML document.

Now, your short script looks like the following:

```
#!/bin/sh
echo "Content-type: text/html";
echo;
echo "<HTML>"
echo "<HEAD><TITLE>My Message Page</TITLE></HEAD>";
echo "<BODY>"
echo "<H1>This is my message.</H1>";
echo "</BODY></HTML>";
```

When you run it, it appears as shown in figure 17.2.

Fig. 17.2
Remember to have
your script include
all of the appropri-
ate tags for an
HTML document!

Troubleshooting

*I put in all of these additions, and all I saw was this plain text of the codes I put into the
script. Why isn't the server parsing this out to show it in HTML like it should?*

If you're seeing the HTML tags, it's most likely because you forgot to tell the server
that the information you're sending is an HTML document. Check the very first lines
you print out, and make sure they're printing out Content-type: text/html, not
Content-type: text/plain.

Creating a Script to Use Other Applications

Say you want to write a script that does something and then outputs the
information it receives. It's pretty easy to write a script that issues the FINGER
command and returns the information through the WWW. Simply put the
finger information in the script, and then send it out again—except wrap it in
a blanket of HTML tags.

The following is a simple PERL program to do this (FINGER.PL):

On the CD

```perl
#!/usr/local/bin/perl
# issue the 'finger' command and put it's output in the array
"data".
@data = 'finger';
# print out the beginning stuff to tell the server you're sending
it
# an HTML document.
print "Content-type: text/html\n\n";
# print out the HTML tags that you want to appear before the output
# from the finger command
print "<HTML><HEAD>\n";
print "<TITLE>finger script</TITLE>\n";
print "</HEAD><BODY>\n";
# make sure you output this as preformatted text
print "<PRE>\n";
#print out the finger command
print @data;
#print out the final HTML tags to complete the document properly.
print "</PRE>\n";
print "</BODY>\n";
print "</HTML>\n";
```

The results of this program are shown in figure 17.3.

Fig. 17.3
The finger script
uses the
preformatted text
elements to make
sure it looks
correct on the
browser.

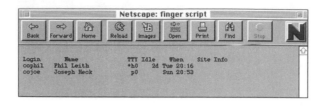

Caution

One of the most common problems you can have (and quickly see) when writing
scripts that take the output from other programs is remembering that you have to
include the <PRE> and </PRE> tags for text that's been preformatted. If you don't,
then your WWW browser will automatically try to wrap all that nice table-like information into a single line or two, which would make it extremely hard to read and, for
the most part, useless.

Writing Scripts to Read in Data from a Form

If you're using PERL, the easiest way to read in data from a form and do
something with it is to use the CGI-LIB.PL Library. If you expect data to be
there, read that data—then process it and return some output. You can get
this at **ftp://ftp.ncsa.uiuc.edu/Web/httpd/UNIX/ncsa_httpd/cgi/
cgi-lib.pl.Z**.

Start the script with the following:

```
do "cgi-lib.pl" || die "Fatal Error: Can't load cgi library";
```

This ensures that you load up CGI-LIB.PL to use as you want. If it can't, it
writes Fatal Error: Can't load cgi library into the server error log. The first
thing you do is read in the data. The line

```
&ReadParse
```

invokes the subroutine ReadParse from the CGI-LIB.PL program and does all
the nasty work for you. From there, all the variables are in the array @in. To
read them out, you can use $in{'name'} to get the data in the variable selected
by name. For example, if you had the data name=Frederick&age=6, then
&ReadParse would allow you to access the value of age with $in{'age'}.
The line

```
print "The age is ${'age'}.\n";
```

would print out the line

```
The age is 6.
```

> **Caution**
>
> When you print out characters from a PERL (or other) script, remember that the symbols for quote ("), backslash (\), exclamation mark (!), and others are special characters. To keep the script from trying to use them as part of the program, make sure you "escape" them out using a backslash (\). For example, if you wanted to print out the line
>
> ```
> <A HREF="http://www.cern.ch/">
> ```
>
> you have to put it into the PERL script as
>
> ```
> print "<A HREF=\"http://www.cern.ch/\">\n";
> ```

Tricks of the Trade

One of the fancier tricks in programming scripts to output HTML data is to have the script present the form you want to receive data from. You can accomplish this by trying to read in the data from the form, and if it's not there, then display the form. The following is a short example of how this might work (FORM.PL):

```perl
#!/usr/local/bin/perl
do "cgi-lib.pl" ¦¦ die "Fatal Error: Can't load cgi library";
#calls subroutine in cgi-lib.pl library (documented in library)
&ReadParse;
print "Content-type: text/html\n\n";
if ($#in>=0) {
  print "<HTML>\n";
  print "<HEAD>\n";
  print "<TITLE>Test Form Results</TITLE>\n";
  print "</HEAD>\n";
  print "<BODY>\n";
  print "<H1>Test Form Results</H1>\n";
  print "<P>\n";
  print "<PRE>\n";
  print "<HR>\n";
  print @in;
  print "<HR>\n";
  print "$in";
  print "<HR>\n";
  print "</PRE>\n";
  print "</BODY>\n";
  print "</HTML>\n";
} else {
  print "<HTML>\n";
  print "<HEAD>\n";
```

```
        print "<TITLE>Test Form</TITLE>\n";
        print "</HEAD>\n";
        print "<BODY>\n";
        print "<H1>Test Form</H1>\n";
        print "<ISINDEX>\n";
        print "</BODY>\n";
        print "</HTML>\n";
    }
```

When this code is called through the server, it tries to read any variables that might be waiting for it (assuming it was being answered by a form). When it doesn't find any, it presents the screen shown in figure 17.4.

Fig. 17.4

The form is presented by the script; it isn't a separate HTML document.

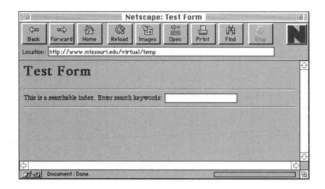

When you type a keyword to search for (the script uses the simple ISINDEX form) and press return, it prints out the results of the query, which are the variables "@in" and "$in" (see fig. 17.5).

Fig. 17.5

The top line shows the results after decoding it from the standard URL format.

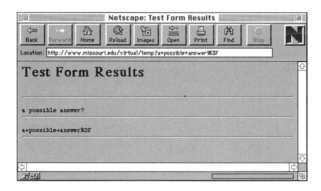

Another common desire is to mail the contents of a form to someone. You can do this by writing out the variables to a file and then mailing that file to someone. Using this method, however, can lead to some problems: it's easy to have two people trying to use the same script at once! A good solution is that when you write the file that you're going to send, you append something onto the file name to make it unique—a process-id number will do the trick. For example, the Perl script below will take anything sent to it from a form and mail it to me@somewhere, as well as displaying the following message for the user (REPLY.PL):

```perl
#!/usr/local/bin/perl
#Includes cgi-lib file; if cgi-lib doesn't exist, returns malformed
#header error to /tmp/httpd_errlog
do "cgi-lib.pl" || die "Fatal Error: Can't load cgi library";
#calls subroutine in cgi-lib.pl library (documented in library)
&ReadParse;
#tells http server incoming data is text html
print "Content-type: text/html\n\n";
#returns acknowledgment of mail submission and provides a link back
print "<H2>Thank you\!  I will process your request as soon as";
print " possible.</H2>\n<p>";
print "<H3>Back to the <A HREF=\"/index.html\">";
print "The Front Page</A></H3>";
#assigns process id to $pid
$pid=$$;
#opens up comment file for writing
open(COMMENTSFILE,">/tmp/my_comment.$pid");
print COMMENTSFILE @in;
close COMMENTSFILE;
#sends comment file as mail to user
$command="mail me@somewhere < /tmp/my_comment.$pid";
system($command);
#erases temp file
unlink("/tmp/my_comment.$pid");
```

Caution

Because this last bit of code goes into issuing UNIX commands from within a script, be *very* careful when taking information from a form of any sort and executing it directly. The above script is meant to specifically circumvent that, preventing some possible UNIX security problems.

It's quite possible for someone to enter in a few special characters to issue another command if you take a user's input directly.

From Here...

Hopefully, this chapter has given you not only some insight, but also some concrete examples of how to write scripts to work with the WWW and forms.

The scripts are small programs that read in variables with the help of some libraries, and present some sort of output to the user. For further information on forms, see the following chapter:

- Chapter 18, "Sample Forms with Code," shows three sets of forms with different types of fields and the scripts to run them from the server.

Sample Forms with Code

The sample forms in this chapter provide some examples from which you can create your own forms. They cover a variety of topics, as well as display a number of different types of form elements.

In this chapter, you learn to

- Set up a customer satisfaction survey and a script to mail the results to you

- Create an online product order form and do some simple error checking before accepting the order

- Set up a user registration form with some simple password checking

Sample Customer Satisfaction Survey

The Customer Satisfaction Survey is a very common form to find on the WWW. A variation of it is a response form that allows browsers that don't support the Mailto tag to send a message to someone. It provides a quick and easy way to send comments back to a specific person.

HTML Document

The Customer Satisfaction Survey form is available on the CD-ROM by the file name SURVEY.HTML. It's a short form with only a few fields that can be expanded to cover a wide variety of needs.

On the CD

Listing 18.1   Customer Satisfaction Survey

```
<HTML>
<HEAD>
<TITLE>Customer Satisfaction Survey</TITLE>
</HEAD>
<BODY>
<H1>Customer Satisfaction Survey</H1>
We would very much like to have your thoughts
on the services we provide. Please help us out
by filling out this form and submitting it.
<HR>
<FORM METHOD="POST" ACTION="http://my.www.server/cgi-bin/
survey.pl">
<P>
<CENTER><I><H2>Optional Information</H2></I></CENTER>
<PRE>
Your Name:           <INPUT TYPE="text" NAME="name" SIZE="20">
Phone Number:        <INPUT TYPE="text" NAME="phone" SIZE="15">
Your E-mail Address: <INPUT TYPE="text" NAME="e-mail" SIZE="50">
<HR>
How would you rate our service?
<INPUT TYPE="radio" NAME="rating" VALUE="Excellent">: Excellent
<INPUT TYPE="radio" NAME="rating" VALUE="Good">: Good
<INPUT TYPE="radio" NAME="rating" VALUE="Reasonable">: Reasonable
<INPUT TYPE="radio" NAME="rating" VALUE="So-so">: So-so
<INPUT TYPE="radio" NAME="rating" VALUE="Poor">: Poor
</PRE>
<BR>
Any Comments on how we can help you further?<BR>
<TEXTAREA NAME="comments" ROWS=6 COLS=60></TEXTAREA>
<P>
<INPUT TYPE="submit" VALUE="Send in the survey!">
</FORM>
</BODY>
</HTML>
```

◄ See "Using the Preformatted Text Tag to Line Up Forms," p. 300

◄ See "Displaying Preformatted Text in Its Original Form," p. 183

This HTML document purposely allows the end user to not specify a rating if they don't want to. If you want to make sure they choose at least one of the ratings, set one of the radio buttons to SELECTED in the form.

To make the form look nicer, I used the <PRE> and </PRE> tags to line up the text fields.

The Associated Server Script

On the CD

The script SURVEY.PL (available on the CD-ROM) is what the server invokes to work with information the end user presented with the survey form. The script is written in PERL and requires the PERL CGI Library. The variables listed in the script also correspond directly to the names that I gave the fields in the file SURVEY.HTML.

The form collects the information, using the CGI Library to decode it. It then writes the information to a file, and mails that file to the e-mail address *me@somewhere*. While the script is creating and mailing this file, it also sends out an HTML document to the browser. Finally, it erases the file it created for this response.

◀ See "Getting Information from the Server," p. 313

◀ See "Writing Scripts to Read in Data from a Form," p. 318

IV

Using Forms

Listing 18.2   SURVEY.PL

```perl
#!/usr/local/bin/perl
#Includes cgi-lib file; if cgi-lib doesn't exist, returns malformed
#header error
do "cgi-lib.pl" || die "Fatal Error: Can't load cgi library";
#calls the subroutine in the cgi-lib.pl library
#to read in the variables from the form and set them up
#as key=value pairs in the array @in
&ReadParse;
#tells http server incoming data is text html
print "Content-type: text/html\n\n";
#returns acknowledgment of mail submission and provides a link back
print "<HTML>";
print "<HEAD><TITLE>Thank You\!</TITLE>";
print "</HEAD><BODY>";
print "<H2>Thank you\!</H2>";
print "We value your input highly\!";
print "<P>";
print "We've mailed off your survey to\n";
print "be collated as soon as possible\n";
print "<HR>";
print "<H3>Back to the <A HREF=\"/index.html\">";
print "Front Page</A></H3>";
print "</BODY></HTML>";
#assigns process id to $pid
$pid=$$;
#opens up comment file for writing
open(COMMENTSFILE,">/tmp/my_comment.$pid");
#enter the form data into the file to be mailed
print COMMENTSFILE "CUSTOMER SATISFACTION SURVEY REPORT\n";
print COMMENTSFILE "- - - - - - - - - - - - - - - - - -\n";
print COMMENTSFILE "optional information:\n";
print COMMENTSFILE "   Name:  $in{'name'}\n";
print COMMENTSFILE "   Phone: $in{'phone'}\n";
print COMMENTSFILE "   E-mail: $in{'e-mail'}\n";
print COMMENTSFILE;
print COMMENTSFILE "Rating: $in{'rating'}\n";
print COMMENTSFILE;
print COMMENTSFILE "Comments:\n";
print COMMENTSFILE "$in{'comments'}";
#close out file to be mailed
close COMMENTSFILE;
#sends comment file as mail to user
$command="mail me@somewhere < /tmp/my_comment.$pid";
system($command);
#erases temp file
unlink("/tmp/my_comment.$pid");
```

Viewer Interpretation

Figure 18.1 shows the end user's view of Listing 18.1.

Fig. 18.1
The survey form shows two separate areas of the form: one for comments and one to provide information about yourself.

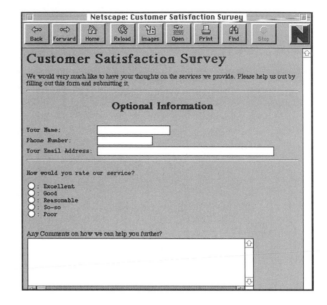

Script Output

The end result of submitting the form, the code shown in Listing 18.2, is shown in figure 18.2.

The mail the script sent is shown in Listing 18.3:

Fig. 18.2
The SURVEY.PL script provides an HTML document with a link to another page so the end user doesn't have to flip back through the documents.

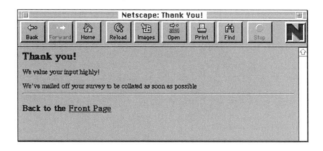

Listing 18.3   E-Mail from the Survey Form

```
Date: Mon, 1 Mar 1995 00:14:45 GMT
To: me@somewhere
CUSTOMER SATISFACTION SURVEY REPORT
- - - - - - - - - - - - - - - - - -
optional information:
   Name:   My Name
   Phone:  (111) 555-1212
   E-mail:  me@somewhere
Rating: Good
Comments:
I'm very glad you made this available!
```

Sample Online Product Order Form

The Online Product Order form is another common form, and it's getting more popular by the day. The variations on this form include any sort of standard request for specific items, including a simple test.

HTML Document

The Online Product Order form is available on the CD-ROM by the file name ORDER.HTML. Similar to the Survey form, this is a short form with only a few fields that you can expand as needed.

On the CD

Listing 18.4   Online Product Order Form

```
<HTML>
<HEAD>
<TITLE>Online Product Order Form</TITLE>
</HEAD>
<BODY>
<H1>Online Product Order Form</H1>
<HR>
<FORM METHOD="POST" ACTION="http://my.www.server/cgi-bin/order.pl">
<H2>Costumer Information</H2>
<PRE>
Your Name:       <INPUT TYPE="text" NAME="name" SIZE="40">
Phone Number:    <INPUT TYPE="text" NAME="phone" SIZE="15">
Street Address:  <INPUT TYPE="text" NAME="address1" SIZE="40">
Street Address:  <INPUT TYPE="text" NAME="address2" SIZE="40">
City:            <INPUT TYPE="text" NAME="city" SIZE="40">
State:           <INPUT TYPE="text" NAME="state" SIZE="2">
Zip Code:        <INPUT TYPE="text" NAME="zip" SIZE="10">
</PRE>
<H2>Widget's Available</H2>
please select number and size of widgets to be ordered
```

◀ See "Checkbox and Radio Button Layouts," p. 304

(continues)

Listing 18.4   Continued

```
<PRE>
Round Widget              Number: <INPUT NAME="num_round" SIZE="6"> </PRE>
Small:<INPUT TYPE="radio" NAME="r_size" VALUE="small">
Medium:<INPUT TYPE="radio" NAME="r_size" VALUE="medium">
Large:<INPUT TYPE="radio" NAME="r_size" VALUE="large">
<P>
<PRE>
Square Widget             Number: <INPUT NAME="num_square"
                                  SIZE="6">
</PRE>
Small:<INPUT TYPE="radio" NAME="sq_size" VALUE="small">
Medium:<INPUT TYPE="radio" NAME="sq_size" VALUE="medium">
Large:<INPUT TYPE="radio" NAME="sq_size" VALUE="large">
<P>
<PRE>
Triangular Widget         Number: <INPUT NAME="num_triangle"
                                  SIZE="6">
</PRE>
Small:<INPUT TYPE="radio" NAME="tr_size" VALUE="small">
Medium:<INPUT TYPE="radio" NAME="tr_size" VALUE="medium">
Large:<INPUT TYPE="radio" NAME="tr_size" VALUE="large">
<HR>
<INPUT TYPE="submit" VALUE="Send in the order">
<INPUT TYPE="reset" VALUE="Clear the form">
</FORM>
</BODY>
</HTML>
```

Figure 18.3 shows the end user's view of the form ORDER.HTML.

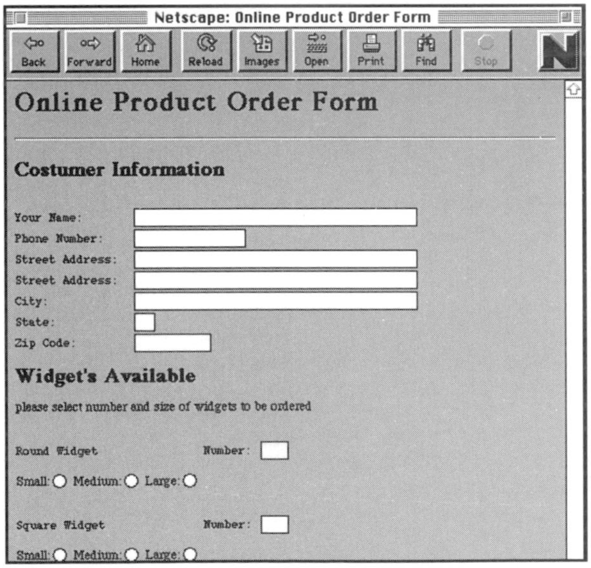

Fig. 18.3

A combination of preformatted text and normal text can make a very compact form.

The Associated Server Script

The script ORDER.PL (available on the CD-ROM) is what the server invokes to read in the form's information. As with the SURVEY.PL code, this script is written in PERL and requires the PERL CGI Library. The variables listed in the script also correspond directly to the names I gave the fields in the file ORDER.HTML.

On the CD

IV

Using Forms

The form uses the CGI Library to retrieve and decode the information from the form. It then does some simple checking to make sure that one of the fields (Name) has been completed. If it hasn't, it sends back an HTML document saying so. If the Name field was completed, the form does a little more error checking to make sure the numbers make sense and writes the verified information to a file. After this, it follows the same kind of setup as the SURVEY.PL: it mails that file to the e-mail address *me@somewhere,* sends an HTML document to the browser, and then erases the file it created for this order.

◀ See "Getting Information from the Server," p. 313

◀ See "Writing Scripts to Read in Data from a Form," p. 318

Listing 18.5   ORDER.PL

```perl
#!/usr/local/bin/perl
#Includes cgi-lib file; if cgi-lib doesn't exist, returns malformed
#header error
do "cgi-lib.pl" || die "Fatal Error: Can't load cgi library";
#calls the subroutine in the cgi-lib.pl library
#to read in the variables from the form and set them up
#as key=value pairs in the array @in
&ReadParse;
#do a simple check to make sure the necessary fields are
#completed.
$name = $in{'name'};
unless ($name > 0) {
  #tells http server incoming data is text html
  #sends back NO-GO for order form
  print "Content-type: text/html\n\n";
  print "<HTML>";
  print "<HEAD><TITLE>Can not process order</TITLE>";
  print "</HEAD><BODY>";
  print "<H1>Sorry\!</H1>";
  print "We are unable to process your order at this\n";
  print "time because we did not receive your name.\n";
  print "<P>";
  print "<H2><I>Widget Manufacturer's Inc.</I></H2>";
  print "<HR>";
  print "<H3>Back to the <A HREF=\"/index.html\">";
  print "Front Page</A></H3>";
  print "<H3>Back to the <A HREF=\"/order.html\">";
  print "Order Form</A></H3>";
  print "</BODY></HTML>";
```

(continues)

Listing 18.5   Continued

```
    #quit the script - not enough information was present to
    #place an order.
    exit;
}
# Do any error checking you need...
$round = $in{'num_round'};
if ($round < 1) {
  $round = 0;
}
$square = $in{'num_square'};
if ($square < 1) {
  $square = 0;
}
$tri = $in{'num_triangle'};
if ($tri < 1 ) {
  $tri = 0;
}
#assigns process id to $pid
$pid=$$;
#opens up comment file for writing
open(ORDER,">/tmp/order_info.$pid");
#enter the form data into the file to be mailed
print ORDER "          WIDGET ORDER FORM\n";
print ORDER "- - - - - - - - - - - - - - - - - - -\n";
print ORDER "   Name:  $in{'name'}\n";
print ORDER "  Phone:  $in{'phone'}\n";
print ORDER "Address:  $in{'address1'}\n";
print ORDER "       :  $in{'address2'}\n";
print ORDER "   City:  $in{'city'}\n";
print ORDER "  State:  $in{'state'}\n";
print ORDER "    Zip:  $in{'zip'}\n";
print ORDER "- - - - - - - - - - - - - - - - - - -\n";
print ORDER;
print ORDER "$in{'name'} ordered:\n";
print ORDER "     $round $in{'r_size'} Round Widgets\n";
print ORDER "     $square $in{'sq_size'} Square Widgets\n";
print ORDER "     $tri $in{'tr_size'} Triangular Widgets\n";
print ORDER;
print ORDER "- - - - - - - - - - - - - - - - - - -\n";
#close out file to be mailed
close COMMENTSFILE;
#sends comment file as mail to user
$command="mail me@somewhere < /tmp/order_info.$pid";
system($command);
#erases temp file
unlink("/tmp/order_info.$pid");
#tells http server incoming data is text html
#acknowledges receipt of information
```

```
print "Content-type: text/html\n\n";
print "<HTML>";
print "<HEAD><TITLE>Thank You\!</TITLE>";
print "</HEAD><BODY>";
print "<H2>Thank you\!</H2>";
print "According to our information, you ordered:\n";
print "<PRE>\n";
print "      $round $in{'r_size'} Round Widgets\n";
print "      $square $in{'sq_size'} Square Widgets\n";
print "      $tri $in{'tr_size'} Triangular Widgets\n";
print "</PRE>\n";
print "<P>";
print "We will contact you by phone for payment\n";
print "instructions\n";
print "<P>";
print "<H2><I>Widget Manufacturer's Inc.</I></H2>";
print "<HR>";
print "<H3>Back to the <A HREF=\"/index.html\">";
print "Front Page</A></H3>";
print "</BODY></HTML>";
```

When the user completes the form with no errors, you receive the HTML document shown in figure 18.4.

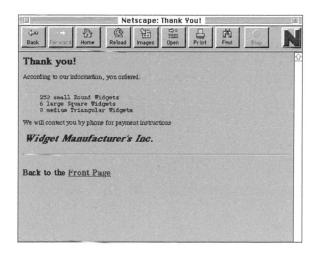

Fig. 18.4
The completed message verifies the order, and provides a link to another page.

If the program finds any errors in the order form, you receive the HTML document shown in figure 18.5.

Fig. 18.5
Because there could be multiple problems in filling out the forms, the error message is as specific as possible.

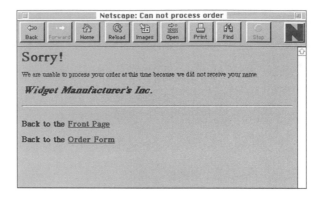

Script Output

Listing 18.6 shows the information you receive through e-mail when the end user correctly completes the order form.

Listing 18.6   E-Mail from the Survey Form

```
              WIDGET ORDER FORM
- - - - - - - - - - - - - - - - - - - -
    Name:  My Name
   Phone:  (111) 555-1212
 Address:  123 My Street
       :
    City:  Rockville
   State:  ZZ
     Zip:  12345-6789
- - - - - - - - - - - - - - - - - - - -
My Name ordered:
     253 small Round Widgets
     6 large Square Widgets
     0 medium Triangular Widgets
- - - - - - - - - - - - - - - - - - - -
```

You can easily modify the script to print order forms directly to your printer (in UNIX) by changing the line:

```
$command="mail me@somewhere < /tmp/order_info.$pid";
```

to:

```
$command="lpr -P Office_Printer < /tmp/order_info.$pid";
```

Sample User Registration and Validation System

The User Registration and Validation System is a form that expands upon the previous examples. You can use a variation of this form for anything that requires limited access.

HTML Document

The User Registration and Validation System is available on the CD-ROM by the file name REGISTER.HTML. As with the survey and order form, it's a form designed to be expanded to fit your needs.

On the CD

Listing 18.7   User Registration and Validation Form

```
<HTML>
<HEAD>
<TITLE>User Registration and Validation System</TITLE>
</HEAD>
<BODY>
<H1>User Registration and Validation</H1>
<HR>
<FORM METHOD="POST" ACTION="http://.my.www.server/cgi-bin/register.pl">
<PRE>
ID:       <INPUT TYPE="text" NAME="id" SIZE="15">
Password: <INPUT TYPE="password" NAME="password" SIZE="15">
</PRE>
<P>
What classes would you like to register for?
<SELECT NAME="classes" SIZE=6 MULTIPLE>
<OPTION VALUE="html101"> [HTML 101] The Internet and the World Wide Web
<OPTION VALUE="html151"> [HTML 151] How HTML Documents Reach Your Desktop
<OPTION VALUE="html201"> [HTML 201] Using Forms in HTML Documents
<OPTION VALUE="html210"> [HTML 210] HTML3.0
<OPTION VALUE="html211"> [HTML 211] Document Aesthetics
<OPTION VALUE="html301"> [HTML 301] Sample HTML applications
<OPTION VALUE="html310"> [HTML 310] HTML Editors and Style Sheets
<OPTION> — Advanced Classes —
<OPTION VALUE="html320"> [HTML 320] HTML Editors and Style Sheets 2
<OPTION VALUE="html401"> [HTML 401] Creating the Customer Satisfaction Survey
<OPTION VALUE="html402"> [HTML 402] Creating the Online Product Order Form
<OPTION VALUE="html403"> [HTML 403] Creating the Registration and Validation System
</SELECT>
<P>
Please select the reference materials you wish to have available:
<BR>
<INPUT TYPE="checkbox" NAME="ref" VALUE="ref">HTML Elements Reference
<BR>
<INPUT TYPE="checkbox" NAME="biblio" VALUE="biblio">WWW Bibliography
<BR>
```

(continues)

Listing 18.7   Continued

```
<INPUT TYPE="checkbox" NAME="cdrom" VALUE="cdrom">What's on the CD-ROM
<BR>
<INPUT TYPE="checkbox" NAME="html2" VALUE="html2">HTML Level 2 Definition
<BR>
<INPUT TYPE="checkbox" NAME="html3" VALUE="html3">HTML Level 3 Definition
<HR>
<INPUT TYPE="submit" VALUE="Register">
<INPUT TYPE="reset" VALUE="Clear all selections">
</FORM>
</BODY>
</HTML>
```

The result of this code is shown in figure 18.6.

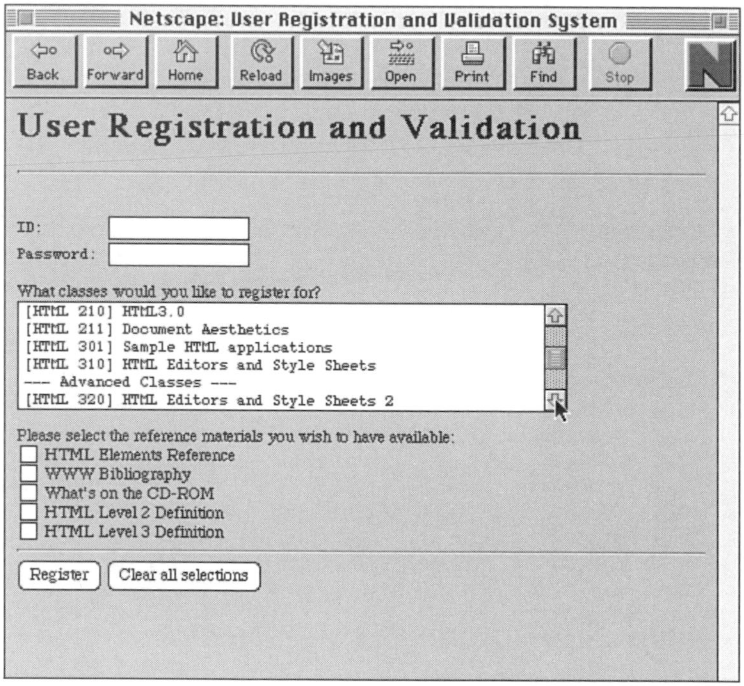

Fig. 18.6

The Registration form uses the most complex layout, incorporating text and password fields, a selection box, and five checkboxes.

The Associated Server Script

The script REGISTER.PL (available on the CD-ROM) is what the server invokes
to read in and check the information from the form. As with the SURVEY.PL
and ORDER.PL code, this script is written in PERL and requires the PERL CGI
Library. The variables listed in the script also correspond directly to the
names I gave the fields in the file REGISTER.HTML.

After the form retrieves and decodes the information from the form, it makes
sure both an ID and password are entered. If one isn't entered, the form returns an HTML document specifically stating that, and the form stops there.
If both an ID and password are entered, the script attempts to look up the
password for the ID. If the ID doesn't exist, an HTML document is sent out
with that information. If it does exist, the script tries to match the password
to the one in the file. If it doesn't match, another HTML document is sent
out with that error.

If all has gone well to this point, the script sends out the information put
into the form in an HTML document. You can modify this last section to add
some information to a database, or perhaps send an e-mail message like
SURVEY.PL and ORDER.PL.

◄ See "Getting
Information
from the
Server," p. 313

◄ See "Writing
Scripts to Read
in Data from a
Form," p. 318

Listing 18.8 REGISTER.PL

```perl
#!/usr/local/bin/perl
# this is a variable which points to the location of the user/password file
# on the current system. This would definitely need to be modified to fit
# any other systems.
$userfile = 'users.file';
#Includes cgi-lib file; if cgi-lib doesn't exist, returns malformed
#header error
do "cgi-lib.pl" || die "Fatal Error: Can't load cgi library";
#calls the subroutine in the cgi-lib.pl library
#to read in the variables from the form and set them up
#as key=value pairs in the array @in
&ReadParse;
#Gather the ID & Password into simple string variables
$id = $in{'id'};
$password = $in{'password'};
# Make sure both the ID and Password were entered...
$test = $id && $password;
if (length($test) < 1) {
  #Refuses to continue if there is no name or password
  print "Content-type: text/html\n\n";
  print "<HTML>";
  print "<HEAD><TITLE>Invalid Registration</TITLE>";
  print "</HEAD><BODY>";
  print "<H1>Invalid Registration</H1>";
```

(continues)

Listing 18.8 Continued

```
print "<P>";
print "You have either not entered a name or password.\n";
print "<P>";
print "<H2><I>—School of the Internet</I></H2>";
print "<HR>";
print "<H3>Back to the <A HREF=\"/index.html\">";
print "Front Page</A></H3>";
print "<H3>Back to the <A HREF=\"/register.html\">";
print "Registration Form</A></H3>";
print "</BODY></HTML>";
#quit the script - not enough information was present to
#process the registration.
exit;
}
# I'm assuming that there is a simple file that consists of
# ID:Password entries and that it's not encrypted in any way.
#
# This would normally be unlikely, and the following code could
# of course be modified to include encryption with the "crypt" command
# in PERL.
# get the user's entry from the password file
# In using the "look" command, I'm assuming that the password file
# is sorted by ID (which could be done with a 'sort -t: -o users.file'
# command from the UNIX prompt)
$_ = 'look -f $id $userfile';
# check to make sure we found an entry in the user file
# by checking the length of the $_ variable. If it's less
# than 1, we didn't find anything.
if (length($_) < 1) {
  #Refuses to continue if the password doesn't match up
  print "Content-type: text/html\n\n";
  print "<HTML>";
  print "<HEAD><TITLE>Invalid Registration</TITLE>";
  print "</HEAD><BODY>";
  print "<H1>Invalid Registration</H1>";
  print "<P>\n";
  print "Your entry isn't listed in our user file.\n";
  print "<P>";
  print "<H2><I>—School of the Internet</I></H2>";
  print "<HR>";
  print "<H3>Back to the <A HREF=\"/index.html\">";
  print "Front Page</A></H3>";
  print "<H3>Back to the <A HREF=\"/register.html\">";
  print "Registration Form</A></H3>";
  print "</BODY></HTML>";
  #quit the script - An invalid password or ID was entered
  exit;
}
#split off the password from the rest of the data
@user_data = split(/:/);
#remove the linefeed at the end of the password
chop(@user_data[1]);
```

```
#check the password entered against entry in password file
unless ($password eq @user_data[1]) {
  #Refuses to continue if the password doesn't match up
  print "Content-type: text/html\n\n";
  print "<HTML>";
  print "<HEAD><TITLE>Invalid Registration</TITLE>";
  print "</HEAD><BODY>";
  print "<H1>Invalid Registration</H1>";
  print "<P>\n";
  print "You have entered an invalid name or password.\n";
  print "<P>";
  print "<H2><I>—School of the Internet</I></H2>";
  print "<HR>";
  print "<H3>Back to the <A HREF=\"/index.html\">";
  print "Front Page</A></H3>";
  print "<H3>Back to the <A HREF=\"/register.html\">";
  print "Registration Form</A></H3>";
  print "</BODY></HTML>";
  #quit the script - An invalid password or ID was entered
  exit;
} else {
#password matches the entry in the file, go ahead and do
#something with this verification.
  print "Content-type: text/html\n\n";
  print "<HTML>";
  print "<HEAD><TITLE>Registration Confirmation</TITLE>";
  print "</HEAD><BODY>";
  print "<H1>Registration Confirmation</H1>\n";
  print "<H2>You've registered for the following classes:</H2>\n";
  print "<PRE>\n";
  #break down the classes into an array
  @classes = split(/\\0/,$in{'classes'});
  #print out the array of classes
  for each (@classes) {
    print "       ";
    print;
    print "\n";
  }
  print "</PRE>";
  # Note:
  # We could do similar pattern matching here to get class names
  # for the courses listed, or add the information into a simple
  # database by writing it to a file. A more complex program could
  # also read that database and produce a document from it, allowing
  # students to update their files automatically (with the proper
  # password...)
  # Go through the list of checkbox'd materials that have been
  # requested...
  print "<H2>You've requested the following materials:</H2>\n";
  print "<UL>\n";
  if ($in{'ref'} eq "ref") {
    print "<LI> HTML Elements Reference\n";
  }
```

(continues)

Listing 18.8   Continued

```
if ($in{'biblio'} eq "biblio") {
  print "<LI> WWW Bibliography\n";
}
if ($in{'cdrom'} eq "cdrom") {
  print "<LI> What's on the CD-ROM\n";
}
if ($in{'html2'} eq "html2") {
  print "<LI> HTML Level 2 Definition\n";
}
if ($in{'html3'} eq "html3") {
  print "<LI> HTML Level 3 Definition\n";
}
print "</UL>";
print "<H2><I>—School of the Internet</I></H2>";
print "<HR>";
print "<H3>Back to the <A HREF=\"/index.html\">";
print "Front Page</A></H3>";
print "</BODY></HTML>";
}
```

Figure 18.7 shows the result of one of the error messages from the previous code.

Fig. 18.7
Other possible messages include `Your entry isn't listed in our user file` and `You have entered an invalid name or password.`

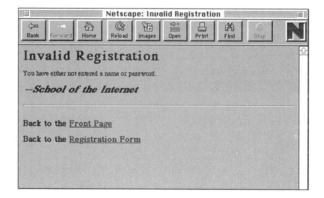

Script Output
When the form is completed correctly, the script sends out the HTML document shown in figure 18.8.

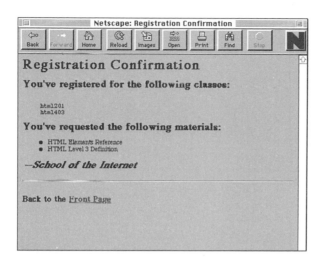

Fig. 18.8
The completed form uses preformatted text and list tags to display the information sent in on the form.

From Here...

The examples presented in this chapter have covered very simple and moderately complex forms. The most common form today is the simplest—just getting some information and passing it along somewhere else (in this case, using e-mail). Another common form is the survey, where the script does some basic error checking and returns an error if the form isn't filled out correctly. The third (and most complex) form includes multiple error checking steps, as well as verification of information in the form.

■ Chapter 15, "Elements of Forms," describes the various elements and tags used in creating forms, and how to use each of the elements and their options.

■ Chapter 16, "Form Layout and Design," shows how to set up forms to be easy and fun while still getting the needed information.

■ Chapter 17, "Server Scripts and Applications," goes over how to create scripts and how to make them work with forms.

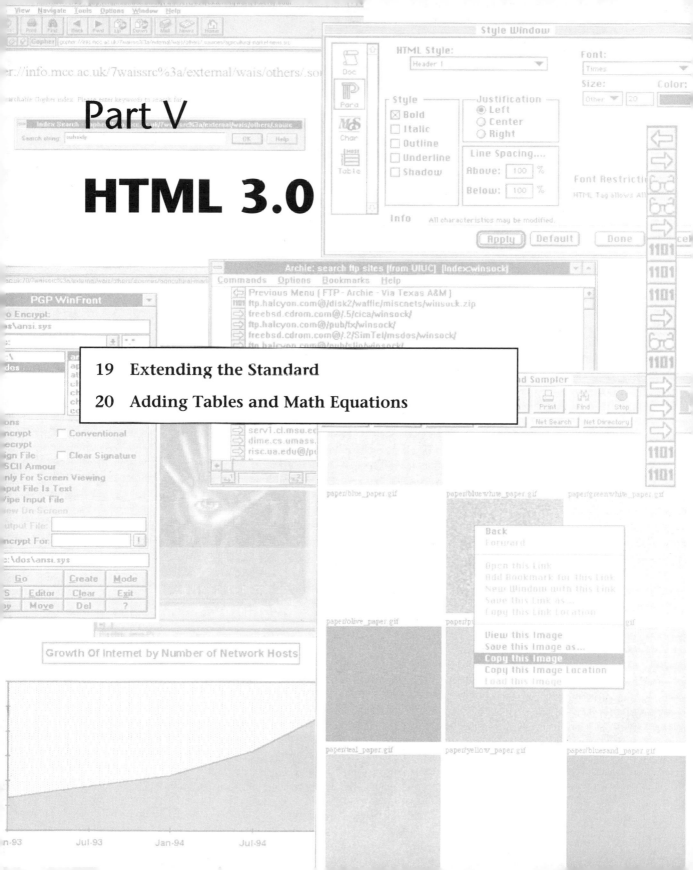

Part V

HTML 3.0

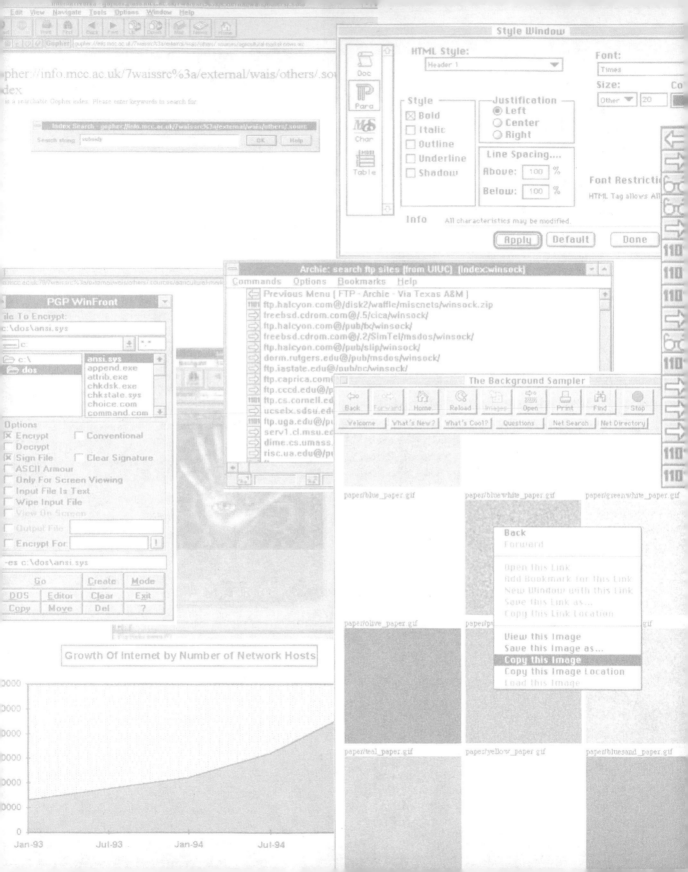

Chapter 19

Extending the Standard

HTML's popularity is a testament to its ease of use, its wide application, and its acceptance as the standard for Web-based documents and information. Few other development platforms can boast such wide support for a single language by its authoring community. Even Netscape's extensions to HTML do not interfere with the language's ability to deliver information to every Web-compatible client (regardless of their support for the Netscape code).

This chapter answers these questions:

- Who is developing HTML 3.0?

- When will it be available for authors and viewer developers?

- What new features will it support?

- Can I get a peek at the upcoming version of Netscape Navigator?

V

HTML 3.0

Who Is Developing HTML 3.0?

The evolution of the HTML standard is very much a public process; users can offer suggestions and commentary about the current standard and proposals for the upcoming levels. The explosion of Web-based development has spawned many debates and suggestions for extending HTML functionality.

There is a call from one side for more creator control over the on-screen layout of Web pages. There are also others lobbying for HTML to follow more closely to its older sibling, SGML, by remaining platform-independent. The W3 Consortium, charged with developing the upcoming HTML 3.0 (also called HTML Level 3), is working to address as many concerns as possible without losing HTML's focus on content delivery.

◀ See "HTML's DTD," p. 67

Availability of HTML 3.0

◀ See "Origins of
the Web," p. 30

Tip

If you haven't filled
out a form recently
(or ever), point
your Web viewer to
the GVU User
Survey Page
(**http://www-
survey.cc.gatech.
edu/cgi-bin/
Entry**) and fill
one out.

The DTD (Definition Type Document) is targeted to be published towards the
end of 1995. This document declares the HTML 3.0 features and describes
their acceptable uses (in SGML, of course). The Internet Engineering Task
Force (IETF), the appointed architects of the HTML standards, will continue
developing for the next level (presumably HTML 4.0).

Does this mean that the features of HTML 3.0 won't be available for use until
then? Of course not. Some of the HTML 3.0 features are already in general
use—remember that form you filled out on a Web site recently? That's an
implementation of a major "new" feature of Level 3. Forms and tables (to a
lesser extent) are supported by a wide range of WWW clients, and they use
the proposed Level 3 elements and tag syntax (see fig. 19.1).

There is very little chance that the proposed HTML will change before the
DTD publication—unless there's a strong and compelling reason.

Fig. 19.1

Forms have
become so
commonplace that
users and authors
often do not
realize they're
not "standard"
HTML yet.

Troubleshooting

I've heard that not too many clients can display HTML 3.0 yet. Is it dangerous to use HTML 3.0 coding in your documents?

Not really. HTML 3.0 will be completely backwards-compatible with version 2.0 (some of the deprecated or obsolete HTML 1.0 elements such as PLAINTEXT and XMP might drop out of the standard at this point). If a viewer comes across coding it doesn't understand, it's supposed to ignore it, formatting the information as though the tag is not present. This can make for an ugly presentation of your data, but the data *will* reach the end user's screen.

Tip
For a look at a draft of the HTML Level 3 Description Type Document on the World Wide Web, see Appendix E.

Proposed New Features

Considering the goals of the HTML architects, Level 3 promises cutting edge advanced and innovative features. Besides officially describing forms support (with enhancements beyond the current description), other new features will include:

- Tables

- Mathematical equations

- Style sheets

- FIG, a new enhanced element for embedded text and images

- Fixed BANNER inline images

- Greater text display control in conjunction with images

- Author-customized lists

- Text tabs

- Horizontal alignment control

- New text containers for greater support of content types

The HTML 3.0 features will give authors a monumental leap in control over their information. Take a look at some of these advances.

V

HTML 3.0

Style Sheets

Style sheets are a dramatic turn for HTML. Until now, HTML has been letting viewers define styles for text layouts, including font size, color, and style. HTML 3.0 will support the optional use of style sheets, giving authors enough creative control to literally bring desktop publishing to the Web.

HTML style sheets can be based on a subset of the Document Style Semantics and Specification Language (DSSSL) being promoted by the SGML Open Consortium. This add-on to HTML will control viewer aspects such as window size and the font text it's displayed with. The DSSSL subset (dubbed "DSSSL Lite") has not been created yet—it's under development—so authors have something yet to wish for.

BANNER Element

One complaint with the current state of HTML documents is that, if the document is longer than users set their viewer window, they must scroll the window to read all of the information. Authors use anchor links to named anchors in the document to speed up the process of finding specific locations in the extended text. But, after the reader is finished reading the data at this internal location in the document, how do they get back to the top of the document, or to the last document location?

Authors resorted to inserting navigation controls at the end of every section in the text. Aesthetically, this was not a preferable choice. Besides repeating the same functions over and over in the same document, they tended to "break the flow" of information in the document; text became compartmentalized and disjointed. Why not attach a floating menu bar to the top of the viewer window, with the navigation controls always at reach?

Tip
The BANNER feature lets Web site administrators add constant on-screen advertising to commercial Web pages.

◀ See "Using the IMG Element," p. 231

That's what the BANNER element will do, and more. The BANNER will support text and graphics in a fixed position in the viewer window. Whatever the author wants to put in there is up to him or her: a graphic logo, advertisements, navigation buttons, help buttons, and so on. This essentially lets the author create a toolbar for the Web pages, and each page can have custom controls and text.

FIG Element

The current HTML model limits the author's ability to merge text and graphics seamlessly in Web documents, making them perform elaborate tricks to create the illusion of wrapping text and providing no support at all for overlapping images. The FIG container element, with its corresponding OVERLAY and CAPTION options, will provide the author this control and more.

First, all FIG images will be required to have descriptions for nongraphical users (score one for the text-only users!). Along with descriptions, a CAPTION can be associated with each figure as a text label, aligned along the top, bottom, left, or right of the figure.

The OVERLAY will allow figures to have other graphics lay on top of them, allowing authors to combine images dynamically without creating composite images separately. Overlays will have defined hot spots just as other inline image maps, and they can be used to impose a new set of links to an existing image map (the topmost overlay supersedes all other image maps, so adding a new overlay to a stack of images introduces new hot spots and their defined links).

Tip

And IMG will not go away, but inherit additional features, such as the Netscape WIDTH and HEIGHT attributes.

◀ See "Just What Is an Image Map?" p. 272

Horizontal Tabs

Web authors have long complained about the lack of tab controls in HTML body text sections. HTML 3.0 will introduce the TAB element to provide more control of on-screen text. Tabs will be *programmable:* the author will define the positioning of as many tabs as he wants, and then give the <TAB> tag a value relating to the TAB definition he wants. An additional ALIGN attribute will let you place text flush against both margins with blank space between them.

Tip

Currently, only Netscape's non-standard extensions allow authors to align inline images with the right margin, but not text.

◀ See "Using the Anchor Element," p. 253

Footnotes

New text containers will provide authors with greater control over how their content is defined. The FN element will let authors create footnotes for text references. They will act much like anchor links to named anchors, but with one exception: where supported, the viewer will be able to display the FN value in a pop-up window on top of the current document. Authors will no longer have to make readers jump back and forth in a document to read footnote information (or have to insert footnotes near the referenced text, thereby breaking the flow of the text).

Preview of HTML Support in Netscape's Navigator 1.1

As the only commercial developer who has pushed the HTML language beyond its current standard (and has become the overwhelming favorite client on the market as a result), Netscape's beta testing for its new version of Navigator is worth a quick look.

V

HTML 3.0

Navigator 1.1 will provide support for the HTML Level 3 standard (in its final form, they assure), as well as provide additional display control for HTML authors. Included in these controls will be support for tables and document background images (see fig. 19.2).

Fig. 19.2
Navigator 1.1 allows users and authors to control the viewing window's background color. It's set to white here.

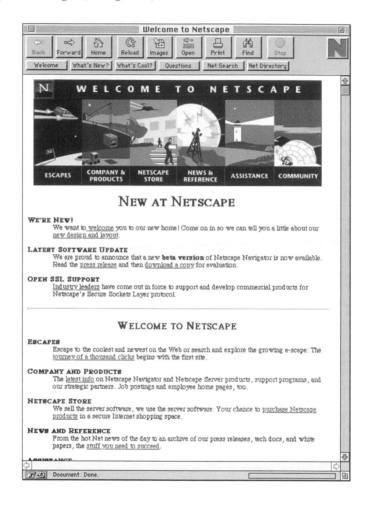

While it's argued that the current version of Navigator has the best news and mail interface, version 1.1 will make the news and mail readers even better. The UseNet News interface now allows for text searches and hierarchical newsgroup browsing, and the mail reader supports MIME (Multipurpose Internet Mail Extensions), letting users mix data types in outgoing mail messages and receive mail with data attachments (see fig. 19.3).

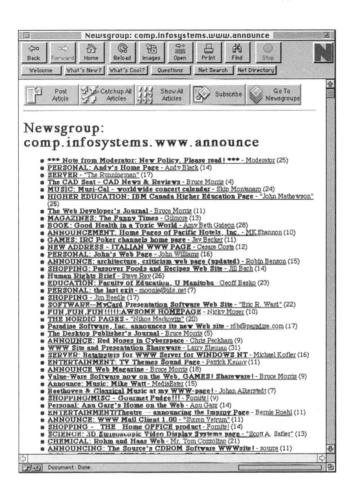

Fig. 19.3
Navigator comes with the best UseNet Network News interface found in a Web viewer.

V

HTML 3.0

Another feature that is ground-breaking for Navigator 1.1 is the use of pop-up menus. By right-clicking (or clicking and holding, for one-button users) an inline image or link, Navigator pops up a menu of user options, such as page navigation, adding links to the bookmark list, copying the current link, and copying or saving inline images to the local hard disk (see fig. 19.4).

Netscape's new version of Navigator will continue to set the pace for the rest of the commercial viewer industry. Features such as pop-up menus and background images, when combined with HTML 3.0, will promise to delight and empower the millions of Web users and HTML authors.

Navigator 1.1 will be available in 32-bit versions for Microsoft Windows 95 and Windows NT users, as well as a PowerPC version for PowerMac users.

Tip
Netscape 1.1 pop-up menus are time-saving short-cuts to options only available from the pull-down menus.

Fig. 19.4
Navigator's pop-up menu simplifies Web browsing and provides new save and copy features.

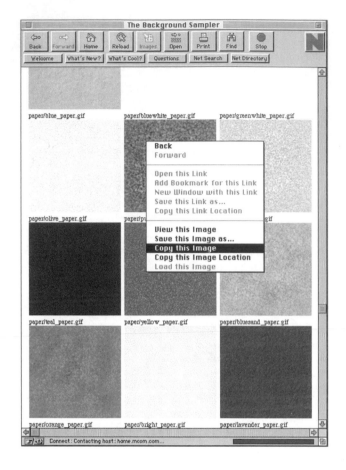

From Here...

The HTML 3.0 standard is still a work in progress, and these features—and the DTD—will most likely change in small ways by the time the standard is published. Many of the features are already in use by some viewers, especially forms support. To learn about other HTML 3.0 features coming into use, or to get advice on creating HTML documents, refer to the following chapters:

■ Chapter 20, "Adding Tables and Math Equations," describes why table support is important for distributing many types of data, and discusses how HTML 3.0 will provide support for customizable tables, and what support exists today.

- Chapter 21, "Managing Your Text," talks about the design issues surrounding how text and HTML elements can be used for consistent and creative purposes in Web documents.

- Chapter 22, "Managing Your Images," discusses the design issues surrounding inline images and how to use them best in HTML applications.

- Part VII, "Sample HTML Applications," details the creation of two HTML applications from the concept stage to going online the World Wide Web.

V

HTML 3.0

Chapter 20

Adding Tables and Math Equations

As a tool for government, commercial, educational, and personal Web applications, HTML has quite a few needs and expectations to meet. It's the language for what is becoming the standard interface to the Internet, and as such is required to support a much greater range of uses today than perhaps its original creators had first imagined.

HTML 3.0's level of sophistication will be head and shoulders above the current standard, and will accommodate a wider range of user needs. Two deficiencies in HTML 2.0 were the lack of support for tables and mathematical equations. HTML 3.0 will encompass both features with robust support.

◀ See "Proposed New Features," p. 345

This chapter answers the following questions:

- How does HTML 3.0 define tables?

- Do any current viewers support tables?

- How do I create a table in my HTML document?

- How are math equations supported by HTML?

- Can equations created with other software programs be used by Web pages?

> **Note**
>
> This information is based on public texts and discussions regarding the development process for HTML 3.0. This new version is not a finished product (at the time of this writing), so any specific notations or expressions may change drastically before the new standard is finalized. This information is being provided to give you a sense of the direction HTML is taking, and how you can begin to visualize your own needs being served by these additional capabilities.

Using Tables

◀ See "Creating a Numbered List," p. 203

◀ See "FIG Element," p. 346

HTML 3.0 defines tables in much the same way it defines list containers. The TABLE element is the container for the table's data and layout. A caption can be included, using the CAPTION container.

HTML tables are composed row by row: you separate the data with either the <TH> (table header) or <TD> (table data) tags, and indicate a new row with the <TR> (table row) tag. Think of the <TR> tag as a line break, signaling that the following data starts a new table row. Table header data is generally shown in bold by WWW viewers, and table data information in the standard body text format. <TH> supports the ALIGN attribute, which aligns your text in a cell. ALIGN values are LEFT, CENTER (the default), or RIGHT.

Tip
Tables are necessarily uniform, with equal numbers of cells in each row and in each column. No Tetris-looking tables allowed here!

Cells do not necessarily have to contain data, either. To create a blank cell, just do not enter any data text before defining the next cell (such as, <TH><TH>data here). It's not really necessary to create blank cells if the rest of the cells on the row are going to be blank; the TR element signals the start of a new row, so the Web viewers automatically fill in blank cells to even out the row with the rest of the table.

> **Note**
>
> If you're concerned about viewers displaying your header text correctly (as emphasized text, preferably in a bold font), you can use style tags to force the issue. Be careful what you wish for, though: if you want an italicized font but the viewer automatically formats the text bold, you can wind up with bold italicized headers.

Rows and columns can be *spanned,* meaning that they're combined with adjacent cells to create larger cells for the data. The other columns or rows will continue to use the same number of cell division, leaving you with one cell that spans or extends over the area of two or more cells.

> **Note**
>
> When you create larger cells in an HTML table, you might find that your cell data acts a bit unruly: not breaking properly, wrapping text when it shouldn't, crowding too close to the cell divisions. Like other HTML documents, tables support internal HTML elements such as BR (to create a line break in the data), hyperlink anchors, inline images, and even forms. Use an HTML table in the same manner you would a spreadsheet: for data display, creating data layouts (such as inventory lists or business invoices), and for calculation tables (when combined with a CGI script that can take your form input and generate output data that's displayed in your HTML table). The uses for tables are limited only by your data and your creativity.

To span two adjacent cells on a row, use the ROWSPAN attribute with <TH>, as follows:

    <TH ROWSPAN=2>

To span two adjacent cells in a column, use the COLSPAN attribute to <TH>, as follows:

    <TH COLSPAN=2>

> **Note**
>
> By default, tables are composed without lines separating the data cells. To have the viewer show the table cell lines, include the BORDER attribute in the <TABLE> tag:
>
>   <TABLE BORDER>

Tip

Don't forget to close your table data with the </TABLE> closing tag.

> **Troubleshooting**
>
> *I created a table with a fill-in form in it, but I can't see the Submit button or fill-in fields. What's happening?*
>
> You're probably using a viewer with incomplete table support. According to the NCSA Mosaic Tables tutorial (**http://www.ncsa.uiuc.edu:80/SDG/Software /Mosaic/Tables/tutorial.html**), forms are legal within tables and are fully supported (and they will even print correctly). Update your viewer or try another client, such as Mosaic 2.0.

Viewer Support for Tables

◀ See "Preview of HTML Support Netscape's Navigator 1.1," p. 347

Only the beta versions of Mosaic and Netscape currently support tables, as does Arena—the "test bed" UNIX viewer for the HTML 3.0 development team. Both Mosaic and Netscape support tables very well, as shown in figure 20.1. Because Navigator doesn't recognize blank cells, you have to use false data (PRE containers that consist of two blank spaces) as a placemarker in Netscape tables. It's not very neat or pretty; hopefully, the second Netscape beta will correct this shortcoming.

Fig. 20.1

Netscape Navigator 1.1b (the next beta version) supports HTML Level 3 table features and provides a stylistic border definition for table cells.

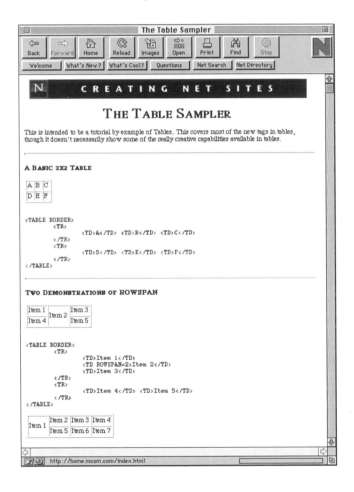

As HTML 3.0 is formalized, tables will be readily supported by all updated WWW clients. Additional customizing attributes may also be available, such as attributes that define the look of individual cells (3D recessed, extruded, or shaded, for example).

Using Math Equations

HTML Level 3 will provide full support for creating mathematical equations in the body of text in HTML documents. The basic element will be the MATH element, and it will contain attributes that define the formula expressions and numerical data (and variables). HTML's MATH will display mathematical elements in a plain font and numerical variables in italicized text. The HTML standard will borrow heavily from the LaTeX UNIX application, so if you have experience using LaTeX to create mathematical content for documents, you'll have a leg up on the HTML 3.0 implementation.

The MATH container will support elements for brackets, delimiters, the proper display of numerators and denominators (the former placed above the latter); superscript and subscript text, and matrices and other arrays. HTML entities will be provided for mathematical functions, Greek letters, operators, and other math symbols.

Math Equations for Viewers without HTML 3.0 Support

No commercial viewers offer math equation support. Arena is the only viewer that supports equations, and it's primarily a testing location for the HTML 3.0 development process. How then can equations be used in Web documents that anyone can access and display?

Through inline images. Many word processors include math equation editors. Create your math formulae in your favorite word processor, setting the font size, style, and color to the proper size in relation to your Web document text (see fig. 20.2).

Use a screen capture utility (such as Capture on the Macintosh, or even Windows Alt+Print Screen function) to copy the screen image to the Clipboard or to a Capture file. Open this file in your favorite graphics editor (or paste the Capture into a new document), crop the image to just the formula and save the new image as a GIF file (see fig. 20.3).

If you make the background transparent, the formula text will appear as part of the normal flow of text when displayed in your Web viewer (see fig. 20.4).

Fig. 20.2

Word processors like Word for Windows allow you to create math formulas directly in your document text.

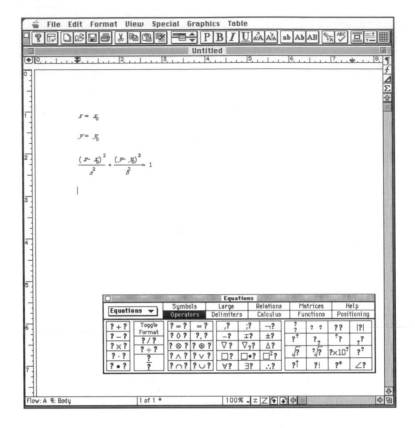

Fig. 20.3

Use the cropping for effect: crop closely if you don't want the text to stand apart from your flow of text, or crop wider to create a natural space around the displayed equations.

◄ See "Aligning Graphics and Text," p. 237

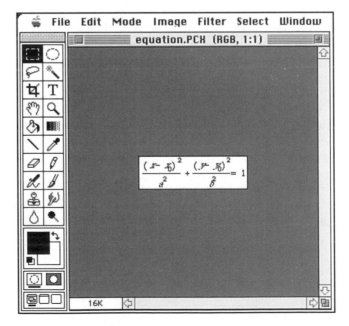

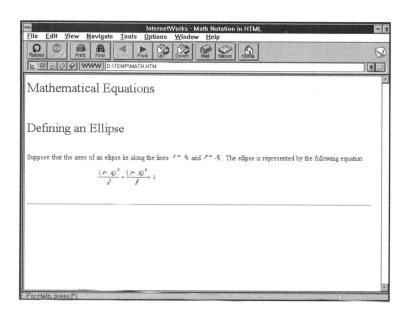

Fig. 20.4
Use the IMG ALIGN attribute for the formula graphics to control the position of the images within the text.

Incorporating math formulae for users without HTML 3.0-compatible viewers (and who has one?) requires a little more work than just entering text into a Web page. If you maintain your equations in a single source file you can always go back and edit or re-use your math "code" in future HTML documents.

Tip
Use colors in your equations to highlight specific variables and values for your audience.

From Here...

Table support is growing among the various WWW clients. When the HTML 3.0 standard is published, this support will become a standard feature of HTML. Mathematical equation support is much farther away than table support, and the current solutions are a stopgap until a more standardized usage is proposed. At this point, the breadth of the HyperText Markup Language and where it's development efforts are going have been explored. For design advice on creating HTML documents, or to see real-world applications of HTML, refer to the following:

- Chapter 21, "Managing Your Text," discusses the design issues surrounding how text and HTML elements can be used for consistent and creative purposes in Web documents.

- Chapter 22, "Managing Your Images," describes the design issues surrounding inline images and how they are best used in HTML applications.

- Part VII, "Sample HTML Applications," details the creation of two HTML applications from the concept stage to going online the WWW.

- Part VIII, "HTML Editors and Style Sheets," provides a look into the most widely used HTML document tools, including stand-alone editors and add-ons for popular word processors.

Part VI

Document Aesthetics

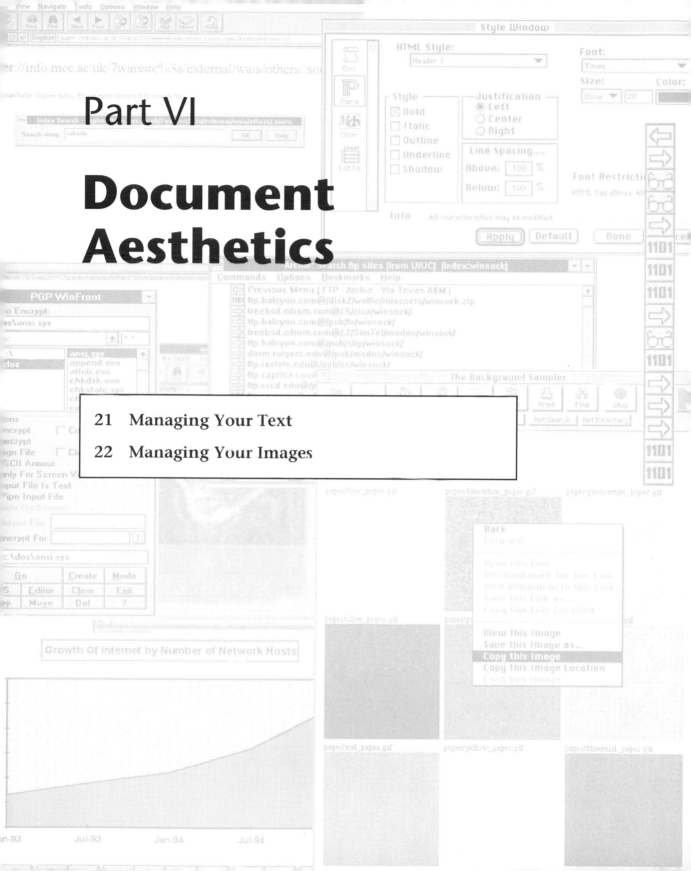

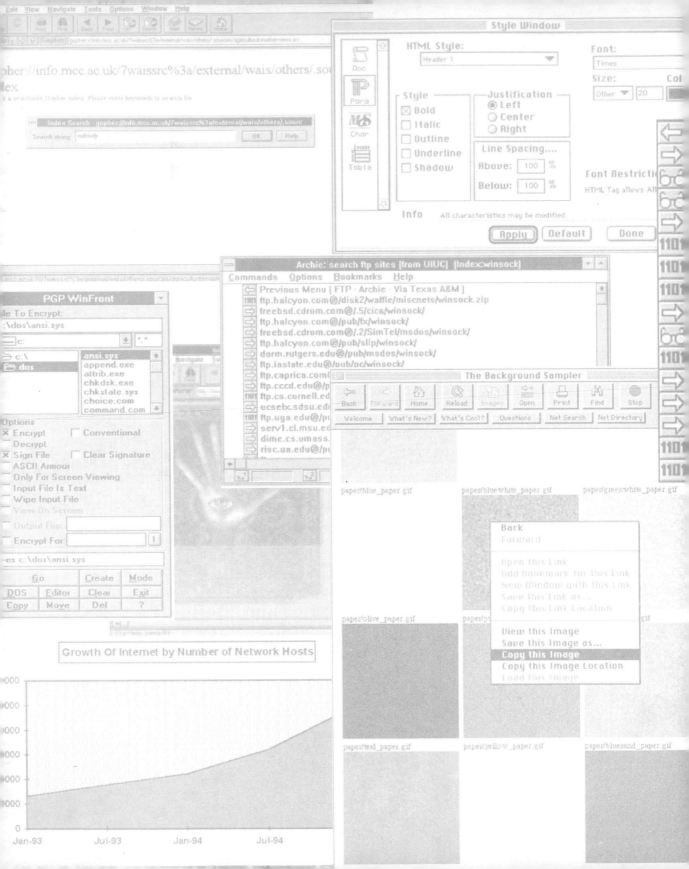

## Chapter 21

Managing Your Text

"Language is an aesthetic as well as an analytical tool. And to slur language is as painful to the well-tempered ear as to slur music."

—William F. Buckley, Jr.

"That's not writing, that's typing."

—Truman Capote

At its simplest level, the World Wide Web is a system for distributing information. This system was built on a tradition of text-based data, and is only now creating a new paradigm of communication that includes text, images, sounds, and moving pictures. The only thing missing is a way to transmit tastes, but I'm sure they're working on it already.

This chapter answers the following questions:

- How do I use logical and physical styles concurrently?

- Can I use lists for information other than listed data?

- How should I use horizontal rules?

- Why do I want to control text line breaks?

- How can I use internal links?

- How can I create navigational links in my documents (and why should I)?

- What's a good rule of thumb for choosing font sizes in Netscape?

Communicating Your Message

As content providers, Web authors have the formidable task of taking a message and communicating it to users around the world—and do so in a manner that conveys the point of the whole transmission.

That's the same task writers throughout human history have had to contend with. Literature is a body of human endeavors that attempts, in as many and various ways as possible, to communicate any number of messages. "Man is inherently good"; "love is all you need"; "carpe diem." Whatever message is chosen, written language is its vehicle.

So how does this relate to HTML and the World Wide Web? "I mean, all I'm doing is telling people how much my merchandise costs." (Or, "all I'm doing is advertising our services." Or, "all I'm doing is showing the world my two goldfish, Merckle and Flip.") The simplicity of the message isn't relevant. It's when this simplicity is lost in the medium, that messages fail to come through—when "writing" becomes "typing."

There are a few simple steps you should follow when creating an HTML document:

1. Know what you want to communicate.

2. Can you explain it to a six-year old? Can you explain it to a colleague? Who's your audience? (Don't laugh, it could be both.) Your language needs to approach the level of your audience.

3. Get it on paper (or on-screen, if you're environmentally conscious). Make sure you use direct and active language.

4. Organize your information. Remember to build ideas (don't skip around a subject until it makes little sense no matter which way you read it).

5. Divide the organization into pages. Here's where you make the first conscious decision regarding the structure of your Web application.

6. Adapt the information to HTML. Mark up the text, and insert links and inline images.

Sometimes, you can skip a step here or there; people with strong communication skills need less guidance at times. After you have your message clearly written, clearly organized, and properly adapted to HTML, you've just gone 95 percent of the way toward creating a good Web application. The rest is creativity.

Using Text Creatively in HTML

"Words themselves, more than any other visual symbols, have the power to completely describe the invisible realm of senses and emotions."

—Scott McCloud, *Understanding Comics*

When friends found out I was writing this book, they were pretty excited. Many of them had seen my fiction in one form or another, and they were anticipating being a part of my writing process again. When I told them it was a computer book they all had the same reaction: "Oh. That's nice." Meaning, "What's creative about that?" They had little appreciation for this mode of communication.

I hear the same thing from prospective Web users and authors alike. Many dread the task of having to convert the company's emergency evacuation plan (or some other such "trivial" information) to Web documents. My answer is always to take them out on the Web and show them around. Show them companies like Sun Microsystems and IBM—not the traditional bastions of mirth—doing some personable and interesting things with their Web sites. Your information doesn't have to be hip or wacky to be presented in an interesting way—but it helps if there's a little of that in you.

Creativity is an energy source that you can apply to any endeavor. The Web is no exception. You don't think an emergency plan home page can be interesting? How about including a link to a fire engine siren sound clip? Or using Netscape's BLINK element (which should rarely be used) to highlight the "Exit" text? Or enlisting the help of a coworker who can doodle half-decently and get her to do little sketches of various employees, and insert their pictures into the floor plan where appropriate? The point is, when you make a task interesting for you to do, it will be interesting for the people who will read it on the Web. *You* are the very first member of your audience.

So far in this chapter I've talked about communication theory, basic Web development guides, and creativity. Where's all the really handy stuff about using HTML in text documents? I was hoping you'd ask that.

Mixing Logical and Physical Styles

One of the first things you'll notice about text styles in HTML is that there are two different kinds of markup: logical and physical styles. The *logical styles* define how text functions within the context of the document. *Physical styles* define how text is absolutely represented. The ongoing debate between

◀ See "Using
Logical Style
Elements,"
p. 192

◀ See "Using
Physical Style
Elements,"
p. 191

◀ See "Using
PRE," p. 183

authors who favor one or the other for whatever reasons stops being important at a certain point. What is important is how these styles function separately, and how they work together. Can you have both?

You can if you use the logical styles at all. There are times when the text you
want highlighted in some manner doesn't fit the basic definitions of the
logical elements (emphasize, strong, cite). What is the text, then? The straight
advice is: use the style that best suits your needs. If you want to give the Web
viewers control over how the text looks (if how it looks is immaterial against
how the text relates to the rest of the document body), or if your primary
audience is using a text-only viewer, use logical styles. If you're creating a
rough table using a PRE container and want the column and row headers to
be bold, use the bold style (see fig. 21.1).

Fig. 21.1
PRE containers
retain all of the
spacing and line
breaks of the
original text and
also allow HTML
styles to apply.

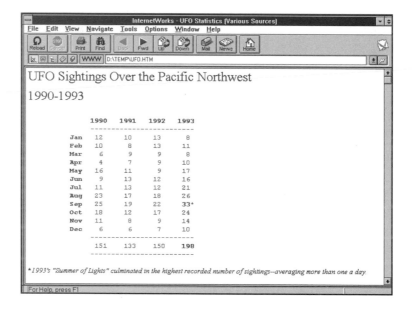

There's nothing wrong with marking document text so that it does what you
want it to. Just think about how your audience will be reading the Web page.

Using Lists for Effect

In HTML, lists are defined a lot like logical text styles; they represent list
types, and don't necessarily describe how the lists look (bulleted lists are
called unnumbered lists—try to figure out what *that* looks like). As a Web

author, however, look at lists as the closest thing in HTML to a "sure thing"—practically every viewer, graphical or text-based, uses the same on-screen definition for these elements. You might find slight differences in the spacing between lines, but they're almost uniformly formatted with the same marker styles (with the exception of bullet markers, but they all appear in the same place and at about the same size).

◄ See "Creating a Bulleted List," p. 203

Lists are the next best formatting tool after tables in HTML. They provide a variety of screen styles you can combine for eye-catching effects. Numbered lists are somewhat limited in the rolls they can play, but bulleted and definition lists are quite versatile. The purist school of thought resists the idea of lists being used for any purpose other than their explicitly defined role—numbered lists catalog items with consecutive numbers, definition lists represent terminology and their respective text definitions, and so on. To use lists in a creative context is a lot like facing the wrong direction in an elevator—it's not proper HTML.

My favorite list type to play with is the definition list. It's best used as an indented text container. Figure 21.2 shows a series of HTML examples using definition lists, and figure 21.3 shows how a typical viewer would display them.

◄ See "Creating Definition Lists," p. 215

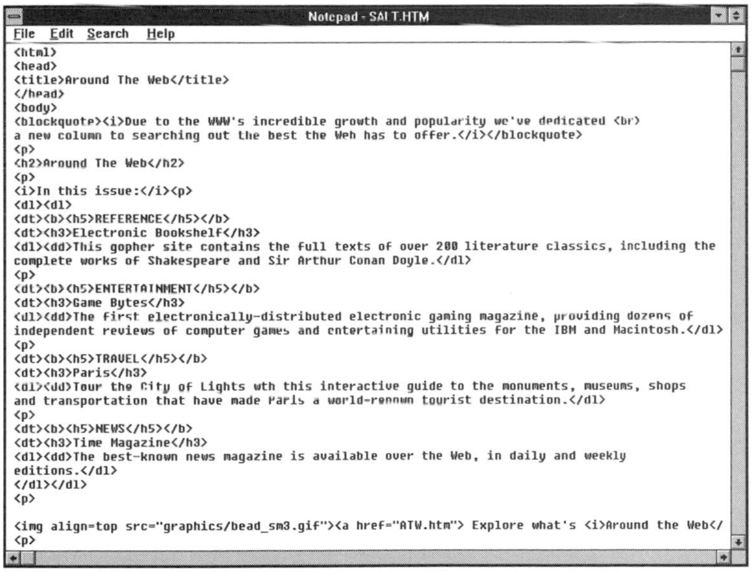


```
<html>
<head>
<title>Around The Web</title>
</head>
<body>
<blockquote><i>Due to the WWW's incredible growth and popularity we've dedicated <br>
a new column to searching out the best the Web has to offer.</i></blockquote>
<p>
<h2>Around The Web</h2>
<p>
<i>In this issue:</i><p>
<dl><dl>
<dt><b><h5>REFERENCE</h5></b>
<dt><h3>Electronic Bookshelf</h3>
<dl><dd>This gopher site contains the full texts of over 200 literature classics, including the
complete works of Shakespeare and Sir Arthur Conan Doyle.</dl>
<p>
<dt><b><h5>ENTERTAINMENT</h5></b>
<dt><h3>Game Bytes</h3>
<dl><dd>The first electronically-distributed electronic gaming magazine, providing dozens of
independent reviews of computer games and entertaining utilities for the IBM and Macintosh.</dl>
<p>
<dt><b><h5>TRAVEL</h5></b>
<dt><h3>Paris</h3>
<dl><dd>Tour the City of Lights wth this interactive guide to the monuments, museums, shops
and transportation that have made Paris a world-rennwn tourist destination.</dl>
<p>
<dt><b><h5>NEWS</h5></b>
<dt><h3>Time Magazine</h3>
<dl><dd>The best-known news magazine is available over the Web, in daily and weekly
editions.</dl>
</dl></dl>
<p>

<img align=top src="graphics/bead_sm3.gif"><a href="ATW.htm"> Explore what's <i>Around the Web</
<p>
```

Fig. 21.2
Close each definition list with the </DL> tag to preserve your intended formatting.

VI

Document Aesthetics

Fig. 21.3

It's legal HTML to embed other HTML elements or lists in definition lists.

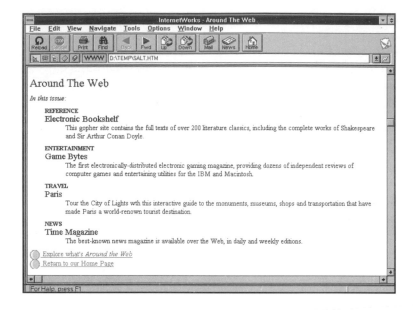

Using Horizontal Rules

One of the most overused HTML elements is the horizontal rule. Authors just love these things; there are hundreds of Web sites filled with page after page of items separated by such rules. And pity poor Netscape users! With Netscape's capability to display rules of different widths and heights, there are Web pages with monstrous stylistic problems.

◀ See "Separating Paragraphs with Horizontal Lines," p. 195

It's time to step back and take a look at horizontal rules from a creative and functional perspective. Authors have to know what horizontal rules are doing before they can properly implement them in HTML documents. Without knowing why something should (or should not) be done, there is no conscious decision, just random behavior. As an author, this is what you need to know:

■ What do horizontal rules represent?

■ What effect do they create in a Web document?

What Rules Represent

A horizontal rule represents a separation, a change of direction or subject, a new beginning, a shifting of gears. It can represent (in a fictional context) the passage of time or a change of location. Whatever it represents, one thing is clear: horizontal rules tell the reader to consider the content that follows as something new or different. However, they must be used sparingly (see fig. 21.4).

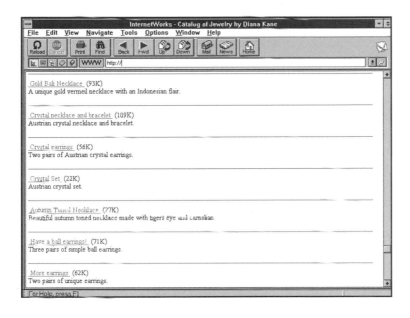

Fig. 21.4
This product catalog weakens its presentation and format with an over-reliance on horizontal rules.

How do you protect the effectiveness of horizontal rules? By establishing a clear logic to their use, to begin with. Only use horizontal rules where they apply in your internalized "style sheet" and be consistent. Don't arbitrarily break your own stylistic rules simply for effect.

Caution

The overuse of any stylistic element can distract the reader and detract from the message you are trying to convey.

When you establish these horizontal rules, use a critical aesthetic eye. Does it make sense to use three rules for every section break? Do you like the way you double underline every heading with two horizontal rules? Your own taste and sense of what "works" will steer you away from these errors that are far too common on the Web.

VI

Document Aesthetics

Creating Effects with Rules

Some authors want to use horizontal rules as though they're on-screen graphics. If you don't use horizontal rules to indicate a change, can they work as screen objects? Of course they can. The trick here, again, is to formulate a clear understanding of how such rules are functioning. This way, your intentions will be clear to the audience.

This is where the Netscape extensions to rules are so effective. Netscape allows you to make rules shorter and taller, and to make them two-dimensional objects by leaving off the drop shadow. "Objectifying" rules lets them be objects—an <HR> tag is just a horizontal rule in an HTML document. Your definition of its purpose is the key to how or whether it works.

What are some interesting graphical uses of rules? How about using rules to define an area of the screen as not part of the text; a series of navigation buttons at the bottom of a page, enclosed between two rules, looks like a button bar to me. You can even create this effect with text-based navigation links (see fig. 21.5).

Fig. 21.5
Text navigation links can look like buttons, or they can have a style all their own.

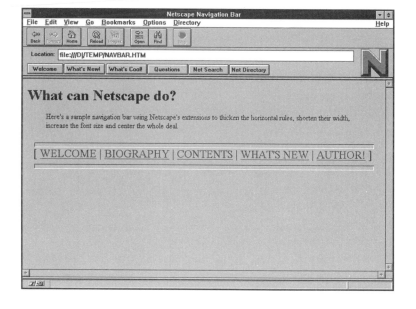

You can also use multiple horizontal rules to create a graphic banner, separating or highlighting important information. In Netscape, these banners can be accomplished with one or two rules. The danger is that you risk losing the effect for your non-Netscape audience; however, the effects can be very striking (see fig. 21.6).

Fig. 21.6
Netscape's versatile control over horizontal rules leads to some creative and effective Web document presentation.

Controlling Text Breaks

HTML provides two elements for inserting breaks into text: BR, the line break element, and P, the paragraph break element. BR stops the current line of text and continues the text against the left margin of the next line. P stops the current line of text and begins a new paragraph a double space beneath the previous line. What effects can you make with these elements?

Paragraph breaks in lists add an interesting touch—they insert white space between list items (or, in the case of definition lists, between paragraphs in the <DD> tagged text). A list with white space between two items is construed as being broken into two or more groups of items. In a definition list, it can simply indicate a new paragraph, but the new text maintains the same indented properties, leading to a nice stylistic layout (see fig. 21.7).

◀ See "The Paragraph Break," p. 178

◀ See "The Forced Line Break," p. 179

VI

Document Aesthetics

Fig. 21.7
Web viewers ignore sequential paragraph breaks after the first one. To force additional white space, you must insert blank text (using a PRE container) to mark the paragraph as valid.

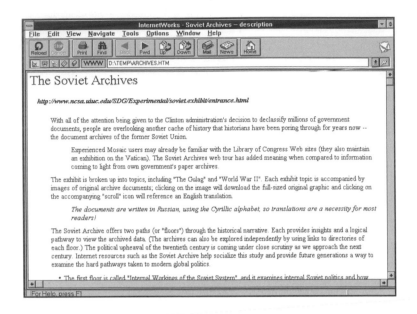

Line breaks are much less graceful. If you use a break in the middle of a sentence and a user has set his viewer window width narrower than the line of text, the text will wrap to the next line before breaking, creating an unattractive layout.

If you use line breaks in your text, do it for effect. I prefer to take a section of body text and use a Macintosh utility called Add/Strip to shorten the lines to a defined number of characters (say, 25). I then add a line break to the end of each line. When this text displays in a Web page, it creates a narrow vertical column of text. Wrap this next to an inline graphic to create a newspaper-type effect. Wrap it beside a transparent place-holder graphic and you have a "floating" text paragraph (see fig. 21.8). You can also accomplish this by formatting a <PRE> container to display the text in the same manner; however, most viewers define PRE text as a non-proportional font and different from the rest of the body text.

◀ See "Using PRE," p. 183

Using Internal Links in HTML

◀ See "What Are Hypertext Links?" p. 252

The WWW's intuitive nature is not a boon granted by the system—people have to create the links to allow users to wander the Web's wealth of documents. This data can be located in the same document, in different documents in the same application, or on different files on remote Web hosts. In Chapter 14, I covered what links are and how to use them to access Web and other Internet information systems. The question now is, when should you use them?

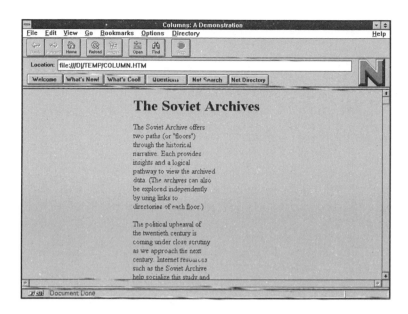

Fig. 21.8
You can display
text columns at
any point in the
Web page.

A good link jumps right out at you. The first thing you notice is that it relates directly to another document or section in the current document. Other times you have to make a connection between what the text is saying and how the other resource will benefit the reader. The main concept here is to limit your links to those that enhance the current information, and to provide every link possible to enhance the reader's experience.

> **Note**
>
> Watch out for blank spaces that creep into your links; they may be displayed in the viewer as part of the link text, giving you a link that looks like this:
>
> `E-mail me at Webmaster@mall.com_.`

The intersection of these two ideas is not as complex as it may sound. In any Web document, there are going to be obvious links (to software products you mention, or to other services or Web sites). The less obvious links are those that connect, for example, a reference to grail mythology to the Arthurian Home Page.

The key to using links is to balance the possible detours for a reader's attention with the material at hand. Try to place links at the end of thoughts, not smack dab in the middle, so that the natural progression from your idea to the link reference and back is an easy transition (because you do want people to come to your page sometimes).

VI

Document Aesthetics

Creating Navigation Text Links

Tip
When creating text links, avoid self-referential references to the linking action. Stay away from such phrases as "click here" to indicate a link—users can see that there's a link. Be descriptive with what it links to, not just what it is.

Web documents don't have any natural internal navigation capabilities. Web viewers provide the user with buttons and keyboard shortcuts that allow them to move forwards and backwards along the document path they've been following. Authors, however, can use links as navigation aids.

Most people are already familiar with navigation aids. VCRs with on-screen programming have "press 'menu' to return to main menu" and day of the week on-screen options. User's manuals (and this book) have references (just like links) to other information in the text, as well as guides at the end of chapters to direct you to your next topic of interest. These kinds of tools should be made available to Web users as well.

Navigation links are easy to create. Figure 21.9 shows how I formed a series of text links that create button-like interfaces for Web documents.

Fig. 21.9
In general, navigation links should provide access to higher-level documents, such as the application's main Web page, and optionally to services like e-mail and information indexes.

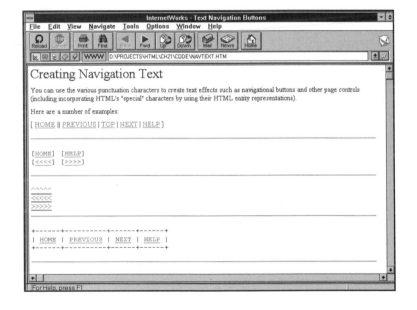

Depending on your needs, you might want to limit your in-page navigation controls to links to the previous and next pages in a series (if your information is being presented in a linear fashion across a number of HTML documents) or strictly to a "main menu" Web page. As the author, it's in your power to decide where the user should be encouraged to travel.

Controlling Netscape's Variable Font Sizes

Netscape provides control over the actual size of the on-screen text. The definition is created with the <FONT SIZE=> code. The value can be set to an absolute size (numerically 1 through 7) or it can be a size relative to the base (or standard) font in the text containers (using the + and – symbols).

The Netscape text control is a nice touch to HTML, and should become a standard fixture in the future. Using FONT SIZE, it's possible to create the following:

- *A small capital letters effect in your text.* Just capitalize all of the body text and raise the first letter of each capitalized word by +1.

- *Large initial capital letters.* Set the value of the first letter to 5 or 6, depending on how large you want the cap to be.

- *A receding text effect.* Set all of the text to size 7, then reduce the final characters by one until you reach the value of one for the last letter.

- *An approaching text effect.* Begin with a font size of one and increase each letter by one until all of the remaining text is in size 7.

Figure 21.10 shows a few Netscape text effects. Remember, these are only visible in Netscape Navigator and other Netscape-compatible viewers, so be sure your audience can appreciate the time and effort you put into these effects.

Tip
To change the entire document's base font size in Netscape, use the <BASEFONT SIZE= > coding. The value can range from 1 through 7; the default text size has a value of 3.

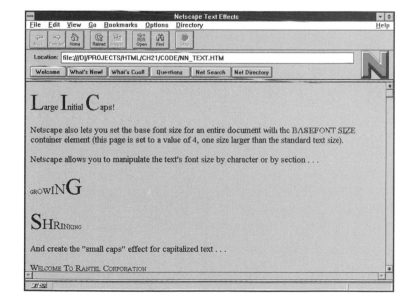

Fig. 21.10
Don't be too fancy with your effects— a single effect at the appropriate time will have much more impact than a document loaded with all sorts of text manipulation (that betrays a lack of any sort of critical eye).

VI

Document Aesthetics

From Here...

This chapter discussed HTML design issues regarding text and HTML elements. Other references on document layout and page design are available from any bookstore or library and are invaluable for extending the practices of print publishing to the WWW. To learn about the design issues regarding inline images in Web pages, or to see how these guidelines are put to use, refer to the following chapters:

- Chapter 8, "HTML Standards and Practices," describes how HTML authoring has accumulated a set of common practices for the benefit of both authors and end users. This chapter discusses these "good habits" of HTML development.

- Chapter 22, "Managing Your Images," discusses the design issues surrounding inline images and how they are best used in HTML applications.

- The chapters in Part VII, "Sample HTML Applications," detail the creation of two HTML applications from the concept stage to online the World Wide Web.

- Part VIII, "HTML Editors and Style Sheets," provides a look into the most widely used HTML document tools, including stand-alone editors and add-ons for popular word processors.

Chapter 22

Managing Your Images

"Painting isn't an aesthetic operation; it's a form of magic designed as a mediator between this strange hostile world and us, a way of seizing the power by giving form to our terrors as well as our desires."

– Pablo Picasso

"Painting can do for the illiterate what writing does for those who can read."

—Pope Gregory the Great

In the history of human communication, the image—any sort of graphic expression—has been the companion of spoken and written words since humans first learned how to express themselves. From cave paintings tens of thousands of years ago to modern-day graffiti, art transcends many of the barriers that hamper other modes of communication.

Before this starts to sound like an Art Criticism course, let's ground this in the discussion of using images on the World Wide Web. As an international information system, the Web's capability to incorporate graphical data is absolutely critical in breaking down language and cultural differences. If the audience doesn't understand you, there's something wrong with your message! Text can only get you so far, and if your audience doesn't understand your language—a definite possibility on the global Web—the graphical information you choose and how you integrate it into your textual information can be the key to making your message understood.

This chapter answers the following questions:

- What can I do to best use large graphic images in my Web pages?

- Is it possible to control where graphics align in a document?

- What are interlaced GIFs (and why should I care)?

■ How do transparent GIFs work?

■ Should I use navigation buttons in my documents?

■ Can I scale graphics without having to physically resize them?

How to Use Graphics in Web Pages

◀ See "Just What
Is an Image
Map?" p. 272

Icons are used to represent the text they're associated with or to replace functions (such as how hyperlinked images work), as shown in figure 22.1. Images can completely replace the conventional text interface, as with image maps, and must communicate the entire message alone—that's why so many image maps include text labels in them; it's hard for a single image to replace a series of actions or choices.

Fig. 22.1
ReZ.n8's home
page is aestheti-
cally pleasing and
professional-
looking, but
confusing for the
first time reader.
What do the
icons do?

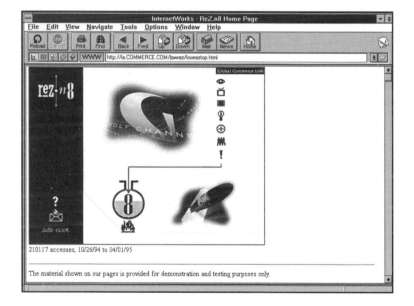

Choose Your Images Carefully

How are authors successful in using graphics to enhance, rather than detract from, their mode of communication? They achieve success by choosing images that draw on a common set of meanings. For example, everyone knows that a question mark (?) represents an idea; if an author places a button on a page that is only a question mark, the user will understand that, if they are confused by what to do in this page, the question mark will provide help or additional information.

Symbols are everywhere in our society: traffic signs, map legends, even company logos (who in the world is not going to recognize the McDonald's golden arches?). Organizations exist to establish common meanings to sets of international and regional symbols. These are tools that authors can draw on and feel fairly sure that their audience will "get the picture" (see fig. 22.2).

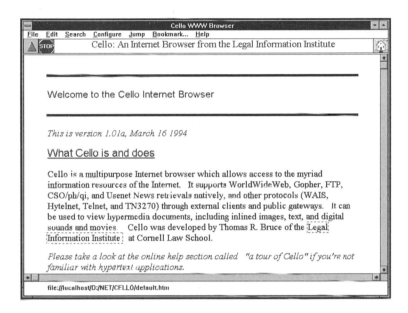

Fig. 22.2
Web viewers have standardized button graphics for certain universal functions, such as the "stop sign" for stopping the transfer of files; if a viewer detours from these conventions, the audience has to work harder to use the software.

Why Use Images at All?

"Pictures can induce strong feelings in the reader, but they can also lack the specificity of words. Words, on the other hand, offer that specificity, but can lack the immediate emotional charge of pictures, relying instead on a gradual cumulative effect."

"Together, of course, words and pictures can work miracles."

–Scott McCloud, *Understanding Comics*

There is a reason why the WWW, when introduced with its multimedia capabilities, struck such a chord in the global masses of the Internet. It's Picasso's magical mediator, Pope Gregory's messenger of meaning to the illiterati, McCloud's miraculous synthesis of ideas. People are enchanted—and delighted—the first time they see information on the WWW. They can't believe that the Internet has made the leap from being trapped in a textual

VI

Document Aesthetics

communication mode to a visual, layered, and engaging medium (see fig. 22.3). Actually, they just think the graphics are cool and like clicking the mouse on things. The effect is the same, even if something is lost in the interpretation!

Fig. 22.3
This page contains links to thousands of Web sites. Sure, people like things to click on, but this is taking that idea a little too far!

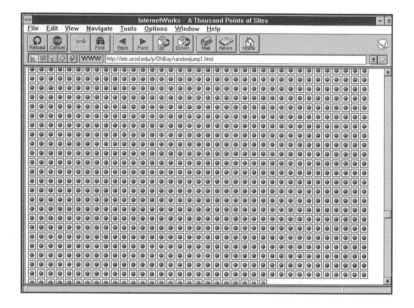

Getting Down to Business

Armed with some knowledge of how and why images are so important to the popularity and success of the Web is one thing—knowing how to make it work for you is another. It's time to deal with the brass tacks and show you how images can enhance your Web pages.

Using Large Graphics in HTML

Many of the uses for the WWW involve presenting large quantities of images. It's a foregone conclusion that, once the Web became a social atmosphere, coffee table books and personal adventures through the hinterlands (with hundreds of photographs, of course) would be widely available. I may be poking a little fun here, but there are some absolutely well-done Web applications like this. Two such sites are Philip Greenspun's "Travels with Samantha" (**http://martigny.ai.mit.edu/samantha/travels-with-samantha.html**) and Lee Liming's "A Tourist Expedition to Antarctica" (**http://http2.sils.umich.edu/Antarctica/Story.html**).

There are also online art galleries and artist resources that maintain hundreds of full-size images.

So how do you incorporate large images into Web pages? With smaller images, of course. *Thumbnail images* are small (or reduced) representations of larger images. They're typically 5 to 10K in size, and you can use quite a few of them before you push the patience of even 14.4K baud users. A good rule of thumb is to break the images into categories and try to maintain more documents with fewer inline thumbnails than fewer pages with more images.

◄ See "What's a Picture Worth?" p. 222

> **Note**
>
> An *inline image* is inserted directly into a document, rather than having to download it separately for viewing with an additional application. Inline images are useful because they add considerably to a Web page, either by making it visually more appealing, or by adding to some page element, such as a "clickable" button.

Use the thumbnails as links to the full-sized image. If a user wants to see the larger image, a click of the mouse retrieves only that file, saving a tremendous amount of time. Figure 22.4 shows how the "Travels with Samantha" Web site uses thumbnails to represent links to the full-sized images.

Fig. 22.4
This Web site has more than 220 full-sized JPEG images, and uses inline thumbnails to allow users to retrieve only the full-sized images they want to see.

VI

Document Aesthetics

◀ See "Just What Is an Image Map?" p. 272

A second method for incorporating thumbnails is to create an image map GIF with the thumbnails as a part of the image. This model is limited; to make any changes, you have to edit the composited image map GIF—instead of just replacing the necessary thumbnails in your thumbnail directory and making sure the Web page inline image statement points to the new images.

> **Note**
>
> If you use larger images for a Netscape audience, take advantage of the IMG element's LOWRSC extension. This lets a single link define both the smaller, low resolution version and the larger high resolution version of the image.
>
> On the first pass through the document, Netscape Navigator loads the image defined by the LOWSRC attribute. Then, after all images have been loaded, it returns and loads all images defined by the SRC statement. This allows users to wait to see the better-looking image after getting an idea of what's on the page.
>
> Try this trick with black-and-white LOWSRC images and color SRC images. Viewers that don't understand the LOWRSC attribute simply ignore it.

Controlling Graphic Alignment

◀ See "Aligning Graphics and Text," p. 237

HTML provides a number of options for aligning images in Web documents. The most common alignment is to let the viewer do it—just throw the images into the document and the viewer will wrap them in the viewer window depending on the size of the window and the graphics. Text is used the same way.

Authors generally like a little more control over the display of their hard work. Controlling how images will be displayed can be tricky, because you have no clue what size the viewer window will be. Users might leave their viewers at their default start-up size, they might use them full-screen (and at different resolutions), and they might tile them on their desktop with other open windows and applications. You just don't know, so don't assume anything.

Most authors take it on good faith that users want to read Web pages. One way to give them the best experience is to provide a guideline graphic that tells the user "size your viewer to the width of this graphic" (see fig. 22.5).

This kind of approach is a little broach of HTML's platform independent philosophy—what if the user's display isn't wide enough for the image? What if they aren't using graphics? It's a tricky request but one that is occurring with more regularity on the Web.

Fig. 22.5
How wide should
your viewer be?
This site lets you
know.

Other means of controlling alignment is to incorporate other HTML elements that lend control to Web page layout. Paragraph breaks assure that a series of images are aligned vertically; PRE containers assure the horizontal spacing between images. Try displaying images inside lists (definition and bulleted lists are especially interesting) and in lists inside lists. For Netscape users, the CENTER container does just that for any graphics and text. See figure 22.6 for some creative alignment.

◀ See "The Paragraph Break," p. 178

◀ See "Using PRE," p. 183

Fig. 22.6
The Paris home
page formats its
image links in a
non-conforming
and visually
pleasing manner.

VI

Document Aesthetics

Interlaced and Transparent GIFs

Incorporating graphics into Web pages is no small feat for the graphic designer. HTML doesn't provide many tools to control how images are displayed. Much of the work has to take place before the images reach the Web server.

Tip

Use an Internet search engine to locate graphics utilities available on the Net. A browser such as Netscape comes with a directory button that offers a selection of search engines to choose from.

Such is the case for two vital image effects that are supported by Web viewers. The first effect, *interlacing,* enhances the end user's experience by displaying an image in stages as it's retrieved.

An interlaced image is much like an American television signal where each picture (or frame, in video lingo) is composed of two "fields" that contain alternating lines of information. When a video signal is received by a television, it first displays one field a line at a time, then goes back to the top of the frame and displays the missing alternate lines one at a time, until a complete frame is displayed. The television does this 30 times in a second, creating the illusion of motion through persistence of vision—but that's a discussion for another field of study.

Tip

Make the background color of a transparent GIF graphic light gray. If a viewer doesn't support transparent GIF files, the GIF still looks transparent against the viewer's default background (if the user didn't change the viewer background to another color).

Interlaced GIF images do the same thing, but on a much slower scale—a single "pass" can take four or five seconds, and GIFs use more than two alternating fields to create the complete image. When you watch an interlaced GIF being displayed in a Web page, one of two effects will happen: the image will look like horizontal blinds opening, and you can see each visible line in the normal resolution, or the image will look like a *rack focus,* where it changes from a blocky low resolution image to the normal resolution image (see fig. 22.7). There are advantages and disadvantages to both, but the author has no control over this process at all.

The second effect, *transparency,* is a creative enhancement for GIF images. There are two GIF formats available today: GIF 87a and GIF 89a. The earlier version, 87a, does not support transparency. The newer GIF standard, 89a, lets authors create a transparent "channel" by assigning a color from the image's color palette to the background. This allows transparent GIFs to "float" above a background and psychologically breaks the confinements of the image "box."

Any GIF (or other graphic file, for that matter) can be converted to the 89a format with one of dozens of utilities. For the Macintosh, Transparency and GIF Converter fit this bill. For Windows, LView Pro and Paintshop Pro can convert and edit GIF files. For UNIX, xv is one of the most capable image editing utilities around.

Fig. 22.7
InternetWorks
uses the horizontal
blinds method
of displaying
interlaced GIFs.

Figure 22.8 shows a Web page with a graphic with and without the transparency characteristic.

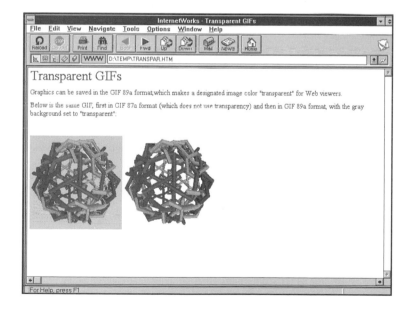

Fig. 22.8
Any one image
color can be made
transparent,
creating images
with holes or with
non-rectangular
edges.

VI

Document Aesthetics

Troubleshooting

I want users who are reading my Web page to be able to create GIFs on-the-fly that will be displayed to them. What can I do?

Thomas Boutell has written a program library, gd, for generating GIFs on-the-fly. The library allows users to manipulate polygon fills, line styles, shape tiling, interlacing, and many more characteristics. To implement this feature, you use a form on your Web page that gives users the characteristics they can manipulate and then submits the form to a CGI script. The script takes the parameters and generates a new GIF image with the gd library, and then generates another Web page with the new GIF or replaces an inline image in the current page and reloads the same page on the WWW viewer.

The gd 1.1 library is available at **http://siva.cshl.org/gd/gd.html**.

Creating Navigation Buttons

Web users are a smart bunch, but they're rarely psychic. When they're maneuvering through a Web site, they probably won't remember the URL for each of your different application pathways. And, although it may be easy for them to travel back to where they've been before (using the viewer's navigation buttons or document history list), they won't know how to get somewhere new.

Tip
There's also a problem with authors shifting the navigating tasks to the Web users—the harder you make them work to read your information, the less likely they'll explore much or return to your Web site later.

Provide the user with the navigation tools they need right in the Web document. By including graphics with links to your section heads (or the introduction, index, or feedback pages), you empower the users to follow their inquisitive natures. You create navigation tools with inline images. There are two choices for incorporating inline images as navigation tools in a Web document: as a series of hyperlink images or as a single image map.

The advantage of using a series of navigation graphics is that they provide you with the freedom to pick and choose what controls will appear on what pages, and you can order and align them in a number of ways. They're easy to edit or replace and, in HTML 3.0, will be able to provide the same linked functionality to text-only users (by incorporating links in the ALT text, which is not supported in HTML 2.0). Figure 22.9 shows a series of uses for separate navigation graphics.

The advantage of using an image map is that you're allowed greater freedom to create navigation tools that don't conform to the "square button" syndrome. Links can be whimsical, they can incorporate text and composited graphics, and they can be horizontal or vertical (for Netscape audiences) within the body of text. You can easily transport image maps from one document to the next.

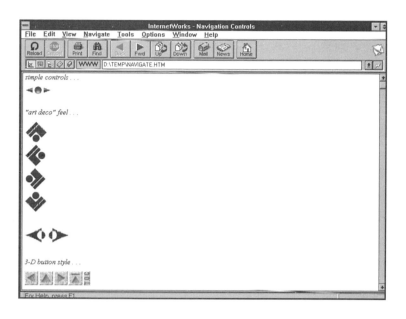

Fig. 22.9
Different techniques are applicable to different styles of Web pages—the creative choice is yours.

Figure 22.10 shows a Web page that incorporates an image map for navigating the Web site. When creating image maps, you're required to determine the *x*-axis and *y*-axis pixel coordinates of your "hot spots." Web utilities like Mapedit let you draw hot spot shapes onto an image and save the results to a text file.

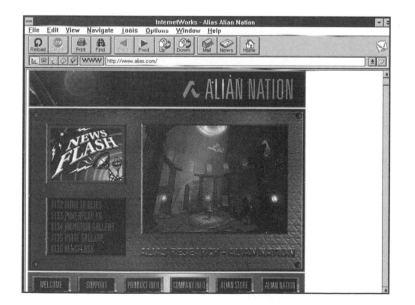

Fig. 22.10
Image maps can use text to represent a hot spot or navigational link.

Scaling Graphics in Netscape

Netscape Navigator supports a feature that lets you define both the HEIGHT and WIDTH of an image in your HTML document. The primary function of these dimensions is to let Navigator map out the page layout faster when retrieving a Web page, thus displaying the text information much sooner than it normally would.

A secondary function (and much more interesting, from a graphic design perspective) is to use HEIGHT and WIDTH to scale the image to new dimensions. If you set these values to pixel sizes that are different from the actual image size (say, to twice as large, or to half the size), Navigator scales the images to fit the new dimensions. This will be very useful some day for letting the Web server scale images on-the-fly to match the current size of the Web viewer accessing a document with graphics, such as a navigation bar or logo banner.

Figure 22.11 shows a Web page that demonstrates a "normal" GIF display and the same GIF scaled with the IMG extensions.

Fig. 22.11

Scaling images in Netscape can create distortions—test all Web pages that use auto-scaling to make sure the image is still acceptable.

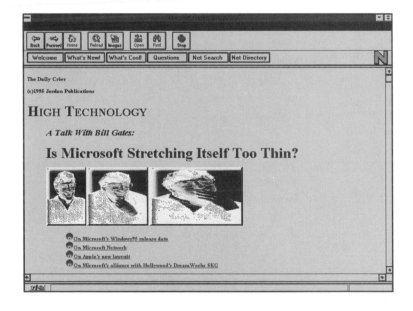

Troubleshooting

I just decided to physically resize all of my page images. Is there a utility that will make changes to an entire group of graphic files at once?

Yes! MegaMedia's shareware Batch Image Processor (or BIP) for Windows can make global changes to a selected group of files. It can rescale all of the images to the same dimensions, as well as apply textures and image effects (such as parchment and soften) to the entire group. This is a fantastic utility for managing a collection of graphic images that need to have a uniform look.

From Here...

There are plenty of other materials available that can give you general advice towards better graphic design—check your local bookstore or library in the desktop publishing and graphic illustration sections. For "tips and tricks" about using text creatively in HTML documents, or to see how these guidelines are put to use in real-world applications, refer to the following chapters:

- Chapter 8, "HTML Standards and Practices," describes how HTML authoring has accumulated a set of common practices for the benefit of both authors and end users. This chapter discusses these "good habits" of HTML development.

- Chapter 21, "Managing Your Text," discusses the design issues surrounding how text and HTML elements can be used for consistent and creative purposes in Web documents.

- The chapters in Part VII, "Sample HTML Applications," detail the creation of two HTML applications from the concept stage to online the World Wide Web.

- Part VIII, "HTML Editors and Style Sheets," provides a look into the most widely used HTML document tools, including stand-alone editors and add-ons for popular word processors.

VI

Document Aesthetics

Part VII

Sample HTML Applications

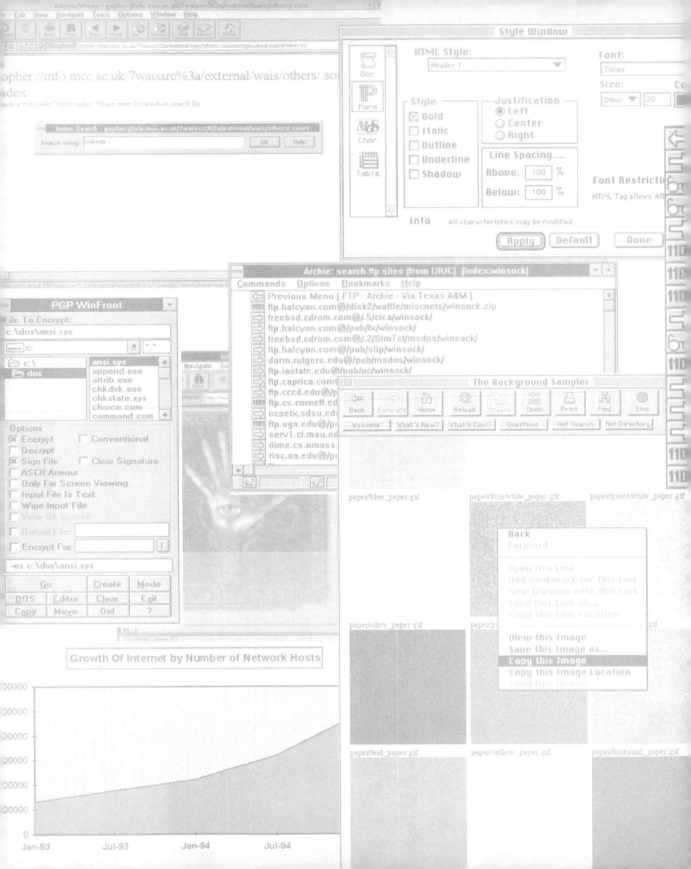

Chapter 23

Online Visitor's Guide to Jubilee Falls State Park

People use the World Wide Web in hundreds of ways every day. One of the most popular is searching the Web for information about a travel destination or to learn about someone else's travel experiences. Regions and communities are getting online in an effort to attract these new "cyber tourists." To successfully promote a tourist location online, cities and states have to catch the Web audience's interest and communicate the "local flavor" to tempt them into participating in the local tourist trade.

This chapter presents the step-by-step development process for a Web-based guidebook and travel reference for a fictitious Pacific Northwest state park. The process includes the following:

- Defining the goals of the application
- Outlining the structure of the application
- Creating the guidebook's body text
- Designing the guide's graphics and images
- Creating the response forms and scripts
- Putting it together in HTML documents

Defining Goals

Jubilee State Park is a scenic getaway in the Pacific Northwest, encompassing parts of a mountain range, lakes, waterfalls, and broad forests. The state park administration has made the resources available to produce a guidebook for the park. Their goals include the following:

- To provide an electronic guide complete with seasonal information and park maps

- To broadcast the guidebook over the WWW in an effort to attract tourists

- To display the guidebook on the park's visitor information kiosks

- To provide current information without incurring the costs of reprinting literature

- To increase the park's attendance while managing budget costs

Tip
Kiosks are stand-alone information machines, many with touch screens for ease of use. They're often used to provide guidance to services or activities, such as in a library or shopping mall.

As one of many local and federal facilities trying to increase their seasonal business, and in online competition with larger "name" locations such as the Grand Canyon and the Napa Valley region, Jubilee Falls needs to make a concerted effort to promote and advertise its presence on the Internet. First, the Guidebook will be publicized on the Web's popular new site references, including the NCSA "What's New on the WWW" page and by post in the UseNet newsgroup **comp.infosystems.www.announce**. Second, the park's designated "Web master" (the person creating the assets for the Web site and managing it when the site is finished) will maintain an online presence in UseNet discussion groups that might be interested to know about the park's facilities, such as **alt.rec.camping**, **rec.outdoors.fishing**, **rec.travel.usa-canada**, **rec.climbing**, **misc.kids.vacation**, and **rec.animals.wildlife**.

> **Note**
>
> Authors are discovering that HTML and a Web viewer are powerful replacements for traditional multimedia and computer-based training (CBT) software tools. A sophisticated Web application can provide most of the functions and features of a product created with other proprietary and expensive software authoring systems. These uses for HTML and Web clients will continue to expand as the Web standards mature further.

Outlining the Application

The park has identified four sections for their Web application: the introduction, with a list of services and interactive maps to the park's facilities; the park's seasonal schedules and fee and reservation information; a "what's there to do" section, with a list of activities indexed to the park location and when the activity is recommended; and a scenic tour of park images to give users a glimpse of the park's highlights.

The park creates a flow chart for each section to flesh out the form of Web site struture. These charts show only the individual pages or sub-group of pages, not the intuitive links users will expect when the pages are distributed online. Figure 23.1 shows the layout of the introduction section, figure 23.2 shows the seasonal schedules and fees section, figure 23.3 shows the index of activities, and figure 23.4 shows the scenic tour.

VII

Sample Applications

Tip
Web applications, although non-linear from the end users' perspective, actually do have a clearly-defined structure. When planning a new application, take the time to lay out the structure and content.

Fig. 23.1
This chart represents the structure of the introduction text and map documents on the Web site.

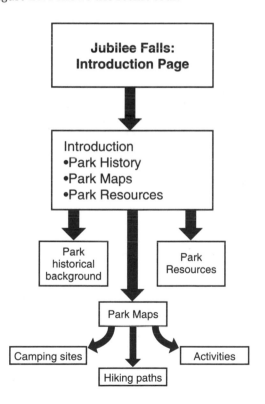

Fig. 23.2
This chart shows
the schedules and
fees sub-group of
documents.

Fig. 23.3
Here you can see
the index of
activities pages.

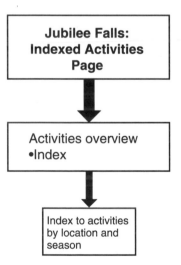

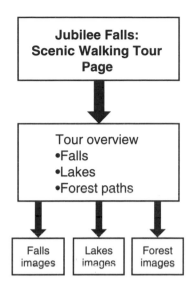

VII

Sample Applications

Fig. 23.4
This chart
represents the
scenic tour image
pages.

Creating the Body Text

After creating a visual guide to give this Web site a general shape, the park creates the content for these documents. These documents are strictly text only—adding the HTML formatting comes later.

As a public facility and a destination for foreign tourists, it's imperative that the language is direct and easy to understand. The point is to attract visitors, not discourage them from finding the details they'll need to plan their vacations. Communicating the park's seasonal calendar and hours is almost more important than showing off the facilities themselves. Figure 23.5 shows the plain text for the introduction page.

Tip
A clear focus on the information followed by good organization are the key to a successful Web site; know what your audience expects to find and deliver them the goods in a way that's clear and accessible.

Fig. 23.5
The text is organized into short paragraphs and the text that will be used for the links to other pages clearly describes the content referenced by the link—a good sign.

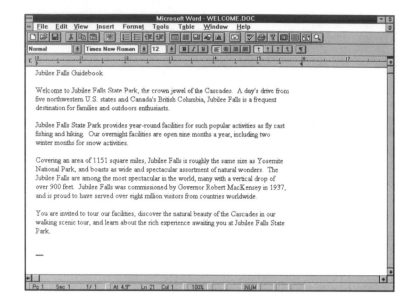

Creating the Graphics and Images

The park administrators (and the state Parks and Recreation department) have a traditional image or reputation for how the facilities are represented. This includes a standardized logo for brochures and other literature, and the state government has an official seal. It's necessary to incorporate these elements into the graphic design for the Web application.

Unfortunately, the park does not have any of these resources in an electronic format that the "Web master" can readily use. So she turns to a combination of commercial and shareware software programs to create the look for the Web pages.

> **Note**
>
> Graphic design is more than just "making pictures"; it entails choosing an overall organizing purpose and graphical "feel." Mixing unrelated graphic types, mismatched color schemes, and inconsistent elements betrays a novice approach to graphic design.

Knowing that all graphical Web viewers can display GIF graphic files, she selects PhotoMagic, the paint program that came with Micrografix Designer, to create the new graphics. Programs like PhotoMagic give complete control over the size, resolution, color depth, and graphic effects of each image. Figure 23.6 shows the new park logo.

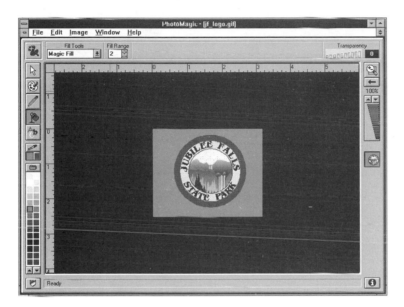

Fig. 23.6
The logo uses simple text and color combinations for a pleasing, professional effect.

Many of the Web pages will display color photo images of scenic sights and activities. The Web master hires a photographer to document the park's natural beauty. These images are supplied on a CD-ROM disk in the Kodak PhotoCD format. The Web master manages the photos with an image catalog utility—in this case, Collage Image Manager (see fig. 23.7).

After the images have been cataloged, the Web master sorts them out, selecting the images for the scenic tour and for the activities index. She also picks an image for the welcome page that represents the park's namesake.

Some images need to be edited to fit into the Web page design. The Web master uses Collage to crop and convert the images into a format best supported over the Web. In this case, because she's using photo-realistic images, she opts for the JPEG graphic format (it supports more than 256 colors, which are better suited for the GIF file format).

Last, she creates a set of unique navigation GIF images to add a nice touch to the Web pages.

Fig. 23.7
Collage Image
Manager displays
the PhotoCD
images with
thumbnails,
simplifying
finding and
previewing the
collection of
image files.

Troubleshooting

The HTML documents and graphics I'm using are copyrighted by my organization. How do we protect our intellectual property over the Web?

Truthfully, you can't. If someone wants to steal from you bad enough, they will. What's prudent, though, is to protect the accidental misuse of your work. This happens when users include links from their Web pages to pages on your server that are "inside" the application, away from the main page that usually contains the author's information and company affiliation. For the best protection, include copyright statements on each page (using the smallest heading size, H6, to keep them unobtrusive) and LINK statements in the documents' head sections to identify the author and the originating organization. You can also add copyright statements in fine print to graphics if necessary.

Creating the Input Forms

The Jubilee Falls Guidebook is primarily intended to deliver information; an on-site kiosk is less complicated if users aren't asked to input information (and a keyboard isn't necessary). But, for the online audience, a form that can be filled out to receive additional park information by mail is a great idea; these people are most likely not from the local area, and probably don't have access to the Park Service's printed materials. A response form is the perfect way to get feedback on the park's efforts to provide an informative Web site. The Web master decides to plan out the form in her word processor (see fig. 23.8).

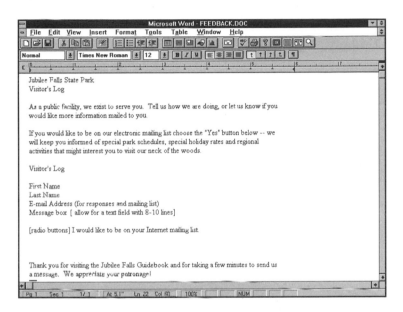

Fig. 23.8
You can use the information form to receive feedback on specific questions pertaining to the park's service.

The form is written in HTML as follows.

```
<HTML>
<HEAD>
<TITLE>Jubilee Falls Visitor's Log</TITLE>
</HEAD>

<BODY>
<IMG ALIGN=middle SRC="../graphics/jf_logo.gif"><H1>Jubilee Falls State Park</H1>
<H2>Visitor's Log </H2>
<P>
As a public facility, we exist to serve you. Tell us how we are doing, or
let us know if you would like more information mailed to you.
<P>
If you would like to be on our electronic mailing list choose the "Yes"
button below -- we will keep you informed of special park schedules,
special holiday rates and regional activities that might interest you to
visit our neck of the woods.
<P>
<HR>
<FORM METHOD=POST ACTION="http://www.jubilee.org/cgi-bin/log_script">
```

```
<H3>Visitor's Log</H3>
<P>
First Name: <INPUT TYPE="text" NAME="fname" SIZE=25 VALUE=""><BR>
Last Name: <INPUT TYPE="text" NAME="lame" SIZE=25 VALUE=""><BR>
Mailing address: <BR><TEXTAREA NAME="message" ROWS="4" COLS="30"> </TEXTAREA>
<P>
E-mail address (for responses and mailing list):
<BR>
<INPUT NAME="email" SIZE=25 VALUE="">
<P>
I would like to receive <SELECT NAME="mailer">
<OPTION SELECTED VALUE="nothing"> Nothing
<OPTION VALUE="brochure"> Jubilee Falls brochure
<OPTION VALUE="calendar"> Jubilee Falls Calendar
<OPTION VALUE="activities"> Jubilee Falls Activities Schedule
<OPTION VALUE="stateparks"> Oregon State Parks catalog
<OPTION VALUE="everything"> All information
</SELECT>
<P>
Enter a message if you wish:
<P>
<TEXTAREA NAME="message" ROWS="10" COLS="60"></TEXTAREA>
<P>
I would like to be on your Internet mailing list.
<INPUT TYPE="radio" NAME="list" VALUE="yes">Yes
<INPUT TYPE="radio" NAME="list" VALUE="no">No
</FORM>
<HR>
<P>
Thank you for visiting the Jubilee Falls Guidebook and for taking a few
minutes to send us a message. We appreciate your patronage!
<P>
<A HREF="http://www.jubilee.org/cgi-bin/menu"><IMG SRC="../graphics/
menubar.gif" ISMAP></A>
<H6>(c) 1995 Jubilee Falls State Park</H6>
</BODY>
</HTML>
```

Putting It All Together

To avoid having the Web page contents look different from viewer to viewer, the Web master decides to create the HTML documents in strict accordance with HTML 2.0 (with the exception of the Web application's feedback form, which is a feature of HTML 3.0 that most current viewers already support). When HTML 3.0 is released, she will return to the documents and add tables for the seasonal calendars and image dimension attributes to speed up the display of Web pages with inline images. She uses a stand-alone editor, HTML Assistant, to mark up the existing text documents.

The following code is the Jubilee Falls State Park home page in HTML (INDEX.HTM). The results are shown in figure 23.9.

On the CD

```html
<HTML>
<HEAD>
<TITLE>Jubilee State Park Guidebook</TITLE>
</HEAD>
<BODY>
<A HREF="http://www.jubilee.org/cgi-bin/main"><IMG SRC="../graphics/
jubilee.gif"
ALT="Welcome to the Jubilee Falls State Park Guidebook" ISMAP
BORDER=0></A>
<P><PRE> </PRE>
<P>
Select a menu option:
<PRE>
   <A HREF="intro.htm">[Introduction]</A>    <A HREF="schedule.htm">
[Schedules and Fees]</A>
   <A HREF="activity.htm">[Park activities]</A> <A HREF-"tour.htm">
[Scenic walking tour]</A>
</PRE>
<P>
<HR>
<H6>(c) 1995 Jubilee Falls State Park</H6>
</BODY>
</HTML>
```

Fig. 23.9
The Jubilee Falls State Park home page includes both an image map and text hyperlinks to access the linked Web pages.

On the CD

The following code is the Jubilee Falls State Park welcome page in HTML (INTRO.HTM). The results are shown in figure 23.10.

```
<HTML>
<HEAD>
<TITLE>Jubilee Falls Guidebook</TITLE>
</HEAD>
<BODY>
<IMG ALIGN=bottom SRC="../graphics/thmb_psh.gif"><H1>Jubilee Falls
Guidebook</H1>
Welcome to Jubilee Falls State Park, the crown jewel of the Cascades. A
day's drive from five northwestern U.S. states and Canada's British
Columbia, Jubilee Falls is a frequent destination for families and
outdoors enthusiasts.
<P>
Jubilee Falls State Park provides year-round facilities for such popular
activities as fly cast fishing and hiking. Our overnight facilities are
open nine months a year, including two winter months for snow activi-
ties.
<P>
Covering an area of 1151 square miles, Jubilee Falls is roughly the same
size as Yosemite National Park, and boasts as wide and spectacular
assortment of natural wonders. The Jubilee Falls are among the most
spectacular in the world, many with a vertical drop of over 900 feet.
Jubilee Falls was commissioned by Governor Robert MacKensey in 1937, and
is proud to have served over eight million visitors from countries
worldwide.
<P>
You are invited to <A HREF="facility.htm">check out our facilities</A>,
discover the natural beauty of the Cascades in our
<A HREF="tour.htm">walking scenic tour</A>, and learn about the
<A HREF="activity.htm">rich experience</A> awaiting you at Jubilee Falls
State Park.
<P><PRE> </PRE>
<P>
<A HREF="jubilee.htm"><IMG ALIGN=bottom SRC="../graphics/intro.gif"></A>
<A HREF="schedule.htm"><IMG ALIGN=bottom SRC="../graphics/schedfee.gif"></A>
<A HREF="activity.htm"><IMG ALIGN=bottom SRC="../graphics activity.gif"></A>
<A HREF="tour.htm"><IMG ALIGN=bottom SRC="../graphics/tour.gif"></A>
<A HREF="feedback.htm"><IMG ALIGN=bottom SRC="../graphics/ feedback.gif"></A>
<P>
<H6>(c) 1995 Jubilee Falls State Park</H6>
</BODY>
</HTML>
```

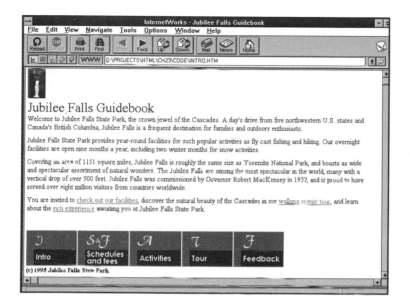

Fig. 23.10
Menu links are provided on this page with a row of separate linked images, using standard anchored hyperlinks and GIFs.

The following code is the Jubilee Falls State Park Schedules and Fees page in HTML (SCHEDULE.HTM). The results are shown in figure 23.11.

On the CD

```
<HTML>
<HEAD>
<TITLE>Jubilee Falls State Park Schedules and Fees</TITLE>
</HEAD>
<BODY>
<IMG ALIGN=middle
SRC="d:/projects/html/ch23/graphics/jf_logo.gif"><H1>Schedules and Fees</H1>
<P>
<B>Jubilee Falls Day Areas</B>
<P>
Open 365 days a year, including major holidays. These areas include
the hiking trails and boat slips on the McKensie riverhead. Day use
rates and activity fees are available <A HREF="fees.htm">here</A>.
<P><PRE> </PRE>
<P>
<B>Jubilee Falls Overnight Areas</B>
<P>
The overnight areas, including the powered RV slips and rustic
camping sites, are available on a seasonal basis. The following
calendar is for the 1995 season:
<P>
<BLOCKQUOTE><I>Jan. 1 through February 28</I>: No overnight areas
available due to potentially hazardous winter weather
conditions.<BR>
```

```
<I>March 1 through March 31</I>: Overnight only permitted in
powered RV slips. Limited shower and bathroom services
available.<BR>
<I>April 1 through October 31</I>: Overnight available in all
areas. Full shower and bathroom services available. Weather adviso-
ries may close the camping sites, so check with the local weather
information before planning your stay.<BR>
<I>November 1 through November 30</I>: Overnight only permitted in
powered RV slips. Limited shower and bathroom services
available.<BR>
<I>December 1 through December 31</I>: No overnight areas available
due to potentially hazardous winter weather conditions.</ BLOCKQUOTE>
<P><PRE> </PRE>
<P>
<H2>Activities Calendar</H2>
Jubilee Falls hosts many events year-round for outdoors enthusi-
asts. The following activities have been scheduled. Please
<A HREF="feedback.htm"> contact us</A> for late-breaking events and
calendar changes.
<P>
<DL>
<DT><B>May 13-14</B><BR>
<B>Couples Caravan Weekend</B>
<DD>Jubilee Falls throws a party for adult couples, including our
nightly chuckwagon banquet and music under the stars. Midnight
walking tours are held and all water activities are included in the
registration fees.
<P>
<DT><B>June 24</B><BR>
<B>Lightning Bug Races</B>
<DD>Overnighters can participate in Jubilee Falls' renown Lightning
Bug Races. This evening activity is open to children of all ages
and features prizes galore.
<P>
<DT><B>July 1</B><BR>
<B>Falls Jubilee</B>
<DD>The holiday weekend features the Falls Jubilee, a celebration
of the natural landmarks that make our park special. Walking tours
and public swimming are available in the high pools, underneath the
Widow Falls, the tallest waterfalls in the park.
<P>
<DT><B>August 26-27</B><BR>
<B>Kids Camp Jubilee</B>
<DD>A weekend for pre-teens, Jubilee Falls hosts over a dozen local
teen groups for fun in the sun. The weekend's highlight is the
McKensie Olympics, pitting teams of water-logged kids in seven
competitive events.
</DL><P>
<HR>
<IMG ALIGN=bottom SRC="../graphics/menubar.gif">
<P>
(c)1995 Jubilee Falls State Park
</BODY>
</HTML>
```

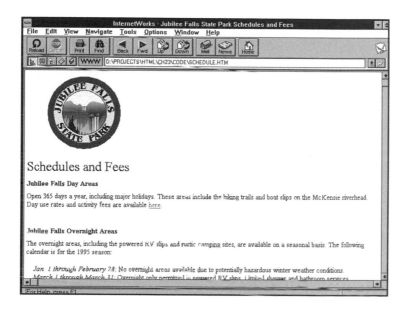

Fig. 23.11
When mixing italicized and normal text on the same line, watch out for the tendency of viewers to crowd them together.

VII

Sample Applications

The following code is the Jubilee Falls State Park Campsite Map page in HTML (CAMPMAP.HTM). The results are shown in figure 23.12.

On the CD

```
<HTML>
<HEAD>
<TITLE>Jubilee Falls Campsite Map</TITLE>

</HEAD>
<BODY>
<H1>Campsite Map</H1>
<P>
Use the following map to get information about the various overnight
camping areas at Jubilee Falls State Park. Click on a yellow triangle
(rustic campsite) or pink rectangle (Recreational Vehicle slip) for the
area's facilities and nearby activities. The black rectangle is the Park
Lodge — click on it for its operational hours and services.
<P>
<A HREF="http://www.jubilee.org/cgi-bin/campsites"><IMG SRC="../graph-
ics/campmap.gif" ALT="" ISMAP BORDER=0></A>
<P>
<HR>
<A HREF="camptxt.htm">Text-only listings</A> of the park's camp sites by number.
<HR>
<P>
(c) 1995 Jubilee Falls State Park
</BODY>
</HTML>
```

Fig. 23.12
Image map hot spots can be defined in any shape and size.

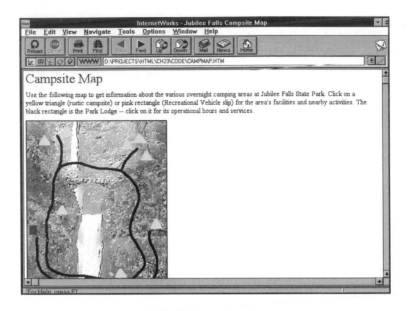

The following code is the Jubilee Falls State Park Activities Index page in HTML (ACTIVITY.HTM). The result of this code is shown in figure 23.13.

```
<HTML>
<HEAD>
<TITLE>Jubilee Falls State Park Activities Index</TITLE>

</HEAD>
<BODY>
<IMG ALIGN=middle SRC="d:/projects/html/ch23/graphics/
jf_logo.gif"><H1>Activities Index</H1>
<P>
Jubilee Falls offers a wide variety of activities for everyone from
the avid outdoorsman to the weekend nature lover. This index
provides the following for park activities:
<DL><DT><UL>
<LI>Location
<LI>Seasonal availability
<LI>Available park resources
<LI>Fees required
<LI>Recommended experience
</UL></DL>
<P><PRE> </PRE>
<P>
<A HREF="file://../graphics/activity.qtw"><IMG ALIGN=middle
SRC="../graphics/activity.jpg"></A>A short QuickTime video shows
many of our most popular activities.
<P><PRE> </PRE>
<P>
<H2>Index Starting Point</H2>
```

```
Choose a category to begin your search from. You can return to this
menu at any time by clicking the Index button: <IMG ALIGN=middle
SRC="../graphics/indx_psh.gif">
<P>
<DL>
<DT><B>By Season</B>
<DD><A HREF="winter.htm">Winter Season</A>
<DD><A HREF="summer.htm">Summer Season</A>
<DD><A HREF="yearly.htm">Year-round</A>
</DL>
<DL>
<DT><B>By Location</B>
<DD><A HREF="mckensie.htm">McKensie Riverhead</A>
<DD><A HREF="deschute.htm">Deschutes Riverhead</A>
<DD><A HREF="mt_jef.htm">Lower Mt. Jefferson</A>
<DD><A HREF="up_falls.htm">Upper Falls</A>
<DD><A HREF="low_falls.htm">Lower Falls</A>
<DD><A HREF="vista.htm">Vista Lake</A>
<DD><A HREF="jacob.htm">Jacob Lake</A>
<DD><A HREF="trail.htm">Forest Trails</A>
</DL>
<P>
<HR>
<IMG ALIGN=bottom SRC="../graphics/menubar.gif">
<P>
(c)1995 Jubilee Falls State Park
</BODY>
</HTML>
```

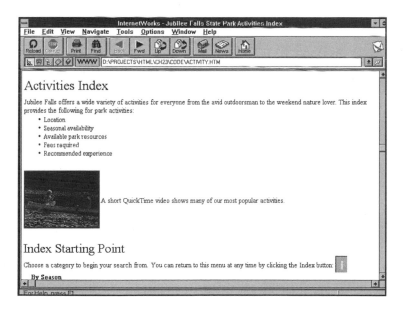

Fig. 23.13

A captured frame from the movie file acts as a clickable link to the actual QuickTime file.

On the CD

The following code is the Jubilee Falls State Park Scenic Walking Tour page in HTML (TOUR.HTM). The results are shown in figure 23.14.

```
<HTML>
<HEAD>
<TITLE>Jubilee Falls State Park Scenic Walking Tour</TITLE>
</HEAD>
<BODY>
<IMG ALIGN=middle SRC="d:/projects/html/ch23/graphics/
jf_logo.gif"><H1>Scenic Walking Tour</H1>
<P>
Jubilee Falls is a place of great natural beauty. Don't believe us, or
want to see more? Then join us on a walking tour of the park. You can
let us lead the way or choose your own path to explore the wonders of
Jubilee Falls State Park.
<P><PRE> </PRE>
<P>
<A HREF="path1.htm"><IMG ALIGN=middle
SRC="d:/projects/html/ch23/graphics/thmb_psh.gif"></A>Follow the park's
guide down the wooded path.
<P><PRE> </PRE>
<P>
Choose a path for yourself:
<P>
<DL><DT><UL>
<DD><A HREF="path1.htm"><IMG ALIGN=middle SRC="../graphics/path1.jpg">
Walk the forest paths</A>
<DD><A HREF="falls1.htm"><IMG ALIGN=middle SRC="../graphics/falls1.jpg">
Do you hear falling water?</A>
<DD><A HREF="river1.htm"><IMG ALIGN=middle SRC="../graphics/river1.jpg">
Water rushing into rivers</A>
<DD><A HREF="lake1.htm"><IMG ALIGN=middle SRC="../graphics/alone.jpg">
Alone on a lakeshore</A>
<DD><A HREF="sunset.htm"><IMG ALIGN=middle SRC="../graphics/sunset.jpg">
Until tomorrow . . .</A>
</UL></DL>
<P><PRE> </PRE>
<P>
<HR>
<IMG ALIGN=bottom SRC="../graphics/menubar.gif">
<P>
(c)1995 Jubilee Falls State Park
</BODY>
</HTML>
```

Fig. 23.14
Use unique elements (such as the recessed falls button) to indicate special options in the Web page.

The following code is the Jubilee Falls State Park Walking Tour: The Falls page in HTML (FALLS.HTM). The results are shown in figure 23.15.

On the CD

```
<HTML>
<HEAD>
<TITLE>Walking Tour: The Falls</TITLE>
</HEAD>
<BODY>
<B>Scenic Walking Tour</B>
<P>
<H1>The Falls</H1>
<P>
The highlight of Jubilee Falls State Park are its namesake, the
Jubilee Falls. This series of water drops begins in the Upper
Falls, where the park's tallest waterfall is located, and continues
with the Lower Falls, where the series of small drops creates a
chain of swimming holes with dense forest undergrowth.
<P>
The park's namesake, which also is represented in the park's
emblem, can be seen from many vantage points, but this rest stop is
the most dramatic.
<P>
<IMG ALIGN=bottom SRC="../graphics/falls0a.jpg"><BR>
<A HREF="../graphics/falls0.jpg"><IMG ALIGN=middle SRC= "../
graphics/thm2_psh.gif"></A> Click this button to see a larger
version of the Jubilee Fall (<I>note: this file is 370K</I>).
<P><PRE> </PRE>
<P>
The Lower Falls is filled with the sound of falling water. These
small drops are a main outflow of snow-bound water from the local
segment of the Cascade mountain range.
```

```
<P>
<IMG ALIGN=bottom SRC="../graphics/falls2.jpg"><IMG ALIGN=bottom
SRC="../graphics/falls3.jpg"><IMG ALIGN=bottom SRC="../graphics/
falls4.jpg"><IMG ALIGN=bottom SRC="../graphics/falls5.jpg"><IMG
ALIGN=bottom SRC="../graphics/falls1.jpg"><IMG ALIGN=bottom
SRC="../graphics/falls_a.jpg">
<P><PRE> </PRE>
<P>
<HR>
<IMG ALIGN=bottom SRC="../graphics/menubar.gif">
<P>
(c)1995 Jubilee Falls State Park
</BODY>
</HTML>
```

Fig. 23.15

You can link the smaller embedded image to the full-screen image for users to retrieve if they want.

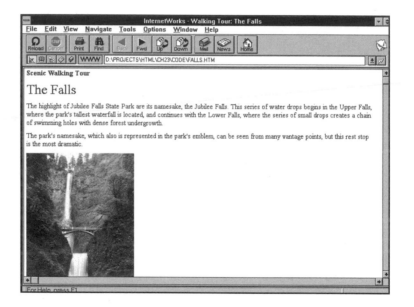

The Jubilee Falls Visitor's Log, as interpreted by InternetWorks, is shown in figure 23.16.

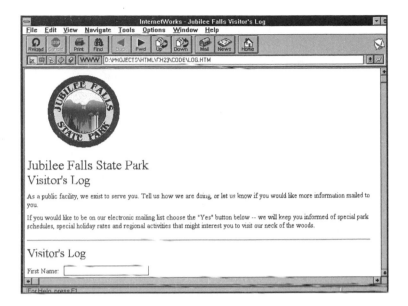

Fig. 23.16
Use separators,
such as horizontal
lines, to emphasize
the boundaries of
an HTML input
form.

From Here...

The Jubilee Falls Guidebook, complete with source code and images, is available on the CD-ROM. For additional application examples, and tips and tricks
on using HTML effectively, see the following chapters:

- Chapter 8, "HTML Standards and Practices," shows how HTML
  authoring has accumulated a set of common practices for the benefit of
  both authors and end users. This chapter discusses these "good habits"
  of HTML development.

- Chapter 21, "Managing Your Text," discusses the design issues surrounding how text and HTML elements can be used for consistent and
  creative purposes in Web documents.

- Chapter 24, "WWW Catalog for Paul Thompson Jewelers," describes
  how to create an online HTML commercial application for a retail
  catalog.

- Part VIII, "HTML Editors and Style Sheets," provides a look into the
  most widely-used HTML document tools, including stand-alone editors
  and add-ons for popular word processors.

Chapter 24

WWW Catalog for Paul Thompson Jewelers

The Internet's commercial traffic is increasing rapidly. When the W3 Consortium adopts a standard, secured HTTP protocol (allowing merchants and customers to send sensitive information without fear of it being stolen), the consumer market will open wide. WWW users will become hard-sought consumers.

This chapter presents a step-by-step development process for a fictitious Web-based customer catalog for a fine jewelry store that is interested in attracting national and international business. The process includes:

- Defining the application's goals

- Outlining the structure of the application

- Creating the body text of the catalog

- Creating the catalog's graphics and images

- Creating the response forms and scripts

- Putting it together in HTML documents

Tip
To be successful online, a company has to use the medium correctly to attract and keep customers.

Defining Goals

Paul Thompson Jewelers (PTJ) offers a wide range of products and services, from custom jewelry design and manufacturing to carrying jewelry items on consignment for local customers. PTJ also provides in-house certified appraisal services. PTJ wants to attain the following goals:

- Increase its customer base for retail fine jewelry by offering a range of products in varying price ranges to maximize customer interest

- Market "estate" jewelry and consignment products to an international audience

- Offer secured jewelry and collectibles appraisal services based on the company's professional certification and established industry reputation

- Measure consumer interest in other products and services, such as antiques, gift items, and fine stationery

- Build an international electronic mailing list for future direct promotions

As an independent store without an affiliation to a national or regional jewelry store chain, PTJ has the task of establishing a presence in this global marketplace. Besides publicizing the new Web site on NCSA's "What New on the WWW" and in the UseNet newsgroup **comp.infosystems.www.announce**, PTJ will participate in discussions on various UseNet newsgroups, including **rec.crafts.jewelry**, **rec.collecting**, and **rec.antiques**. PTJ will refrain from advertising its services in these discussion groups, but the sharing of knowledge (and a message signature that includes the URL of the commercial site) will let Net users become familiar with PTJ's staff and expertise.

> **Note**
>
> If you're creating a commercial HTML application, your focus has to be wider than just the application—you have to know where your audience will be and how to best advertise your presence without, for instance, ruffling anyone's feathers with blatant commercial postings on UseNet.

Outlining the Application

PTJ identified three separate sections for the Web site:

- *The introductory text,* with documents that discuss how jewelry is graded and valued, what services are available from PTJ, and defining some jewelry and antique purchasing tips for the electronic community

■ *The electronic catalog,* with thumbnail images and links to full-sized graphics

■ *The ordering and user feedback section,* which will also collect mailing list data

After the document creation stage is started, these three sections will be broken down further into smaller documents. But for now, the broad strokes are what's important.

PTJ creates a basic flow chart for each section—these charts don't show the nonlinear links between document text (they'll be added as the document content is clarified) but they do all point back to the primary Welcome home page. Figure 24.1 shows the text section, figure 24.2 shows the catalog section, and figure 24.3 shows the customer input section.

VII

Sample Applications

Tip
Adding information to an existing Web document structure requires only that new links be added to the existing pages that point to the new documents.

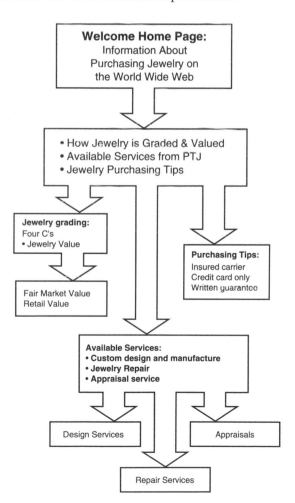

Fig. 24.1
This chart represents the structure of the informative documents on the Web site; items with bullets are links that lead to the connecting pages.

Fig. 24.2
This chart shows the basic form of the jewelry catalog.

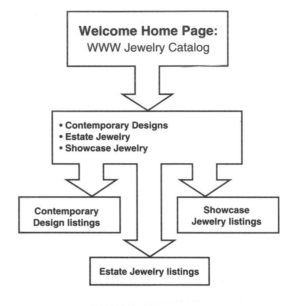

Fig. 24.3
This chart shows how the various input forms will relate to each other.

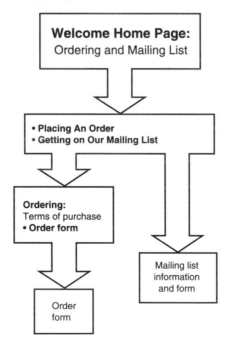

Creating the Body Text

After the overall structure is in place for each section, PTJ writes the body text for each document. Figure 24.4 shows the main home page text. Notice that headings, lists, and hyperlinks are included but not yet marked with HTML tags—this is the place to concentrate on the message, not how it is delivered.

> **Note**
>
> This is the most time-intensive step in Web authoring—you aren't writing for yourself, but for your audience. Make sure the text is easy to understand, that any jargon and unfamiliar phrases are explained, and that you write the text in manageable, frequent paragraphs for easy reading.

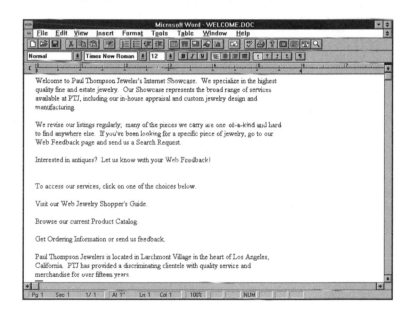

Fig. 24.4
You can use any word processor to create the body text for documents.

Remember to refer to the document outline for transitions in and out of the text; the content must lead naturally from one page to another or you risk confusing (and losing!) your audience.

Creating the Graphics and Images

As is true with most businesses, PTJ already has an existing company image that is reflected in its advertising, company literature, and even business cards. It's fairly easy to incorporate a company's style into HTML documents;

Tip
Use an HTML filter or style sheet with your favorite word processor to simplify the content creation process, or save your documents as plain text files to edit in a stand-alone HTML editor.

it's even easier if you have the company logo and representative text (such as a statement of purpose) in a digital graphic format.

In this case, PTJ has its company letterhead in a CorelDRAW! graphic format. Knowing that no WWW viewers support this data format, PTJ uses a common graphics utility to convert the metafile into a GIF file (the most widely supported format around). Figure 24.5 shows the PTJ letterhead after it has been converted in Lview Pro, a graphics utility that is often used by Web viewers as the external viewer for JPEG images. One of Lview's features is the capability to convert standard GIF images to transparent GIF format; here Lview sets the color white in the logo to the background, which will be transparent in the viewer window.

Fig. 24.5
After setting the background color, save the file in the GIF89a format to create a transparent GIF.

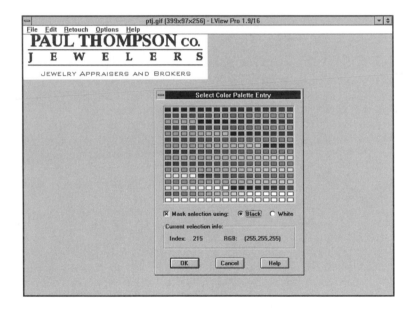

Tip
Save the proof sheets of image thumbnails created by your image cataloging software for easy reference in the future—you won't have to keep reloading the individual image files.

After the company graphic has been converted and prepped for use, PTJ selects the current inventory to display in the Web application. PTJ uses a 35mm camera (normally used for photographing appraisal jobs) to photograph each piece and has the film lab store the pictures on a CD-ROM in the Kodak PhotoCD format. PTJ uses its store computer system to open the CD-ROM disk and view the images in Jasc Media Center, a shareware graphics cataloging application frequently used to manage large collections of graphic files.

One great advantage of using PhotoCD is that the images are stored in multiple size formats. This gives PTJ a shortcut for creating small images for the online catalog that can be linked to large images if the customer wants a closer look. After selecting the images for the catalog, PTJ converts them to JPEG format (using Jasc Media Center). Figure 24.6 shows the converted inventory as thumbnails in Jasc Media Center.

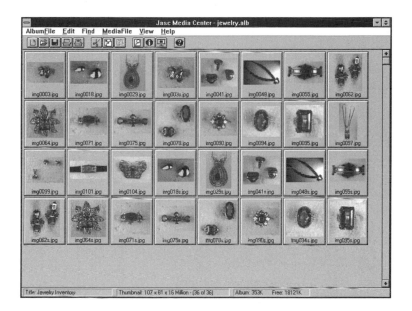

Fig. 24.6
Jasc Media Center can open files in 38 graphic file formats (including animation and digital video) and can convert files to any of 24 graphic file types.

When the images have been converted and labeled, PTJ uses Lview Pro once again to edit each JPEG file: cropping them to make them as small as they can be and reducing the retrieval times for the Web users (a few seconds can really add up when you have lots of files).

Finally, PTJ decides to use some additional GIFs for aesthetic value. They choose a unique button icon and a patterned separator graphic to enhance the layout of the Web pages.

Troubleshooting

Some viewers don't support transparent GIFs. How do I "simulate" transparency to keep my images looking as consistent as possible in all viewers?

The vast majority of Web viewers set the background color of the viewer window to a default color, somewhere from 20 to 35 percent gray. Fill in your transparent background areas with a gray value so that viewers that don't display the color as transparent will display a gray similar to their default background.

Creating the Input Forms

PTJ has planned for two forms: one for online product ordering and another for sending in mailing list requests and other Web feedback. The first step to planning a form is to put it on paper; because PTJ is an environmentally conscious company and tries to keep its office as paper-free as possible, it decides to map out the forms on its word processor. Figure 24.7 shows how the order form looks on-screen, and figure 24.8 shows the Web feedback form page.

Fig. 24.7
The order form will require a mixture of different form input field types.

Fig. 24.8
You can use the Web Feedback form for many purposes, including product search requests and mailing list additions.

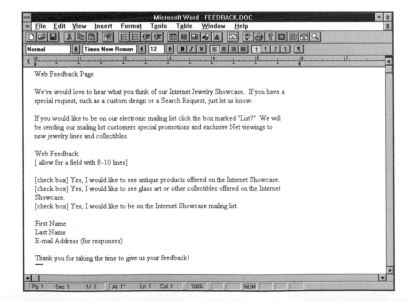

Putting It All Together

PTJ decides that it would like to use some of the basic enhancements that Netscape provides for HTML, including centering images, defining their height and width, and using custom horizontal rules. PTJ decides to use Quarterdeck's Web Author to edit the existing Word documents into Web pages. The rest of this chapter shows the HTML coding used to create each page, and the corresponding interpretations by Netscape 1.0N.

The following code creates the Paul Thompson home page in HTML (WELCOME.HTM). The result of this code is shown in figure 24.9.

On the CD

```
<!doctype html public "-//IETF//DTD HTML//EN">
<HTML>
<HEAD>
<TITLE>Welcome to the Internet Showcase</TITLE>
<META NAME="GENERATOR" CONTENT="Internet Assistant for Word 1.00">
<META NAME="AUTHOR" CONTENT="Thomas V. Savola">
</HEAD>
<BODY>
<P>
<CENTER><IMG src="PTJ.GIF" alt="Paul Thompson Co.">
<P>
<IMG src="JEWELBAR.GIF">
<P>
<FONT SIZE=+2>Welcome to Paul Thompson Jeweler's Internet Showcase.
</FONT></CENTER>
<P>
We specialize in the highest quality fine and estate jewelry.
Our Showcase represents the broad range of services available
at <B>PTJ</B>, including our in-house appraisal and custom jewelry
design and manufacturing.
<P>
We revise our listings regularly; many of the pieces we carry
are <I>one-of-a-kind</I> and hard to find anywhere else. If you've
been looking for a specific piece of jewelry, go to our
<A HREF="feedback.htm">Web  Feedback</A>
page and send us a Search Request.
<P>
<IMG SRC="question.gif" ALT="Q:" ALIGN="MIDDLE"> Interested in
antiques? Let us know with your <A HREF="feedback.htm">Web Feedback!</A>
<P>
<CENTER><FONT SIZE=+1><I>To access our services, click on one
of the choices below.</FONT> </CENTER></I>
<P>
<IMG SRC="in_cone.gif" ALIGN=MIDDLE ALT="----------">Visit our
<A HREF="guide.htm">Web Jewelry Shopper's Guide </A>.<BR>
<IMG SRC="in_cone.gif" ALIGN=MIDDLE ALT="----------">Browse our
current <A HREF="catalog.htm">Contemporary Catalog </A>and our
<A HREF="estate.htm">Estate Collection</A>.<BR>
<IMG SRC="in_cone.gif"ALIGN=MIDDLE ALT="----------">Get
```

(continues)

```
<A HREF="orders.htm">Ordering Information</A>
or send us <A HREF="feedback.htm">Feedback</A>.
<P>
<CENTER><IMG src="JEWELBAR.GIF"> </CENTER>
<P>
Paul Thompson Jewelers is located in Larchmont Village in the
heart of Los Angeles, California. <B>PTJ</B> has provided a discriminat-
ing clientele with quality <A NAME="DDE_LINK2">service and merchandise
for over fifteen years. </A><HR>
<P>
Questions? Contact the <A HREF="mailto:savola@holonet.net">PTJ
Webmaster</A>.
<HR>
</BODY>
</HTML>
```

Fig. 24.9

The home page in Netscape. Notice the clean look of the transparent graphics.

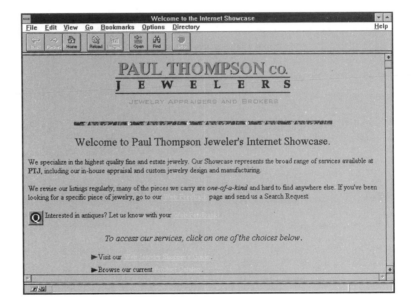

On the CD

The following code creates the HTML version of the Shopper Guide (GUIDE.HTM). The result of this code is shown in figure 24.10.

```
<!doctype html public "-//IETF//DTD HTML//EN">
<HTML>
<HEAD>
<TITLE>Shopper's Guide</TITLE>
<META NAME="GENERATOR" CONTENT="Internet Assistant for Word 1.00">
<META NAME="AUTHOR" CONTENT="Thomas V. Savola">
```

```
</HEAD>
<BODY>
<P>
<IMG SRC="ptj_sm.gif" ALT="PTJ" ALIGN="BOTTOM">
<P>
<IMG SRC="guide.gif" ALT="Shopper's Guide" ALIGN="BOTTOM">
<BR>
<IMG SRC="jewelbar.gif" ALIGN="BOTTOM">
<P>
Purchasing merchandise over the Internet can be a risky proposition.
It takes preparation as a consumer to guarantee that you are fully
protected in the event that what you order is not what you get.
It also takes trust in the vendor that they will stand behind
their products and services. The following topics provide information
on:
<P>
<IMG SRC="cone2.gif" ALIGN="MIDDLE"><FONT SIZE=+1><A
HREF="grading.htm">Jewelry grading
and valuation</A></FONT>.
This section provides a guide to the jewelry industry's
&quot;jargon&quot; and practices regarding how the quality of jewelry is
described, and how asking prices are reached.
<P>
<IMG SRC="cone2.gif" ALIGN="MIDDLE"><FONT SIZE=+1><A
HREF="tips.htm">Jewelry purchasing tips</A></FONT>. Learn how to protect
yourself when making any substantial purchase over the Internet.
<P>
<IMG SRC="cone2.gif" ALIGN="MIDDLE"><FONT SIZE=+1><A
HREF="services.htm">Customer Services</A></FONT>.
PTJ provides a wide range of services for our customers, including
design and manufacturing, repair and value appraising.
<P>
<CENTER>
<P>
<A HREF="grading.htm"><IMG SRC="next.gif" ALIGN="BOTTOM"></A>
<BR>
<A HREF="welcome.htm"><IMG SRC="home.gif" ALIGN="BOTTOM"></A>
<BR>
<A HREF="help.htm"><IMG SRC="help.gif" ALIGN="BOTTOM"></A><A
NAME="DDE_LINK4"></A>
<HR>
[ <A HREF="grading.htm">NEXT PAGE</A> ] [ <A HREF="welcome.htm">HOME
PAGE</A>
] [ <A HREF="help.htm">HELP</A> ] <HR>
<P>
</CENTER>
</BODY>
</HTML>
```

Fig. 24.10

By using a custom font size, Netscape aligns the text properly with the colored bullets.

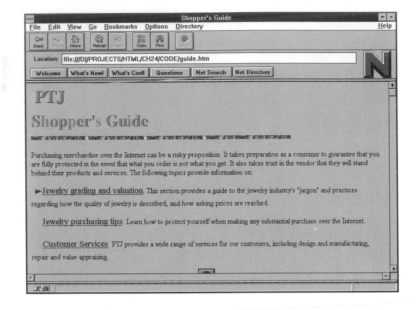

The following code creates the Jewelry Grading page in HTML (GRADING.HTM). The result of this code is shown in figure 24.11.

```
<!doctype html public "-//IETF//DTD HTML//EN">
<HTML>
<HEAD>
<TITLE>Jewelry Grading</TITLE>
<META NAME="GENERATOR" CONTENT="Internet Assistant for Word 1.00">
<META NAME="AUTHOR" CONTENT="Thomas V. Savola">
</HEAD>
<BODY>
<P>
<IMG SRC="ptj_sm.gif" ALT="PTJ" ALIGN="BOTTOM">
<P>
<IMG SRC="grading.gif" ALIGN="BOTTOM"> <BR>
<IMG SRC="jewelbar.gif" ALIGN="BOTTOM">
<P>
Jewelry is graded according to strict guidelines. Yet, jewelry
grading is a subjective process, relying on the skills and training
of professional gemologists to judge the characteristics of a
gemstone accurately. For the highest confidence in jewelry grading,
make sure that the jewelry you purchase is evaluated by a gemologist
certified by the Gemological Institute of America, the world-wide
authority on gemological testing and education.
<P>
The following topics are available:
<P>
<IMG SRC="in_cone.gif" ALIGN="MIDDLE"><A HREF="#Diamonds">Grading
diamonds: the Four C's</A>
<P>
<IMG SRC="in_cone.gif" ALIGN="MIDDLE"><A HREF="value.htm">Determining
```

```
The Value of Jewelry</A>
<P>
<CENTER>
<P>
<A HREF="value.htm"><IMG SRC="next.gif" ALIGN="BOTTOM"></A>
<BR>
<A HREF="welcome.htm"><IMG SRC="home.gif" ALIGN="BOTTOM"></A>
<BR>
<A HREF="help.htm"><IMG SRC="help.gif" ALIGN="BOTTOM"></A>
<P>
<HR>
<P>
[ <A HREF="services.htm">NEXT PAGE</A> ] [ <A HREF="welcome.htm">HOME
PAGE</A>
] [ <A HREF="help.htm">HELP</A> ] <HR>
<P>
</CENTER>
<H1><A NAME="Diamonds"></A>Diamond Grading</H1>
<P>
At first glance, diamonds may look alike, but the truth is they
can be very different. Although they may be of equal size, each
diamond has unique characteristics that may lead to very different
values.<A NAME="Top"></A>
<P>
The difference between diamonds can be subtle. Gemologists use
four measurements of a diamond -- the four C's -- to determine
the value of a diamond. The four C's are <A HREF="#Cut">Cut</A>,
<A HREF="#Color">Color</A>, <A HREF="#Clarity">Clarity</A> and
<A HREF="#Carat">Carat</A>.
<HR SIZE=15>
<H2><A NAME="Cut"></A>Cut</H2>
<P>
Many people confuse cut with the shape of a diamond. The shape
you select is a matter of individual taste, and today your choice
is only limited by the skill and imagination of the craftsman.
It is their efforts during every stage of the fashioning process
that reflects the maximum amount of light back to the eye. Most
round, brilliant-cut or fancy-shaped diamonds possess 58 carefully
angled flat surfaces, called facets. It is the precision of each
facet's placement that will affect the amount of fire, brilliance
and ultimate beauty of your diamond.
<P>
<A HREF="#Top"><IMG SRC="index.gif" ALIGN="MIDDLE"> Return to Four C's
List</A>
<HR SIZE=15>
<H2><A NAME="Color"></A>Color</H2>
<P>
The most prized diamonds are colorless diamonds, because their
beauty depends entirely upon their remarkable optical properties.
In such diamonds, all the colors of the rainbow are reflected
back to your eye. While the majority of gem diamonds appear to
be colorless, others can contain increasing shades of yellow to
brown, some of which are referred to as champagne diamonds. Other
diamonds of exceptional color, red, blue, green, pink, and amber,
are known as &quot;Fancies&quot;.
<P>
```

(continues)

```
The color grading scale varies from totally colorless to light
color or tinted. The difference between one grade and its neighbor
is very subtle. Experts never try to remember color; they use
master diamonds of known color for comparison.
<P>
<A HREF="#Top"><IMG SRC="index.gif" ALIGN="MIDDLE"> Return to Four C's
List</A>
<HR SIZE=15>
<H2><A NAME="Clarity"></A>Clarity</H2>
<P>
Because of their unique optical properties, diamonds, more than
any other gemstones, are capable of producing the maximum amount
of brilliance. While minute crystals of diamond or other minerals
are contained in almost all diamonds, a diamond that is virtually
free of inclusions and surface markings will be judged as flawless.
In these diamonds, nothing interferes with the passage of light
nor spoils the beauty. But these diamonds are extremely rare and
will command a high price.
<P>
To determine a diamond's clarity grading, it must be examined
under a 10x magnification by a trained, skilled eye. What minute
inclusions there may be make every diamond unique. These are,
in fact, nature's fingerprints and do not mar the diamond's beauty
or endanger its durability. Without high magnification, you
may never see these inclusions. However, the fewer there are,
the rarer your diamond will be.
<P>
<A HREF="#Top"><IMG SRC="index.gif" ALIGN="MIDDLE"> Return to Four C's
List</A>
<HR SIZE=15>
<H2><A NAME="Carat"></A>Carat</H2>
<P>
As with all precious stones, the weight and therefore the size
of a diamond is expressed in carats. One carat is divided into
100&quot;points&quot; so that a diamond of 25 points is described
as a quarter of a carat or 0.25 carats. Size is the most obvious
factor in determining the value of a diamond, but now you know
that two diamonds of equal size can have very unequal prices depending
on their quality. However, remember that diamonds of high quality
can be found in all size ranges.
<P>
<A HREF="#Top"><IMG SRC="index.gif" ALIGN="MIDDLE"> Return to Four C's
List</A>
<HR SIZE=15>
<P>
<CENTER>
<P>
<A HREF="value.htm"><IMG SRC="next.gif" ALIGN="BOTTOM"></A>
<BR>
<A HREF="welcome.htm"><IMG SRC="home.gif" ALIGN="BOTTOM"></A>
<BR>
<A HREF="help.htm"><IMG SRC="help.gif" ALIGN="BOTTOM"></A>
<HR>
[ <A HREF="services.htm">NEXT PAGE</A> ] [ <A HREF="welcome.htm">HOME
PAGE</A>
```

```
] [ <A HREF="help.htm">HELP</A> ] <HR>
<P>
</CENTER>
</BODY>
</HTML>
```

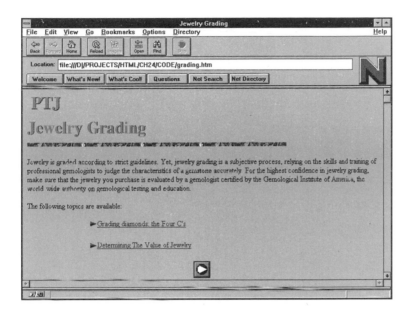

Fig. 24.11
The Jewelry Grading page includes the Four C's diamond grading guide in a single document.

The following code creates the Available Services page in HTML (SERVICES.HTM). The result of this code is shown in figure 24.12.

On the CD

```
<!doctype html public "-//IETF//DTD HTML//EN">
<HTML>
<HEAD>
<TITLE>PTJ Services</TITLE>
<META NAME="GENERATOR" CONTENT="Internet Assistant for Word 1.00">
<META NAME="AUTHOR" CONTENT="Thomas V. Savola">
</HEAD>
<BODY>
<P>
<IMG SRC="ptj_sm.gif" ALT="PTJ" ALIGN="BOTTOM">
<P>
<IMG SRC="services.gif" ALT="Services" ALIGN="BOTTOM">
<BR>
<IMG SRC="jewelbar.gif" ALIGN="BOTTOM">

<P>
Paul Thompson Jewelers provides a full compliment of professional
services for our customers. Select from the following list of
topics for more information:
<P>
```

(continues)

```
<IMG SRC="in_cone.gif" ALIGN="MIDDLE"><A HREF="design.htm">Custom
Jewelry Design and Manufacture</A>
<P>
<IMG SRC="in_cone.gif" ALIGN="MIDDLE"><A HREF="repairs.htm">Jewelry
Repair</A>
<P>
<IMG SRC="in_cone.gif" ALIGN="MIDDLE"><A HREF="appraise.htm">Jewelry
Appraisal Services</A>
<P>
<CENTER>
<P>
<A HREF="tips.htm"><IMG SRC="next.gif" ALIGN="BOTTOM"></A>
<BR>
<A HREF="welcome.htm"><IMG SRC="home.gif" ALIGN="BOTTOM"></A>
<BR>
<A HREF="help.htm"><IMG SRC="help.gif" ALIGN="BOTTOM"></A>
<P>
<HR>
<P>
[ <A HREF="catalog.htm">NEXT PAGE</A> ] [ <A HREF="welcome.htm">HOME
PAGE</A>
] [ <A HREF="help.htm">HELP</A> ] <HR>
<P>
</CENTER>
</BODY>
</HTML>
```

Fig. 24.12

The page's straightforward and clutter-free design makes it easy to navigate.

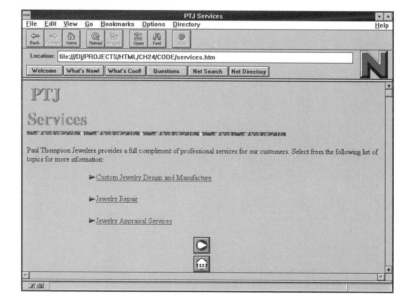

The following code creates the Jewelry Catalog page in HTML (CATALOG.HTM). The result of this code is shown in figure 24.13.

```
<!doctype html public "-//IETF//DTD HTML//EN">
<HTML>
<HEAD>
<TITLE>Contemporary Catalog</TITLE>
<META NAME="GENERATOR" CONTENT="Internet Assistant for Word 1.00">
<META NAME="AUTHOR" CONTENT="Thomas V. Savola">
</HEAD>
<BODY>
<P>
<IMG SRC="ptj_sm.gif" ALT="PTJ" ALIGN="BOTTOM">
<P>
<IMG SRC="catalog.gif" ALIGN="BOTTOM"> <BR>
<IMG SRC="jewelbar.gif" ALIGN="BOTTOM">
<P>
Paul Thompson carries a full selection of contemporary designs
from industry-leading manufacturers and designers.
<P>
Browse the following categories:
<P>
<IMG SRC="in_cone.gif" ALIGN="MIDDLE"><A HREF="#ears">For the ears</A>
<P>
<IMG SRC="in_cone.gif" ALIGN="MIDDLE"><A HREF="#hands">For the hands</A>
<P>
<IMG SRC="in_cone.gif" ALIGN="MIDDLE"><A HREF="#neck">For the neck</A>
<HR>
<P>
<CENTER>
<PRE>
<A HREF="estate.htm"><IMG SRC="next.gif" ALIGN="BOTTOM"></A>
<A HREF="welcome.htm"><IMG SRC="home.gif" ALIGN="BOTTOM"></A>
<A HREF="help.htm"><IMG SRC="help.gif" ALIGN="BOTTOM"></A>
</PRE>
<HR>
<P>
[ <A HREF="estate.htm">NEXT PAGE</A> ] [ <A HREF="welcome.htm">HOME
PAGE</A>
] [ <A HREF="help.htm">HELP</A> ] <HR>
<H2></CENTER><I><A NAME="ears"></A>For the Ears</I> </H2>
<P>
<IMG ALIGN=left HSPACE=10 SRC="../graphics/img018s.jpg"> 14K
YELLOW GOLD EARRINGS<BR>
Product Code 0018<BR>
$225<BR CLEAR=all>
<IMG ALIGN=bottom HSPACE=10 SRC="jewelbr2.gif">
<P>
<IMG ALIGN=left  HSPACE=10 SRC="../graphics/img099s.jpg"> 18K
WHITE GOLD DIAMOND EARRING STUDS PLUS PENDANT<BR>
Product Code 0099<BR>
$10,000<BR CLEAR=all>
<IMG ALIGN=bottom HSPACE=10 SRC="jewelbr2.gif">
<P>
<IMG ALIGN=left HSPACE=10 SRC="../graphics/img062s.jpg"> 18K
WHITE GOLD AQUAMARINE AND DIAMOND EARRINGS<BR>
Product Code 0062<BR>
$15,000<BR CLEAR=all>
<HR>
```

(continues)

```
<P>
<A NAME="hands"></A>
<H2><I>For the Hands</I> </H2>
<P>
<IMG ALIGN=left HSPACE=10 SRC="../graphics/img094s.jpg"> 18K
YELLOW GOLD AND CITRINE RING<BR>
Signed Tiffany<BR>
Product Code 0094<BR>
$3750<BR CLEAR=all>
<IMG ALIGN=bottom SRC="jewelbr2.gif">
<P>
<IMG ALIGN=left HSPACE=10 SRC="../graphics/img095s.jpg"> 18K
YELLOW GOLD AND AQUAMARINE RING<BR>
Product Code 0095<BR>
$4500<BR CLEAR=all>
<IMG ALIGN=bottom SRC="jewelbr2.gif">
<P>
<IMG ALIGN=left HSPACE=10 SRC="../graphics/img090s.jpg"> 18K
YELLOW GOLD EMERALD AND DIAMOND RING<BR>
Product Code 0090<BR>
$18,000<BR CLEAR=all>
<HR>
<P>
<A NAME="neck"></A>
<H2><I>For the Neck</I> </H2>
<P>
<IMG ALIGN=left HSPACE=10 SRC="../graphics/img097s.jpg"> 18K YELLOW
GOLD AQUAMARINE PENDANT WITH SNAKE CHAIN<BR>
Product Code 0097<BR>
$11,000<BR CLEAR=all>
<IMG ALIGN=bottom SRC="jewelbr2.gif">
<P>
<IMG ALIGN=left HSPACE=10 SRC="../graphics/img029s.jpg"> EDWARDIAN
PLATINUM EMERALD AND DIAMOND NECKLACE<BR>
Product Code 0029<BR>
$16,000<BR CLEAR=all>
<HR>
<P>
<CENTER>
<P>
<A HREF="estate.htm"><IMG SRC="next.gif" ALIGN="BOTTOM"></A>
<BR>
<A HREF="welcome.htm"><IMG SRC="home.gif" ALIGN="BOTTOM"></A>
<BR>
<A HREF="help.htm"><IMG SRC="help.gif" ALIGN="BOTTOM"></A> <HR>
<P>
[ <A HREF="estate.htm">NEXT PAGE</A> ] [ <A HREF="welcome.htm">HOME
PAGE</A>
] [ <A HREF="help.htm">HELP</A> ] <HR>
<P>
</CENTER>
</BODY>
</HTML>
```

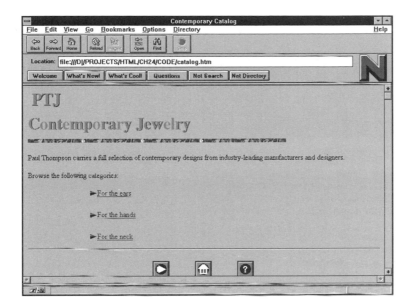

Fig. 24.13
The catalog page uses Netscape's capability to wrap text next to an image to create a compact and eye-pleasing layout.

The following code creates the Estate Jewelry page in HTML (ESTATE.HTM). The result of this code is shown in figure 24.14.

On the CD

```
<!doctype html public "-//IETF//DTD HTML//EN">
<HTML>
<HEAD>
<TITLE>Estate Collection</TITLE>
<META NAME="GENERATOR" CONTENT="Internet Assistant for Word 1.00">
<META NAME="AUTHOR" CONTENT="Thomas V. Savola">
</HEAD>
<BODY>
<P>
<IMG SRC="ptj_sm.gif" ALT="PTJ" ALIGN="BOTTOM">
<P>
<IMG SRC="estate.gif" ALIGN="BOTTOM"><IMG SRC="jewelbar.gif"
ALIGN="BOTTOM">
<P>
Paul Thompson sells jewelry from years past in our Estate Collection.
Many pieces are &quot;one of a kind&quot; are available for a
limited time. This selection will change often, so remember to
check back with us to see what we're currently displaying.
<P>
The Collection:
<P>
<IMG SRC="in_cone.gif" ALIGN="MIDDLE"><A HREF="#Hands">For the hands</A>
<P>
<IMG SRC="in_cone.gif" ALIGN="MIDDLE"><A HREF="#Wrist">For the wrist</A>
<P>
```

(continues)

```
<IMG SRC="in_cone.gif" ALIGN="MIDDLE"><A HREF="#Misc">Miscellaneous</A>
<HR>
<P>
<CENTER>
<PRE>
<A HREF="orders.htm"><IMG SRC="next.gif" ALIGN="BOTTOM"></A>
<A HREF="welcome.htm"><IMG SRC="home.gif" ALIGN="BOTTOM"></A>
<A HREF="help.htm"><IMG SRC="help.gif" ALIGN="BOTTOM"></A>
</PRE>
<HR>
<P>
[ <A HREF="orders.htm">NEXT PAGE</A> ] [ <A HREF="welcome.htm">HOME
PAGE</A>
] [ <A HREF="help.htm">HELP</A> ] <HR>
</CENTER>
<H2><I><A NAME="Hands"></A>For the Hands</I> </H2>
<P>
<IMG ALIGN=left HSPACE=10 SRC="../graphics/img003s.jpg"> 14K YELLOW
GOLD SERPENT RING<BR>
Product Code 0003<BR>
$1750<BR CLEAR=all>
<IMG ALIGN=bottom SRC="jewelbr2.gif">
<P>
<IMG ALIGN=left HSPACE=10 SRC="../graphics/img071s.jpg"> ART DECO
PLATINUM AND DIAMOND
<BR>
Product Code 0071<BR>
$3250<BR CLEAR=all>
<HR>
<H2><I><A NAME="Wrist"></A>For the Wrist</I> </H2>
<P>
<IMG ALIGN=left HSPACE=10 SRC="../graphics/img041s.jpg"> ART DECO
PLATINUM AND DIAMOND (8.0 CTS OF FULL CUT AND SINGLE CUT DIAMONDS)<BR>
Product Code 0041<BR>
$12,500<BR CLEAR=all>
<IMG ALIGN=bottom SRC="jewelbr2.gif">
<P>
<IMG ALIGN=left HSPACE=10 SRC="../graphics/img101s.jpg"> ART DECO
PLATINUM AND DIAMOND WATCH ON RIBBON<BR>
Product Code 0101<BR>
$3800<BR CLEAR=all>
<HR>
<H2><I><A NAME="Misc"></A>Miscellaneous</I> </H2>
<P>
<IMG ALIGN=left HSPACE=10 SRC="../graphics/img078s.jpg"> 18K YELLOW GOLD
GIRL PIN<BR>
Product Code 0078<BR>
$475<BR CLEAR=all>
<IMG ALIGN=bottom HSPACE=10 SRC="jewelbr2.gif">
<P>
<IMG ALIGN=left HSPACE=10 SRC="../graphics/img055s.jpg"> HAND CARVED
SHELL CAMEO, UNMOUNTED
<BR>
```

```
Product Code 0055<BR>
$125<BR CLEAR=all>
<IMG ALIGN=bottom HSPACE=10 SRC="jewelbr2.gif">
<P>
<IMG ALIGN=left HSPACE=10 SRC="../graphics/img075s.jpg"> VICTORIAN
CARVED CARNELIAN AND ENAMEL PIN<BR>
Product Code 0075<BR>
$1150<BR CLEAR=all>
<HR>
<P>
<CENTER>
<P>
<A HREF="orders.htm"><IMG SRC="next.gif" ALIGN="BOTTOM"></A>
<BR>
<A HREF="welcome.htm"><IMG SRC="home.gif" ALIGN="BOTTOM"></A>
<BR>
<A HREF="help.htm"><IMG SRC="help.gif" ALIGN="BOTTOM"></A> <HR>
<P>
[ <A HREF="orders.htm">NEXT PAGE</A> ] [ <A HREF="welcome.htm">HOME
PAGE</A>
] [ <A HREF="help.htm">HELP</A> ] <HR>
<P>
</CENTER>
</BODY>
</HTML>
```

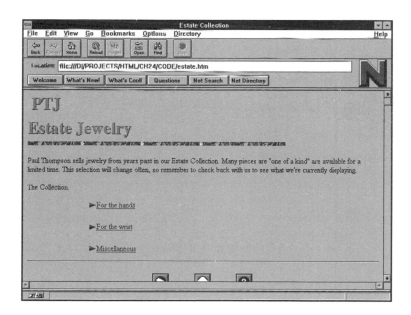

Fig. 24.14
The three collection options are linked to locations within the same document.

The following code creates the Order form page in HTML (ORDERS.HTM). The result of this code is shown in figure 24.15.

On the CD

```
<!doctype html public "-//IETF//DTD HTML//EN">
<HTML>
<HEAD>
<TITLE>Placing an Order</TITLE>
<META NAME="GENERATOR" CONTENT="Internet Assistant for Word 1.00">
<META NAME="AUTHOR" CONTENT="Thomas V. Savola">
<META NAME="OPERATOR" CONTENT="Thomas V. Savola">
</HEAD>
<BODY>
<P>
<A NAME="DDE_LINK6"><IMG SRC="ptj_sm.gif" ALT="PTJ" ALIGN="BOTTOM"></A>
<P>
<IMG SRC="order.gif" ALT="Services" ALIGN="BOTTOM">
<P>
<IMG SRC="jewelbar.gif" ALIGN="BOTTOM">
<P>
Fill out the information below. Include your e-mail and local
telephone number. Do not include any payment information! When
your order is submitted, our system will generate a Verification
Code that will be displayed to you. After receiving your code,
call our Internet Sales hotline at (800) 555-9753. Our sales
associate will be able to take your payment information over the
phone and verify the total billed amount at that time. Your credit
card will not be billed until your order ships.
<FORM >
<P>
<CENTER><H1>Order Form</H1>
<P>
<H2>Personal Information</H2></CENTER>
<P>
<FORM METHOD=POST ACTION="http://www.ptj.com/cgi-bin/mailto">
<B>First Name</B> <INPUT NAME="firstname" VALUE=""SIZE="15" >
<BR>
<B>Last Name</B> <INPUT NAME="lastname" VALUE="" SIZE="15" >
<BR>
<B>Street Address</B> <INPUT NAME="address1" VALUE="" SIZE="25" >
<BR>
<B>(line 2)</B> <INPUT NAME="address2" VALUE="" SIZE="25" >
<BR>
<B>City</B> <INPUT NAME="city" VALUE=""SIZE="15" > <B>State</B> <INPUT
NAME="state" VALUE="" SIZE="2" > <B>ZIP Code</B> <INPUT NAME="zip"
VALUE="" SIZE="5" >
<BR>
<B>Daytime Phone</B> (<INPUT NAME="areacode" VALUE="" SIZE="3">) <INPUT
NAME="prefix" VALUE="" SIZE="3">-<INPUT NAME="number" VALUE="" SIZE="4">
<P>
<B>E-mail address</B> <I>(optional)</I> <INPUT NAME="email" VALUE=""
SIZE="20" >
<P>
Will your shipping and billing addresses be the same? <INPUT
TYPE="RADIO" NAME="billship" VALUE="yes" CHECKED>Yes
<INPUT TYPE="RADIO" NAME="billship" VALUE="no">No
<P>
<CENTER><H2>Products Ordered </H2></CENTER>
<P>
```

```
(for multiple items enter the quantity in the last final field;
blank responses are assumed to be a quantity of 1):
<P>
Code for Item 1 <INPUT NAME="code1" VALUE="" SIZE="4" > Size/Options?
<INPUT NAME="item1" VALUE="" SIZE="25" >
<BR>
Code for Item 2 <INPUT NAME="code2" VALUE="" SIZE="4" > Size/Options?
<INPUT NAME="item2" VALUE="" SIZE="25" >
<BR>
Code for Item 3 <INPUT NAME="code3" VALUE="" SIZE="4" > Size/Options?
<INPUT NAME="item3" VALUE="" SIZE="25" >
<BR>
Code for Item 4 <INPUT NAME="code4" VALUE="" SIZE="4" > Size/Options?
<INPUT NAME="item4" VALUE="" SIZE="25" >
<BR>
Code for Item 5 <INPUT NAME="code5" VALUE="" SIZE="4" > Size/Options?
<INPUT NAME="item5" VALUE="" SIZE="25" >
<BR>
Code for Item 6 <INPUT NAME="code6" VALUE="" SIZE="4" > Size/Options?
<INPUT NAME="item6" VALUE="" SIZE="25" >
<BR>
Code for Item 7 <INPUT NAME="code7" VALUE="" SIZE="4" > Size/Options?
<INPUT NAME="item7" VALUE="" SIZE="25" >
<BR>
Code for Item 8 <INPUT NAME="code8" VALUE="" SIZE="4" > Size/Options?
<INPUT NAME="item8" VALUE="" SIZE="25" >
<BR>
Code for Item 9 <INPUT NAME="code9" VALUE="" SIZE="4" > Size/Options?
<INPUT NAME="item9" VALUE="" SIZE="25" >
<P>
<INPUT TYPE="SUBMIT" VALUE="Send Order"><INPUT TYPE="RESET">
<P>
<I>Note: Customers in California will be charged 8.25% sales
tax.</I>
</FORM>
<H3>Thank you for your order!</H3>
<P>
<CENTER>
<P>
<A HREF="welcome.htm"><IMG SRC="home.gif" ALIGN="BOTTOM"></A><BR><A
HREF="help.htm">
<IMG SRC="help.gif" ALIGN="BOTTOM"></A><HR>
<P>
[ <A HREF="catalog.htm">CONTEMPORARY CATALOG</A>  ] [ <A
HREF="estate.htm">ESTATE COLLECTION</A>
 ] [ <A HREF="welcome.htm">HOME PAGE</A> ] [ <A
HREF="welcome.htm">HELP</A>
 ] <HR>
<P>
</CENTER>
</BODY>
</HTML>
```

Fig. 24.15
The order form
lets users tab
between the text
fields when
entering
information.

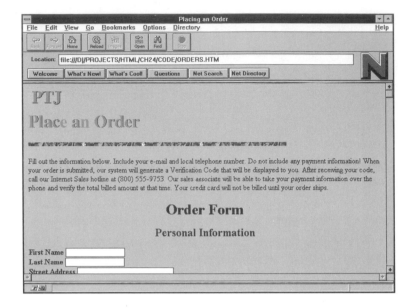

On the CD

The following code creates the Web Feedback page in HTML
(FEEDBACK.HTM). The result of this code is shown in figure 24.16.

```
<!doctype html public "-//IETF//DTD HTML//EN">
<HTML>
<HEAD>
<TITLE>Send us Feedback!</TITLE>
<META NAME="GENERATOR" CONTENT="Internet Assistant for Word 1.00">
<META NAME="AUTHOR" CONTENT="Thomas V. Savola">
</HEAD>
<BODY>
<P>
<IMG SRC="ptj_sm.gif" ALT="PTJ" ALIGN="BOTTOM">
<P>
<IMG SRC="feedback.gif" ALT="Services" ALIGN="BOTTOM">
<P>
<IMG SRC="jewelbar.gif" ALIGN="BOTTOM">
<P>
We've would love to hear what you think of the Internet Jewelry
Showcase. If you have a special request, such as a custom design
or a Search Request, just let us know.
<P>
If you would like to be on our electronic mailing list click the
box below marked &quot;<B>List</B>?&quot; We will be sending
our mailing list customers special promotions and exclusive Net
viewings to new jewelry lines and collectibles.
<CENTER><H1>Web Feedback Form</H1></CENTER>
<P>
<FORM METHOD=POST ACTION="http://www.ptj.com/cgi-bin/mailto">
To: <INPUT NAME="SendTo" VALUE="PTJ Webmaster" ><P>
Your name: <INPUT NAME="name" SIZE=35 VALUE="">
<BR>
```

```
Your e-mail: <INPUT NAME="from" SIZE=30 VALUE="">
<BR>
Subject: <INPUT NAME="subject" VALUE="" SIZE="20" ><HR>
<P>
<TEXTAREA NAME="body" ROWS="8" COLS="45"></TEXTAREA>
<HR>
<P>
<INPUT TYPE="CHECKBOX" NAME="Antiques" >Yes, I would like to see antique
products offered on the Internet Showcase.
<BR>
<INPUT TYPE="CHECKBOX" NAME="Collectibles" >Yes, I would like to see
glass art or other collectibles offered on the Internet Showcase.
<BR>
<INPUT TYPE="CHECKBOX" NAME="Maillist" >Yes, I would like to be on the
Internet Showcase mailing list.
<P>
<INPUT TYPE="SUBMIT" VALUE="Send Message"><INPUT TYPE="RESET"
VALUE="Clear Message">
</FORM>
<P>
Thank you for taking the time to give us your feedback!
<P>
<CENTER>
<P>
<A HREF="welcome.htm"><IMG SRC="home.gif" ALIGN="BOTTOM"></A><BR><A
HREF="help.htm">
<IMG SRC="help.gif" ALIGN="BOTTOM"></A><HR>
<P>
[ <A HREF="welcome.htm">HOME PAGE</A> ] [ <A HREF="welcome.htm">HELP</A>
 ]
<P>
</CENTER>
</BODY>
</HTML>
```

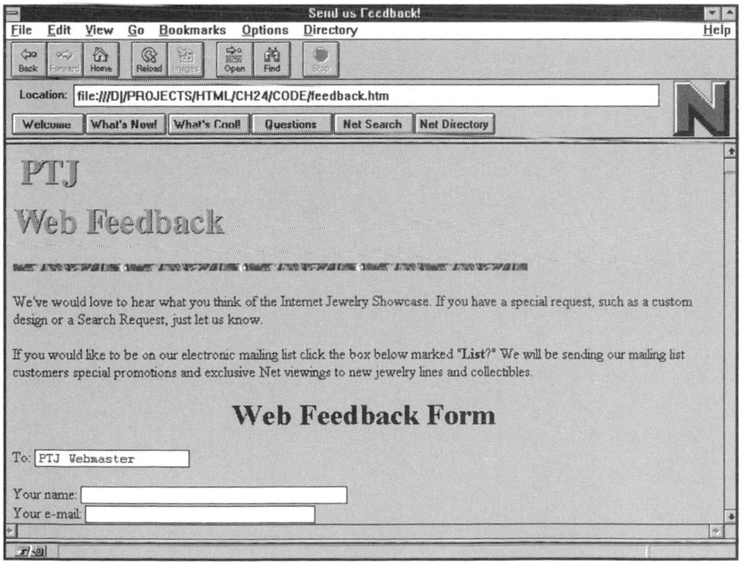

Fig. 24.16
HTML forms let you designate a default text (such as "PTJ WebMaster" in this form) for any input field.

From Here...

On the CD

The Paul Thompson Jewelers Internet Showcase, complete with source code and images, is available on the CD-ROM. For additional application examples and tips and tricks on using HTML effectively, check out the following chapters:

- Chapter 8, "HTML Standards and Practices," describes the set of common practices HTML authoring has accumulated for the benefit of both authors and end users. This chapter discusses these "good habits" of HTML development.

- Chapter 21, "Managing Your Text," discusses the design issues surrounding how text and HTML elements can be used for consistent and creative purposes in Web documents.

- Chapter 23, "Online Visitor's Guide to Jubilee Falls State Park," follows the creation of an online HTML application for a State Park.

- Part VIII, "HTML Editors and Style Sheets," provides a look into the most widely used HTML document tools, including stand-alone editors and add-ons for popular word processors.

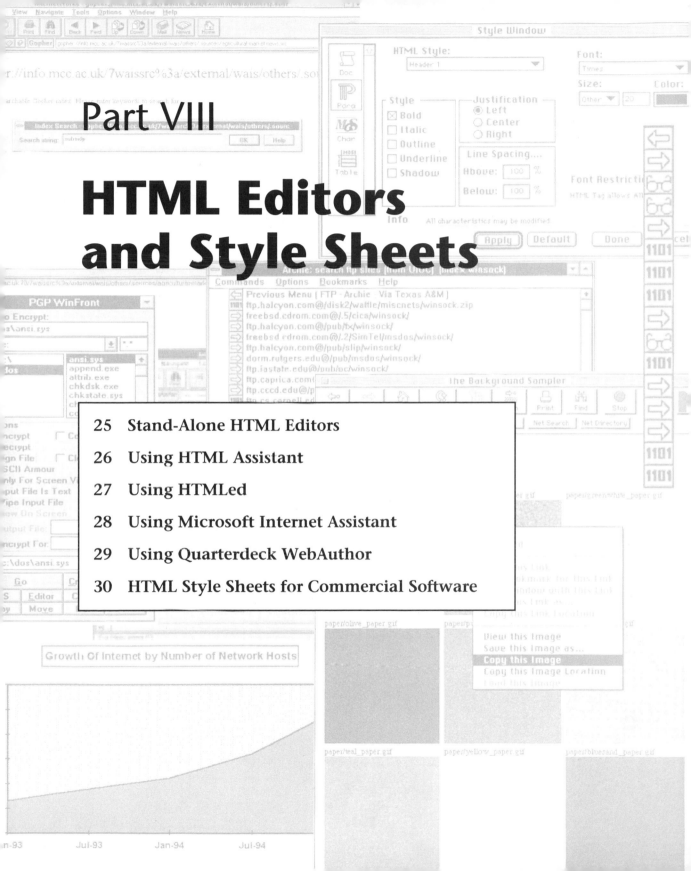

Part VIII

HTML Editors and Style Sheets

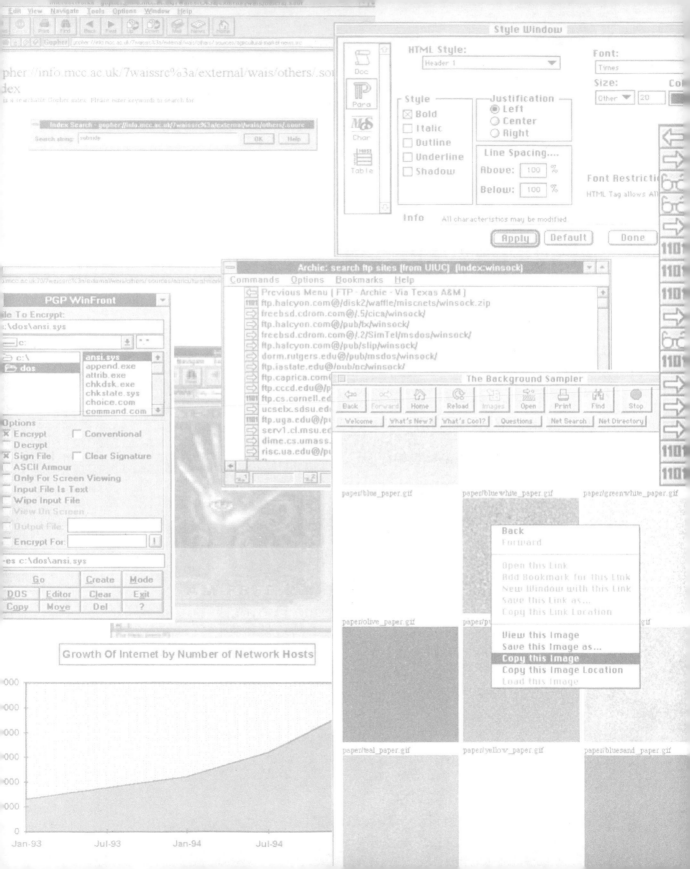

Chapter 25

Stand-Alone HTML Editors

"I wish people who have trouble communicating would just shut up."

—Tom Lehrer

For all of its relative simplicity, HTML can be a bear to master. Remembering which elements are containers and require closing tags (and which don't), trying to remember which break forces one and two line feeds, forgetting the syntax of anchor statements, and being boggled by the variety of URL descriptions—sometimes it can be too much to take! The answer for people who have trouble writing solid HTML is not to throw in the towel and "shut up," but to arm themselves—with the proper tools.

In Part IV, I discussed some of the tricks of the trade and presented them with the various software tools that allow many of these tricks to work. In HTML document creation, there are similar tools that can simplify your task of writing consistent and legal web pages. These tools are *stand-alone* HTML editors (separate applications that allow you to mark up new or existing text files). Other tools can be integrated into word processing applications you're already familiar with: these are style sheets. Most require that you also use a Web viewer to preview your documents; only one here combines the two functions, Microsoft Internet Assistant. And all of the tools use a WYSIWYG (What You See Is What You Get) interface.

This chapter answers the following questions:

- What's a stand-alone HTML editor?

- What's the advantage to using an HTML editor?

- Are there any disadvantages?

- How do they provide compatibility for the different levels of HTML and non-standard extensions?

> **Note**
>
> Choose an editing tool based on the criteria important to you. Ease of use, application features, document compatibility, and developer support are some of the qualities HTML tools can provide. You might think of others that are more or less important to you as well.

Stand-Alone Editors

Over the years, computer software development has been driven by the independent programmers. In the last few years, the "majors" have accelerated a trend of combining many different features and tools into one package (often called a "suite") to entice end user dollars. The fierce competition for providing the most features and tools at lower and lower prices has dampened the independent software market—but not killed it. With the advent of HTML, and the success of programmers such as the NCSA Mosaic team, a strong wave of independent development rose to provide solutions for the growing army of Web authors.

Besides HTML viewers, the most active development field has been in HTML editors. These applications provide a familiar document interface and pre-written menu options and button bars that put the various HTML tags at your command with the click of the mouse. Many allow you to import an existing text document and by selecting sections of text, apply formatting and containers to your documents. Practically every editor also allows you to designate a "test viewer" that launches and automatically loads your document for previewing—all at the touch of a button or menu choice. The crop of stand-alone HTML tools has matured lately, and they're a valuable asset that you can take advantage of.

Advantages of Using a Stand-Alone Editor

What's the advantage of any single-function utility? The first is speed, speed, and more speed. Stand-alone editors, such as HTML Writer, which is provided on this book's CD-ROM, are lightning fast at opening text and HTML formatted documents, scrolling through them, and saving page changes (see fig. 25.1). They don't require the same amount of system overhead as a full-featured mega-package, in either hard disk space or RAM memory necessary to run the program. This allows you to keep the tools loaded in memory while you work in other applications; there's no danger that they're taking up much of your precious system resources.

On the CD

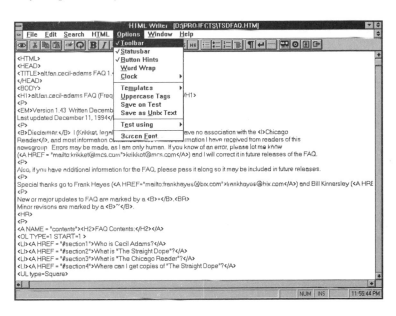

Fig. 25.1
HTML Writer has a lot of features and allows you to customize your document work space.

VIII

Editors & Styles

Stand-alone editors also have a tremendous advantage in that they're capable of providing a unique editing interface that is particular to creating Web documents. Integrated tools or style sheets are locked into interface conventions that must be functional (and intuitive) for many tasks.

A stand-alone utility can give you pull-down menus, button or icon bars, floating palettes, floating menus, floating text clipboards—you name it, they can do it. And most let you choose which features to use and which to turn off, further customizing the tools to suit your needs.

Finally, one distinct advantage that stand-alone editors from independent software developers have that virtually no corporate software provides is prompt developer response. It's not uncommon for user feedback to a small developer to be incorporated into the next software release. I've seen interface and feature suggestions incorporated almost overnight. Software shortcomings (and bugs) have been addressed in days and weeks—not months or years. No major software developer can afford to release new product every few weeks to meet the needs of end users. This is where the relationship between end users and independent developers really shines, and it's the main reason they should be supported and encouraged.

Disadvantages of Using a Stand-Alone Editor

The disadvantages of a stand-alone editor may be enough to make you choose an integrated solution, such as a word processor style sheet or add-on. The primary weakness for separate utilities is their reliance on external Web viewers (such as Mosaic and Netscape) to preview documents. Sure, WYSIWYG looks great in the edit window, but a document has to be seen in a real-world situation—in a viewer window—to make sure it "works." Currently, the only product that allows you to switch between edit and preview mode is Microsoft Internet Assistant, because it's the only editing tool that can also act as a full-featured browser.

Tip

Use the customize features in your edit tools to change the interface menus and icon bars to support any nonstandard HTML elements, including Level 3 and Netscape-specific tags. Now they'll be at your fingertips when you need them!

> **Note**
>
> Novell has announced plans to ship a similar package for its WordPerfect word-processing program. WordPerfect Internet Publisher will provide styles and macros to make creating and converting documents to HTML quick and easy, along with a custom version of Netscape for viewing your work.

Another disadvantage is the flip-side to one of the advantages listed previously. While being able to customize and tailor the editor's interface to the task at hand is a benefit, it also requires the user to learn a new set of commands, icons, and menu arrangements. The lack of standardization— or the necessary price, some might say—is a learning curve. Some users may avoid this curve by staying near to what they know best, like their current word processor.

HTML Compatibility

Writing good HTML is not just the purpose of the author, but can also be a function of the editor. Most editors today provide all of the standard HTML 2.0 tags; some have incorporated support for such approaching 3.0 features as forms and image maps (see fig. 25.2).

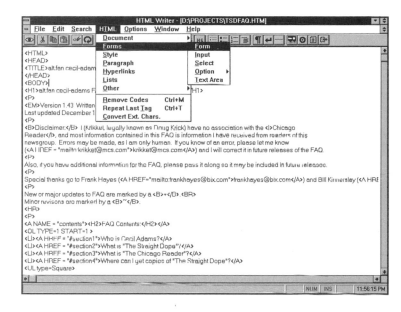

Fig. 25.2
HTML Writer provides tools for creating forms, a feature of the unpublished HTML 3.0 that is widely used today.

VIII

Editors & Styles

On the CD

Some editors and add-ons have a built-in HTML *validation process*, comparing an HTML-formatted document with the current definition of HTML (some allow you to choose the Level for compatibility purposes). The validation test flags illegal HTML and allows you to change the code. Some also let you enter your own deviations so they are not considered "errors" by the test function. Two HTML tools that provide this support are HoTMetaL (provided on this book's CD-ROM) and Quarterdeck's Web Author. For details on Web Author, see Chapter 29, "Using Quarterdeck Web Author."

Compatibility for non-standard HTML (such as the Netscape HTML extensions) can be added as a part of the customizing process. None of the current validation tests allows for Netscape extensions without being told to allow them. The actual tags and attributes for Netscape features should be added to a floating tag palette or pull-down menu for easy access.

A Look at Some High-Powered Packages

The editors covered in the next four chapters are powerful and full of features to make your Web publishing jobs easy. Each one has a different set of strengths and weaknesses, but all are capable tools.

HTML Assistant

HTML Assistant is a stand-alone program that really lets you customize your environment for the tasks at hand. You can also access cool features like an automatic converter that changes Mosaic Hotlists to HTML documents.

Another strong point is the URL Manager. This is a database of URLs that you can reuse in your documents without having to look them up (and type them over and over).

HTMLed

HTMLed is for the power user. There isn't a lot of WYSIWYG display to get in your way, just tools to let you do the tags and markup as quickly and easily as possible.

A nice thing about HTMLed is it's MDI design. This allows you to work on several HTML documents at once, and switch between them with a mouse click or shortcut key.

Another feature is Intelligent Tag Insert. This great idea makes adding tags a lot easier than it is in other editors. If you choose to insert a tag anywhere in a line, HTMLed automatically parses through the text and chooses the appropriate place to start and end the tags. This is terrific for people who don't like using the mouse a lot.

Microsoft Internet Assistant

If you can write a document in Word, you can create HTML. Microsoft Internet Assistant lets you create (or open) a Word document, then create links to other documents using a handy toolbar. Save as HTML, and you're ready to go.

Internet Assistant also includes a full working Web browser right in the package. Based on InternetWorks by BookLink technology, this tool gives you one-click access to a browser to see how your document looks in its final form.

Quarterdeck Web Author

This is a great editor and does a good job of converting existing documents. The feel is very friendly, with lots of Wizard-like, step-by-step processes to help beginners through the rough stuff.

Web Author has a very professional interface and excellent online help. Its interface can be customized enough to allow lots of help for beginners without getting in the way of HTML power users.

From Here...

Choosing a set of tools that you feel comfortable with is the most important first step in HTML authoring. Giving the various applications a "test drive" is the best way to determine what will work best for you—and why these tools (and more) are included on this book's CD-ROM disk. For a detailed look at some of the more popular applications, refer to the following:

- Chapter 26, "Using HTML Assistant," takes a look at HTML Assistant, a WYSIWYG editor for Windows that allows the author to customize the editing tools to suit his or her needs.

- Chapter 27, "Using HTMLed," describes how HTMLed, a WYSIWYG editor for Windows, can provide a well-designed menu and button interface with floating palettes to aid in document authoring.

- Chapter 28, "Using Microsoft Internet Assistant," details the long anticipated Internet Assistant. This is Microsoft's add-on product for its Word 6 for Windows word processor that combines authoring tools with a robust Web browser interface.

- Chapter 29, "Using Quarterdeck WebAuthor," shows you the ins and outs of this add-on for Microsoft Word 6 for Windows; the authoring tool makes creating new HTML documents or converting existing Word documents to HTML a snap.

- Chapter 30, "HTML Style Sheets for Commercial Software," provides an overview of other style sheet add-ons available for Microsoft Word and WordPerfect.

VIII

Editors & Styles

## Chapter 26

Using HTML Assistant

HTML Assistant is a Visual Basic application from Howard Harawitz of Brooklyn North Software Works in Bedford, Nova Scotia, Canada. HTML Assistant is a very useful WYSIWYG editing tool that uses a Web browser for the document-preview functions of the editing process.

Aside from creating new Web pages, HTML Assistant makes converting your Mosaic or Cello URL "hotlists" to HTML pages quick and easy, allowing anyone to create customized HTML menus for any Web browser. Converting your hotlist to a Web page is like having a customized, active table of contents to the entire World Wide Web: you can go to your favorite places with a simple click of the mouse.

In this chapter, you learn to

- Install HTML Assistant
- Convert your URL hotlists to HTML documents
- Create and manage simple URL databases
- Create a simple HTML document
- Use HTML Assistant formatting tools
- Preview and test your HTML document using your favorite browser
- Create custom HTML formatting tools

Installing HTML Assistant

HTML Assistant is available on most Internet FTP archives as HTMLASST.ZIP, or you can get it directly from Brooklyn North Software Works. This archive contains everything needed to run the program, except for the VBRUN300.DLL

VIII

Editors & Styles

run-time module that any Visual Basic application requires. (If you have Visual Basic, or any other Visual Basic application or shareware on your system, you have probably already got this file.) If you don't have the VB run-time module, it is readily obtainable from most archives, BBSes, and online services.

To install HTML Assistant, follow these steps:

1. Create a directory for HTML Assistant.

2. Copy the HTMLASST.ZIP file into it.

3. Decompress the file using your favorite archiving utility (for example, PKUNZIP.EXE or WINZIP).

4. Create an icon for HTML Assistant in the appropriate Program Manager group for your Internet or editing tools.

Starting HTML Assistant

When you're ready to create your Web page, simply double-click the HTML Assistant icon you've created. The HTML Assistant screen will appear, as shown in figure 26.1.

Fig. 26.1
HTML Assistant opens with its opening screen, menu, and main tool bar.

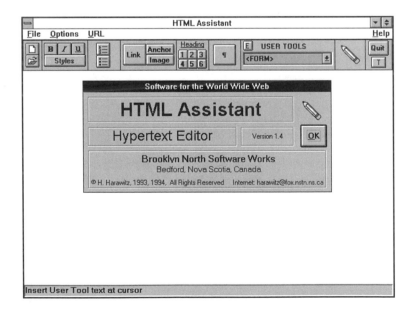

Click the **O**K button and you're on your way. Note that HTML Assistant's menus look fairly sparse. Like some other applications, HTML Assistant won't display its full menus until you create or load a document. HTML Assistant uses Microsoft's icon buttons.

To start a new document in HTML Assistant, choose the **F**ile, **N**ew command from the HTML Assistant menu or click the New File button. HTML Assistant displays its full menus and an Untitled document window, as shown in figure 26.2.

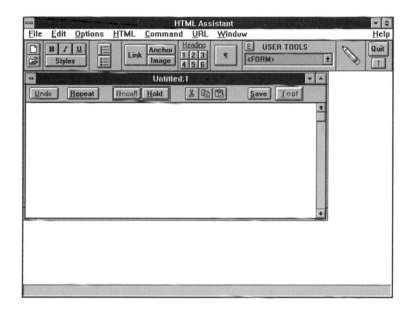

Fig. 26.2
HTML Assistant offers a wide variety of editing tools.

VIII

Editors & Styles

Creating an HTML Document with HTML Assistant

While HTML Assistant won't support all of the advanced features of other HTML editors, it has several excellent tools designed for quick creation of pages, and can be customized or extended, in the sense that it allows you to define custom tools at will for special needs.

Quick-Starting from the URL Menu

One of the really nice touches in HTML Assistant is the **U**RL menu, which allows fast creation of pages via automatic conversion of other file types—specifically, the common bookmark files of the Cello and Mosaic browsers.

To create a page from a Mosaic file:

1. Choose **U**RL, **A**utoconvert File to HTML. HTML Assistant displays the menu shown in figure 26.3.

Fig. 26.3
HTML Assistant
makes it easy to
convert common
hotlists to Web
pages.

Tip
If you use HTML
Assistant to con-
vert your hotlist,
you probably want
to set it up as your
default home page
in your Web
browser. HTML
Assistant can't do
that for you, so see
your browser for
particulars. Most
have a simple
menu option for
this feature.

Fig. 26.4
HTML Assistant
lets you select the
desired INI file
for automatic
conversion.

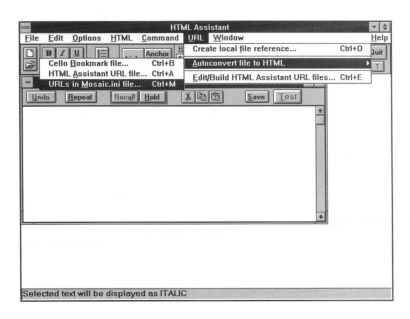

2. Choose URLs in **M**OSAIC.INI File, if that is the viewer you're converting from. HTML Assistant displays the Select Mosaic Initialization File dia-log box (see fig. 26.4).

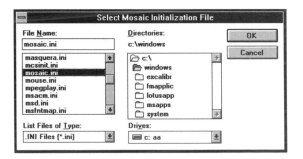

3. Using the dialog box controls, navigate to the directory containing the MOSAIC.INI file and highlight it. Then click the OK button. HTML Assistant displays the converted file in the Untitled window.

4. Save the file, under a new name, to the directory of your choice using either the File, Save or File, Save As commands.

You can also use the URL menu to automatically create local file references, converting the local system path and file references to a tagged HTML URL for insertion in your Web document. In addition, HTML Assistant lets you save collections of URLs via a feature called the URL Manager.

To use the URL Manager:

1. Choose URL, Edit/Build HTML Assistant URL Files. HTML Assistant displays the URL Manager [New File] window shown in figure 26.5.

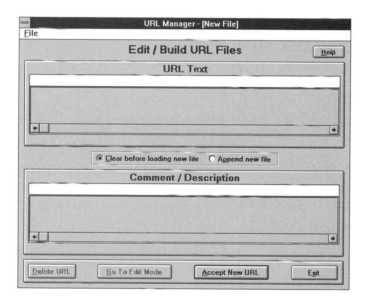

Fig. 26.5
HTML Assistant lets you manage URL databases via the URL file format and URL Manager feature.

VIII

Editors & Styles

2. Select File from the URL Manager [New File] window. HTML Assistant displays the menu shown in figure 26.6.

Notice the similarity of the menu options here to the Autoconvert menu item described previously. While the same import options are in both places, the URL Manager lets you store and retrieve from other file types (by default, the URL type). You can append multiple files, add comments to the URLs in the file, and edit from the URL Manager window as well. You can easily combine URLs from many different sources to create your master hotlist database, and export them to other file types as well.

Fig. 26.6
You can create new URL databases from the URL Manager menu.

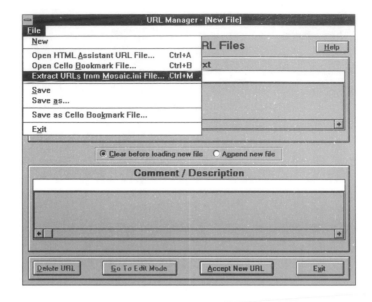

Starting a Page from Scratch with HTML Assistant

If you're going to use HTML Assistant to create brand-new Web pages, or add other text or graphics to your hotlist pages, there are many more useful features available. HTML Assistant makes these tools readily available in its toolbars. (You can activate the toolbar by selecting **O**ptions, making sure Hide **L**ower Tool Bar isn't checked. If it is, click it, and the toolbar will appear just below the main menu, as shown in figure 26.7.)

Fig. 26.7
The HTML Assistant toolbar allows quick access to formatting tools.

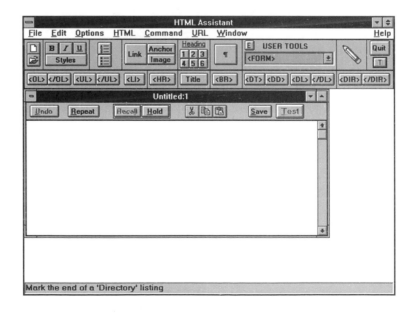

The toolbar contains buttons for most HTML elements. HTML Assistant supports three main tool types:

- Tools used to mark selected text (Type 1 tools)

- Tools used to insert HTML elements at the cursor (Type 2 tools)

- User Tools (defined by the user)

Tools in the main HTML Assistant toolbar are Type 1 tools, used on selected text, except for the end-of-paragraph tool, and the toggle tool for the second formatting toolbar.

You will reveal the second HTML Assistant toolbar when you click the T button on the main toolbar (on the right, just underneath the Quit button). All of the tools here will insert HTML markings at the current cursor point of insertion. Clicking an item will insert the displayed marking.

User Tools allow you to keep your Web pages current by exploiting the latest HTML features. I discuss customizing HTML Assistant User Tools later in this chapter, in the section "Creating Custom HTML Tags with User Tools."

> **Note**
>
> While HTML Assistant does a good job of providing most of the common HTML tag tools on the toolbar, you may find yourself searching for a few of the major (but infrequently used) ones the first time you use the program. Don't sweat—if you can't find a tag type on the toolbar, chances are they're all readily available under the **C**ommand menu (TITLE, BODY, HEAD, HTML, and Horizontal Rule). There's also a handy **R**epeat Last Command command.

To create a new page with HTML Assistant, follow these steps:

1. Choose the **F**ile, **N**ew command from the HTML Assistant menu.

   HTML Assistant displays its full menus and an Untitled document window.

2. Before you begin your page, you'll want to insert the standard HTML page minimum template. HTML Assistant provides this automatically via the **C**ommand, **D**isplay Standard Document Template command from the main menu.

   HTML Assistant inserts the minimum template, as shown in figure 26.8.

Fig. 26.8
HTML Assistant
provides a
minimum HTML
template with a
single command.

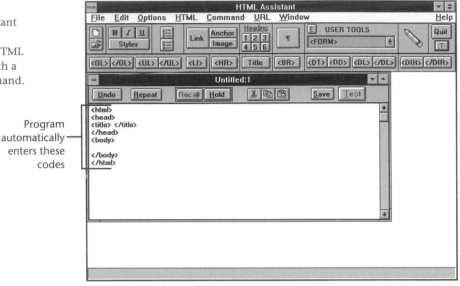

Program
automatically
enters these
codes

3. You can type directly into the HTML Assistant document window, insert a file, or paste from the Windows Clipboard. To insert a file, choose
   File, **I**nsert File at Cursor, as shown in figure 26.9.

Fig. 26.9
HTML Assistant
imports files with
a simple menu
option.

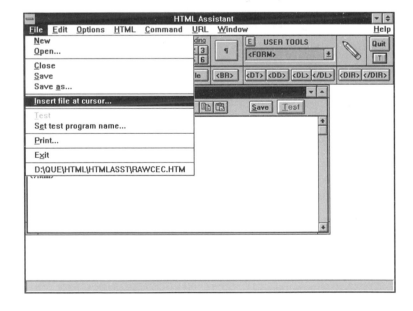

4. When you've typed or otherwise inserted your text, you're ready to start formatting. Highlight the text you wish to format (for example, the main headline of the page) and click the appropriate heading button on the toolbar.

HTML Assistant inserts the command, as shown in figure 26.10.

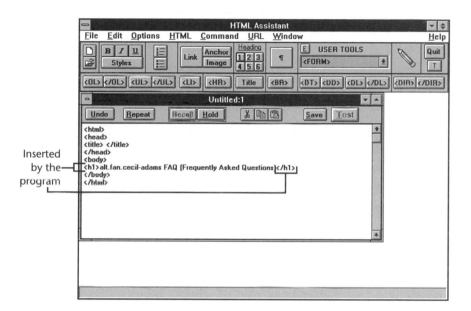

Inserted by the program

Fig. 26.10
HTML Assistant inserts the HTML tags for the highlighted text.

Tip
The Insert File at Cursor option is a great way to use *boilerplate* (often-used, seldom-changing) text in your Web pages. If you use the same information again and again on different pages, taking advantage of this feature can save you many minutes and protect your tired typing fingers.

VIII

Editors & Styles

Adding Hypertext Links

Once you've got the majority of your raw text in your Web page, you'll want to add the hypertext links. HTML Assistant makes this simple by providing a single command for converting your URL text to a fully tagged link reference.

To set up a link in your page, follow these steps:

1. Enter the URL for your link into the document at the appropriate place.

2. Highlight the URL text, and choose **C**ommand, Create Formatted Lin**k** from the main HTML Assistant menu.

HTML Assistant inserts the appropriate HTML codes.

Troubleshooting

Why does HTML Assistant insist that my files are UNIX files? I'm not within a mile of a UNIX system.

You probably opened a word processing file, such as a Word for Windows document, using HTML Assistant. The embedded codes and line formatting in the DOC file resemble UNIX control characters.

HTML Assistant really isn't designed to convert file formats. If you must import your Word document, save it as text first (use the Word **F**ile, Save **A**s command), or use Windows cut and paste via the Clipboard. Don't worry about losing your formatting; it's still intact in your original Word document, and HTML Assistant can't use it anyway.

Previewing Documents with HTML Assistant

You don't have to wait to complete your document to see how it's looking. HTML Assistant allows you to preview your Web page at any point in the production process with simple menu commands.

To set up HTML Assistant for previewing with your favorite browser, follow these steps:

1. Choose **F**ile, **S**et Test Program Name from the HTML Assistant menu.

2. The first time you use the HTML Assistant, it displays a dialog box asking whether you want the selected browser to be used permanently. Answer yes to avoid repeating this step in the future.

3. To assign a browser, use the mouse and the dialog box controls, navigate to your browser directory, and highlight the browser main program name. Click the OK button to accept the file name.

4. When HTML Assistant returns you to the main program window, save your HTML file using the **F**ile, **S**ave commands from the main menu, or click the Save button in the document window toolbar.

5. To preview your file, choose **F**ile, **T**est, or click Test in the document window toolbar.

   HTML Assistant runs your browser and displays your test file, as shown in figure 26.11.

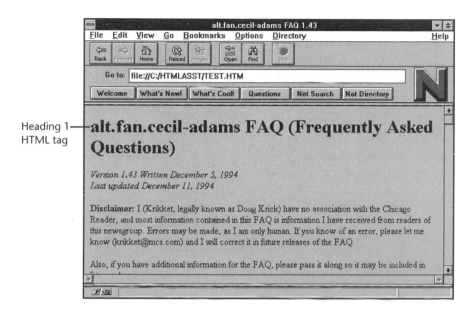

Heading 1
HTML tag

Fig. 26.11
HTML Assistant
makes it simple
to preview your
HTML documents.

VIII

Editors & Styles

Caution

Be sure to choose **O**ptions, **A**utosave Before Testing. Windows will occasionally have a "bad hair day" during a test, and you don't want to lose that Web page you worked so hard on, do you?

If you don't choose **A**utosave or save manually, HTML Assistant will display a warning dialog box as a gentle reminder.

Troubleshooting

Why doesn't HTML Assistant test documents with my company's browser? I set it up just the way the instructions indicated, but the page never appears when the browser loads.

To test a file, HTML Assistant simply calls the browser you've specified with the name of the current file as an argument on the browser command line. If your browser can't support command-line variables, HTML Assistant can't use the browser.

To test your browser, use Program Manager's **F**ile, **R**un commands, and enter a line in the following format:

```
[drive:]\[path]\[browsername] [drive:]\[path]\[HTMLfilename]
```

(continues)

(continued)

For example, if you're using the generally unsupported WebWeasel browser on your drive C:, and your HTML file is also in a directory on that drive, the command line will look something like this:

```
C:\WWEASEL\WWEASEL.EXE C:\HTML\HOME.HTM
```

If this fails, you can't use the browser with HTML Assistant. Why can't some browsers do this? The designers probably didn't see it as a priority at the time, or never thought anyone would want to do it. Most of the major browsers will work just fine.

Creating Custom HTML Tags with User Tools

Because HTML is an evolving set of standards, you'll probably want to alter some of the markings on your pages over time. HTML Assistant lets you do this quickly and easily by defining new HTML markings and storing them in the program for easy retrieval and use.

HTML Assistant lists User Tools in a drop-down list box on the main toolbar. When you click an item in the list, it's inserted in the text at the cursor insertion point.

Creating new User Tools, or editing old ones, is simple. To create or edit a User Tool, follow these steps:

1. Click the E button in the User Tools section of the HTML Assistant toolbar.

HTML Assistant displays the Edit User Tools dialog box shown in figure 26.12.

2. To create a new custom tag, place the cursor in the edit box at the top of the Edit User Tool window. Enter the tag information.

3. To use an existing tag as the beginning for a new one, highlight it and click the Copy button at the right side of the dialog box.

4. When you've entered or altered the tag information, select the location of the new tag in the tag list by highlighting an area of the list box. You can insert the new tag above the existing highlighted one, append it to the end of the list, or replace the highlighted tag using the buttons at the right of the dialog box.

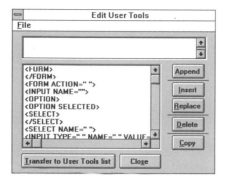

Fig. 26.12
The HTML
Assistant User Tool
editor allows easy
customization of
HTML tags.

5. When you've entered all of your tag information, be sure to click the
Transfer to User Tools List button so HTML Assistant will update the list
box on the main toolbar.

From Here...

In this chapter, you've learned how to create, edit, and maintain HTML documents using HTML Assistant. For more information on and examples of using HTML, see these chapters:

■ Chapters 23 and 24 detail the creation of two HTML applications from the concept stage to online the World Wide Web.

■ Chapter 25, "Stand-Alone HTML Editors," gives an overview of the stand-alone HTML editors that are available and tells the advantages and disadvantages of each.

■ Appendix A, "HTML Elements Reference," lists the elements and gives their usage.

VIII

Editors & Styles

## Chapter 27

Using HTMLed

HTMLed is an MDI (multiple-document interface) HTML editor for Microsoft Windows with many useful and unique features. Written by I-Net Training & Consulting Ltd., New Brunswick, Canada, HTMLed presents a wealth of formatting tools in a clean, well-designed interface. While it doesn't support all of the most current HTML tag types (and has no forms support in the reviewed version), it is a solid performer if creating a few basic Web pages is your goal.

In this chapter, you learn to do the following:

- Install HTMLed
- Convert your Mosaic hotlist to an HTML page
- Create a simple HTML document using HTMLed
- Use HTMLed formatting tools
- Preview and test your HTML document using Mosaic

Installing HTMLed

HTMLed is available on most Internet FTP archives as HTMED12.ZIP, or direct from I-Net Training & Consulting Ltd. The program is distributed as shareware, so you have a 30-day trial period for evaluating HTMLed. If you continue to use it after the trial period, you need to register it with the authors (for a modest fee of $39.00 US).

To install HTMLed, follow these steps:

1. Create a directory for HTMLed.

VIII

Editors & Styles

2. Copy the HTMED12.ZIP file into it.

3. Decompress the file using your favorite MS-DOS or Windows unarchiving utility (for example, PKUNZIP.EXE or WINZIP).

4. Create an icon for HTMLed in the appropriate Program Manager group for your Internet or editing tools.

Starting HTMLed

When you're ready to create Web pages, simply double-click the HTMLed icon you've created in Program Manager, or double-click the file HTMLED.EXE from File Manager. The HTMLed screen appears, as shown in figure 27.1.

Fig. 27.1
HTMLed opens with its opening screen, menu, and main tool bar.

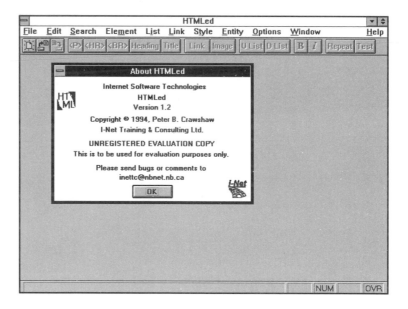

Click the OK button and you're on your way. HTMLed won't display its full menus until you create or load a document, so the first thing to do is create a new file.

Creating a New HTML Document with HTMLed

To start a new document in HTMLed, Choose **F**ile, **N**ew from the HTMLed menu. HTMLed displays its full menu and an Untitled document window (see fig. 27.2).

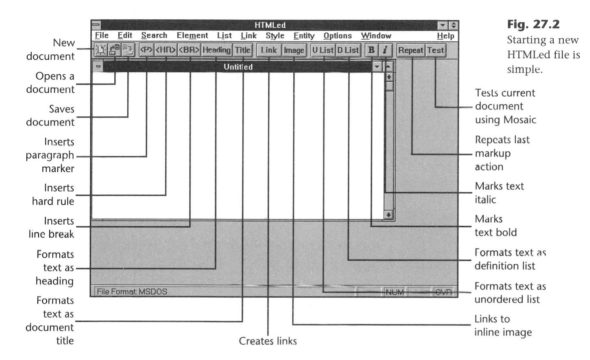

Fig. 27.2
Starting a new HTMLed file is simple.

Labels (left, top to bottom): New document; Opens a document; Saves document; Inserts paragraph marker; Inserts hard rule; Inserts line break; Formats text as heading; Formats text as document title; Creates links

Labels (right, top to bottom): Tests current document using Mosaic; Repeats last markup action; Marks text italic; Marks text bold; Formats text as definition list; Formats text as unordered list; Links to inline image

VIII

Editors & Styles

Just like other HTML editors, HTMLed lets you create a Web page from your Mosaic hotlist. To transform your Mosaic hotlist into an HTML document, follow these steps:

1. Choose **O**ptions, **C**onvert Mosaic.ini to HTML File. HTMLed displays the Mosaic.ini File to Convert dialog box, as shown in figure 27.3.

2. Using the dialog box controls, navigate to the directory containing the MOSAIC.INI file and highlight it. Then click the OK button.

   HTMLed displays another dialog box, asking you to give the new file a name, and displays the converted file in a new window.

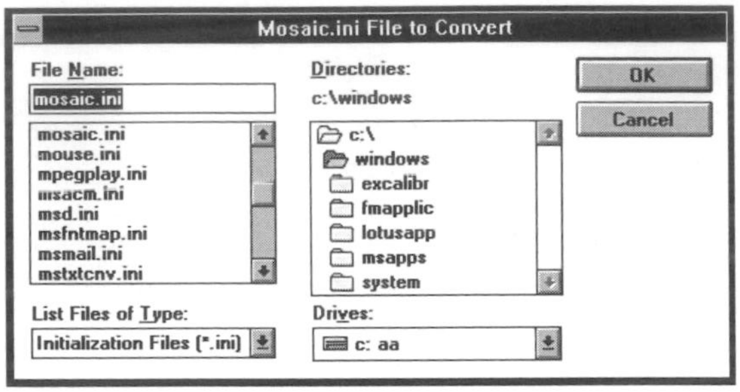

Fig. 27.3
Select the INI file you want to convert, and HTMLed does the rest.

Tip
If HTML tag types are intimidating or hard to remember, create a guide document by using each tag type on a line of text that describes it, and contains the literal tag characters. Print out the page for a quick reference, or keep it in your browser hotlist.

Formatting a New HTML Document with HTMLed

HTMLed works just like any other text editor. You can type directly into the HTMLed document window or paste from the Windows Clipboard. There aren't any special import tools for merging documents, but because HTMLed is a multiple-document interface application, it's easy to cut-and-paste from window to window using the Clipboard.

When you've typed or otherwise inserted your text, you're ready to start formatting. Highlight the text you want to format (for example, the main title of the page) and click the appropriate tool on the toolbar. HTMLed inserts the command, as shown in figure 27.4.

Fig. 27.4
HTMLed makes inserting the HTML tags easy, quick, and consistent.

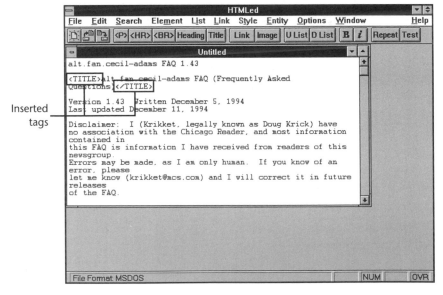

Inserted tags

Besides the basic tag types on the primary menu bar, there are a wide variety of other codes supported in HTMLed.

Troubleshooting

I selected my favorite font for my HTML document by choosing Option, Font in HTMLed. Now, when I preview the page using my browser, the text looks totally different! What am I doing wrong?

You're not doing anything wrong, you're just not understanding a basic function of HTML. In HTML, the browser settings determine the final presentation of the page, including the fonts used for each HTML heading type. The HTML editor simply allows you to pick a pleasing font for the editing process.

Using the Element Menu

HTMLed provides the most common container commands (those that wrap around the text they apply to) in the Element menu. For any of these tag types, you should first highlight the text string you want to tag, and then select the appropriate menu option.

Using the List Menu

HTMLed automates many tasks for you. The List menu functions are a slick way to create various types of lists quickly and easily. Just as with other HTML editors, you can format text in a variety of list types, as shown in figure 27.5.

Fig. 27.5
HTMLed automatically formats these list types for you.

To format a list, highlight the list items, and select a type from the menu. HTMLed will even handle whitespace in the text (HTMLed assumes white spaces are part of the previous line).

Adding Hypertext Links

After you have the majority of your raw text in your Web page, you'll want to add the hypertext links. HTMLed makes this simple by providing a set of

VIII

Editors & Styles

commands for converting your URL text to fully-tagged link references, inserting inline graphics, and setting text anchors within documents.

To set up a link in your page, follow these steps:

1. Place your cursor at the insertion point for the hypertext link.

2. Choose **L**ink, **M**ake Link from URL from the main HTMLed menu. HTMLed displays the Link to URL dialog box (see fig. 27.6).

Fig. 27.6

Place the cursor where you want your link, point to the document, and HTMLed does the rest.

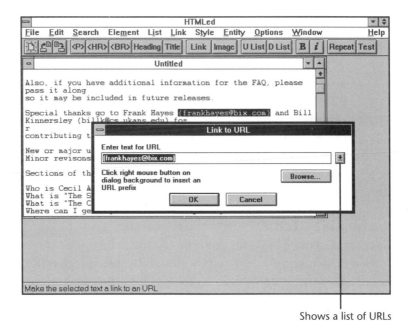

Shows a list of URLs

3. Click the OK button, and HTMLed inserts the appropriate HTML link codes.

Inserting Graphics

After you've got the majority of your raw text in your Web page, you'll want to add the inline graphics.

To insert inline graphics in your page, follow these steps:

1. Place your cursor at the insertion point for your inline graphic.

2. Choose **L**ink, **I**mage from the main HTMLed menu.

HTMLed inserts the appropriate HTML codes.

Note

HTMLed also offers a great tool in its Intelligent Tag Insert feature. You don't have to highlight each portion of a line or lines in a document you want to update; HTMLed lets you simply select the line you want the tag to effect, and it uses its intelligent parsing routines to identify the target text automatically. You can select the lines to be affected by specifying Starting With, Containing, or Ending With radio buttons.

Troubleshooting

I've finished marking up my HTML document, inserting links, and I've placed it on my server. Why don't any of the inline graphics load when I view the page?

Make sure the links you inserted in your Web document point to the actual location of the graphics on the server, not the system you authored on. Be sure your linked graphic images are moved to the server when the page is, and the links are correct in the new relative locations.

Tip

Be careful to not specify large graphics files on your pages. Not all users have high-speed connections, and complex graphics really slow down a Web page transfer.

VIII

Editors & Styles

Other HTMLed Tools

HTMLed opens with a standard Windows menu and a fairly straightforward toolbar. Less obvious are the wealth of other tools stashed behind this deceptively plain facade. Passing the mouse cursor over the toolbar will reveal additional layers of control features. For example, when you click the Heading toolbar button (refer to fig. 27.2), it "morphs" into a list tool for choosing a header type, as shown in figure 27.7.

While this isn't truly Windows GUI-standard design, it works well and it's fast.

In addition to the primary toolbar, HTMLed offers some floating toolbars for other formatting functions. From the **O**ptions menu, you can toggle the **H**eadings, **C**ommon Tags, and **E**xtended Characters toolbars, as shown in figure 27.8.

Fig. 27.7
The Heading button changes to a list when you click it, hiding itself and the Title button.

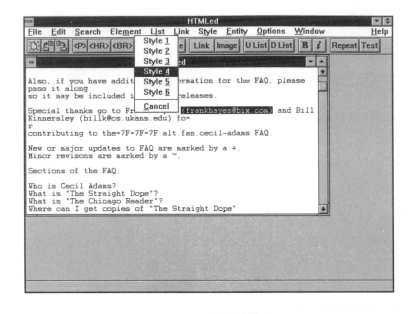

Fig. 27.8
You can toggle the HTMLed floating toolbars from the **O**ptions menu.

There's also a programmable Custom toolbar you can use to extend the current set of HTML tags supported by HTMLed, ensuring that you can keep your pages current with the ever-changing "standards" of HTML+, HTML 2.0, and the emerging HTML 3.0. You can create a custom toolbar entry by following these steps:

1. Choose **O**ptions, **C**onfigure Custom Toolbar from the main HTMLed menu.

   The Custom Toolbar dialog box appears, as shown in figure 27.9.

2. Click the New button to enter the button text you want to appear on the toolbar button.

3. Enter your custom HTML codes for the button in the First Tag and Second Tag windows of the Custom Toolbar dialog box.

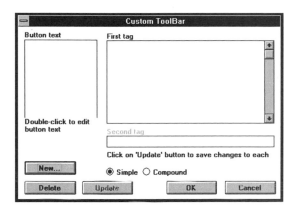

Fig. 27.9
Creating custom
tag codes is easy,
and helps you
keep your pages
current as Web
standards evolve.

4. Click the Update button to save the change, and the OK button to exit
the dialog box.

5. You'll need to restart HTMLed for the changes to take effect.

Previewing Documents with HTMLed

You don't have to wait to complete your document to see how it's looking.
HTMLed allows you to preview your Web page at any point in the production
process with simple menu commands. Unfortunately, unlike some other
editors, you can't specify which browser you want (actually you can, as long
as it's Mosaic). If you don't have the "preferred brand," you will have to perform the preview manually using your browser menu, or drag-and-drop if it
supports it (later versions of Netscape and InternetWorks do this beautifully).

Here's how to do the preview manually:

1. Choose **F**ile, **T**est HTML Document from the HTMLed menu.

2. If you haven't already saved the document, HTMLed asks you to. It's a
wise thing to do so at this point, in case Windows or your browser decides to misbehave at a critical time.

HTMLed executes Mosaic and displays your page.

Note

If you don't use NCSA Mosaic, you can still test documents pretty quickly. Most
newer browser versions (such as Netscape and InternetWorks) support Windows
drag-and-drop. Simply open File Manager, go to the directory your HTML file is in,
and drag it onto the browser interface. The document opens automatically.

VIII

Editors & Styles

Special HTMLed Features

In addition to the standard set of editing tools, HTMLed contains bonus features designed to make the task of maintaining a Web site quicker and easier, such as exporting your HTML to UNIX systems, cleaning up imported text, and supporting special character requirements for languages other than English.

Multi-Platform File Support

HTMLed offers a great set of options for saving files. Many Web server administrators find themselves doing page maintenance for UNIX Web servers from Windows or MS-DOS workstations. HTMLed allows them to save their HTML files in UNIX format, with automatic end-of-line conversion, allowing a simple merge to the server file structure without additional file-conversion steps.

Troubleshooting

I opened an HTML file from my UNIX server and all the text is there, but it runs out of the HTMLed window. Is this how it will appear in my browser? How can I edit this text without endless scrolling?

HTML files are saved as text. MS-DOS text files use both carriage returns and line feed characters at the end of each line; UNIX text files only use the line feed characters. That's why the UNIX HTML file looks different.

You can fix this in HTMLed by simply using automatic line wrap for your files. HTMLed will "wrap" the line on the fly according to your current editor window size. Simply choose **O**ptions, **S**etup and make sure Word Wrap In Editor is checked (under the Other section of the Setup dialog box).

Cleaning Up HTML with HTMLed

HTMLed has two features that may not be of obvious benefit, but will really appeal to anyone doing conversion to-and-from HTML from other document applications, or needing to save pages in raw ASCII for other document management or distribution systems.

If you have an HTML page you want to totally restructure, you'll find the **E**dit, Remove HTML Tags command very useful. By combining this with the **E**dit, Select All command you can quite quickly clean out all commands in a document.

If you need to save your documents in both tagged and raw ASCII formats, you can do so easily. The File, Save without HTML Tags command lets you accomplish this in a snap.

Foreign Character Support with HTMLed

Web-site management eventually creates a deeper awareness of the truly international nature of the Internet and the World Wide Web. If you're a responsible Web administrator, you'll plan for international versions of the information you're providing, even if you primarily target your information at specific "overseas" markets.

What this means in terms of page design and maintenance is that you'll probably be using characters that aren't part of the standard 7-bit ASCII set. HTMLed has good tools for dealing with this issue in its Entity menu and Extended Character Set Toolbar. For example, you can alter character attributes for special language needs such as the grave, umlaut, acute, and circumflex accents.

From Here...

In this chapter, you learned to install and configure HTMLed and use it to convert existing hotlists to HTML pages. You also learned to create, edit, and preview HTML documents. For more HTML information, examples, and tools, see:

- Chapters 23 and 24 detail the creation of two HTML applications from the concept stage to online the World Wide Web.

- Chapter 25, "Stand-Alone HTML Editors," gives an overview of the stand-alone HTML editors that are available and tells the advantages and disadvantages of each.

- Appendix A, "HTML Elements Reference," lists the elements and gives their usage.

VIII

Editors & Styles

Chapter 28

Using Microsoft Internet Assistant

Authoring HTML documents with Internet Assistant is a piece of cake. One of the reasons is that, unlike the other tools out there, Internet Assistant is also a full-featured WWW browser. This gives you a much better representation of what the document will look like in final form.

Internet Assistant, an HTML converter, is an add-on for Microsoft Word 6 for Windows. It consists of two document templates that facilitate viewing and authoring documents for the WWW and a browser engine accessed through Object Linking and Embedding (OLE). The browser is actually InternetWorks from BookLink Technologies. It does the work in the background while Word provides its own user interface. The result is a single environment where you can create your documents and then try them out, complete with links and references to resources at other locations. Pretty cool, huh?

Note

Microsoft Internet Assistant requires that you have the U.S. version of Word 6.0a for Windows. Earlier versions (including 6.0) won't work. Internet Assistant works well with all English, French, and German versions of 6.0a or later.

Internet Assistant lacks some of the user-friendly features of WebAuthor, but the inclusion of the browser makes up the difference. If you're new to HTML, Internet Assistant simplifies the process of creating simple documents without putting a lot of roadblocks in the way of creating documents full of advanced features.

In this chapter, you learn the following:

- The HTML features supported by Internet Assistant

- The features that make creating and editing documents easier

- How to create an HTML document with advanced formatting, graphics, and hyperlinks

- How to use the features already in Word 6 to speed up the creation of your HTML documents

- How to use Internet Assistant as a browser

Installing Internet Assistant

Internet Assistant is available via the Internet, either from Microsoft's WWW site, or their FTP server. Here are the exact locations:

- FTP: **ftp.microsoft.com** in the /deskapps/word/winword-public/ia directory as WORDIA.EXE

- WWW: **http://www.microsoft.com/pages/deskapps/word/ia/ default.htm**

After you download the file, copy it to a temporary directory on your hard disk. Run the program by double-clicking WORDIA.EXE in File Manager, then follow these steps:

1. Double-click SETUP.EXE to run the setup program.

2. Click Complete Installation to begin the installation.

3. If you want to install the browser components, click Yes when you're prompted; otherwise, click No.

When the installation is complete, click OK to exit the setup program.

Internet Assistant HTML Features

Because this is a book about HTML, I'll stick to the features of Internet Assistant that apply to creating HTML documents. The Web browser is a cool thing—it's discussed at the end of this chapter.

Using Internet Assistant, you can create documents in HTML format that support most of the features and extensions of HTML 2.0. Doing so is simple if you have a basic understanding of the elements of HTML.

The following sections cover the different HTML elements supported by Internet Assistant.

◀ See "The Elements of HTML," p. 68

The HEAD Element and Related Elements

Internet Assistant will automatically generate a series of tags for the beginning of an HTML document, including the following:

■ The document type definition (DTD)

■ The <HTML> tag

■ The <HEAD> tag

■ A series of <META> tags that contain the document author name, comments, date and time created, and version. This information comes from the document summary information

■ The <TITLE> tag

■ The </HEAD> end tag

Each of these elements—except <TITLE>—are created when Internet Assistant saves a document in HTML format.

Basic Formatting Tags

Most HTML documents you create will use only a few tags and most of those will be for formatting the text in the document. Internet Assistant has support for all the tags in the HTML 2.0 specification, including these popular ones:

■ The <HEADING> tags, from H1 to H6

■ The <PRE> and <PRE WIDE> tags for displaying preformatted, monospaced text

■ The <STRONG> and <EM> (emphasis) tags for displaying text in **bold** and *italics*

■ The <CITE> tag for displaying the names of publications

■ The <CODE> tag for displaying computer programs

■ The <BODY> tag for displaying plain old text

Tip

While most browsers will adequately render pages that contain none of the above elements, it's good practice to include them (especially the TITLE element).

VIII

Editors & Styles

These six tags allow you control over the formatting of key elements with any browser.

List Elements

If you want to present information in the form of a list, or a series of steps in a particular order, you can use HTML's list tags to create a series of numbered and bulleted lists. You can also create menus and lists of terms or definitions.

Internet Assistant can create lists using the following tags:

- The <UL> tag to begin an unordered (bulleted) list

- The <OL> tag to begin an ordered (numbered) list

- The <MENU> tag to create a menu list of items

- The <DIR> tag to create a directory list

- The <DFN> tag to add definitions to a directory list

- The <LI> tag to specify items in a list

The great thing about the list elements is that Internet Assistant allows you to use the familiar Word 6 for Windows toolbar to create numbered and bulleted lists.

Advanced Formatting

One of the most common elements you'll see in an HTML document is the horizontal rule: a simple horizontal line that breaks up different sections of a page. Internet Assistant lets you insert a horizontal rule by either choosing the <HR> style tag, or clicking the horizontal rule button on the toolbar.

You can also insert any HTML tags you like by choosing **I**nsert, **H**TML Markup. This way, you can add tags (<CENTER>, for example) that aren't supported by Internet Assistant.

Graphics

Internet Assistant supports inline images in either GIF or JPEG format. You can align text to an image (with the ALIGN modifier) and choose to make an image a clickable map (ISMAP). There's no support for centering images, or for wrapping text around a graphic. Both of these features are expected in HTML 3.0, and are currently supported by other browsers. You can always add the tags and modifiers yourself if it's something you need.

Using graphics as links in an anchor is also supported, and it's as easy as picking a file name from a list.

Hyperlinks and Anchors

One of the benefits of HTML is being able to link one page to another. Internet Assistant does a terrific job of helping you create links to other documents on your machine, other places in the same document, or other documents on other machines anywhere on the Internet.

Internet Assistant lets you create hyperlinks using text, graphics, or both. You can also specify advanced link information, including custom HREFs, URNs, and METHODs (when you have a link to submit a form, for example).

Forms

Forms can add a tremendous amount of usefulness to your HTML document. Unfortunately, forms are also the least understood and most confusing element of HTML.

Internet Assistant allows you to generate forms with the following elements and options:

- Text boxes (single line only)
- Checkboxes
- Drop-down lists
- Submit and Reset buttons

Adding form elements is very straightforward. While there isn't a large level of support (no radio buttons, for example), the basics do get covered.

Internet Assistant Usability Features

One of the areas where Internet Assistant really shines is its interface with the user. It sports a number of features to make it easy for beginners to figure out, and a number more to give experienced users all the power they need.

Custom Toolbars

Word 6 for Windows has several toolbars you can turn on and off and drag around the screen; they give you access to most of the program's features. Internet Assistant adds separate toolbars for browsing the WWW, formatting HTML documents, and creating forms.

VIII

Editors & Styles

It's pretty tough to make a 16 × 16 pixel button convey much of a message, but the Internet Assistant toolbars do a pretty good job. Some of the buttons and associated functions (such as cut, copy, and paste) you already know from Word. Others are specific to creating and viewing HTML documents; they appear and disappear as you need them.

The functions chosen for the toolbar buttons are useful and, for the most part, the buttons are indicative of what they do (clicking a picture of a link of a chain to insert a link, for example).

The toolbars also support ToolTips, a Microsoft feature that makes a small label pop up over the buttons. When you hold the mouse over a button for more than a second, the label describes its function.

Property Sheets

Property sheets are tabbed dialog boxes that let you quickly switch between settings for groups of options. An example of this is the Insert Hyperlink property sheet, which lets you set attributes for either a local link (residing on the same server), a URL (on another machine), or a bookmark (a jump in the same document).

Certain options, such as text to display or an image file, remain constant no matter what tab you choose. Others change depending on the type of link chosen.

Two-Stage Dialog Boxes

You can often insert a graphic or form element by specifying a minimum of information (such as the file name of a picture). There may be other times when you want complete control over the way an image is aligned or an action is taken in response to a click of a hyperlink.

To keep the interface simple and to avoid confusing beginning users, most dialog boxes have an **A**dvanced button that displays another dialog box with additional options.

A good example of this is the Insert Picture dialog box. The only options needed in most instances are the name of the graphic file and the text to be displayed as an alternative if the browser can't load the image. The **A**dvanced button brings up a second dialog box where you can specify how you want text aligned to the graphic and whether to treat the image as a clickable map.

Using Internet Assistant to Create an HTML Document

In this section, you learn how to create an HTML document using Internet Assistant. For this example, you create a page with links to several different broadcast and cable TV networks.

Open a New HTML Document

To open a new HTML document, follow these steps:

1. Choose **F**ile, **N**ew. Clicking the New button on the toolbar creates a new document from the default template, which isn't what you want.

2. Choose the HTML template (see fig. 28.1). Click OK.

Fig. 28.1
Select HTML as the template to base your new document on.

3. Click the Title button and type a title for your document. For the example, I called it TV Networks.

4. Save the document by choosing **F**ile, Save **A**s, and typing a name in the dialog box. I used TVNET.HTM.

Putting in Some Headings

Here you add a level 1 and a couple of level 2 headings, with some horizontal rules to separate them:

1. Type the level 1 heading for the document and choose Heading 1 (H1) from the Style drop-down list. I used Welcome to the TV Networks Page.

2. Press Enter and click the Horizontal Rule button in the toolbar to add a line that separates your big heading from the rest of the page.

3. Type your first level 2 heading and choose Heading 2 (H2) from the Style drop-down list. I made this heading Broadcast Networks.

Tip
Save the document before you try to create any hyperlinks. Internet Assistant can't create a link without a reference point to the document's location.

Tip
If you don't want
to use the mouse
to select the styles
from the list, press
Ctrl+Shift+S, type
the name of the
style, and then
press Enter.

4. Press Enter to move to a new line, and add another level 2 heading (I called this one Cable Networks).

Adding Some Links

Now that you've got the basics in place, add a few links. This is a good place to use an unordered (bulleted) list:

1. Move the insertion point to the Broadcast Networks line and press Enter to create a blank line.

2. Click the Insert Bullets button.

3. Click the Insert HyperLink button. The HyperLink dialog box appears (see fig. 28.2).

Fig. 28.2
Here, you can
control how your
link looks and
behaves.

4. Choose the To **U**RL tab to specify a document on another machine.

5. In the Te**x**t to Display field, type CBS Television.

6. In the URL field, type **http://www.cbs.com**.

7. Click OK. Your first link is created to the CBS World Wide Web server.

8. Repeat these steps with **http://www.pbs.org** and **http:// www.eden.com/users/my-html/fox.html** for PBS and FOX, respectively.

9. Now move the insertion point to the Cable TV line and press Enter to create another blank line.

10. Repeat the steps above to add links for these URLs:

http://www.discovery.ca for The Discovery Channel

http://www.ftms.com/vidiot/upn.html for UPN

http://www.scifi.com for the Sci-Fi Channel

http://www.delphi.com/fx/fxtop.html for FX

Adding a Graphic

Now just add a picture and your page will be complete. To add a graphic of your choosing to the level 1 heading, follow these steps:

1. Move the insertion point to the end of the level 1 heading line.

2. Click the Insert Picture button to display the Insert Picture dialog box (see fig. 28.3).

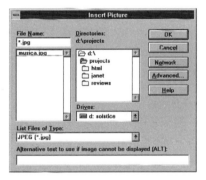

Fig. 28.3
Here, you can insert a graphic and specify how it will be loaded, along with making it an image map.

VIII

Editors & Styles

3. Choose the GIF or JPEG graphic file you want to add.

4. Click OK.

The graphic is added right below the heading.

Saving Your Work

That's all there is to it! You've created a page using Internet Assistant in a lot less time than it would have taken doing it by hand.

Choose File, Save to save your work and you're finished.

Browsing the Web with Internet Assistant

The additional power offered by having a built-in browser makes Internet Assistant one of the most versatile and easy-to-use tools available. You can load your documents as you work to make sure the formatting you wanted is the formatting you got. It's also handy to be able to check the validity of any links you're working on.

Here are the basics you'll need to use the browser capabilities as you create and edit HTML documents.

> **Note**
>
> Even though Internet Assistant is a WYSIWYG editor, it's still possible for you to in-clude more formatting than HTML can preserve. Centered text and graphics, for example, are not supported by most browsers. It's a good idea to check your work periodically by loading it back into Internet Assistant as an HTML document just to see how it looks.

Opening Documents

To start the Internet Assistant browser, choose **F**ile, Browse **W**eb (see fig. 28.4). The default Internet Assistant home page appears, with links to inter-esting places around the Web.

Fig. 28.4

The Browse **W**eb option appears on the File menu in Word 6 for Windows after installation.

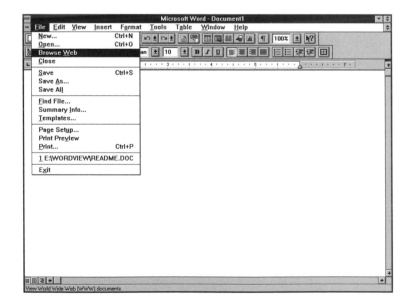

You can choose to follow any of these links you want, or open your own (either locally or from anywhere on the Internet). To open a local document, follow these steps:

1. Choose File, Open.

2. In the List Files of Type drop-down list, choose All Files (*.*).

3. Select the HTM file you want to open and click OK.

4. When the Convert File dialog box appears, confirm that you want to open a Hypertext Markup Language (HTML) file.

To open a document on the Internet using a URL, follow these steps:

1. Choose File, Open URL to display the Open URL dialog box shown in figure 28.5.

Fig. 28.5
To open any document on the WWW, type its URL here.

2. In the Open URL dialog box, type the URL you want to load.

3. Click OK.

Following Links and Going to Favorite Places

Following a link in Internet Assistant works just like it does in other browsers. Click the link you want to follow, and Internet Assistant transfers the HTML file and displays it. GIF and JPEG images are displayed as well.

Internet Assistant maintains a list of Favorite Places so you have a quick reference of places that you want to visit again. To access the Favorite Places page, click the Open Favorite button. Now you can click any of the links in the page and jump right to them.

To add the current document to the Favorite Places page, click the Add Favorite button. A link is then created on the Favorite Places page.

From Here...

In this chapter, you learned how to use Internet Assistant to view, create, and edit HTML documents. For more information on creating and editing documents for the World Wide Web, check out these chapters:

VIII

Editors & Styles

- Chapter 30, "HTML Style Sheets for Commercial Software," describes other tools you can use to create and edit HTML documents.

- Appendix A, "HTML Elements Reference," details the elements of HTML.

Chapter 29

Using Quarterdeck WebAuthor

WebAuthor is a WYSIWYG (What You See Is What You Get) authoring tool for creating and editing multimedia hypertext documents for the World Wide Web. WebAuthor works with Microsoft Word 6 for Windows, taking advantage of Word's WYSIWYG editing capabilities to allow you to create HTML documents quickly and easily. If you know Word, then you can be creating beautiful Web pages in a snap with WebAuthor.

Before you can use WebAuthor, you must have Word 6 for Windows installed on your system. If you have Word 2.0, don't despair; Quarterdeck didn't have a version of WebAuthor for 2.0 at the time of this writing, but it will be available soon.

In this chapter, you learn to do the following:

- Install WebAuthor
- Start WebAuthor from within Word 6 for Windows
- Create a simple HTML document
- Add inline images to your HTML document
- Use HTML forms
- Support HTML 2.0 and 3.0 features in your pages

Installing WebAuthor

Unlike many Web tools available online, WebAuthor is a commercial product and must be obtained from a retail dealer, mail order, or direct from Quarterdeck Office Systems, Inc.

WebAuthor is not part of Word; it's an *add-on*. Before you can start creating Web masterpieces, you need to "add it on." This is a very simple operation that only takes a few minutes.

To install WebAuthor, follow these steps:

1. Insert the WebAuthor disk in the appropriate drive. This example uses drive A.

2. From the Program Manager, choose **F**ile, **R**un.

3. Type **a:install** and press Enter.

4. Answer the questions the WebAuthor Install program asks, and follow the directions for installation.

Starting WebAuthor

After the installation process is complete, starting WebAuthor is as simple as starting Word.

With Word open on-screen, follow these steps:

1. From Word, Choose **F**ile, **N**ew.

2. Select HTML60. The Word menu changes, adding the <WebAuthor> menu item just to the left of the Help menu. The WebAuthor v1.0 dialog box appears, allowing you to choose from three basic initial actions (see fig. 29.1).

3. Choose Create a **N**ew HTML Document. WebAuthor displays the Document Title dialog box shown in figure 29.2.

4. Type the title for your document and press Enter. WebAuthor displays a blank document with a gray title header containing your title text.

The document title you provide is placed in the document head, an undisplayed part of your Web page that contains information for use by the Web browser software. While this information doesn't appear as part of the

HTML page, it does appear in the title bar of the browser window (and in any hotlists the user creates). Choose wisely, Grasshopper!

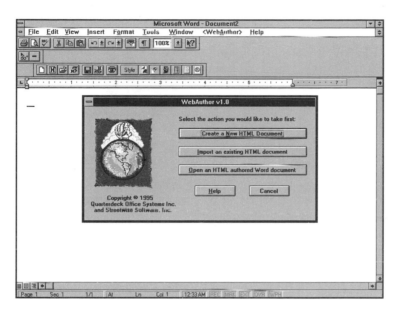

Fig. 29.1
WebAuthor will ask you some basic questions before you begin formatting your HTML document.

Fig. 29.2
WebAuthor needs a document title to begin your new HTML page.

VIII

Editors & Styles

Note

Use descriptive titles when you're creating documents. Think of a title that will appeal to a Web browser user. "Ted's Excellent, Most Majestic, and Profound Home Page" will probably appeal to a user's sense of curiosity more than "Ted Page Number 1." Remember, if your design is a success, it will appear in thousands of hotlists on desktops around the world.

WebAuthor Document Types

WebAuthor works with two main document types:

- HTML documents in Word format
- HTML files in ASCII format

WebAuthor uses *HTML Word documents* (files stored in DOC format) to save, edit, and preview HTML pages because it's faster, and you get WYSIWYG without having to load a real browser. But if you want to view the DOC file with a real browser, you need to save it in HTM format first.

HTML files in raw text, or *ASCII,* contain all of the same formatting information, but WebAuthor has to "translate" the codes for Word to provide WYSIWYG.

When you're ready to put a WebAuthor document on a Web server, you need to save it as an HTM file in ASCII format. Until then, leave it in DOC format so WebAuthor can load it quickly and provide WYSIWYG.

Troubleshooting

Why can't I get to WebAuthor Help when I hit the F1 key? Also, sometimes WebAuthor Help appears under the Word Help menu, and then it's gone! What gives?

It's okay to be confused a little on this one. Word reserved the F1 key for its own help system, so when you're editing a WebAuthor document, use the Ctrl+F1 key combination to call WebAuthor Help. This key combination doesn't work when you're in a Word document (and Word's F1 Help is disabled when you're in a WebAuthor document).

WebAuthor also replaces Word's Help menu with its own menu when you're editing a WebAuthor document. Return to a Word document, and Word's Help menu entries will reappear.

WebAuthor Tools for Formatting HTML Documents

Now that you've started WebAuthor, you can enter the text content of the page. WebAuthor lets you treat the HTML page just like any other Word document: you can type in the raw text and format it later, or format it as you go using the powerful style controls Word offers. WebAuthor's magic consists of automating the application of HTML style tags via Word's standard style template tools. If you know these Word functions already, you're halfway there.

There are two basic kinds of HTML styles:

- Paragraph styles (that change entire paragraphs)

- Character styles (that alter just the selected text)

HTML uses two main styles for characters:

- Physical (specifies a particular font, but not the purpose of the text)

- Logical (specifies the purpose, but leaves the font specifications to the browser application)

Using style controls is simple in WebAuthor. Because HTML styles are so different from Word styles, WebAuthor removes the Style drop-down list from the Word formatting toolbar when WebAuthor is active (don't worry, your Word styles are still loaded, just not active for the current document; when you switch back to a Word document, they'll reappear automatically).

Instead of the Style drop-down list, WebAuthor has a Style button on its own toolbar (to the right of the toolbar button with the eye). When you click this button, WebAuthor displays the Paragraph Styles dialog box (see fig. 29.3).

Fig. 29.3
Applying HTML paragraph styles is simple with WebAuthor.

Bold, italic, and other character formats are also handled a little differently in WebAuthor. The Format Character button on the WebAuthor toolbar (to the right of the Style button) is great for quickly altering character styles (see fig. 29.4).

Note

HTML currently doesn't support hyphenation or full justification of text, so you won't find these features when Word is in WebAuthor mode. HTML *does* support automatic word-flow, so you don't have to plan the length of your text lines for a specific display system.

VIII

Editors & Styles

Tip
Beware of specifying physical font characteristics that might not be supported on the viewer's system — logical specifications may backfire in certain situations as well. Logical fonts will be displayed with whatever settings the viewer's browser supports.

Fig. 29.4
WebAuthor offers the full gamut of HTML character styles via the Character Formatting Selector dialog box. You can easily select the appropriate physical or logical styles.

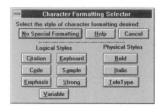

Adding Hypertext Links

Adding hypertext links, or URLs, is a snap. WebAuthor supports three types of links:

- Internal (link points to a location in the current document)

- Local (link points to another file on the same computer or local network)

- Remote (link points to an address on a server across a TCP/IP network, the Internet, or otherwise)

WebAuthor handles all the peculiarities of address syntax for you; you don't have to worry about the forward slash versus backslash problem, and so on.

Follow these steps to create a hypertext link in your document:

1. Highlight the text you want the user to select as the link.

2. Choose **I**nsert, Hypertext **L**ink. WebAuthor displays the New Anchor dialog box (see fig. 29.5).

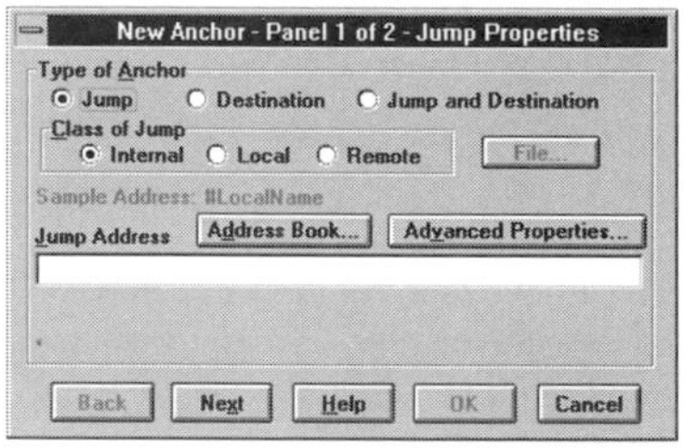

Fig. 29.5
WebAuthor offers a variety of options and controls for quickly adding new HTML anchors. Taking advantage of the address book feature really speeds up the linking process.

3. Select the Jump radio button.

4. Select the radio button for the Jump class you want (Internal, Local, or Remote).

5. In the Jump Address field, type the name of the target file (if it's on the local network, just enter the file name; if it's on a TCP/IP network or the Internet, type HTTP or the appropriate service type, followed by the URL for the file).

6. Click the Next button.

7. When the second dialog box appears, select the appropriate display properties for the page (Text, Image Only, or Text and Image) and click the OK button.

Using Inline Images

You may also want to add graphics to your Web pages—the best pages use graphics to add zest to the layout, and draw the user's eye to specific objects of interest.

Follow these steps to add a graphic to your page:

1. Place the cursor at the location on the page where you want the graphic to be placed.

2. From the Word menu, choose Insert, Image. WebAuthor displays the New Graphic Image dialog box, as shown in figure 29.6.

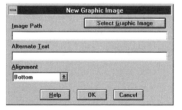

Fig. 29.6
You can quickly specify the image location in the New Graphic Image dialog box, or choose the Select Graphic Image button to browse (if your image is local).

3. If your viewer's browser is not set up for inline image display, you can specify alternate text using the Alternate Text field. Click in the field and type the message you want these users to see (make it descriptive— remember, they won't see the image).

4. You can choose the position of the graphic relative to the page text using the Alignment drop-down list.

5. When you finish specifying the graphic location, click OK. WebAuthor will insert a thumbnail representing the graphic into the document.

VIII

Editors & Styles

Troubleshooting

I can't seem to import graphics into my WebAuthor pages. What's wrong?

If you can't get your document to read GIF files, make sure Word has this import filter installed. Try opening a new document with the Normal style template, and choosing **I**nsert, **P**icture. If Word can't import the image, run Word Setup and install the filter.

Using Forms

HTML 2.0 supports improved form display, and WebAuthor makes it very easy to add forms to your Web pages.

Follow these instructions to create a form:

1. Place the cursor where you want the form to begin.

2. Choose **I**nsert, **F**orm. WebAuthor displays the Form Manager dialog box (see fig. 29.7). Choose **Y**es.

Fig. 29.7
Simply answer **Y**es to create a new form in your HTML document. WebAuthor will guide you through the particulars of form design quickly and easily.

3. WebAuthor displays the Form Attributes dialog box. Enter the URL of the server handling the form requests and select the form type (POST or GET). WebAuthor inserts the Start Form and End Form bars in your document (see fig. 29.8).

Now you can add radio buttons, checkboxes, inline graphics, or any other legal HTML document format or object to your form.

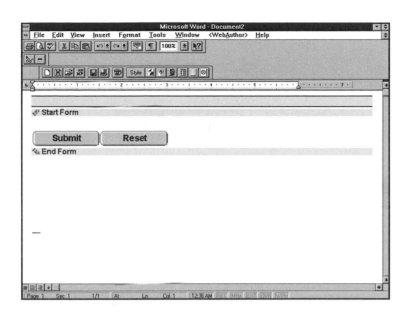

Fig. 29.8
WebAuthor
provides a clear
and simple
template for
designing your
HTML form.

VIII

Editors & Styles

Using WebAuthor to Edit Existing HTML Files

WebAuthor is just as valuable a tool for maintaining existing HTML files as it is for creating them from scratch. You can edit other Web pages regardless of what tools were used to create them.

Follow these steps to open an existing HTML document:

1. Place Word in WebAuthor mode (choose **T**ools, We**b**Author or choose **F**ile, **N**ew).

2. Choose **F**ile, **O**pen. WebAuthor displays the Open dialog box (see fig. 29.9).

3. Select the file you want to edit and click OK. WebAuthor displays the File Open (Convert HTML) dialog box, as shown in figure 29.10. Choose **Y**es.

Fig. 29.9
WebAuthor uses the standard, familiar Word Open dialog box for file selection.

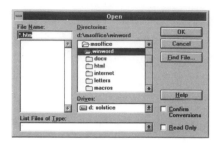

Fig. 29.10
WebAuthor asks whether you want to convert the HTML file to DOC format to enable WYSIWYG editing.

After conversion, WebAuthor displays the file in WYSIWYG format for further editing (see fig. 29.11).

Fig. 29.11
The converted HTM file is now ready for further editing.

Styles and HTML commands display here

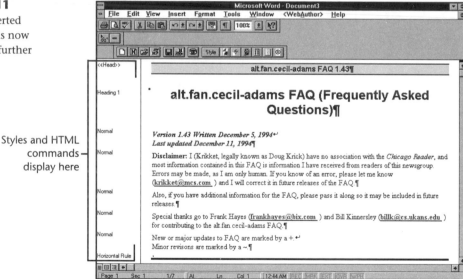

Troubleshooting

Why won't my older Word documents convert correctly when I import them with WebAuthor?

WebAuthor isn't designed to convert existing Word documents to HTML. Quarter-deck plans on adding a conversion utility specifically for Word files at a later date.

You can save your Word document as text, then import it to WebAuthor, but you'll lose all formatting in the Word document. Cut and paste works also, but expect the same loss of all text attributes.

From Here...

For more information on creating and editing HTML documents, see the following chapters:

■ Part III, "Creating HTML Documents," includes chapters exploring the common "standard and practices" in HTML and creating HTML documents from top to bottom.

■ Chapters 25 through 28 discuss some other stand-alone HTML editors you might want to investigate. These include HTML Assistant, HTMLed, and Microsoft Internet Assistant.

Chapter 30

HTML Style Sheets for Commercial Software

In addition to the variety of stand-alone HTML editors, there are a number of very useful style sheets and document templates for commercial word processors like Microsoft Word and Novell's WordPerfect.

There are some good reasons to look at these as alternatives to the higher-powered stuff:

- They're usually free (or at least cheap)

- They're simpler, so there's a quicker learning curve

- They easily let you reuse documents you already have

- They let you create multipurpose documents for conventional and online publishing simultaneously

A style sheet typically consists of a single file that contains special macros, styles, and formatting information specific to working with HTML. The better ones also include a toolbar and online help.

In this chapter, you learn to use popular style sheets for word processors like Microsoft Word and WordPerfect to create and edit HTML documents.

Using Your Word Processor to Create HTML Documents

Chances are good that you already use a word processor like Word for Windows. You're probably familiar with its toolbars, menus, dialog boxes, and commands. It makes sense to build on that knowledge instead of learning completely new software. That's where these style sheets come in. They add functionality to the word processor you already have, making use of their text-editing tools, spell-checker, and so on.

> **Note**
>
> *Style sheet* is the generic term for a built-in set of formatting, macro, and command functions in a document. Different word processing programs call them different things. Word, for example, calls them templates. I use the generic term in this chapter, so you can assume that when you see "style sheet" it applies to a document template in Word.

Using a style sheet is a snap. You simply create a new document based on the style sheet and start typing. Each style sheet gives you at least rudimentary clues about adding graphics, anchors, and rules. It's easy because you still use your word processor commands for saving, spell-checking, and the like. You just access the HTML features you need as you go.

Installation and use instructions are covered in the sections on each style sheet, along with examples of creating and editing HTML documents.

Making Multi-Purpose Documents

Tip

Any time you have information that needs to be distributed on the Web and in printed form, a style sheet makes it quick and easy.

Creating multi-purpose documents is one of the biggest benefits of using style sheets. For example, say that you write job postings for your company. You have a pre-defined style, with specific fonts and sizes for headings, titles, and descriptions. These documents are posted internally on bulletin boards, placed in a shared e-mail folder, and printed and sent to the newspaper for ad placement. By adding one of these style sheets, you can make the document ready to be added to your company's WWW server with just a few clicks of the mouse.

You can also use these style sheets to reuse all of your existing documents. A large company may have hundreds of faxable documents for customer support or sales information purposes. They can all be converted to HTML and placed on a WWW server in a matter of a few minutes. Add some anchor tags, and you can convert your entire arsenal of faxable documents to a powerful hypertext library in one afternoon.

Using Style Sheets with Word for Windows

Note

These document templates are designed for use with Microsoft Word for Windows. There are no versions specific to the Macintosh, but you can use at least some of the features in Word 6 for the Macintosh.

There are several Word document templates floating around on the Internet. In this section, I cover five of the more popular ones, each with varying features and ease of use. Some are better suited to converting existing documents than creating new ones.

ANT_HTML

ANT_HTML is a template created by Jill Swift and offered as reasonably priced shareware (see fig. 30.1). Its strong points include easy conversion of existing documents and good online documentation (in the form of an HTML file, of course!). It includes its own custom ANT menu, a colorful (if not terribly attractive) toolbar, and useful dialogs that give some help to users unfamiliar with HTML.

VIII

Editors & Styles

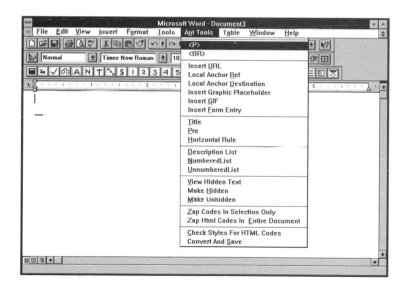

Fig. 30.1
ANT DEMO is the demonstration version of ANT_HTML. It has an extensive toolbar and custom menus with just about every HTML command you could want.

Installing and Setting Up ANT_HTML

This part is really easy. To install and set up ANT_HTML, follow these steps:

1. Create a temporary directory on your hard disk for the files.

2. Unzip the ANT_DEMO.ZIP file into the directory you created.

3. Start Microsoft Word.

4. Choose **F**ile, **O**pen and then choose ANT_INST.DOC from the directory you created.

5. When the document opens, double-click the red Double-Click Here box.

When you do this, the installer copies ANT_DEMO.DOT and ANTDEMO.HTM to your Microsoft Word templates directory and creates a preferences file named ANT_HTML.INI in your Windows directory.

That's all there is to it. Installation is completely painless. Now you're ready to start using the style sheet to create and convert your own documents.

Creating an HTML Document

To create a new HTML document using ANT_HTML, follow these steps:

1. Start Word and choose **F**ile, **N**ew.

2. Choose ANT_DEMO as the template to base the document on and click OK.

3. Create your document as you normally would, using the Heading 1 through Heading 6 styles to specify headings and the Normal style to specify normal text.

4. When you're done, save your document and then choose **A**nt tools, Convert and Save.

You now have a copy of your document in Word format, and a copy in HTML format with an HTM extension.

Converting Existing Documents to HTML

This is a little clunky, but it works:

1. Select your entire document by choosing **E**dit, Select **A**ll.

2. Choose **E**dit, **C**opy to copy the entire document to the Clipboard.

3. Choose **F**ile, **N**ew and select ANT_DEMO.

4. Choose **E**dit, **P**aste to paste the Clipboard contents into the new HTML document.

5. Save the document and choose **A**nt tools, **C**onvert and Save.

This converts the Word document to HTML with all the style tags intact.

Working with HTML Elements

Adding style tags is pretty effortless. There are buttons on the toolbar for the common HTML styles. If you want to assign a title style to a line of text, for example, select the text and click the Title button. The same applies for any of the heading styles or any other HTML style tag.

Supported tags include title, heading 1 through 6, address, preformatted, keyboard, numbered and unnumbered lists, strong and emphasis, line break, and forms.

Working with Anchors, Graphics, and URLs

To add an inline graphic, place the cursor where you want the graphic to appear and click the GIF button in the toolbar. Select the file name and click OK.

> **Note**
>
> ANT_HTML doesn't actually display the graphic, just a placeholder. You have to open your document in a viewer to see the graphic on the page.

To add a link to another location, select the word you want to be the anchor and click the URL button in the toolbar. Type the URL and click OK. ANT_HTML creates the appropriate anchor for you.

Working with Forms

ANT_HTML lets you add forms support to your HTML document by clicking the Form Entry button and specifying the type of field you want to add. The unregistered version of ANT_HTML only supports get and post methods, along with checkboxes.

CU HTML

CU HTML is written by Kenneth Wong and Anton Lam at the Chinese University of Hong Kong's Computer Services Center. It's actually written for Word 2.0, but will work fine with Word 6.

Tip

The Select Graphic dialog box only shows GIF files. Even though ANT_HTML doesn't let you include JPEG files, you can still type a JPEG file name in the dialog box. It appears correctly in your HTML document.

VIII

Editors & Styles

CU HTML is simpler than ANT_HTML and a little easier to use (see fig. 30.2). It supports inline images (GIF format only) and a basic set of tags and anchors.

Installing and Setting Up CU HTML

To install CU HTML, follow these steps:

1. Copy the CUHTML.ZIP file to a temporary directory on your hard disk and unzip it.

2. Copy CUHTML.DLL and GIF.DLL to your \windows\system directory.

3. Copy CU_HTML.DOT to your Word template directory.

That's all there is to it. Installation is complete.

Creating an HTML Document

To create an HTML document with CU HTML, follow these steps:

1. Start Word.

2. Choose **F**ile, **N**ew and choose CU_HTML as the template. If you're using Word 6, you need to choose **V**iew, **T**oolbars and select the Word 2.0 toolbar.

3. Type your document as you normally would. Apply any styles you want to the text using the Styles drop-down list box.

4. If you want to use the <STRONG> and <EMPH> tags, use Word's **bold** and *italic* commands.

5. Save your document.

6. Click the Write HTML button on the toolbar. This saves the document as an HTML file, with an HTM extension.

Working with Graphics and Links

To insert an inline image, place the insertion point in the document where you want the graphic to be. Click the GIF button in the toolbar and select the GIF file from the dialog box. Click OK and you're done.

To create a link to a URL, select the word you want to use as a link and click the URL button in the toolbar. Type the URL and click OK.

Using WPTOHTML

WPTOHTML is a public-domain WordPerfect macro that converts WordPerfect documents to HTML. It runs on the DOS and VAX VMS platforms, and is available for versions 5.1 and 6.0 of WordPerfect.

> **Note**
>
> WPTOHTML is available via anonymous FTP at: **oak.oakland.edu/SimTel/msdos /wordperf/wpt51d10.zip**.

> **Note**
>
> There are currently no style sheets available for the Windows, OS/2, or UNIX versions of WordPerfect. Novell is planning to release WordPerfect Internet Publisher for Windows in the near future. This will be an add-in to WordPerfect with similar features and functionality to Microsoft Internet Assistant for Word, with a viewer based on Netscape.

Installing and Setting Up WPTOHTML

Installing WPTOHTML is straightforward. Unzip the file in your WordPerfect macro directory (probably \WP60\MACROS) and then copy the PRS file to your printer files directory.

Converting Existing Documents

WPTOHTML doesn't have any features for creating and editing HTML documents, but it does let you convert documents you already have.

The macro makes arbitrary decisions about what HTML tag to apply to which text, based on the relative font sizes in the structure of the document. You need to experiment to get the best results.

To run the macro, load (or create) the document you want to convert, then press Alt+F10, type the name of the macro (WPTOHTML), and press Enter. The macro inserts HTML tags as it goes through the document. When it's finished, it asks you to save the newly marked-up file with an HTM extension.

VIII

Editors & Styles

Limitations of WPTOHTML

This macro is good for batch-converting large numbers of documents, but lacks a number of important features that must be tagged by hand. These include the following:

- Ordered lists

- Unordered lists

- Definition lists

- Inline graphics

From Here...

In this chapter, you learned how to use document templates and style sheets with a word processor to easily create and edit HTML documents. For information about alternatives to these tools, check out these chapters:

- Chapter 25, "Stand-Alone HTML Editors," gives alternatives to style sheets, including powerful HTML authoring systems for Microsoft Word.

- Appendix A, "HTML Elements Reference," provides information on the elements of HTML and a comprehensive reference.

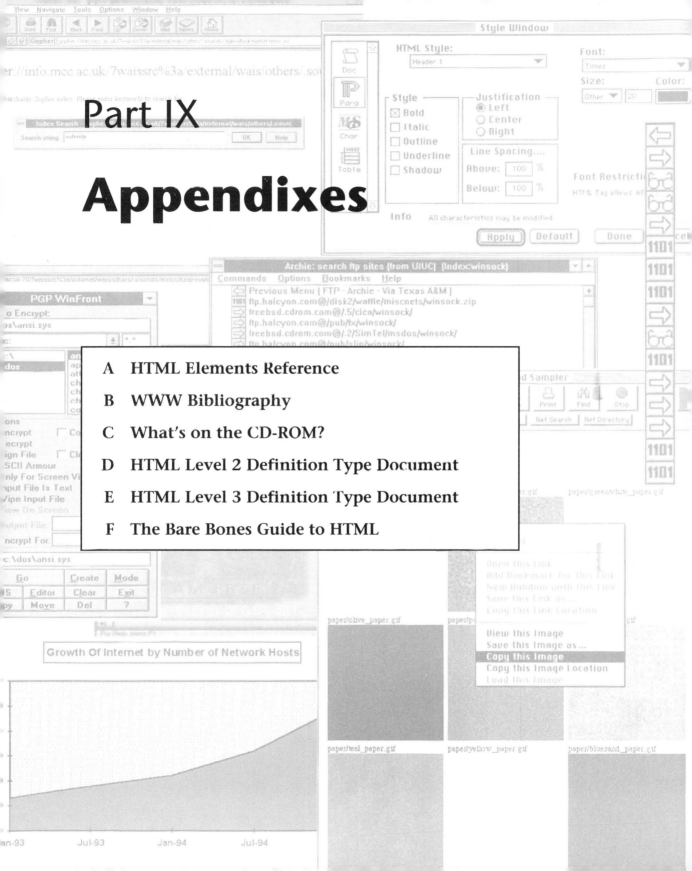

Part IX

Appendixes

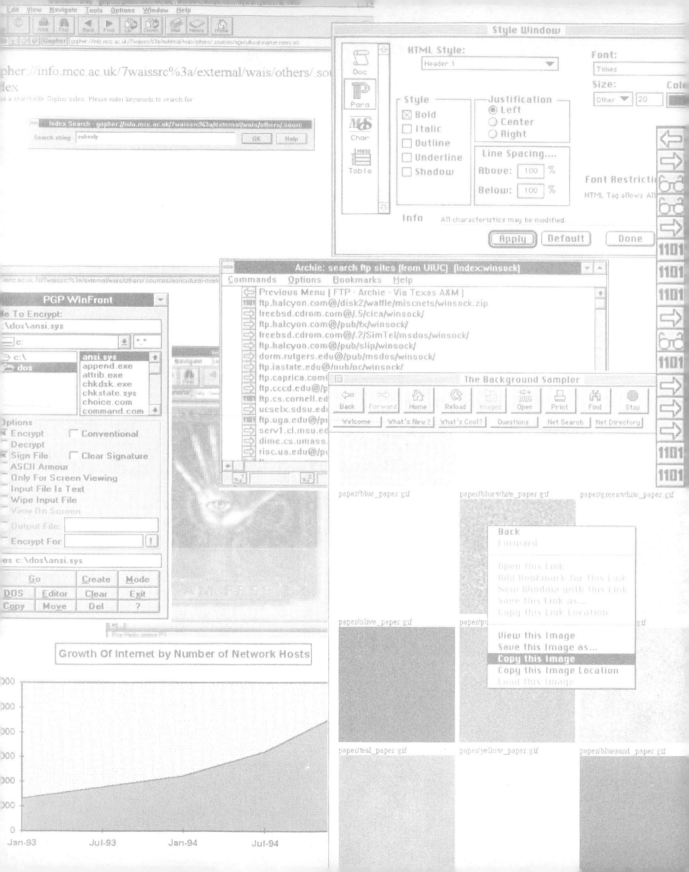

Appendix A

HTML Elements Reference

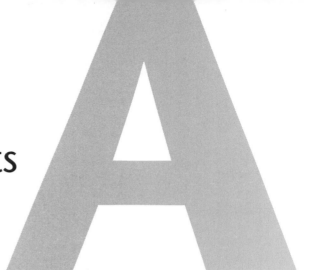

This appendix presents the HTML 2.0 elements by their appropriate usage in Web documents. HTML 3.0 elements are included and noted if they're supported by any available Web clients. Netscape extensions are also included and noted as such (including the version compatibility of Netscape required).

The standard format of an entry is:

ELEMENT
Element description

Container or empty element?

Syntax of usage

Attributes
Attribute description

Syntax of usage

Attribute option and option description

Usage
Legal uses of current element

The following is an example:

P

Inserts a paragraph break at the current point in the document, beginning the next line of text or inline graphic against the left margin two lines beneath the current text.

Empty element, requiring no closing tag.

Syntax: <P>

Attributes

ALIGN   HTML 3.0 revision of P element, using it as a container and applying alignment to all of the content within the container.

Syntax: <P ALIGN=center> ... </P>

Usage

Body section—stand-alone and within lists, pre-formatted text, and forms containers.

Whole Document Elements

BODY

Defines the body section in an HTML document.

Container element, requiring </BODY> closing tag.

Attributes

BACK-   Netscape 1.1 extension to the standard HTML, specifying
GROUND   a graphic image to be used for the background of the current document.

Syntax: <BODY BACKGROUND=*URL*> (where *URL* is a graphic URL)

BGCOLOR   Netscape 1.1 extension specifying a color to be used for the current document.

Syntax: <BODY BGCOLOR=*value*> (where *value* is a color notation)

Color notation: "$*xyz*" (where *x* is the value for the red color component, *y* is the value for the green color component, and *z* is the value for the blue color component; values range from 0–9)

TEXT   Netscape 1.1 extension specifying a color to be used for the body content text.

Syntax: <BODY TEXT=*value*> (where *value* is a color notation)

Color notation: "$*xyz*" (where *x* is the value for the red color component, *y* is the value for the green color component, and *z* is the value for the blue color component; values range from 0–9)

LINK   Netscape 1.1 extension specifying a color to be used for body content hyperlinks.

Syntax: <BODY LINK=*value*> (where *value* is a color notation)

Color notation: "$*xyz*" (where *x* is the value for the red color component, *y* is the value for the green color component, and *z* is the value for the blue color component; values range from 0–9)

VLINK   Netscape 1.1 extension specifying a color to be used for visited body content hyperlinks.

Syntax: <BODY VLINK=*value*> (where *value* is a color notation)

Color notation: "$*xyz*" (where *x* is the value for the red color component, *y* is the value for the green color component, and *z* is the value for the blue color component; values range from 0–9)

ALINK   Netscape 1.1 extension specifying a color to be used for active body content hyperlinks.

Syntax: <BODY ALINK=*value*> (where *value* is a color notation)

Color notation: "$xyz" (where *x* is the value for the red color component, *y* is the value for the green color component, and *z* is the value for the blue color component; values range from 0–9)

Usage
Enclose all HTML content that is part of the document's body data that is to be displayed by Web clients, including text, inline images, and hyperlink anchors.

Comment Coding
Non-standard HTML container for inserting hidden comments in HTML documents, which are not displayed in Web viewers.

Container element, requiring closing tag.

Syntax: <!—...—>

Attributes
None

Usage
Any document section and in containers if required.

HEAD
Defines the head section in an HTML document.

Container element, requiring </HEAD> closing tag.

Attributes
None

Usage
Encloses all HTML content that isn't a part of the body data in a document, including the document's title and link relationships.

HTML
Defines the HTML content in a document on a Web server.

Container element, requiring </HTML> closing tag.

Syntax: <HTML>...</HTML>

Attributes

None

Usage

Encloses all content in a document that should be recognized as HTML by Internet applications (such as Web viewers).

Head Section Elements

BASE

Indicates the URL of the current document. This helps Web viewers process relative hypertext links within the document.

Empty element, requiring no closing tag.

Syntax: <BASE HREF=*URL*> (where *URL* is specific for the current document)

Attributes

None

Usage

Head section only, not within containers.

ISINDEX

Indicates that the current Web page can be searched with the Web client's search feature. Requires server-side index search capabilities.

Empty element, requiring no closing tag.

Syntax: <ISINDEX>

Attributes

PROMPT   Netscape 1.0 extension, customizes text message in search dialog box or window.

Syntax: <ISINDEX PROMPT="*value*"> (where *value* is the new text message)

Usage

Head section only, not within containers. Requires the server-side capability to service searches.

LINK

Establishes a relationship between the current document and another document. Can be used more than once to define multiple relationships.

Empty element, requiring no closing tag.

Syntax: <LINK *attribute* HREF=*URL*> (where *attribute* is the applicable relationship, and *URL* is the other party in the relationship)

Attributes

REL   Defines the relationship between the current document and the URL.

Syntax: <LINK REL=*relationship* HREF=*URL*> (where *relationship* is the type of relationship being defined)

Options:

PRECEDE. The current document precedes the resource in the *URL* value

PREV. The *URL* value resource precedes the current document

USEINDEX. The *URL* document is a related index used in searches in the current document

USEGLOSSARY. The *URL* document is an index used for glossary queries in the current document

ANNOTATION. The *URL* document provides secondary information (such as margin notes) for the current document

REPLY. The *URL* document provides primary information for the current document

PRECEDES. Defines the ordered relationship between the two documents, where the current document comes before the *URL* document

SUBDOCUMENT. Defines the hierarchical relationship between two documents, where the current document is higher than the *URL* document

PRESENT. States that whenever the current document is retrieved, the *URL* document must be retrieved as well (but not vice versa)

SEARCH. States that when the *URL* document is accessed, a search is carried out on it before its content is retrieved

SUPERSEDES. The *URL* document is a previous version of the current document

HISTORY. The *URL* document contains a documented history of the versions of the current document

MADE. The *URL* value in the e-mail address is the creator of the current document

OWNS. The *URL* value defines the owner of the current document

INCLUDES. The current document includes (as a grouping) the *URL* value

REV   Defined the relation between the URL and the current document (the reverse relationship of REL).

Syntax: <LINK REV=*relationship* HREF=*URL*> (where *relationship* is the type of relationship being defined)

Options: Use the same as with REL, but reverse the defined relationships

Usage
Head section only, not within containers.

META
Contains additional information about the current document that isn't displayed by Web viewers.

Empty element, not requiring a closing tag.

Syntax: <NEXTID = *value*> (where *value* is a unique number)

Attributes
None

IX

Appendixes

Usage
Head section only, not within containers.

NEXTID
Indicates the NEXTID value to use for link name.

Container element, requiring </TITLE> closing tag.

Syntax: <TITLE>...</TITLE>

Attributes
None

Usage
Head section only, not within containers.

TITLE
Indicates the document's title, which is displayed in Web viewers but not in the body of the document text.

Container element, requiring </TITLE> closing tag.

Syntax: <TITLE>...</TITLE>

Attributes
None

Usage
Head section only, not within containers.

Body Section Elements

A
Indicates a document anchor, used to create links to other resources or to define a location that can be linked to.

Container element, requiring </A> closing tag.

Options:

Creating a hyperlink to a WWW resource:

Syntax: <A HREF="*URL*">...</A> (where *URL* describes a valid WWW resource)

Attributes: None

Usage: Body section, stand-alone or within text, form, and table containers. Text between the anchor tags is clickable and will appear in the viewer's currently defined link color. Clicking the link text activates the link and accesses the specified Web resource.

Defining a named anchor location:

Syntax: <A name="*value*">...</A> (where *value* is a unique anchor name for the current document)

Attributes: None

Usage: Body section, stand-alone or within text, form, and table containers. Text between the anchor tags is not highlighted or clickable.

Creating a hyperlink to a named anchor:

Syntax: <A HREF="*URL#value*">...</A> (where *URL* describes a valid WWW document and *value* is a named anchor within that document)

Attributes: None

Usage: Body section, stand-alone or within text, form, and table containers. Text between the anchor tags is clickable and will appear in the viewer's currently defined link color. Clicking the link text activates the link and accesses the specified location in the specified Web page.

Creating a hyperlink to a named anchor in the same document:

Syntax: <A HREF="#*value*">...</A> (where *value* is a named anchor within the same document)

Attributes: None

Usage: Body section, stand-alone or within text, form, and table containers. Text between the anchor tags is clickable and will appear in the viewer's currently defined link color. Clicking the link text activates the link and accesses the specified location in the same Web page.

ADDRESS

Defines the address of the document author and is displayed in Web viewers.

Container element, requiring </ADDRESS> closing tag.

Syntax: <ADDRESS>...</ADDRESS>

Attributes
None

Usage
Body or form sections, stand-alone, or within containers.

B

Formats the container text as bold text. Requires HTML break elements for text breaks. Can be combined with active HTML style elements.

Container element, requiring </B> closing tag.

Syntax: <B>...</B>

Attributes
None

Usage
Body section, stand-alone, and within list and form containers.

BASEFONT

Defines the default document text size to a value from 1–7 (3 is the common default). Requires Netscape support. Affects relative FONT element use.

Empty element, does not require a closing tag.

Syntax: <BASEFONT SIZE=n> (where n is a font size value from 1–7)

Attributes
None

Usage

Body section, stand-alone, and within list and form containers.

BLINK

Makes the container text blink on and off in the WWW client window. Requires Netscape support. Can be combined with active HTML style elements.

Container element, requiring </BLINK> closing tag.

Syntax: <BLINK>...</BLINK>

Attributes

None

Usage

Body section, stand-alone, and within list and form containers. Support is very limited and the element is unpopular with readers. Use sparingly.

BLOCKQUOTE

Defines the container text as a quotation from another source, using the viewer's current text settings. Retains all natural line and paragraph breaks in the text and indents both right and left margins. Can contain active HTML style elements.

Container element, requiring </BLOCKQUOTE> closing tag.

Syntax: <BLOCKQUOTE>...</BLOCKQUOTE>

Attributes

None

Usage

Body section, stand-alone, and within list and form containers.

BR

Inserts a line break at the current point in the document, beginning the next line of text or inline graphic against the left margin one line beneath the current text.

Empty element, requiring no closing tag.

Syntax:

Attributes

CLEAR   Netscape 1.0 extension, defining where the content can begin the next line in the document.

Syntax: <BR CLEAR=*value*> (where *value* is a valid option)

Options:

LEFT. The content can continue on the next available line whose left margin is clear

RIGHT. The content can continue on the next available line whose right margin is clear

ALL. The content can continue on the next available line where both margins are clear

Usage

Body section—stand-alone and within lists, pre-formatted text, and form containers.

CENTER

Aligns the container text relative to the current container. Requires Netscape 1.0 support. Can be combined with active HTML style elements.

Container element, requiring </CENTER> closing tag.

Syntax: <CENTER>...</CENTER>

Attributes

None

Usage

Body section, stand-alone, and within list and form containers. Will be superseded by HTML 3.0's ALIGN attribute to the P and H elements.

CITE

Defines the container text as a text citation, using the viewer's current text settings. Requires HTML break elements for text breaks. Can be combined with active HTML style elements.

Container element, requiring </CITE> closing tag.

Syntax: <CITE>...</CITE>

Attributes

None

Usage

Body section, stand-alone, and within list and form containers.

CODE

Defines the container text as computer code text, using the viewer's current text settings. Requires HTML break elements for text breaks. Can be combined with active HTML style elements.

Container element, requiring </CODE> closing tag.

Syntax: <CODE>...</CODE>

Attributes

None

Usage

Body section, stand-alone, and within list and form containers.

DD

Formats subsequent body text as a text definition. Provides additional space when it is superseded by a new element. Can contain active HTML elements.

Empty element, does not require a closing tag.

Syntax: <DD>

Attributes

None

Usage

Body section, a component of definition lists (DL), generally following a definition term (DT).

DFN

Defines the container text as definition text, using the viewer's current text settings. Requires HTML break elements for text breaks. Can be combined with active HTML style elements.

Container element, requiring </DFN> closing tag.

Syntax: <DFN>...</DFN>

Attributes
None

Usage
Body section, stand-alone, and within list and form containers. Support by current Web viewers is inconsistent (not recommended for use).

DIR

Formats the container text as a file directory list. Contains list items (LI). Can contain active HTML elements. Intended to format text in compressed columns, but viewer support is rare.

Container element, requiring </DIR> closing tag.

Syntax: <DIR>...</DIR>

Attributes
None

Usage
Body section, stand-alone, or within other list, form, and table containers.

DL

Formats the container text as a definition list. Contains definition term (DT) and definition text (DD). Provides a double-spaced closing text break.

Container element, requiring </DL> closing tag.

Syntax: <DL>...</DL>

Attributes
None

Usage
Body section, stand-alone, or within other list, form, and table containers.

DT

Formats subsequent body text as a definition term. Provides additional space after the term. Can contain active HTML elements.

Empty element, does not require a closing tag.

Syntax: <DT>

Attributes

None

Usage

Body section, a component of definition lists (DL).

EM

Defines the container text as emphasized, using the viewer's current text settings. Requires HTML break elements for text breaks. Can be combined with active HTML style elements.

Container element, requiring </EM> closing tag.

Syntax: <EM>...</EM>

Attributes

None

Usage

Body section, stand-alone, and within list and form containers.

FONT

Formats the container text to the specific or relative font size indicated. Requires Netscape support. Does not affect the use of any other HTML elements.

Container element, requiring </FONT> closing tag.

Syntax: <FONT SIZE=*value*>...</FONT> (where *value* is an absolute or relative font size)

Attributes

None

Usage
Options:

Absolute font size. Font will be displayed at a specific size ranging from 1–7 (one being the smallest font and seven the largest)

Syntax example: <FONT SIZE=5>...</FONT>

Relative font size. Font will be displayed at a size relative (using the plus and minus symbols) to the current base font, which is normally a size 3.

Syntax example: <FONT SIZE=–2>...</FONT>

Usage
Body section, stand-alone, and within list and form containers.

H*n*

Defines the container text as a heading, using the viewer's current text settings. Requires HTML break elements for text breaks. Can be combined with active HTML style elements.

Container element, requiring </H*n*> closing tag.

Syntax: <H*n*>...</H*n*> (where *n* corresponds to the heading level)

Level values of 1–6 are valid and each will have unique text definitions; in general, the lower the level number, the larger and more prominent the display text will be.

Attributes

ALIGN   HTML 3.0 revision of H element, applying on-screen alignment to all of the content within the container.

Syntax: <H*n*ALIGN=*value*>...</H*n*> (where *value* is a valid alignment option and *n* corresponds to the heading level)

Options:

LEFT. The content is aligned against the left text margin

RIGHT. The content is aligned against the right text margin

CENTER. The content is centered between the left and right text margins

Usage

Body section, stand-alone, and within list and form containers. Headings define logical relationships; for example, H2 is a sub-heading of H1 and a super-heading of H3. Alignment options are relative to the current container.

HR

Displays a horizontal rule in the WWW client window. The rule fills the current container from the left to the right margins. Does not affect other HTML elements in use.

Empty element, does not require a closing tag.

Syntax: <HR>

Attributes

WIDTH   Netscape 1.0 extension, defines the actual or window percentage length of the horizontal rule.

Syntax: <HR WIDTH=*value*> (where *value* is a pixel measurement or a percentage, as in 50 percent)

SIZE   Netscape 1.0 extension, defines the height or thickness of the horizontal rule.

Syntax: <HR SIZE=*n*> (where *n* is a pixel measurement)

NOSHADE   Netscape 1.0 extension, displays the rule as a solid black line with no drop shadow.

Syntax: <HR NOSHADE>

ALIGN   Netscape 1.0 extension, aligns the horizontal rule relative to the current container.

Syntax: <HR ALIGN=*value*> (where *value* is a valid alignment option)

Options:

LEFT. The rule is aligned against the left text margin

RIGHT. The rule is aligned against the right text margin

CENTER. The rule is centered between the left and right margins

Usage

Body section, stand-alone, and within text containers.

I

Formats the container text as italicized text. Requires HTML break elements for text breaks. Can be combined with active HTML style elements.

Container element, requiring </I> closing tag.

Syntax: <I>...</I>

Attributes

None

Usage

Body section, stand-alone, and within list and form containers.

IMG

Displays inline images and image maps in the document body.

Empty element, does not require a closing tag.

Syntax: <IMG SRC="*URL*"> (where *URL* describes a valid graphic image file)

Attributes

SRC   Defines the source of the associated image file.

ALT   Defines a text string to be displayed by a WWW client if inline graphic support is not available.

     Syntax: <IMG SRC="*URL*" ALT"*value*"> (where *URL* is a valid graphic file and *value* is a text message)

ISMAP Defines the inline image as an image map.

     Syntax: <IMG SRC="*URL*" ISMAP> (where *URL* is a valid graphic file)

ALIGN Applies a specific alignment to text on the same line as the current inline graphic.

     Syntax: <IMG SRC="*URL*" ALIGN=*value*> (where *URL* is a valid graphic file and *value* is a valid alignment option)

Options:

TOP. Aligns the top of the image with the line's text

MIDDLE. Aligns the middle of the image with the line's text

BOTTOM. Aligns the bottom of the image with the line's text (default)

LEFT. Netscape 1.0 extension, aligns the graphic along the left-hand margin and allows text to flow beside the image

RIGHT. Netscape 1.0 extension, aligns the graphic along the right-hand margin and allows the text to flow beside the image

TEXTTOP. Netscape 1.0 extension, aligns the top of the image with the top of the tallest text on the line

ABSMIDDLE. Netscape 1.0 extension, aligns the middle of the image with the middle of the line's text

BASELINE. Netscape 1.0 extension, aligns the bottom of the image with the baseline of the line's text

ABSBOTTOM. Netscape 1.0 extension, aligns the bottom of the image with the bottom of the line's text

HSPACE Netscape 1.0 extension, defines the space along the horizontal edges of an inline graphic between the graphic and the adjacent text.

Syntax: <IMG SRC="*URL*" HSPACE=*n*> (where *URL* is a valid graphic file and *n* is the measurement of the blank space in pixels)

Usage: Often used in conjunction with VSPACE.

VSPACE Netscape 1.0 extension, defines the space along the vertical edges of an inline graphic between the graphic and the adjacent text.

Syntax: <IMG SRC="*URL*" VSPACE=*n*> (where *URL* is a valid graphic file and *n* is the measurement of the blank space in pixels)

Usage: Often used in conjunction with HSPACE.

WIDTH   Netscape 1.0 extension, defines the width of the inline image for the convenience of the WWW client; used with HEIGHT.

HEIGHT   Netscape 1.0 extension, defines the height of the inline image for the convenience of the WWW client; used with WIDTH.

Syntax: <IMG SRC="*URL*" WIDTH=*n1* HEIGHT=*n2*> (where *URL* is a valid graphic file, *n1* is the measurement of the width of the image in pixels, and *n2* is the measurement of the height of the image in pixels)

Usage: The WIDTH and HEIGHT values can be purposefully different than the image's actual measurements to force the image to "scale" to the new dimensions.

BORDER   Netscape 1.0 extension, determines the size of the client-provided border for an inline image.

Syntax: <IMG SRC="*URL*" BORDER=*n*> (where *URL* is a valid graphic file and *n* is the thickness of the border in pixels)

LOWSRC   Netscape 1.0 extension, defines a "low resolution" version of the inline image to be displayed at initial retrieval of the document, before the primary image is retrieved.

Syntax: <IMG SRC="*URL1*" LOWRSC="*URL2*"> (where *URL1* is a valid graphic file and *URL2* is a valid low resolution substitution for *URL1*)

Usage

Body or form sections, stand-alone or within containers.

KBD

Defines the container text as keyboard input text, using the viewer's current text settings. Requires HTML break elements for text breaks. Can be combined with active HTML style elements.

Container element, requiring </KBD> closing tag.

Syntax: <KBD>...</KBD>

Attributes

None

Usage

Body section, stand-alone, and within list and form containers.

LI

Defines a new item in a list.

Empty element, does not require a closing tag.

Syntax: <LI>

Attributes

TYPE   Netscape 1.0 extension, defines the current list type
                (regardless of the list container).

                Syntax: <LI TYPE=*value*> (where *value* is a valid type
                option)

                Options:

                CIRCLE. Defines the unordered list marker type as filled
                circles

                SQUARE. Defines the unordered list marker type as filled
                squares

                DISC. Defines the unordered list marker type as unfilled
                circles

                A. Defines the ordered list numbering characters as capital
                letters

                a. Defines the ordered list numbering characters as lower-
                case letters

                I. Defines the ordered list numbering characters as capital
                Roman numerals

                i. Defines the ordered list numbering characters as lower-
                case Roman numerals

                1. Defines the ordered list numbering characters as num-
                bers (default)

VALUE   Netscape 1.0 extension, defines the new beginning sequential value for the container's current and subsequent list items.

Syntax: <LI VALUE=*n*> (where *n* is a sequential value)

Usage
Body section, in ordered lists (OL) and unordered lists (UL).

LISTING

Defines the container text as a computer text list, using the viewer's current text settings. Retains all natural line and paragraph breaks in the text. Does not recognize internal HTML style elements.

Container element, requiring </LISTING> closing tag.

Syntax: <LISTING>...</LISTING>

Attributes
None

Usage
Body section, stand-alone, and within list and form containers. This element is deprecated and support by current Web viewers is inconsistent (not recommended for use).

MENU

Formats the container text as a menu list. Contains list items (LI). Can contain active HTML elements.

Container element, requiring </MENU> closing tag.

Syntax: <MENU>...</MENU>

Attributes
None

Usage
Body section, stand-alone, or within other list, form, and table containers.

NOBR

Prevents the container text from wrapping in the viewer window. Requires Netscape 1.0 support. Can be combined with active HTML style elements.

Container element, requiring </NOBR> closing tag.

Syntax: <NOBR>...</NOBR>

Attributes

None

Usage

Body section, stand-alone, and within list and form containers.

OL

Formats the container text as an ordered list. Sequentially numbers each enclosed list item (LI). Requires HTML break elements for text breaks. Can contain active HTML style elements.

Container element, requiring </OL> closing tag.

Syntax: <OL>...</OL>

Attributes

TYPE   Netscape 1.0 extension, defines the marker type for items in the contained list.

Syntax: <UL TYPE=*value*> (where *value* is a valid marker option)

Options:

A. Defines the numbering characters as capital letters

a. Defines the numbering characters as lowercase letters

I. Defines the numbering characters as capital Roman numerals

i. Defines the numbering characters as lowercase Roman numerals

1. Defines the numbering characters as numbers (default)

IX

Appendixes

START   Netscape 1.0 extension, defines the starting sequential value for the container's list items.

Syntax: <OL START=*n*> (where *n* is the starting value for the listed items)

Usage

Body section, stand-alone and within other containers. Uses the LI element to identify list items.

P

Inserts a paragraph break at the current point in the document, beginning the next line of text or inline graphic against the left margin two lines beneath the current text.

Empty element, requiring no closing tag.

Syntax: <P>

Attributes

ALIGN   HTML 3.0 revision of P element, using it as a container and applying alignment to all of the content within the container.

Syntax: <P ALIGN=*value*> ... </P> (where *value* is a valid option)

Options:

LEFT. The content is aligned against the left text margin

RIGHT. The content is aligned against the right text margin

CENTER. The content is centered between the left and right text margins

Usage

Body section—stand-alone and within lists, pre-formatted text and forms containers. ALIGN values are relative to the current container.

PLAINTEXT

Defines the subsequent text as unformatted text, using the viewer's current text settings. Retains all natural line and paragraph breaks in the text. Does not recognize internal HTML style elements.

Empty element, requiring no closing tag.

Syntax: <PLAINTEXT>

Attributes

None

Usage

Body section, stand-alone. This element has no closing tag, and all subsequent content (including HTML elements) is displayed as plain text. This element is deprecated and support by current Web viewers is *very* inconsistent (not recommended for use).

PRE

Defines the container content as "pre-formatted" and is displayed with the viewer's current text settings (usually a standard proportional font). Retains all natural line and paragraph breaks within the text. Can contain active HTML style elements.

Container element, requiring </PRE> closing tag.

Syntax: <PRE>...</PRE>

Attributes

WIDTH   Defines the width of a pre-formatted text container, in characters.

Syntax: <PRE WIDTH=*n*>...</PRE> (where *n* is the number of characters per line)

Usage

Body section, stand-alone, and within lists and form containers.

S

Formats the container text with strikeouts. Requires HTML break elements for text breaks. Can be combined with active HTML style elements.

Container element, requiring </S> closing tag.

Syntax: <S>...</S>

Attributes
None

Usage
Body section, stand-alone, and within list and form containers. Support by current Web viewers is rare (will become more common with the adoption of HTML 3.0).

SAMP

Defines the container text as sample output text, using the viewer's current text settings. Requires HTML break elements for text breaks. Can be combined with active HTML style elements.

Container element, requiring </SAMP> closing tag.

Syntax: <SAMP>...</SAMP>

Attributes
None

Usage
Body section, stand-alone, and within list and form containers.

STRONG

Defines the container text as strongly emphasized, using the viewer's current text settings. Requires HTML break elements for text breaks. Can be combined with active HTML style elements.

Container element, requiring </STRONG> closing tag.

Syntax: <STRONG>...</STRONG>

Attributes
None

Usage

Body section, stand-alone, and within list and form containers.

TT

Formats the container text as typewriter-style text (monospaced font). Requires HTML break elements for text breaks. Can be combined with active HTML style elements.

Container element, requiring </TT> closing tag.

Syntax: <TT>...</TT>

Attributes

None

Usage

Body section, stand-alone, and within list and form containers.

U

Formats the container text as underlined text. Requires HTML break elements for text breaks. Can be combined with active HTML style elements.

Container element, requiring </U> closing tag.

Syntax: <U>...</U>

Attributes

None

Usage

Body section, stand-alone, and within list and form containers. Support by current Web viewers is inconsistent (will become more common with the adoption of HTML 3.0).

UL

Formats the container text as an unordered list. Mark each enclosed list item (LI) with a viewer-defined bullet. Requires HTML break elements for text breaks. Can contain active HTML style elements.

Container element, requiring </UL> closing tag.

Syntax: <UL>...</UL>

Attributes

TYPE   Netscape 1.0 extension, defines the marker type for items in the contained list.

Syntax: <UL TYPE=*value*> (where *value* is a valid marker option)

Options:

CIRCLE. Defines the marker type as filled circles

SQUARE. Defines the marker type as filled squares

DISC. Defines the marker type as unfilled circles

Usage

Body section, stand-alone, and within other containers. Uses the LI element to identify list items.

VAR

Defines the container text as a text variable, using the viewer's current text settings. Requires HTML break elements for text breaks. Can be combined with active HTML style elements.

Container element, requiring </VAR> closing tag.

Syntax: <VAR>...</VAR>

Attributes

None

Usage

Body section, stand-alone, and within list and form containers.

WBR

Indicates a possible "break point" in the text. Requires Netscape 1.0 support. Is often used with the NOBR container elements.

Empty element, does not require a closing tag.

Syntax: <WBR>

Attributes

None

Usage

Body section, stand-alone, and within list and form containers.

XMP

Defines the container text as a text example, using the viewer's current text settings. Retains all natural line and paragraph breaks in the text. Does not recognize internal HTML style elements.

Container element, requiring </XMP> closing tag.

Syntax: <XMP>...</XMP>

Attributes

None

Usage

Body section, stand-alone, and within list and form containers. This element is deprecated and support by current Web viewers is inconsistent (not recommended for use).

Table Elements (HTML 3.0 Features)

CAPTION

Defines the table's caption text. Can contain active HTML elements.

Container element, requiring the </CAPTION> closing tag.

Syntax: <CAPTION>...</CAPTION>

Attributes

ALIGN   Defines the alignment of the caption text with the table.

Syntax: <CAPTION ALIGN=*value*> (where *value* is a valid alignment option)

Options:

TOP. Aligns caption above the table

Syntax: <CAPTION ALIGN=TOP>

BOTTOM. Aligns caption below the table

Syntax: <CAPTION ALIGN=BOTTOM>

Usage

Body section, within table containers only.

TABLE

Defines the container text as a table. Contains rows (TR), cells (TD), headers (TH), and captions (CAPTION). Can contain active HTML elements, including forms.

Container element, requiring </TABLE> closing tag.

Syntax: <TABLE>...</TABLE>

Attributes

BORDER — Defines the line weight of the border around the table cells.

Syntax: <TABLE BORDER=n> (where n is a number representing the chosen line weight)

Usage: If no border attribute is included, table will display cells without borders.

CELL-SPACING — Netscape 1.1 extension, defines horizontal spacing between adjacent cells.

Syntax: <TABLE CELLSPACING=n> (where n is the number of pixels between adjacent cells)

CELL-PADDING — Netscape 1.1 extension, defines vertical spacing between adjacent cells.

Syntax: <TABLE CELLPADDING=n> (where n is the number of pixels between adjacent cells)

WIDTH — Netscape 1.1 extension, defines width of table cells in pixels or as a percentage of the container's width.

Syntax: <TABLE WIDTH=*value*> (where *value* is the number of pixels or the percentage, expressed as n percent, of the width of the individual cells)

Usage

Body section, stand-alone, or within other list and form containers.

TD

Defines the text in individual table cells. Supports active HTML elements.

Container element, requiring </TD> closing tag.

Syntax: <TD>...</TD>

Attributes

ALIGN   Defines the text's horizontal alignment within the specific table cell.

Syntax: <TD ALIGN=*value*> (where *value* is a valid alignment option)

Options:

LEFT. Aligns the text with the cell's left edge

RIGHT. Aligns the text with the cell's right edge

CENTER. Centers the text in the cell

VALIGN   Defines the text's vertical alignment within the specific cell.

Options:

TOP. Aligns the header text with the top of the cell

MIDDLE. Aligns the header text with the middle of the cell

BOTTOM. Aligns the header text with the bottom of the cell

NOWRAP   Instructs the viewer not to wrap the text within the table cell.

Syntax: <TD NOWRAP>

COLSPAN   Instructs the viewer to span the specified number of table columns.

Syntax: <TD COLSPAN=*n*> (where *n* is a number of table columns to span)

IX

Appendixes

ROWSPAN   Instructs the viewer to span the specified table rows.

Syntax: <TD ROWSPAN=*n*> (where *n* is the number of table rows to span)

WIDTH   Netscape 1.1 extension, defines the width of the specific table cell.

Syntax: <TD WIDTH=*value*> (where *value* is either the number of pixels or the percentage, expressed as *n* percent, of the width of the table header)

Usage
Body section, within table row containers only.

TH

Defines header text in a table. Does not support additional HTML elements.

Container element, requiring </TH> closing tag.

Syntax: <TH>...</TH>

Attributes
ALIGN   Defines the horizontal alignment of the header text within the table cell.

Syntax: <TH ALIGN=*value*> (where *value* is a valid alignment option)

Options:

LEFT. Aligns the header text with the cell's left edge

RIGHT. Aligns the header text with the cell's right edge

CENTER. Centers the header text in the cell

VALIGN   Defines the vertical alignment of the header text within the cell.

Options:

TOP. Aligns the header text with the top of the cell

MIDDLE. Aligns the header text with the middle of the cell

BOTTOM. Aligns the header text with the bottom of the cell

NOWRAP   Instructs the viewer not to wrap the header text within the table cell.

Syntax: <TH NOWRAP>

COLSPAN   Instructs the viewer to span the specified number of table columns.

Syntax: <TH COLSPAN=*n*> (where *n* is a number of table columns to span)

ROWSPAN   Instructs the viewer to span the specified table rows.

Syntax: <TH ROWSPAN=*n*> (where *n* is the number of table rows to span)

WIDTH   Netscape 1.1 extension, defines the width of the table header cell within the table.

Syntax: <TH WIDTH=*value*> (where *value* is either the number of pixels or the percentage, expressed as *n* percent, of the width of the table header)

Usage
Body section, within table containers only.

TR
Defines a row within a table.

Container element, requiring </TR> closing tag.

Syntax: <TR>...</TR>

Attributes
ALIGN   Defines the horizontal alignment of the text within the table row.

Syntax: <TR ALIGN=*value*> (where *value* is a valid alignment option)

Options:

LEFT. Aligns text to the left edge in the row's cells

IX

Appendixes

RIGHT. Aligns text to the right edge in the row's cells

CENTER. Centers text in the row's cells

VALIGN   Defines the vertical alignment of the text within the row's cells.

Options:

TOP. Aligns the text with the top of the row's cells

MIDDLE. Aligns the text with the middle of the row's cells

BOTTOM. Aligns the text with the bottom of the row's cells

Usage
Body section, within table containers only.

Form Elements (HTML 3.0 Features)

FORM
Defines the container text as a form. Contains input fields (INPUT), selection lists (SELECT) and input boxes (TEXTAREA). Can contain active HTML elements.

Container element, requiring </FORM> closing tag.

Syntax: <FORM>...</FORM>

Attributes
ACTION   Defines the program that will process the current form.

METHOD   Defines the procedure for passing information to the ACTION URL.

Syntax: <FORM ACTION="*URL*" METHOD=*value*>
(where *URL* is a valid Web resource and *value* is a valid method option)

Options:

GET. Program retrieves data from current document

POST. Web page sends the data to the processing program

Usage

Body section, stand-alone, or within list or table containers.

INPUT

Defines an input field where the user may enter information on the form.

Empty element, does not require a closing tag.

Syntax: <INPUT>

Attributes

TYPE   Defines the format of input data.

           Syntax: <INPUT TYPE=*value*> (where *value* is a valid type option)

           Options:

           TEXT. Defines input type as character data

           PASSWORD. Defines input type as character data

           CHECKBOX. Defines input type as a checkbox

           RADIO. Defines input type as a radio button

           SUBMIT. Defines input type as a submit form data button

           RESET. Defines input type as a reset form data button

NAME   Establishes the symbolic name for this input field.

           Syntax: <INPUT NAME=*value*> (where *value* is a text name)

           Usage: Required for all INPUT types except SUBMIT and RESET.

CHECKED   Indicates that this input field is checked by default.

           Syntax: <INPUT CHECKED>

SIZE   Defines the physical size of the input field.

           Options:

           For single-line input fields

IX

Appendixes

Syntax: <INPUT SIZE=*n*> (where *n* is the number of characters for the field)

For multi-line input fields

Syntax: <INPUT SIZE=*x,y*> (where *x* is the number of characters per line and *y* is the number of lines in the input field)

MAX-LENGTH — Establishes the maximum number of characters of input that can be entered into an input field.

Syntax: <INPUT MAXLENGTH=*n*> (where *n* is the number of characters allowed in the input field)

Usage
Body section, form container only.

OPTION

Defines a selection item in a selection list; does not support HTML elements.

Empty element, does not require a closing tag.

Syntax: <OPTION>

Attributes
SELECTED — Indicates the selection list option that is selected by default.

Syntax: <OPTION SELECTED>

Usage
Body section, form container, within a SELECT list only.

SELECT

Defines a list of options that can be selected from a pull-down list in the current form; can contain active HTML elements.

Container element, requires </SELECT> closing tag.

Syntax: <SELECT>...</SELECT>

Attributes

NAME Establishes the symbolic name for this selection list.

Syntax: <SELECT NAME=*value*> (where *value* is a text name)

SIZE Defines the number of options or choices that will be available in the selection list.

Syntax: <SELECT SIZE=*n*> (where *n* is the number of available selections)

MULTIPLE Indicates that multiple selections are allowed from the selection list.

Syntax: <SELECT MULTIPLE>

Usage

Body section, form container only.

TEXTAREA

Defines a multi-line input field; does not support HTML elements.

Container element, requires </TEXTAREA> closing tag.

Syntax: <TEXTAREA>...</TEXTAREA>

> **Note**
>
> Default text to be displayed in the input field is filled between the tags.

Attributes

NAME Establishes the symbolic name for this selection list.

Syntax: <TEXTAREA NAME=*value*> (where *value* is a text name)

ROWS Defines the number of rows the input field will display.

Syntax: <TEXTAREA ROWS=*n*> (where *n* is the number of input field rows visible)

COLS   Defines the width (in characters) of the text input area.

       Syntax: <TEXTAREA COLS=*n*> (where *n* is the number of columns or characters of the input field's width)

       Usage: Regularly combined with ROWS to specify the text input field's display dimensions.

Usage
Body section, within a form container only.

HTML 2.0 Entities

Note: These escape sequences must be entered in lowercase.

Accented Characters

Æ   for capital AE diphthong (ligature)

Á for capital A, acute accent

Â   for capital A, circumflex accent

À for capital A, grave accent

Å   for capital A, ring

Ã   for capital A, tilde

Ä   for capital A, dieresis or umlaut mark

Ç   for capital C, cedilla

Ð   for capital Eth, Icelandic

É   for capital E, acute accent

Ê   for capital E, circumflex accent

È   for capital E, grave accent

Ë   for capital E, dieresis or umlaut mark

Í   for capital I, acute accent

Î   for capital I, circumflex accent

Ì   for capital I, grave accent

Ï   for capital I, dieresis or umlaut mark

Ñ   for capital N, tilde

Ó   for capital O, acute accent

Ô   for capital O, circumflex accent

Ò   for capital O, grave accent

Ø   for capital O, slash

Õ   for capital O, tilde

Ö   for capital O, dieresis or umlaut mark

Þ   for capital THORN, Icelandic

Ú   for capital U, acute accent

Û   for capital U, circumflex accent

Ù   for capital U, grave accent

Ü   for capital U, dieresis or umlaut mark

Ý   for capital Y, acute accent

á   for small a, acute accent

â   for small a, circumflex accent

æ   for small ae diphthong (ligature)

à   for small a, grave accent

å   for small a, ring

ã   for small a, tilde

ä   for small a, dieresis or umlaut mark

ç   for small c, cedilla

é   for small e, acute accent

ê   for small e, circumflex accent

è   for small e, grave accent

ð   for small eth, Icelandic

ë   for small e, dieresis or umlaut mark

&iacute;	for small i, acute accent
&icirc;	for small i, circumflex accent
&igrave;	for small i, grave accent
&iuml;	for small i, dieresis or umlaut mark
&ntilde;	for small n, tilde
&oacute;	for small o, acute accent
&ocirc;	for small o, circumflex accent
&ograve;	for small o, grave accent
&oslash;	for small o, slash
&otilde;	for small o, tilde
&ouml;	for small o, dieresis or umlaut mark
&szlig;	for small sharp s, German (sz ligature)
&thorn;	for small thorn, Icelandic
&uacute;	for small u, acute accent
&ucirc;	for small u, circumflex accent
&ugrave;	for small u, grave accent
&uuml;	for small u, dieresis or umlaut mark
&yacute;	for small y, acute accent
&yuml;	for small y, dieresis or umlaut mark

ASCII Characters

&#n;   (where n is the specified ASCII code)

Reserved HTML Characters

&lt;	for < character
&gt;	for > character
&amp;	for & character
&quot;	for " character
&reg;	Netscape 1.0 extension, for registered trademark symbol
&copy;	Netscape 1.0 extension, for copyright symbol

Appendix B

WWW Bibliography

The following bibliographical references are all available over the World Wide Web; they constitute the majority of the information available regarding HTML and the standards process (as well as references to topics such as Perl, UseNet, and the WWW itself). Some of these documents will move over time—the Web isn't a fixed environment. If you have trouble finding a specific document listed here, use a Web searching facility (such as Web Search) to see whether the document has been relocated or is maintained elsewhere.

The quality of the information in these documents varies as the quality of any data on the Internet does. Consider the source before you take the accuracy of any information for granted. Many documents also include links to other documents on this list. In this manner, the WWW lives up to its reputation as a sort of spider's web, or a maze, and it's very easy to find yourself at the same place after a long, convoluted search.

HTML Documentation
http://www.utirc.utoronto.ca/HTMLdocs/NewHTML/htmlindex.html

Dr. Ian Graham, University of Toronto

World Wide Web Frequently Asked Questions
http://sunsite.unc.edu/boutell/faq/www_faq.html

Thomas Boutell

A Beginner's Guide to HTML
http://www.ncsa.uiuc.edu/General/Internet/WWW/HTMLPrimer.html

National Center for Supercomputing Applications (pubs@ncsa.uiuc.edu)

HTML Quick Reference
http://kuhttp.cc.ukans.edu/lynx_help/HTML_quick.html

Michael Grobe, The University of Kansas

Composing Good HTML
http://www.willamette.edu/html-composition/strict-html.html

James "Eric" Tilton (jtilton@willamette.edu)

HyperText Markup Language (HTML)
http://info.cern.ch/hypertext/WWW/MarkUp/MarkUp.html

Daniel W. Connolly, World-Wide Web Consortium (W3C) in the Laboratory for Computer Science, MIT

HyperText Markup Language Specification Version 3.0
http://www.hpl.hp.co.uk/people/dsr/html/CoverPage.html

Dave Raggett, W3C

A Beginner's Guide to URLs
http://www.ncsa.uiuc.edu/demoweb/url-primer.html

Marc Andreessen (mosaic@ncsa.uiuc.edu)

Crash Course on Writing Documents for the Web
http://www.pcweek.ziff.com/~eamonn/crash_course.html

Eamonn Sullivan, *PC Week*

Elements of HTML Style
http://bookweb.cwis.uci.edu:8042/Staff/StyleGuide.html

J.K. Cohen, UC Irvine (jkcohen@uci.edu)

Hypertext Terms
http://info.cern.ch/hypertext/WWW/Terms.html

The Common Gateway Interface
http://hoohoo.ncsa.uiuc.edu/cgi/

Rob McCool, NCSA (robm@ncsa.uiuc.edu)

Style Guide for Online Hypertext
http://info.cern.ch/hypertext/WWW/Provider/Style
/Overview.html

Tim Berns-Lee, W3C (timbl@w3.org)

Entering the World Wide Web: A Guide to Cyberspace
http://www.eit.com/web/www.guide/

Kevin Hughes, Enterprise Integration Technologies

A Basic HTML Style Guide
http://guinan.gsfc.nasa.gov/Style.html

Alan Richmond, NASA GSFC

IETF HyperText Markup Language (HTML) Working Group
ftp://www.ics.uci.edu/pub/ietf/html/index.html

The HTML 3.0 Hypertext Document Format
http://www.w3.org/hypertext/WWW/Arena/tour/start.html

Daniel W. Connolly's Welcome Page
http://www.w3.org/hypertext/WWW/People/Connolly/

Daniel W. Connolly

The WWW Virtual Library
http://info.cern.ch/hypertext/DataSources/bySubject
/Overview2.html

vlib@mail.w3.org

IX

Appendixes

SGML (Standard Generalized Markup Language)
http://nearnet.gnn.com/wic/comput.39.html

The World Wide Web
http://www.w3.org/hypertext/WWW/TheProject.html

Tim Berns-Lee, W3C (timbl@w3.org)

Authoring WWW Documents—Overview
http://rsd.gsfc.nasa.gov/users/delabeau/talk/

Jeff de La Beaujardière (delabeau@camille.gsfc.nasa.gov)

HTML-Writers-Guild
http://ezinfo.ucs.indiana.edu/~awooldri/www-writers.html

awooldri@indiana.edu

The Web Developer's Journal
http://www.awa.com/nct/software/eleclead.html

NCT Web Magazine

Markland Communities, Inc.

WAIS, A Sketch of an Overview
Jeff Kellem, Beyond Dreams (**composer@Beyond.Dreams.ORG**)

World Wide Web Primer
http://www.vuw.ac.nz/~gnat/ideas/www-primer.html

Nathan Torkington

The Internet Index
http://www.openmarket.com/info/internet-index/current.html

Win Treese (treese@OpenMarket.com)

HTML Documents: A Mosaic Tutorial
http://fire.clarkson.edu/doc/html/htut.html

Wm. Dennis Horn, Clarkson University

How to Create High-Impact Documents
http://home.mcom.com/home/services_docs/impact_docs /creating-high-impact-docs.html

Netscape Communications Corporation

Bad Style Page
http://www.earth.com/bad-style/

Tony Sanders (sanders@bsdi.com)

The Web Communications Comprehensive Guide to Publishing on the Web
http://www.webcom.com/html/

Web Communications (support@webcom.com)

WebTechs and HTML
http://www.hal.com/~markg/WebTechs/

Mark Gaither, HaL Computer Systems (markg@hal.com)

SGML
http://info.cern.ch/hypertext/WWW/MarkUp/SGML.html

Tim Berns-Lee, W3C (timbl@w3.org)

Perl FAQ
http://www.cis.ohio-state.edu/hypertext/faq/usenet/perl-faq /top.html

Stephen P. Potter and Tom Christiansen (perlfaq@perl.com)

PERL—Practical Extraction and Report Language
http://www-cgi.cs.cmu.edu/cgi-bin/perl-man

Larry Wall (lwall@netlabs.com)

University of Florida's Perl Archive
http://www.cis.ufl.edu/perl/

Steve Potter,Varimetrix Corporation (spp@vx.com)

IX

Appendixes

Appendix C

What's on the CD-ROM?

If you've read other chapters in this book, you probably read about a program or utility that you are ready to install. Or, if you're like many users, you turned to this chapter first because you want to see what's on HTMLCD and then dive right in. Regardless, this chapter should help you find the software you need to make the most of the Net and make your HTML documents shine.

HTMLCD contains software for PCs running DOS or Windows, Macintoshes, and workstations running UNIX. For the convenience of Windows and DOS users, we've expanded the archives for these files so they're ready to install—directly from the CD. Unfortunately, we can't do the same for the UNIX software. To include DOS and UNIX files on the same CD and preserve the long file names allowed in UNIX, we've kept these archives compressed and given them file names that are legal in DOS. The Mac software is in a separate part of the CD and has all of the normal long file names and folder structure Mac users are familiar with.

HTMLCD has a wide variety of software for creating, editing, and managing HTML documents. You'll find that HTMLCD is packed with software you can use with the WWW and the rest of the Internet. We spent scores of online hours over the past few months gathering the best freeware, shareware, and public-domain software available. I hope these efforts save you a significant amount of online time and money. Throughout the book, when you see the HTMLCD icon (as shown in the margin here) you'll know that the software being discussed is on the CD.

Many of the examples of HTML documents from this book are included on HTMLCD too. You can use these documents as templates to get started creating HTML code quickly and efficiently.

Finally, a large collection of useful documents about the Internet is included on HTMLCD. You can find all the RFCs, STDs, and FYIs on HTMLCD. Also included are lists of service providers, some selected FAQs, and other documents of special interest.

So drop HTMLCD in your CD-ROM drive and get ready to load the best collection of HTML and Net utilities anywhere.

This appendix covers the following topics:

- What is shareware?
- How to get new versions of software on HTMLCD
- How to install programs from HTMLCD
- Software for creating HTML documents
- Software for connecting to the Net
- World Wide Web software
- Graphics and multimedia viewers to use with Mosaic and other Web browsers
- Software for UseNet News, FTP, Archie, Gopher, Internet Relay Chat, Telnet, and many other Internet applications and utilities
- Example code from the book
- Internet documents

What Is Shareware?

Much of the software on HTMLCD is shareware. *Shareware* is software you can try before you buy; it's not free software, but it is a neat idea.

Shareware software is written by talented and creative people. Quite often, the software provides the same power as programs you can purchase at your local computer or software store. You have the advantage, however, of knowing what you're getting before you buy it.

> **Note**
>
> In the case of the Internet, shareware was often the only choice before traditional retail software vendors recognized the large market for products. Shareware software was part of the large driving force in opening the Internet for your use.

All shareware software on HTMLCD comes with a text file (or instructions in the software itself) that tells you how to register the software. You are obligated to register any shareware software you plan to use regularly.

What benefits do you gain by registering the shareware? First, you have a clean conscience, knowing that you've paid the author for the many hours spent in creating such a useful program.

Second, registering the software gives you additional benefits, such as technical support from the author, a printed manual, and additional features available only to registered users. Consult the individual programs for details about what bonuses you may receive for registering.

Next, registering your shareware usually puts you on the author's mailing list. Registration enables the author to keep you up to date about new versions of the software, bug fixes, compatibility issues, and so on. Again, the benefits of registration vary from product to product. Some authors even include in the cost of registration a free update to the next version.

Finally, if the license agreement states that you must pay to continue using the software, you are violating the license if you don't pay. In some cases, unregistered use may be a criminal offense. Although an individual user is not likely to be arrested or sued for failing to pay registration for shareware, the small possibility of repercussions is no excuse for violating the license. Wise corporations and businesses register shareware to avoid any chance of legal problems.

> **Note**
>
> Several of the authors and companies that provided software for HTMLCD asked that a notice of their copyright, shareware agreement, or license information be included in this book. The lack of such a statement printed in this book does not mean that the software is not copyrighted or does not have a license agreement. Please see the text or help files for any program for which you need copyright or licensing information.

Getting Updates for Software on HTMLCD

The advantage is simple. Putting all of this great software on HTMLCD saves you many hours of looking for and downloading the software yourself. The only downside is that as new versions of software become available, HTMLCD stays the same.

As a result, we created a special FTP site to enable users of this book to get new versions of the software on HTMLCD. As soon as we receive an update, we'll post it on the FTP site. You can download by anonymous FTP. The FTP address for this site is **ftp.mcp.com**. (MCP stands for Macmillan Computer Publishing, the company that owns Que, which is the publisher of this book.) The directory for Windows and UNIX software in this book is /pub/que/net-cd. Look for Mac software in /pub/que/macnet-cd. Any time you want, you can log onto this FTP site and look for new software.

What if you want to be told when new software is posted? Your time will be wasted if you look and find nothing new that interests you. Well, Que thought about that, too. You can subscribe to the HTMLCD mailing list by sending an e-mail message to **majordomo@misl.mcp.com**. The body of the message should be **subscribe HTMLCD**.

> **Note**
>
> You also can subscribe to the HTMLCD mailing list by visiting the MCP Web site at **http://www.mcp.com**. From there, choose the Reference Desk; then click Information Super Library Reports. Enter your name, e-mail address, and company name (if appropriate). Select HTMLCD and then click Send.

The Macmillan site and mailing list are not the only ways to keep up to date. Many of the programs on HTMLCD are regularly updated at several of the major software FTP sites. Sites (and directories) to check out for Windows Internet software include the following:

ftp.cica.indiana.edu in /pub/pc/win3/winsock

archive.orst.edu in /pub/mirrors/ftp.cica.indiana.edu

ftp.ncsa.uiuc.edu in /Web

oak.oakland.edu in /SimTel/win3/winsock

For large collections of Macintosh software, check out these sites:

> **sumex-aim.stanford.edu** in /info-mac
>
> **ftp.apple.com** in /dts/mac
>
> **amug.org** in /pub/peterlewis
>
> **mac.archive.umich** in /mac

Some of the best UNIX sites are

> **ftp.uu.net** in /systems/UNIX
>
> **sunsite.unc.edu** in /pub/packages
>
> **wuarchive.wustl.edu** in /systems/UNIX

Note

Many of the authors and companies asked that an e-mail or postal address where they can be contacted be included in this book. If you don't find a specific e-mail address listed here, you can find an e-mail address for nearly every program on HTMLCD in the documentation that comes with the program or in the program.

Installing Windows Software from HTMLCD

Before using any of the software on HTMLCD, you need to install it. Many of the programs come with their own installation program. If a program includes an installation program, the description of it in this chapter gives you the directions you need to get it installed.

For programs that don't have an installation program, the installation process is straightforward. To install a program that doesn't have an installer, follow these steps:

1. Create a directory on your hard drive for the software.

Note

Create one main directory in the root of your hard drive for all of your Web software, for example c:\web, and then create subdirectories for individual programs in that directory. That keeps the root directory of your hard drive less cluttered.

IX

Appendixes

2. Copy all of the files and subdirectories from the program's directory on HTMLCD to the directory you created on your hard drive. The easiest way to do this in Windows is to select all of the files and subdirectories to copy in File Manager and drag them from the window for your CD to the directory on your hard drive (see fig. C.1).

> **Note**
>
> A directory name appears after the name of each program in this chapter. The directory name is where you can find the software on HTMLCD.

Fig. C.1

If you're copying subdirectories, be sure to answer Yes when prompted if you want to create the new subdirectories.

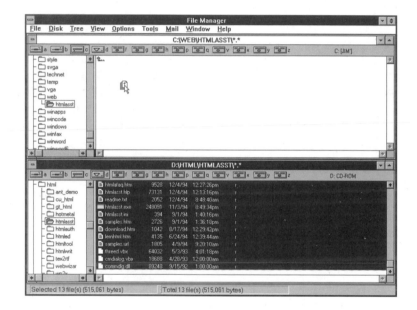

3. If you used File Manager to copy the files, you need to turn off the read only attribute. To do this, select all of the files in the directory you copied them to and then choose **F**ile, Proper**t**ies. In the Properties dialog box, deselect **R**ead Only and choose OK (see fig. C.2).

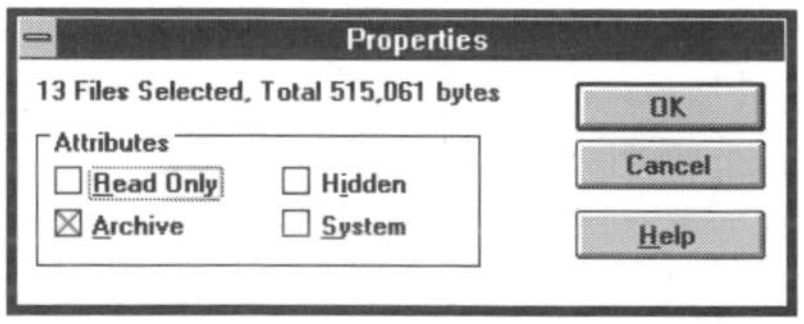

Fig. C.2

Click the Read Only box so that no X or shading appears. When you choose OK, the Read Only attribute will be turned off for all files.

4. After all of the files are copied, create an icon to run the program from Program Manager (if you plan to run the program in Windows). The easiest way to do this is to drag the program file from the directory on your hard drive in File Manager to the Program Manager and drop it in the program group where you want the icon (see fig. C.3).

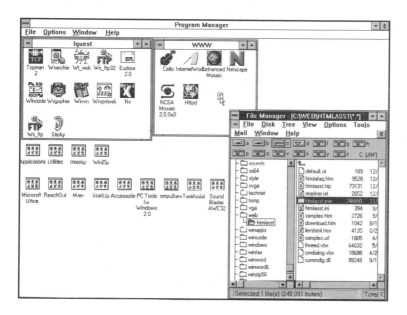

Fig. C.3
Dragging a file from File Manager to Program Manager doesn't move it, it just creates a program icon in Program Manager.

That's all there is to it. Repeat these steps for any software you want to install.

Tip
Create a new program group to hold all of your Web software program icons. In Program Manager, choose **F**ile, **N**ew, and then click Program **G**roup to do this.

Installing Macintosh Software on HTMLCD

Installing the Macintosh software on HTMLCD is a very simple process. We've expanded the compressed files, so you simply need to copy the software from its folder on HTMLCD to a folder on your hard drive. If you want quick and easy access to any of these programs, add an alias on your Apple Menu or put an alias on your desktop.

There are a few programs that come with an installer. For those, we'll tell you what you need to do to get started with them along with the description of the programs in this chapter.

Installing UNIX Software on HTMLCD

To install software for UNIX, you first need to decompress the archives. Most of the UNIX programs are compressed using gzip or UNIX Compress. Gzip compressed files have a GZ extension and UNIX Compress files have a Z extension. Gzip is included on the CD just in case you don't already have it. Most of the compressed files contain the source code for the program in a TAR archive. After restoring the TAR archive, compile a binary for your platform from the included source.

HTML

HTML documents are at the heart of the Web and they're the reason you bought this book. Whether you're creating a Web site for a major corporation or just putting up a few personal pages, you need an HTML editor or translator that suits the way you work. This area has seen a flood of good programs and we've got most of them here for you.

ANT_HTML (Windows and Mac)

Windows: \html\ant_demo

Mac: HTML:ant_demo

◄ See
"ANT_HTML,"
p. 503

ANT_DEMO.DOT is a template designed to work in Word 6 for Windows and Word 6 for Macintosh to facilitate the creation of hypertext documents. You can insert HTML codes in any new or existing Word document or any ASCII document. ANT_DEMO is a demonstration version of the ANT_PLUS conversion utility and the ANT_HTML package. Both ANT_HTML and ANT_PLUS work in all international versions of Word 6.

For directions on installation and use see Chapter 30, "HTML Style Sheets for Commercial Software."

> **Note**
>
> ANT_HTML.DOT and ANT_DEMO.DOC are copyright © 1994 by Jill Swift. For more information, contact Jill Swift, P.O. Box 213, Montgomery, TX, 77356, **jswift@freenet.fsu.edu**.

BBEdit HTML Extensions (Mac)

HTML:BBEdit HTML Extensions

This is a set of extensions for creating HTML documents with the popular BBEdit shareware on the Mac. The version included here is release 9. This release includes a Preview extension that opens Netscape via Apple Events and displays your document and template function for including some boilerplate elements at the beginning of each document.

To install these extensions, drag the Extensions folder onto the BBEdit extensions folder that comes with BBEdit. (A "lite" version and a demo of BBEdit are included on HTMLCD. These are covered in "Multimedia Viewers and Editors" later in this chapter.)

CU_HTML (Windows)

\html\cu_html

This template enables you to write hypertext (HTML) documents in Word for Windows 2 and 6.0. The version included here is version 1.5. Chapter 30 describes this package in some detail, along with installation directions.

◀ See "CU HTML," p. 505

> **Note**
>
> CU_HTML was developed by Kenneth Wong Y.P. and Anton Lam S.Y., of the Computer Services Centre of The Chinese University of Hong Kong. The package can be distributed freely, except in conjunction with any commercial or for-fee product. You must obtain permission from the authors if the package is to be included in any commercial or for-fee product, and you must distribute the following copyright notice with the software.
>
> The software is provided as is. Currently, no warranty exists, and no support in any form will be entertained. You use this software at your own risk. You can, however, send comments and wish lists to **anton-lam@cuhk.hk**.

Frame to HTML (UNIX)

/UNIX/frame2ht.z

This HTML filter converts Framemaker documents to HTML.

IX

Appendixes

> **Note**
>
> Frame to HTML is used by permission of Telenor Research and Jon Stephenson von Tetzcherner. Telenor Research owns the rights to the software, but MacDonald Dettwiler and Duncan Fraser have contributed substantially.

GT_HTML (Windows)

\html\gt_html

This is another Word 6 template for creating HTML documents. It currently supports only a small number of HTML tags. The ones included, however, are the most common tags and should be useful for many basic HTML documents.

For installation instructions and a more complete description, please see Chapter 30.

HomeMaker (Mac)

HTML:HomeMaker 1.0b5 Blank

HomeMaker is a HyperCard-based application that helps you create a simple home page about yourself. It's a very simple application for a single purpose without many options. However, if you need to get HTML pages from a group of users that don't know HTML and you want them all to look similar, this is a very useful application.

Hotlist2HTML (Mac)

HTML:Hotlist2HTML0.7.2 folder

Hotlist2HTML converts an NCSA Mosaic for Mac or EINet MacWeb hotlist into an HTML file. You can leave the HTML links in the file in the order they appear in the hotlist or sort them alphabetically. You can also import this output to Netscape as bookmarks.

Hotlist-HTML (Mac)

HTML:HHconv 1.1

Hotlist-HTML is a HyperCard stack that will convert Mosaic or MacWeb hotlists to HTML documents. It also converts TurboGopher bookmarks to HTML.

HTML Assistant for Windows

\html\htmlasst

This program is a simple shareware HTML document editor. Most commands are implemented via a huge toolbar. The program is a good editor for small documents, but this version limits file size to 32K. (A pro version that loads larger documents is available; see the help file for order information.) One neat feature of note is the program's capability to covert files that contain URLs (for example, Cello bookmarks and Mosaic INI files) to HTML documents that can be read with any Web browser.

For installation instructions and a more complete description, please see Chapter 25, "Stand-Alone HTML Editors."

HTML Author (Windows)

\html\htmlauth

This is another template for creating HTML documents in Word 6 for Windows. To use HTML Author, copy all of the files from this directory to a directory on your hard drive as explained in the section "Installing Windows Software on HTMLCD," then copy the HTMLAUTH.DOT template to your Microsoft Word for Windows templates directory (usually the directory is C:\WINWORD\TEMPLATE). To create an HTML source document, just start up Microsoft Word for Windows and create a new document, selecting HTMLAUTH.DOT as the template. For more complete directions, see the manual included in Word and HTML formats.

> **Note**
>
> The HTML Author Software and its associated manual are copyright © 1995 Grahame S. Cooper. You may copy and use them provided you do not modify them (other than to change the paragraph styles).
>
> The HTML Author software is provided AS-IS without warranty or guarantee. Neither Grahame S. Cooper nor the University of Salford accept any liability for errors or faults in the software or any damage arising from the use of the software.
>
> New versions and updates of the software may be obtained from the University of Salford at the following World Wide Web address:
>
> **http://www.salford.ac.uk/docs/depts/iti/staff/gsc/htmlauth/summary.html**

IX

Appendixes

HTML.edit (Mac)

HTML:HTML.edit.1.5bl

HTML.edit is a Hypercard-based HTML editor. HTML.edit makes managing a large number of HTML documents easy by managing all of your HTML as master files that you then export to individual documents. All of the files are exported directly as HTML (plain ASCII text) and are not saved as binary files. This editor performs structural error checking to ensure that your HTML will work correctly, it has shortcuts for entering special characters, and it supports previewing the documents in a WWW browser.

HTML Editor (Mac)

HTML:HTML_Editor_1.0 folder

This is a shareware HTML Editor for the Mac. It has menus and buttons for inserting most common HTML tags, and a palette of tags you can edit. It can switch to Mosaic or MacWeb and show a preview of the current document. HTML Editor imports documents from other applications and automatically applies formatting.

HTMLed (Windows)

\html\htmled

◀ See "Using HTMLed," p. 465

HTMLed is a powerful shareware HTML document editor. The interface features a toolbar for ease of use, and the abundant and clear menus make it easy to find the features you need.

For installation instructions and a complete description, please see Chapter 27, "Using HTMLed."

HTML Pro (Mac)

HTML:HTML_Pro_1.07 Folder

HTML Pro is an HTML editor that displays documents almost as they appear on-screen in a Web browser. HTML Pro uses two editing windows. The source window shows the HTML source text. The HTML window shows the formatted text as it will appear in a Web browser. You can edit in either window. You can format text with either the Styles menu or by entering the tags manually in the source window. HTML Pro also allows you to define macros for entering tags that are not part of its menus.

HTML Web Weaver (Mac)

HTML:HTML Web Weaver 2.5 *f*

HTML Web Weaver is a stand-alone HTML editor. It comes with a very nice set of documentation in HTML format. It supports all the commonly used HTML tags via menus, and even has menus for special characters and forms. It's very flexible and allows you to add more tags to the interface as you become more experienced with HTML. (Presumably, this would allow the addition of new tags as new HTML specifications are adopted, although I don't see this mentioned specifically.)

LaTeX2HTML (UNIX)

/UNIX/latex2ht.tar

This utility is a handy way to convert LaTeX files to HTML in UNIX. The LaTeX format is very popular for files created in print and online, and is also a common language used for technical documents. LaTeX2HTML can break documents into pieces as you specify, handle equations, footnotes, tables, and other elements frequently found in technical documents. It also translates cross-references into hyperlinks.

RTF To HTML (Windows and Mac)

Windows: \html\rtf2html

Mac: HTML:rtfto–html–mac

This utility converts documents from the RTF format to HTML. Many word processors, including Word for Windows, can import and export RTF (Rich Text Format). The package includes a Word 2 for Windows template for writing HTML.

When installing the Windows version, after copying this program from HTMLCD to a directory on your hard drive, move RTFTOHTM.DLL to somewhere in your path. The best place for it is your \windows directory. Move HTML.DOT to your Word template directory (usually \winword\template). You can then open a new document in WinWord using HTML.DOT as the template.

HTML Writer (Windows)

\html\htmlwrit

HTML Writer is a stand-alone HTML authoring program. You can insert most HTML tags via an extensive set of menu choices. It has a nice toolbar for implementing many HTML tags. Another good feature is the support of templates: you can use templates to help design and create HTML documents with a consistent look and feel.

Microsoft Word Internet Assistant (Windows)

\html\wordia

◀ See "Browsing the Web with Internet Assistant," p. 486

This can be in the HTML category and in the Web browser category, because it's used for both purposes. This is the Word 6 (for Windows only) add-in that lets you create HTML documents and cruise the Web from within the familiar confines of Word 6. Chapter 28, "Using Microsoft Internet Assistant," discusses this add-in completely.

Simple HTML Editor (Mac)

HTML:simple-html-editor Folder

Despite its unassuming name, Simple HTML Editor has a full set of features. It's a HyperCard-based application that has menus for including most common HTML tags and a special menu for creating HTML forms. There's a small palette of buttons for creating the most common tags and when you first open a document, it inserts the standard heading and body tags.

SoftQuad HoTMetaL (Windows and UNIX)

Windows: \html\hotmetal

UNIX: \UNIX\sq-hotme.z

This freeware program is a full-featured, professional-quality HTML editor for Windows and UNIX. With this program, you can edit multiple documents at the same time, use templates to ensure consistency between documents, and use the powerful word-processor-like features to do such things as search and replace.

> **Note**
>
> The commercial version of HoTMetaL PRO 2.0 fully supports HTML standards and most Netscape extensions, including HTML 3.0 experimental tables.
>
> Version 2.0's improved user interface design and enhanced feature set is geared to providing Web publishers with more power, flexibility, and control over the creation of their Web documents.
>
> Features of version 2.0 include:
>
> - An import filter that allows users to import and convert many popular text formats including MS-Word, WordPerfect, Lotus AMI Pro, and MS-RTF
>
> - Version 2.0 takes up less disk space, less memory, and will provide more streamlined performance
>
> - A new toolbar from which markup elements and common operations can be performed
>
> - Key stroke and dialog enhancements that are designed to make document markup even easier
>
> - Enhanced URL support, including the ability to import hotlists and point-and-click linking
>
> - Improved support for easier insertion of special characters
>
> - Enhanced previewing capability through the use of multiple browsers

Tex2RTF (Windows and UNIX)

Windows: \html\tex2rtf

UNIX: /UNIX/tex2rtfs.z

This utility handily converts LaTeX files to HTML in Windows or UNIX. It also converts LaTeX to Windows Help file format if you need that capability. The LaTeX format is very popular for files created in print and online, and is a common language for technical documents. This program has a very good help system; read through it to make the most of the program. The file list above for UNIX contains the source code. Precompiled versions for Sun Motiff (tex2rtsm.z) and HP (tex2rtfh.z) are also included.

tkHTML (UNIX)

/UNIX/tkhtml22.gz

This is a WYSIWYG HTML editor. To use this program, you also need wwwish (WWWISH.GZ) which is included on HTMLCD. You should also see TKHTML.REA (the author's tkHTML.README file) and CHANGE.LOG (the author's ChangeLog file) for information on contacting the author and a pointer to the WWW home page.

txt2html (UNIX)

/UNIX/txt2html.pl

This is a Perl script for converting existing UNIX text documents to HTML. The author states that there are probably better programs for creating new HTML. Because this is a Perl script, you can also use it with the DOS version of Perl to convert DOS text files to HTML.

Web Wizard (Windows)

\html\webwiza

This is an HTML authoring system that works as a template in Word 6 for Windows. It adds a new toolbar with some HTML commands and a new Web Wizard menu to the Word 6 menu bar when loaded.

To install Web Wizard, run the \html\webwiza\setup.exe file in Windows and follow the on-screen directions. After you load it, use it by opening a new file and selecting WEB.WIZ (which should be in the Word templates directory) as the template. This template name does not end with the DOT extension. To see this in the list, you have to select to show all files in the Attach Templates dialog box.

The documentation provided here (in the \html\webwiza\doc directory on HTMLCD) is for a larger commercial version of this product, called SGML TagWizard, but the two products function in the same way. HTML is a subset of the SGML, so Web Wizard is a subset of the SGML product. If you need an SGML document creator, see the README.TXT file for information about contacting the creator of this product.

WP2x (UNIX)

/UNIX/wp2x_23.gz

This program coverts Word Perfect documents created on the UNIX platform to HTML.

All-in-One Suites

If you're looking for a quick and easy solution to most of your Internet software needs, one of these suites may be exactly what you need. Some suites include connection software; others include just the applications. (For the latter packages, you also need connection software, that's listed in the section "Software for Connecting to the Internet (TCP/IP)," later in this appendix.) Some suites are front-end interfaces to special service providers.

Internet Chameleon with Automatic Internet (Windows)

\suites\chameleo

Internet Chameleon version 4.1 is a complete Internet Windows-based application. Chameleon supports FTP transfer, Telnet logins to remote computers over the Internet or standard TCP/IP connections, e-mail sending and receiving, remote pinging of Internet servers, and World Wide Web browsing.

Before installing Internet Chameleon, close any other applications you're using. You have to close Windows and restart your machine before using the software after you install it; it modifies your AUTOEXEC.BAT file. To begin the installation, run SETUP.EXE (in Windows) in the \suites\chameleo\disk1 directory. (When you're prompted for disks 2 and 3 during installation, enter the path name for these directories on HTMLCD.)

After you run the installation, you still have to register the software before you can use it. The registration process is automated and sets up the software immediately. You have the option of registering to use the software for a free 30-day trial period or you can purchase a full license to use the software when you register. You can also set it up to work with an existing service provider's account or to register for a new account with one of several providers that have joined with NetManage to provide instant access. Some of these providers offer free trials, others don't. Read the information for each provider before proceeding.

> **Note**
>
> To register the software, you must provide a credit card number, even if you're just registering for the trial time period. The registration takes place over phone lines, not over the Internet so you don't worry about the safety of your credit card number. If you don't provide a valid card number, you can't use the software.

For complete directions on completing the installation and registering the software, see the file INETCHAM.WRI in the \disk1 subdirectory.

> **Note**
>
> If you've used an older version of the NetManage Chameleon Sampler, you'll notice some major differences in this version. First, the software now includes all the features of the retail version. Second, you can use this trial version for only 30 days. To continue using the software after 30 days, you must register and purchase the full retail version. Finally, you can't install this software over the older sampler.

NetCruiser (Windows)
\Suites\netcruis

NetCruiser is another all-in-one connectivity package you may want to check into. It includes all of the application software needed for the Internet and Web access as well as an automatic setup process through NetCom, one of the nation's leading service providers.

To install this, run SETUP.EXE in Windows from this directory.

Pipeline (Windows)
\suites\pipeline

This software connects you to The Pipeline, a custom service provider. The Pipeline software provides access to e-mail, Gopher, WWW, FTP, and UseNet News through The Pipeline's service. In addition to providing access to the Internet, The Pipeline also allows their users to create Web pages on their system, and provides software to do this.

To install the software for Windows, run the program SETUP.EXE from The Pipeline directory. The version included on HTMLCD is version 2.08.

> **Note**
>
> The Pipeline was recently acquired by PSINet. PSINet has local numbers in many US cities and The Pipeline customers will soon be able to access The Pipeline through these numbers instead of SprintNet In those cities. You might also want to check for a Mac version; a new version was being developed just as this book went to press.

Instant InterRamp (Mac)

Suites:InterCon

Instant InterRamp includes TCP/Connect II Remote, which is a full suite of Internet applications including e-mail, UseNet News, FTP, World Wide Web, and more. TCP/Connect II Remote includes a SLIP/PPP dialer for connecting to the Internet.

With Instant InterRamp, you get all of the features of TCP/Connect II and a special setup that connects you to Performance Systems International (PSI), a large national Internet service provider. If you don't already have Internet service, this software provides an easy way to get connected and have all of the software you need. To install Instant InterRamp, double-click InterRamp and follow the on-screen directions. When you sign up with Instant InterRamp, you get a free seven-day trial of the software and PSI's service. After the trial period, you have to pay for the software and the service through PSI.

Software for Connecting to the Internet (TCP/IP)

If you want to connect to the Internet, you need software. Whether you use a modem to dial up a SLIP or PPP account or connect from your LAN at work, the software here can make the connection.

Core Internet-Connect 2.0 Trial Version (Windows)
\tcpip\inetcon2

This program, that provides WinSock and TCP/IP for networks, is designed to help end users connect; it's also designed for developers who want to build other TCP/IP applications based on it.

To run the automatic installation, run SETUP.EXE (in Windows) in the \tcpip\inetcon2 directory.

> **Note**
>
> This package contains the Internet-Connect © Trial Copy program. Internet-Connect is a registered trademark of Core Systems. Internet-Connect is developed and marketed by Core Systems, 245 Firestone Drive, Walnut Creek, CA, 94598, (510) 943-5765.

Crynwr Packet Drivers (Windows/DOS)
\tcpip\crynwr\pktd11, \tcpip\crynwr\pktd11a,
\tcpip\crynwr\pktd11b, \tcpip\crynwr\pktd11c,
\tcpip\crynwr\exp16116

Most DOS-based (and some Windows-based) Internet applications require this collection of drivers. The collection serves as an interface between established network software and packet-based Internet connections. These archive files include a wide range of drivers for most popular network packages, such as Novell's NetWare and Artisoft's LANtastic. The source code for each driver is also included. If you are experienced enough to alter the code for a driver, you can reassemble these drivers to function differently or better than they do in their current form.

To install the Crynwr Packet Drivers, copy only the files you need. You'll find all the documentation for these drivers in the \pktd11 subdirectory. Please read the documentation for this and your applications to determine what files you need.

MacPPP (Mac)
TCP/IP:macppp2.0.1 folder

If you have a PPP account with your service provider, or if you're convinced that PPP is the future and you want to switch from your old SLIP account to a PPP account, MacPPP is a good choice for you.

Note

Of related interest are three useful MacPPP utilities, found in the TCP/IP folder. First is Control PPP in the Control PPP ƒ folder. This is a control strip module that lets you connect and disconnect MacPPP and open the MacTCP and MacPPP control panels to change the dialup number (a useful feature if you travel with your Mac or have more than one account). The icon for the program also shows you if MacPPP is open, in case you have an internal modem.

The other similar utility is MacPPP QuicKeys in the MacPPP QuicKeys 3.0 folder. These allow QuicKeys to open and close MacPPP and test if it is open or closed. To install this, double-click the installer script icon.

Finally, MacPPP Add-ons includes some ResEdit resources for changing the MacPPP icons and connection dialog. You need to know how to use ResEdit to use these.

Note

Copyright © 1993-1995 by Merit Network, Inc. and The Regents of the University of Michigan.

MacPPP was developed at, and is copyrighted by, the Merit Network, Inc. and the University of Michigan. Merit and the University of Michigan grant an unlimited license for use and redistribution of the executable program provided that it is not sold for profit, whether as is or as part of another product. Charges to recover the cost of duplication and distribution are permitted. This PPP program is offered "as is"—neither Merit nor the University of Michigan make any guarantees about the performance or reliability of the software.

The PPP core software engine is based on public domain code written by William Allen Simpson, taken from KA9Q. All modifications to the PPP core software engine necessary to develop MacPPP and bring the implementation to compliance with RFCs 1331, 1332, and 1334 have been performed by Merit Network, Inc. and the University of Michigan.

In recognition of his original work, William Allen Simpson has been granted copyright for the PPP core software engine. The TCP header compression routines used in MacPPP were written by Van Jacobsen and are copyright © 1989 Regents of the University of California. These routines were heavily modified by Katie Stevens and William Allen Simpson.

(continues)

IX

Appendixes

(continued)

Primary development of MacPPP at Merit Network, Inc. and the University of Michigan was performed by Larry J. Blunk. Eric Schneider wrote many of the "LAP" interface routines necessary for a MacTCP mdev, as well as additional support code. Glenn McGregor provided additional code, as well as valuable input on the project. Many other individuals also provided input, and their support is appreciated.

MacTCP 2.0.6 (Mac)

TCP/IP:MacTCP

MacTCP is the basis for connecting a Mac to the Internet. If you have System 7.5, it includes this program (although you might want to see whether this is a newer version). If you're on a LAN, MacTCP is probably the only software you need to get connected. If you're connecting via a modem, you also need SLIP or PPP software such as InterSLIP or MacPPP.

To install MacTCP, copy the MacTCP control panel to the Control Panels folder in your system folder. Copy the Hosts file to your system folder, but leave it in the system folder not it a folder inside the system folder.

To configure and use MacTCP, you need to know a lot of information about your Internet connection. You can get this information from your network administrator or technical support at your service provider. You can also look at a book that details how to connect a Mac to the Internet such as *The Internet Starter Kit for Macintosh 2nd Edition* or *Special Edition Using the Internet with Your Mac*.

NetDial (Windows)

\tcpip\netdial

NetDial is an Internet dialup program with many features: NetDial can call, connect to your Internet host, log you in, and run your TCP/IP program at the click of a mouse. Other features include baud-rate support to 256K baud, up to 99 redial attempts, automatic dialing on startup, sound support, up to five separate configurations, cumulative timer window (tracks all time online), built-in call log viewer/editor, up to five startup programs on startup, and additional modem support.

To install NetDial, run \tcpip\netdial\setup.exe in Windows. For more information about the program and installation, see the files READ.ME and INSTALL.TXT.

Slipper/CSlipper (Windows/DOS)

\tcpip\slippr

Slipper/CSlipper version 1.5 is a DOS-based replacement application for
SLIP8250. Slipper and CSlipper were written to provide Internet connections
through a packet-driver interface. Both applications are very small and com-
mand-line-driven. For information about using Slipper or CSlipper and their
options, see SLIPPER.DOC.

Trumpet Winsock (Windows)

\tcpip\twsk21f

Trumpet Winsock is the most widely used shareware WinSock package.
The software supports modem and network connections. At this writing,
TWSK20B.ZIP is the officially released, working version. This version, which
was recently released, includes new features such as firewall support, improved scripting, and routing capabilities. Trumpet also fixes the minor problems in version 1 and fixes a bug with PPP in the first release of version 2.

After copying this program to your hard drive, you need to provide IP
address information. If you're using this program over a modem, you need
to modify LOGIN.CMD to work with your service provider. You also may
need to add the directory that contains Trumpet to your path statement in
AUTOEXEC.BAT. The file INSTALL.DOC contains installation and configuration information.

> **Note**
>
> The Trumpet Winsock is currently distributed as shareware. You may use the Trumpet
> Winsock for 30 days to evaluate its usefulness. If at the end of that time you are
> satisfied with the Trumpet Winsock as a product, you should register it.
>
> Trumpet Winsock version 2.0b has a "Send Registration" option that will automati-
> cally post encrypted credit card details to Trumpet Software International. Choose
> **F**ile, **R**egister to take advantage of this feature.

World Wide Web

It's amazing how much software is available for use with the World Wide
Web. Even though the WWW is one of the newest developments on the
Internet, there's an abundance of good software relating to it. Dig in and
enjoy.

CERN httpd (UNIX)

/UNIX/wwwdaemo.z

NCSA's Web server isn't the only game in town for setting up a Web server in UNIX. The creators of the Web, CERN, have also released CERN httpd, their Web server, into the public domain. The source code for version 3 is included here. For more information on this and for some precompiled versions see **http://info.cern.ch/hypertext/WWW/Daemon/Status.html**.

CGIWrap (UNIX)

/UNIX/cgiwrap.tar

This is a CGI gateway for providing secure access to CGI with NCSA httpd.

DocFinder (UNIX)

/UNIX/docfinde.tar

Doc Finder is a suite of scripts and programs based on freeWAIS that you use to create indexes and HTML documents, and then do searches against this index database to locate the HTML documents. It requires freeWAIS (included as FREEWAIS.GZ).

Get URL (Mac)

WWW:Get URL Folder

This extension for BBEdit retrieves a Web Page from a URL in BBEdit. It opens MacWeb to retrieve the page. Get URL also works in Easy View and can also open Anarchie and retrieve a file or directory.

Gwstat (UNIX)

/UNIX/gwstat.gz

The program processes the output from wwwstat (discussed in the section "wwwstat (UNIX)" later in this chapter) and generates GIF graphs of your server traffic data. To run this program, you need the following programs— that are also included on HTMLCD (the file name on HTMLCD follows the program name):

Perl5 (PERL5000.GZ)

wwwstat (WWWSTAT-.Z)

ImageMagick (IMAGEMAG.GZ)

Ghostscript (GHOSTSCR.GZ)

You also need Xmgr, which is not on HTMLCD. You can get it by ftp at **ftp.ccalmr.ogi.edu/CCALMR/pub/acegr/xmgr-3.01.tar.Z**.

The TAR file you should expand from the GZ file is named GWSTAT1.12.TAR. After that, look at **http://dis.cs.umass.edu/stats/gwstat.html** for detailed installation directions.

> **Note**
>
> There's information on using Gwstat in Linux at http://www.sjs.cam/stats/gwstat.html. To use it, you also need the files in LIBJPEG-.GZ to use this version.

Hyper MapEdit (Mac)
WWW:HyperMapEdit_Folder

Hyper MapEdit is a program for creating interactive, clickable graphics, known as ISMAP images, to use on the Web. This is a HyperCard Application. To use an image, you must first convert it to PICT format. (There are several applications that perform this conversion listed in the "Multimedia Viewers and Editors" section later in this chapter.)

Launcher (Windows)
\www\launcher

This freeware program is a neat utility that allows you to launch a Windows application from a link in a Web browser such as Mosaic. This feature allows you to open an application (such as WordPerfect or Excel) without having to create a link to a particular document. The source code is supplied; see the file READ.ME for directions on using it.

Lynx (DOS)
\www\lynx

This program is a WWW client for DOS machines. Lynx is an alpha release and does not support forms at present. On the positive side, each URL you access is opened in a separate window so you can have several documents open at once. It also support has for displaying inline images. See the README.TXT file for information on configuring DOS Lynx to work with your Internet connection.

Mac ImageMap (Mac)

WWW:Mac-ImageMap 1.3 folder

Mac ImageMap aids in the creation of clickable image maps from GIF images for use on the World Wide Web. It requires MacHTTP 2.0. In addition to creating standard rectangular clickable regions, you can define circular, elliptic, and polygonal regions.

MapMaker (UNIX)

\UNIX\mapmaker

You can access the MapMaker home page from any platform, as discussed in Chapter 14. If you want to set up your own MapMaker page, see the documentation with the MapMaker page and use the software and scripts in this directory.

Momspider (UNIX)

/UNIX/momspide.z

This program for checking hyperlinks is a Perl script. It roams the Web, following each link. It can build a map of the links it follows.

> **Note**
>
> This software has been developed by Roy Fielding as part of the Arcadia project at the University of California, Irvine. Copyright © 1994 Regents of the University of California. All rights reserved. Redistribution and use in source and binary forms are permitted, subject to the restriction noted below, provided that the above copyright notice and this paragraph and the following paragraphs are duplicated in all such forms and that any documentation, advertising materials, and other materials related to such distribution and use acknowledge that the software was developed in part by the University of California, Irvine. The name of the University may not be used to endorse or promote products derived from this software without specific prior written permission. THIS SOFTWARE IS PROVIDED "AS IS" AND WITHOUT ANY EXPRESS OR IMPLIED WARRANTIES, INCLUDING, WITHOUT LIMITATION, THE IMPLIED WARRANTIES OF MERCHANT ABILITY AND FITNESS FOR A PARTICULAR PURPOSE.

NCSA Web Server (UNIX)

/UNIX/ncsahttp/source.z

This is a Web server for UNIX. It supports a wide range of advanced features including scripting and forms support. If you want to set up a Web server for a demanding business application, this is a good choice.

All of the file names in this directory have been shortened by removing the httpd_ that precedes the given name at the NCSA site. In addition to the source files, the following platforms have documentation and binaries:

> DECAXP
>
> DECMIPS
>
> HP
>
> RS6000
>
> SGI
>
> SUN4

Perl (Windows/DOS, UNIX, and Macintosh)

Windows/DOS: \www\dosperl

UNIX: /UNIX/perl5000.gz

Mac: WWW:Mac_Perl

This is version 5 of the Perl script processing language used for processing input from forms and other purposes with a Web server. See Chapter 18, "Server Scripts and Applications," for details on scripts. Version are included for DOS (used with Windows httpd), UNIX, and Macintosh (version 4). All of these versions include source code.

> **Note**
>
> A Windows NT version of Perl is also included in \www\winntprl.

IX

Appendixes

SlipKnot (Windows)

\www\slipknot

SlipKnot is a graphical World Wide Web browser specifically designed for Microsoft Windows users who have UNIX shell accounts with their service providers. SlipKnot's primary feature is that it does not require SLIP or PPP or TCP/IP services. It also allows background retrieval of multiple documents, and storage of complete documents on users' local hard disks.

To install SlipKnot, run \www\slipknot\setup.exe in Windows and follow the on-screen directions. The READ.ME file contains some information about possible installation glitches should you encounter trouble.

Web4ham (Windows)
\www\web4ham

Web4ham is a World Wide Web server for Windows. The program enables your Windows PC to act like a WWW site that other WWW users can access with any Web client software.

Windows httpd 1.4
\www\whttpd

If you're setting up your own Web server in Windows and need most of the power and features of a UNIX Web server, take a look at this software. Please note that earlier versions of this software were freeware, but this version is shareware and requires a payment after a 30-day trial period for continued use. See INDEX.HTM for details of this agreement.

To install this software, create a \httpd directory on your hard drive. (Don't use another directory name.) Use PKUnzip or Winzip to expand the compressed file into that directory and select the option to preserve the directory structure. In PKUnzip, you do this by adding the -d parameter at the end of the command line. In WinZip, choose the **U**se Directory Names option from the Extract dialog box.

For complete details on setting up and maintaining a Web server in Windows or UNIX, see the book *Running a Perfect Web Site*.

URL Grabber Demo (Windows)
\www\grabdemo

Have you ever read an article in a UseNet newsgroup or an e-mail message and seen a URL that you wanted to save for further reference? Sure, you can copy and paste the URL into a browser and then save it in a hotlist or book-mark, but this handy little utility makes this process even easier. The URL Grabber toolbar enables you to grab a URL from documents as you read them and then save a collection of addresses as HTML documents that you can open in any WWW browser. You will then have a Web document that contains all the links to the URL addresses you saved, enabling you to jump to those URLs quickly and easily.

In this demo version, you're limited to grabbing three addresses each time you run the program. For information about ordering the full version, which doesn't have this limit, see the help file.

wwwstat (UNIX)

/UNIX/wwwstat-.z

This program keeps usage statistics about accesses to your Web site. In combination with Gwstat, you can produce graphs of the statistics.

Multimedia Viewers and Editors

If you frequently download graphics or sound files, you need software to view or listen to these files. Although a commercial graphics program may have more power and versatility than the programs listed here, you sometimes may prefer to use a smaller, simpler program.

In addition to programs for graphics and sound, the following sections list text editors and other file-viewing programs.

While no one is likely to use all of these programs, we've included quite a few with similar features to give you more choices. What is right in one situation may not be right in others.

All JPEG (Mac)

Viewers:All JPEG1.0fat folder

All JPEG is a freeware program for converting PICT files to QuickTime Photo-JPEG PICT. This is a FAT version and is accelerated for Power Mac. You have control over the type of compression and the quality of the compressed images.

BBEdit Lite 3.0 and BBEdit 3.1.1 Demo (Mac)

Viewers:Bare Bones Software

BBEdit is a popular text editor. You will find many online documents saved in BBEdit format. There are two versions of the software included here. In addition to the usual functions you expect in a simple text editor, BBEdit Lite 3.0 supports stationery documents that are used as templates, the capability

IX

Appendixes

to open several files at once, multiple file searching, and third-party extensions. (One such extension is the HTML Extension discussed earlier in this chapter.)

The full version of BBEdit adds native support for Power Macs, AOCE support, scripting, and many other advanced features. BBEdit 3.1.1 Demo is a demonstration version of this fuller version of the software.

BijouPlay (Mac)

Viewers:BijouPlay 2.0GM

BijouPlay is a freeware QuickTime movie player for the Mac. It's designed for use with System 7.5 and QuickTime 2.0 and supports the use of scripting with AppleScript. It's optimized for speed on a Power Mac. You can use it to create slide shows, edit music tracks, and to save movies to videotape.

GhostScript (Mac)

Viewers:MacGS 2.5.2B3 Runtime *f*

Ghostscript for Mac can be used to view printer files that conform to GhostScript 2.6 or later standards. GhostScript is an interpreter for the PostScript page-description language used by many laser printers. GhostView also can print GhostScript embedded documents. Source code for this application is part of the archive. GhostView is the interpreter that NCSA recommends for use with Mosaic for viewing PostScript files with GhostScript.

GhostView (Windows)

\viewers\gsview

GhostView v1.0, a Windows 3.1 application, is used to view printer files that conform to GhostScript 2.6 or later standards. GhostScript is an interpreter for the PostScript page-description language used by many laser printers. GhostView can also print GhostScript-embedded documents. Source code for this application is part of the archive. GhostView is the interpreter that NCSA recommends for use with Mosaic for viewing PostScript files. See GSVIEW.DOC for installation and setup directions. (You also need the GhostScript 2.61 files which are on HTMLCD in the directory \viewers \gsview\gscript. See USE.DOC in that directory for installation and setup directions.)

GrabIt Pro (Windows)

\viewers\grabpro

This is a Windows screen capture utility. If you're putting together Web pages for software documentation, you'll find this an invaluable aid in creating pages with embedded screen shots. (It does not save files in GIF format, so if you want to use saved images as inline images, you need to convert them using one of the other utilities discussed in this section.) There is a Windows 3.1 and Windows NT version, both of which are included here.

To install GrabIt Pro, run the GPSETUP.EXE program in Windows from either the win31 or winnt directory and follow the directions on-screen.

Graphic Converter (Mac)

Viewers:GraphicConverter 2.0.7 (US)

Graphic Converter converts pictures to different formats and has some features for manipulating images. It imports graphics in PICT, JPEG, GIF, PCX, TIFF, and many other formats. Its export formats are more limited but PICT, JPEG, GIF, PCX, TIFF, and about a dozen other formats are still supported. In addition to converting individual pictures, an entire folder can be converted from one picture format to another.

Image'n'Bits (Windows)

\viewers\ima

This is a graphics manipulation and conversion utility. Among the formats supported are BMP and GIF. Some of the special effects it includes are dithering, pixelize, and solarize just to name a few. If you're working with artistic images or photographs as Web images, this is very useful.

To install this program, run \viewers\ima\setup.exe in Windows and follow the directions on-screen.

Imagery (Mac)

Viewers:Imagery192a

This is a collection of simple utilities for working with TIFF images.

Jasc Media Center (Windows)

\viewers\jascmedi

If you have a large collection of multimedia files you have collected from the Web, use this program to keep them organized. It supports 37 file formats including GIF, JPEG, MIDI, WAV, and AVI. You can still use formats that aren't supported if you have an external file filter for them.

To install Jasc Media Center, run \viewers\jascmedi\setup.exe in Windows.

JPEGView (Mac)
Viewers:JPEGView 3.3 *f*

JPEGView displays images in JPEG, PICT, GIF, and several other image formats. It has a screen show option and can automatically scale images to fit your screen. This viewer is recommended by NCSA for use with Mosaic.

LView (Windows)
\viewers\lview

This is one of the best all around graphics viewers and utilities. NCSA recommends this viewer for both GIF and JPEG images with Mosaic. It also supports TIFF, PCX, and several other image formats. In addition to viewing these files, you can retouch images by adjusting their color balance, contrast, and many other attributes.

MacAnim Viewer
Viewers:MAV_1.0.5_Only Folder

MacAnim Viewer displays GL, FLI, FLX, DL, GIF, and PCX files. It also unzips ZIPed files to look for files in the format that it can display.

Media Blastoff (Windows)
\viewers\blastoff

This viewer provides support for several popular graphics formats as well as sound and movies. The file formats that will probably be of most use to you with the Internet are GIF, AVI, and WAV.

To install this, run \viewers\blastoff\setup.exe in Windows and follow the directions on-screen.

MegaEdit (Windows)
\viewers\megaedit

MegaEdit version 2.08 is a Windows text file editor that has many of the standard features that you might find in a DOS-based text editor. This application works for multiple or large files. MegaEdit provides internal support for the original IBM OEM (original equipment manufacturer) font set. This support means that MegaEdit has the capability to correctly display extended

IBM characters, such as the line sets with which other Windows-based editors have problems.

> **Note**
>
> This version of MegaEdit is a shareware version that's limited to files of 5,000 lines or less. The full version has no file-size limit except for the limits placed on it by the amount of virtual memory you have in Windows.

MooVer (Mac)

Viewers:MooVer 1.1

MooVer creates QuickTime movies from a sequence of PICT files. You can also add sound tracks and subtitles to the movie you create.

MpegPlay (Windows)

\viewers\mpegwin

This is an MPEG movie player for Windows. This current version requires Win32 to run. (See the section "Win32s" later in this appendix.) MpegPlay is the viewer recommended by NCSA for use with Mosaic. This latest version adds a Save As feature so that there is now a way to save movies downloaded by Mosaic. If you've used older versions of this with Mosaic, you'll appreciate this new feature. This is an unregistered shareware version and will not play files larger than 1M; the limitation is removed if you register.

To install this product, run \viewers\mpegwin\setup.exe in Windows and follow the directions on-screen.

NIH Image (Mac)

Viewers:NIH Image

NIH Image is a digital image processing tool. You can use it to view and edit images in TIFF, PICT, PICS, and MacPaint format. It can acquire images from a digital capture board using PhotoShop compatible plug-ins.

Paint Shop Pro (Windows)

\viewers\paintshp

This is a powerful graphics viewing and editing utility. It supports about 20 different graphics file formats including the common GIF and JPEG formats found on the Web. It has a host of features for editing and manipulating graphics, and rivals commercial packages with the number and variety of filters and special effects. It also includes a screen capture program.

IX

Appendixes

To install this, run \viewers\paintshp\setup.exe in Windows and follow the directions on-screen.

Peter's Player (Mac)

Viewers:Peter's Player 1.1

This is a simple but fast QuickTime player signed for the smoothest possible movie playback. It's accelerated for Power Mac and runs quickly on 68K Macs too. If you have enough memory, it can load an entire movie to memory (to speed up playback).

PhotoCapture (Mac)

Viewers:PhotoCapture folder

Using an AV capable Mac, you can use PhotoCapture to capture PICT images from a video input source. This is similar to the Apple Video Monitor but yields higher quality images and gives you the chance to name your saved files instead of having the video monitor save them for you.

PICTcompare (Mac)

Viewers:PICTcompare folder

PICTcompare compares digitized images in PICT format to see if they are identical or similar. You can use it to compare files even if one is gray scale, the size or aspect rations are different, or if they have other digitized differences.

PICTify (Mac)

Viewers:PICTify 1.5 *f*

PICTify is a control panel for capturing your screen as a PICT file. You can capture the whole screen or only parts of it. To install this, copy it to your Control Panel folder.

PICTshow (Mac)

Viewers:PICTshow

PICTshow is much more than the name suggests. It plays or views PICTS, GIFS, QuickTime, and sound files.

Play Wave (Windows)

\viewers\playwav

Play Wave is a simple Windows application for playing WAV sound files. The program requires few mouse clicks for playing waves and can be set to loop a wave file continuously. The author states that this application may not work on all systems. To use it, just use the File Manager to "associate" WAV files with PlayWave, not the Sound Recorder. Then, when you double-click WAV file names, PlayWave comes up, not the Sound Recorder. To use it with Mosaic, just designate it as the viewer for WAV files and when you download a WAV format sound it will start.

QuickTime 2.0 (Windows and Mac)

Windows: \viewers\qtime20
Mac: Viewers:QuickTime 2.0

This is the new and improved version of QuickTime that Apple released with System 7.5. If you already have System 7.5 or you have another application that installed QuickTime 2.0, you don't need this. If you don't have it, install this to enjoy faster QuickTime playback at larger image sizes with your Quick-Time applications. Use PowerPlay if you have a Power Macintosh computer.

To install this, drag the QuickTime extension to the Extensions folder in your System folder. You need to restart the Mac afterwards.

The Windows version includes a player application for viewing QuickTime movies. To install the Windows version, run SETUP.EXE and follow the directions on-screen. If you already have an older version installed, you will be prompted to delete it.

Video for Windows

\viewers\vid4win

This is the Microsoft Video for Windows run-time version that you need to view Video for Windows (AVI) files. This is the latest version, 1.1d. Even if you have Video for Windows installed, you should check the version to see if it is older. This newer version runs significantly faster and better than some older versions.

The installation program will restart Windows when done, so save anything you are working on and exit all applications before starting the installation. To install Video for Windows run \viewers\vid4win\setup.exe in Windows and follow the directions on-screen.

VuePrint (Windows)

\viewers\vueprint

Here's a useful combination if you get a lot of UUEncoded graphics from the Internet. VuePrint is a graphics viewer that opens, saves, and prints graphics in JPEG and GIF formats, as well as several other popular formats. It also has a built-in UUEncoder and UUDecoder. This makes it the closest thing to an all-in-one graphics solution for the Internet that I've seen.

To install this, just copy the files from either the \win31 or \winnt directory to your hard drive as described earlier in this appendix in "Installing Windows Software from HTMLCD." The first time you run this, it installs the screen saver for you. There are also menu options for uninstalling and reinstalling the screen saver.

WinJPEG (Windows)

\viewers\winjpg

WinJPEG is a Windows-based, graphics-file viewer and converter. You can read and save TIFF, GIF, JPG, TGA, BMP, and PCX file formats with this viewer/converter. WinJPEG has several color-enhancement and dithering features that allow the user to alter a graphics file slightly. The program also supports batch conversions and screen captures.

WinECJ (Windows)

\viewers\winecj

WinECJ is a fast JPEG viewer. The program has the capability to open multiple files and has a slide-show presentation mode.

WinLab (Windows)

\viewers\winlab

This is a powerful graphics viewer and editor. In addition to the image processing features, it has built-in twain and network support and it has a WinSock-compliant application for sending and receiving images.

WPlany (Windows)

\viewers\wplany

This sound utility plays sound files through a Windows Wave output device (such as a SoundBlaster card). NCSA recommends WPlany for use with Mosaic. The program supports several sound-file formats (including most formats used on the Net) and is very easy to use.

xv (UNIX)

\UNIX\XV-3_10a.z.

xv is an image editor for UNIX. This program is discussed in Chapter 22.

E-Mail

E-mail is one of the most popular applications on the Internet. A freeware version of Eudora and several other popular programs are included on HTMLCD.

Eudora (Windows and Mac)

Windows: \email\eudora

Mac: Email:Eudora

Eudora is an e-mail package that offers many features. Private mailboxes, reply functions, periodic mail checking, and many more features make this software one of the best mail packages on the market. Included here are versions 1.4.4 for Windows and 1.5.1 for Mac. (There are two Mac versions here, a 68K version and a FAT version for use with PowerMacs or 68K Macs.)

> **Note**
>
> You can get information about Eudora 2, the commercial version, on the Web page for Qualcomm's QUEST group. The URL is **http://www.qualcomm.com/quest/QuestMain.html**. Alternately, you can get information about the commercial version by sending e-mail to **eudora-sales@qualcomm.com** or by calling (800) 2-EUDORA—that is, (800) 238-3672. You can find the latest version of the freeware version at **ftp.qualcomm.com** in the directory quest/eudora/windows/1.4.

LeeMail (Mac)

Email:LeeMail 2.0.4 Folder

This Macintosh mail client supports multiple users and aliases. This program has some features that make it better suited for network than dialup use. You can copy this onto the hard drive in order for it to work.

Pegasus Mail (Windows)

\email\pegasus

Pegasus Mail is a powerful and easy to use e-mail program. Several add-ins for Pegasus make it easier to send attachments of popular document types, such as Ami Pro and Word for Windows. One of these add-ins, Mercury (a mail

IX

Appendixes

transport system), is included in the install2\email\pegasus\mercury directory. Pegasus is free software that can be used without restriction.

RFD MAIL (Windows)

\email\rfdmail

RFD MAIL is a Windows offline mail reader that supports many online services, including CompuServe, Delphi, GEnie, MCI Mail, World UNIX, The Direct Connection, MV Communications, Panix, The Well, The Portal System, NETCOM, CRL, INS, and The Internet Access Company. The program's other features include support for scripts; an address book; folders with drag, drop, and search capability; backup and restore capability; polling; and multiple signature blocks.

Registration grants you the code to unlock the shareware version, a free update, and technical support via e-mail. To install the program, run \email\rfdmail\install.exe in Windows.

Transfer Pro (Windows)

\email\xferpro

Transfer Pro is a Windows-based shareware tool that allows you to send text, application data, messages, images, audio, video, executable files, and other data types via e-mail, using the latest MIME 1.0 standards according to RFC1341. The program supports UU and XX encoding and decoding.

To install the program, run \email\xferpro\setup.exe in Windows.

UseNet News

If you plan to read UseNet News on a regular basis, you'll want to use one of the excellent newsreaders listed in this section. Although most of the Web browsers discussed throughout this book include some newsreader functions, you'll probably find that for frequent news reading, you need a dedicated newsreading program. Newsreaders are available for both Windows and Mac.

Internews (Mac)

News:Internews 1.0.6

Internews is a simple newsreader for Macs. It has all of the features for reading, replying, and posting articles that you would expect. It has a 32K file size limit, so it isn't really suitable for working with large binary files. It does allow you to sort newsgroups and articles several different ways, and it has a find feature to search for groups or content in articles.

News Xpress (Windows)

\news\nxpress

This is one of the newest Windows newsreaders and it's quickly becoming very popular. It has all of the features found in the traditional leaders in this category and adds a more pleasant interface.

Nuntius (Mac)

News:Nuntius 2.0.3 *f*

This Mac-based newsreader has several features worth looking at. You can set it up with multiple subscription lists so that if you share a Mac, each person using it has their own subscription. The newsgroup list is hierarchically structured which makes it easier to find the group you are looking for. You can use it with your favorite text editor or mail program for creating articles or sending mail.

Trumpet News Reader (Windows)

\news\wt_wsk

This program is a full-featured shareware Winsock newsreader for Windows. You can use this program to perform all the expected functions, such as reading, posting, and replying (as a follow-up post or by e-mail). You also can save messages and decode attached files.

After copying this to your hard drive, you have to provide information about your news server and your Internet account the first time you run it.

> **Note**
>
> Three other versions of this software are available for other types of Internet connections. WT_LWP requires Novell LWP DOS/Windows and is located in the directory \news\wt_lwp. WT_ABI requires the Trumpet TSR TCP stack and is located in the directory \news\wt_abi. WT_PKT works with a direct-to-packet driver (internal TCP stack) and is located in the directory \news\wt_pkt. All these versions are similar in function to the WinSock version.

IX

Appendixes

WinVN NewsReader (Windows)

\news\winvn

This program is a full-featured, public-domain Winsock newsreader for Windows. Like the Trumpet program, this program provides all the expected features. You need to provide information about your news server and Internet account the first time you run it. There is also a 32-bit version for Windows NT in the \news\winvn32 directory. If you're running Windows 3.1 with Win32s installed, you will probably find that the 16-bit version runs better for you.

> **Note**
>
> You'll find new versions of this program at **ftp.ksc.nasa.gov** in the /pub/win3/ winvn directory. New releases are posted at that site rather frequently.

Gopher

Several good Gopher clients are available, offering varying degrees of features and varying degrees of complexity. You're sure to find a program that suits your needs. (Unfortunately, several of the Gopher clients couldn't be licensed for use with this book, so if you want WS_Gopher, a popular Windows Gopher client, or Turbo Gopher for the Mac, you have to get them off the Internet yourself.)

Although you can access all of Gopherspace through the WWW with a Web browser, you'll want to use one of the Gopher applications if you spend a lot of time Gophering.

Gopher for Windows (Windows)

\gopher\wgopher

The Chinese University of Hong Kong created this simple little Gopher client. If you're looking for something fancy, this program may not be the ticket for you. If you want something fast and simple, though, this program is the perfect Gopher client.

FTP and Archie

If you plan to perform many file transfers on the Internet, you'll want to find an FTP client you like. You also need a good Archie client to help you find the files you want to transfer. Although you can use just about any Web browser for FTP, and although some Web pages perform Archie searches, an Archie program and an FTP client are must-haves if you download many files.

Anarchie (Mac)

FTP:Anarchie-140

This is a clever application that combines an FTP client and an Archie front end into one program. It comes preconfigured with bookmarks for some of the most popular FTP sites and software of interest to Mac users. You can add your own bookmarks and edit existing bookmarks. This program also works with other applications like NewsWatcher or InterNews to retrieve files based on URLs in text in the other program. Advanced features include firewall support and an option to automatically decode downloaded files (if you have Stuffit Expander or some other application that decodes files).

Fetch (Mac)

FTP:Fetch 2.1.2 Folder

This is a very solid FTP program that has been around for a while. It performs all of the usual FTP functions, allows you to create bookmarks for favorite FTP sites, and has a view function that lets you view text files. It also keeps track of the directories you have been in during the current session and allows you to return to a previous directory on the list.

FTPd (Mac)

FTP:FTPd-240

If you're setting up a Web server on your Mac and are considering giving users access to files on your Mac, you may want to look at using FTPd as an FTP server for your FTP needs. FTPd is an FTP and Gopher server. It has some security features and supports MacBinary and BinHex transfers.

WSArchie (Windows)

\ftp\wsarchie

WSArchie is a WinSock-compliant Archie program that allows you to connect to an Archie server and search for a file by using the familiar Windows interface. The program comes preconfigured with the locations of several Archie servers. You can configure WSArchie to transfer files directly from the list of found files so that you don't have to open your FTP client manually and then re-enter the address and directory information. The software doesn't work this way, however, with the current version of WS_FTP32.

IX

Appendixes

WS_FTP (Windows)

\ftp\ws_ftp16

This is the very popular WS_FTP FTP freeware client for Windows. WS_FTP makes it very easy to use FTP in a Windows point-and-click fashion that is as easy to understand as File Manager. It comes with configurations for connection to several popular FTP sites and you can add more to the list. It has support for advanced features such as firewalls. There is also a 32-bit version in the \ftp\ws_ftp32 directory.

WinFTP (Windows)

\ftp\winftp

If you have used WS_FTP, you'll recognize WinFTP; the author based his work on the source code from WS_FTP, and for the most part, the operation is the same. WinFTP offers a few nice additional features. With the History dialog box you can select a directory that you have already visited, without having to traverse the entire directory tree. There are filters to allow you to look for specific file types, such as *.TXT, or *.ZIP, in the local and remote hosts, and many other features. This directory contains a 16-bit and 32-bit version.

Windows FTP Daemon

\ftp\wftpd

This may be useful to you if you want to run an FTP site in Windows in addition to your Web site. This is a shareware WinSock-compliant server for FTP that allows you to use your Windows PC as an FTP server. It allows both anonymous FTP and FTP using accounts with login names and passwords. There are some security features, and you can keep a log of logins and activity. This version responds to FTP requests from Mosaic, Cello, and Netscape.

Internet Relay Chat

Internet Relay Chat is a real-time way to carry on a conversation with one person or several people via computer over the Internet. Whatever you type, everyone else will see. Little software is available for Windows or Mac for IRC, but the programs included in this section are very good.

Homer (Mac)

IRC:Homer IRC 0.93.4 folder

This is the most interesting IRC client I've seen for Mac or Windows. It allows multiple chat sessions on different channels in separate windows as do most IRC clients; it has buttons for changing many of your attributes in IRC; and it does most everything else you need from IRC. It's most unique feature is the use of small icons of photos you can associate with the people you chat with.

WSIRC (Windows)

\irc\wsirc

This product comes in several styles: a freeware version, a shareware version that provides more functions when it's registered, and retail versions for personal and corporate use. The author also can custom-design an IRC client for special needs. The freeware and shareware versions are both included on HTMLCD. In this release, the shareware version has all the features enabled, but only for a limited time; after 30 days, you must register the shareware version to continue using it. The freeware version has no such limitations.

Other Internet Applications and Useful Utilities

All of the main categories of Internet software were covered previously in this appendix, but a great deal of software doesn't fit any of the major categories. The following sections cover the programs that just didn't fit anywhere else.

ArcMaster (Windows)

\other\arcmastr

This is a handy utility for compressing and decompressing files using many popular compression formats. Support formats include ZIP, LHZ, and ARJ. You need to have the file compression/decompression utilities for each of these because this is just a front end to make it easier to use the DOS utilities. It supports drag and drop, allows you to conveniently manipulate compressed files, and converts files from one compression format to another.

ArcShell (Windows)

\other\arcshell

ArcShell is a Windows shell for ZIP, LHZ, ARC, and ARJ compression files. You need to have the file compression/decompression utilities for each of these because ArcShell is just a front end to make it easier to use the DOS utilities.

Batch UUD for DOS (DOS)

\other\batchuud

As the name implies, this program is a batch UUDecoder that runs in DOS. With UUD, all you have to do is run UUD *.* in DOS or with the Windows File, Run, and all saved files in UUEncoded format are decoded. The program is smart as well: by alphabetizing all entries, UUD can make a logical guess at the order of split files.

> **Note**
>
> UUEncoding converts binary files (programs and archives) to text so that they can be transmitted over the Internet via messages. After receipt, the message files must be converted back to their original binary form.

COMt (Windows)

\other\comt

COMt is a shareware program that allows a standard Windows-based communication program to act as a Telnet client in a TCP/IP environment. It allows you to use the more powerful features of your communication program in a Telnet session.

Run \other\comt\ INSTALL.EXE (in Windows) to run the automatic installation or read README.TXT to install the program manually.

Compact Pro (Mac)

Other:Compact Pro Package (English)

Compact Pro is a file compression utility for Macs. Its files end with a CPT extension by default. It can create self-extracting archives for distribution to users that don't have Compact Pro.

Crip for Windows

\other\cripwin

This is a Windows-based text encryption program. It was designed for use over the Internet and has options for dealing with PC linefeeds in files that will be sent over the Internet. (See the README file for information on this.)

Crypt (Mac)

Other:Crypt-04 folder

There are two different encryption utilities here. One is a desk accessory for encrypting text or PICT files to be sent by e-mail. The other is a simple text editor with an encryption option.

Daemon (Mac)

Other:Daemon-100

If you're running a server that others have access to, Daemon provides you several additional daemons. With this, you can run Finger, Whois, Ident, NTP, and Daytime servers. (See the Daemon Documentation file for details on setting these up.)

DeHQX (Mac)

Other:DeHQX-201

This is an application for decoding BinHex encoded documents. It can ignore headers and works with multiple and split files.

DeSEA (Mac)

:Other:DeSEA 1.5

DeSEA is used to convert self-extracting code from self-extracting compressed archives. This makes the archives smaller and saves transmission time. If the user receiving the file has the program for uncompressing the archive, the self-extracting archive adds unnecessarily to the file size. DeSEA works with self-extracting archives created with Compact Pro, Disk Doubler, StuffIt, and NOW Compress.

Disinfectant (Mac)

Other:Disinfectant

This is a virus detector and cleaner for the Mac. It can recognize most non-HyperCard viruses and their variations. It's a good idea to keep up a current copy of this. As new viruses are created, new versions of Disinfectant are released to combat them.

Drag And Zip (Windows)

\other\dragzip

Drag And Zip is a set of utilities that makes Windows 3.1 File Manager into a file manager for creating and managing ZIP, LZH, and GZ files. With its built-in routines to zip and unzip files, Drag And Zip makes it very easy to compress files into ZIP files and to extract files from ZIP files from any Windows file manager that supports Drag and Drop. Drag And Zip also supports use of your copies of PKZIP, LHA, and GUNZIP, to manage compressed files. Drag And Zip has a built-in virus scanner you can use to scan the files in the compressed file for possible viruses.

To install Drag And Zip, run \other\dragzip\dzseup.exe in Windows and follow the directions on-screen.

Easy View (Mac)
Other:Easy View 2.50 *f*

Use Easy View to browse collections of structured text files, such as collections of Info-Mac digests, Eudora mail, and TidBITS. An extension menu has been added to allow for external extensions. The extension feature is compatible with BBEdit. (See "Get URL" in the World Wide Web section of this appendix for an extension that works with this.)

Enigma for Windows
\other\enigma

This is a file encryption program that supports the DES encryption standard used by many US government agencies. While it isn't designed for sending encrypted messages via Internet e-mail, you can use it for transferring files through any protocol that supports binary transfer. So you can encrypt files on an FTP site, you can send encrypted files as attachments to e-mail using UUEncode or MIME, and you can make encrypted files available via the WWW as links from an HTML document. This is not a public key system so the same password is used to encode and decode files. This does limit its security for Internet usage because anyone receiving a file needs your password.

To install this, run \other\enigma\install.exe in Windows.

EWAN Emulator without a Good Name (Windows)
\other\ewan

Despite the fact that this emulator does not have a good name, it's a good product. In a typical setting, this program is used primarily for Telnet; you can save configurations for several different Telnet sites. The program supports a capture log, and you can perform the usual copy and paste operations from the text to the capture log.

To install EWAN, run \install1\other\ewan\install.exe.

Extract (Windows)

\other\extract

Extract version 3.04 is a Windows application for encoding and decoding UU-embedded files.

> **Note**
>
> The documentation with this software is slightly out of date. The author requests that e-mail regarding the product be sent to **dpenner@msi.cuug.ab.ca**. His surface mail address is Eau Claire Place II, 650, 521 - 3rd Avenue S.W., Calgary, Alberta, T2P 3T3.

Finger (Mac)

Other:finger-150

This is a simple application that is both a Finger server and client. You can finger someone else to find out what information they have set up about themselves in their server (which is useful for finding a particular e-mail address at another host) and you can set it up to tell others what you want when they finger you. The server needs to be connected to respond so you'll probably need a network connection to use this as a server.

Finger (Windows)

\other\finger10

Finger 1.0 is a simple but functional Finger client. Enter a host and user name, and the program reports information about the user, as determined by the host. (This feature is useful for finding e-mail addresses and other information at a given host computer.)

GetMyAddress (Mac)

Other:GetMyAddress

This simple utility tells you the address information about your Mac. It reports your Zone name, Ethernet address (if applicable), and your IP address as well as other information. You can copy the information to the Clipboard to paste into other applications.

gzip (UNIX)

/UNIX/gzip124.tar

You use this program to uncompress all of the gzip files on HTMLCD, just in case you don't already have it. This is version 1.2.4—the latest version at the time this book went to press.

IP Manager (Windows)

\other\ipmgr

Do you have trouble keeping track of IP addresses? If this is something you need help with, IP Manager is the solution. It helps you keep track of IP addresses, ensure you don't have duplicate addresses, and you can even launch FTP and Telnet sessions from it.

This trial version is limited to only 25 devices. You may try IP Manager for 21 days. If at the end of the trial period you decide not to purchase IP Manager, you should delete it.

MacGzip (Mac)

Other:MacGzip

This is a compression utility for compressing and expanding files in the GNU Zip format. This is a common format for UNIX files on the Internet.

MacTCP Switcher (Mac)

Other:MacTCP Switcher 1.0

MacTCP Switcher makes it easy to save and switch between different MacTCP configurations. The software author states that this is useful for PowerBook users that may use a dialup SLIP or PPP account on the road and a LAN in the office. It's also useful if you have Internet accounts with more than one service provider even if you don't have the luxury of a PowerBook.

MacTCP Watcher (Mac)

Other:MacTCP Watcher

This utility monitors the TCP activity on your Mac. It reports on all of the current connections and any errors.

Name Server Lookup Utility (Windows)

\other\nslookup

This program is a simple but powerful little utility for looking up information about a specific machine or domain on the Internet. The program reports the numeric IP address and other information for the site or machine name.

StuffIt (Mac)
Other:StuffIt

This folder contains three popular versions of the StuffIt compression utilities. StuffIt expands compressed files. Drop Stuff with Expander Enhancer adds the capability to expand ZIP, Gzip, Z, and other compressed formats, and adds drag and drop functionality. StuffIt Lite is a reduced function version of the popular StuffIt Delux program that creates and extracts stuffed files. To install any of these, double-click the installer.

Tar for the Macintosh (Mac)
Other:tar folder

This program reads and writes TAR (Tape Archive) files. This is a popular archive format for UNIX users on the Internet.

TekTel (Windows)
\other\tektel

TekTel is a simple Telnet application with Textronix T4010 and VT100 emulation. The program, which is written in Visual Basic, is still a little rough around the edges. The source code is included.

Time Sync (Windows)
\other\tsync

Time Sync version 1.4 is a Windows-based application that is designed to synchronize your PC's clock with the time on a UNIX host. This program, which relies on an established WinSock connection, is written in Visual Basic.

To install Time Sync, run \other\tsync\setup.exe in Windows.

Translation Package (Mac)
Other:Translation Package v1.5.2

This handy package performs a large number of format translations for graphics and text files for use with Apple File Exchange. Some of the supported translations include TIFF from IBM to Mac, Windows BMP to PICT, and EPSF from IBM to Mac. See the documentation for directions on installing these translators for use with AFE.

IX

Appendixes

U2D (Windows)

\other\u2d

This handy program converts UNIX text file line endings to DOS text file format. All you have to do is drag a file (or files) from File Manager to the U2D icon to process them.

UUCode (Windows)

\other\uucode

UUCode is a Windows-based application used to decode UUEncoded files sent over the Internet in messages. This application also encodes a binary file in UUCode so that it can be inserted into a message and sent over the Internet in this manner. The program's configuration options include file overwriting, default file names, and status messages.

To install UUCode, run \other\uucode\setup.exe in Windows.

UULite (Mac)

Other:UULite

This is a UUEncoder and UUDecoder for the Mac. It can handle multiple part files and multiple files. It supports drag-and-drop and can handle very large files. It's file size limit is based only on your hard drive, not available memory.

Visual Basic Run Time DLLs (Windows)

\other\vbrun

Many of the Windows programs included on HTMLCD are written in Visual Basic and require one of these files to run. Most of the time, these files will be installled by the program or will have been installed by something else. But, if you ever get an error message that says something like Cannot run, cannot find vbrunx00.dll, just copy the missing Visual Basic Run Time file from here to your \windows\system directory.

VoiceChat (Windows)

\other\ivc

VoiceChat is a great example of a cutting-edge Internet application. This program enables two users connected to the Internet to talk to each other via their PCs. The program requires both PCs to have sound cards, microphones, and speakers.

The current version of IVC does not transmit the conversation in real time. It waits for a pause (such as the pause at the end of a sentence) and transmits the whole phrase at once. Audio quality is not effected by a SLIP connection, but you can choose a lower sampling rate to speed transmission. Even so, the sound should be telephone-quality or better. If you use Trumpet Winsock, be sure to upgrade to version 2.0b; IVC is not compatible with earlier versions. See the IVC.FAQ file for more information about using this interesting application.

If you register this program, you get additional features, such as answering-machine and fax modes. After copying the program from HTMLCD, move the files from the \ivc\windows\system directory to your \windows\system directory.

> **Note**
>
> Internet VoiceChat is copyright © 1994, Richard L. Ahrens. You can use the unregistered version of IVC on an evaluation basis for no more than 30 days. Continued use after the 30-day trial period requires registration, which is $20 for individual users. Site licenses are negotiable. Contact the author at 7 Omega Court, Middletown, NJ, 07748.

Win32s (Windows)

\win32s

Several Windows programs on HTMLCD require Win32s to run. If you're running Windows 3.1, Windows 3.11, or Windows for Workgroups 3.11, you need to install Win32s to make these programs run. The version here is Win32s 1.25 with OLE 2.02, which is the correct version to use with NCSA Mosaic version 2 and other programs that require Win32 will work with this version. To install Win32s, run \win32s\disk1\setup.exe in Windows and follow the directions on screen. The setup may require you to restart Windows, so you should close any open applications before beginning.

> **Note**
>
> You may not redistribute Win32s without the permission of Microsoft.

IX

Appendixes

WinCode (Windows)

\other\wincode

WinCode is a great utility for UUEncoding and UUDecoding files. A couple of really nice features are the way the program handles multiple files (effortlessly) and its capability to tie its menus to other programs. The program decodes many poorly encoded programs that other decoders can't handle.

To install WinCode, run the \other\wincode\setup.exe in Windows

Windows Sockets Host (Windows)

\other\wshost

Windows Sockets Host is a simple utility that determines a host computer's name based on a numeric IP address, or vice versa.

Windows Sockets Net Watch (Windows)

\other\ws_watch

This program makes active checks on Internet hosts that are listed in its database file. This is useful for monitoring a host to see if it's functioning. This program is designed to work on any Winsock DLL but the documentation notes which Winsocks it works best with and which it has problems with.

Windows Sockets Ping

\other\ws_ping

Ping is an uncomplicated Windows application used to test an Internet connection. The author wrote the program to test whether his two computers were connected on the Internet; you can use it to do the same thing. The source code is included in the archive, and the author grants you permission to alter it, if necessary. There are Windows 3.1 and Windows NT versions included here.

> **Note**
>
> Because Ping uses nonstandard WinSock calls, this application may not run on every WinSock stack.

WinZip (Windows)

\other\winzip

WinZip version 5.6 is a fantastic Windows ZIP archive-managing program that no Internet user should be without. This application provides a pleasant graphical interface for managing many archive-file formats, such as ZIP, ARJ, ARC, and LZH. WinZip allows you to extract text files from an archive directly to the screen, so you can read a file in an archive without actually extracting it. Another feature in this version enables you to uninstall a program soon after you install it.

Version 5.6 has added support of archives that use the GZIP, TAR, and Z formats that are very common on the Internet. You can now manage these files just as easily as ZIP files. It's common to find files on the Internet that have been stored as TAR files and then compressed with GZIP or Z. WinZip handles these multiple formats with no problems. This support is unique among the other ZIP file utilities discussed in this chapter.

WinZip is shareware and well worth the $29 registration fee for an individual user.

To install WinZip, run \other\winzip\setup.exe in Windows.

YAWTELNET (Windows)

\other\yawtel

YAWTELNET (Yet Another Windows Socket Telnet) is a freeware Telnet client designed specifically to work well with Mosaic. Many of the menu commands are not functional, but you can select text in the active window and copy it to another application.

> **Note**
>
> YAWTELNET is copyright © 1994, Hans van Oostrom. Refer to LICENSE.TXT in the yawtel directory for complete copyright information.

IX

Appendixes

ZipIt (Mac)

other:ZipIt

This compression utility for the Mac zips and unzips files in the popular ZIP format. It's fully compatible with PKZip version 2.0g, the standard format used by most PKZip users. It supports drag and drop.

Zip Master (Windows)

\other\zipmastr

ZMW is a stand-alone Windows 3.1 ZIP utility. PKZip and PKUnzip are not required to use this, which sets it apart from most other Windows based ZIP utilities. You can use it to add to, freshen, or update existing ZIP files; create new ZIP files; extract from or test existing ZIP files; view existing ZIP file contents; and many other functions.

Zip Manager (Windows)

\other\zipmgr

This is another Windows ZIP utility that doesn't require you to also have PKZip or PKUnzip. It is 100 percent PKZip 2.04 compatible and the compression utilities are designed specifically for Windows. ZMZIP and ZMUNZIP are built in to Zip Manager.

To install this, run \other\zipmgr\zmsetup.exe in Program Manager.

> **Note**
>
> You must run the ZMSETUP program to expand them before the program can be used. You must run MSETUP.EXE from the Windows Program Manager. Other shells such as the Norton Desktop or PC Tools for Windows are not 100 percent compatible with our setup program and may cause it to fail when attempting to create the Zip Manager Group.

Examples from *Special Edition Using HTML*

Windows: \examples

Mac: Examples

Throughout this book there are many examples of HTML code. All of the longer examples and code used for figures are included in this directory.

Internet Documents

The final group of files on HTMLCD is a large collection of documents about the Internet. I hope you find all of this information useful. HTMLCD doesn't install any of these documents. Any documents that were zipped are now expanded; you can read them in a text viewer or word processor directly from HTMLCD, or you can copy them.

RFCs

Windows: \docs\rfc

Mac: Internet Documents:RFC

More than 1,000 RFCs (Request for Comments) are available on HTMLCD. These RFCs—the working notes of the committees that develop the protocols and standards for the Internet—are numbered in the order in which they were released. (Zeros were added to the beginning of the number part of the file names for the ones numbered below 1,000 so that they display in numerical order in File Manager. For example, rfc3 was changed to rfc0003.) Some numbers are skipped. These numbers represent RFCs that are outdated or that have been replaced by newer ones.

STDs

Windows: \docs\std

Mac: Internet Documents:STD

If an RFC becomes fully accepted, it becomes a standard and is designated an STD (Internet Activities Board Standards). STDs tend to be technical.

FYIs

Windows: \docs\fyi

Mac: Internet Documents:FYI

FYIs (For Your Information) are a subset of RFCs; they tend to be more informative and less technical.

Appendix D

HTML Level 2 Definition Type Document

What follows is the public text of the current DTD for HTML 2.0. This document is formatted in SGML, a machine-level markup language. Although HTML Level 2 is the current standard, the DTD is still undergoing minor revisions to clarify language and accepted uses.

```
<!--    html.dtd
Document Type Definition for the HyperText Markup Language
                (HTML DTD)
     $Id: html.dtd,v 1.1 1995/03/07 05:50:35 connolly Exp $
     Author: Daniel W. Connolly <connolly@hal.com>
     See Also: html.decl, html-0.dtd, html-1.dtd
     http://www.hal.com/%7Econnolly/html-spec/index.html
     http://info.cern.ch/hypertext/WWW/MarkUp2/MarkUp.html
-->
<!ENTITY % HTML.Version
        "-//IETF//DTD HTML 2.0//EN"
        -- Typical usage:
            <!DOCTYPE HTML PUBLIC "-//IETF//DTD HTML//EN">
            <html>
            ...
            </html>

        --
        >
<!--============ Feature Test Entities ========================-->
<!ENTITY % HTML.Recommended "IGNORE"
        -- Certain features of the language are necessary for
           compatibility with widespread usage, but they may
           compromise the structural integrity of a document.
           This feature test entity enables a more prescriptive
           document type definition that eliminates
           those features.
        -->
<![ %HTML.Recommended [
        <!ENTITY % HTML.Deprecated "IGNORE">
]]>
```

```
<!ENTITY % HTML.Deprecated "INCLUDE"
        -- Certain features of the language are necessary for
           compatibility with earlier versions of the specification,
           but they tend to be used and implemented inconsistently,
           and their use is deprecated. This feature test entity
           enables a document type definition that eliminates
           these features.
        -->
<!ENTITY % HTML.Highlighting "INCLUDE"
        -- Use this feature test entity to validate that a
           document uses no highlighting tags, which may be
           ignored on minimal implementations.
        -->
<!ENTITY % HTML.Forms "INCLUDE"
        -- Use this feature test entity to validate that a document
           contains no forms, which may not be supported in minimal
           implementations
        -->
<!--=============== Imported Names ===============================-->
<!ENTITY % Content-Type "CDATA"
        -- meaning an internet media type
           (aka MIME content type, as per RFC1521)
        -->
<!ENTITY % HTTP-Method "GET ¦ POST"
        -- as per HTTP specification, in progress
        -->
<!ENTITY % URI "CDATA"
        -- The term URI means a CDATA attribute
           whose value is a Uniform Resource Identifier,
           as defined by
        "Universal Resource Identifiers" by Tim Berners-Lee
        aka RFC 1630
        Note that CDATA attributes are limited by the LITLEN
        capacity (1024 in the current version of html.decl),
        so that URIs in HTML have a bounded length.
        -->
<!--========= DTD "Macros" =====================-->
<!ENTITY % heading "H1¦H2¦H3¦H4¦H5¦H6">
<!ENTITY % list " UL ¦ OL ¦ DIR ¦ MENU " >
<!--======= Character mnemonic entities ==================-->
<!ENTITY % ISOlat1 PUBLIC
  "ISO 8879-1986//ENTITIES Added Latin 1//EN//HTML">
%ISOlat1;
<!ENTITY amp CDATA "&#38;"     -- ampersand          -->
<!ENTITY gt CDATA "&#62;"      -- greater than       -->
<!ENTITY lt CDATA "&#60;"      -- less than          -->
<!ENTITY quot CDATA "&#34;"    -- double quote        -->
<!--======= SGML Document Access (SDA) Parameter Entities ====-->
<!-- HTML 2.0 contains SGML Document Access (SDA) fixed attributes
in support of easy transformation to the International Committee
for Accessible Document Design (ICADD) DTD
        "-//EC-USA-CDA/ICADD//DTD ICADD22//EN".
ICADD applications are designed to support usable access to
structured information by print-impaired individuals through
```

```
Braille, large print and voice synthesis.  For more information on
SDA & ICADD:
            - ISO 12083:1993, Annex A.8, Facilities for Braille,
              large print and computer voice
            - ICADD ListServ
              <ICADD%ASUACAD.BITNET@ARIZVM1.ccit.arizona.edu>
            - Usenet news group bit.listserv.easi
            - Recording for the Blind, +1 800 221 4792
-->
<!ENTITY % SDAFORM  "SDAFORM  CDATA  #FIXED"
          -- one to one mapping       -->
<!ENTITY % SDARULE  "SDARULE  CDATA  #FIXED"
          -- context-sensitive mapping -->
<!ENTITY % SDAPREF  "SDAPREF  CDATA  #FIXED"
          -- generated text prefix     -->
<!ENTITY % SDASUFF  "SDASUFF  CDATA  #FIXED"
          -- generated text suffix     -->
<!ENTITY % SDASUSP  "SDASUSP  NAME   #FIXED"
          -- suspend transform process -->
<!--========== Text Markup =====================-->
<![ %HTML.Highlighting [
<!ENTITY % font " TT ¦ B ¦ I ">
<!ENTITY % phrase "EM ¦ STRONG ¦ CODE ¦ SAMP ¦ KBD ¦ VAR ¦ CITE ">
<!ENTITY % text "#PCDATA ¦ A ¦ IMG ¦ BR ¦ %phrase ¦ %font">
<!ELEMENT (%font;¦%phrase) - - (%text)*>
<!ATTLIST ( TT ¦ CODE ¦ SAMP ¦ KBD ¦ VAR )
        %SDAFORM; "Lit"
        >
<!ATTLIST ( B ¦ STRONG )
        %SDAFORM; "B"
        >
<!ATTLIST ( I ¦ EM ¦ CITE )
        %SDAFORM; "It"
        >
<!-- <TT>        Typewriter text                 -->
<!-- <B>         Bold text                       -->
<!-- <I>         Italic text                     -->
<!-- <EM>        Emphasized phrase               -->
<!-- <STRONG>    Strong emphasis                 -->
<!-- <CODE>      Source code phrase              -->
<!-- <SAMP>      Sample text or characters       -->
<!-- <KBD>       Keyboard phrase, e.g. user input -->
<!-- <VAR>       Variable phrase or substitutable -->
<!-- <CITE>      Name or title of cited work     -->
<!ENTITY % pre.content "#PCDATA ¦ A ¦ HR ¦ BR ¦ %font ¦ %phrase">
]]>
<!ENTITY % text "#PCDATA ¦ A ¦ IMG ¦ BR">
<!ELEMENT BR    - O EMPTY>
<!ATTLIST BR
        %SDAPREF; "&#RE;"
        >
<!-- <BR>        Line break      -->
<!--========== Link Markup =====================-->
<![ %HTML.Recommended [
        <!ENTITY % linkName "ID">
```

```
        ]]>
        <!ENTITY % linkName "CDATA">
        <!ENTITY % linkType "NAME"
                -- a list of these will be specified at a later date -->
        <!ENTITY % linkExtraAttributes
                "REL %linkType #IMPLIED
                REV %linkType #IMPLIED
                URN CDATA #IMPLIED
                TITLE CDATA #IMPLIED
                METHODS NAMES #IMPLIED
                ">
        <![ %HTML.Recommended [
                <!ENTITY % A.content    "(%text)*"
                -- <H1><a name="xxx">Heading</a></H1>
                        is preferred to
                   <a name="xxx"><H1>Heading</H1></a>
                -->
        ]]>
        <!ENTITY % A.content    "(%heading¦%text)*">
        <!ELEMENT A     - - %A.content -(A)>
        <!ATTLIST A
                HREF %URI #IMPLIED
                NAME %linkName #IMPLIED
                %linkExtraAttributes;
                %SDAPREF; "<Anchor: #AttList>"
                >
        <!-- <A>            Anchor; source/destination of link    -->
        <!-- <A NAME="...">  Name of this anchor                  -->
        <!-- <A HREF="...">  Address of link destination          -->
        <!-- <A URN="...">   Permanent address of destination     -->
        <!-- <A REL=...>     Relationship to destination          -->
        <!-- <A REV=...>     Relationship of destination to this  -->
        <!-- <A TITLE="..."> Title of destination (advisory)      -->
        <!-- <A METHODS="...">Operations on destination (advisory) -->
        <!--========== Images ============================-->
        <!ELEMENT IMG    - O EMPTY>
        <!ATTLIST IMG
                SRC %URI; #REQUIRED
                ALT CDATA #IMPLIED
                ALIGN (top¦middle¦bottom) #IMPLIED
                ISMAP (ISMAP) #IMPLIED
                %SDAPREF; "<Fig><?SDATrans Img: #AttList>#AttVal(Alt)</Fig>"
                >
        <!-- <IMG>           Image; icon, glyph or illustration   -->
        <!-- <IMG SRC="..."> Address of image object              -->
        <!-- <IMG ALT="..."> Textual alternative                  -->
        <!-- <IMG ALIGN=...> Position relative to text            -->
        <!-- <IMG ISMAP>     Each pixel can be a link             -->
        <!--========== Paragraphs=======================-->
        <!ELEMENT P     - O (%text)*>
        <!ATTLIST P
                %SDAFORM; "Para"
                >
```

```
<!-- <P>           Paragraph       -->
<!--========== Headings, Titles, Sections ===============-->
<!ELEMENT HR     - O EMPTY>
<!ATTLIST HR
        %SDAPREF; "&#RE;&#RE;"
        >
<!-- <HR>          Horizontal rule -->
<!ELEMENT ( %heading )  - -  (%text;)*>
<!ATTLIST H1
        %SDAFORM; "H1"
        >
<!ATTLIST H2
        %SDAFORM; "H2"
        >
<!ATTLIST H3
        %SDAFORM; "H3"
        >
<!ATTLIST H4
        %SDAFORM; "H4"
        >
<!ATTLIST H5
        %SDAFORM; "H5"
        >
<!ATTLIST H6
        %SDAFORM; "H6"
        >
<!-- <H1>          Heading, level 1 -->
<!-- <H2>          Heading, level 2 -->
<!-- <H3>          Heading, level 3 -->
<!-- <H4>          Heading, level 4 -->
<!-- <H5>          Heading, level 5 -->
<!-- <H6>          Heading, level 6 -->
<!--========== Text Flows =====================-->
<![ %HTML.Forms [
        <!ENTITY % block.forms "BLOCKQUOTE ¦ FORM ¦ ISINDEX">
]]>
<!ENTITY % block.forms "BLOCKQUOTE">
<![ %HTML.Deprecated [
        <!ENTITY % preformatted "PRE ¦ XMP ¦ LISTING">
]]>
<!ENTITY % preformatted "PRE">
<!ENTITY % block "P ¦ %list ¦ DL
        ¦ %preformatted
        ¦ %block.forms">
<!ENTITY % flow "(%text¦%block)*">
<!ENTITY % pre.content "#PCDATA ¦ A ¦ HR ¦ BR">
<!ELEMENT PRE - - (%pre.content)*>
<!ATTLIST PRE
        WIDTH NUMBER #implied
        %SDAFORM; "Lit"
        >
<!-- <PRE>             Preformatted text              -->
<!-- <PRE WIDTH=...>   Maximum characters per line    -->
<![ %HTML.Deprecated [
<!ENTITY % literal "CDATA"
```

```
                           -- historical, non-conforming parsing mode where
                              the only markup signal is the end tag
                              in full
                           -->
<!ELEMENT (XMP|LISTING) - - %literal>
<!ATTLIST XMP
         %SDAFORM; "Lit"
         %SDAPREF; "Example:&#RE;"
         >
<!ATTLIST LISTING
         %SDAFORM; "Lit"
         %SDAPREF; "Listing:&#RE;"
         >
<!-- <XMP>                 Example section          -->
<!-- <LISTING>             Computer listing         -->
<!ELEMENT PLAINTEXT - O %literal>
<!-- <PLAINTEXT>           Plain text passage       -->
<!ATTLIST PLAINTEXT
         %SDAFORM; "Lit"
         >
]]>
<!--========== Lists ==================-->
<!ELEMENT DL    - -  (DT | DD)+>
<!ATTLIST DL
         COMPACT (COMPACT) #IMPLIED
         %SDAFORM; "List"
         %SDAPREF; "Definition List:"
         >
<!ELEMENT DT    - O (%text)*>
<!ATTLIST DT
         %SDAFORM; "Term"
         >
<!ELEMENT DD    - O %flow>
<!ATTLIST DD
         %SDAFORM; "LItem"
         >
<!-- <DL>                  Definition list, or glossary   -->
<!-- <DL COMPACT>          Compact style list             -->
<!-- <DT>                  Term in definition list        -->
<!-- <DD>                  Definition of term             -->
<!ELEMENT (OL|UL) - -  (LI)+>
<!ATTLIST OL
         COMPACT (COMPACT) #IMPLIED
         %SDAFORM; "List"
         >
<!ATTLIST UL
         COMPACT (COMPACT) #IMPLIED
         %SDAFORM; "List"
         >
<!-- <UL>                  Unordered list           -->
<!-- <UL COMPACT>          Compact list style       -->
<!-- <OL>                  Ordered, or numbered list -->
<!-- <OL COMPACT>          Compact list style       -->
<!ELEMENT (DIR|MENU) - -  (LI)+ -(%block)>
<!ATTLIST DIR
```

```
          COMPACT (COMPACT) #IMPLIED
          %SDAFORM; "List"
          %SDAPREF; "<LHead>Directory</LHead>"
          >
<!ATTLIST MENU
          COMPACT (COMPACT) #IMPLIED
          %SDAFORM; "List"
          %SDAPREF; "<LHead>Menu</LHead>"
          >
<!-- <DIR>              Directory list              -->
<!-- <DIR COMPACT>      Compact list style          -->
<!-- <MENU>             Menu list                   -->
<!-- <MENU COMPACT>     Compact list style          -->
<!ELEMENT LI     - O %flow>
<!ATTLIST LI
          %SDAFORM; "LItem"
          >
<!-- <LI>               List item                   -->
<!--========= Document Body ===================-->
<![ %HTML.Recommended [
          <!ENTITY % body.content "(%heading¦%block¦HR¦ADDRESS¦IMG)*"
          -- <h1>Heading</h1>
            <p>Text ...
                 is preferred to
            <h1>Heading</h1>
            Text ...
          -->
]]>
<!ENTITY % body.content "(%heading ¦ %text ¦ %block ¦
                          HR ¦ ADDRESS)*">
<!ELEMENT BODY O O %body.content>
<!-- <BODY>     Document body    -->
<!ELEMENT BLOCKQUOTE - - %body.content>
<!ATTLIST BLOCKQUOTE
          %SDAFORM; "BQ"
          >
<!-- <BLOCKQUOTE>       Quoted passage  -->
<!ELEMENT ADDRESS - - (%text¦P)*>
<!ATTLIST  ADDRESS
          %SDAFORM; "Lit"
          %SDAPREF; "Address:&#RE;"
          >
<!-- <ADDRESS> Address, signature, or byline  -->
<!--======= Forms ====================-->
<![ %HTML.Forms [
<!ELEMENT FORM - - %body.content -(FORM) +(INPUT¦SELECT¦TEXTAREA)>
<!ATTLIST FORM
          ACTION %URI #IMPLIED
          METHOD (%HTTP-Method) GET
          ENCTYPE %Content-Type; "application/x-www-form-urlencoded"
          %SDAPREF; "<Para>Form:</Para>"
          %SDASUFF; "<Para>Form End.</Para>"
          >
<!-- <FORM>                  Fill-out or data-entry form    -->
<!-- <FORM ACTION="...">     Address for completed form     -->
```

```
<!-- <FORM METHOD=...>        Method of submitting form    -->
<!-- <FORM ENCTYPE="...">     Representation of form data  -->
<!ENTITY % InputType "(TEXT ¦ PASSWORD ¦ CHECKBOX ¦
                       RADIO ¦ SUBMIT ¦ RESET ¦
                       IMAGE ¦ HIDDEN )">
<!ELEMENT INPUT - O EMPTY>
<!ATTLIST INPUT
        TYPE %InputType TEXT
        NAME CDATA #IMPLIED
        VALUE CDATA #IMPLIED
        SRC %URI #IMPLIED
        CHECKED (CHECKED) #IMPLIED
        SIZE CDATA #IMPLIED
        MAXLENGTH NUMBER #IMPLIED
        ALIGN (top¦middle¦bottom) #IMPLIED
        %SDAPREF; "Input: "
        >
<!-- <INPUT>                  Form input datum             -->
<!-- <INPUT TYPE=...>         Type of input interaction    -->
<!-- <INPUT NAME=...>         Name of form datum           -->
<!-- <INPUT VALUE="...">      Default/initial/selected value -->
<!-- <INPUT SRC="...">        Address of image             -->
<!-- <INPUT CHECKED>          Initial state is "on"        -->
<!-- <INPUT SIZE=...>         Field size hint              -->
<!-- <INPUT MAXLENGTH=...>    Data length maximum          -->
<!-- <INPUT ALIGN=...>        Image alignment              -->
<!ELEMENT SELECT - - (OPTION+) -(INPUT¦SELECT¦TEXTAREA)>
<!ATTLIST SELECT
        NAME CDATA #REQUIRED
        SIZE NUMBER #IMPLIED
        MULTIPLE (MULTIPLE) #IMPLIED
        %SDAFORM; "List"
        %SDAPREF;
        "<LHead>Select #AttVal(Multiple)</LHead>"
        >
<!-- <SELECT>                 Selection of option(s)       -->
<!-- <SELECT NAME=...>        Name of form datum           -->
<!-- <SELECT SIZE=...>        Options displayed at a time  -->
<!-- <SELECT MULTIPLE>        Multiple selections allowed  -->
<!ELEMENT OPTION - O (#PCDATA)*>
<!ATTLIST OPTION
        SELECTED (SELECTED) #IMPLIED
        VALUE CDATA #IMPLIED
        %SDAFORM; "LItem"
        %SDAPREF;
        "Option: #AttVal(Value) #AttVal(Selected)"
        >
<!-- <OPTION>                 A selection option           -->
<!-- <OPTION SELECTED>        Initial state                -->
<!-- <OPTION VALUE="...">     Form datum value for this option-->
<!ELEMENT TEXTAREA - - (#PCDATA)* -(INPUT¦SELECT¦TEXTAREA)>
<!ATTLIST TEXTAREA
        NAME CDATA #REQUIRED
        ROWS NUMBER #REQUIRED
        COLS NUMBER #REQUIRED
```

```
            %SDAFORM; "Para"
            %SDAPREF; "Input Text -- #AttVal(Name): "
            >
<!-- <TEXTAREA>                An area for text input        -->
<!-- <TEXTAREA NAME=...>       Name of form datum            -->
<!-- <TEXTAREA ROWS=...>       Height of area                -->
<!-- <TEXTAREA COLS=...>       Width of area                 -->
]]>
<!--======= Document Head =====================-->
<![ %HTML.Recommended [
        <!ENTITY % head.extra "META* & LINK*">
]]>
<!ENTITY % head.extra "NEXTID? & META* & LINK*">
<!ENTITY % head.content "TITLE & ISINDEX? & BASE? &
                        (%head.extra)">
<!ELEMENT HEAD O O  (%head.content)>
<!-- <HEAD>     Document head   -->
<!ELEMENT TITLE - -  (#PCDATA)*>
<!ATTLIST TITLE
        %SDAFORM; "Ti"    >
<!-- <TITLE>    Title of document -->
<!ELEMENT LINK - O EMPTY>
<!ATTLIST LINK
        HREF %URI #REQUIRED
        %linkExtraAttributes;
        %SDAPREF; "Linked to : #AttVal (TITLE) (URN) (HREF)>"    >
<!-- <LINK>             Link from this document          -->
<!-- <LINK HREF="...">Address of link destination        -->
<!-- <LINK URN="..."> Lasting name of destination        -->
<!-- <LINK REL=...>   Relationship to destination        -->
<!-- <LINK REV=...>   Relationship of destination to this  -->
<!-- <LINK TITLE="...">Title of destination (advisory)    -->
<!-- <LINK METHODS="...">Operations allowed (advisory)    -->
<!ELEMENT ISINDEX - O EMPTY>
<!ATTLIST ISINDEX
        %SDAPREF;
   "<Para>[Document is indexed/searchable.]</Para>">
<!-- <ISINDEX>         Document is a searchable index    -->
<!ELEMENT BASE - O EMPTY>
<!ATTLIST BASE
        HREF %URI; #REQUIRED    >
<!-- <BASE>             Base context document            -->
<!-- <BASE HREF="...">Address for this document          -->
<!ELEMENT NEXTID - O EMPTY>
<!ATTLIST NEXTID
        N %linkName #REQUIRED    >
<!-- <NEXTID>          Next ID to use for link name      -->
<!-- <NEXTID N=...>    Next ID to use for link name      -->
<!ELEMENT META - O EMPTY>
<!ATTLIST META
        HTTP-EQUIV   NAME    #IMPLIED
        NAME         NAME    #IMPLIED
        CONTENT      CDATA   #REQUIRED    >
<!-- <META>                    Generic Metainformation     -->
<!-- <META HTTP-EQUIV=...>    HTTP response header name     -->
```

```
<!-- <META HTTP-EQUIV=...>      Metainformation name           -->
<!-- <META CONTENT="...">       Associated information         -->
<!--======= Document Structure ==================-->
<![ %HTML.Deprecated [
        <!ENTITY % html.content "HEAD, BODY, PLAINTEXT?">
]]>
<!ENTITY % html.content "HEAD, BODY">
<!ELEMENT HTML O O  (%html.content)>
<!ENTITY % version.attr "VERSION CDATA #FIXED '%HTML.Version;'">
<!ATTLIST HTML
        %version.attr;
        %SDAFORM; "Book"
        >
<!-- <HTML>                            HTML Document    -->
```

Appendix E

HTML Level 3 Definition Type Document

This appendix contains the exact text of the current proposed DTD for HTML 3.0. This document is formatted in SGML, and does not make for good reading. But it is the best map to the features and support that have been proposed for HTML Level 3.

```
<!--
        html3.dtd
     Document Type Definition for the HyperText Markup Language (HTML DTD)
        Draft: Tues 21-Mar-95 10:16:50
        Author: Dave Raggett <dsr@hplb.hpl.hp.com>
        W3O is developing a testbed browser to provide practical
        experience with HTML 3.0 before it becomes a standard.
        See:  http://www.w3.org/hypertext/WWW/Arena/
```

This is an open process and comments are welcomed on the WWW-HTML mailing list. Please use the following MIME content type:

Content-Type: text/html; version=3.0

This will allow clients to distinguish HTML 3.0 from current HTML documents. This is most easily achieved by saving files with the extension ".html3" or ".ht3" so that servers can easily distinguish these files from HTML 2.0 files.

The entity HTML.Recommended can be used to give a more rigorous version of the DTD suitable for use with SGML authoring tools. The default version of the DTD offers a laxer interpretation, e.g., allowing authors to omit leading <P> elements. You can switch on the more rigorous version of the DTD by including the following at the start of your HTML document:

```
<!DOCTYPE HTML PUBLIC "-//IETF//DTD HTML 3.0//EN//"
[ <!ENTITY % HTML.Recommended "INCLUDE"> ] >
```

Design Objectives:

- Backwards compatibility with 2.0

- Tighten up HTML.Recommended and move more things to HTML.Deprecated

- Keep HTML simple—don't compete with CALS

- Make it practical for people to edit HTML 3.0 documents directly, i.e., avoid long names

- Tables, figures and math from HTML+ with tweaks based on recent experience

- Client-side event handling for figures and graphical form selection menus

- Add limited presentational controls with a view to use of linked style sheets (style overrides are supported)

- Compatibility with ICADD as per Yuri's suggestions

HTML 3.0 relies on linked style info to give authors control over the appearence of documents. Such info is placed in a linked style sheet, or as overrides in the HTML document head, using the STYLE element. The generic CLASS attribute can be used to subclass elements when you want to use a different style from normal, e.g., you might use <h2 class=bigcaps> for headers with enlarged capital letters. Note that the class attribute has a wider scope than just style changes, e.g., browsers could provide the means for searching through documents, restricting a search according to element class values.

The DTD contains a small number of attributes for direct control of basic alignment parameters: column widths for tables, support for custom bullets, sequence numbering for lists and headers, and text flow. These attributes offer control over appearance which would be inconvenient to express exclusively via associated style sheets.

The MD attribute for each hypertext or inline link specifies a message digest such as MD5 for the linked object and is needed to ensure someone hasn't tampered with a linked document.

```
-->
<!ENTITY % HTML.Version
        "-//IETF//DTD HTML 3.0//EN"
        -- Typical usage:
           <!DOCTYPE HTML PUBLIC "-//IETF//DTD HTML 3.0//EN">
           <html>
           ...
           </html>
        --
        >
<!--================== Flags for Marked Sections ==============-->

<!ENTITY % HTML.Recommended "IGNORE"
```

— Certain features of the language are necessary for compatibility with wide-spread usage, but they may compromise the structural integrity of a document. This feature test entity enables a more prescriptive document type definition that eliminates the above features.

```
     -->
<![ %HTML.Recommended [
        <!ENTITY % HTML.Deprecated "IGNORE">
]]>
<!ENTITY % HTML.Deprecated "INCLUDE"
```

— Certain features of the language are necessary for compatibility with earlier versions of the specification, but they tend to be used and implemented inconsistently, and their use is deprecated. This feature test entity enables a document type definition that eliminates these features.

```
     -->
<!ENTITY % HTML.Obsoleted "IGNORE"
```

— The XMP, LISTING and PLAINTEXT tags are incompatible with SGML and derive from very early versions of HTML. They require nonstandard parsers and will cause problems for processing documents with standard SGML tools.

```
        -->
<!--================== Imported Names ===================-->
<!ENTITY % Content-Type "CDATA"
        -- meaning a MIME content type, as per RFC1521
        -->
<!ENTITY % HTTP-Method "GET | POST"
        -- as per HTTP specification
        -->
<!ENTITY % URI "CDATA"
```

— The term URI means a CDATA attribute whose value is a Uniform Resource Identifier, as defined by "Uniform Resource Identifiers" by Tim Berners-Lee aka **http://info.cern.ch/hypertext/WWW/Addressing/URL /URI_Overview.html** aka RFC 1630. Note that CDATA attributes are limited by the LITLEN capacity (1024 in the current version of html.decl), so that URIs in HTML have a bounded length.

```
    -->
<!ENTITY % Misc.Relations "stylesheet¦node¦path">
<!ENTITY % FLOAT "CDATA" -- floating point numbers (not in SGML) -->
<!ENTITY % SHAPE "CDATA"
```

— Shape of hotzone in image. All coordinates are assumed to be numbers in the range 0 to 1 and interpreted as fractional width/height and measured from the top left corner of the associated image.

The attribute value is a string taking one of the following forms:

"default"

Used to define a default link for the figure background.

"circle x, y, r"

(x, y) define the center and r the radius.

"rect x, y, w, h"

(x, y) defines upper left, and w and h the width and height.

"polygon x1, y1, x2, y2, ..."

Given n pairs of x, y coordinates, the polygon is closed by a line linking the n'th point to the first. Intersecting polygons use the nonzero winding number rule to determine if a point lies inside the polygon.

```
    -->
<!-- 3.0 Parameter Entities -->
<!ENTITY % heading "H1¦H2¦H3¦H4¦H5¦H6">
<![ %HTML.Obsoleted [
    <!ENTITY % preformatted "PRE ¦ XMP ¦ LISTING">
]]>

<![ %HTML.Deprecated [
    <!ENTITY % list "UL ¦ OL ¦ DIR ¦ MENU">
    <!ENTITY % blockquote "BLOCKQUOTE ¦ BQ">
]]>
<!ENTITY % list "UL ¦ OL">
<!ENTITY % blockquote "BQ">
<!ENTITY % preformatted "PRE">
```

<!— The CLASS attribute is used to subclass HTML elements for rendering purposes, when used with style sheets, e.g., DSSSL lite.—>

```
<!ENTITY % attrs  -- common attributes for elements --
 'id       ID     #IMPLIED -- as target for hrefs (link ends) --
 lang      CDATA  "en.us"  -- ISO language, country code --
 class     NAMES  #IMPLIED -- for subclassing elements --'>
```

<!— SGML standard forces different NAMES for all attribute values in the same element, regardless of the attribute name! As a result, CDATA is used for the CLEAR attribute to avoid clashing with the ALIGN attribute.—>

```
<!--
```

When text flows around a figure or table in the margin, you sometimes want to start an element like a header, paragraph or list below the figure rather than alongside it. The CLEAR attribute allows you to move down unconditionally:

clear=left	move down until left margin is clear
clear=right	move down until right margin is clear
clear=all	move down until both margins are clear

Alternatively, you can decide to place the element alongside the figure just so long as there is enough room. The minimum width needed is specified as:

clear="40 en"	move down until there is at least 40 en units free
clear="100 pixels"	move down until there is at least 100 pixels free

The style sheet (or browser defaults) may provide default minimum widths for each class of block-like elements.

```
-->
<!ENTITY % needs -- Attributes for controlling text flow. Used in
headers and other elements to guarantee sufficient room --
       'clear  CDATA #IMPLIED'>

<!--
```

The following attribute may be included wherever a URL can be given:

```
md        message digest e.g. md="md5:jV2OfH+nnXHU8bnkPAad/mSQlTDZ"
```

where the digest is base64-encoded and preceded by a prefix denoting the algorithm (in this case MD5).

```
-->

<!ENTITY % url.link -- Attributes associated with URL based links --
        "md      CDATA  #IMPLIED  -- message digest for linked object --">

<!--===============Character mnemonic entities=============== -->
```

<!— The HTML list of Latin-1 entities includes the full range of characters in widely available Latin-1 fonts, and as such is a mixture of ISOlat1 and other ISO publishing symbols. —>

```
<!ENTITY % HTMLlat1 PUBLIC
  "-//IETF//ENTITIES Added Latin 1 for HTML//EN">
%HTMLlat1;

<!--===============Entities for special symbol===============-->

<!ENTITY emsp    SDATA "[emsp  ]" -- em space -->
<!ENTITY ensp    SDATA "[ensp  ]" -- en space (1/2-em) -->
<!ENTITY mdash   SDATA "[mdash ]" -- em dash -->
<!ENTITY ndash   SDATA "[ndash ]" -- en dash (1/2-em) -->
<!ENTITY nbsp    SDATA "[nbsp  ]" -- nonbreaking space -->
<!ENTITY shy     SDATA "[shy   ]" -- soft hyphen -->
<!ENTITY copy    SDATA "[copy  ]" -- copyright sign -->
<!ENTITY trade   SDATA "[trade ]" -- trademark sign -->
<!ENTITY reg     SDATA "[reg   ]" -- registered sign -->

<!--===============Entities for standard icons===============-->
```

<!— A range of standard icons such as &folder; for use in speeding up display of directory listings, etc. —>

```
<!ENTITY % HTMLicons PUBLIC
  "-//IETF//ENTITIES icons for HTML//EN">
%HTMLicons;

<!--===============Entities for math symbols===============-->

<!-- ISO subset chosen for use with the widely available Adobe math
font -->

<!ENTITY % HTMLmath PUBLIC
  "-//IETF//ENTITIES Math and Greek for HTML//EN">
%HTMLmath;

<!--===================Text Markup===================-->

<!ENTITY % font " U ¦ S ¦ TT ¦ I ¦ BIG ¦ SMALL">

<!ENTITY % phrase "EM ¦ STRONG ¦ CODE ¦ SAMP ¦ KBD ¦ VAR ¦ CITE">

<!ENTITY % misc "Q ¦ LANG ¦ AU ¦ DFN ¦ PERSON ¦ ACRONYM ¦ ABBREV ¦ INS ¦ DEL">
```

```
<!ENTITY % special "TAB ¦ MATH ¦ A ¦ IMG ¦ BR">

<!ENTITY % notmath "%font ¦ %phrase ¦ %special ¦ %misc">

<!ENTITY % text "#PCDATA ¦ SUB ¦ SUP ¦ B ¦ %notmath">


<!ENTITY % pre.exclusion "TAB¦MATH¦IMG¦BIG¦SMALL¦SUB¦SUP">

<!ELEMENT (%font¦B¦%phrase¦%misc) - - (%text)+>
<!ATTLIST (%font¦B¦%phrase¦%misc) %attrs;>

<!-- Subscripts and superscripts. The ALIGN attribute is only used for math -->

<!ELEMENT (SUB¦SUP) - - (%text)+>
<!ATTLIST (SUB¦SUP)
        %attrs;
        align (left¦center¦right) #IMPLIED
        >

<!-- Forced line break -->

<!ELEMENT BR      - O EMPTY>
<!ATTLIST BR
        %attrs;
        %needs; -- for control of text flow --
        >

<!-- Named left, center and right tab stops (independent of '\t'
char) -->

<!ELEMENT TAB - O EMPTY>
<!ATTLIST TAB
        id       ID       #IMPLIED  -- defines named tab stop --
        indent   NUMBER   0          -- en units before new tab stop --
        to       IDREF    #IMPLIED  -- jump to named tab stop --
        align    (left¦center¦right¦decimal) left
        dp       CDATA    #IMPLIED  -- decimal point e.g. dp="," --
        >

<!-==================Link Markup====================-->

<!--
```

With HTML 3.0 you can use ID attributes on most elements for named link ends. The use of the NAME attribute on anchors is deprecated.

Do we want to support arbitrary elements for link starts? This would involve adding HREF and related attributes to most elements.

```
-->

<![ %HTML.Deprecated [
    <!ENTITY % linkName "name CDATA #IMPLIED -- named link end -->
]]>

<!ENTITY % linkName "">


<!ENTITY % ToolBar "home¦toc¦index¦glossary¦copyright¦
                    up¦previous¦next¦help¦bookmark"
```

— LINK RELationship values which are used to create toolbar buttons or menu items for navigation, where toc stands for table of contents and bookmark provides for an open ended set of links, i.e., you can use multiple bookmarks for key entry points. Use the optional TITLE attribute to override default names.

```
    -->

<!ENTITY % linkType "NAME"
```

— A definitive list will be specified at a later date.

They are used

   a) by stylesheets to control how collections of html nodes are rendered into printed documents.

   b) for document-specific toolbars/menus when used with the LINK element in the document head:

        "home|toc|index|glossary|copyright|

        up|previous|next|help|bookmark"

       where toc stands for table of contents and bookmark provides for an open ended set of links, i.e., you can use several bookmarks for key entry points. Use the optional TITLE attribute to override default names.

   c) for hypertext paths or guided tours, with REL=NODE and REL=PATH.

   d) to make a link to a style sheet, e.g., rel=style (used only with the LINK element).

```
        -->


<!ENTITY % linkExtraAttributes -- URN moved to %url.link --
        "rel %linkType #IMPLIED -- forward relationship type --
        rev %linkType #IMPLIED -- reversed relationship type
```

```
                                        to referent data --
            title   CDATA #IMPLIED -- advisory only --
            methods NAMES #IMPLIED -- supported public methods of the object:
                                            TEXTSEARCH, GET, HEAD, ... --
            ">

<![ %HTML.Deprecated [
    <!ENTITY % A.content  "(%heading¦%text)+">
]]>

<!ENTITY % A.content    "(%text)+">

<!ELEMENT A      - - %A.content -(A)>

<!ATTLIST A
        %attrs;
        href   %URI;  #IMPLIED
        %url.link;      -- standard link attributes --
        %linkName;        -- name attribute is deprecated; use ID instead --
        shape %SHAPE; #IMPLIED -- for shaped hotzones in FIGs --
        %linkExtraAttributes;
        >

<!--===================Images===================-->
```

<!— Desired widths are used for negotiating image size with the module responsible for painting the image.

align=left or right causes image to float to margin and for subsequent text to wrap around image —>

```
<!ELEMENT IMG     - O EMPTY --  Embedded image -->
<!ATTLIST IMG
        %attrs;
        src %URI; #REQUIRED  -- URI of image to embed --
        %url.link;               -- standard link attributes --
        alt CDATA   #IMPLIED  -- for display in place of image --
        align  (top¦middle¦bottom¦left¦right) top -- relative to baseline
        --          width  NUMBER #IMPLIED -- desired width in en's or pixels --
        height NUMBER #IMPLIED -- desired height in en's or pixels --
        units  (en¦pixels) pixels -- units for width and height --
        ismap (ismap) #IMPLIED -- pass clicks to server --
        >

<!--===================Paragraphs===================-->

<!ELEMENT P     - O (%text)+>
<!ATTLIST P
        %attrs;
        align  (left¦center¦right¦justify) #IMPLIED
        %needs; -- for control of text flow --
        nowrap (nowrap) #IMPLIED -- disable wordwrap --
        >
```

```
<!--===============Headings, Titles, Sections================-->

<!ELEMENT HR     - O EMPTY -- customizable horizontal rule -->
<!ATTLIST HR
        %attrs;
        src     %URI;    #IMPLIED -- URI of custom rule graphic --
        %url.link;                 -- standard link attributes --
        %needs; -- for control of text flow --
        >

<!--
```

Headers can be numbered, although this is a matter for style sheets. The style sheet controls the numbering style:

a) whether the parent numbering is inherited, e.g., 5.i.c where 5 is the current sequence number for H1 headers, and 1 is the number for H2 headers and 3 for H3 headers.

b) what style is used for current sequence number, e.g., arabic, upperalpha, loweralpha, upperroman, lowerroman, or a numbering scheme appropriate for the current language.

The skip attribute is used to skip over sequence numbers for items which have been left out of the list, e.g., skip=3 advances the sequence number past 3 omitted items. The seqnum sets the sequence number to a specified value. Note that the style sheet may take advantage of the sequence number for higher level headers.

The dingbat or src attributes may be used to specify a bullet-like image to be placed adjacent to the header. Defining this in the header element simplifies the document markup and avoids the need to use the clear or needs attribute in the following element to prevent it flowing around this image.

```
-->
<!ELEMENT ( %heading )  - -  (%text;)+>
<!ATTLIST ( %heading )
        %attrs;
        align   (left¦center¦right¦justify) #IMPLIED
        %needs; -- for control of text flow --
        seqnum  NUMBER    #IMPLIED  -- starting sequence number --
        skip    NUMBER    0         -- skip seqnums for missing items --
        dingbat ENTITY    #IMPLIED  -- dingbat entity from HTMLicons --
        src     (%URI;)   #IMPLIED  -- bullet defined by graphic --
        %url.link;                  -- standard link attributes --
        nowrap  (nowrap)  #IMPLIED -- disable wordwrap --
        >

<!ELEMENT TITLE - -  (#PCDATA)
```

— The TITLE element is not considered part of the flow of text. It should be displayed, for example, as the page header or window title.

```
        -->

<!--===================Text Flows===================-->

<!ENTITY % block
      "P ¦ %list ¦ DL
         ¦ %preformatted
         ¦ %blockquote
         ¦ FORM ¦ ISINDEX ¦ FN
         ¦ TABLE ¦ FIG ¦ NOTE">

<!--
```

((%block)* | (%text)*) would be much nicer as it would avoid the need for a <P> tag when all you want is a few words of text. The problem is that it also prevents "<LI> <P>some text" since it forbids PCDATA and hence the white space between the <LI> and the <P>.

```
    -->

<![ %HTML.Recommended [
    <!ENTITY % flow "(%block)*">
]]>

<!ENTITY % flow "(%text ¦ %block)*">

<!ELEMENT PRE - - (%text)* -(%pre.exclusion)>

<!ATTLIST PRE
        %attrs;
        width NUMBER #implied
        %needs; -- for control of text flow --
        >

<![ %HTML.Obsoleted [

<!ENTITY % literal "CDATA"
```

— Special nonconforming parsing mode where the only markup signal is the end tag in full. This will cause problems for standard SGML tools!

```
        -->

<!ELEMENT XMP - - %literal>
<!ELEMENT LISTING - - %literal>
<!ELEMENT PLAINTEXT - O %literal>

]]>
```

```
<!--====================Lists====================-->

<!ELEMENT DL     - -  (LH?, (DT|DD)+) -- this is perhaps too lax? -->
<!ATTLIST DL
        %attrs;
        %needs; -- for control of text flow --
        compact (compact) #IMPLIED -- more compact style --
        >

<!ELEMENT DT     - O  (%text)+>
<!ELEMENT DD     - O  %flow;>
<!ATTLIST (DT|DD)
        %attrs;
        %needs; -- for control of text flow --
        >


<!ELEMENT (OL|UL) - -  (LH?, LI+) -- should we allow a list header ? -->
```

<!— Style sheet controls numbering style

    a) whether the parent numbering is inherited, e.g. 5.1.c.

    b) what style is used for current sequence number, e.g. arabic, upperalpha, loweralpha, upperroman, lowerroman, or a numbering scheme for the current language.

```
-->
<!ATTLIST OL
  %attrs;
  %needs; -- for control of text flow --
  continue (continue)  #IMPLIED   -- don't restart sequence number --
  seqnum    NUMBER      #IMPLIED   -- starting sequence number --
  compact (compact)     #IMPLIED   -- reduced interitem spacing --
  >
```

<!— Unordered lists:

■ single or multicolumn with horizontal or vertical wrapping

■ plain or bulleted list items

■ bullets can be customised via:

    - entities (dingbats in HTMLicons)

    - external graphic via URL

    - individual attributes on LI tags

```
-->
<!ATTLIST UL
```

```
        %attrs;
        %needs; -- for control of text flow --
        wrap (vert¦horiz¦none) none -- multicolumn list style --
        plain   (plain)  #IMPLIED   -- suppress bullets --
        dingbat  ENTITY  #IMPLIED   -- dingbat entity from HTMLicons --
        src      (%URI;)  #IMPLIED  -- bullet defined by graphic --
        %url.link;                  -- standard link attributes --
        compact (compact) #IMPLIED  -- reduced interitem spacing --
        >

<!ELEMENT LH - O (%text;)+ -- list header -->
<!ATTLIST LH %attrs;>

<!--
```

For unordered lists, you can override the standard bullet with a custom
graphic specified via a URI, e.g., src="splash.gif" or a reference to one of the
HTMLicons graphics, e.g., dingbat=folder. The skip attribute is used with
ordered lists to skip over sequence numbers for items which have been left
out of the list, e.g., skip=3 advances the sequence number past 3 omitted
items.

```
        -->

<!ELEMENT LI - O %flow; -- list item -->
<!ATTLIST LI
        %attrs;
        %needs; -- for control of text flow --
        dingbat ENTITY #IMPLIED -- dingbat entity from HTMLicons --
        src (%URI;) #IMPLIED    -- custom bullet graphic --
        %url.link;              -- standard link attributes --
        skip NUMBER 0           -- skip seq nums for missing items --
        >
```

<!-- DIR and MENU are now subsumed by UL with type=plain. Use the wrap
attribute to control wrapping style for multicolumn lists. -->

```
<![ %HTML.Deprecated [
    <!ELEMENT (DIR¦MENU) - - (LI)+ -(%block)>
    <!ATTLIST (DIR¦MENU)
        compact (compact) #IMPLIED>
]]>


<!--===================Document Body====================-->

<![ %HTML.Recommended [
        <!ENTITY % body.content "(DIV¦%heading¦%block¦HR¦ADDRESS)*"
        -- <h1>Heading</h1>
          <p>Text ...
                is preferred to
          <h1>Heading</h1>
          Text ...
        -->
]]>
```

```
<!ENTITY % body.content "(DIV ¦ %heading ¦ %text ¦ %block ¦ HR ¦ ADDRESS)*">

<!ELEMENT BODY O O  (BANNER?, %body.content) +(SPOT)>
<!ATTLIST BODY
        %attrs;
        background %URI; #IMPLIED  -- texture tile for document background --
        >
```

```
<!--
```

The BANNER element is used for a banner section which appears at the top of the window and doesn't scroll with window contents. This can be used for corporate logos, copyright statements and disclaimers, as well as customized navigation/search controls.

```
      -->
<!ELEMENT BANNER - - %body.content>
<!ATTLIST BANNER %attrs; >

<!-- SPOT is used to insert IDs at arbitrary places
     e.g. for end points of a marked range (see RANGE) -->
<!ELEMENT SPOT - O EMPTY>
<!ATTLIST SPOT id ID #REQUIRED>

<!ELEMENT (%blockquote) - - (%body.content, CREDIT?)>
<!ATTLIST (%blockquote)
        %attrs;
        %needs; -- for control of text flow --
        nowrap   (nowrap)  #IMPLIED -- disable wordwrap --
        >

<!ENTITY % address.content "((%text;)* ¦ P*)">

<!ELEMENT ADDRESS - - %address.content>
<!ATTLIST ADDRESS
        %attrs;
        %needs; -- for control of text flow --
        >
```

```
<!--
```

DIV can be used with the CLASS attribute to represent different kinds of containers, e.g., chapter, section, abstract, appendix.

```
      -->

<!ELEMENT DIV - - %body.content>
<!ATTLIST DIV
        %attrs;
```

```
        %needs; -- for control of text flow --
        align   (left¦center¦right) left -- alignment of following text --
        nowrap  (nowrap)  #IMPLIED -- disable wordwrap --
        >

  <!--====================Forms====================-->

  <!--
```

As HTML 2.0 plus a few extensions:

a) A RANGE control which varies between a pair of values specified with the size attribute, e.g., SIZE="1, 10"

b) FILE widget for uploading one or more files to a server

c) SCRIBBLE on image widget that sends the "ink" to the server

d) AUDIO widget for playing and recording audio samples

e) SUBMIT/RESET buttons can now be customized with an image. This subsumes the IMAGE type which is now deprecated.

f) Graphical SELECTion menus are now supported, using the new SHAPE attribute on OPTION elements.

Further extensions are in the pipeline (e.g., table entry, multiple data formats for TEXTAREA fields and client-side scripts with custom widgets) but will have to wait until the backlog of implementation work diminishes.

```
        -->

  <!ELEMENT FORM - - %body.content -(FORM) +(INPUT¦SELECT¦TEXTAREA)>
  <!ATTLIST FORM
          action %URI #REQUIRED -- server-side form handler --
          method (%HTTP-Method) GET -- see HTTP specification --
          enctype %Content-Type; "application/x-www-form-urlencoded"
          script %URI #IMPLIED -- link to client-side script --
          >

  <![ %HTML.Deprecated [
      <!ENTITY % InputType "(TEXT ¦ PASSWORD ¦ CHECKBOX ¦ RADIO ¦ SUBMIT ¦ RESET
                  ¦ RANGE ¦ AUDIO ¦ FILE ¦ SCRIBBLE ¦ HIDDEN ¦ IMAGE)">
  ]]>

  <!ENTITY % InputType "(TEXT ¦ PASSWORD ¦ CHECKBOX ¦ RADIO ¦ SUBMIT ¦ RESET
                  ¦ RANGE ¦ AUDIO ¦ FILE ¦ SCRIBBLE ¦ HIDDEN)">

  <!ELEMENT INPUT - O EMPTY>
  <!ATTLIST INPUT
        %attrs;
        type %InputType TEXT
        name  CDATA #IMPLIED       -- required for all but submit and reset --
```

IX

Appendixes

```
     value CDATA #IMPLIED
     src   %URI  #IMPLIED        -- for fields with background images --
     %url.link;                  -- standard link attributes --
     checked (checked) #IMPLIED -- for radio buttons and check boxes --
     size CDATA #IMPLIED    -- like NUMBERS,
                                        but delimited with comma, not space --
     maxlength NUMBER #IMPLIED
     align  (top¦middle¦bottom¦left¦right) top
     >

<!--
```

SRC attribute added for graphical selection menus. The WIDTH, HEIGHT and UNITS attributes apply to the image specified by the SRC attribute.

```
  -->

<!ELEMENT SELECT - - (OPTION+) -(INPUT¦TEXTAREA¦SELECT)>
<!ATTLIST SELECT
     %attrs;
     name CDATA #REQUIRED
     multiple (multiple) #IMPLIED
     src  %URI  #IMPLIED    -- for graphical selection menus --
     %url.link;             -- standard link attributes --
     width  NUMBER #IMPLIED -- desired width in en's or pixels --
     height NUMBER #IMPLIED -- desired height in en's or pixels --
     units  (en¦pixels) pixels -- units for width and height --
     align  (top¦middle¦bottom¦left¦right) top
     >

<!ELEMENT OPTION - O (#PCDATA)>
<!ATTLIST OPTION
     %attrs;
     selected (selected) #IMPLIED
     value  CDATA  #IMPLIED -- default to element content --
     shape %SHAPE; #IMPLIED -- for graphical selection menus --
     >

<!--
```

Multiline text input field. Align=left or right causes the field to float to the margin and for subsequent text to wrap around the field.

```
  -->

<!ELEMENT TEXTAREA - - (#PCDATA) -(INPUT¦TEXTAREA¦SELECT)>
<!ATTLIST TEXTAREA
     %attrs;
     name CDATA #REQUIRED
     rows NUMBER #REQUIRED
     cols NUMBER #REQUIRED
     align  (top¦middle¦bottom¦left¦right) top
     >
```

```
<!--===================Captions===================-->

<!ELEMENT CAPTION - - (%text;)+ -- table or figure caption -->
<!ATTLIST CAPTION
         %attrs;
         align (top|bottom|left|right) #IMPLIED
         >
<!--===================Tables===================-->

<!--
```

Tables and figures can be aligned in several ways:

bleedleft	flush left with the left (window) border
left	flush left with the left text margin
center	centered (text flow is disabled for this mode)
right	flush right with the right text margin
bleedright	flush right with the right (window) border
justify	when applicable the table/figure should stretch to fill space between the text margins

Note:

Text will flow around the table or figure if the browser judges there is enough room and the alignment is not centered or justified. The table or figure may itself be part of the text flow around some earlier figure. You can in this case use the clear or needs attributes to move the new table or figure down the page beyond the obstructing earlier figure. Similarly, you can use the clear or needs attributes with other elements such as headers and lists to move them further down the page.

```
-->

<!ENTITY % block.align
         "align  (bleedleft|left|center|right|bleedright|justify) center">

<!--
```

The HTML 3.0 table model has been chosen for its simplicity and the ease in writing filters from common DTP packages.

By default the table is automatically sized according to the cell contents and the current window size. Specifying the column widths using the colspec attribute allows browsers to start displaying the table without having to wait for the last row.

The colspec attribute is a list of column widths and alignment specifications. The columns are listed from left to right with a capital letter followed by a number, e.g., COLSPEC="L20 C8 L40". The letter is L for left, C for center, and R for right alignment of cell contents. J is for justification, when feasible; otherwise this is treated in the same way as L for left alignment. Column entries are delimited by one or more space characters.

The number specifies the width in en's, pixels or as a fractional value of the table width, as according to the associated units attribute. This approach is more compact than the one used with most SGML table models and chosen to simplify hand entry. The width attribute allows you to specify the width of the table in pixels, en units, or as a percentage of the space between the current left and right margins.

To assist with rendering to speech, row and column headers can be given short names using the AXIS attribute. The AXIS attribute is used to explicitly specify the row and column names for use with each cell. Otherwise browsers can follow up columns and left along rows (right for some languages) to find the corresponding header cells.

Table content model: Braille limits the width of tables, placing severe limits on column widths. User agents need to render big cells by moving the content to a note placed before the table. The cell is then rendered as a link to the corresponding note.

To assist with formatting tables to paged media, authors can differentiate leading and trailing rows that are to be duplicated when splitting tables across page boundaries. The recommended way is to subclass rows with the CLASS attribute. For example: <TR CLASS=Header>, <TR CLASS=Footer> are used for header and footer rows. Paged browsers insert footer rows at the bottom of the current page and header rows at the top of the new page, followed by the remaining body rows.

```
-->

<!ELEMENT TABLE - - (CAPTION?, TR*) -- mixed headers and data -->
<!ATTLIST TABLE
        %attrs;
        %needs; -- for control of text flow --
        border (border) #IMPLIED -- draw borders --
        colspec CDATA   #IMPLIED -- column widths and alignment --
        units   (en¦pixels¦relative) en -- units for column widths --
        dp      CDATA   #IMPLIED -- decimal point e.g. dp="," --
        width NUMBER    #IMPLIED -- absolute or percentage width --
        %block.align;   -- horizontal alignment --
        noflow (noflow) #IMPLIED -- noflow around table --
        nowrap (nowrap) #IMPLIED -- don't wrap words --
        >
```

```
<!ENTITY % cell      "TH ¦ TD">
<!ENTITY % horiz.align "left¦center¦right¦justify">
<!ENTITY % vert.align  "top¦middle¦bottom¦baseline">

<!--
```

Browsers should tolerate an omission of the first <TR> tag as it is implied by the context. Missing trailing <TR>s implied by rowspans should be ignored.

The alignment attributes act as defaults for rows overriding the colspec attribute and being in turn overridden by alignment attributes on cell elements. Use valign=baseline when you want to ensure that text in different cells on the same row is aligned on the same baseline regardless of fonts. It only applies when the cells contain a single line of text.

```
-->

<!ELEMENT TR - O (%cell)* -- row container -->
<!ATTLIST TR
        %attrs;
        align  (%horiz.align) #IMPLIED -- horizontal alignment --
        valign (%vert.align)  top  -- vertical alignment --
        dp     CDATA    #IMPLIED  -- decimal point e.g. dp="," --
        nowrap (nowrap)  #IMPLIED  -- don't wrap words --
        >

<!--
```

Note that table cells can include nested tables. Missing cells are considered to be empty, while missing rows should be ignored, i.e., if a cell spans a row and there are no further TR elements then the implied row should be ignored.

```
-->

<!ELEMENT (%cell) - O %body.content>
<!ATTLIST (%cell)
        %attrs;
        colspan NUMBER    1       -- columns spanned --
        rowspan NUMBER    1       -- rows spanned --
        align  (%horiz.align) #IMPLIED -- horizontal alignment --
        valign (%vert.align) top -- vertical alignment --
        dp       CDATA    #IMPLIED  -- decimal point e.g. dp="," --
        nowrap (nowrap)  #IMPLIED  -- don't wrap words --
        axis CDATA #IMPLIED -- axis name, defaults to element content --
        axes CDATA #IMPLIED -- comma-separated list of axis names --
        >

<!--===================Figures====================-->

<!--
```

The element contains text for use in nongraphical displays. Note that you can use the shape attribute in anchors to specify hotzones on images. This provides for local processing of pointer clicks and a unified method for dealing with graphical and nongraphical displays.

Text is flowed around figures when the figure is left- or right-aligned. You can request the browser to move down until there is enough room for the next element—see the CLEAR and NEED attributes (in %needs).

Figures offer a path towards embedding arbitrary information formats via some kind of OLE/OpenDoc mechanism.

```
-->

<!ELEMENT FIG - - (OVERLAY*, CAPTION?, %body.content;, CREDIT?) -(FIG|IMG)>
<!ATTLIST FIG
        %attrs;
        %needs;                     -- for control of text flow --
        src  %URI;  #REQUIRED       -- URI of document to embed --
        %url.link;                  -- standard link attributes --
        %block.align;               -- horizontal alignment --
        noflow (noflow) #IMPLIED    -- noflow around figure --
        width NUMBER #IMPLIED       -- desired width in units --
        height NUMBER #IMPLIED      -- desired height in units --
        units (en|pixels) pixels    -- specifies units as en's or pixels --
        imagemap (%URI) #IMPLIED    -- pass background clicks to server --
        >

<!--
```

Figure overlays. When combined with local caching, overlays provide a cheap way of modifying a larger base image sent as part of a previous page.

```
-->

<!ELEMENT OVERLAY - O EMPTY -- image overlay -->
<!ATTLIST OVERLAY
        src  %URI;  #REQUIRED      -- URI of image overlay --
        %url.link;                 -- standard link attributes --
        units (en|pixels) pixels   -- specifies units as en's or pixels --
        x        NUMBER   0        -- offset from left in units --
        y        NUMBER   0        -- offset from top in units --
        width  NUMBER #IMPLIED     -- desired width in units --
        height NUMBER #IMPLIED     -- desired height in units --
        imagemap (%URI) #IMPLIED   -- pass background clicks to server --
        >

<!ELEMENT CREDIT - - (%text;)* -- source of image -->
<!ATTLIST CREDIT
        %attrs;
        >
```

```
<!--===================Notes====================-->

<!--
```

The NOTE element is used for admonishments. The CLASS attribute is used to differentiate NOTEs, e.g., Note, Caution, or Warning.

```
-->

<!ELEMENT NOTE - - %body.content; -- admonishment -->
<!ATTLIST NOTE
        %attrs;
        src %URI;    #IMPLIED  -- URI of custom graphic --
        %url.link;             -- standard link attributes --
        %needs; -- for control of text flow --
        >

<!--==================Footnotes===================-->

<!--
```

Typically rendered as popup note. These elements are referenced by hypertext links specified with the anchor element.

```
-->
<!ELEMENT FN - - %body.content;>
<!ATTLIST FN %attrs;>

<!--=================Math====================-->

<!-- Use     etc for greater control of spacing. -->

<!-- Subscripts and Superscripts

  <SUB> and <SUP> are used for subscripts and superscripts.

                                       i j
      X <SUP>i</SUP>Y<SUP>j</SUP>  is  X Y
```

i.e., the space following the X makes the binding clear. The align attribute can be used for horizontal alignment, e.g., to explicitly place an index above an element:

```
                                         i
      X<sup align=center>i</sup>  produces  X
```

Short references are defined for superscripts, subscripts and boxes to save typing when manually editing HTML math, e.g.:

x^2^ is mapped to x²

y_z_ is mapped to y_z

{a+b} is mapped to <box>a + b</box>

Note that these only apply within the MATH element and can't be used in normal text!

```
-->
<!ENTITY REF1    STARTTAG    "SUP">
<!ENTITY REF2    ENDTAG      "SUP">
<!ENTITY REF3    STARTTAG    "SUB">
<!ENTITY REF4    ENDTAG      "SUB">
<!ENTITY REF5    STARTTAG    "BOX">
<!ENTITY REF6    ENDTAG      "BOX">

<!USEMAP MAP1    MATH>
<!USEMAP MAP2    SUP>
<!USEMAP MAP3    SUB>
<!USEMAP MAP4    BOX>

<!SHORTREF MAP1  "^" REF1
                 "_" REF3
                 "{" REF5 >

<!SHORTREF MAP2  "^" REF2
                 "_" REF3
                 "{" REF5 >

<!SHORTREF MAP3  "_" REF4
                 "^" REF1
                 "{" REF5 >

<!SHORTREF MAP4  "}" REF6
                 "^" REF1
                 "_" REF3
                 "{" REF5 >

<!--
```

The inclusion of %math and exclusion of %notmath is used here to alter the content model for the B, SUB and SUP elements, to limit them to formulae rather than general text elements.

```
-->

<!ENTITY % mathvec "VEC¦BAR¦DOT¦DDOT¦HAT¦TILDE" -- common accents -->
<!ENTITY % mathface "B¦T¦BT" -- control of font face -->
<!ENTITY % math "BOX¦ABOVE¦BELOW¦%mathvec¦ROOT¦SQRT¦ARRAY¦SUB¦SUP¦%mathface">
<!ENTITY % formula "#PCDATA¦%math">

<!ELEMENT MATH - - (#PCDATA)* -(%notmath) +(%math)>
<!ATTLIST MATH
     id      ID      #IMPLIED
     model   CDATA   #IMPLIED>
```

<!— The BOX element acts as brackets. Delimiters are optional and stretch to match the height of the box. The OVER element is used when you want a line between numerator and denominator. This line is suppressed with the alternative ATOP element. CHOOSE acts like ATOP but adds enclosing round brackets as a convenience for binomial coefficients. Note the use of { and } as shorthand for <BOX> and </BOX> respectively:

$$1 + X$$

{1 + X<OVER>Y} is _____

$$Y$$

$$a + b$$

{a + b<ATOP>c – d} is

$$c – d$$

The delimiters are represented using the LEFT and RIGHT elements, as in:

{[<LEFT>x + y<RIGHT>]} is [x + y]

{(<LEFT>a<RIGHT>]} is (a]

{||<LEFT>a<RIGHT>||} is || a ||

Use { and } for "{" and "}" respectively as these symbols are used as shorthand for BOX, e.g.:

{{<LEFT>a+b<RIGHT>}} is {a+b}

You can stretch definite integrals to match the integrand, e.g.:

{∫_a^b<LEFT>{f(x)<over>1+x} dx}

```
    b
    /  f(x)
    ¦  ---- dx
    / 1 + x
    a
```

Note the complex content model for BOX is a work around for the absence of support for infix operators in SGML.

You can get oversize delimiters with the SIZE attribute, for example <BOX SIZE=large>(<LEFT>...<RIGHT>)</BOX>

Note that the names of common functions are recognized by the parser without the need to use "&" and ";" around them, e.g., int, sum, sin, cos, tan, ...

```
-->

<!ELEMENT BOX - - ((%formula)*, (LEFT, (%formula)*)?,
                   ((OVER¦ATOP¦CHOOSE), (%formula)*)?,
                   (RIGHT, (%formula)*)?)>
<!ATTLIST BOX
        size  (normal¦medium¦large¦huge) normal -- oversize delims -->

<!ELEMENT (OVER¦ATOP¦CHOOSE¦LEFT¦RIGHT) - O EMPTY>

<!-- Horizontal line drawn ABOVE contents
```

The symbol attribute allows authors to supply an entity name for an accent, arrow symbol, etc. Generalization of LaTeX's overline command.

```
-->

<!ELEMENT ABOVE - - (%formula)+>
<!ATTLIST ABOVE symbol ENTITY #IMPLIED>

<!-- Horizontal line drawn BELOW contents
```

The symbol attribute allows authors to supply an entity name for an arrow symbol, etc. Generalization of LaTeX's underline command.

```
-->

<!ELEMENT BELOW - - (%formula)+>
<!ATTLIST BELOW symbol ENTITY #IMPLIED>

<!-- Convenience tags for common accents:
     vec, bar, dot, ddot, hat and tilde
-->

<!ELEMENT (%mathvec) - - (%formula)+>

<!--
```

T and BT are used to designate terms which should be rendered in an upright font (& boldface for BT)

```
-->

<!ELEMENT (T¦BT) - - (%formula)+>
<!ATTLIST (T¦BT) class NAMES #IMPLIED>

<!-- Roots  e.g. <ROOT>3<OF>1+x</ROOT> -->

<!ELEMENT ROOT - - ((%formula)+, OF, (%formula)+)>
<!ELEMENT OF - O (%formula)* -- what the root applies to -->

<!ELEMENT SQRT - - (%formula)* -- square root convenience tag -->
```

<!— LaTeX-like arrays. The COLDEF attribute specifies a single capital letter for each column determining how the column should be aligned, e.g., coldef="CCC"

"L"	left
"C"	center
"R"	right

An optional separator letter can occur between columns and should be one of +, –, or =, e.g., "C+C+C+C=C". Whitespace within coldef is ignored. By default, the columns are all centered.

The ALIGN attribute alters the vertical position of the array as compared with preceding and following expressions.

Use LDELIM and RDELIM attributes for delimiter entities. When the LABELS attribute is present, the array is displayed with the first row and the first column as labels displaced from the other elements. In this case, the first element of the first row should normally be left blank.

Use &vdots; &cdots; and &ddots; for vertical, horizontal, and diagonal ellipsis dots. Use &dotfill; to fill an array cell with horizontal dots (e.g., for a full row). Note &ldots; places the dots on the baseline, while &cdots; places them higher up.

```
    -->
    <!ELEMENT ARRAY - - (ROW)+>
    <!ATTLIST ARRAY
        align (top¦middle¦bottom) middle -- vertical alignment --
        coldef  CDATA    #IMPLIED  -- column alignment and separator --
        ldelim  NAMES    #IMPLIED  -- stretchy left delimiter --
        rdelim  NAMES    #IMPLIED  -- stretchy right delimiter --
        labels (labels) #IMPLIED  -- TeX's \bordermatrix style -->

    <!ELEMENT ROW - O (ITEM)*>
    <!ELEMENT ITEM - O (%formula)*>
    <!ATTLIST ITEM
        align   CDATA  #IMPLIED  -- override coldef alignment --
        colspan NUMBER 1         -- merge columns as per TABLE --
        rowspan NUMBER 1         -- merge rows as per TABLE -->

    <!--====================Document Head====================-->

    <![ %HTML.Deprecated [
       <!ENTITY % head.content "TITLE & ISINDEX? & BASE? & STYLE?
                                & META* & LINK* & RANGE* & NEXTID?">
    ]]>
```

```
<!ENTITY % head.nextid "">

<!ENTITY % head.content "TITLE & ISINDEX? & BASE? & STYLE
                                & META* & LINK* & RANGE*">

<!ELEMENT HEAD O O  (%head.content)>

<!ELEMENT LINK - O EMPTY>
<!ATTLIST LINK
        href %URI #REQUIRED
        %linkExtraAttributes; >

<!ELEMENT RANGE - O EMPTY>
<!ATTLIST RANGE
        id     ID    #IMPLIED  -- for naming marked range --
        class CDATA #IMPLIED  -- for subclassing --
        from   IDREF #REQUIRED -- start of marked range --
        until IDREF #REQUIRED -- end of marked range --
        >

<!ELEMENT ISINDEX - O EMPTY>
<!ATTLIST ISINDEX
        href   %URI  #IMPLIED -- server handling queries --
        prompt CDATA #IMPLIED -- prompt message -->

<!--
```

The BASE element gives the base URL for dereferencing relative URLs, e.g.:

```
    <BASE href="http://foo.com/images">
    ...
    <IMG SRC="bar.gif">

The image is dereferenced to

    http://foo.com/images/bar.gif
-->

<!ELEMENT BASE - O EMPTY>
<!ATTLIST BASE
        id     ID    #IMPLIED
        href %URI; #REQUIRED
        >

<![ %HTML.Deprecated [
    <!ELEMENT NEXTID - O EMPTY>
    <!ATTLIST NEXTID N CDATA #REQUIRED>
]]>

<!ELEMENT META - O EMPTY      -- Generic Metainformation -->
<!ATTLIST META
        http-equiv  NAME    #IMPLIED  -- HTTP response header name  --
        name        NAME    #IMPLIED  -- metainformation name       --
        content     CDATA   #REQUIRED -- associated information      --
        >

<!--
```

A style sheet can be associated with the document using the LINK element, e.g., <LINK rel=style href="housestyle.dsssl">. Style overrides can be placed in the document head using the STYLE element, e.g.:

```
<style notation=dsssl-lite>
    dsss-lite stuff
</style>
```

Later on in the document you can use:

```
<h2 class=bigcaps>Header with bigger than normal capitals</h2>
<p class=abstract>A paragraph with a unique style of its own
...
```

Statements in the given style notation.

The tag names, class and id attributes are used in the style sheet notation to describe how to render matching elements.

```
    -->

    <!ENTITY % style-notations "dsssl-lite | w3c-style">
    <!NOTATION dsssl-lite PUBLIC
        "ISO/IEC 10179:1995//NOTATION DSSSL Style Language//EN">

    <!NOTATION w3c-style PUBLIC "-//IETF//W3C Style Language//EN">

    <!ELEMENT STYLE - O (#PCDATA)>
    <!ATTLIST STYLE
        notation NOTATION (%style-notations;) #REQUIRED
    >

    <!--===================Document Structure===================-->

    <!ENTITY % html.content "HEAD, BODY">

    <!ELEMENT HTML O O  (%html.content)>
    <!ENTITY % version.attr 'VERSION CDATA #FIXED "%HTML.Version;"'>

    <!-- suggested roles are: TOC, DOC, DOCPART, HITLIST, DIALOG -->

    <!ATTLIST HTML
            %version.attr;          -- report DTD version to application --
            urn  CDATA    #IMPLIED  -- universal resource name for this document --
            role NAMES    #IMPLIED  -- role of this document, e.g. table of contents --
            >

    <!-- The END -->
```

The Bare Bones Guide to HTML

This guide was prepared by Kevin Webach © 1995 and is redistributed with his permission. You can get updates to this guide at **http://www.access.digex.net/~werbach/barbone.html**.

```
SYMBOLS USED
-----------------------------------------------------------------------
URL URL of an external file (or just file name if in the same directory)
?   Arbitrary number (i.e. <H?> means <H1>, <H2>, <H3>, etc.)
%   Arbitrary percentage (i.e. <HR WIDTH=%> means <HR WIDTH=50%>, etc.)
*** Arbitrary text (i.e. ALT="***" means fill in with text)
$$$ Arbitrary hex (i.e. BGCOLOR="#$$$" means BGCOLOR="#00FF1C", etc.)
¦   Alternatives (i.e. ALIGN=LEFT¦RIGHT¦CENTER means pick one of the three)


COMPATIBILITY (As of 3/29/95; remember that HTML is constantly evolving)
-----------------------------------------------------------------------
        (no notation) In the HTML 2.0 spec; should work on all browsers
N1.0    Probably works only in Netscape 1.0N and later versions
N1.1    Probably works only in Netscape 1.1b1 and later versions
3.0     Proposed HTML 3.0 tag; may work in some browsers


=======================================================================
=======================================================================


GENERAL   (all HTML documents should have these)
-----------------------------------------------------------------------
    Document type    <HTML></HTML>      (beginning and end of file)
    Title            <TITLE></TITLE>    (document name; must be in header)
    Header           <HEAD></HEAD>      (descriptive info, such as title)
    Body             <BODY></BODY>      (bulk of the page)
```

```
HARD FORMATTING  (user specifies text appearance)
------------------------------------------------------------------------
         Bold           <B></B>
         Italic         <I></I>
3.0      Underline      <U></U>                (not widely implemented yet)
3.0      Strikeout      <S></S>                (not widely implemented yet)
         Typewriter     <TT></TT>              (display in a monospaced font)
N1.0     Blinking       <BLINK></BLINK>        (the most derided tag ever)


SOFT FORMATTING  (controlled by the browser's style definitions)
------------------------------------------------------------------------
      Headings          <H?></H?>              (the spec. defines 6 levels)
      Emphasis          <EM></EM>              (usually displayed as italic)
      Strong Emphasis   <STRONG></STRONG>      (usually displayed as bold)
      Preformatted      <PRE></PRE>            (display text as-is)
      Width             <PRE WIDTH=?></PRE>    (in characters)
      Pre/No Tags       <XMP></XMP>            (like PRE but no embedded tags)
      Citation          <CITE></CITE>          (usually italics)
      Code              <CODE></CODE>          (for source code listings)
      Sample Output     <SAMP></SAMP>
      Keyboard Input    <KBD></KBD>
      Variable          <VAR></VAR>
      Definition        <DFN></DFN>            (not widely implemented)
N1.0  Font Size         <FONT SIZE=?></FONT>   (ranges from 1-7)
N1.0  Base Font Size    <BASEFONT SIZE=?>      (from 1-7; default is 3)


ALIGNMENT
------------------------------------------------------------------------
         Block indent   <BLOCKQUOTE></BLOCKQUOTE>
N1.0     Center         <CENTER></CENTER>         (for both text and images)
3.0      Align text     <P ALIGN=LEFT¦CENTER¦RIGHT></P>
3.0      Align heading  <H? ALIGN=LEFT¦CENTER¦RIGHT></H?>


LINKS AND GRAPHICS
------------------------------------------------------------------------
      Link something    <A HREF="URL"></A>
      Link to target    <A HREF="URL#***"></A>    (If in another document)
                        <A HREF="#***"></A>       (If in current document)
      Define target     <A NAME="***"></A>
      Display Image     <IMG SRC="URL">
      Alignment         <IMG SRC="URL" ALIGN=TOP¦BOTTOM¦MIDDLE>
N1.0  Alignment         <IMG SRC="RUL" ALIGN=LEFT¦RIGHT¦TEXTTOP¦ABSMIDDLE¦
                        BASELINE¦ABSBOTTOM>
      Alternate         <IMG SRC="URL" ALT="***"> (if image not displayed)
      Imagemap          <IMG SRC="URL" ISMAP)   (requires a script)
N1.0  Dimensions        <IMG SRC="URL" WIDTH="?" HEIGHT="?">   (in pixels)
N1.0  Border            <IMG SRC="URL" BORDER=?>                (in pixels)
N1.0  Runaround Space   <IMG SRC="URL" HSPACE=? VSPACE=?>       (in pixels)
N1.0  Low-Res Proxy     <IMG SRC="URL" LOWSRC="URL">
```

```
DIVIDERS
-----------------------------------------------------------------
     Paragraph         <P>              (a double return)
     Line Break        <BR>             (a single carriage return)
N1.0 Clear textwrap    <BR CLEAR=LEFT|RIGHT|ALL
     Horizontal Rule   <HR>
N1.0 Alignment         <HR ALIGN=LEFT|RIGHT|CENTER>
N1.0 Thickness         <HR SIZE=?>  (in pixels)
N1.0 Width             <HR WIDTH=?>  (in pixels)
N1.0 Width Percent     <HR WIDTH=%>  (as a percentage of page width)
N1.0 Solid Line        <HR NOSHADE>  (without the 3D cutout look)
N1.0 No Break          <NOBR>           (prevents line breaks)
N1.0 Word Break        <WBR>            (where to break a line if needed)


LISTS   (lists can be nested)
-----------------------------------------------------------------
     Unordered List  <UL><LI></UL>        (<LI> before each list item)
N1.0 Bullet Type      <UL TYPE=DISC|CIRCLE|SQUARE>  (for the whole list)
                      <LI TYPE=DISC|CIRCLE|SQUARE>  (this & subsequent)
     Ordered List    <OL><LI></OL>        (<LI> before each list item)
N1.0 Outline Type     <OL TYPE=A|a|I|i|1>      (for the whole list)
                      <LI TYPE=A|a|I|i|1>      (this & subsequent)
N1.0 Starting number <OL VALUE=?>            (for the whole list)
                      <LI VALUE=?>            (this & subsequent)
     Definition List <DL><DT><DD></DL>  (<DT>-term, <DD>-definition)
     Menu List       <MENU><LI></MENU>  (<LI> before each list item)
     Directory List  <DIR><LI></DIR>    (<LI> before each list item)


BACKGROUNDS AND COLORS
-----------------------------------------------------------------
N1.1 Bkground Color <BODY BGCOLOR="#$$$">    (order is red/green/blue)
N1.1 Texture        <BODY BACKGROUND="URL">
N1.1 Text Color     <BODY TEXT="#$$$">
N1.1 Link Color     <BODY LINK="#$$$">
N1.1 Visited Link   <BODY VLINK="#$$$">
N1.1 Active Link    <BODY ALINK="#$$$">


SPECIAL CHARACTERS  (these must all be in lower case)
-----------------------------------------------------------------
     ASCII code      &#?;                (where ? is the ASCII code)
     <               &lt;
     >               &gt;
     &               &amp;
     "               &quot;
     Registered      &#174;
N1.0 Registered TM   &reg;
     Copyright       &#169;
N1.0 Copyright       &copy;
(Complete list at http://www.w3.org/hypertext/WWW/MarkUp/Entities.html)
```

```
FORMS   (generally require a script on your server)
- - - - - - - - - - - - - - - - - - - - - - - - - - - - - - - - - - - - - - - - - - - - - -
        Define Form       <FORM ACTION="URL" METHOD=GET¦POST></FORM>
        Input field       <INPUT TYPE="TEXT¦PASSWORD¦CHECKBOX¦RADIO¦
                          SUBMIT¦RESET">
         Field name       <INPUT NAME="***">
         Checked?         <INPUT CHECKED>   (checkboxes and radio boxes)
         Field size       <INPUT SIZE=?>        (in characters)
         Max Length       <INPUT MAXLENGTH=?>   (in characters)
        Selection List    <SELECT></SELECT>
         Name of List     <SELECT NAME="***"></SELECT>
         # of Options     <SELECT SIZE=?></SELECT>
         Multiple Choice  <SELECT MULTIPLE>      (can select more than one)
        Option            <OPTION>              (items that can be selected)
         Default Option   <OPTION SELECTED>
        Input box size    <TEXTAREA ROWS=? COLS=?></TEXTAREA>
         Name of box      <TEXTAREA NAME="***"></TEXTAREA>


TABLES
- - - - - - - - - - - - - - - - - - - - - - - - - - - - - - - - - - - - - - - - - - - - - -
3.0   Define Table    <TABLE></TABLE>
3.0   Table Border    <TABLE BORDER></TABLE>     (either on or off)
N1.1  Table Border    <TABLE BORDER=?></TABLE>  (you can set the value)
N1.1  Cell Spacing    <TABLE CELLSPACING=?>
N1.1  Cell Padding    <TABLE CELLPADDING=?>
N1.1  Desired width   <TABLE WIDTH=?>            (in pixels)
N1.1  Width percent   <TABLE WIDTH=%>            (percentage of page)
3.0   Table Row       <TR></TR>
3.0   Alignment  <TR ALIGN=LEFT¦RIGHT¦CENTER VALIGN=TOP¦MIDDLE¦BOTTOM>
3.0   Table Cell      <TD></TD>         (must appear within table rows)
3.0   Alignment  <TD ALIGN=LEFT¦RIGHT¦CENTER VALIGN=TOP¦MIDDLE¦BOTTOM>
3.0   No linebreaks   <TD NOWRAP>
3.0   Columns to span <TD COLSPAN=?>
3.0   Rows to span    <TD ROWSPAN=?>
N1.1  Desired width   <TD WIDTH=?>     (in pixels)
N1.1  Width percent   <TD WIDTH=%>     (percentage of table)
3.0   Table Header    <TH></TH>   (same as data, except bold centered)
3.0   Alignment  <TH ALIGN=LEFT¦RIGHT¦CENTER VALIGN=TOP¦MIDDLE¦BOTTOM>
3.0   No linebreaks   <TH NOWRAP>
3.0   Columns to span <TH COLSPAN=?>
3.0   Rows to span    <TH ROWSPAN=?>
N1.1  Desired width   <TH WIDTH=?>     (in pixels)
N1.1  Width percent   <TH WIDTH=%>     (percentage of table)
3.0   Table Caption   <CAPTION></CAPTION>
3.0   Alignment       <CAPTION ALIGN=TOP¦BOTTOM> (above or below table)
```

```
MISCELLANEOUS  (generally not necessary for basic page design)
- - - - - - - - - - - - - - - - - - - - - - - - - - - - - - - - - - - - - - - - - - - - - - - - - - - - - - - -
Comment           <!-- *** -->          (not displayed by the browser)
Author's address  <ADDRESS></ADDRESS>
Searchable        <ISINDEX>             (indicates a searchable index)
N1.0    Prompt    <ISINDEX PROMPT="***">   (text to prompt input)
Send search       <A HREF="URL?***"></a> (use a real question mark)
URL of this file  <BASE HREF="URL">  (must be in header)
Relationship      <LINK REV="***" REL="***" HREF="URL">  (in header)
Meta information  <META>              (must be in header)
Identifier        <NEXTID>            (must be in header)
```

Index

A

B

S

X-Y-Z

GET CONNECTED
to the ultimate source of computer information!

The MCP Forum on CompuServe

Go online with the world's leading computer book publisher!
Macmillan Computer Publishing offers everything
you need for computer success!

Find the books that are right for you!
A complete online catalog, plus sample
chapters and tables of contents give
you an in-depth look at all our books.
The best way to shop or browse!

➤ Get fast answers and technical support for
  MCP books and software

➤ Join discussion groups on major computer
  subjects

➤ Interact with our expert authors via e-mail
  and conferences

➤ Download software from our immense
  library:

  ▷ Source code from books
  ▷ Demos of hot software
  ▷ The best shareware and freeware
  ▷ Graphics files

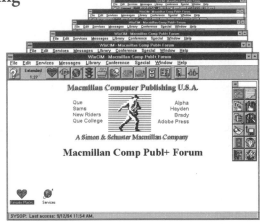

Join now and get a free CompuServe Starter Kit!

To receive your free CompuServe Introductory Membership, call **1-800-848-
8199** and ask for representative #597.

The Starter Kit includes:
➤ Personal ID number and password
➤ $15 credit on the system
➤ Subscription to *CompuServe Magazine*

Once on the CompuServe System, type:

GO MACMILLAN

for the most computer information anywhere!

MACMILLAN
COMPUTER
PUBLISHING

 **CompuServe**

EASIEST WAY TO GET ON THE INTERNET.

NetCruiser Software

EASIEST WAY TO STAY THERE.

40 PEAK HOURS FREE EACH MONTH!

NetCruiser Service

ONLY $19.95 A MONTH!
- **FREE** SERVICE ACTIVATION!*
- 420+HRS/MO. AT NO CHARGE!

800-353-6600

How can you get the best Internet access software <u>and</u> the best nation-wide Internet service? Easy. Just pick up the phone and order NetCruiser™ for Windows™ from NETCOM.

NetCruiser Internet Service gives you 40 peak-time hours, and hundreds of week-end and off-peak hours, every month for under $20. That's enough access time for just about anybody who's planning a stay on the Internet.

"NetCruiser...the hands-down favorite of our first-time Internet users."
PC World

"...NetCruiser from NETCOM is one of the most comprehensive Internet packages available. This one-stop interface will have you on the Internet within minutes..."
LAN Times

MONTHLY COST OF INTERNET SERVICE

SERVICE PROVIDER	20 HRS/MO	30 HRS/MO	40 HRS/MO
NETCRUISER	**$19.95**	**$19.95**	**$19.95**
AMERICA ONLINE	$54.20	$83.70	$113.20
COMPUSERVE	$105.95	$153.95	$201.95
PRODIGY	$29.95	$44.70	$74.20

Cost comparison based on published monthly fees and prime hourly charges for Internet service as of 5/24/95.

Plus NetCruiser includes World-Wide Web, IRC, Gopher, FTP, Usenet, Telnet, E-mail—all the most popular Internet resource discovery tools.

Best of all, with NetCruiser service you get NetCruiser software FREE. It's fun. It's easy. And, with simple point-and-click icons to guide you along the way, it can have you up and running in only minutes.

Order now and we'll even give you FREE activation too. So call us today. It just doesn't get any easier than this.

NETCOM
The Leading Internet Service Provider

*For PC/Windows systems only. Offer subject to change/credit card required. You can get more information on NETCOM's services at info@netcom.com. NetCruiser is a trademark of NETCOM. Windows is a trademark of Microsoft Corporation. ©1995 NETCOM Inc.

SOFTWARE LICENSE

1. GRANT OF LICENSE. MACMILLAN COMPUTER PUBLISHING grants to you a non-exclusive, royalty-free right to make and use an unlimited number of copies of the software provided with this Agreement (Software), provided that each copy shall be a true and complete copy, including all copyright and trademark notices.

2. COPYRIGHT. The SOFTWARE is owned by MACMILLAN COMPUTER PUBLISHING or its suppliers and is protected by United States copyright laws and international treaty provisions. Therefore, you must treat the SOFTWARE like any other copyrighted material (e.g., a book or musical recording) except that you may either (a) make one copy of the SOFTWARE solely for backup or archival purposes, or (b) transfer the SOFTWARE to a single hard disk provided you keep the original solely for backup or archival purposes.

3. OTHER RESTRICTIONS. This License is your proof of license to exercise the rights granted herein and must be retained by you. You may not reverse engineer, decompile, or disassemble the SOFTWARE, except to the extent the foregoing restriction is expressly prohibited by applicable law.

LIMITED WARRANTY

NO WARRANTIES. MACMILLAN COMPUTER PUBLISHING expressly disclaims any warranty for the SOFTWARE. The SOFTWARE and any related documentation is provided *as is* without warranty of any kind, either expressed or implied, including, without limitation, the implied warranties or merchantability, fitness for a particular purpose, or noninfringement. The entire risk arising out of use or performance of the SOFTWARE remains with you.

NO LIABILITY FOR CONSEQUENTIAL DAMAGES. In no event shall MACMILLAN COMPUTER PUBLISHING or its suppliers be liable for any damages whatsoever (including, without limitation, damages for loss of business profits, business interruption, loss of business information, or any other pecuniary loss) arising out of the use of or inability to use this MACMILLAN COMPUTER PUBLISHING product, even if MACMILLAN COMPUTER PUBLISHING has been advised of the possibility of such damages. Because some states/jurisdictions do not allow the exclusion or limitation or liability for liability for consequential or incidental damages, the above limitation may not apply to you.

U.S. GOVERNMENT RESTRICTED RIGHTS

The SOFTWARE and documentation are provided with RESTRICTED RIGHTS. Use, duplication, or disclosure by the Government is subject to restrictions as set forth in subparagraph (c)(1)(ii) of The Rights of Technical Data and Computer Software clause at FARS 252.227-7013 or subparagraphs (c)(1) and (2) of the Commercial Computer Software-Restricted Rights at 48 CFR 52.227-19, as applicable.

Microsoft's Internet Assistant was reproduced by Macmillan Computer Publishing on the accompanying CD-ROM under a special arrangement with Microsoft Corporation. For this reason, Macmillan Computer Publishing is responsible for the product warranty and for support. If your CD-ROM is defective, please return it to Macmillan Computer Publishing, which will arrange for its replacement. PLEASE DO NOT RETURN IT TO MICROSOFT CORPORATION. Any product support will be provided, if at all, by Macmillan Computer Publishing. PLEASE DO NOT CONTACT MICROSOFT CORPORATION FOR PRODUCT SUPPORT. End users of this Microsoft program shall not be considered registered owners of a Microsoft product and therefore shall not be eligible for upgrades, promotions, or other benefits available to registered owners of Microsoft products.